UMKHONTO WE SIZWE

WE SIZWE

THE ANC'S ARMED STRUGGLE

UMKHONTO WE SIZWE

THE ANC'S ARMED STRUGGLE

THULA SIMPSON

PENGUIN BOOKS

Published by Penguin Books
an imprint of Penguin Random House South Africa (Pty) Ltd
Reg. No. 1953/000441/07
The Estuaries No. 4, Oxbow Crescent, Century Avenue, Century City, 7441
PO Box 1144, Cape Town, 8000, South Africa

www.penguinbooks.co.za

First published 2016

1 3 5 7 9 10 8 6 4 2

Publication © Penguin Random House 2016
Text © Thula Simpson 2016

PUBLISHER: Marlene Fryer
EDITOR: Robert Plummer
PROOFREADER: Bronwen Maynier
COVER AND TEXT DESIGNER: Ryan Africa
TYPESETTER: Monique van den Berg
INDEXER: Sanet le Roux

Set in 10.5 pt on 14 pt Minion

Printed by novus print, a Novus Holdings company

MIX
Paper from
responsible sources
FSC
www.fsc.org   FSC® C022948

This book is printed on FSC® certified and controlled sources. FSC (Forest Stewardship Council®) is an
independent, international, non-governmental organization. Its aim is to support environmentally
sustainable, socially and economically responsible global forest management.

ISBN 978 1 77022 841 2 (print)
ISBN 978 1 77022 842 9 (ePub)
ISBN 978 1 77022 843 6 (PDF)

Contents

Preface vii

PART I: THE STRUGGLE 1
Acts of Treason 3
Violence and Non-Violence 20

PART II: SABOTAGE 43
The Opening Phase 45
Soldiers of Mandela 57
Adversity and Retreat 93
External Mission in Command 109

PART III: GUERRILLA WARFARE 117
Invasion 119
The Wankie and Sipolilo Campaigns 133
By Land, Sea and Air 166
Rebuilding the Underground 186

PART IV: ARMED PROPAGANDA 205
Soweto Generation 207
The Anvil and the Hammer 226
Battlefield Southern Africa 271
Planning for People's War 311

PART V: PEOPLE'S WAR 333
Township Rebellion 335
Taking the War to White Areas 355
Season of Violence 403
Interregnum 435

PART VI: ENDGAME 457
Homecoming 459
Transition 483
Victory 501

Notes 515
Abbreviations 569
Index 571

Preface

This book tells the story of the armed struggle waged by the ANC's military wing, Umkhonto we Sizwe (MK), which stands as the longest sustained insurgency in South African history. From its beginnings in the 1950s, the rebellion lasted for almost four decades, culminating in the inauguration of MK's first commander-in-chief, Nelson Mandela, as South African president in 1994. The rebellion unfolded over a vast area, for while MK conducted operations across South Africa, its largest campaigns and heaviest engagements occurred outside the country's borders, and it was also able to draw on support from individuals, organisations and governments across the globe, testifying to the international resonance of the basic issues at stake in the conflict.

I have tried to provide an account of the struggle in all its diversity. The magnitude of the topic and the size of the task were considerable. My research has taken me to a number of countries, including Zambia, Zimbabwe, Botswana, Swaziland and the United Kingdom, as well as throughout South Africa. The sources I consulted ranged from newspaper reports, trial records and oral history collections to the archives of a number of individuals, organisations and governments party to the conflict.

While writing, my approach has been to try as far as possible to recount the events of the armed struggle through the experiences of those who participated in them, for three main reasons. Above all, I wanted the book to rest on as solid a foundation of fact as possible, and only participant accounts can claim first-hand knowledge, rather than hearsay, as the basis for their version of events. At the same time, in order to avoid the pitfalls of relying on single-source testimonies, I have generally ensured that facts are verified by at least two corroborating sources. Only two exceptions have been made to this preference for eye- and ear-witness testimony. The first has been for accounts from expert witnesses regarding the interpretation of material evidence (which I have utilised in an attempt to explain some of the technical details in the participant witness accounts), and, secondly, to place events in context, I have also cited documents of governments and organisations in which their official policy positions are outlined.

Basing the narrative on the perspective of participants has also allowed me to focus on the practical aspects of the armed struggle. The sources include accounts from insurgents about the challenges they faced in conducting operations; from counter-insurgents who used various methods – both conventional and non-conventional – to try to suppress the revolt; and from non-combatants about the life-changing experience of being caught in the crossfire. Such perspectives offer important insights into the tactical and strategic dimensions of the conflict by identifying some of the problems operatives faced when putting the abovementioned official policies into practice on the ground. I have meanwhile considered a variety of operations, large and small, successful and unsuccessful. While unsuccessful missions might be considered inconsequential by some, I feel they are important in that they illustrate the limitations of certain approaches, and in the history of the armed struggle it was ultimately such operations that served as catalysts for the revision of existing policies. For this reason they merit careful consideration.

Finally, utilising participant accounts enables a consideration of the role of 'subjective' factors in shaping historical outcomes. Many of the sources offer records not just of events witnessed, but also of individual reactions and responses to them. They include accounts of willpower sustained in the face of resistance, resolution (or disintegration) in adversity, and, conversely, the hubris that so often accompanies victory. It is the uncertain, never fully predictable outcome of the encounter between subjective actors and objective facts that gives events the dramatic character that is such a conspicuous feature of lived experience. When the effects of these events are finally felt or perceived, they provide further tests of character that introduce both heroic and tragic features into the narrative, all carrying consequences of their own, and which in turn shape future developments. Some of the accounts provided in this book in which these features appear can be ranked among the most poignant and stirring in all South African history.

I have opted to narrate this book in the present tense in order to preserve a sense of the momentous, real-time dilemmas with which those embroiled in the conflict were confronted. While the usual direction of historical reflection is from the present to the past, and involves offering praise or blame for the decisions of those whose actions are being considered, from reading the accounts of those who lived through the events discussed in this book it is often difficult to tell, even with the advantage of hindsight, what one could or would have done differently if confronted with the same choices.

Although I have relied chiefly on primary sources, it would be unfortunate if this were to obscure the value of previous studies on the history of the armed struggle. Among these, special mention must be made of the pioneering studies of Howard Barrell, which first stimulated my inquiries in this field. The large number of memoirs by veterans of the struggle also added greatly to the store of participant perspectives available to me while developing my account.

This book is structured into six sections, corresponding to the major strategic phases of the insurgency. The shift from non-violent mass protest to armed struggle is dealt with first (Part I). Then we pass successively to sabotage (Part II), guerrilla warfare (Part III), armed propaganda (Part IV), people's war (Part V) and negotiations (Part VI). The narrative as a whole charts the progression from the height of the Defiance Campaign during the 1950s to the negotiated settlement of the 1990s that marked the accomplishment of the anti-apartheid struggle's basic political objectives, which MK had been established to help achieve.

*

I owe acknowledgements to my mother, Felicia Ntshangase; to Cathy and Jason Laye-Sion for accommodating me during an earlier phase of this project; and to Dr Hilary Sapire for her academic mentorship then and since.

At Penguin Random House, thanks are due firstly to Marlene Fryer, who was a decisive supporter of the project; to the production team involved in design, type-setting, proofreading, indexing and photographic research; and foremost to managing editor Robert Plummer, for his constructive input regarding ways in which the manuscript as a whole could be recast to make it more accessible to the reader.

I dedicate this book to my wife, Genevieve, who offered a life beyond manuscript development; for this, the greatest thanks are owed to her. The aspects of duration and loss that are such prominent features in this story were not wholly absent, either, during the writing process, as my father, Robert Theodore Simpson, who assisted me in more ways and on more occasions than can be recounted here, passed away just before its long-promised publication. I dedicate this book to him as well.

The usual disclaimer about the author's ultimate responsibility for the content of the work applies here, but I welcome amendments and corrections of the errors that must, unfortunately but inevitably, be present in a book representing the consilience of thousands of sources.

T.W.S.
WATERKLOOF, PRETORIA
JANUARY 2016

I

THE STRUGGLE

ACTS OF TREASON

At Port Elizabeth's North End Station at 1 p.m. on 18 October 1952, railway employee Frans Gerber sees two Natives approach his cabin, look round, sit by the door, and start eating fish.

Two and a half hours later, the Cradock train pulls in. One of the Natives grabs a tin of paint. Gerber tells him to leave it, but the men ignore him. One stands next to the drum while the other merges into the crowd of around forty waiting to board the train.

Gerber telephones the next station, New Brighton, to report the theft. Constable J.F. Burger, the recipient of the call, proceeds to Platform Two.

At about 3.45 p.m. the Cradock train reaches New Brighton. Two Natives are among those who step out of Third Class. One of them is carrying a tin of paint.

Burger approaches them and says he has information the paint is stolen. Unless they can give him a suitable explanation, he says he will arrest them.

The larger of the two men (the one carrying the tin) says: 'Find out for yourselves.' When Burger moves in to perform an arrest, the two resist. Burger manages to handcuff the larger man, but in the process the smaller of the two escapes.

At this point, men on the platform try to prise the captive out of Burger's grasp. The constable is hit from behind and dragged off the platform onto the railway line. A section of the thousand-or-so Natives on the platform begin to pelt him with stones. In response, he fires a shot into the air.[1]

*

At Emloteni Square in New Brighton, the local ANC Youth League branch is holding a public meeting when two men arrive and draw members of the Youth League executive aside.

A while later, Milner Ntsangani of the executive returns to inform the gathering that the meeting will have to close because there is a problem at New Brighton Station. Ntsangani departs with six or seven others.

As they approach the station, they see that its roof has been stoned. They immediately take up position in front of the station in order to address the crowd.

After they have finished speaking, they try, with the assistance of members of the crowd, to disperse those assembled. Ntsangani then hears the sound of gunfire, which comes from a contingent of police reinforcements who have arrived.[2]

Most of the crowd flees, but rather than go home, some take up positions at other points in New Brighton.

From their vantage point at the station, the police see a lorry on fire some 400 metres away. When they arrive at the vehicle, they find inside it the mutilated corpse of a white man, Mr Laas.[3]

*

Two days later, at Burghersdorp in the Cape Province, South Africa's minister of native affairs, H.F. Verwoerd, tells a National Party meeting that Port Elizabeth is the only city in the Union where 'control measures' have not been properly enforced.

The city thought it could handle native affairs better in its own way, with the consequence that it has become the 'fountainhead' of the 'Defiance Campaign'. He is referring to the Defiance of Unjust Laws Campaign, coordinated by a Joint Action Committee of ANC and South African Indian Congress (SAIC) members, which began on 26 June and which involves groups of 'volunteers' courting arrest by openly contravening racially discriminatory laws.[4]

Verwoerd is keen to draw a link between the rioters and the volunteers. He says proper control measures will have to be enforced in Port Elizabeth in the future, even if this requires special legislation.

The following night, Verwoerd tells another National Party meeting, this time in Dordtrecht, what he feels are the larger issues at stake. He says that in fifty years' time there will, conservatively reckoning, be nineteen million Natives and six million Europeans. If the Natives are not relocated to the reserves by that time, the resulting chaos can only be imagined.[5]

*

Port Elizabeth's town clerk, Mr G. Brewer, says on 28 October that following its meeting earlier in the day, the City Council has decided to ask the minister of native affairs to impose a 9 p.m. to 5 a.m. curfew in the city for an emergency period.

He adds that the council is *not* requesting a curfew for New Brighton, because that location is a 'free area'.[6]

*

Four days later, the Eastern Cape Regional Committee of the ANC issues a press statement serving notice that it will lead a strike on 10 November against Port Elizabeth's plans to ban non-religious public meetings and to impose the curfew.[7]

*

A 9 p.m. to 5 a.m. curfew is introduced in Port Elizabeth on the night of 7 November, according to the next day's *Rand Daily Mail*. The article mentions that the national government has also banned all (non-religious) gatherings of non-Europeans in Port Elizabeth, Uitenhage, Peddie, East London and King William's Town for a month.[8]

Donald Card is among a posse of uniformed policemen at Fleet Street Station in East London at 2 p.m. the following day. They are instructed by their commanding officer to investigate what is happening at Bantu Square in the city's East Bank location.[9]

The policemen arrive at Bantu Square about an hour and a half later. They find around 1,500 people gathered, including a man purporting to be a preacher. A policeman steps in to search the minister's Bible. Concluding that it is not a religious gathering, the commanding officer tells the crowd they have five minutes to disperse.

Parts of the audience start leaving, while some of the ANC members begin dismantling the loudspeaker. While they are doing this, a group of Native policemen charge at them with batons.[10]

The *Rand Daily Mail* reports the following morning that in the night's rioting in East London, three Europeans (identified as Dr Elsie Quinlan, a nun; a Scottish doctor named Cahoon; and an insurance official, Mr A. Forster) were killed, along with 'at least eight Natives' (who go unnamed in the article).[11]

*

On the same morning, the ANC Secretariat in Johannesburg releases a statement undersigned by Dan Tloome and Nelson Mandela, offering commentary on the East London events. It reads:

> We realize that these are tense and difficult times for the Native people, in which small incidents often lead to violent outbursts; we realize that tempers are high and that there is often provocation; we realize that no attempt is being made by the authorities to come to an understanding with the Native people or to give sympathetic attention to their grave problems. Nevertheless, we cannot condone outbursts of this kind, which are damaging to the cause of the Natives themselves.

They state that the ANC is proud that 'the defiance campaign was planned as a peaceful campaign and had been conducted peacefully'. They call on ANC members to now go among the people and tell them: 'Do not be provoked. Do not be hasty. Keep courage and remain quiet. It is of the utmost importance that the Native people set an example of courage and restraint in these tragic days.'[12]

*

The 10th of November is the day of the ANC's planned strike against the curfew and the ban on meetings in Port Elizabeth.

At 6.45 a.m. the New Brighton train arrives in Port Elizabeth. Only twenty people get out.[13]

The South African Press Association reports later that day that a mere 10 per cent of the black labour force turned up for work in Port Elizabeth.[14]

From 6.30 a.m. on the 11th, blacks begin streaming into Port Elizabeth by bus and train for work. At the New Brighton housing scheme, however, workers find a notice informing them that the project has been suspended. The message instructs them to ask the ANC for alternative jobs or for the difference between the salaries they were receiving and those they will now get as recruits.

Meanwhile, at the city engineer's yard in Kensington, workers are verbally informed that they have been fired, and that while they will be paid off, they must now go home. As the gates are shut, the laid-off workers start shouting in protest. The police arrive shortly thereafter in troop carriers. The officer in charge gives the workers five minutes to disperse. When they fail to do so, the police advance. The workers flee.

A dispatch in the Johannesburg *Star* later in the day says that by 9 a.m. scores of jobless workers had returned home and the North End location streets were lined with idle men sitting in the gutter or against walls, waiting in the hope that their employers would take them back.[15]

*

On the following day in Groutville, near Stanger, some forty-five miles from Durban, Major Liefeldt, the Stanger magistrate and area native commissioner, informs a meeting of the Amakholwa tribe that the government is terminating Chief Albert Luthuli's appointment as chief.

Liefeldt reads a letter from the Department of Native Affairs. He says Luthuli was invited to Pretoria at the government's expense, and there it was explained to him that as a chief he was part of the government of the country. He was told that he could not at the same time take part in agitation encouraging people to defy the laws of the land.

Luthuli was given a fortnight to choose between his chieftaincy and his role as ANC president in Natal, but Luthuli said he felt there was no conflict between the two roles. Therefore, Liefeldt says, the government is dismissing him.[16]

*

Crown prosecutor Mr P.S. Claassen tells a court on 26 November that the evidence to be led against the accused, namely James Moroka (president of the ANC), Dr Yusuf Dadoo (president of the SAIC) and eighteen others (including Walter Sisulu, Dan Tloome, Nelson Mandela, Moses Kotane and Ahmed Kathrada), is that they were party to a plan aimed at bringing about full equality between Europeans and non-Europeans in South Africa, including the franchise for all.[17]

*

Six days later at the Rand Criminal Sessions, Mr Justice Rumpff says: 'it is not for me to judge the wisdom of legislation, but only to interpret it. That is the province of the legislature.' He then finds the twenty accused leaders of the Defiance Campaign guilty of contravening the Suppression of Communism Act.

He sentences each to nine months' imprisonment, but suspends this for two years, 'because I accept the evidence that you have consistently advised your followers to avoid violence and I know that the implications of the Act are complex'.

Following the verdict, James Moroka enters the witness box. As he does so, Rumpff clarifies that the offence for which he and the other accused have been found guilty is 'statutory communism'. He adds: 'The charge has nothing to do with communism as it is commonly known.'

Moroka nonetheless proceeds to plead for mitigation of his sentence.[18]

*

At the ANC's annual conference in December 1952, Albert Luthuli challenges and defeats James Moroka to become the organisation's president.[19]

*

Moving the second reading of the Public Safety Bill in the House of Assembly in Cape Town in February 1953, justice minister C.R. Swart says that the friends of the Opposition – certain members of the ANC – have produced a law of the jungle, and it is impossible to fight the law of the jungle with the ordinary rule of law.

Swart says there have been a number of significant statements from Native leaders recently. For example, Z.K. Matthews, formerly of the Native Representative Council, said that the logical outcome of the non-cooperation movement would be a policy of African nationalism and Africa for the Africans. Swart says this is an indication of the direction in which Native opinion is heading.[20]

Swart also quotes statements in his possession culled from court trials and ANC meetings. He offers some samples:

> It would take about a minute to kill all the whites. I will repeat it before a Magistrate. If we fight against the Europeans it will last about a minute.

> God created the white man and placed him overseas. He created the black man and placed him in this country. It is therefore Europeans who are breaking the law by coming to this country.

> The white people robbed our ancestors of this country and they cannot produce the title deeds. We will train our armies at night and you will be instructed in due course.[21]

*

Nineteen-fifty-three is a general election year in South Africa.

At a rally in Queenstown on the night of 17 March, H.F. Verwoerd challenges the opposition United Party's election slogan, 'Vote for the right to vote again'. He dismisses it as scaremongering and asks the audience: 'Have you ever lived in a state of less fear than today?'[22]

*

The election results are announced on 18 April. The *Rand Daily Mail* reports that the 'United Front' of the United and Labour Parties has secured 54.4 per cent of all votes cast – some 130,000 more votes than the National Party. But this translates into only 61 seats versus the Nationalists' 94. The National Party won 24 seats with majorities of under 1,000 and the United Party only three.[23]

*

At a press conference in Johannesburg two days later, Albert Luthuli announces that the Defiance Campaign will continue.

Shortly afterwards he receives a banning order from C.R. Swart, prohibiting him from attending public meetings or visiting any of the country's cities for a year.[24]

*

On 28 June, scores of policemen assemble outside the Odeon Cinema in Sophiatown, at the corners of Good Street and Main Road, and Good Street and Victoria Road. Nelson Mandela and Walter Sisulu are on the street conversing with Father Trevor Huddleston. A police officer approaches and tells Mandela and Sisulu that they are banned individuals who have no right to be there. He orders his officers to arrest them.

'No, you can't arrest them,' Huddleston says, adding that their bans have expired. 'No, you must arrest me instead, my dears.'

A policeman orders Huddleston to step aside. Huddleston refuses, only to be manhandled out of the way.

Mandela then tells the policemen: 'You must make sure whether we are under a ban or not. Be careful, because it would be a wrongful arrest to take us in if our bans have expired. Now, do you think we would be here tonight talking to you if our bans had not expired?'

The officer hesitates and then instructs his men to pull back. Huddleston, Mandela and Sisulu enter the Odeon.

There are approximately 1,500 people in the hall as Mandela chairs.

Yusuf Cachalia, national secretary of the South African Indian Congress, addresses the conference. He is violating a ban placed on him speaking at public gatherings. After he has finished, two Special Branch detectives enter the hall, mount the platform and approach the speakers.

'Me?' says Nelson Mandela.

'No,' replies one of the policemen, a Major Prinsloo.

The other policeman reaches Cachalia, twists his hand and forces him down the platform to the doorway. In their way at the exit are Ahmed Kathrada, Babla Saloojee and T.N. Naidoo, all members of the credentials committee.

Robert Resha exits the hall alongside Mandela. As they emerge they see a line of policemen standing, rifles aimed. There are about a hundred policemen altogether. One of them warns the delegates that if they come out they will be shot.

Mandela and Resha urge the delegates to return inside. The conference resumes, but Kathrada, Naidoo and Saloojee are arrested for obstructing the police.[25]

*

Shortly after the Odeon incident, Sisulu informs Mandela that he has been invited to Bucharest to attend the World Festival of Youth and Students for Peace and Friendship as a guest of honour. Mandela encourages him to go.[26]

*

At the ANC's Cape Provincial Congress, which takes place in Cradock on 15 August 1953, Z.K. Matthews delivers the presidential address. He tells the delegates: 'one phase of our struggle has come and gone, but contrary to popular belief in some quarters the struggle is by no means at an end'.

He notes that 'various groups in the country as you know are considering the idea of a National Convention at which all groups might be represented to consider our national problems on an all-inclusive basis'.

He asks 'whether the time has not come for the African National Congress to consider the question of convening a National Convention, a Congress of the People, representing all the people of this country irrespective of race or colour to draw up a Freedom Charter for the democratic South Africa'.[27]

*

When Nelson Mandela and Walter Sisulu meet again, Mandela suggests that while abroad Sisulu should visit China to discuss whether Peking would be willing to supply the ANC with weapons in the event of an armed struggle in South Africa. Sisulu welcomes the idea and promises to pursue it.[28]

*

When Nelson Mandela arrives to take a case at the courthouse in the town of Villiers in the Orange Free State on 3 September, he finds a group of policemen waiting. One of them serves him an order under the Suppression of Communism Act.

Under the terms of the ban, Mandela cannot attend gatherings for two years, so, on 21 September, when the ANC's Transvaal Provincial Conference meets, Andrew Kunene, a colleague on the regional executive, reads the presidential address on his behalf.[29]

Titled 'No Easy Walk to Freedom', the speech reflects on the achievements of the Defiance Campaign. Mandela writes: 'By the end of July last year, the campaign had reached a stage where it had to be suppressed by the government or it would impose its own policies on the country.'

That said, the 'tide of defiance was bound to recede, and we were forced to pause and to take stock of the new situation'. Under the new contingencies of struggle, 'old methods of bringing about mass action through public mass meetings, press statements, and leaflets calling upon the people to go to action have become extremely dangerous and difficult to use effectively'.

Looking forward, Mandela writes:

Our immediate task is to consolidate these victories, to preserve our organisations, and to muster our forces for the resumption of the offensive. To achieve this important task the National Executive of the ANC in consultation with the National Action Committee of the ANC and the SAIC formulated a plan of action popularly known as the 'M' Plan and the highest importance is attached to it by the National Executives. Instructions were given to all provinces to implement the 'M' Plan without delay.

The aims of the M-Plan are to consolidate the Congress machinery; to enable important decisions taken at the national level to be transmitted to every member of the organisation without having to call public meetings, issue press statements or print circulars; to build up local branches of the ANC; to extend and strengthen links between Congress and the people; and to consolidate Congress leadership.[30]

*

In a discussion in Peking with the heads of the Chinese Communist Party's Youth League and International Department, who are both members of the party's Central

Committee, Walter Sisulu says he is sure that armed struggle will come, and that the South Africans would like assistance and advice.

The two Chinese officials express serious doubts about the wisdom of this course of action.

Sisulu protests that in South Africa there are outstanding personalities, veterans, men who are trained in the international situation, and who can therefore give direction, so it is *not* some ill-considered move that they are undertaking lightly.[31]

Despite this plea, the Chinese officials remain unswayed, and Sisulu returns to South Africa empty handed.

*

On 27 December 1954, the first notices are served in Sophiatown calling on people to prepare to be moved from the area between 7 and 12 February 1955.[32]

*

At 4 p.m. on 8 February 1955, members of the Special Branch arrive at the home of Robert Resha, the ANC secretary in the Transvaal. They serve him a notice to the effect that public assemblies of more than twelve people have been banned in the magisterial districts of Johannesburg and Roodepoort.

That afternoon, Resha reads in the press that the deadline for the completion of the Sophiatown removals has been brought forward to the following day.

In the evening he travels to Sophiatown and finds fully armed policemen on almost every street corner. He proceeds to an open square on the corner of Meyer and Victoria Roads. Between 3,000 and 5,000 people have gathered there, as well as a score of uniformed police.

A policeman approaches Resha and tells him that they are trying to disperse the people and have issued them notices that public gatherings are banned. Another officer asks Resha, as the leading ANC official in the area, to help.

Resha agrees. He tells the crowd that meetings are banned and that the day of removal has been brought forward to Wednesday. He calls upon them to go home and do nothing until the ANC gives further instructions.

The crowd begins to disperse.[33]

*

At 6.20 a.m. the following morning, army truck U42156 begins the Sophiatown removals when it transports the first residents out of the location.[34]

The clearance of Sophiatown, home to 65,000 inhabitants, will take five years to complete. The majority of the residents are relocated to Meadowlands on Johannesburg's south-western outskirts, which henceforth will be the new mecca of black urban life in South Africa.[35]

*

The Congress of the People called for by Z.K. Matthews in 1953 meets on Sunday 26 June 1955.

Beneath a stage adorned by a banner featuring a green 'Freedom Wheel' with four spokes, 2,884 delegates assemble in Kliptown, Soweto. The event has been organised by the Congress Alliance, an alliance of the ANC, the SAIC, the Congress of Democrats (consisting of white activists) and the South African Congress of Trade Unions (SACTU). To the rear of the crowd are Special Branch detectives seated on empty lemonade boxes.

At about 3.30 p.m. some fifteen detectives, escorted by a group of policemen armed with Sten guns, storm the delegates' enclosure. As they approach the platform, Piet Beyleveld, the conference chairman, announces from the stage: 'Armed police are approaching. We don't know what they want. Please keep your seats.'

Beyleveld then asks the crowd to rise and sing 'Nkosi Sikelel' iAfrika'.

With the delegates in full voice, the policemen and detectives mount the platform. At the same time, some policemen on horseback and others armed with rifles form a double cordon round the conference enclosure.

One of the officers on the platform demands that the meeting be closed. Beyleveld requests that, before complying, the meeting be allowed a vote on the document they have been discussing. The police grant this concession.

The document in question is the 'Freedom Charter'. Its preamble begins: 'We, the people of South Africa declare for all our country and the world to know: That South Africa belongs to all who live in it, black and white, and that no government can justly claim authority unless it is based on the will of all the people.' The main body of the document consists of ten sections, headed 'The people shall govern!', 'All national groups shall have equal rights!', 'The people shall share in the country's wealth!', 'The land shall be shared among those who work it!', 'All shall be equal before the law!', 'All shall enjoy equal human rights!', 'There shall be work and security!', 'The doors of learning and of culture shall be opened!', 'There shall be houses, security and comfort!' and 'There shall be peace and friendship!', which collectively offer a vision of a post-apartheid South Africa.

The Congress of the People adopts the document unanimously.[36]

*

In the company of two assistants, Theodore Moeller, a detective sergeant in the South African Police, searches the ANC's offices at 38 Market Street, Johannesburg, on the morning of 27 September 1955. Robert Resha is the only member of the ANC present at the time. He is body-searched.

On the same day, Albert Luthuli is stopped and searched by F.C. Swanepoel of the police. A document is recovered from the ANC president, bearing his handwriting. From its heading it appears to be a speech to be delivered at the ANC's annual conference in December.

It reads: 'In discharge of my duty as Leader of Congress I feel it necessary for me in guiding conference to point out the implications of the Charter as I see it.'

Further on: 'My advice to Conference would be to accept the Charter with the qualification that it does not commit itself at present until [there is] further discussion on the principle of nationalisation, of means of production, as visualised in section 3 of the Charter.'[37]

*

The Transvaal Provincial Conference of the ANC is held the following month.

The conference reveals divisions that have opened up within the ANC over the Congress Alliance and the Freedom Charter. Potlako Leballo argues that the struggle is being deflected by 'foreign ideologies' and that Congress has abandoned the basis of its nationalism, which is the policy of 'Africa for the Africans'.

His speech is interrupted by a delegate from Springs, who rises to say that Leballo no longer belongs to the ANC. His place should rather be in the breakaway Bantu National Congress: 'That is where such views and policies are discussed.'[38]

*

The *New Age* reports on 29 March 1956 that Nelson Mandela has been served with fresh banning orders confining him to Johannesburg for the next five years and prohibiting him from attending gatherings for that period.[39]

*

Three days later, Ruth First attends a special ANC conference in Johannesburg. She does so as a reporter for *New Age*.

During a debate on the pass laws, a total of about sixteen self-styled 'Africanists' scattered around the hall denounce the ANC National Executive Committee's (NEC) 'cowardly' stance on the issue. A group of about ten women march to Potlako Leballo's seat and attempt to physically eject him. ANC officials intervene to prevent this happening.

After this, the 'Africanists' depart *en bloc*.

Ruth First's report on the meeting appears in the 5 April issue of *New Age*. She notes in it that the conference saw the ANC officially adopt the Freedom Charter as a policy document.[40]

*

On the last evening of April 1956, C.R. Swart informs the House of Assembly in Cape Town that, consequent to the nationwide police raids the previous September, 200 people will be prosecuted for treason, breaching the Suppression of Communism Act and other offences. The charges will be based on documents seized during the raids, but for now information from the documents is still being 'correlated'.[41]

*

In December 1956, the state makes its move.

At 5 a.m. on the 5th, policemen arrive at the offices of the ANC and the Transvaal Indian Congress on the corner of Market and Diagonal Streets in Johannesburg.

The office doors only open at 9 a.m. When they do, the police enter and conduct a thorough search of the premises, confiscating books and documents in the process.

In the evening, at the Johannesburg Magistrate's Court, staff reporters from the *Rand Daily Mail* can hear the voices of men and women singing 'Afrika, Mayibuye' from cells below the court. Dr Ronald Press, national secretary of the Textile Workers Industrial Union, then emerges from the cells wearing a blazer embellished with a Wits University badge. He stumbles over the top step. As he regains his balance he turns to the crowded non-European public gallery and gives the thumbs-up sign.

Still smiling, he turns towards the magistrate, Mr M.R. Hartogh, who says: 'Listen, you are in a court of law now, do you understand? I will not permit you to do anything like that.'

Press, looking sheepish, says, 'Sorry, your honour.'

In their report the following day, the *Rand Daily Mail* correspondents write that 140 men and women were arrested on the 5th. Of these, 110 were being held in the court cells, while the remainder, who were arrested in areas outside Johannesburg, were being brought to the Rand.[42]

*

The spectre of further legal proscription dogs the ANC in 1957. On 3 March the political correspondent of the *Sunday Times* reports from Cape Town that he understands that justice department officials and Special Branch detectives have been tasked with investigating whether grounds exist to ban the organisation under the Suppression of Communism Act.[43]

Two weeks later, the correspondent reports that he has been informed that the government is rethinking imposing an organisational ban on the ANC after having been told by the police that such a move would be insufficient as individual leaders would be able to remain in the towns and cities and continue to cause trouble under alternative political guises. The police advised that banishing *individuals* from urban areas would be more effective, and they sent a list to C.R. Swart of activists they wanted to round up. The report says police action is expected soon.[44]

The ANC responds in a statement published in the *New Age* on 28 March which recalls the organisation's prediction when the Suppression of Communism Act was first piloted in 1950, that the legislation was 'only the first step in the Nationalist plan to destroy all its opponents'. The statement says it would be a 'tragedy' if the government were to succeed in banning and destroying the ANC, because 'the ANC is no threat to the existence and welfare of the Whites in the Union of South Africa since it works through non-violent methods for the realisation of a common society in the Union where all its people shall live in peace and friendship as equals'.[45]

*

Meanwhile the estrangement of the Africanists from the ANC accelerates. At the annual ANC Transvaal Provincial Congress meeting in October, during a discussion of disputes in the branches, Africanists denounce what they claim is the takeover of the movement by leaders and ideologies hostile to African nationalism. In the end, amidst shouts of 'We stand by our leaders', loyalist delegates pass a resolution to re-elect the previous years' leadership, many of whom are in the Drill Hall facing treason charges.[46]

At the ANC's annual conference held in Orlando from 14 to 16 December, the Africanists use a debate about a National Executive Committee memorandum 'on the place of the 1949 Programme of Action in present-day ANC policy' to berate the Freedom Charter. They accuse the present ANC leadership of 'selling out' the African nationalism of the 1949 document. The loyalists again rally: one charges the African-ists of advancing 'Broederbond racialism'; another says, 'We don't want any worms in our apple.'

Ultimately, a majority of the three hundred and five delegates approve the memo-randum's conclusion that the Freedom Charter and the Programme of Action are 'complementary'.[47]

*

Albert Luthuli writes a letter to South African prime minister J.G. Strijdom on 19 December 1957 requesting negotiations between the ANC and the government.[48]

On 10 March the following year, he gets an answer, of sorts. Speaking before a crowd at Johannesburg City Hall, Strijdom says that from reading articles in pro-United Party newspapers and speeches by United Party spokesmen, 'hostile non-white organizations like the ANC can come to only one conclusion, and that is that the United Party support them in their action against the government'.

The opposition candidate Sir de Villiers Graaff said in 1953 that the Natives would put the government in its place, and United Party newspapers and speakers incited the 1957 bus boycott called by residents of Alexandra to protest the raising of bus tariffs between the township and Johannesburg. The United Party and its news-papers, 'who constantly convince the Natives that their wages are too low', will have to bear responsibility for the threat to paralyse the country with strikes.[49]

*

Nineteen-fifty-eight is another general election year in South Africa.

On 14 March, at a meeting in the new constituency of North-West Rand, H.F. Verwoerd, still the native affairs minister, announces: 'yesterday, I signed a proclamation which was sent to the governor-general for his signature. Through this, I accept the power to declare the African National Congress as a prohibited organisation in any Native area of which I have control, and where the abovemen-tioned organisation prepares to make trouble.'

He hastens to add that the ANC 'has already been considerably curbed by the government', but 'through this measure, the minister obtains power to control it in the areas where it wants to make trouble'.[50]

*

On the weekend of 15–16 March, some 2,000 delegates of the Congress Alliance meet in Johannesburg. They decide to commence a programme of mass action on 14 April, two days before voting begins in the election.[51]

*

Having obtained the governor-general's assent, Verwoerd moves quickly to exercise the powers he demanded on the 14th. Under a proclamation published in a Government Gazette on 17 March, the ANC is banned from the African reserves of the Marico district, which includes Zeerust, as well as from the Sekhukhuneland reserves and Ramagoep's location in the Soutpansberg.[52]

*

The ANC's call for mass action meanwhile only serves to aggravate its internal divisions.

On 26 March, a political correspondent with the Johannesburg *Star* writes that 'responsible Native leaders', speaking on condition of anonymity, told him that while the delegates at the 15–16 March meeting 'may have been genuinely under the impression that they were somehow exposing the failure' of National Party native administration policies,

> nobody has any doubt that behind the scenes people from the other congress movements – the Indian Congress and the Congress of Democrats – were encouraging the Natives to make this decision for quite other motives. They knew perfectly well that Native demonstrations at election time would drive white voters to vote Nationalist. And they want the Nationalists to stay in power because racial friction and bitterness suit their purposes.[53]

Potlako Leballo is willing to go on record with his opposition to the proposed mass action. Interviewed by a *Rand Daily Mail* reporter on 1 April, he says: 'we are against this protest because it is left-wing inspired. We do not want to stay away from work. Why should we? But many of us fear assault and intimidation if we do go to work and for that reason, I think many of us will stay at home. I shall do so myself.'[54]

Six days later the *Rand Daily Mail* conveys a response by Albert Luthuli. He says the ANC wishes to refute interpretations by certain leaders that the planned protests are designed to return the National Party to office.

The ANC is convinced, Luthuli says, that the 'immediate problem before South Africans is to get rid of the Nationalist Government', but it has 'never considered the United Party to be the real opposition to the Nationalists. It has seen it vote, time and again, with the Nationalist Government on a crucial issue – e.g. for the Public Safety Act and the Criminal Law Amendment Act.'

Therefore, the ANC feels compelled to 're-assert its demands for a real break with past policies and to give expression to the needs of the non-European people. The only political power the non-Whites can use to assert their claims is protests and demonstrations.'[55]

*

With the elections approaching, the state feels it is winning.

Speaking in Pretoria on 10 April, police commissioner Major General Rademeyer expresses satisfaction that the Natives seem to 'have tumbled to the fact that they are being exploited by groups of communists and agitators. I want to say to the Natives – you won't find any European, Indian or Coloured agitators on strike on Monday. They will be urging you to strike. You will have to go it alone – as in the past.'[56]

*

On the 11th, Special Branch detectives raid the ANC and Transvaal Indian Congress's Johannesburg offices.[57]

*

The *Star* reports on the same day that Minister Verwoerd has signed a Government Gazette Extraordinary in Pretoria banning gatherings of more than ten Natives in all urban centres in order 'to prevent irresponsible elements from trying to fan the feelings of workers over a stoppage of work' during election week.[58]

*

On Monday 14 April, the date on which the mass action campaign is planned to begin, the *Star* reports that the ANC's strike has failed. Even in Johannesburg, 'where it was expected that the effect of the protest would be most apparent, not one in 10 workers stayed at home'.[59]

In the evening, the ANC admits defeat. Its secretary-general Oliver Tambo issues a statement calling off the strike. Workers are advised to return to their jobs the following day. The strike's failure is attributed to 'punitive' measures by government and 'economic pressure and propaganda' by employers.[60]

*

On Friday 18 April, the final election results are released. The United Party has won 53 seats and the National Party 103, but, again, the United Party received more votes (708,283) than the Nationalists (617,468).[61]

*

On the morning of 24 August 1958, Prime Minister J.G. Strijdom dies at the Volks Hospital in Cape Town after his condition suddenly deteriorates following a period of illness. C.R. Swart was appointed to act for Strijdom on the 21st, but it is H.F. Verwoerd who is elected by the National Party in early September to be Strijdom's successor.[62]

*

The ANC's internal divisions, painfully exposed during the elections, lead to schism by the end of the year. Albert Luthuli addresses the Transvaal Provincial Conference of the ANC in Orlando, Johannesburg, on the afternoon of 1 November 1958. He accuses the government of injecting the 'virus of prejudice and sectionalism' into the African community.

'Continuous harping on race by the Nationalists has caused some non-whites to emulate them and preach exclusive control of South Africa by one racial group. We have seen developing, even though it is in its embryonic stage, a dangerously narrow African nationalism, which itself tends to encourage us to go back to a tribalism men-tality.' Luthuli says that whatever apartheid might do to disturb racial peace in South Africa, the ANC will never pursue the same 'disastrous' course of narrow nationalism.

While Luthuli is speaking, a large group of Africanists, some of whom are dressed in Basotho blankets and carrying sticks, enter the hall.

In the ensuing debate, when speakers from the roughly 600-strong audience rise to support Luthuli, a section of about fifty Africanists at the back of the hall heckle them. A declaration by a female speaker that 'Africa is for all' receives particularly loud boos. The Africanists declare that 'Africa is for the Africans and the white man must go back to Europe'.

On the morning of the 2nd, a crowd of at least a hundred ANC volunteers gathers behind the conference hall, some armed with sticks and lengths of iron. A comparably sized contingent of Africanists gathers at the front. Some are similarly armed.

As the screening of delegates begins, volunteers loyal to the Luthuli leadership are posted to the doors of the hall while Security Branch detectives and policemen watch from a distance.

The Africanists hold consultations among themselves while elections begin inside.

They then deliver a document to the door of the conference hall. The document says they are not prepared to settle their dispute with the ANC by violence, but they are also not prepared to remain any longer in an organisation that has the Freedom Charter as its policy.[63]

*

On 8 November the Africanists confirm that they have seceded from the ANC.[64]

*

The January–March 1959 issue of the journal *Africa South* features an article by Michael Harmel, introduced to readers as a 'Johannesburg Journalist', but who is in fact also a member of the Secretariat of the clandestine South African Communist Party (SACP), which is banned under the Suppression of Communism Act.

Harmel's article, 'Revolutions are not Abnormal', is a rejoinder to an essay published in an earlier issue of the journal by Wits University professor Julius Lewin, titled 'No Revolution Round the Corner'.

Harmel counters Lewin with the argument that in South Africa the Congress Alliance 'is steadily winning the allegiance of the vast majority of the people. And herein lies the certainty of the defeat of the present form of government and the victory of the South African revolution. For no minority government can endure, however rigid its repression or seemingly powerful its forces, once the great majority of the people have taken the path of resolute resistance and organisation against it.'

He emphasises that the 'revolution need not involve violence'. In fact, 'There have been plenty of examples in history where a combination of factors have been compelling enough to make a ruling class give way for urgent and overdue changes, without dragging the people through the agony of civil war. We can only hope that this may also be the case in South Africa. We cannot tell what exact form the changes will take, how exactly or when they will come.'

Harmel concludes that 'In so far as Mr Lewin was seeking to discourage facile optimism and dispel visions of easy victory, his purpose was worthy. The weakness of his article, however, was that, perhaps under the shadow of the Nationalists' last election victory, he has painted a difficult task as a hopeless one. And that is not true.'[65]

*

But 1959 sees the state place further restrictions on the ANC and its leaders, severely limiting the space available for non-violent protest.

In the first week of June, Albert Luthuli receives a banning order preventing him from attending any gathering at all, and restricting his movement to an area twenty-five miles wide in the vicinity of Stanger for a period of five years.[66]

*

On 12 June Oliver Tambo, now Luthuli's deputy, receives a ban prohibiting him from attending any meetings for five years.[67]

*

In its 10 December issue, the *New Age* reports that defence minister Frans Erasmus has recently declared his intention to reorganise the Defence Force along the lines of the French in Algeria, to maintain 'internal' security.

The article features a rejoinder from Duma Nokwe, the ANC's secretary-general, that 'although the Minister supplied minute details of the reorganisation of the army to meet its new tasks, he made no attempt to justify his belief that there is going to be a civil war in South Africa'.

Nokwe says that the ANC, for its part, 'is convinced that there is no threat of armed rebellion from so-called "subversive elements"'.[68]

*

The 'Executive Report' submitted to the ANC's annual December conference, which in 1959 is held in Durban, warns that 'Dark clouds are threatening our organisation.'

One recommended counter-measure is to 'enrol more new members so that the Congress should enjoy mass support which is necessary for its defence against the onslaught of the reactionary Nationalist regime'.

Another concerns the M-Plan, discussed by Nelson Mandela in 'No Easy Walk to Freedom', but left unimplemented since then. The report says: 'During the year your executive issued a directive to the effect that it was compulsory for all Congress branches to implement this plan. Our aim is to get a proper organisational machinery which can withstand and defeat the savage onslaught of the enemy of the Non-Europeans in South Africa.'[69]

*

Addressing the House of Assembly on 20 January 1960, Prime Minister H.F. Verwoerd announces that a referendum rather than an election will decide whether the country becomes a republic. Legislation will be introduced during the present Parliament to make the existing electoral machinery available for a referendum.[70]

*

By now, the struggle in South Africa is taking place against the backdrop of a rapidly changing Africa. Speaking before a joint sitting of both South African Houses of Parliament on the morning of 3 February, British prime minister Harold Macmillan observes: 'As I have travelled through the Union, I have found everywhere, as I expected, a deep preoccupation with what is happening to the rest of the African continent. I understand and sympathise with your interest in these events and your anxiety about them.'

He continues: 'the most striking of the impressions I have formed since I left London a month ago is of the strength of this African national consciousness. The wind of change is blowing throughout the continent. Whether we like it or not, this growth of national consciousness is a political fact. We must all accept it as a fact. Our national policies must take account of it.'

Macmillan says Britain's response was expressed by its foreign secretary Mr Selwyn Lloyd at the United Nations on 17 September 1959, when he said: 'In those territories where different races or tribes live side by side the task is to ensure that all the people may enjoy security and freedom and the chance to contribute as individuals to the progress and well-being of these countries.'

As for Pretoria's response, Macmillan says: 'as a fellow member of the Common-wealth we have always tried to give South Africa our support and encouragement. But I hope you won't mind my saying frankly that there are some aspects of your policies which make it impossible for us to do this without being false to our own deep convictions about the political destinies of free men.'

Macmillan condemns attempts under way in Britain to boycott South African goods: 'I and my colleagues in the United Kingdom government deplore this proposed boycott and regard it as undesirable from every point of view.'

When Macmillan finishes, Verwoerd responds. He thanks Macmillan for the address, but says, 'I cannot endorse all of it.' It is 'on an occasion like this, when we can be perfectly frank, we can say we differ from you'. There is 'a tendency in Africa for nations to become independent and at the same time justice has to be done to all. There must not only be justice to the black man in Africa but also to the white man.'

On an otherwise sombre day for South Africa's parliamentarians, this draws strong applause.[71]

*

On 22 February the *Rand Daily Mail* reports an ANC boycott campaign that is planned to coincide with the launch of one by the British Labour Party on 1 March.

The report says the ANC's campaign against 'Nationalist goods' will target a brand of cigarettes and a canned fish product. The products are two of a list of fifteen brands so targeted. An ANC spokesman is quoted in the article saying the campaign will end with an 'anti-pass' day on 31 March, when public meetings will be held and deputations of Africans will petition their local authorities with demands for the abolition of the pass system.[72]

*

Robert Sobukwe is the president of the Pan-Africanist Congress (PAC), the new organisation formed by the Africanists who split from the ANC in 1958. Sobukwe informs a press conference on Friday 18 March that the PAC will commence its own sustained, disciplined and non-violent campaign against the pass laws the following Monday.

For the campaign's duration, nobody will go to work, he says. Africans will leave their passes at home and surrender themselves at selected police stations under the leadership of local PAC members. They will tell the police: 'We do not have passes. We will not carry passes again. Millions of our people are arrested under the pass laws so you had better arrest us all now.'

Sobukwe adds: 'These are my orders, and if we must win, these orders must be faithfully carried out.'[73]

VIOLENCE AND NON-VIOLENCE

In its early edition on Monday 21 March 1960, the *Star* reports a serious disturbance unfolding in Vanderbijlpark and the Sharpeville location in Vereeniging.

The trouble apparently began when Natives working in the Vanderbijlpark area staged an impromptu demonstration outside the local police station, only to be dispersed by teargas and baton charges. 'Skiet kommandos' (white army reservists) rushed to the scene, along with white civilians who showed up at the station asking to be signed on. The paper says estimates are that one Native has been killed in Vander-bijlpark and another badly wounded in Vereeniging. Colonel J.C. Lemmer, deputy commissioner of police for the Witwatersrand, describes the situation to the paper as 'very explosive' in both areas.[1]

At around 1.30 p.m. that afternoon, a hastily formed line of police reinforcements on the western side of Sharpeville Police Station opens fire on a group of demon-strators who are pressing against the station's perimeter fence. This causes a chain reaction which spreads to policemen positioned in Saracen tanks in the station yard. They fire on protesters who are trying to flee northwards across open veld. Many are shot in the back. The shooting lasts less than a minute.[2]

The death toll in Sharpeville rises through the day, reaching an eventual official total of 67 Africans dead and 186 wounded.[3]

During the night there is rioting at Langa township outside Cape Town, in which at least two people are killed by the police.[4]

*

Addressing the House of Assembly on 22 March, H.F. Verwoerd claims that the Vereeniging and Cape Town 'riots' resulted from attempts to stage a 'massive revolt'.

Fortunately the police acted firmly, he says, and 'as long as the police act in this manner, I have the fullest confidence that they will be able to prevent such attempts at revolt from succeeding'.[5]

*

Albert Luthuli issues a statement from the ANC's Johannesburg headquarters on the evening of the 23rd. He says that instead of the planned anti-pass demonstration on the 31st, he is calling on 'Africans and all other sections of the people' to observe the 28th as a day of mourning for the dead of Sharpeville and Langa.[6]

*

The government, however, is clear in its intent not to compromise. On Friday 25 March, Frans Erasmus, now justice minister, tells the House of Assembly that he will introduce a bill on Monday that will, inter alia, give the governor-general emergency powers to ban the ANC, the PAC and other organisations if the need arises.[7]

*

A car bearing a Cape Town registration number arrives in Lobatse in the Bechuanaland protectorate at 7.30 a.m. on Monday 28 March.

Oliver Tambo, the passenger, is interviewed by the local district commissioner. Tambo says he is ANC deputy president and his organisation is about to be banned in South Africa. He says he fears action will be taken against him by the Union government. Therefore he hopes to receive political asylum. Tambo says he has in his possession suitcases containing ANC files and he eventually hopes to go to the United Kingdom.[8]

Ronald Segal, the driver, says they left Johannesburg at 3.30 a.m. because they feared Tambo would be detained when the strike planned for later that day occurred.[9]

*

A *Star* correspondent and his colleague are driving in Emdeni, Soweto, at about 3 p.m. that afternoon when they see a group of Natives making a bonfire of their passes. The crowd are jubilant: singing, dancing, posing for photographers, giving the thumbs-up sign and chanting 'Afrika!'

Then an ANC district official approaches the journalist and warns: 'It's time you left, sir. Big trouble is coming to the townships tonight.'

On the road out they see an angry crowd stone a black motorist to death. Other drivers are hauled from their cars to see if they have gone to work.

As their car approaches Phefeni Station, they see a large crowd tearing down rediffusion telegraph poles. The crowd then streams onto the road to block the car's path. One man lashes at the driver with a knobkerrie, missing his skull by a fraction. After being held up for several minutes, the car manages to get clear of the crowd and escape, under a torrent of bricks and stones.[10]

Oscar Tamsen of the *Rand Daily Mail* is driving in Soweto later that afternoon. He is accompanied by a photographer colleague. At sunset, large groups of Africans start patrolling the streets. Many are carrying rocks and threatening passing motorists. Tamsen drives to Dube Railway Station. En route, pedestrians pelt the car with objects.

The station is crowded with shouting people. Some are threatening to kill anybody arriving by train from Johannesburg.

Within minutes, the nearby bridge over the railway line is completely blocked, barring the car's route out of the township. Tamsen and his colleague drive into the veld and escape via a little-used side road before heading to Meadowlands Police Station.[11]

*

Justice minister Frans Erasmus moves the second reading of the Unlawful Organisations Bill in the House of Assembly on 29 March. He says he has included the term 'certain other organisations' to the Bill just in case the ANC and PAC try to reappear under different names. 'I understand the ANC has already adopted what it has called the M-Plan to make provision for the ban,' he says. 'I have no hesitation in saying the acts of the PAC and the ANC border on revolution. They are sailing close to the wind.'[12]

*

That evening Bram Fischer phones his comrade Wolfie Kodesh: 'Look Wolfie,' he says, 'I've just had a call from an anonymous chap who spoke to me in Afrikaans, and he said: "Bram, they are going to raid all over South Africa within the next two hours or so, you better duck it, duck."'

He continues, 'I then asked: "Well, who is speaking?" to which the man said, "Nee wat, don't worry about who is speaking, Bram, I'm telling you. It is going to happen."'

Fischer tells Kodesh to warn as many people as possible.

After putting down the receiver, Kodesh calls colleagues in the underground in Cape Town to warn them to prepare.[13]

*

Around midnight, Jack Hodgson appears at Ben Turok's home. Hodgson says there has been a call from Durban warning that a large number of police cars were seen at Special Branch headquarters and similar activity has been reported in other areas. The advice is that people should leave their homes in case of mass arrests.

Turok packs a small suitcase. His wife Mary drives him to a house in Mons Road in Johannesburg's Observatory suburb. Turok knocks on the door. Ralph Sepal opens and greets him. Turok goes to a prepared bedroom.

Later, in the early hours of the morning, Wolfie Kodesh and Michael Harmel arrive and find Turok and Moses Kotane already there.[14]

*

Pre-dawn raids are conducted that morning in Johannesburg, Pretoria, Durban, Ladysmith, Cape Town, Port Elizabeth, East London, King William's Town, Grahamstown and Pietermaritzburg. Over a hundred activists are arrested, including Albert Luthuli, Nelson Mandela, Walter Sisulu, Ronald Press, Duma Nokwe, Govan Mbeki, Raymond Mhlaba and Moses Mabhida. When the police arrive at Jack Hodgson's home they find that he is gone, but they arrest his activist wife Rica.

On the night of the 30th, a Government Gazette Extraordinary is published declaring a state of emergency under which anybody can be arrested in the interest of public safety and order. The order is made retrospective to cover the arrests made the previous night.[15]

*

A *Star* staff reporter visits the ANC's Transvaal provincial headquarters in Bezuidenhout Street, Johannesburg, on 4 April 1960. He finds an ANC district official standing outside a locked door. The official tells him simply: 'We have gone underground.'[16]

*

Justice minister Erasmus informs Parliament in Cape Town on 8 April that the government has just signed a proclamation under the Unlawful Organisations Act that will see the ANC and PAC banned for a year.

He says a Government Gazette Extraordinary will be issued later in the day proscribing both organisations until 6 April 1961.[17]

*

At Milner Park showgrounds the following afternoon, Prime Minister Verwoerd is among 30,000 people at the Union exposition. It is 3.15 p.m. and he is in the President's Box surrounded by officials of the Witwatersrand Agricultural Show.

A tall, slightly built, brown-haired European man wearing slacks and a green fawn sports jacket pushes his way through the crowd.

The man reaches the Presidential Box at about 3.20 p.m. and asks softly, 'Dr Verwoerd?' upon which Verwoerd turns smiling. The man suddenly produces a .32 automatic pistol from his right trouser pocket, presses it against Verwoerd's right cheek and fires a shot.

After a few seconds of silence, bystanders rush to Verwoerd's aid. The gunman then fires a second shot into Verwoerd's ear.

At this point, Verwoerd, his face covered in blood, slumps forward in his seat, clutching his head in his hands.

The would-be assassin, a fifty-one-year-old farmer named David Pratt, is overpowered by policemen and spectators on the main stage and is taken, struggling, to the police station behind the main grandstand. Pratt is politically unaffiliated, and was driven by a 'feeling' that first came over him the previous day when he saw about a hundred prisoners being loaded into a van and thought to himself: 'What the hell will be happening next? This cannot go on. Where can we see any light?' The thoughts that afflicted him before shooting Verwoerd were: 'What is the country going to do? What is all this leading to?'

Verwoerd is taken to Johannesburg General Hospital where he has an emergency operation. He will survive. In the early evening the three specialists who examined him release an official bulletin describing his condition as satisfactory, adding that there has been no damage to the brain, that he was not unconscious at any time, and that he understood everything that was said to him.[18]

*

The ANC's 'Emergency Committee' plans a general strike from 18 to 25 April. On Thursday 14 April, thousands of pamphlets are distributed in the Rand calling on Africans to stay at home the following week.[19]

*

The *Rand Daily Mail* reports on Tuesday the 19th that most Africans showed up for work the previous day, so it appears that the call for a stayaway has failed.[20]

*

On 16 May, Harold Sacks of the *Rand Daily Mail* writes that the government has devised a contingency plan to deal with future riots. Sacks comments that the plan will doubtlessly be put into operation as soon as possible before 26 June.[21] This day is the anniversary of the beginning of the Defiance Campaign and also the day in 1950 on which the ANC, SAIC, Communist Party of South Africa, the Council of Non-European Trade Unions and the African People's Organisation staged a general strike to protest the passing of the Suppression of Communism Act.

On 27 June, the *Rand Daily Mail* reports that on the 26th, 'formerly the ANC's "day of mourning, protest and rededication"', all was 'quiet and uneventful through-out South Africa'. In Johannesburg's townships it was a normal Sunday as Africans lounged in the sun, in their gardens and on street corners, while sport, funerals and church meetings took place as usual.

That said, in Orlando there were a few slogans painted on walls, one of which read 'Release our leaders'.[22]

*

Moses Kotane, Michael Harmel and Ben Turok are now roommates. Harmel shows Turok a document that he has just completed.

In 'South Africa What's Next?' Harmel outlines his thoughts on the South African revolution's prospects in light of the year's events. He begins: 'The struggle for freedom in South Africa has entered a new phase since the terrible massacre at Sharpeville and other towns on March 21, 1960.'

Following the banning of the ANC and *New Age*, and the subsequent arrests of leaders, 'there was a period of confusion. When the Emergency Committee which the A.N.C. had formed to carry on underground called for a general strike from April 18 to 25, there was a disappointing response.'

A period of rebuilding therefore ensued, and 'On June 26 Congress slogans and posters appeared all over the country'.

Then, on 14 July, the SACP distributed leaflets announcing its existence.

Concerning the future, in a section of the paper titled 'Violent or Non-Violent?' Harmel returns to a question that he left open in 'Revolutions are not Abnormal' the previous year. He notes that the 'Non-White people of this country have consistently, and with unbelievable patience, attempted to find non-violent means of achieving change and redress of grievances ... The answer has been bullets and Saracens.'

If this continues, then despite what some 'theorists' may say, 'the people will have no alternative but to defend themselves' – as is already happening in places like Sekhukhuneland, Pondoland and Zululand, where rural uprisings have taken place against apartheid measures.

The paper continues:

> 'Non-violence' is not an absolute principle. It was correct in the past, and still is today, to warn the people against being provoked into desperate and useless acts of unorganised retaliation. But if the Verwoerd regime continues to butcher unarmed and defenceless people, it will become more and more futile to preach 'non-violence', until the time comes when it will be worse than futile – even treacherous. The stage may be reached in the life of any nation when the stern and sacred duty presents itself to organise for battle.

Harmel argues, however: 'It is still not too late for the democratic and progressive forces, under militant leadership, and taking advantage of the splits within the ruling class and widespread world support for our cause, to remove this hated, minority government by the force of popular pressure on a mass scale.'

Harmel mentions the forthcoming referendum to make the country a republic and argues: 'It is correct to encourage the White electorate to vote NO in the referendum.'

Moses Kotane agrees with the basic thrust of Harmel's document when it is shown to him, and the three men (Harmel, Kotane, Turok) decide to circulate it more broadly within the movement as a discussion paper.[23]

*

The state of emergency ends on 31 August 1960.[24]

*

In the referendum, held on 5 October, the republican cause wins by 73,980 votes, obtaining 52.3 per cent of all valid votes.

Prime Minister Verwoerd addresses the nation at 7.20 p.m. on the evening of the 7th.[25] He suggests that 'Parliament might deem it of value to associate the birth of the republic with an historic date such as May 31'. This is the date in 1910 when the Union of South Africa came into being.[26]

*

On 16 December, a two-day Consultative Conference of African leaders begins in Orlando, Soweto. Altogether thirty-six political, religious, cultural, sports, professional and business people attend.

On the 17th the conference agrees on its resolutions. Among them is the assertion that 'because the African people were denied participation in the republican referendum they do not accept the result', and that the conference calls on the African people to attend an All-In Conference in order to:

(a) demand the calling of a national convention representing all the people of South Africa wherein the fundamental rights of the people will be considered;

(b) consolidate the unity of the African people.[27]

*

In December 1960, Ben Turok drives a minibus containing various individuals to a large vacant house near Zoo Lake in Johannesburg.

On the same evening, Bob Hepple does the rounds collecting people in a closed van. One of the people he picks up is Nelson Mandela.

Hepple takes them to the same house where Turok delivered his passengers. When they arrive, Mandela shakes Hepple's hand and asks, 'How are your parents?'

The occasion is the SACP's annual congress. About twenty people attend. Besides Hepple, Mandela and Turok, Fred Carneson, Bram Fischer, Michael Harmel, Govan Mbeki, Raymond Mhlaba, M.P. Naicker, John Nkadimeng, Walter Sisulu, Joe Slovo and Dan Tloome are there.[28] A marquee has been erected at the property.

Inside a room within the house, Bram Fischer chairs the meeting. Walter Sisulu delivers the main political report, and Michael Harmel delivers a report-back on a conference in Moscow from which he has just returned. A long discussion follows on the differences between the Chinese and Soviet Communist Parties that were manifest at the conference. The discussion overruns.[29]

When it is complete, Rusty Bernstein reads a discussion document. Based on the feedback to Harmel's 'South Africa What's Next?', it recommends that the party 'should create an armed force to prepare for a new phase', because the old ways of struggle are so circumscribed, given the state's willingness to resort to the most extreme forms of repression to defend the system.

A debate on the proposal follows. Nelson Mandela is sitting next to Sisulu at the back of the room. He reminds the delegates that the ANC's policy is against violence and it will be difficult to sell this to the movement, especially to Luthuli.[30]

The prevailing view is in favour of the proposal. This is reflected in an interim decision that is unanimously approved by all those present. The decision endorses the creation by the SACP of specialist armed units, while also calling on the SACP to work to mobilise the broader Congress movement behind a shift in policy away from an exclusive reliance on non-violent methods. The resolution passed consists of three parts. They are:

a. That the peoples' movement could no longer hope to continue along the road of exclusively non-violent forms of political struggle, and to do so would lead to the paralysis of the movement in the face of new government tactics, and to the disillusionment and spread of defeatism amongst the people.

b. That therefore steps should be taken to ensure that the whole peoples' movement reconsidered its tactics of exclusive reliance on non-violent methods, and that a campaign of education and explanation be carried out throughout the movement to prepare for forcible forms of struggle when these became necessary or desirable.

c. That the Party CC [SACP Central Committee] should take steps to initiate the training and equipping of selected personnel in new methods of struggle, and thus prepare the nucleus of an adequate apparatus to lead struggles of a more forcible and violent character.[31]

The original discussion document containing the proposal is burned and the ashes are thrown down a trapdoor. The SACP Congress then disbands.[32]

*

Moses Kotane was not present at the SACP Congress. When Ben Turok informs him of what was decided, he is not happy. While he had agreed to the circulation of Michael Harmel's 'South Africa What's Next' as a discussion document, he fears his more impetuous colleagues have just sent the movement careering towards disaster.

He tells Turok: 'If you break people's windows they're going to come out and break your neck, so don't do it unless you know what you are doing!'[33]

*

On 3 February 1961, the *Star* contains a report mentioning that the date for an 'African People's Conference' to be held in Pietermaritzburg has been set for 25–26 March.[34]

*

The five-year ban on Nelson Mandela attending meetings expires on 14 March.[35]

*

Eleven days later, with two vanloads of police keeping watch outside, Mr Nyembe, the conference chairman, welcomes the roughly 1,500 delegates gathered in Pietermaritzburg's Arya Samaj Hall 'in the name of Congress', but, remembering that this is now a criminal offence, quickly corrects himself.

The first speech is by Nelson Mandela, now sporting a beard.

Maxwell Levy Marwa, a black detective sergeant in the Special Branch, enters the hall during the address and starts taking notes of Mandela's utterances.

Mandela declares that Verwoerd and the Nationalists 'have held a fraudulent referendum to make South Africa a republic, and they overlooked the African majority of the country – he overlooked the African majority and owners of the country. As you all know that on the 31st of May South Africa will be declared a Republic, [to] which we are opposed, I call upon you to reject a white Republic by the minority of Nats.'

He warns that 'if we do not act, we will betray the people of Pondoland, Zeerust and Sekhukhuneland. Our course is to fight shoulder to shoulder for that great idea – the liberation of all the oppressed people in South Africa.'

In the early hours of 26 March, the conference agrees on its resolutions. Central among these is a demand for a National Convention elected by universal adult franchise 'to be called by the Union Government not later than May 31st'.

A warning is conveyed that 'should the minority Government refuse', country-wide demonstrations will be held on the eve of the declaration of the republic.[36]

*

Three days later, the last of the accused in the Treason Trial, which dates back to the December 1956 arrests, are acquitted.

The judges' final word – as contained in a 168-page 'Reasons for Judgement' document submitted to the Court Registrar by Justice Rumpff, who also presided over the 1952 Defiance Campaign trial – is that 'it had not been proved that over the indictment period the African National Congress had, as a matter of policy, decided to use violence as a method to achieve its ends, or to establish a form of state having the fundamental attributes of a Marxist-Leninist state'.[37]

Ironically, given the progress of the debate within the liberation movement since December 1956 concerning the question of armed struggle, many of the accused are now plotting to commit the offence of which they have been acquitted.

According to a report in the *Rand Daily Mail* on 30 March, while there was singing and dancing in Orlando the previous night, 'behind all the excited talk, the handshaking that continued off and on all evening and the congratulations of friends and of strangers was a question that cropped up every few minutes at every party: "What now?"'[38]

*

While performing observation duty on Nelson Mandela on 17 April 1961, Sergeant A.J. Coetzee notices that Mandela has gone missing.[39]

*

Jacobus F. Barnard, private secretary to H.F. Verwoerd, receives a letter in an airmail envelope on 24 April. The postmark reads 'Johannesburg, Fox Street' and bears the date 22 April 1961. On the letterhead is written 'All-In African National Action Council, Makhoza House, 17 Commissioner Street, Johannesburg'.

He looks to see who the author might be and finds, typed, 'N.R. Mandela', below which is a signature and, again typed, 'Honorary Secretary of the All-In African National Action Council'.

Mandela begins: 'I am directed by the All-In African National Action Council to address your government in the following terms.'

Point 1 reads: 'The All-In African National Council was established in terms of a resolution adopted at a Conference …'; point 2: 'Conference noted that your government, after receiving a mandate from a section of the European population[,] decided to proclaim a Republic on May 31st'; point 3: 'It was the firm view of the delegates that your government, which represents only a minority of the population in the country, is not entitled to take such a decision without first seeking the views and obtaining the express consent of the African people'; point 4: 'The Conference feared that under this proposed Republic your Government which is already notorious the world over for its obnoxious policies, would continue to make even more savage attacks on the rights and living conditions of the African people.'

There are thirteen points in all.[40]

*

The government soon displays its determination to prevent any disruption of the republic celebrations.

Shortly after 4 p.m. on 27 April, security police detectives and uniformed policemen launch simultaneous raids on offices and homes on the Rand.

The offices of the All-In African National Action Council, the Congress of Democrats, SACTU and *New Age*, as well as the homes of Nelson Mandela, Duma Nokwe and Walter Sisulu, are among those raided.[41]

*

Then, on the night of 2–3 May, in perhaps the biggest police operation in South African history to date, detectives and uniformed policemen launch raids on fifty-nine homes including those of Bram Fischer, Joe Slovo and Ruth First, Piet Beyleveld, Ben Turok, Moses Kotane, Ahmed Kathrada, Rusty Bernstein and Robert Resha, as well as, once again, Mandela, Nokwe and Sisulu.[42]

*

In an interview conducted on 12 May, Nelson Mandela, who is still operating underground, tells Peter Bruce Hazelhurst of the South African *Sunday Express* that a strike has been called for 29–31 May to coincide with the inauguration of the republic. Mandela says: 'white South Africa has nothing to fear from outside. The main purpose of the three-day demonstrations is to express to the Nationalist government our disapproval of the Republic. It is a Republic of the minority of the people of South Africa.'[43]

The All-In African Council distributes a statement that evening under Mandela's signature, confirming 29–31 May as the date for the anti-republic stay-at-home. Notice is made of the government's evident plan to crush the peaceful protests, throw white South Africans into unreasoning panic, and turn the country into an armed camp/police dictatorship in which any expression of opposition to apartheid will be regarded as treason.

'We protest most vigorously against this disastrous attitude,' the statement reads, 'and reaffirm our determination to strive for a non-violent transition to a free and non-racial South Africa.'[44]

*

Further police raids take place on the 24th, starting at 4 a.m. and continuing for two hours. Among the houses targeted are those of Nelson Mandela, Walter Sisulu, Boy Hashe, Brian Somana and Joe Gqabi.[45]

*

Nelson Mandela calls Benjamin Pogrund of the *Rand Daily Mail* from a public phone box on the evening of 29 May, which was intended to be the first day of the stay-at-home. As was the case during the 1958 elections and the 1960 state of emergency, the call for mass action has failed. 'We are not disheartened,' Mandela says. 'The people did not respond to the stay-at-home to the extent to which we expected them to do.'

But, he continues,

> This is not the end of the matter. We have learnt our lesson. Next time we will not
> be caught napping. The setback will not in any way deter us. The grievances against
> which the people are protesting still remain, and we will continue struggling to
> remove these grievances. The events of today and the reaction of the authorities
> close a chapter as far as our methods of political action are concerned.[46]

*

In an interview conducted at Professor Julius Lewin's house near Zoo Lake in
Johannesburg in the early hours of 31 May, the day of the birth of the Republic of
South Africa, Mandela elaborates to British reporter Brian Widlake of Independent
Television News about what he meant by his statement that a chapter of the struggle
was drawing to a close.

Filmed with soft lighting and blackout material in front of a bare brick wall in
order to conceal his whereabouts, Mandela says:

> There are many people who feel that the reaction of the government to our
> stay-at-home, ordering a general mobilisation, arming the white community,
> arresting ten thousands of Africans, the show of force throughout the country,
> notwithstanding our clear declaration that this campaign is being run on peace-
> ful and nonviolent lines, close a chapter as far as our methods of political struggle
> are concerned. There are many people who feel that it is useless and futile for us
> to continue talking peace and nonviolence against a government whose reply is
> only savage attacks on an unarmed and defenceless people, and I think the time
> has come for us to consider, in the light of our experiences in this stay-at-home,
> whether the methods which we have applied so far are adequate.[47]

*

Justice minister Frans Erasmus releases a statement on 2 June attributing the failure
of the anti-republic stayaway to government measures that put agitators, intimida-
tors and tsotsis out of action, thereby proving that such elements were above all
responsible for the disturbances and riots of the past.[48]

*

The effort to persuade the broader Congress movement to endorse new forms of
struggle beyond non-violence gathers momentum after the failure of the stayaway.

At a meeting of the Working Committee of the ANC's National Executive Committee, Moses Kotane, who did not attend the SACP annual congress the previous
December, cuts Nelson Mandela short, saying the time has not come for armed
struggle.

Kotane then chides him: 'Because of the severe measures taken by the government
you are unable to continue in the old way. The difficulties have paralysed you and
you now want to talk a revolutionary language and talk about armed struggle, when
in fact there is still room for the old method that we are using *if* we are imaginative

and determined enough. You just want to expose people, you see, to massacres by the enemy. You have not even thought very carefully about this.'

Nobody speaks in Mandela's favour, including Walter Sisulu, who is present.[49]

*

Later, in a private meeting, Mandela criticises Sisulu for not having supported him.

Sisulu laughs, saying it would have been as foolish as attempting to fight a pride of angry lions. But he says, 'Let me arrange for Moses to come and see you privately, and you can make your case that way.'[50]

*

When the two men meet, Mandela tells Kotane, 'Sebatana ha se bokwe ka diatla' ('the attacks of the wild beast cannot be averted with only bare hands').

It is now Kotane's turn to face the lion pack. Mandela says his opposition is reminiscent of the Cuban Communist Party under Batista. They too insisted that the appropriate conditions for revolution had not yet arrived, and waited because they were following the prescriptions of Lenin and Stalin. By contrast, Castro did not wait, he acted – *and he triumphed*. If you wait for textbook conditions, Mandela says, they will never occur.

'Here we have to decide from our own situation,' he continues. 'The situation in this country is that it is time for us to consider a revolution, an armed struggle, because people are already forming military units in order to start acts of violence. And if we don't do so, they are going to continue. They haven't got the resources, they haven't got the experience, they haven't got the political machinery to carry out that decision. The only organisation that can do so is the African National Congress which commands the masses of the people. And you must be creative and *change* your attitude because your attitude really is the attitude of a man who is leading the movement in the old way when we were legal, who is not considering leading now in terms of the illegal conditions under which we are operating.'

In response Kotane says, 'Well, I'm not going to promise anything, but raise it again.'[51]

*

At a Working Committee meeting a week later, Mandela again raises the issue of armed struggle.

Following his pitch, Kotane tells the meeting: 'Well I'm still not convinced, but let's give him a chance. Let him go and put these ideas to the Executive, with our support.'

Walter Sisulu just smiles.[52]

*

On 28 June Jacobus Barnard receives another letter from Nelson Mandela.

It begins: 'I refer you to my letter of the 20th April 1961, to which you do not have the courtesy to reply or acknowledge receipt.' He writes that – as he predicted in the earlier correspondence – 'your Government sought to suppress the strike by force'.

He reminds Verwoerd that 'the Pietermaritzburg resolution provided that in addition to the countrywide demonstrations, the African people would refuse to co-operate with the Republic or any form of government based on force ... Failure by your Government to call the Convention makes it imperative for us to launch a full scale and countrywide campaign for non-co-operation with your Government.'

He then warns:

> For our own part, we wish to make it perfectly clear that we shall never cease to fight against repression and injustice, and we are resuming active opposition against your regime. In taking this decision we must again stress that we have no illusions of the serious implications of our decision. We know that your Government will once again unleash all its fury and barbarity to persecute the African people.[53]

*

In Dar es Salaam, Tanganyika, in July 1961, Tennyson Makiwane converses with Wilton Mkwayi and Moses Mabhida.

Makiwane tells them that, following the SACP's December 1960 decision, they will be sent to Prague for military training. They will depart later in the year, but in the meantime one of them must get prepared (in Tanganyika). Makiwane suggests that the party would like Mkwayi to go first to receive training.

Makiwane mentions that somebody from London will be joining them for the training.[54]

*

In London around the same time, Vella Pillay, the SACP's representative in Europe, approaches Nandha Naidoo and says 'our people' in South Africa have issued a request that somebody be sent to study radio technology and communication and then return to teach others.

Naidoo asks how long the course will take.

Pillay says three months, and that Mac Maharaj will also be going to East Germany to study printing.

Naidoo agrees to get involved.

Pillay tells Naidoo to travel to Prague and meet Moses Mabhida and Wilton Mkwayi, who will be in the Atlantic Hotel.[55]

*

The ANC's National Executive Committee meets in Groutville on the same night as the South African Indian Congress executive convenes in Tongaat.

Albert Luthuli criticises Mandela's statement to the *Rand Daily Mail* on 29 May that the ANC was closing a chapter on a phase of the struggle. Luthuli says the statement raised an important matter that should have been discussed by the organisation before a public announcement was made.

Mandela acknowledges the validity of the criticism, but reiterates the basic point that a turn is necessary. The state has left us no alternative to violence, he says; it is wrong and immoral to subject our people to armed attacks by the state without offering them some kind of alternative. Some people have taken up arms on their own initiative, hence violence will occur whether we adopt armed struggle or not.

Would it not be better for the ANC to guide the violence itself, according to principles whereby it saves lives by attacking symbols of oppression rather than people? If the ANC fails to lead at this stage, it will be a latecomer to a process that it will be unable to control.

Luthuli initially opposes Mandela's argument, but the advocates of the turn to violence press their point and eventually the National Executive endorses the Working Committee's preliminary decision.[56]

*

At 8 p.m. the following night at a beach house near Stanger, a meeting of the Congress Alliance joint executives takes place. It includes delegates from the ANC, the Indian Congress, SACTU, the Congress of Democrats, the Coloured People's Congress and the Federation of South African Women.

Luthuli chairs. He mentions the fact that the ANC endorsed its Working Committee's decision on violence the previous night: 'Look we have already taken a decision in the ANC but I would like to request my colleagues that in spite of the fact that we've taken a decision, let's start afresh as if we had taken no decision in the ANC.'

In the ensuing debate, J.N. Singh says: 'Non-violence has not failed us, we have failed non-violence.'

Mandela responds that non-violence *has* in fact failed, because it has failed to stem state violence or change the heart of the oppressors.

The debate continues through the night. At one point, a delegate insinuates that Luthuli is perhaps a pacifist.

'If anybody thinks I'm a pacifist, let him go and take my chickens,' Luthuli replies; 'he will know how wrong he is!'

In the early hours of the following morning, Yusuf Cachalia says, 'Look, I appeal to you, let's not take this decision. Let's not decide to use violence. They will arrest us, they will throw us into jail, they will slaughter us.'

To this, M.D. Naidoo answers – referring in particular to some of his colleagues in the Indian Congress – 'well you people are just afraid of militant action, that's all. That's why you are so articulate[,] you know, loquacious, you are afraid of militancy.' He concludes by saying: 'Ah, you are afraid of going to jail that's all!'

The proponents of non-violence are livid at this comment, pandemonium ensues and the discussion goes back to square one.

Later, an intervention by Moses Kotane, of all people, enables the proponents of armed struggle to recover lost ground. He says, referring to Mandela, 'well, look, *he* has established the need for this organisation. *I* think the solution is that we should allow him to go and start it. But he must not involve us. The ANC is going to be busy applying the policy of non-violence which can only be changed by the National Executive; it can't be changed by us. But he can go and start this organisation, and co-ordinate with others that are in the field. But we don't want him to involve us. But as our member we will not discipline him because of the conditions, and we want him to keep on reporting.'

At about 7 a.m., with dawn approaching, the meeting endorses the ANC's decision of the previous night. The agreed resolution is based on Kotane's suggestion. It gives Mandela authority to build the military organ and join with whomever he wishes in doing so. This military organ will not be subject to direct ANC control. The ANC's policy will remain one of non-violence and only a National Conference decision can change it.[57]

*

Following this decision, Nelson Mandela and Joe Slovo, representing respectively the ANC's NEC Working Committee and the SACP Central Committee, meet to discuss who they want to join them on the 'High Command' of the new military wing, and how they will organise regional commands and urban units.[58]

*

Jack Hodgson visits the house in Springs of Ronald Press, who is his colleague in the Congress of Democrats, an ex-Treason Trialist and a Wits University chemical engineering graduate.

Hodgson asks Press to work on devices that can be used to detonate explosives. Press agrees to help.[59]

*

Denis Goldberg meets Fred Carneson at lunchtime on a bench in the gardens near the Cape Town Art Gallery. Under spring sunshine they feed peanuts to some squirrels and doves. Carneson asks Goldberg if he would be willing to join the Western Cape Regional Command of a newly formed military organ of the movement. Carneson says they need a technical officer: 'You are an engineer Denis, we need your technical skill. Will you join? You must know the risks involved.'

Carneson attempts to outline the risks, but Goldberg stops him short: 'Yes, of course I will join.'

Carneson insists he think about it for a while.

'But you know I have been arguing for at least a year for adding armed actions to our struggle,' Goldberg replies.[60]

*

Jack Hodgson, Nelson Mandela and a pharmacist are passengers in Wolfie Kodesh's 1948 Chevrolet.

The car arrives at an unpopulated area between the suburbs of Primrose, Kempton Park and Edenvale. It is a twenty-acre site that includes a small wood and two brickworks.

Kodesh parks the car out of view before he, Mandela, Hodgson and the pharmacist get out and approach one of the brickworks. At the site there are derelict buildings and several pits.

A black watchman emerges from a galvanised iron building and strides towards them. Mandela signals to his comrades to go and fetch the equipment from the car. Mandela then takes this man, a Zulu-speaker, and engages him in conversation out of earshot of the others. Mandela has him arm around the man's shoulder. After a while the watchman begins nodding his head vigorously, before walking away. When his three colleagues return with the equipment, Mandela explains that he has persuaded the man to accept their presence.

One of the derelict buildings is used to test Molotov cocktails. As the bottles burst into flames, Mandela shakes his head gleefully.

After dousing the last remaining flames, the four move from the building to one of the open pits outside. They bring with them a paraffin tin with the tube of a biro pen inserted into the spout. This tin is placed in one of the pits. The four wait outside, but after twenty minutes nothing has happened.

Kodesh retrieves the tin. Hodgson manipulates the tube and hands the tin back to Kodesh, who returns it to the pit. Kodesh is then pulled out of the hole by the others.

A few seconds later there is an almighty bang from the pit, sending a huge dust cloud into the air and mounds of earth into the ground, completely submerging the tin. The four run back to the Chevy.

In the car, Mandela advises that certain adjustments and alterations must be attended to, but he congratulates his colleagues and thanks them as the vehicle speeds off. While en route home, Mandela recommends that as soon as they are certain that the problem with the timing device has been solved, they must report to the High Command so that every unit in the area can be put on alert and properly briefed on the correct use of the bomb.[61]

*

In Port Elizabeth, Denis Goldberg, Fred Carneson and Archie Sibeko meet in Tolly Bennun's flat. Harold Strachan begins a demonstration with glycerine and permanganate of potash.

Bennun tells Goldberg he discovered this mixture working through texts on World War II explosives in the University of Cape Town library.[62]

*

On 20 October 1961 the *Rand Daily Mail* reports that the National Party has been returned to power with its biggest majority ever in the House of Assembly, where it now holds 105 of 160 seats.

In the same issue, the paper reports Albert Luthuli saying he 'deeply regretted' the outcome, which he fears the National Party will interpret as a mandate to continue its repressive policies.[63]

*

Three days later, there is better news for Luthuli. The Nobel Institute in Oslo, Norway, announces that he has won its Peace Prize for the year 1960. (The prize is awarded in 1961 because the Nobel Committee felt there was no suitable recipient among the nominees shortlisted the previous year.)

Phoned that night at his Groutville home by a *Rand Daily Mail* correspondent, Luthuli says: 'You have a feeling of being happy that some recognition has come your way for the little work you do for furthering the liberation movement in South Africa along non-violent lines.'[64]

*

Andrew Mlangeni tells Abel Mthembu and Joe Gqabi that arrangements have been made for them to receive military training in China.

Mthembu and Gqabi then travel to the Bechuanaland protectorate via Potgiet-ersrust.

In Francistown in Bechuanaland they board an aeroplane to Kasane, and from there they go to Mbeya in Tanganyika.[65]

*

On 31 October, Andrew Mlangeni himself arrives in Bechuanaland with Raymond Mhlaba, and the pair are driven to Lobatse Hotel by John Nkadimeng. At around 5 a.m. the following morning they arrive at an airstrip where they find a plane waiting for them. The plane belongs to a private firm run by Herbert Bartaune, a Belgian former Luftwaffe pilot. Bartaune flies Mhlaba and Mlangeni to Mbeya in Tanganyika.

On 20 November, Mlangeni and Mhlaba arrive in Peking. There they meet up with Joe Gqabi and Abel Mthembu, who are in the company of Wilton Mkwayi and Nandha Naidoo. (This is the same SACP mission for which Mkwayi and Naidoo were approached to travel to Czechoslovakia earlier in the year.)

The six then hold a discussion with Chinese Communist Party members.

Mhlaba speaks for the South Africans. He says they are there to obtain knowledge of military science. On the basis of the conversation, a decision is reached that Gqabi, Mhlaba, Mkwayi and Mthembu will go south to receive guerrilla warfare training at the Nanking Military Academy, while Mlangeni and Naidoo will head north for instruction in radio communications.

For the time being they all remain in Peking.[66]

*

In late November/early December 1961, Duma Nokwe approaches Billy Nair of the South African Indian Congress and asks him to canvass the opinion of people in Durban about joining a 'sabotage committee' that will target government instal-lations.

Nokwe adds that Harold Strachan will be coming to Durban to give the com-mittee a demonstration in the manufacture and use of explosives.[67]

*

At a flat in Ridge Road in Durban, Brian Chaitow, Ronnie Kasrils, Bruno Mtolo, Billy Nair and one other African assemble.

Then, with potassium permanganate, thermite and seasand, Harold Strachan begins a demonstration on how to manufacture explosives.[68]

*

Albert Luthuli delivers the Nobel Laureate Lecture in Oslo on 11 December.

He says that in South Africa, one finds 'a constant drive for more policemen, more soldiers, more armaments, banishments without trial and penal whippings'. Yet 'through all this cruel treatment in the name of law and order, our people, with few exceptions, have remained non-violent'. This is remarkable, he says, given 'how easy it would have been in South Africa for the natural feelings of resentment at white domination to have been turned into feelings of hatred and a desire for revenge'.

He says: 'that it has not done so is no accident. It is because, deliberately and advisedly, African leadership for the past 50 years, with the inspiration of the African National Congress, which I had the honour to lead for the last decade or so until it was banned, had set itself steadfastly against racial vaingloriousness.'[69]

*

At Cyril Jones's home at 11 Cooper Street, Cyrildene, in Johannesburg, Bob Hepple chairs a meeting of the SACP's Johannesburg District Committee on 14 December 1961.

Joe Slovo addresses the gathering on behalf of the SACP Central Committee. He talks about a new organisation, 'Umkhonto we Sizwe', whose function will be sabotage. Its members will be trained both inside and outside South Africa. All those present at the meeting will need to pass the message on to people beneath them so these others know that this organisation exists.

Slovo says Umkhonto we Sizwe's first operations will take place in two days' time. Pamphlets will be printed to publicise the launch. The members of this committee will need to distribute them.

Slovo takes Bartholomew Hlapane, one of those present, aside. He tells Hlapane to return to 11 Cooper Street early on the morning of the 16th, look for Cyril Jones, and ask Jones to give him the pamphlets.[70]

*

At 5.30 p.m. on 15 December, Ronnie Kasrils arrives at Bruno Mtolo's apartment holding a paper carrier bag. From it Kasrils takes out what look like Christmas presents in wrapping paper.[71]

*

That evening, Albert Luthuli and his wife disembark from a Viscount plane at Durban Airport.

Luthuli tells the gathered press corps that senior police officials boarded the plane and informed him he was still under banning orders: 'They reminded me that I was back on South African soil. They dealt courteously with me and asked me not to stop to speak to people.'

Therefore he does not stop and instead walks with his wife to a waiting vehicle.[72]

*

Later that night, Bruno Mtolo, Ronnie Kasrils and a young Indian colleague, Subbiah Moodley, depart from a car which has been parked outside 132 Ordnance Road in Durban.

Mtolo is carrying two five-litre jerry cans. The three men approach a gate. They see a number of policemen sitting there. They go to the rear of the building, where they find a wooden door.

Once in position, they wait, watching the clock. It is before 9 p.m.

Moodley and Kasrils then return to the car. From it they each collect two sandbags. When they get back to the wooden door they place two sandbags on each of the five-litre containers. Mtolo has by now opened the container lids. The sandbags are placed against the door but behind the containers, so as to direct the explosive charges inward.

When Mtolo sees that it is only a few minutes to nine he places glycerine into the containers and puts the lids back on. The three then depart the scene.

At around 9.30 p.m. (by his timekeeping), an African watchman on duty hears a dull thud from the rear of the building. When he investigates he finds a fuse amid some sandbags. Next to the fuse he notices an inflammable substance.

When the police arrive at the building they find a plastic jerry can three-quarters full of thermite. A fragment of the screw-top lid is also found nearby, as is a fuse.[73]

*

Saturday 16 December 1961.

Bruno Mtolo leaves his apartment in the morning and sees some sea sand spilt outside the door.

He travels to Billy Nair's home and finds Ronnie Kasrils has beaten him there. Before Mtolo can say anything, Nair asks, 'Why didn't you put the detonator in that other bomb?' Nair explains that the other bomb, intended for the Coloured Affairs Department building, did not go off. The third explosion also didn't detonate, according to Nair.[74]

*

Later on the 16th, Ben Turok meets Rusty Bernstein and Jack Hodgson at a restaurant in central Johannesburg. Turok has a parcel in his possession. His hands are clammy. Bernstein's hands are shaking uncontrollably.

Turok and Hodgson depart together. Hodgson leads them to his green car and says to Turok, 'You drive. I've got something to do.'

'Jack, *are you going to use your car?*' Turok asks.

'Yes, it's okay, it's only a short drive.'

As Turok pulls off, Hodgson takes objects out of the parcel Turok brought from the restaurant. The parcel contains four canisters usually used for tennis balls and four glass phials. Hodgson begins inserting the glass phials into the canisters.

At the intersection of Market and Eloff Streets, a burst of smoke fills the car, upon which Turok draws the vehicle to a halt, gets out and moves about ten paces away. He sees Hodgson has remained in the car, so he returns.

Hodgson has by now opened the door and kicked the canister emitting the smoke into the street. When it has stopped smoking he bends down and retrieves it. He closes the door and says: 'Get moving!'

By now, however, a traffic officer is at the window. Hodgson winds it open.

'What's going on?' the policeman asks.

'Oh, some fireworks have gone off,' Hodgson replies. The policeman does not pursue the matter.

A crowd has gathered. Turok manages to start the car and drive off down Market Street. Hodgson continues placing the remaining phials into the empty canisters.

'Listen, chum. This probably sounds very bad, but I don't care,' Turok says. 'It's the truth – we must abort. We can't go on like this.'

Hodgson, however, insists that they continue.

They stop at a parking lot in Market Street. There they meet a colleague who takes two phials, puts them in a suitcase and heads off.

Turok then walks up Market Street in the direction of Rissik Street Post Office. He walks in and places the bomb on top of a telephone kiosk.

When he arrives home, Turok's wife immediately asks him what has happened. It is only then that he realises that his eyebrows have been singed, his hair burnt and his suit is full of little burn holes.[75]

*

It is just past 5 p.m. on the 16th when Joe Slovo enters the Johannesburg Drill Hall through a side door. He finds about fifty black cleaners removing chairs and polishing the floors.

Slovo wanders through the complex and makes his way to the Administrative Office, which seems not to have any staff still on duty. He goes inside one of the offices. It has large wooden cupboards. He turns a small bottle whose outlet is sealed by cardboard upside down and is about to place the carrier bag containing it behind one of the cupboards, when he hears a voice behind him: 'Can I do anything for you?'

The man is a sergeant major in the South African Defence Force. Slovo says that his brother has received call-up papers but is about to take an important exam. He asks who he can see about arranging an exemption.

The sergeant major says: Follow me.

Slovo does so, carrying the bottle behind him. He knows the acid in the bottle must now be eating away at the cardboard and that it will explode after about fifteen minutes – if he and Jack Hodgson have calculated correctly when manufacturing the device in the 'laboratory' that they established in the kitchen of the latter's apartment.

When they get to the exemption officer's room, they find it empty. The sergeant major tells Slovo to return another day.

Slovo gives him a sweaty-palmed handshake and walks briskly out.

About three minutes have passed since Slovo first met the man.[76]

*

A call is received at the *Sunday Times* offices in Johannesburg at 8 p.m. that evening. The speaker tells the reporter: 'There is a poster that you will find interesting on the corner of Anderson and Polly Streets.' When the reporter asks for the caller's name, the speaker puts down the phone.

At the said place, the reporter finds a poster headed 'Umkonto we Sizwe' pasted to a wall. The poster is printed in Zulu and English and declares that 'Umkonto we Sizwe will carry on the struggle for freedom and democracy by new methods, which are necessary to complement the actions of the established national liberation organisations.'

In the document the organisation is described as 'a new independent body, formed by Africans'. Reference is made to virtual martial law having been imposed twice in the past eighteen months in order to crush peaceful strike action. The new organisation identifies itself as the 'fighting arm of the people against the Government and its policy of race oppression'.

The poster emphasises that the organisation's actions are as yet warning shots: 'We of Umkonto we Sizwe have always sought – as the liberation movement has sought – to achieve liberation without bloodshed and civil clash. We do so still. We hope – even at this late hour – that our first actions will awaken everyone to the realisation of the disastrous situation to which Nationalist policy is leading. We believe our actions to be a blow against the Nationalist preparations for civil war and military rule.'[77]

*

In Port Elizabeth at around the same time, a car races through the streets of the African townships and bundles of handbills in the name of 'Umkonto we Sizwe' are hurled through the window. Their content is the same as the poster in Johannesburg.[78]

*

At 9 p.m., Sergeant J. Fritz hears explosions coming from the direction of the Brick-makers Kloof electrical substation in the Port Elizabeth flatland. As he approaches the scene he sees a group of people fleeing the power plant in different directions.

One of the men is caught by a white civilian near the Arts Hall at the entrance to St George's Park. He is taken away on the pillion of a traffic policeman's motorcycle, handcuffed to the machine.

The other four or five people are not caught.[79]

*

After his abortive attempt at the Drill Hall earlier in the evening, Joe Slovo is alongside Jack Hodgson and Rusty Bernstein next to a manhole on the Johannesburg–Pretoria road. Underground are the telephone cables connecting the two cities.[80]

The men remove the manhole cover, and Bernstein keeps watch as the other two go down the hole. Bernstein then moves the car to conceal the open manhole. He waits by the car, bonnet open, as if the vehicle has broken down.

After the dynamite has been planted on the cables and the fuses have been lit, Hodgson and Slovo emerge and the three depart, keeping watch for any signs of an explosion behind them. They don't see anything. Slovo then claims he heard something in the distance, but in fact the pack of dynamite that he and Hodgson taped to the underground cables has not exploded.[81]

*

At the Knight's Tavern in Fox Street, Johannesburg, Reggie Vandeyar is working the night shift when he is picked up in a vehicle containing Wolfie Kodesh, Laloo Chiba and Paul Joseph.

After the men plant bombs at two targets, Vandeyar is returned to work just in time to deal with a customer complaining that his chicken has not been properly grilled.[82]

*

Allen Loxton of the *Sunday Times* arrives at Fordsburg Post Office later that evening. He finds glass from two phone booths strewn everywhere. Glass from the front door and sitting-room windows of two semi-detached houses on the other side of the road have also been scattered by the blast.

Loxton sees that the main door at the post office, with its 'Blankes Alleen/Whites Only' sign, has had the inside half blown off. Then, inside the main European hall, he notices an eight-hour clock hanging skew on the wall. The clock tells the time it stopped ticking: 10.22 p.m.[83]

*

Joe Modise is travelling in Soweto by car with Comrade Tladi and another comrade who is chief of ANC volunteers in Alexandra township, when they hear a huge explosion from elsewhere in Soweto.[84]

*

Across Soweto, at the municipal offices in Dube, Benjamin Ramotse is walking across the street, away from the building. The right sleeve of his jacket is burning just under the armpit and the left side of his head is blackened. Behind him there is a flame from an explosion that has just occurred at the gate of the municipal office complex.

Constable Frans Masinda grabs Ramotse by the right arm. In the process he notices that the jacket is burning and also that Ramotse's trousers are torn on his backside with burn marks on both sides of the tear. Masinda leads Ramotse to a tap and removes the jacket. This reveals that Ramotse has injuries just above his right wrist and below his right elbow.

Masinda then takes Ramotse to a building at the rear of the municipal office complex. The Dube municipal police have offices there. Inside they find Corporal Thomas Sigasa. He asks the man with the wounds (which look to Sigasa like holes in his right arm) for his name. He is told: 'Baba Sigasa, don't you know me? I am Ramotse.' Sigasa realises that the man half concealed behind the blackened visage is Benjamin Ramotse, who lives in the same area of Dube as him.

Masinda overhears Ramotse tell Sigasa that he was walking across the street when he saw Molefe and greeted him. The next thing he heard was an explosion and he didn't know what had caused it.

Detective Constable Dlepu arrives at the Dube municipal offices from Orlando Police Station. He finds municipal police officers at the scene. Just outside the main gate and next to a pole there is a man lying on his back with his intestines hanging out. All the fingers and the palm of his left hand have been blown off. He has a reddish-brown glove on his right hand.

Next to the body is a torn rubber or plastic container shaped like a bottle. It has some sort of substance in it.

The fatality – MK's first – is Petrus Molefe.[85]

*

Joe Modise, Comrade Tladi and their colleague reach the post office at Kliptown at about 11.30 p.m.

Equipped with handgloves and pliers, Tladi proceeds to open up a gap in the two-metre-high diamond-mesh wire fence at the rear of the building. While Tladi keeps watch, the other two enter.

Modise uses a piece of clay to position the explosive against the building's wall. The Alexandra comrade lights the fuse by applying a cigarette tip to it. Sparks fly as soon as the fuse is lit. The two run in the direction of the fence.[86]

*

Altogether there are ten explosions recorded by the police that night – five in Johannesburg and five in Port Elizabeth – of which nine were bombs made with plastic explosives and the other, in Johannesburg, with dynamite. Two men are under arrest, namely Benjamin Ramotse and the African seized in St George's Park, while the one fatality is Petrus Molefe.[87]

These are initial estimates; there are a number of devices which have either not exploded or have only lightly exploded, including the dynamite planted by Slovo and Hodgson on the cables connecting Johannesburg and Pretoria, and some cylinders containing chemicals that were deposited by a colleague of Benjamin Turok (two of which have not exploded and still have Turok's fingerprints on them) inside the judges' bench at the Central Native Appeal Court on the first floor of the Rissik Street Post Office building.[88] These will be discovered later and added to the tally, as will the acts of sabotage perpetrated the previous night in Durban.

II

SABOTAGE

THE OPENING PHASE

On 17 December 1961, police recover a bottle filled to the brim with petrol from the Tax Office of the Magistrate's Court in Engcobo in the Transkei.

They notice that inside the petrol there is an unexploded fuse that has apparently 'drowned': the fuse appears to have fallen into the liquid before it could explode. For it to have exploded, there ought to have been a greater gap at the top between the petrol and the lid.[1]

*

Lieutenant A.J. Kruger arrests Sisa Dukada, a known member of the ANC in the Eastern Cape, and finds certain chemicals in his possession.

Dukada leads Kruger to a garage in Port Elizabeth. The garage appears to have been used as a lecture room. There are signs of an explosion in the corner. There are also boxes marked 'Handle with Care'.

Upon closer inspection, the boxes are found to have been addressed to Harold Strachan.[2]

*

When interviewed by a reporter from *Die Transvaler* on 18 December, John Vorster, South Africa's new justice minister, says: 'It's clear for me at this stage that white agitators are behind the sabotage that was committed on Saturday night in Johannesburg and Port Elizabeth.'

'Sabotage of this nature cannot be tolerated,' he contends, adding he considers it his duty in the coming year to take strong legislative action against saboteurs.[3]

*

That night an explosion is heard emanating from a flat in Cuyler Street, Port Elizabeth.[4]

*

On 19 December, the flat in Cuyler Street from which the explosion was heard the previous evening is searched.

It turns out the flat belongs to Harold Strachan.

Detective Sergeant E. Erasmus, Major P.J. Heiberg and other policemen ransack the premises. In a cupboard on the back of the veranda they find a piece of tinfoil and a piece of green plastic. They also unearth an envelope containing a silvery fatty powder. In a bundle of sacks in a small room on the second floor they recover two plastic containers. One of them is small and white and contains a liquid.

In Strachan's car, which is parked in Bird Street, they find plastic foam rubber, papers covered with silvery powder, a ball of string, a carton containing sand, test tubes, corks, a copper pipe, electrical wire, plastic piping and a hacksaw blade. The test tube found in the car has Strachan's fingerprints on it.[5]

*

The following day's *Cape Argus* features an article by a Durban correspondent quoting extracts from an interview with Albert Luthuli.

Concerning the events of the 16th, Luthuli said: 'For myself, I regret anything that is violent, but I have not got the facts, I do not even know who carried on the sabotage – whether it was Africans, Europeans, Coloured people or Indians. I resent the assumption that it was Africans. Until the matter is clear, how can I comment? I condemn no one because I do not know the facts.'[6]

*

The Christmas Eve edition of the *Sunday Times* reports that in the sabotage bill that John Vorster intends introducing in the forthcoming parliamentary session, the death penalty is expected to be included.[7]

*

Joe Gqabi, Raymond Mhlaba, Wilton Mkwayi, Andrew Mlangeni, Abel Mthembu and Nandha Naidoo are still in Peking.

They are taken to a building just off Tiananmen Square. At the door they find Chairman Mao, who, with an interpreter's assistance, greets them all individually.

They all take seats in what is a modestly furnished building.

Raymond Mhlaba briefs Mao about the South African situation.

Then Mao speaks. He says his comments are simply illustrative. He states that everything changes, including Marxism and communism. The South Africans' policies should be based on a study and understanding of their own situation, he says. He nonetheless observes that the South African situation sounds similar to Algeria, so the conflict in that territory might be worth studying.

Mao also raises the issue of the differences between the Soviet and Chinese communist parties. He asks the South Africans for their take on the matter.

Mhlaba indicates that they do not wish to take sides.[8]

*

In a diary entry on Wednesday 3 January 1962, Nelson Mandela refers to a National Executive Committee meeting at 'DR MA' that ended at 11 a.m: 'It is decided that we send delegates to Addis Ababa. Also that I go down and discuss the matter with A.J. We are served with lavish meal.'

On the 7th Mandela writes that he reached Durban at 1.30 p.m. He adds: 'Am extremely anxious to see AJ on same day but Dbn's sense of urgency not as sharp as one would expect.'

At 11 p.m. the following evening he finally gets to see Albert Luthuli. The meeting occurs in a safe house in Groutville.

Luthuli upbraids Mandela for not consulting him about the formation of Umkhonto we Sizwe.

Mandela tries to remind him about the discussions undertaken the previous year about taking up arms.

Luthuli says he doesn't recall them.[9]

In his diary entry for the day, Mandela writes: 'I see AJ. He is in high spirits. Approve of trip; suggests consultation on new Op.'

*

At 11.15 a.m. on 11 January, a motor van with a TJ 130-833 licence plate arrives at the Pioneer Gate border checkpoint between South Africa and Bechuanaland. The driver declares himself in the Border Register as 'M. Ismail' of '10, Main Road, Fordsburg'.[10]

On the afternoon of the 11th, Fish Keitseng is plastering the walls of a room in his house in Lobatse when he sees a car approaching, driven by an Indian man.

Nelson Mandela is the sole passenger, and when he emerges from the vehicle he says to Keitseng: 'Hey man, I'm looking for you. I tried to book at Lobatse Hotel, but they refused. So now I'm looking for you.'[11]

*

At 4 p.m. on 2 February, the Heads of Delegates session at the meeting of the Pan-African Freedom Movement of East, Central and Southern Africa begins in Addis Ababa.

Emperor Haile Selassie opens proceedings. He speaks in Amharic on the theme of African unity. Mentioning South Africa, he says he feels the need for new methods.

In accordance with the National Executive Committee decision in January, Mandela is present. On the following day, he reads the ANC's address. Referring to the ANC's shift in policy he says: 'a leadership commits a crime against its own people if it hesitates to sharpen its political weapons where they have become less effective'. When he adds that 'On the night of 16 December last year, the whole of South Africa vibrated under the heavy blows of Umkhonto we Sizwe', the Ugandan chief minister exclaims: 'Give it to them again!'[12]

*

Curnick Ndlovu and Joe Modise meet in Durban.

Modise says he has been sent by the ANC's National Executive Committee. He explains that the ANC has formed a sabotage committee which has a wing in Durban, and that they want Ndlovu to be a part of it. In fact, they want him to serve as chairman of the Natal Regional Command because they need an 'eye' of the ANC on the committee, to show that it is the child of the ANC.

Ndlovu accepts.

After this, Modise takes Ndlovu to see Billy Nair.

During introductions, Modise tells Ndlovu that Nair is an existing member of the Durban sabotage committee, and he informs Nair that Ndlovu will be chairman of the committee henceforth. Modise says to both that the Johannesburg High Command has now formed 'Umkhonto we Sizwe' which is no longer the old sabotage committee; it is rather a wing of the ANC and Ndlovu will represent the ANC on the committee.[13]

*

On 18 March 1962, Robert Resha and Nelson Mandela depart Rabat in Morocco by train. They head to Oujda, which is the headquarters of the Algerian ALN (Armée de Libération Nationale) in Morocco. They travel in the company of Ahmed Ben Bella and Colonel Parmidian.

When they arrive in Oujda at 8 a.m. on the 19th they are met at the station by an officer who drives them to the ALN's headquarters.

There they are received by Si Abdelhanna, head of the ALN's political section. Later they are introduced to a number of senior ALN leaders, of whom two are introduced as Captain Larbi and Commander Jamal. In their company a searching discussion of the South African situation commences.[14]

When asked by a senior Algerian commander how he envisions the future of the military struggle in South Africa, Mandela answers that he is most impressed by the Cuban example: twelve men landing in a boat, hiding in the mountains and conquering the country.

The Algerian asks if he has looked at a map of South Africa.

Mandela says he knows the country.

The Algerian asks where they would hide. In the end there would only be the mountains of Lesotho. And what would they do from there? There is not a population centre or key area of the country within reach. South Africa is a huge country, and the military and air power of the South African regime is greater than Batista's was. So Cuba cannot be used as an example.[15]

*

Wolfie Kodesh shows up in court as the *New Age*'s reporter on the trial of Benjamin Ramotse.

The Special Branch detective in charge of the case notices him and says, 'Oh, Mr Kodesh, come and sit here.' The other Afrikaans-speaking detectives budge up to make space for him. Kodesh sees that there are exhibits laid out on the table in front of the dock.

The detective who welcomed Kodesh says, 'Ja, very interesting. You see that piece there with the tag on it there?', and he points to it. 'That's the Post Office, you know up there in Vrededorp and Ferreiratown.' He proceeds to identify the source of each piece of evidence.

The description of the exhibits complete, Kodesh sighs, 'Oh, well,' and takes out his notebook. The detective says: 'You know, these fellows think they are clever, they use gloves, but you know we can catch them: our scientists are working how you can even tell the fingerprints inside the glove.'

Kodesh chuckles gingerly while jotting this down.

Then the detective produces a big envelope and says, 'You know, I showed these pictures to Vandeyar.' He pulls out photographs of Petrus Molefe's corpse with one hand blown off and intestines hanging out. 'I showed this to Vandeyar in jail and I don't think he liked it,' he says. 'This is what happens to terrorists.'[16]

*

In the preparatory examination of Benjamin Ramotse at the Johannesburg Magistrate's Court on 29 March 1962, Sergeant Jacobus Visagie tells the magistrate that having compared the typewriting in *Umkonto*, the manifesto distributed on 16 December 1961, with SACP publications like the journal *Inkululeko* and the pamphlet *Who killed Lumumba?*, he feels they were all done on the same machine – each contained the same faults.[17]

*

Bruno Mtolo is riding on a bus between Pinetown and Mariannhill when he notices two red boxes ringed by wire fencing.

He gets off the bus and approaches maintenance men working on the road. He asks one of them what those boxes are.

The man tells him it is where the dynamite is stored.[18]

*

Ronnie Kasrils, Bruno Mtolo and Billy Nair get out of a 1958 Vauxhall Victor on a dirt track near Mariannhill on the evening of Friday 13 April.

Kasrils is carrying a key in his hand and he has a pistol in his belt, while Mtolo and Nair each have large wire cutters and crowbars. When they reach the gate, Kasrils unlocks it.

Sparks fly into the night air as the crowbars are used to prise open the doors of a red explosives box. Inside the magazine, the men find a large number of boxes.

About twenty minutes after their arrival, Emmanuel Isaacs, the driver of the Vauxhall, moves it forward to see where the men have gone. Unable to see them, he returns to his original spot, but on the way he sees Nair emerge from the bushes carrying brown cardboard boxes about eighteen inches long, and one foot high and wide. Mtolo and Kasrils follow carrying boxes of the same type.

Mtolo, Nair and Kasrils place the boxes inside the boot and on the back seat. There are about six boxes in all.

The car travels to Stella Road in Durban's Malvern suburb. Nair gets out and goes to a house.

At the house, Nair tells George Naicker's brother that the parcels in the car belong to George. Keep them safe for a few days, he says, and then I will pick them up again.

The brother agrees.

The containers are then loaded in the garage. On them is written in bold capital letters: 'EXPLOSIVES'.[19]

*

The government publishes John Vorster's long-promised anti-sabotage legislation on 12 May. Known as the General Law Amendment Bill, it makes sabotage subject to the same penalties as treason: namely death, imprisonment, property confiscation and banishment.

Under its terms, if death is not invoked there is a mandatory minimum five-year prison sentence, and leniency for juveniles is prohibited.[20]

*

In the early months of 1962 there have been efforts in various parts of South Africa to get regional MK structures up and running. Joe Modise's trip to Durban earlier in the year to establish a regional command was one example. By mid-year some of the command structures are engaged in recruitment drives.

In May, Oceanic Ngoza is one of about twelve people assembled at Mgqala Mali's house in Kwazakhele outside Port Elizabeth. Mali tells them he has good news: the ANC has a new branch, a fighting branch known as Umkhonto we Sizwe. He says the National Executive Committee wants them to raise money to procure arms: implements such as saws and cutters will be required for sabotaging railway lines and telephone wires, while dynamite will have to be purchased to blow up government buildings.

Mali adds that some of those assembled will be deployed to the new military structure. He mentions Oceanic Ngoza and Meglory Magwayi. He says he does not expect anybody beyond those two to be deployed, but counsels the rest not to be worried if they don't see Ngoza and Magwayi at meetings.[21]

*

In East London the following month, Lizo Lenton Dukashe is one of about fifty people huddled in bushes just below the Esefokweni Golf Club.

Malcolmess Kondoti addresses them. He says each person must fill in volunteer forms and contribute twenty cents to the fund. Washington Bongco and Steve Tshwete begin distributing the forms.

Reginald Mdube fills in his form. After so doing he is sworn in by Kondoti. The ceremony involves Mdube clenching his right fist, raising it and saying, 'Amandla Wetu.'

The process is repeated with each recruit.[22]

*

Meanwhile, Ahmed Kathrada introduces taxi operator Essop Suleiman to Walter Sisulu, explaining that he is an ANC leader and he will want to engage Suleiman's Combis to convey passengers.

Sisulu then tells Suleiman that he wants people conveyed to the border so that they can proceed to Kenya and Tanganyika.[23]

*

Isaac Rani and Alfred Jantjies are both members of the ANC Youth League, which is now operating under the name of the 'African Youth League' due to the ban on the mother organisation. At Bellville Station in the Western Cape on Wednesday 13 June, they are waiting on a platform in the company of a third youngster, Goodman Saula.

At 10.30 a.m. a train arrives from Cape Town and a man named Looksmart Ngudle exits from it. Ngudle joins the youngsters and tells them to be on the look-out for another train that will arrive shortly. On that train will be tickets hanging outside with the names 'Rona', 'Sozo' and 'Mzwake'.

Ngudle buys a packet of cigarettes and writes a Johannesburg address on the inside of the container. He says that if nobody shows up to meet them at the station in Johannesburg, they must proceed to this address. The address is Commissioner Street, Commercial Trading Company, 39B. Ngudle says they must show this to Khandilal Moodley.

The train arrives at 10.55 a.m.

When the train approaches Park Station in Johannesburg the following day, the youngsters are now each wearing black ties and armbands by which they can be identified.

They disembark and wait a while. Concluding that nobody is coming to meet them, they adopt the fall-back suggested by Ngudle and approach a policeman who points them to the place where taxis can be hired.

When the trio arrive at their destination, Khandilal Moodley tells them Sisulu is sick and Hodgson unavailable.

Instead, a man named Khumalo comes to collect them. He escorts them to a place called Marabi Hotel in Orlando, Soweto.

There they find eleven or twelve other recruits originating from Port Elizabeth and Durban, including Nganzile Nkaba, 'Bhengu', Philemon Beyela, Matthews Ngcobo, 'Eric', Alfred Khonza, Maxwell Mayekiso, Ernest Malgaz, Jack Ndzuzo, Matthews Makhalima and Macdonald Masala.[24]

*

Nelson Mandela meets David Astor, the editor of the *Observer*, at his house in London on 15 June. They are in the company of the journalist Colin Legum and the Anglican priest Reverend Michael Scott.

Mandela outlines his perspective on the situation in South Africa. Then the group converses at length about the ANC. Mandela raises his concern about recent editorials in the *Observer* that he feels tilted in the PAC's favour and implied the ANC was a spent force.

Astor meanwhile suggests Mandela speak to certain British politicians during his time in England.

Just after midday two days later, Mandela meets British Labour Party leader Hugh Gaitskell in the company of Labour politician Denis Healey.

Then at 6 p.m. Mandela and Healey meet Jo Grimond, leader of the Liberal Party.[25]

*

By this time, Nelson Mandela is top of the South African Security Branch's most-wanted list. At 10 p.m. on 20 June, two policemen arrive at his house in Orlando. A female relative opens the door. When they indicate they want to search the house, she asks them for a warrant. They don't have one, but proceed to ransack the house anyway. As the policemen try to confiscate some books from a shelf, the relative snatches them back. A dispute ensues, during which a blast is heard emanating from outside.

Winnie Mandela returns home in the company of a neighbour to find the two policemen in the street, brandishing their revolvers. While they were inside the house, the motorcycle on which the policemen arrived was set alight and exploded when the flames reached the petrol tank. The only clues they have are car tyre marks leading away from the wreck. They have no choice but to walk home through the township.

Winnie Mandela tells a *Sunday Times* reporter on Saturday the 23rd that 'The police have been making visits and searches at my house almost every night for three weeks. Whenever my children and I are about to sleep, security branch people arrive. They ask me where my husband is and sometimes search the house. Sometimes they joke and at other times they are aggressive, which frightens the children. There are rumours Nelson is back, but I have not seen or heard from him.'

The interview appears in a report the following day which confirms that an extensive investigation was launched by the Security Branch in May after strong rumours emerged in the townships that Mandela (who, the reporter notes, has been dubbed the 'Scarlet Pimpernel of Africa' by his pursuers because of his exploits across the continent) is either back in the country or seeking temporary refuge in a neighbouring territory.[26]

*

On Tuesday 26 June, Nelson Mandela arrives in Addis Ababa in Oliver Tambo's company, having flown from Khartoum.

Two days later, at the headquarters of the Ethiopian Riot Battalion, Mandela meets Colonel Tadesse, Colonel Bekele and Lieutenant Wondoni Befikadu of the Ethiopian Army.

Mandela's training begins the following day when Lieutenant Befikadu introduces him to demolition work.[27]

*

On Sunday 1 July, Elias Motsoaledi is waiting at the Marabi Hotel when a group including Isaac Rani, Matthews Makhalima, Maxwell Mayekiso, Ernest Malgaz, Jack Ndzuzo and Alfred Khonza returns.

Motsoaledi tells them to have supper first, but that he would like to see them afterwards. He then leaves with Makhalima.

Motsoaledi comes back after supper and tells the youngsters to collect their bags. With him leading the way, a group fourteen to fifteen strong leaves the hotel, turns right, crosses some railway tracks and approaches a tall, double-storey house near the railway lines.

At this house, the group goes upstairs. There they find a group seated, among which are ANC members Johnny Makhathini and Joseph Jack. After waiting for a while the group heads back downstairs.

Outside the building they find a Chevrolet panel van and two Volkswagen Combis. Joe Modise is waiting by the vehicles with Essop Suleiman (the taxi operator enlisted by Ahmed Kathrada), Ebrahim Suleiman (Essop's brother) and a coloured man named Piet Coetzee. There are about thirty recruits waiting to board.

When Alfred Jantjies sees his colleagues boarding the vehicles, he follows suit, entering the Combi behind the panel van.

The vehicles travel in convoy until they reach a pole lying across the road, obstructing further progress. Jantjies's Combi leads the way and is close to the pole when it stops.

The driver has travelled further than the agreed stopping point. It is a mistake he has made before. Shortly afterwards Modise arrives in one of the following vehicles and admonishes the driver: 'Man, you may not drive to here. This is not the first time you have driven to here. Why did you stop here?'

The driver reverses.

The recruits deposit all of their belongings in one of the Combis. Then, in the dark, Modise leads them through the bush on foot and across the South Africa–Bechuanaland border near Zeerust, a short distance from the official crossing.[28]

*

At 1.30 a.m. on 12 July, J.J. Matoti, former chief organiser of the ANC in East London but now Transkei leader Kaiser Matanzima's representative in the city, is woken from his sleep at his home at No. 404 Mtyeku Street when his bedroom window shakes before bursting open.

He goes to the broken window to investigate, and then makes for the bedroom door. Before he gets there, a bottle comes flying through the window and lands under the bed, where it explodes, burning the inside of his left leg.

'It's burning!' he shouts, and opens the door.

He exits his house and sees two people running. He gives chase. Matoti can't make out the identity of the one closest to the fence, but the nearer man looks very much like Malcolmess Kondoti, his former colleague in the ANC.[29]

*

In Dar es Salaam Nelson Mandela meets a group of twenty-one recruits, including some of those who left Marabi Hotel at the end of June.

A ceremony is held at which a goat is slaughtered. Mandela tells them about his experiences in Ethiopia. He says he received training there and has arranged for them to obtain the same.[30]

*

On 20 July, Theophilus 'T.T.' Cholo, Patrick Baphela and Johanna Buthelezi fly from Lobatse to Mbeya in an aeroplane chartered by Bechuanaland Safaris.[31]

On the following morning Cholo waits at Mbeya Airport. He meets Nelson Mandela, who arrives on a plane with Oliver Tambo.[32]

Fish Keitseng is waiting at Mbeya's Railway Hotel when Mandela shows up a while later in Tambo's company. The three hold a discussion that runs through the night.

Keitseng tells them he thinks travelling back through Bechuanaland will be risky because the Boers are everywhere in Lobatse looking for Mandela day and night.

Mandela says he is returning regardless.

Keitseng suggests they land in Kanye rather than Lobatse.[33]

*

On 23 July, Fish Keitseng and Nelson Mandela board a plane piloted by Herbert Bartaune, who lands them in Kanye in southern Bechuanaland. Waiting on the airfield are two men, Mr Innes-Kerr from the Bechuanaland Special Branch, and Mr Grant, the district commissioner of Gaborone.

While disembarking, Mandela overhears Grant saying to Innes-Kerr, 'Who is he? A big man?'

Innes-Kerr speaks for the Bechuanaland officials. He first greets Keitseng and then Mandela, who responds: 'I'm not Mr Mandela. I'm David Motsamayi.'

'No, can you give us your real name?' says Innes-Kerr.

'That's my real name.'

'No, we have come here to meet Mr Mandela. Aren't you Mandela?'

'No, I have given you a name.'

'No, we have instructions to come and meet Mr Mandela, and even to help him. But if of course you are not Mr Mandela then I must arrest you, because you have no permit to enter this country.

'Honestly, Mr Keitseng,' Innes-Kerr continues, 'I know you're coming and I know you're Mr Mandela. I think I must do something about you.'

'Well, if you insist that I am Mandela, then I won't challenge that.'

'No, we expected you yesterday. Can I give you a lift, because I think that your chaps are aware that you are going to land here, but they are late.'

Innes-Kerr drives Mandela, Keitseng and Grant in the direction of Lobatse. Fifteen miles out of Kanye, Mandela and Keitseng see the vehicle that was supposed to collect them at the landing strip approaching.

In that other car are Jonas Matlou and Joe Modise. They follow the car driven by Innes-Kerr, which stops at Jonas Matlou's place in Lobatse.

'Look the South African Police know that you are coming back,' Innes-Kerr tells Mandela. 'Be very careful; I would suggest that you leave tomorrow.' He then drives off with Grant, leaving Mandela behind.

Though Innes-Kerr has been the model of friendliness and cordiality, Mandela doesn't trust him. He says to Matlou and Modise: 'Let me leave tonight. I don't know what they have planned tomorrow.'

Mandela fetches some clothes and leaves the property. He was at Matlou's house for barely five minutes.

A white man named Cecil Williams has come to Bechuanaland. Mandela, who is dressed in a khaki outfit, gets into Williams's car and is driven by him into South Africa.[34]

*

Joe Slovo tells his wife Ruth First that a conference of people working in the SACP and the ANC is about to take place.

The couple travel to Liliesleaf Farm in Rivonia on the morning of Saturday 28 July 1962. Nelson Mandela is there. Among those present while Mandela gives a briefing about his overseas trip are Moses Kotane, Michael Harmel, Duma Nokwe, Rusty Bernstein, Walter Sisulu, Govan Mbeki, Mark Shope, Dan Tloome, J.B. Marks, Ahmed Kathrada and two Africans from Durban.

Mandela offers a general overview of his travels. He itemises the monies received and the offers of training that were extended. He speaks about the reservations that were expressed about the ANC's cooperation with whites, Indians and especially communists.

He explains that Tambo and he feel that the ANC has to appear more independent in order to reassure the organisation's new allies, since they would ultimately be the ones training and financing Umkhonto we Sizwe. Mandela proposes reshaping the Congress Alliance to ensure the ANC is seen to clearly be the leader, particularly on issues affecting Africans directly.

At the conclusion of the conference the following day, Mandela says he wants to report to Chief Luthuli in order to clarify the situation regarding the reports that surfaced while he was away that he had deviated from the ANC's historical position of non-racialism because of criticisms of that policy by African leaders.

When he leaves Liliesleaf Farm for Natal in the company of Cecil Williams later that night, Mandela poses as a chauffeur.[35]

*

When the two leaders meet in a house in Tongaat on 1 August, Albert Luthuli tells Nelson Mandela that he doesn't like the idea of foreign politicians dictating policy. The ANC has developed its policy of non-racialism for good reasons; it should not be changed because it doesn't suit a few foreign politicians.

Mandela replies: It is not that foreign politicians are dictating policy; it's that they don't understand it. He explains that he would like to make cosmetic changes that would render the policy more comprehensible to them. This is necessary because if the African states opt to support the PAC, an insignificant organisation could become a force to be reckoned with.[36]

*

Billy Nair drives his colleagues on the Natal Regional Command to Reservoir Hills, Durban. When the car stops, Nair indicates that they must enter a certain house.

At the house, an Indian woman greets the group. Curnick Ndlovu, the chairman of the Regional Command, is present, as is Bruno Mtolo, who hears Nair speaking to the lady in an Indian language. Then another woman enters. When the members of the command are all seated, Nelson Mandela emerges, clad in a traditional Arabic gown.

'Salaam Alaikum,' he greets them. He then asks whether they are all members of the Regional Command. When they respond in the affirmative, he says he is glad, and also glad that they are young men and not old men.

Mandela says that before he discusses any complaints, he wants to tell them that he has been abroad, where he met leaders of African states who all expressed sympathetic feelings towards the South African people. They asked why the ANC has decided to fight the government. He mentions that he has been to Algeria where he met Ben Bella and was introduced to the Algerian Army. He further states that he has collected £30,000 from those visits.

Turning to the issue of the armed struggle, he says it is not sufficient for Umkhonto we Sizwe to only engage in sabotage; it will need to train people militarily. Sabotage was the first stage of operations, but it is necessary to proceed to guerrilla warfare, which is the second stage. Mandela mentions that he is visiting them on behalf of the National High Command, to whom he will report back.

Concerning the second stage, Mandela says it would not be a campaign to take lives, nor would it be a war against whites; instead it would be aimed at overthrowing the regime. Cadres trained abroad would have to be politicised. He says a first-class military man who is politically unconscious could end up launching indiscriminate attacks.

Mandela tells them that the educational threshold for recruits should be raised to Standard 6 but the age qualification should remain from sixteen upwards.[37]

*

Mandela is wearing his white chauffeur's dust coat on the afternoon of 5 August 1962 as Cecil Williams drives him in an Austin motor car.

They pass through Howick from Durban, and at Cedara, a town just past Howick, Mandela notices a Ford V8 full of white men move to overtake. Mandela looks behind and sees two more cars filled with white men.

When in front of the Austin, the Ford signals to them to stop. There is a steep, wooded bank to the left. Williams slows down, turns to Mandela and asks, 'Who are these men?'

Mandela remains silent.

A tall, thin, unshaven man approaches the car on the passenger's side, and at the window introduces himself to Mandela as Sergeant Vorster of the Pietermaritzburg Police. He produces an arrest warrant and asks Mandela to identify himself.

Mandela says he is David Motsamayi.

Vorster nods and asks a few questions about where they have been and about their destination.

After a while, however, Vorster just says, 'Ag, you're Nelson Mandela, and this is Cecil Williams, and you are under arrest. We'll have to turn back and go to Pieter-maritzburg. The Sergeant – the Major will get into your car, the back of your car. You can just drive back.'[38]

*

In Dar es Salaam on the same day, Isaac Rani is part of a group waiting in the ANC office when Tennyson Makiwane arrives and escorts them to another building in the complex. In this other building they receive injections for yellow fever and smallpox.

Then Joseph Jack comes and takes them to the immigration office, where they have passports made.

Later, while the group eats, Oliver Tambo, Tennyson Makiwane and James Hadebe arrive. Tambo beckons members of the group to him individually.

When Alfred Jantjies's turn comes, Tambo says: 'Look, tomorrow you will depart, you must not tell your friends, even if he sleeps alongside and next to you. You must quietly stand up and go.'

At 5 a.m. the following morning, fifteen recruits, including Rani, Jantjies, Matthews Makhalima, Maxwell Mayekiso, James Chirwa, Ernest Malgaz, Jack Ndzuzo, Alfred Khonza and Macdonald Masala, quietly stand up in their communal sleeping quarters and depart the yard of Princess Margaret Hospital.

Oliver Tambo and Tennyson Makiwane meet them in a car on the tar road, and transport the group to Makiwane's house.

There Makiwane informs them that they will be trained as soldiers in Ethiopia: 'Look, you're going away today, and where you are going, you must show respect.'

The group leave for the bus terminus and board a bus for Nairobi. Upon arrival in the Kenyan capital they are met by Henry Fazzie, who leads them to a hotel, where they meet another smaller group of ANC recruits.

On the evening of 10 August, Macdonald Masala arrives at the hotel to inform the group, which now numbers twenty, that they will depart at seven the following morning.

The next day, at the designated pick-up point, the twenty men are collected in a Combi and taken to the airport.

After filling in various forms, they board an aeroplane that takes them to Debre Zeyit in Ethiopia. When they exit the plane, they are met by 'Lieutenant Kubana', who is accompanied by a man in civilian clothes. The cadres are then taken in a van to a camp where they find Ethiopian soldiers waiting for them.[39]

SOLDIERS OF MANDELA

Oliver Tambo and Tennyson Makiwane are joined by the ANC's other representatives abroad, namely Robert Resha, James Hadebe and Mzwai Piliso, at a meeting held in Dar es Salaam on 15 August.

At the end of this meeting, the five leaders of the ANC's 'External Mission' issue a statement. It reads:

the arrest of Nelson Mandela marks the beginning of a chapter in the bitter struggle for freedom. For Mandela symbolises a historic phase in our struggle. In this situation the African people cannot be expected to fold their arms and look to the skies for help when their very manhood is attacked. It is the sacred duty of the African people to mobilise their forces and resist this tyranny. We know we are facing a ruthless and formidable enemy but the Nationalist Party Government is not invincible and never will be. Thus the certainty of our victory is not in doubt.[1]

*

Peter Mogano, who was chairman of the ANC in Pretoria before it was banned, converses with John Masupye outside the bottle store in Pretoria where Mogano works. Mogano asks whether Masupye has a target that can be attacked.

Masupye suggests the synagogue on the corner of Paul Kruger and Struben Streets. 'Why pick on that?'

Masupye says because Mandela is going to be tried there, as will other members of Umkhonto we Sizwe if arrested. The Treason Trial was also held there. Therefore it should be destroyed if possible. 'What do *you* think about it?' he asks.

'No, I am asking you,' says Mogano.

Masupye confirms that he would like to make it his first target in Pretoria.

Mogano responds: 'You pick your target, and then you spy around your target, and consider everything in the vicinity. The most important consideration is that you must see that there will be no person in the close vicinity or inside that could be killed or injured.'[2]

*

Meanwhile, in Durban, Curnick Ndlovu presides over a meeting of the Natal Command. Billy Nair is present. So are Ronnie Kasrils and Bruno Mtolo, the two command members tasked earlier in the year with establishing four-person cells throughout the region. Kasrils is the member of the command now responsible for liaison with the subordinate cells.

In the meeting it is decided that Kasrils must contact the cells and instruct them to identify targets that can be attacked with petrol bombs to protest the arrest of Mandela.[3]

*

Towards the end of September Kasrils meets Solomon Mbanjwa and informs him that he has been appointed a 'platoon' leader in the Natal region.

When the two meet again early the following month, Kasrils orders Mbanjwa's section to identify some signal wires at Georgedale and Hammarsdale Stations that can be cut the coming Sunday.

At 1 p.m. that Sunday, 14 October, Mbanjwa arrives at a kraal belonging to Joshua Zulu. He finds Zulu and Matthews Meyiwa already there. Mbanjwa's platoon consists of five people including himself. Zakhela Mdlalose and Bernard Nkosi, the remaining two members, arrive at the kraal shortly thereafter.

Later the same day, Natoo Babenia, Ebrahim Ismail Ebrahim, Debanathan Perumal and Sonny Singh depart from Babenia's house in Durban's North Street.

In Alice Street, Singh and Ebrahim proceed to a passage leading on to the offices of A.S. Kajee, a businessman and member of the South African Indian Organisation, which eschews protest in favour of working to obtain the best deal for Indians within the framework of segregated institutions. Perumal waits at the entrance to the passage, and Babenia at the bus stop near the corner of Alice and Albert Streets.

A few minutes later, Ebrahim and Singh come running out in the direction of Grey Street. Babenia follows.

Perumal does the same, but when he enters Grey Street he cannot find the others, so he returns to Albert Street and proceeds to his home in Darby Street.

When Perumal arrives home, Ebrahim emerges at his gate and says Babenia and Singh are waiting at Regent Outfitters.

Perumal asks what happened.

Ebrahim says they were disturbed by a nightwatchman.[4]

*

The evening of the 14th sees the weather turn rainy and misty in the Durban area, so Solomon Mbanjwa opts to stay at home rather than conduct his operation.[5]

*

From the Regent Outfitters, Perumal, Babenia, Ebrahim and Singh head towards the Durban municipal bus depot. They see it is well guarded, so they go to Durban Central Railway Station instead.

At the station, Perumal and Ebrahim look at the train times while Perumal purchases tickets to Effingham on the North Coast line.

At about 9 p.m., the four board the train for Effingham. There are only two passengers in their third-class coach at the time: an Indian and an old African. The four sit next to the door.

As the train leaves the station, Babenia heads to the toilet. When he returns to his colleagues, Ebrahim takes a bottle from him and puts it under the chair opposite them.

The men have by this stage captured the attention of a group of Indians who have entered the same coach on their way home from work.

As the train brakes when pulling in to Churchill Station, Singh, who is hiding his face behind a newspaper, suddenly sees Ebrahim and Babenia running out of the coach. Singh and Perumal also jump out of the coach. They cross an overhead bridge and disappear. Realising something is amiss, the other passengers begin to panic.

Soon after 10 p.m. the bomb explodes inside the coach. The train is moving at the time. No one is hurt and there is only slight damage to the compartment.[6]

*

On 21 October, Wolfie Kodesh buys a copy of the *Sunday Times* bearing the headline 'Police hunt Kathrada and Sisulu' on its front page and brings it to the underground conference which Ahmed Kathrada and Walter Sisulu are also attending.

The report says Kathrada – whom it identifies as being an executive member of the 'Free Mandela' committee – and Sisulu are being sought for house arrest.

When Nelson Mandela's trial begins the following day at the Old Synagogue in Pretoria, Ahmed Kathrada enters the building. Sergeant Dirker recognises him and beckons him, but Kathrada ignores this gesture.

In the gallery of the court during the tea break, Kathrada is speaking to Winnie Mandela when three Special Branch detectives approach.

Kathrada heads to speak to Nelson Mandela in the dock. Sergeant Dirker follows and thrusts a house arrest order at him.

Kathrada asks that Dirker read the restriction out loud.

In faltering English, Dirker says the order will last for five years; that Kathrada's freedom to leave his flat will be limited to between 7 a.m. and 6 p.m.; that he will have to report at Security Branch headquarters between twelve and two o'clock every day; and that he will have to leave the court at once because the order is of immediate effect.[7]

*

Two days later in Lobatse, Walter Sisulu tells G.A. Forrest, an interviewing officer in the Bechuanaland police force, that he entered Bechuanaland through Tlokweng Gate at 10 a.m. the day before, in Govan Mbeki and Daniel Tloome's company. They immediately travelled to Fish Keitseng's house, but upon discovering that he had been arrested in Southern Rhodesia, they proceeded to Jonas Matlou's.

Forrest asks if there will be a meeting in Lobatse.

Sisulu says that the ANC executive decided to hold a private consultative meeting of the movement at Keitseng's house two months earlier. The aim of the meeting will be to finalise arrangements for an international conference to be held in an African territory.

He adds that he is expecting thirty senior members to attend. These include Moses Kotane and Tom Nkobi from South Africa, Joe Matthews and Dr Letele from Bechuanaland, and Oliver Tambo, Robert Resha, Tennyson Makiwane, Mzwai Piliso and Moses Mabhida from overseas. Govan Mbeki will chair the proceedings and all delegates will return home shortly after the meeting.[8]

The day after this interview, Sisulu returns to Johannesburg in order to comply with his house-arrest order.[9]

*

Bechuanaland's security police are in attendance on the morning of Saturday 27 October when the ANC's consultative meeting in Lobatse begins. Govan Mbeki delivers the opening remarks before Oliver Tambo gives a report on the External Mission's work outside the country. Dan Tloome then gives the National Executive Committee's report, followed by addresses from the various heads of the ANC's area committees in the Transkei, Ciskei, Transvaal and Natal on work being done by the organisation in rural areas. When Moses Kotane reads the organisational report, he says the new situation will demand greater loyalty, discipline and vigilance from members, and he warns of the dangers of loose talk and gossip. Mark Shope then reports on trade-union matters. Discussions continue until the meeting's adjournment at 7.30 p.m.

There is a night sitting of the meeting that continues till dawn. This time the police are not in attendance.

On the morning of the 28th, the head of the Bechuanaland Security Branch hands Govan Mbeki, the conference chairman, a transcript of the previous day's proceedings.

But the transcript does not feature information from the night sitting, where delegates discussed the matters that they did not want the British authorities to hear. The conference resumes, with the police in attendance once again. The main topic of discussion on the Sunday is cooperation between the ANC and its Youth League.[10]

*

Owing to Walter Sisulu's house arrest, when Govan Mbeki returns to South Africa he moves from Port Elizabeth to Johannesburg to reinforce the ANC Secretariat.[11]

*

Vuyisile Mini of the MK Port Elizabeth command, who was a delegate at the Lobatse Conference, addresses the East London Regional Committee. Reginald Mdube is present, along with his colleagues Malcolmess Kondoti, Washington Bongco, Douglas Sparks, Steve Tshwete and Lunglo Dwaba.

Mini's briefing touches on matters discussed during the conference's night-time sitting. He tells them that the final agreement at Lobatse was that sabotage should be carried out within the country, with the ANC thereby formally associating itself with the armed struggle and moving beyond the hitherto held position of MK being an autonomous body.

Mini says that the East London structures will have to attack police stations in their area. He asks if Tshwete and Dwaba have prepared the maps.

Kondoti says not yet.

Mini urges that these maps be completed, because firearms needed to attack the police are obtainable from those stations.[12]

*

The Natal Regional Command also meets. Billy Nair, Curnick Ndlovu, Ronnie Kasrils and Bruno Mtolo are present.

They are also under pressure from above to step up their activity. Nair says he has received a letter from the National High Command asking what they are waiting for. They have everything – dynamite and detonators – and ought to be using them.[13]

*

When Billy Nair arrives by car at George Naicker's place on 1 November, he finds Ronnie Kasrils and Bruno Mtolo are already there waiting for him. Nair has keys for the garage. Inside, Nair goes to the bin and retrieves three cardboard containers. He hands Mtolo and Kasrils one each and takes the third himself. The three men then depart.

Between seven and eight that evening, Solomon Mbanjwa and Bafana Duma are waiting by a road near an electricity pylon in New Germany when a black motor car arrives, driven by Ronnie Kasrils. Bruno Mtolo emerges from it with a kitbag slung over one shoulder and a brown parcel in the other hand.

Kasrils departs, after which Mtolo leads Mbanjwa and Duma into the bush. There Mtolo tells them in a light whisper that the work on the pylon must be complete by nine o'clock and that the explosion must coincide with Ronnie's in Pinetown and Billy's in Montclair.

At about 8 p.m. George Naicker, Ebrahim Ismail Ebrahim and Kisten Moonsamy are waiting across the road from the Indian School in Mobeni. Billy Nair arrives driving a black Morris 1000. The three enter the car and see a large sealed carton box in the back seat.

Nair drives the group to Umhlatuzana Road. The four get out, and as soon as they do so, Nair produces four pairs of rubber gloves. The group then take it in turns carrying the box up to the pylon.

At the pylon the box stands open and Naicker sees it contains dynamite sticks. They are brownish in colour, ten inches long and an inch in diameter. They resemble candles. Some have holes about the width of a lead pencil running through the middle.

These sticks are then divided into those with holes running through and those without. Both types are given to each member.

Using black insulation tape, they each form bundles of sticks and begin taping them to the feet of the concrete and the steel pylons.

This done, cordtex is threaded through those sticks of dynamite that have holes.

Meanwhile, between 8 and 8.30 p.m, Bruno Mtolo leads Bafana Duma and Solomon Mbanjwa to the pylon in New Germany.

When they arrive, Mtolo puts the kitbag and parcel down. From the kitbag he withdraws three pairs of rubber gloves. He, Duma and Mbanjwa each put on a pair. Mtolo then withdraws three sticks of dynamite with holes in them. He threads long cordtex wires through each of the sticks.

Later, when he has finished attaching the sticks to the pylons, Mtolo produces a plastic capsule and pours acid from a bottle into it. He closes the capsule and inserts it into a larger capsule, which he places on a small dish containing powder. The group then collect their belongings and run in the direction of Claremont bus rank.

On the way there, Duma disappears.

Mbanjwa and Mtolo wait at the bus rank. At about ten o'clock, they hear an explosion from the direction of the pylon. Despite taking damage, the pylon has not been overturned by the blast.

At approximately the same time, in the leg of the operation overseen by Ronnie Kasrils, an eighty-foot pylon carrying 88,000 volts near the Umgeni power station in Pinetown is dynamited. The explosion likewise fails to fell the pylon, but damages three of its four steel legs, causing a power failure lasting up to an hour in several parts of the city.

In Montclair, the pylon attacked by Billy Nair's group has been overturned by the dynamite explosion.[14]

*

The state imposes further restrictive measures on opposition activists. Walter Sisulu and Ahmed Kathrada had been served with overnight house-arrest orders in October.

On 9 November the government issues its first twenty-four-hour house-arrest orders. Among the affected are Michael Harmel and Jack Hodgson.[15]

*

At around 8 p.m. on 17 November 1962, Victor Tonjeni, an ambassador of Chief Matanzima in East London, goes to bed at his home at No. 717 Meki Street in Duncan Village.

Washington Bongco and Reginald Mdube of the East London MK Regional Committee are in the company of a number of youngsters in the bush at Gubasama on the outskirts of Duncan Village.

Following the pattern of the attack on J.J. Matoti earlier in the year, the plan is again to assault homes belonging to individuals whom they associate with the system. Bongco divides the recruits into two groups and says that one section will go to Tonjeni's and the other to Dyani's. The groups must burn the houses to the ground with their petrol bombs because Tonjeni and Dyani are informers. Bongco says that after the operations they should gather at Mdube's place.

Bandile Magxengane is part of the group that departs for the operation on Tonjeni's house. At one point in their advance, Monde, another member of the unit, points to a house about twenty yards away. He says to Magxengane: That's Tonjeni's. At this point, however, a motor car approaches, upon which Magxengane lies flat on the ground while his colleagues run for cover.

With Magxengane no longer present, Siduma Tanana, another member of the group, continues with the operation alongside two other colleagues, namely Zola Mjo and Nkoko. Tanana takes a bottle and moistens it with a cloth. He gives the bottle to Mjo, who lights a match and tosses the cocktail at a window of the house.

It is about midnight and Victor Tonjeni is woken by the sound of a window breaking in his living room. He sees the house burning but manages to escape the flames.[16]

*

The sabotage campaign has thus far been waged by units trained internally, often in the use of self-made weapons. This pattern is about to change. In November in Debre Zeyit, the Fazzie–Rani–Jantjies–Chirwa group of twenty are addressed by an Ethiopian colonel, having completed their three-month training course. He greets them and thanks them for the way they have behaved. He says henceforth they are brothers and that should there be any problems they must let him know.

He then departs.[17]

*

The operations in Natal on 14 October, which inaugurated the post-Mandela-arrest phase of the armed struggle in the province, were not wholly successful. On 9 December, the Regional Command endeavours to put that right.

At 5 p.m., about five minutes after planting explosives next to the door of the offices of A.S. Kajee in Alice Street, Natoo Babenia, Ebrahim Ismail Ebrahim, Debanathan Perumal and Sonny Singh run through the busy streets of Durban. Moments later they hear a huge explosion, which destroys Kajee's offices.

Then, just after 6 p.m., Solomon Mbanjwa heads to the railway line near Webber's Store. He is carrying an old cocoa tin. He is first to arrive. Later Bernard Nkosi, Matthews Meyiwa, Joshua Zulu and Zakhela Mdlalose join him.

The five walk past a pylon, and then up to the top of a bank, where they sit. Mbanjwa takes two pairs of rubber gloves out of his pocket and hands one of them to Bernard Nkosi. After Mbanjwa has put the other pair on himself, he takes out two sticks of dynamite as well as cordtex from the parcel the others have brought with them. He threads the cordtex into one stick of dynamite until the metal point at the end of the cordtex is reached. He then ties the cordtex to the dynamite stick with insulation tape.

This is all done while they are sitting at the top of the bank together. When the wiring is complete, Mbanjwa and Nkosi take leave of the others and proceed down to the target.

With Nkosi's aid, Mbanjwa plasters bundles of dynamite to the pylon's two uprights. While they are doing this, a black man appears along the railway line, walking towards Cliffdale from Hammarsdale. A colleague from the bank shouts that a person is coming.

Mbanjwa tells Nkosi they should turn their backs so the person cannot see their faces.

They do this.

When the person reaches the scene he stands, looks at the cordtex, looks at the group, and appears as though he is going to speak, but he says nothing. He follows the path that leads past Meyiwa, Zulu and Mdlalose's position on the bank.

When he is gone, Nkosi and Mbanjwa carry on.

When finished they pick up everything and head up to the little knoll which offers a vantage point overlooking the scene.

Twenty minutes later they see a fire on the pylon. At that exact time a passenger train passes from Cliffdale to Hammarsdale. As the train passes it looks as though the fire has been extinguished, but shortly after the train has passed there is an explosion.

Then the five all flee towards their respective homes.[18]

*

With MK's first anniversary approaching, Washington Bongco, Reginald Mdube, John Mynute, 'Zola', 'Majojo', 'Monte' and 'Mbuse' of the MK structure in East London gather at Tamsanqa Selani's home at No. 907 Gubusana Street in Duncan Village. It is the evening of Thursday 13 December.

Mdube is in possession of two bottles and he asks Selani if he has a third. Selani does have one and he hands it over before returning to the Primus stove where his food is cooking.

From the kitchen Selani smells petrol. He turns and sees Bongco in the other room pouring petrol into the bottles from a one-gallon tin.

Bongco comes to the kitchen and asks for three cups of water. Selani obliges.

At about 11.30 p.m. two days later, Inkie Hoyi, the East London representative of Chief Archibald Velile Sandile of the Rharhabe branch of the Xhosa royal house, retires to bed at his home at No. 774 Kwinana Street in Duncan Village. The windows of the house are closed, as are both kitchen doors, the door to his bedroom and that of the bedroom next to his room. In this adjacent bedroom, his granddaughter Linda and niece Daphne, aged ten and fourteen, are asleep.

A policeman is seated just outside the house's front door. His tunic and helmet are inside the property. Only the lower half of the front door is closed; the upper half stands open.

During the night, Hoyi is woken by a bang, and after a second thud he gets out of bed. He realises his blankets are burning and he can smell petrol. He runs to the bedroom where the two girls are. Through the gaps in the closed door he can see that the room is engulfed in flames. He can smell the smoke. Hoyi tries to open the door and shouts 'Open the door!' in expectation that the policeman at the front door will hear. Hoyi eventually manages to open the door but suffers burns on his hands and upper lip in the process.

He gets the children out alive, but they have suffered severe burns. To her uncle, Daphne Hoyi's face looks 'like a piece of meat' (she has burns over 85 per cent of her body and will die five days later; Linda will die in just over a year).

Shortly after exiting the bedroom he meets the policeman in the living room on his way to investigate. The policeman tries to blow his whistle, but Hoyi says, 'it's no good now, it is too late; I have been calling you for a long time.'

Minutes after midnight, Donald Card arrives at Hoyi's home. Card finds three panes of glass have been broken out of a large window. The rest of the panes are charred black. Both inside and outside the room he finds pieces of what appear to be brandy bottles. He recovers the tops of two bottles. He can see they have been sealed with corks that were tied on to the bottles with string. There is a strong smell of petrol inside the room. The bedding, clothing and furniture have all been burnt.[19]

*

When the National High Command issues a statement marking Umkhonto we Sizwe's first anniversary, many points from the previous year's founding manifesto are reprised, such as there being no alternative to armed struggle 'because almost every avenue of legal and constitutional struggle has been closed by the State'.

But there is an important difference. The hope expressed on 16 December 1961 that the first attacks might serve as a warning that would induce the government to negotiate, are replaced by a resigned acceptance of the inevitability of civil war.

The High Command calls on the masses to prepare for this second stage, saying: 'We do not believe that the acts of sabotage which we have carried out in the past year will, in themselves, crush white supremacy. We see this activity as only the beginning of a movement which will grow in size and scope and which will confront the state with a people able to resist its force and ultimately crush it.'

They conclude with the following vow, directed at the minister of justice: 'We will show you, Mr. Vorster, that the people you despise and humiliate and whom you consider as inferior, will lead S.A. to freedom, against the most barbaric regime history has seen. With all your power and strength you are a frightened man because you know it is only a matter of time.'[20]

*

On Boxing Day 1962, Caswell Nboxele is a passenger in a car heading to Mowbray Station in Cape Town. There are a number of other youngsters in the vehicle with him.

At the station they find a group from Langa waiting for them, as well as Looksmart Ngudle, with a soldier's overcoat, a beret and a military-type backpack over his shoulders. He instructs them to get into a lorry waiting nearby.

Soon afterwards another group of six arrives. They also board the vehicle. There are now twenty-three youths in the lorry altogether.

Then a white man wearing spectacles arrives. Ngudle tells them that this is one of their comrades, Denis Goldberg.

Each of the passengers has been equipped with a blanket, plate, spoon and rug. Goldberg greets them and proceeds to the front of the lorry, which pulls away.

They stop at Cardiff Marney's house in Lansdowne, where five more people board the vehicle. Four tents and a motor-car engine are also loaded.

From there they proceed to a farm in Mamre, a town to the north of Cape Town, where Goldberg instructs them to offload the tents.

When Goldberg departs again to pick up more people and equipment, Ngudle orders those left behind to erect the tents.

Later at the farm in Mamre, with the tents erected, wood removed and ground cleared, the youngsters line up in rows of five as Denis Goldberg stands facing them.

Goldberg addresses them in English, with Ngudle interpreting. He says the camp is to be run on strict military lines. They will learn how to stand to attention, and about how petrol engines, field telephones and duplicating machines work. Knowledge of all these things will be needed in a revolution.

Goldberg then forms them into two lines and says: 'I've been asked by the committee of the congressmen to take responsibility. We will have sergeants. There are all of us, and there will be sergeants. In each tent there will be a sergeant. We are going to be here ten days.'[21]

*

Three days into MK's first training camp on South African soil, on the morning of 29 December, Cardiff Marney departs to buy some food at a nearby store.

The trip alerts the local community to the group's presence.

Soon afterwards an official from the Mamre Moravian Mission Station arrives at the camp and informs the group that they are camping on trust land without permission.

The official accepts their apology.[22]

Later that day, Cardiff Marney is delivering a lecture on the operation of a petrol engine when a white man arrives. Goldberg introduces the man as Albie Sachs.

In the oppressively hot tent, Sachs delivers a lecture on the history of South Africa from the people's point of view. He speaks about the riches of the country being controlled by a minority and of the need to gain control of the mines. He mentions imports and exports and the need to make South Africa a country of the working people after freedom has been gained.

At one point in the lecture one of the trainees dozes off, upon which Ngudle flicks his arm with a thin branch to wake him up.

'If the teacher makes them fall asleep, you should hit the teacher,' Sachs quips.[23]

*

Word of the camp has spread, however. Later that day, a large police contingent led by Detective Sergeant Johannes van Wyk travels about thirty miles north of Cape Town before turning off the main road and proceeding for about two and a half miles on a dirt track through the bush. After reaching some hilltops they travel across loosely ploughed ground and descend until they reach a ravine. A fence with barbed wire blocks the vehicles' further advance, so the policemen disembark, climb over the fence and get to the other side of the ravine. They march until they see five military-type tents in the distance. There is a group of black and coloured youths at the camp. One of the tents is flapped open, and Van Wyk approaches it.

Hanging on the pole is a notice that contains a daily programme. It indicates that those at the camp begin their daily tasks at 6 a.m. every morning. Thereafter, there is a period of fifteen to thirty minutes for washing and then they partake in twenty minutes' light training led by the 'Comrade Commandant', who personally supervises the bodily exercises. There are seven or eight lectures during the day and after lunch they listen to the news. A discussion is held after the news, during which notes must be taken. At 6 p.m. everybody takes supper. They then wash and from 8 to 10.30 p.m. further lectures are offered. Judo and Karate are also offered at the camp.

The tent with the notice is filled with boxes containing tinned food. In front of the tent is an engine for a lorry as well as various cards with drawings of engines. Behind one tent Van Wyk finds a hundred wine bottles. At the farm all bushes have been cleared and there are three parallel stripes that look as though they have been created by people marching in rows.

Denis Goldberg is taken aside for questioning.

He returns a while later and calls all the recruits together. He asks them to withdraw to their respective tents. Following his request, four groups take form. Altogether there are nineteen Africans, seven coloureds and one white man, Denis Goldberg. The groups each depart to one of the four tents.

In the tents Van Wyk takes their names and addresses, and searches them thoroughly. He finds that almost all have two pairs of trousers on. The concealed trousers have been fastened with rope, and in practically every case, either a dagger or a knife has been attached to the rope.[24]

After taking down all the names of the camp attendees, a policeman tells the group to either pack up or be arrested.

They decide to pack up.

On Sunday 30 December, the day after the police search, the lorry that brought the recruits to Mamre arrives to collect them.

Denis Goldberg travels with them in the back of the vehicle. He tells them they may have another opportunity to have another picnic.

On the drive home they sing 'Amajoni' ('I'm a soldier').

The youngsters are dropped off at Langa. They then form themselves into a platoon and march into the township, with one of them beating time on a paraffin tin.[25]

*

At the beginning of 1963, Joe Gqabi, Raymond Mhlaba, Wilton Mkwayi and Abel Mthembu – four of the six recruits who received training in China – are in Bechuanaland. They are minus Nandha Naidoo and Andrew Mlangeni, who went on to obtain radio training in northern China.

Joe Modise arrives to collect them in a Volkswagen, and transports them to Liliesleaf Farm in Rivonia.

Early on the morning after their arrival, they are met by Joe Slovo, who briefs them on how the work of Umkhonto we Sizwe is proceeding. He says they will have to enter various departments of MK. He instructs Abel Mthembu to join the Johannesburg Regional Command alongside Jack Hodgson and Elias Motsoaledi.[26] Then he tells Raymond Mhlaba that they have been waiting for him as, after Mandela's arrest, the position of commander of Umkhonto we Sizwe has been set aside for him.

Moses Mabhida attends another meeting at the farm shortly afterwards. Raymond Mhlaba gives the China-trained group's feedback on their experiences abroad.

He says they didn't like the way the movement's affairs were being administered in Dar es Salaam. Specifically, there was no proper recording by Tennyson Makiwane of monies received from African governments. Mhlaba claims that some ANC members are starving and Makiwane is pocketing the money. He accuses Makiwane of taking advantage of the fact that he preceded Tambo out of the country and thus formed prior links and contacts with the African governments, consequently forcing Tambo to work through him.

Mhlaba suggests sending Duma Nokwe and Moses Kotane to reinforce Tambo and ensure proper financial accounting at the Dar es Salaam headquarters.[27]

As a consequence of this meeting, Moses Kotane and Duma Nokwe arrive in Lobatse in a car driven by Joe Modise on the morning of 10 January 1963. A fourth man, Levy Mbatha, is also in the vehicle.[28]

*

Three days later, in Port Elizabeth, Sipho Irving Mango, who has agreed to be a witness in a pending sabotage trial of Umkhonto we Sizwe members, is shot and killed by a four-man assault team acting on the instructions of MK's Port Elizabeth Regional Committee, which consists of Wilson Khayingo, Zinakile Mkaba, Vuyisile Mini and one other.[29]

*

Justice Mpanza, Shadrack Maphumulo and Michael Mvula are at the back of the Argyle Hotel on Clarke Street in Durban on the evening of 18 January. A paper carrier bag with cords on top lies open in front of them. It contains red rubber gloves, a green cord and a rectangular black parcel that is three by eight inches, and four inches high. Maphumulo tries to put on the gloves but struggles, so Mvula assists.

The group then proceeds to Umbilo Road, where Mpanza and Maphumulo creep towards a building that houses the National Party's regional offices as well as its newspaper in the province, the *Nataller*. Mvula is on the other side of the road. Mpanza and Maphumulo see a nightwatchman sitting on the opposite side on a wooden box. He doesn't seem to be paying attention.

At the target building, Mpanza places five cylindrical sticks of dynamite against the front wall. He then attaches a detonator with a fuse, and leads the fuse along the wall of the building. He does this out of sight of traffic.

While Maphumulo holds the fuse, Mpanza slices it at close to a forty-five-degree angle. Mpanza fills a capsule with acid and places it into a match box containing white powder. He then clamps the cut part of the fuse into the match box.

'We have ten minutes,' Mpanza says, placing the box carefully on the floor. They swiftly depart.[30]

*

Eric Stanley, his wife and their children are singing hymns as they walk down Umbilo Road on their way back from church at 9.20 that evening.

All of a sudden they hear a bang from a nearby explosion. Mrs Stanley suffers a cut on her leg. Eric Stanley picks her up, dashes round the corner, places her on the bonnet of a car, and tells his daughter to phone for an ambulance. He then stops the first car that comes. The driver has a first-aid kit and bandages Stanley's wife's foot.

At the scene of the explosion, the *Nataller* newspaper's printing room, which lies below ground level, is damaged. Five heavy concrete louvres from the building are lying in the street. There is wrecked office equipment inside and the surrounding cars and buildings have been extensively damaged.[31]

*

Oliver Tambo and Tennyson Makiwane meanwhile arrive at a house just outside Dar es Salaam. It is approaching midday.

The group of twenty who trained in Ethiopia the previous year are there. Makiwane picks out nine, namely Henry Fazzie, Isaac Rani, James Chirwa, Alfred Jantjies, Alfred Khonza, Matthews Makhalima, Ernest Malgaz, Maxwell Mayekiso and Jack Ndzuzo. He appoints Fazzie their leader.

Fazzie then takes the group aside and explains that they are to go to Palapye where they will receive further instructions from Motsamai Mpho. They will be able to get explosives in the Bechuanaland protectorate that they can then take into South Africa. Once back in the republic each man must train fifteen others.

The group departs Dar es Salaam for Mbeya, each with £25.

From Mbeya they take a bus to Tunduma, on the border between Tanganyika and Northern Rhodesia. At the border, eight members of the group get off the bus while Fazzie stays on, along with the luggage belonging to the rest.

Those who decamp proceed on foot across the border into Northern Rhodesia and wait on the side of the road.

When the bus crosses the border, the driver tells Fazzie to get off. He complies. At this stage, the other eight are further down the road. The bus heads off towards them, leaving Fazzie behind. They try to stop the vehicle, but it passes them.

Soon afterwards a policeman in civilian clothes approaches the bush area where the cadres are now stranded. He first meets James Chirwa and Ernest Malgaz.

When Jantjies sees the policeman with Chirwa and Malgaz, he ducks and approaches the scene through the bush. He cannot discern much of what they are saying. Eventually he decides to turn tail and return to Tunduma. On his way he meets Makhalima. They proceed together and meet Fazzie. The three men get back to a hotel in Tunduma.

They are met a while later by Rani and Ndzuzo. Then, in the evening, Maxwell Mayekiso and Alfred Khonza also arrive,[32] and eventually the whole contingent regroups in Tunduma.

*

On the following night, eight of the nine are again in Northern Rhodesia waiting by the side of the road after crossing the border illegally. This time the crossing is successful. As arranged in Tunduma, a lorry collects them and heads towards Lusaka.

Jack Ndzuzo is the exception. He has remained behind. He gets to Lusaka by bus the following day.[33]

*

John Masupye, Nelson Diale and Levy Molefe walk towards two unoccupied dwellings at the corner of Struben and Paul Kruger Streets in Pretoria.

Molefe goes over the fence first and Masupye passes him the paper bag and the tin of oil that the group have brought with them. Masupye then climbs the fence. Diale waits behind as lookout. When on the other side, Masupye picks up the tin and Molefe carries the paper bag. They pass by the rear of the Old Synagogue and proceed until they come to a window.

Masupye takes a stone and breaks the window. He then opens the window and places the tin containing the oil into the building. With the tin inside, Masupye pulls a string attached to it so it tips over and the oil spills out.

Then out of the paper bag Masupye retrieves a smaller tin. He searches around it for a moment, until he notices a small string protruding from a hole in the bottom.

When Masupye starts pulling the string, Molefe admonishes him that he must handle the contraption with gloves, and hands him a pair. Masupye puts them on. Masupye then takes a razor blade from his pocket. But when he tries to cut the string with it, the blade breaks.

Masupye asks Molefe if he perhaps has a knife. Molefe says no, and heads to the fence to ask Diale if he has one. While Molefe and Diale are away, Masupye succeeds in cutting the string with the broken blade.

Molefe returns. He is smoking. Masupye says: 'Give me that cigarette.'

Molefe complies.

Then, crouched, Masupye ignites the string with the cigarette. When he hears a sizzling sound and smells burning, he throws the tin through the window and into the synagogue, before running away alongside Molefe.[34]

The operation is not successful. On 24 January, the *Pretoria News* notes that there was an attempt to explode a dynamite charge at the Old Synagogue the night before. A window at the back of the courtroom was broken and sticks of dynamite were placed inside, but there was no explosion.[35]

*

Two days later, acting on information received from the Northern Rhodesia Police, Detective Inspector Roderick Ivy of Southern Rhodesia's British South Africa Police heads to Bulawayo Central Railway Station.

At 7.10 p.m. the inbound train from Northern Rhodesia arrives. From it emerge James Chirwa, Henry Fazzie, Alfred Jantjies, Alfred Khonza, Matthews Makhalima, Ernest Malgaz, Maxwell Mayekiso, Jack Ndzuzo and Isaac Rani of the group trained in Ethiopia.

They will not make it to Motsamai Mpho in Palapye. Ivy introduces himself as a police officer and says he has reason to believe they are prohibited immigrants in the Federation of Rhodesia and Nyasaland. He asks them to accompany him to the Criminal Investigations Department (CID) offices.

On the following day, Detective Duncan McDermot of Bulawayo CID transports the nine under police escort to the Messina border post, where Warrant Officer Holmes of the South African Police takes them into custody.[36]

*

Harry Bambani is in a Combi with thirteen others on 24 February. Their vehicle is part of a three-Combi convoy in which a total of thirty-seven ANC members are being transported northwards from Johannesburg towards Bechuanaland.

They proceed until they reach a board that reads, in capital letters, 'TRANSVAAL BORDER'.

It is dark. Freddie Tyulu steps out of the last Combi. All thirty-six of his colleagues do the same. When the group sees the lights of a vehicle approaching from the rear, they retreat into the bush, as do the Combis, but the car passes without incident.

The Combis then return to Johannesburg while Joe Modise leads the thirty-seven by foot through the bush. They approach a place where there is a boom gate for cars. The small hut next to the gate is deserted at this time, and they walk past it.

On the following day, Joe Modise visits the thirty-seven in a plantation on the Bechuanaland side of the border. He takes aside Joe Gqabi (one of the six trained in Mao's China), who is to pilot the group, and converses with him. Modise then leaves, while Gqabi addresses the recruits. He says they must go to the immigration offices in Lobatse and sign certain documents.

The group then marches out of the bush in the direction of the town.

On Wednesday the 27th, a lorry arrives to collect the recruits. They all board. Joe Modise arrives a while later in a car. He once again takes Gqabi aside and chats with him on the road.

Then Modise comes up to address the youngsters who are now seated on the truck. Gqabi stands next to Modise.

Modise says that he feels very bad that the children of South Africa have to leave the country for training. He adds that he is nonetheless glad that they will receive training and return to fight for their country. They will be taught to be soldiers where they are going. They should behave themselves and remember that the people of the republic depend on them. They are going to go to Tanganyika and Joe Gqabi will see that they get food and generally supply them with whatever else they need.

Gqabi then enters the front cabin of the lorry, which departs while Modise stays behind.

On its route northwards, the lorry passes a number of townships. Morale is high. The recruits sing a variety of songs, including 'Mandela is coming. He has strength'.[37]

*

The ANC possesses a residence called Luthuli Camp in an area called Ukonga near Dar es Salaam Airport. Early one morning towards the end of February 1963, Peter Mfene is among thirty-six recruits who board a bus waiting outside.

They are then driven in the bus towards Nairobi.

Close to midnight, the vehicle breaks down on a dirt road. The group and driver decide to cut their losses for the night and get some sleep.

At about 9 a.m. the following morning, the driver is able to revive the engine and resume the advance towards Kenya.[38]

*

The lorry with the cadres sent from Lobatse by Joe Modise on the 27th reaches the Zambezi River four days later. While the vehicle returns to Lobatse, they cross the Zambezi by boat.

On the other side, Joe Gqabi gives each of them £5. When he comes to Gladstone

Makamba, he says the money should be used to buy tickets at Livingstone Railway Station.

With the disbursement complete, Gqabi departs to make arrangements for further travel.

A short while later a Land Rover comes to collect the recruits. After two trips, Gladstone Gaxkana is part of a final group of seven still waiting on the banks of the river.

The Land Rover collects them and they are conveyed to Livingstone Station. Gaxkana's group find their thirty colleagues already on the platform. They all wait for their train to arrive.

Instead, the Northern Rhodesian Police arrive, arrest the group, and lead them to the local police station.[39] As with the arrest of the group led by Henry Fazzie, cooperation between the police forces of the Rhodesias and South Africa once again leads to the deportation of the recruits to South Africa. On 4 March the thirty-seven are handed over to Detective Sergeant François Smith at the Beitbridge border post. He leads them to Jan Glas, the passport control officer on the South African side of the checkpoint.[40]

*

The group that departed Luthuli Camp in Dar es Salaam late in February still hasn't reached Nairobi, despite having spent three days on the road. Six private cars and a Combi are dispatched to collect them. The thirty-six are then sped away in smaller groups.

The seven 'taxis' race past Nairobi, their destination Juba in the Sudan. Their route passes through Uganda. Throughout the journey, the roads are terrible – there are dongas everywhere as a result of water having swept away the soil on what are largely dirt roads.

About eighteen kilometres from the terminus, one of the 'taxis' suffers mechanical problems after it hits a donga and starts losing oil. The driver carries on for a bit, but the engine soon packs up.

By this time, other vehicles in the convoy are returning from the Nile, having made their drop-offs. On their way back they approach the broken-down vehicle. The stranded cadres try to flag down the other motors, but the drivers of the taxis – who in these cases are white (though not all the taxi drivers in the convoy are) – speed past. We can't sleep on the roadside, the drivers say; we have to sleep in Nairobi.

Eventually one of the black taxi drivers approaches. He does stop, and ferries this last group of cadres towards the Nile.

They reach Juba at 8.45 p.m. – moments too late for the last boat to Kosti, which has just departed. On the river bank the MK men find their colleagues, who have stayed behind in order for the group to leave as one.

The reunited thirty-six spend the night on the river bank.[41]

*

Late on the evening of 3 March, Andrew Masondo, Nelson Dick, 'Vakala' and 'Mdingi' are standing by a pylon that they have sawed. They give the pole a push, only to be electrocuted in the process. One of the cables lands on Dick's thigh and burns him. He manages to flee with the rest, however.

An area of about 100 miles spanning King William's Town, Alice, Bedford and Fort Beaufort is deprived of power following this act of sabotage.[42]

At Masondo's house the group disperses. They are all wet and muddy.

Masondo's wife tells him the police visited.

Masondo hands his muddy shoes to a friend who is occupying the servant's quarters and tells him to give them to a worker friend of his.[43]

*

Donald Card proceeds from Alice Police Station to the scene of the sabotage. There he notices shoe prints in the mud. Card and colleagues proceed to a construction site located at the University of Fort Hare. They start searching the workers' huts.

Shortly thereafter, a colleague, Detective Coen Scheepers, says he has found something.

Inside the hut is a wet pair of size-10 suede shoes, with grass on the laces. There is also a handsaw with tar marks lying nearby.

The police question the owner of the hut, an old, frail man who is five foot three inches tall. He claims that the size-10 shoes are his.

To this Card says, 'Well if you claim these shoes belong to you, we are going to have to arrest you and charge you with a very serious crime.'

The policemen depart, upon which the old man rushes after them. He says the shoes belong to a teacher who asked him to hide them.

Donald Card and the Police Sabotage Squad arrive at Andrew Masondo's house at 4 p.m. the following day. The old construction worker is with them.

During the search, Card finds in the laundry basket a pair of trousers still wet around the lower legs, with wood, tar, sawdust and grass seed fragments embedded in the turn-ups.

Masondo is arrested.[44]

*

After a week in Juba, the group that left Dar es Salaam in February finally board a boat to Kosti. Their numbers have been reduced slightly because three of the original group are recuperating in hospital after a bout of malaria.

The boat that the remaining thirty-three board is a steamer that can carry about 150 people. One of its notable features is that it has no steering. It just goes forward in a straight line until it hits a river bank. Then it goes backwards, before going forwards again.

On their way up the Nile, the cadres notice locals emerging from the adjacent bush. These southern Sudanese are naked from head to toe. Not knowing what else to do, the South Africans take underwear from their luggage and throw it to them. It seems as though the locals have never worn clothing before by the way they fumble with the undergarments, putting them on backwards, puzzling over them for a while, and only resolving the riddle by trial and error.

But they are not merely seeking handouts; they want to escape. When the steamer hits the river bank as it periodically must, they try to board, only to be sjambokked away by Sudanese soldiers on the boat.

The ANC men protest, but to no avail.[45]

*

Donald Card visits ELCO appliance store in Church Street, East London. While he is walking the store's aisles, a voice booms out: 'Reggie!' Card registers the appearance of the short, dark man who responds to the summons. Soon afterwards, Card leaves the shop.

At the end of the working day, Card waits in his car by the Wool Exchange Building opposite the ELCO store.

Just after 5 p.m. the man he saw earlier leaves ELCO, walks up Church and then turns right into Oxford Street. Card follows him. At the intersection of Oxford and Fleet Streets, Card double-parks, jumps out and pulls the man in.

'Stay down! It's for your own good.'

Card takes the car into the Quigney area of the city and parks in a narrow street leading off the side of the Marine Hotel.

The man arrested is Reginald Mdube.

Card asks him what he knows about the events in Duncan Village.

Mdube says he doesn't know anything.

Card replies that he knows Mdube was involved in the attack on Inkie Hoyi's house.

This is also denied.

Card then says: 'Either you work for me or I charge you for murder.'

After a silence of a few seconds, Mdube says: 'I die either way.'

'Not necessarily; if you work with me I can offer you protection.'

Mdube does not answer.

'You don't have to answer me now. Go home and discuss the matter with your wife – Sarah.'[46]

*

Towards the end of March the group of thirty-three including Peter Mfene that left Dar es Salaam in February arrives by aeroplane in Algiers from Cairo. They are met in Algeria by Johnny Makhathini, Robert Resha and Jonas Matlou.

After being put up in a hotel and then a transit camp, the final leg of their journey sees them travel (without Jimmy Magoafela, who is kept behind in Algiers for disciplinary reasons) westwards in army trucks. Their destination is another camp located in Maghnia near Algeria's border with Morocco.

In Maghnia they find a group of about ten ANC members who earlier received training in Ethiopia. This group is led by Macdonald Masala, and includes among its members Thami Sindelo, Jakes Goniwe, Zinakile Mkaba, 'Zoni' and 'Rashidi'. They are in Algeria for further guerrilla warfare training.[47]

*

At dawn on 3 April, Walter Sisulu is served a twenty-four-hour banning order by Security Branch detectives.

Under it he cannot leave his house or communicate 'in any manner whatsoever' with anyone other than his wife, children and a sister-in-law who lives with him. The only other exemption is for magistrates and doctors.[48]

*

Two days later, in Moscow, Oliver Tambo meets members of the Communist Party of the Soviet Union (CPSU) at CPSU headquarters.

Tambo briefs them on the South African situation and the movement's needs arising from it. It is the first meeting between the Soviets and the leadership of the ANC (as opposed to the SACP, with whom the Soviets have longstanding relations).

Of the struggle in South Africa, Tambo says the government has failed to heed the limited violence of the first Umkhonto we Sizwe actions as a warning of the need for change. The ANC leadership consequently has had to alter its plans and commence immediate preparations for guerrilla warfare. The ANC recognised earlier that this would be necessary, Tambo says, but hesitated because it realised that a civil war in a country polarised along racial lines would be particularly dangerous.

Concerning the ANC's needs arising from its decision, he says that the urgent task is to obtain training abroad for activists. Large-scale training of fighters inside South Africa has proven impossible, despite the many efforts initiated. It is in connection with obtaining such large-scale training that Tambo is visiting the Soviets.[49]

*

At a house belonging to Johannes Letoboko in Lady Selborne, a township servicing Pretoria, Peter Mogano, John Masupye, Jackson Ntsoane, Enoch Matibela, Petrus Nchabeleng and Joseph Mampane of the MK Pretoria command gather on Easter Monday 1963.

Mogano begins by introducing Andrew Mashaba to them as one of the higher officials from Johannesburg. Then Mogano tells Mashaba: 'These men are my men here in Pretoria.' He says Masupye is the section leader of Pretoria itself, Nchabeleng for Atteridgeville, Matibela of the Iscor area, Mampane for Vlakfontein (also known as Mamelodi), and Jackson Ntsoane of Lady Selborne.

Mashaba tells the men there is something he is going to teach them. He produces certain articles from a brown paper bag. The first item is saltpetre, which he puts down on the table and asks if anybody knows what it is.

Masupye says he knows because he uses it in the hotel where he works.

Mashaba asks what Masupye does with it.

He says he uses it for preparing meat.

'But I use it for something else and I am going to show you.'

Mashaba then produces another packet wrapped in paper. He says there is sulphur in it. He asks if anybody knows what that is.

Mogano says he does.

Next comes black charcoal. The same question.

This time, nobody claims knowledge.

Johannes Letoboko then enters and reports that the fire is ready outside.

Ntsoane goes out to check, and when he returns, he says: 'Yes, the fire is ready.' He asks if he can bring it inside.

'Yes, you can bring it in,' says Mashaba.[50]

*

Indres Naidoo sees a pair of soft, crepe-soled shoes on the floor, and puts them on. He then sees a black jersey and takes it. Finally he spots a set of gloves lying around; he picks these up as well.

At 11 p.m., just before he departs with Shirish Nanabhai, Naidoo's mother asks where he is going at this time of night.

Naidoo and Nanabhai arrive at the café where Reggie Vandeyar works as a waiter. Vandeyar says immediately that he is not happy with the behaviour of Gammat Jardien. But Jardien arrives by car soon afterwards, cutting the discussion short.

Naidoo, Vandeyar and Nanabhai get into the car and are driven to Vandeyar's.

Naidoo and Vandeyar get out and go into the house. There, Vandeyar gives Naidoo a rod and says that with the first false move Jardien makes, hit him hard.

They return to the car and travel to Riverlea, Johannesburg, where they stop. Nanabhai and Naidoo go to the signal post and Jardien to the toolshed, while Vandeyar stands guard ten or fifteen metres away.

A strange noise like a long hooter suddenly sounds, causing the men to look up towards the main road, which is about 150 metres away. But the sound dies and no car is seen, so they continue.

It is shortly after midnight on the bitterly cold morning of 17 April. Sergeant M.D. Kruger is on observation duty next to the railway line between Crown and New Canada Stations. From his vantage point he sees Naidoo help Vandeyar break open the door of the toolshed with a crowbar before the two go inside with a cardboard box.

Naidoo then returns to the signal post and he and Nanabhai start fiddling with it.

Vandeyar hears Jardien making a lot of noise at the door of the shed and then sees him light a small fire. Vandeyar goes to Nanabhai and Naidoo and tells them something is wrong.

At this point Naidoo and Nanabhai are fixing dynamite to the signal post. Naidoo shouts at Jardien asking what the hell he is doing. Vandeyar in turn shouts at Naidoo to light the bloody fuse. Naidoo does so, but immediately thereafter he hears a whistle, after which hand-held torches light up the surrounding veld. Vandeyar tells his colleagues to run for their lives. In the attempted escape, Naidoo runs towards a fence that is over a metre high.

Lieutenant Theunis Swanepoel is one of the policemen at the scene. He sees three men running towards him. When they are about ten metres away he blows his whistle and commands: 'Put up your hands. Stand still.'

Vandeyar, Nanabhai and Naidoo comply. Almost immediately afterwards Naidoo hears a shot. Only when he looks down and sees blood does he realise he has been hit.

Swanepoel, heavy set with a thick red face and short crew-cut hair, yells in Afrikaans, 'What are you doing here?' The three shout virtually simultaneously: 'We came with Gammat Jardien.'

'Ah, soldiers of Mandela,' Swanepoel says, before hitting Naidoo in the chest with his rifle butt. The three are surrounded by dozens of policemen wearing railway balaclavas.

Jardien is nowhere to be seen.

Shortly after hearing the gunfire, Sergeant Kruger hears a tremendous explosion from the toolshed. Pieces of wood and zinc sheets fly through the air, landing on the railway line near where he has been concealed.

Soon after that comes a soft explosion from the signal box.[51]

*

On the following day, Paul Maré, a seventy-something retired police detective is at his smallholding in Rivonia that stands on a hill overlooking Liliesleaf Farm.

He sees a panel van carrying three Indians stop in the vicinity of an old disused well near Liliesleaf.

Maré informs Rivonia Police Station that these Indians might be connected with the previous day's attempted sabotage of the New Canada–Booysens line.

But nothing is found in the well when it is searched by the police.[52]

*

On the afternoon of 19 April, Albertina Sisulu returns home to find Security Branch detectives waiting for her.

When they ask her about her husband's whereabouts, she tells them: 'When I left home in the morning, Walter was here. He did not say anything about leaving.'[53]

*

Govan Mbeki also goes into hiding in April after being placed under house arrest. He makes his way to Liliesleaf Farm.[54]

*

On 23 April the government publishes its detention without trial bill. Under its stipulations, anyone can be arrested without warrant and held for ninety days of interrogation without the right to see any legal advisers, and no court will be able to order the person's release. Any commissioned officer who suspects an offence connected with furthering communism or conducting sabotage can perform an arrest without warrant. A person can be detained at 'any place' the officer thinks fit until he or she answers questions 'satisfactorily'. The person has to be released after ninety days but can be immediately rearrested and held for another ninety days, *ad infinitum*.[55]

*

At Liliesleaf Farm, Govan Mbeki converses with Arthur Goldreich, a member of the Congress of Democrats who in 1948 fought with the Palmach, the military wing of the Jewish National Movement, in Palestine.[56] Goldreich says that following discussion among some groups in Umkhonto we Sizwe, he was asked to draw up a document on guerrilla warfare for submission to the National High Command.

Mbeki departs the farm and meets Walter Sisulu at the latter's hideout. There he conveys the information communicated by Goldreich.

Sisulu asks Mbeki to call an urgent National High Command meeting where these plans for guerrilla warfare can be discussed officially.[57]

*

On the final day of April, Ahmed Kathrada vacates Flat 13, Kholvad House, in Market Street. Bob Hepple drives him to Liliesleaf Farm, where Arthur Goldreich works on the disguise that will transform Kathrada into 'Pedro Perreira'.[58]

*

Yet more activists escape from house arrest. On May Day 1963 in Lobatse, W.A. Knight of the Bechuanaland Protectorate Police writes to the chief immigration officer in Mafikeng, advising him to find Mr and Mrs Hodgson's 349 Forms attached.[59]

In his form, Jack Hodgson says that he left South Africa with his wife because it was impossible for them to move about and consequently to earn a living. He says that he has R520 in cash and can get more. He further states that he and his wife 'have taken a flat in Lobatsi and would like to earn our living either by working for someone or by starting a business here. We will not leave the B.P. unless required to leave officially.'

Hodgson explains that they arrived in the protectorate by car through Martin's Drift, in the company of Michael Harmel.[60]

*

Ruth First arrives at a servant's quarters in Pearse Street, Doornfontein, where Mac Maharaj, who returned to South Africa earlier in the year after completing his training in East Germany, is staying. She asks him to go to Natal, contact 'Steve' Naidoo, find out his circumstances, examine how he could be integrated into MK, and make arrangements for him to come to Johannesburg.[61]

During May 1963, Maharaj visits the Naidoo family farm about ten miles inland from Stanger. There he meets Nandha Naidoo, who has been staying there since his return to South Africa in mid-December 1962 after his radio training in China. Maharaj tells Naidoo that the leadership want him in Johannesburg.

Naidoo responds reticently, saying his dad needs help on the farm. He says this puts him in a fix: he can't get into a situation where he makes his father dependent on him while at the same time making himself available for political work. Naidoo adds that he would also need to get a job both as cover and to provide him with an income.

Maharaj is understanding and says he will see what he can do.[62]

*

The MK National High Command meets at Liliesleaf Farm between the end of the first and the beginning of the second week of May 1963.

Goldreich delivers a presentation on guerrilla warfare. He speaks about the simultaneous landing by ship or air of groups of thirty men in four areas, namely Port Elizabeth to Umzimkulu, Port Shepstone to Swaziland, North Western Transvaal bordering Bechuanaland and the Limpopo, and the North Western Cape to the South West.

These men would have to be sufficiently equipped to be self-supporting for at least a month. Each group of thirty would be split into platoons ten people strong that would operate in areas contiguous to the zones designated for guerrilla warfare. These platoons would link their activities with prearranged local groups.

The goal is that the local groups be 2,000 strong in the first three of the above-mentioned areas, and 1,000 strong in the fourth.

Arms would need to be supplied to the guerrilla groups to enable them to arm the local population, which would then become integrated with the armed units.

Attacks would be launched by the guerrillas on pre-selected targets so as to take the enemy by surprise, cause chaos and confusion in their ranks, and inspire the local populace to join the revolution.

Prior to these operations a political authority will need to be established by the movement in a friendly territory in order to supervise the struggle in its internal and external aspects. This authority will in due course become a provisional revolutionary government.

The immediate duties of the National High Command in relation to the guerrilla areas will be to employ ten full-time organisers in each area. These organisers, who will be accountable to the National High Command for their work, will have to map out the regions and then organise regional and district commands and Umkhonto we Sizwe units in the four zones. Finally, the High Command will have to recruit and arrange external training for at least 300 men in the coming two months.

After completing the presentation, Goldreich urges the adoption of the plan. He says it could be implemented in a relatively short time.[63]

*

Under a tree in a churchyard in Claremont in Cape Town on the evening of 7 May, Jack Leibowitz collects Denis Goldberg and transports him to Bellville Railway Station.

Goldberg's train approaches Johannesburg the following day, but he disembarks at Krugersdorp. From there he takes a regional train into Johannesburg.

A couple of days later, at Johannesburg's Skyline Hotel, Goldberg meets Joe Slovo, who asks him to stay in South Africa (Goldberg was planning to leave the country) to investigate the manufacture of weapons that will be needed by Umkhonto we Sizwe.

Goldberg immediately agrees to the proposal.[64]

*

On 21 May, twenty-year-old Chris Hani is part of an eighteen-strong group that crosses the Zambezi River into Kazungula in Northern Rhodesia.[65]

They hide for most of the day in the bush on the banks of the Zambezi. They do not move, because a police van drives by regularly.

In the late afternoon, Mark Shope departs from the group to catch a bus to Livingstone.

At about 5 p.m. the police van comes one last time, collects the policeman guarding the ferry landing stage, and departs.

At 6.30 p.m. two black males unknown to the group arrive in a Land Rover. The cadres board the vehicle and are driven to a house in Livingstone. There they meet up again with Mark Shope.

That same evening, they are driven to Zimba Railway Station outside Livingstone. At 9 p.m. they board a train for Lusaka.

On the following morning, as the train nears Kafue, just south of Lusaka, a group of well-dressed African males instruct all passengers who boarded at the station just outside Livingstone to move to one side of the coach. The eighteen do so and their tickets are checked.

When the train arrives at Kafue at 8 a.m. on the 22nd, uniformed police board the train. Their plain-clothed counterparts point out certain light-skinned men in the cabin. Eight members of the South African group, specifically Joseph Nduli, Mark Shope, Chris Hani, Sydney Thunzi, Pat Molefe, Steve Belle, David Ngwenya and Alfred Khombisa are removed.

The ten who are not identified at Kafue, namely Leonard Nkosi, Archie Sibeko, Do Mahlasela, Mcebisi Mkokwana, Lawrence Sibongi, Kenneth Malinga, Justice Mpanza, Jackson Mbali, George Mothusi and Leslie Sondezi, remain on board. But they are recognised soon afterwards by the plain-clothes policemen and herded into a corner under guard. When the train arrives in Lusaka at 9 a.m. the same uniformed policemen who made the arrests at Kafue are seen waiting at the ticket barrier. On the other side of the barrier, the ten can see their eight arrested colleagues in a police van. The police round up the remaining ten.

Later that morning, when the group of ten arrive at the immigration offices, they are formally arrested by a European official. While being escorted to the truck that is to lead them to Lusaka central prison, however, Justice Mpanza, Jackson Mbali and George Mothusi escape.[66]

*

In contrast to the Fazzie- and Gqabi-led groups in February and March, these recruits will not be surrendered to South Africa. The new outcome is a consequence of Harold Macmillan's 'Wind of Change' sweeping through Northern Rhodesia.

At a joint press conference on 23 May in Lusaka's Ridgeway Hotel, the United National Independence Party (UNIP) and the North Rhodesian African National Congress issue a press statement demanding the immediate release of the refugees. They dismiss the argument that the men are prohibited immigrants by asserting 'no African is a foreigner in Africa'.[67]

They also reject the argument that the men should be deported. (The argument was based on the rationale that immigration was a federal affair in the then existent Central African Federation binding Northern and Southern Rhodesia with Nyasaland. It was this reasoning that led to Federal Police cooperation in the arrest and subsequent deportation to South Africa of the groups earlier in the year.)

In the statement, the two organisations declare the federation dead. They also 'warn that if these people are deported, race relations in Northern Rhodesia will deteriorate'.

They say deporting anybody to South Africa is immoral because the republic is 'hell on earth for all men of conscience – Black or White'.[68]

*

Anthony Delius is present as *Rand Daily Mail* correspondent in Africa Hall, Addis Ababa, on the following day when he witnesses an even greater flex of African nationalist muscle. Algerian prime minister Ahmed Ben Bella strides up to the rostrum, tosses his notes aside and addresses the assembled African heads of state.

He calls for the establishment of an African 'blood bank' of human beings ready to shed their blood to 'liberate our brothers in dependent territories'. He says that over 10,000 experienced Algerian volunteers are waiting for the chance to fight in Portuguese Angola. He says: 'Let us be ready to die a little, so that African unity should not be a vain word.'

After Ben Bella, Julius Nyerere of Tanganyika heads for the podium with his walking stick. 'It is unnecessary,' he says, 'for me to prophesy that it will not be recorded in history that "But for the stubbornness and non-cooperation of Tanganyika the Addis Ababa conference would have been a success."'

Nyerere says that Tanganyika wants to assure 'our gallant brother from Algeria, Brother Ben Bella, that we are prepared to die a little for the final removal of the humiliation of colonialism from the face of Africa'.

For Nyerere, 'the real humiliating truth is that Africa is not free and therefore it is Africa which should take the necessary collective measures to free Africa'.

On 25 May the African heads of state pass a resolution establishing a coordinating committee to be headquartered in Dar es Salaam that will harmonise assistance from African states to the liberation movements in the parts of the continent remaining under European colonial or white settler rule. Under this plan, the African states are to allocate 1 per cent of their national budgets to support a special fund with this aim.

Anthony Delius notes that Oliver Tambo, Duma Nokwe, Robert Resha, Joe Matthews and Tennyson Makiwane are attending the conference on the ANC's behalf.[69]

*

At a meeting of ANC and SACP members at Liliesleaf Farm, Joe Slovo leads the discussion on the guerrilla warfare plan. He speaks of parachute drops.

Bram Fischer interrupts, asking, 'How on earth could people be dropped?' Where would they establish a base?

The response comes that South Africa is a very large country, so parachute drops are theoretically possible, and that MK could not expect to possess bases in territories neighbouring South Africa, so there is no alternative.

Slovo then speaks of the four areas previously mentioned by Goldreich – Port Elizabeth to Umzimkulu, Port Shepstone to Swaziland, the North Western Transvaal bordering Bechuanaland and the Limpopo, and the North Western Cape to the South West – as areas where guerrillas could be infiltrated in order to attack pre-selected targets.

Fischer cuts in that in the last of these areas there are no targets and no population on which to have an impact – there is probably not a single ANC man in that North West Cape area. Furthermore, it is ridiculous to talk of landing thirty men by aeroplane in the North Western Transvaal.

Slovo replies that once the forces land in the republic they will definitely have the support of the masses, even if there are not members of the ANC present.

Another delegate asks where the plane making the drop in the North West Cape will depart from.

Slovo says it is not difficult for planes to fly across Bechuanaland, drop people and fly back. Also, he says, the sea could be used to drop people and sail back.[70]

*

In Pietermaritzburg, Billy Nair tells Bruno Mtolo that if no one meets him in Germiston, he must take a train to Johannesburg and go to His Majesty's Building and ask there for Advocate Slovo.

Mtolo boards a train to Johannesburg on 30 May.

At His Majesty's Building, Mtolo asks a white lady in white uniform where Advocate Slovo might be found.

She tells him to go to Innes Chambers opposite the Supreme Court.

At the entrance to Innes Chambers, Mtolo sees Slovo's name on a board. He gets into a lift, goes up, and finds his way to a reception office. He asks a white lady where Advocate Slovo might be reached. She makes a call, and after putting down the receiver gives him directions to Slovo's office.

Mtolo introduces himself to Slovo, saying he is from the Durban Regional Command and Billy Nair told him that if nobody from the High Command met him at the station, he should come and see Slovo.

'That is all right – sit down,' Slovo says, before making a phone call. When finished, he asks Mtolo if he knows anybody in the townships who can accommodate him.

Mtolo mentions Levy Seloro.

Slovo answers that if Mtolo knows him well, he should go and stay there.[71]

*

On 1 June Solomon Mbanjwa tells Zazi Ngcongo and Jacob Zuma that they will soon leave the country for military training. They must take two shirts, two pairs of trousers, one coat or overcoat, a pair of shoes and two pairs of undervests.

He warns them not to trust anybody, even relatives, and not to resign from any jobs they may have, because it will just cause suspicion.[72]

*

On the following day at Botshabelo location outside Bloemfontein, Herbert Sitilo and Solomon Montwedi arrive at a house belonging to Caleb Matshabe.

They have a discussion with Matshabe and a Reverend Mokwena, who explains how they should behave when they are away at 'school'. He tells them they will leave Bloemfontein on the 7th.[73]

*

The same day, Joe Slovo and J.B. Marks arrive by car in Lobatse and immediately head north to Francistown, where they complete the immigration formalities.[74]

*

Bruno Mtolo and Abel Mthembu are passengers in a car driven by Brian Somana.

It is dark, between 7 and 8 p.m., and Mtolo keeps an eye on passing landmarks. The car stops at a garage where he sees the word 'Rivonia'.

Not long after leaving the station, Mthembu calls on Somana to stop the car on the road. He then tells his colleagues they must get out. The three walk back a short distance in the direction from which they have come. From the road they turn into an open field on which there are visible traces of tyre tracks. At the end of the veld they approach what look like servants' rooms. They pass between two of them and see what appears to be a main building with a thatched roof.

Mthembu knocks on the door, but there is no response, so he just opens it.

As they enter, Mtolo sees Walter Sisulu to his left, sitting on a chair.

Also in the room are Govan Mbeki, Ahmed Kathrada and Wilton Mkwayi. Mthembu performs the introductions – of Sisulu as 'Allah', Mbeki as 'Dhlamini', and Kathrada as 'Pedro'.

Sisulu asks Mtolo where Solomon Mbanjwa is.

Mtolo says that he was surprised to hear from Mthembu earlier that Mbanjwa was expected to come instead of himself.

Pleasantries concluded, Sisulu says he has to leave, and immediately departs.[75]

*

Levy Mbatha and Andrew Mlangeni visit Essop Suleiman's house on 6 June to arrange transport for the 9th.[76]

*

Around this time, some fourteen days after being first detained in Lusaka central, Leonard Nkosi, Do Mahlasela, Mcebisi Mkokwana, Lawrence Sibongi, Kenneth Malinga and Leslie Sondezi are released following a court order.

When they leave the prison they find UNIP vehicles waiting for them. Northern

Rhodesian Police are also there, trying to re-arrest them. The ANC recruits board one of the UNIP cars, a Land Rover, which drives away while the others obstruct the police vehicles. The convoy's destination is a private residence in Lusaka's Matero location. There the cadres meet Archie Sibeko, Elias Matlase and Sam Masemula.

Two days later, the group are in the ANC's office in Dar es Salaam. From there they are driven in two motor cars – a Simca and a Morris – to the city's Ukonga location, where the ANC's transit residence 'Luthuli Camp' is situated. There they meet the eleven colleagues they last saw in Northern Rhodesia: the eight arrested in Kafue and the three who escaped in Lusaka on 23 May.[77]

*

At roughly midnight on 9 June, Detective Sergeants Uys and Ferreira are passengers in a car in which Colonel van Niekerk occupies the driver's seat. The vehicle is parked in the bush a few miles from Groot Marico on the road leading to Zeerust.

A Zodiac Zephyr passes them, followed by two Combis. Van Niekerk follows the vehicles. The policemen notice the distance between the vehicles ahead increasing. In Zeerust, the Zodiac and the first of the Combis cease to be visible. The second Combi, which the policemen can still see, then turns right onto the road to Lobatse. The police car turns right as well. As it does so, Detective Sergeant Ferreira notices the Zodiac pull out of a garage on the road to Mafikeng that they have just left.

The police car continues following the Lobatse-bound Combi through Zeerust. Suddenly this vehicle turns off the road and then heads back so as to retrace its course. The policemen stop the Combi, and Ferreira and Uys climb into it. They see that the vehicle has an Indian driver and African passengers. The Combi heads off with the two policemen on board.

They eventually reach a road block where they hand the driver and passengers over to members of the Uniform Branch.

Ferreira and Uys then drive another police car in the direction of the main Johannesburg road in order to find the other vehicles that are still at large.

Just before leaving Zeerust, Ferreira notes that other members of the Detective Service have stopped the other Combi. At the scene he sees that this Combi is also driven by an Indian and likewise has a large contingent of Africans on board.

Those apprehended are taken to Zeerust Police Station.[78]

*

At Zeerust Police Station Ferreira is interrogating the passengers of the two Combis stopped earlier when he receives information that prompts him, Sergeant Uys and two members of the Uniform Section to depart immediately for Groot Marico.

Just outside Groot Marico, they stop a Combi. Ferreira climbs into it and asks its inhabitants where they are going.

The coloured driver says they are going to a football match.

All the people on the bus are arrested and taken to Groot Marico Police Station.[79]

*

When Ferreira arrives at Rustenburg Police Station at 6 a.m. the following morning he sees a Zodiac Zephyr outside the building. Inside the station he finds Levy Mbatha, Essop Suleiman and an African woman.

From the four vehicles (the three Combis and the Zephyr) apprehended during the night, in excess of fifty people have been arrested. Essop Suleiman and all the drivers used by him to transport ANC recruits to the Bechuanaland border on this and previous occasions are among them. So too are Zazi Ngcongo and Jacob Zuma, who were part of a group of eight sent by Solomon Mbanjwa from Natal. Likewise Herbert Sitilo and Solomon Montwedi, who were sent by Caleb Matshabe from Bloemfontein. There are other recruits from other parts of the country, including a group sent from the Western Cape by Looksmart Ngudle. They are taken to Pretoria, where they are held under the ninety-day detention law.[80]

With these arrestees and the groups repatriated from the Rhodesias earlier in the year, the South African security forces now have in their custody a large number of prisoners who possess a wealth of information about the composition of the MK underground in most of its regions in the country. Unless these mostly young, untrained recruits can hold out under indefinite detention, the intelligence gathered from them will provide the basis for nationwide police operations against the revolutionary underground. Taken together, the arrests mark a turning point in the conflict.

*

Bram Fischer has a conversation with Bob Hepple, his colleague on the SACP Secretariat. Fischer says that the Umkhonto we Sizwe National High Command has sent Joe Slovo and J.B. Marks abroad to present a plan for guerrilla warfare to the external leadership. Fischer stresses that neither the internal ANC nor the SACP have seen or adopted the plan and he is visibly unhappy about it.[81]

*

A reporter from the *Bulawayo Chronicle* is in the company of Joe Slovo and J.B. Marks in Francistown on 20 June.

Marks tells him: 'I foresee guerrilla warfare starting up in South Africa within the next two years, both internally and externally. I know that the Europeans are armed to the teeth. But we also have access to modern weapons. I won't say where they will come from, but our supplier is an Eastern Bloc country.'

For his part, Slovo is much more circumspect. His only words are: 'In a very short time I am convinced I will be a more worthy citizen of South Africa than either Dr Verwoerd or Mr Vorster. That is how confident I am of the future.'

The article appears the following day under the title 'Guerrilla warfare will start soon—S.A. refugee'.[82]

On the same day Marks and Slovo leave Francistown on a chartered Dakota plane along with twenty-six other ANC refugees.[83]

*

In Dar es Salaam's Palace Hotel, Joe Slovo presents the guerrilla warfare plan to Oliver Tambo.

While reading it, Tambo's eyes start darting from side to side in what Slovo will learn to recognise as a characteristic sign of excitement from the leader of the External Mission. Tambo then does a jig of joy around the room.[84]

It seems as though the plan will pass the test of acquiring the External Mission's approval.

*

In Paris on 24 June, the philosopher Jean-Paul Sartre announces the formation of a French anti-apartheid committee.

Sartre tells the press conference that South Africans are involved in a struggle that jeopardises their very existence, so the ANC is obliged to resort to any means possible in its fight. The point of the committee will be to extend useful help to the South African liberation movements. Sartre says he expects the committee to put pressure on public opinion to compel the French government to stop exporting arms to South Africa.

Raymond Kunene, ANC representative in London for Europe and Latin America, also addresses the briefing. He says South Africa is on the brink of one of the bloodiest revolutions in history.[85]

*

On 24 June, Elias Motsoaledi is arrested.[86]

*

Bartholomew Hlapane is brought in for questioning the same day.[87]

*

Abel Mthembu is also arrested on the 24th.[88]

*

John Nkadimeng is detained, again on the 24th.[89]

*

As is Peter Mogano.[90]

*

On the following day, Mzwai Piliso, the ANC's Cairo representative, tells a correspondent from *Xinhua*, the Chinese press agency, that 'the period of non-violent struggle in South Africa has definitely gone and our struggle for freedom has entered a new stage, the stage of armed struggle'.

Accounting for the shift in policy, Piliso says: 'It is not from personal choice but because of existing conditions in my country; conditions that defy a peaceful solution of our problems. Thus it becomes our conviction.'[91]

*

On the 26th, *Xinhua*'s Kao Liang delivers a dispatch concerning the day's commemorations of South African 'Freedom Day' in Dar es Salaam.

Liang says that in interviews he conducted with some ANC leaders on the eve of the celebrations, one claimed that 'very soon revolutionary armed struggle will be unfolded over the vast plain on a larger scale'. Another said that 'as far as the masses in my country are concerned, it is their common understanding that this is a day for preparations for new battles'.[92]

*

On 26 June, Solomon Mbanjwa is arrested on a bus in Durban's Berea Road.[93]

*

Late on the afternoon of the 26th, Lionel Gay, a thirty-two-year-old lecturer in physics at Wits University, goes to the home of Jack Levitan in Empire Road, Johannesburg.

At about 5 p.m. Gay is in the sauna next to the swimming bath, working with Denis Goldberg on the installation of an apparatus. Goldberg has brought some aluminium piping, spray-painted grey-black, for them to work with.

Gay returns to the house later that evening to make final adjustments to the antennae, then leaves again.

About fifteen minutes later, Cyril Jones is in the garden of the house with a torch, while Ivan Schermbrucker patrols the premises with a walkie-talkie connected to Denis Goldberg, who plugs in a tape recorder and presses play.[94]

Then, in a broadcast heard over large stretches of Johannesburg, it is said: 'This is Radio Liberation! This is the Radio of the African National Congress!'

The voice continues: 'Our radio talks to you for the first time today, June 26, but not for the last time. There will be more broadcasts.'

Mention is made of the house-arrest order placed on Walter Sisulu. Of this it is said: 'We could not accept this. We are not afraid of jail or even death in the struggle. Even in jail the struggle goes on, but those in jail are there as captives of the government. Our Congress decided that Walter Sisulu should leave his home. His house was being used by Vorster to imprison him. Today he continues to lead our organisation and the people. He leads from underground. Here from underground is Walter Sisulu to speak to you.'

Sisulu begins: 'Friends, Comrades, Sons and Daughters of Africa, I am speaking to you from somewhere in South Africa. I have not left the country.'

He says that by order of 'my organisation, the African National Congress', I am resuming the position of secretary-general that I relinquished in 1954: 'Those who succeeded me have now been allocated other duties overseas.'

Sisulu's final words are:

We warn the government that drastic laws will not stop our struggle for liberation. Throughout the ages men have sacrificed – they have given their lives for their ideals. And we are also determined to surrender our lives for our freedom. In the face of violence, men struggling for freedom have had to meet violence with violence. How can it be otherwise in South Africa? Changes must come, changes for the better, but not without sacrifice. Your sacrifice, my sacrifice. We face tremendous odds. We know that. But our unity, our determination, our sacrifice, our organisation are our weapons. We must succeed. We will succeed! AMANDLA![95]

*

A savingram, sent on 27 June 1963 by the police commissioner of Bechuanaland to the protectorate's government secretary, reads that a 'reliable but most delicate source, which must be protected', has reported Jack Hodgson's intention of organising a series of lectures at 'the Farm' since his flat is now 'under suspicion'.

The subjects of the lectures will be 'How to detect informers', 'How to awaken the Bechuana to Revolution' and 'How to teach the tactics of Revolution'.[96]

*

Towards the end of June, Lieutenant Willie van Wyk, a Security Branch detective, tells his superior, Colonel George Klindt, that he has received information from an African claiming that Walter Sisulu is living in Rivonia with a man known to the source only as 'the Caretaker'.

Klindt instructs Van Wyk to locate the hideout whatever the cost.[97]

*

The Umkhonto we Sizwe National High Command gathers at the beginning of July to hear Arthur Goldreich submit a Logistics Committee report on the production requirements of the guerrilla warfare plan.

Govan Mbeki makes notes during the discussion that follows. The first entry reads: 'Incorrect to say liberation movement given itself to military methods'. This is written when an argument that the entire liberation movement should be thrown behind the shift to guerrilla warfare receives the rebuttal that there is still a lot of political work to do and hence it is wrong to advocate that the liberation movement be given over wholly to military methods.

When the advocates of guerrilla warfare are asked, 'How? Where? We have no friendly borders', they respond that the movement could obtain a place in the protectorates to which guerrillas can retreat. This draws the objection that such a notion is totally unrealistic, upon which Mbeki jots down 'cross border of protectorates'.

A critic tells the proponents of the plan that it would be incorrect to undertake this action without taking into consideration the other components of the Congress Alliance. Mbeki writes 'Liberation movement not ignored'.

When a supporter says that the government is arming, and the only way of meeting this is also to take up arms and adopt guerrilla warfare, an opponent responds that the government is not arming out of strength but because it feels the pressure of the mass political organisations, thus making it necessary to step up *that* method of pressure. Mbeki writes 'Government not resorting to arms out of strength. It is not a happy choice. Compelled by nature of the struggle.'[98]

*

Lieutenant Willie van Wyk and his African informer undertake an unsuccessful attempt to locate Sisulu's Rivonia hideout.[99]

*

As a member of the SACP Central Committee, Bartholomew Hlapane attended meetings at Liliesleaf Farm; as a member of the MK Johannesburg Regional Command, Abel Mthembu travelled to and from Liliesleaf. With both men in police custody since 24 June (along with Elias Motsoaledi, Mthembu's colleague in the Johannesburg Command), the farm has to be classified as a security risk by their colleagues.

On 4 July 1963, Denis Goldberg goes to live in a cottage in Johannesburg's Mountain View suburb.[100]

On the same day, Raymond Mhlaba and Govan Mbeki take up residence at Travallyn Farm, in the district of Krugersdorp.[101]

*

A savingram sent from Bechuanaland's police commissioner to the territory's government secretary on 5 July says that, during Joe Slovo's stay in the country, he visited Jack Hodgson in Lobatse and, according to sources, discussed arrangements for wholesale airlifts via Bechuanaland of South African 'refugees' who would be headed to Tanganyika for sabotage training.

The correspondence also notes that Slovo tried but failed to contact Motsamai Mpho of the opposition Bechuanaland People's Party (BPP). Mpho was absent from the country at the time. Slovo nonetheless did manage to meet most of the BPP leaders in the territory.[102]

*

Billy Nair is arrested at his Durban home at about 2 a.m. on 6 July 1963.[103]

*

At Liliesleaf Farm, Ian David Kitson says to his colleagues gathered for a meeting: 'I'm surprised to see you here, because I thought you were moving', to which Walter Sisulu responds, 'This is the last time we're coming here.'[104]

*

At a meeting held at Liliesleaf on Saturday 6 July, Rusty Bernstein argues that the plan is a serious mistake. He puts forward an alternative centred on limited attacks on isolated border outposts, after which guerrillas will retreat into bases in the British protectorates, leading to an international incident that will precipitate strikes and a serious political crisis. Bernstein says the only alternative to this is a protracted guerrilla war, which won't succeed given the might of the South African state and its friends.

Govan Mbeki counters that armed invasion and guerrilla war is the only way the regime can be removed.[105]

The meeting runs out of time. Bernstein has to leave. Denis Goldberg says they can't disperse without a venue for the follow-up meeting on Thursday because it will be so difficult to get people back together again.[106]

Bob Hepple suggests returning to Liliesleaf Farm, to which Bernstein says, 'Never again!'

Hepple urges, 'Just this once! The very last time!'

It is near 6 p.m. and dark outside. Bernstein has to go, so he says, 'But definitely never again!' and runs for his car.

He arrives home just in time to meet his house-arrest conditions. He finds his family standing looking anxiously out the living-room windows.[107]

*

On the 10th Lieutenant van Wyk is again driving in Rivonia with his African informant. This time the informant says that he recognises a church.[108]

*

Thursday 11 July 1963.

Ruth First meets Bob Hepple at his house and asks him to give some messages to Sisulu and Mbeki.

They discuss the ongoing debate over guerrilla warfare. Hepple says the existing plan is crazy and will provoke brutal repression that will retard for many years the main task of building up an effective political and trade union organisation among the people. He points out that South Africa is not like Cuba under Batista; it is instead a highly armed state, supported by the white population and backed by the United States in the Cold War. The plan has no chance of succeeding and will only bring suffering.

First acknowledges the dangers, but says: 'For the first time in years we are getting things done.' She compares the achievement of the armed underground in a few months with that of years of committee work by the legal organisations.[109]

*

On the morning of the 11th, Lieutenant van Wyk briefs a group of policemen and tells them about a plan to use a dry-cleaning van to deceive the suspects.[110]

*

Denis Goldberg collects Govan Mbeki, Walter Sisulu and Raymond Mhlaba from Travallyn in the early afternoon and drives them in a Volkswagen Combi to Rivonia.

At Liliesleaf Farm they see a car with a white man inside. Sisulu leaves the Combi to speak to this man. A few moments later Sisulu walks with the man through the kitchen door and into the main house. The time is 2.40 p.m.

The man, who is a dentist, is Arthur Goldreich's brother-in-law Reeve Arenstein. He attends to Sisulu in the house.

As soon as they see Sisulu and Arenstein disappear into the kitchen, Mbeki and Mhlaba step out of the Combi and walk to a room in a thatched outbuilding to the side of the house, where they find Goldberg, who has already left the car, in conversation with Ahmed Kathrada. As Mbeki enters, he says he has to look for a certain document that Goldreich should have left in the store.

While Mbeki conducts this search, Mhlaba puts on overalls.

Mbeki returns to the room with the document and sits at the table. Mhlaba walks up, stands behind Mbeki, and reads the document over Mbeki's shoulder.

After finishing with the dentist, Sisulu leaves the main house and enters the outbuilding. A few minutes later Rusty Bernstein arrives and also enters this out-building, which is a kind of servants'-quarters-cum-cottage.[111]

*

A bakery van and a dry-cleaner's van with the name 'Trade Steam Pressers' on its side enter Liliesleaf Farm at 3 p.m. Both are full of policemen.

Detective Warrant Officer J.H.J. Kennedy is in the dry-cleaner's van. He hears a colleague say that nobody is home, but Lieutenant van Zyl then says: 'We are clos-ing in.'[112]

In the side cottage, Govan Mbeki goes to the window after hearing a van coming down the driveway. 'It's a dry cleaning van,' he says. 'I've never seen it before.'

Rusty Bernstein rushes to the window and tells his colleagues: 'My God, I saw that van outside the police station on the way here!'

The group look at the van through the window as its rear doors open up.[113]

Forty policemen emerge from the two vans and fan out to surround the main house and outbuildings.

When Bob Hepple sees the policemen he says, 'The police are here', and closes the door. Sisulu heads to the window.

At this moment J.H.J. Kennedy enters the outbuilding. He sees Sisulu's frame exiting the window.

However, two police dogs have already been placed at the rear of the servants' quarters, and one of the dogs, 'Cheetah', snarls aggressively at Sisulu, who aborts his escape attempt and returns inside.

In the living room of the main building, Denis Goldberg is leafing through a note-book full of information on such topics as where to find casting for hand grenades or buy chemicals for explosives. Suddenly a number of police officers descend on the room. Goldberg runs for the toilet with the notebook, but policemen intercept him before he gets there.

Back in the outbuilding, everybody present is immediately handcuffed, except for Kathrada, who refuses. The police cuff him anyway. J.H.J. Kennedy notices that Sisulu and Mbeki have had their hair dyed.[114]

Lying open on a table in the outbuilding where Bernstein, Hepple, Kathrada, Mbeki, Mhlaba and Sisulu have been arrested is a six-page document that begins: 'PART 1 The white state has thrown overboard every pretence of rule by democratic process. Armed to the teeth it has presented the people with only one choice and that is its overthrow by force and violence.' Further on, 'PART II' is titled 'OPER-ATION MAYIBUYE'. It begins with a subsection 'AREAS', which are described as 'Port Elizabeth – Mzimkulu', 'Port Shepstone – Swaziland', 'North Western Trans-vaal, bordering respectively Bechuanaland and Limpopo' and 'North Western Cape – South West'.[115]

Shortly afterwards, Arthur Goldreich enters the driveway. When he notices the policemen he immediately starts reversing. Three policemen jump onto his car and one of them points a revolver at him through the window. Goldreich stops the car and is arrested.

Goldreich looks on as policemen tear the car apart. Secreted in one of the hubcaps they find a copy of *Operation Mayibuye*.

Detective Warrant Officer Kennedy finds Goldreich in the company of some policemen saying he knows nothing about the occupants of the outbuilding and the farm. Goldreich says he only hired the main building from the company Navian (Pty) Ltd. He does, however, admit ownership of a duplicating machine and photographs found in the outbuilding; Goldreich says he stored equipment in those rooms. He denies he has a key to a built-in cupboard in the house.

In the main building, the police force the door of the built-in cupboard and find a wall safe inside. Goldreich denies all knowledge of its existence. The police blow the safe open and find money inside.[116]

The police also search a coal shed in the main house and there they find, hidden under the floor, a number of journals of Nelson Mandela, including the diary of his 1962 African trip. They also find Mandela's false passport and a number of handwritten documents authored by him, including one titled 'How to be a good Communist', and a letter referring to a proposed escape plan, saying it would be too difficult for MK to execute now as a young army, but adding that after his conviction the police would relax, so it could be attempted later. This letter includes a written request by Mandela, 'Please destroy as soon as you have finished reading'.[117]

ADVERSITY AND RETREAT

Wilton Mkwayi arrives in Rivonia by taxi at dusk on the 11th. He tells the driver he is going to the flats near the post office to look for somebody.

The taxi passes the gate of Liliesleaf Farm and stops at the flats, where Mkwayi gets off and pays. When the car is out of sight, he turns back and walks towards Liliesleaf.

He passes along a footpath that runs through the bushes on a neighbour's property. When he reaches Liliesleaf, Mkwayi sees two big dogs but no people. He changes his route away from that entrance and heads for the main gate instead.

While walking on the main road towards the gate, he sees another dog. When he reaches the main gate, with tall trees marking the entrance, he steps inside but sees more dogs behind the tree trunks.

Moving away from the property altogether, he takes a footpath towards the river. He sees more dogs near the river so he jumps the fence into another farm where there are cattle. He moves slowly across the field and past the cattle, and then across some bushes. From there he marches briskly towards Alexandra.[1]

*

On 18 July, South Africa's police commissioner Lieutenant General J.M. Keevy tells a *Rand Daily Mail* correspondent that the banned Johannesburg attorney Harold Wolpe was arrested the day before near the border with Bechuanaland. Pressed for further details regarding the circumstances of the arrest, Keevy declines to comment.[2]

Wolpe was arrested in disguise, with his beard shaven and his hair dyed auburn, in a vehicle driven by Mike Michaelis, the husband of his wife's cousin. Michaelis was driving two Norwegian friends to the border area for a picnic. The idea was that Wolpe would cross into Bechuanaland on foot during lunch. The plan came unstuck when Michaelis drove up to a group of black workers led by two white overseers. One of the overseers was a border policeman. The group had no papers and were taken to the local police station. There, Wolpe gave a fake name and address, but said he was a lawyer. This was followed up and the security police were called in.[3]

*

In East London on the 18th, Donald Card receives an unsigned scribbled note from Reginald Mdube affirming that Washington Bongco still lives in Princess Alice Drive.

That evening, Card, in the company of another informer (not Mdube), goes to Number 48 Princess Alice Drive, a double-storey building with a garage below. He tells the informer to remain in the car.

Card knocks on the door for a long time, but there is no response. He tests the door and finds that it is locked. He lies on his stomach and shines his torch under the door but sees no sign of life. When he knocks on the door of an adjacent room, the maid opens and tells him there is nobody in the other room.

Card returns to the first room and again shines his torch under the door. He sees part of a garment that was not there before. He stands up and forces the door open with a shoulder barge. He finds a woman on the bed in her night clothes and a man halfway out the window. Card grabs him by the leg, causing the man to lose grip of the gutter he was clinging on to. Card alone is between the man and a fifteen-foot drop to the concrete driveway below. Card tries but fails to pull the man back into the room, so he shouts at the woman to get the man from the car.

The informer arrives and he and Card manage to haul Washington Bongco into the room.[4]

*

In Lobatse on 20 July, Fish Keitseng takes possession of a new Land Rover, registration BPF 320.[5]

*

Jack Hodgson writes to Oliver Tambo four days later and says that since the Rivonia arrests communications with South Africa have broken down.

There are, however, 'indications that some of our chaps are still available', so 'it may be necessary for some of us to go back in to re-organise'.

As for Bechuanaland, Hodgson says that after great difficulty owing to the fact that the South African government had purchased every such car in the republic, a

Land Rover was bought from Southern Rhodesia for Fish Keitseng. Hodgson says he has given Keitseng an intensive driving course and he should be able to qualify for his driver's licence in another week or so.[6]

*

A black man enters Fleet Street Police Station in East London and asks to speak to Detective Sergeant Card.

In an interrogation room, the man tells Donald Card that Chief Makeleni of the Kwelera area has sent him.

At roughly 2 a.m. on 31 July, Card is outside a hut in a kraal in Chalumna, a tribal hamlet near Hamburg, about an hour's drive from East London. He kicks open the lower portion of the door and sees a man hiding behind two 44-gallon tins. A blanket is lying loose on the ground.

The man, Malcolmess Kondoti, says in Xhosa, 'You've got me.'[7]

*

Stephen Mtshali is arrested at his aunt's home in Durban on the morning of 3 August 1963.

He is interrogated by Detective Warrant Officer Nicolaas J. Grobler in offices at Wentworth Police Station.

On the same morning, at a house in Durban's Windsor Park suburb, Ronnie Kasrils gives Bruno Mtolo some money and tells him to use it to go to Kloof, buy some meat and vegetables, meet Stephen Mtshali and bring him to the new hideout.

Mtolo leaves at 11 a.m. When he reaches Kloof Railway Station, Officers Grobler and Wessels pounce and take him to Pinetown Police Station.[8]

*

On 7 August, a team of Security Branch policemen led by Lieutenant Steenkamp arrests Sonny Singh at the Durban restaurant where he works as a waiter.[9]

*

Two days later, a pair of Security Branch detectives enter the premises of the University of the Witwatersrand.

They go to the main section of the library where they find Ruth First searching for books.

Then, with students looking on in silence, they arrest her under the ninety-day clause.[10]

*

In the second week of August, Lawrence Phokanoka and Leonard Nkosi are part of a group of thirty including Archie Sibeko, Chris Hani, Justice Mpanza and Mark Shope who are flown on a British Overseas Airways Corporation plane from Dar es Salaam to Khartoum.

From the Sudan they fly on a Russian aeroplane to Moscow. There they are met by Russian officials in civilian clothes, who take them in two buses to a double-storey building surrounded by bushes about five miles outside Moscow.[11]

The house has a high wooden fence around it. They are welcomed by a Soviet colonel and a major.[12]

*

At roughly 1.30 a.m. on 11 August, prison warder Johannes Greeff leads Mosie Moolla, Harold Wolpe, Abdulhai Jassat and Arthur Goldreich down a flight of stairs at Marshall Square prison in Johannesburg. Greeff unlocks a door which leads into a storage room. At the other end is a door leading onto a car park. Moolla, Wolpe, Jassat and Goldreich each give Greeff a grateful pat on the shoulder before disappearing into the night.

Greeff then goes upstairs to Goldreich's cell and butts his head against the bars in an attempt to obtain plausible injuries.

Lieutenant Willie van Wyk, whose source provided the information leading to the Rivonia raid, arrives at Marshall Square later that morning. He asks to see Greeff. Almost immediately, the very lightly injured Greeff makes a confession during which he admits the prisoners offered him R4,000 to help them escape.[13]

*

Arrests of members of the underground continue throughout the country.

At about 4 p.m. on 19 August, Detective Sergeant P. Ferreira arrests three men at a house in Elsie's River near Cape Town. One of them is Looksmart Ngudle.

In a room in the house Ferreira finds a paper bag containing a roll of toilet paper, a bottle of Vaseline, plastic bags, charcoal, flowers of sulphur, potassium nitrate, icing sugar and several eye droppers. He also finds political pamphlets, a typewriter, ten hacksaw blades and a pistol.

Ngudle admits that all the articles are his.[14]

*

A Swazi Air Cessna plane lands in Lobatse at 12.30 p.m. on the 27th.

The pilot signs in his name as 'Truter' on the refuelling log. He tells the engineer on duty that he discharged two passengers at the north end of the runway but they disappeared into the bush.

At 2.45 p.m., Inspectors Smith and Coxon track down two white men dressed as religious ministers, but who are in fact Arthur Goldreich and Harold Wolpe.[15]

On the following day, Fish Keitseng drives Goldreich and Wolpe from Lobatse to Francistown.

In Francistown, Goldreich grants an interview to Allister Sparks of the *Rand Daily Mail*. Goldreich boasts: 'At no time did the police get anywhere near us. All those police statements about the net closing were so much nonsense.'

He is keen to give credit to the underground: 'Obviously we did not do this alone. In spite of what Mr Vorster says about me I am not a one-man band. I cannot say anything at all which may endanger people still in South Africa.'[16]

At about 2.15 a.m. the following morning, Keith Munger, an air transport and security officer, is lying in bed at his house on Francistown's airfield, trying to get to sleep. Hearing a large explosion, he springs up and runs to the window. He cannot see the runway directly from this vantage point, but observes a large column of flame and black smoke rising from behind a neighbour's house. He grabs his jersey and runs out of the house.

Munger sees his neighbour, Hendrik Ferreira, approaching and calling for him. The two reach the scene of the explosion along with two black security guards. With a fire tender they spray the starboard side of the plane (an East African Airways Dakota) where the explosion occurred, but they see the flames spreading towards the port wing, where the petrol tanks are stored.

There is a smaller private plane next to the burning Dakota. They push this aircraft out of range.

Just as they get it to a safe distance, the Dakota's petrol tank explodes.[17] It was the plane on which Goldreich and Wolpe were planning to flee Bechuanaland later that morning.

*

On 4 September, Magistrate J.J. Marais is in the Pretoria North Police Station doing his weekly rounds checking on the condition of ninety-day-law detainees. Looksmart Ngudle is one of them. He complains to Marais that he has been assaulted to get him to make a statement, and that he has been coughing up blood.

Ngudle is found the following day dead in his cell, hanging by the cord of his pyjama trousers and a jersey.[18]

*

A *Rand Daily Mail* correspondent phones Arthur Goldreich at 1.15 a.m. on 6 September.

Goldreich is in protective custody in a Francistown jail. The reporter says that the back-up relief plane Goldreich and Wolpe were expecting from Dar es Salaam has crashed in Mbeya.

'Good God!' are Goldreich's first words.[19]

*

Later the same day in Vereeniging prison, Denis Goldberg pushes a wad of paper into his cell door as he is being locked in. During the lunch break, with most of the warders off duty, he forces the door open and proceeds to the exercise yard, where he climbs a drainpipe leading onto the roof of the single-storey prison. He is, however, spotted by a fellow prisoner before making the six-metre jump to freedom on the other side.

About forty-five minutes into his escape, Goldberg hears a police siren. His heart sinks. He is stopped in an alleyway in Vereeniging by two prison guards. One stands over him with a rifle while the other gives his ribs a kicking.[20]

*

At 4.30 a.m. on 8 September comes the third instalment in the Goldreich–Wolpe escape saga. In the company of an American reporter, they slip out of Francistown jail and are then transported in a vehicle driven by an officer of the Bechuanaland Special Branch. A police truck follows as a safety precaution. The vehicles speed towards Palapye.

At 8 a.m. a Cessna four-seater aircraft belonging to TIMAIR of Tanganyika lands at Palapye airfield. Goldreich and Wolpe signal to it with a sheet draped over their car.

The four-seater plane spends only two minutes on the ground before taking off with them.[21]

*

Outside Fish Keitseng's house in Peleng Village, Lobatse, on the night of 17 September, the Land Rover bought by Jack Hodgson for Keitseng's use is extensively damaged by explosives.[22]

*

Jack and Rica Hodgson are deported from the Bechuanaland protectorate four days later. They are accompanied by a Bechuanaland police inspector on a plane chartered by the protectorate's administration, and they land in Mbeya, Tanganyika, on the afternoon of 22 September.[23]

*

Ian David Kitson and Lionel Gay meet at the latter's house. Kitson asks if Gay would be willing to serve on an ad hoc committee to keep Umkhonto we Sizwe functioning. Kitson clarifies that the committee would keep MK's activities going on a day-to-day basis until the liberation movement could decide a new policy following the Rivonia arrests. He says that he expects to be arrested at any time, but that Gay is probably not suspected by the police. Kitson stresses that nobody will think badly of him if he chooses to withdraw.

Gay agrees to help.[24]

*

On 1 October, Bob Hepple meets state prosecutor Dr Percy Yutar at Security Branch headquarters in Pretoria. Yutar says five or six 'leading persons' are making statements and he wants to wait and see what they will say about Hepple before deciding what to do next.

Six days later, the two men meet again. Yutar says he has made a decision to use Hepple as a state witness. Hepple responds that he wants to contact the Johannesburg Bar Council and his family.

Advocates H.D. Nicholas and J.D. Schwartz immediately arrive to see him, after which Hepple meets his wife and family and gives them a copy of a typewritten statement made by him on 5 August. In the statement he said that he was at Rivonia on 11 July because Walter Sisulu asked to see him in hiding to discuss matters such as the ninety-day law and Sisulu's appeal against a Regional Court conviction. Hepple claimed in the statement that it was his first visit to Rivonia and he was surprised to find others there.

He asks his family to give the statement to Bram Fischer.

(The police also possess a second, more incriminating tape-recorded statement by Hepple, which was produced three days after the first. In this declaration he said he had been recruited by Joe Slovo, and that in 1962 he had couriered letters at Slovo's request to Liliesleaf Farm, where he met Govan Mbeki and Walter Sisulu, while he drove to the farm on another occasion in Ahmed Kathrada's company.)

Hepple meets Yutar again following the meeting with his family. He says he is still undecided about testifying as a state witness. Yutar says that if that is the case he will be charged along with the others.[25]

*

Security Branch teams of five and six are positioned at the corners of the old granite Supreme Court building overlooking Church Square in Pretoria, while colleagues in similarly sized groups guard the surrounding streets. Uniformed police reinforcements meanwhile congregate around two vans in the square itself. It is around 9.30 a.m. on 9 October 1963. Some five minutes later a large, dusty police van with Security Branch vehicles in front and behind it enters the court's rear entrance.

At 10 a.m. Nelson Mandela, Walter Sisulu, Denis Goldberg, Govan Mbeki, Ahmed Kathrada, Rusty Bernstein, Raymond Mhlaba, James Kantor, Elias Motsoaledi, Andrew Mlangeni and Bob Hepple appear in the court. They are there to have charges read to them in this the opening sitting of *The State versus the National High Command and Others*, which will soon be better known as the 'Rivonia Trial'.[26]

*

A South African Military Intelligence report dated 21 October 1963 estimates that over 400 ANC members have been flown out of Dar es Salaam and most of them are in Moscow, 'probably for military training'.[27]

A further group of twenty Umkhonto we Sizwe cadres arrives in Moscow for military training towards the end of the month. They meet up with the Hani–Sibeko–Phokanoka group of thirty that came in August.[28]

*

On 30 October, during the tea adjournment on the second day of the Rivonia Trial, Percy Yutar calls Bob Hepple into his office. Yutar says he has decided to release him.

After the adjournment, when the judge asks to be addressed by Hepple (who is representing himself), Yutar intervenes and says the charges are being withdrawn against Hepple, who will be asked to testify for the state.[29]

*

On 7 November, the *Rand Daily Mail* carries a South African Press Association–Reuters dispatch that in Washington D.C. the day before, American officials confirmed reports that a Soviet plane recently transported a group of South African refugees from Dar es Salaam to Moscow.

The Americans, however, said that they could not confirm claims that this was for guerrilla warfare training.[30]

*

When Bob Hepple and Bram Fischer meet at a clandestine location, Hepple is told that the accused in the Rivonia Trial have spent more time discussing his situation than anything else, and they agree that leaving the country is the only viable alternative to him becoming a state witness.

Fischer tells Hepple to leave in eight days' time, and adds that he should go with his wife to avoid her being held as a hostage by the police.

Eight days later, towards the end of November, Bob and Shirley Hepple cross a border fence and enter Bechuanaland illegally with the assistance of two colleagues.[31]

*

Around the beginning of December, a meeting takes place at Lionel Gay's house in Parkhurst, Johannesburg. It is attended by Ian David Kitson, Wilton Mkwayi and Gay himself.

Kitson says that they comprise the new National High Command. He adds that the representative of the politicians told him that in view of the shortages of personnel caused by arrests, detention and departures, the new command can't go running to the politicians every five minutes, but have to act as independently as possible within the framework of existing policy.

Kitson says it is desired by the movement that sabotage be carried out to send the message that Umkhonto we Sizwe is still alive.[32]

*

A group of forty youngsters are in a big Morris truck driven alternately by Mzewu Ntsele, Johannes Tau-Tau and Joe Modise from Dar es Salaam through Nairobi, Kenya, and on to Juba in the Sudan in December 1963.

From Juba they are escorted by riverboat along the Nile to Khartoum.

On their fifth day in Khartoum, one of the group, Eleazor Maboya, says that the next day they will fly to Odessa for training as freedom fighters.

The following afternoon, the forty are flown by the Russian carrier Aeroflot to Cairo, and from there to Odessa.

When their plane lands in the Ukraine, they are met by a Russian official. They are then driven to the camp of the Military Academy of the Soviet Union, approximately five miles east of Odessa's Black Sea harbour.

At the Military Academy there are two sections. One contains Red Army soldiers while the other, which is much smaller, holds freedom fighters from various parts of the world.

The forty ANC men are divided into three groups upon arrival: those with education below Standard 6 are assigned to the infantry; those with qualifications up to a junior certificate (Standard 8) are to be trained in radiology, engineering and the manufacture, use and identification of explosives; while the last group, with qualifications above Standard 8, are to be trained as commanders.

The following day the groups are addressed at their quarters by camp commandant Colonel Zscizserin and his lieutenant, Colonel Pronibrakiz, with the aid of an interpreter from Russian to English, and with Eleazor Maboya translating from English to Zulu.

Colonel Zscizserin says that they are going to be trained for nine months in guerrilla warfare. Colonel Pronibrakiz adds that after completing the training they will return to South Africa to fight.[33]

*

The MK region in Pretoria has been relatively unscathed by the wave of arrests thus far (though its leader Peter Mogano is in prison, having been convicted in a trial held in November–December 1963). But this is about to change.

On the evening of 16 January 1964, Bernard Mochesane is walking the streets of Mamelodi when he comes across a drinking party at a private house. He walks inside and sees about fifteen people.

Nobody notices him, so he declares aloud that the Congress is a good thing; the people of Basutoland are about to get their independence as a result of the Congress. (He means the Basutoland Congress Party and is referring to that territory's impending independence from Britain.)

The men continue to ignore him – with the exception of one man, who takes him aside. Mochesane introduces himself to this man as 'Lucas Mokele' and says he has come from the Free State and is working at Iscor.

The man says in response: 'I am Mampane, I am a member of Umkhonto we Sizwe.' He says he is awaiting a certain man who he works with in blowing places up. He adds that another person will bring explosives that they will use to blow up a chief's guesthouse in Mamelodi.[34]

*

On Monday 27 January, Bernard Mochesane is with Joseph Mampane and Levy Molefe, the colleague Mampane referred to on their first meeting. They are in Mampane's house in Mamelodi.

Molefe says they haven't got any oil or petrol. He orders his colleagues to go and buy some.

Mampane says he hasn't got any money.

Mochesane says the same but adds that he knows somebody who lives quite close by from whom he can borrow cash.

Molefe tells him to go to that person, borrow the money and bring the oil and petrol – about half a gallon.

At about 9 p.m. Thomas Kgwele, a senior detective sergeant in the South African Police, is in the house of a colleague in Mamelodi when another member of the force walks in. It is Constable Bernard Mochesane.

When Mochesane has finished his report, Kgwele hands him fifty cents and tells him to use it to make the purchases. Kgwele also gives him a tin. Before Mochesane leaves, they set their watches to exactly the same time.

When Mochesane returns to Mampane's house he hands two tins over to Molefe.

The trio depart at about 9.30 p.m. Molefe carries a briefcase and a green tin, and Mochesane a tin containing petrol. They leave the kitchen door, exit the front gate, walk across an open space and turn slightly to the right. Just before they reach the next block in the location, a car drives past, flashing its lights as it overtakes them, and parks.

Molefe asks who those people are.

Mochesane tells him not to worry; they are just people getting out of their car.

The three walk past the vehicle: Mochesane is on the left-hand side, Molefe in the middle and Mampane on the right. At this point Detective Sergeant Kgwele, Detective Constable Simon Majinga and colleagues exit the vehicle.

Sergeant Kgwele grabs Molefe. Maintaining his cover, Constable Mochesane drops his tin and runs. Mampane also flees.

Sergeant Kgwele leaves Molefe in Majinga's hands and chases Mampane. Kgwele fires two shots in Mampane's direction, but he misses and Mampane gets away.[35]

*

Later that evening, Sergeant P.A. Ferreira (who was involved in the interception of the convoy headed to the Bechuanaland border in Essop Suleiman's Combis in June 1963) arrives at Vlakfontein Police Station in Mamelodi. In one of the offices he meets Levy Molefe and tells him he is being detained in terms of the ninety-day clause and will be held until he gives a satisfactory statement about his knowledge of Umkhonto we Sizwe activities in Pretoria.

Ferreira is in the passenger seat, while a black detective sits directly behind him in the back seat alongside Molefe, in a vehicle being driven to Pretoria by Sergeant Uys (who was with Ferreira during the arrests the previous year). As Uys turns left into Fountain Lane, Molefe suddenly says in Afrikaans: 'Daar kom Masupye.'

Walking towards them on the side path on the other side of the road is John Masupye, who assumed the role of MK commander in Pretoria following Peter Mogano's arrest on 24 June 1963. Masupye is walking alongside another person. Sergeant Uys stops the car, climbs out and arrests Masupye.

When Masupye enters the vehicle he sees Levy Molefe in handcuffs and also notices the tin of gunpowder that was to be used in the operation on the chief's guesthouse that Masupye sent Molefe to conduct earlier that evening.

Ferreira and Uys had no knowledge that Masupye was even a suspect. This unravelling of the MK command followed Constable Mochesane's random search for troublemakers in the Mamelodi tavern eleven days previously.[36]

*

At the ANC's office in Dar es Salaam, chief representative James Hadebe is present when Patrick Baphela and T.T. Cholo (who left South Africa together in July 1962), Samuel Balekeng, Lucky Sitole, Michael Diro, Peter Metshane and Mnyamane Hlaya are told by Duma Nokwe that they must go to China for military training.

On 30 January, the seven cadres arrive by plane in Kunming in China, having flown from Rangoon. They are met at the airport by a man who introduces himself in fluent English as Lee Shang from the Chinese Peace Committee.

On the 31st, Mr Shang accompanies them on a flight to Peking. There they are introduced to a 'Mr Chen' who says through an interpreter that he is vice president of the Chinese Afro-Asian Solidarity Committee.

The ANC cadres depart for Nanking by train on 5 February in the company of Mr Chen and the interpreter.

Three days later they are met at the station by the president of the Military Academy of Nanking. He declares that they have come to China to share some of the experiences of the Chinese revolution as well as to receive training in the making of explosives and rifle shooting. They will be studying from 16 February to the end of April.[37]

*

In March 1964, Fish Keitseng, Johannes Rantau, Henderson Tshepe, Ronald Letsholonyane, Tennyson Makiwane, Oliver Tambo, Moses Mabhida and Duma Nokwe attend a meeting in Livingstone, Northern Rhodesia.

Nokwe presides. He says that Russia has committed R40,000; Czechoslovakia R34,000; Red China R36,000; the Anti-Apartheid Committee in England R24,000; the ANC journals *Mayibuye* and *Spotlight* R14,000; and the Organisation of African Unity's (OAU) Liberation Committee in Dar es Salaam R14,000 to the 'African Aid Fund'.

Nokwe says that he is going to give them instructions regarding the purposes for which they will spend the Fund's money. They must account every six months regarding disbursements, and funds will be allocated according to expenses incurred.

The funds are to be used for, firstly, the transportation and maintenance of refugees, whether going abroad for military or educational training or returning home after this training; secondly, to cover travelling expenses for organisers and to provide gifts for contacts recruited along the borders (but Nokwe stresses that gifts given to contacts will be limited to a maximum of R16 and a minimum of R10); thirdly, buying South African newspapers for the ANC office in Dar es Salaam; fourthly, for communications; and lastly, for covering staff salaries.

Regarding roles in Bechuanaland, the meeting delegates Johannes Rantau to work out escape routes and recruit contacts on the southern borders of the protectorate; Letsholonyane is to buy food and clothing; Fish Keitseng is to see refugees through at the immigration offices in Lobatse and ensure that they get through to Northern Rhodesia – he is to be assisted by Ramatshwiritlha Mokgosi in this; Henderson Tshepe meanwhile is to see refugees through the immigration offices in Francistown and likewise ensure their safe passage to Northern Rhodesia.[38]

*

In the same month, Michael Dingake and Johannes Rantau meet Martiens Mogotsi at his home in Gopane Village, which is near Zeerust and a few miles from South Africa's border with Bechuanaland.

When they have finished their pitch to him, Martiens asks what he will get in return for helping people cross the border.

Afterwards, Dingake takes Mogotsi to Lobatse and then to Johannesburg, where they meet a man by the name of William Senna.[39]

*

The white and non-white galleries of the Pretoria Supreme Court are packed on 20 April when Bram Fischer, QC, informs Judge President Quartus de Wet that 'The defence case will commence with a statement from the dock by Accused No. 1, who personally took part in the establishment of Umkhonto, and who will be able to inform the Court of the beginnings of that organisation, and of its history up to August, when he was arrested.'

Percy Yutar, the state prosecutor, says the accused should be apprised of the fact that a statement from the dock does not carry the same weight as evidence under oath, though he is sure the accused (as a legal practitioner himself) knows this.

Accused No. 1, Nelson Mandela, gestures that he is indeed aware of this.[40]

During his statement, Mandela identifies the anti-republic stay-at-home of May 1961, and the state's reaction to it, as the *casus belli*. He says the strike was planned to be peaceful, and accordingly careful instructions were conveyed to organisers and members to avoid violence. Despite this,

> The government's answer was to introduce new and harsher laws, to mobilise its armed forces, and to send Saracens [tanks], armed vehicles and soldiers into the townships in a massive show of force designed to intimidate the people. This was an indication that the government had decided to rule by force alone, and this decision was a milestone on the road to Umkhonto.

Regarding what the liberation movement is fighting *for*, towards the end of his address Mandela says: 'Above all, we want equal political rights, because without them our disabilities will be permanent.' He says white fears over granting the vote to the African majority 'cannot be allowed to stand in the way of the only solution which will guarantee racial harmony and freedom for all'.

At the end of his four-hour speech Mandela says:

> During my lifetime I have dedicated myself to this struggle of the African people. I have fought against white domination, and I have fought against black domination. I have cherished the ideal of a democratic and free society in which all persons live together in harmony and with equal opportunities. It is an ideal which I hope to live for and to achieve. But if needs be, it is an ideal for which I am prepared to die.[41]

The sitting is attended by Leslie Minford, the consul-general of the United Kingdom, and John Miles, the counsellor of the United States embassy.[42]

*

On 30 April Patrick Baphela, T.T. Cholo, Samuel Balekeng, Lucky Sitole, Michael Diro, Peter Metshane and Mnyamane Hlaya fly to Shanghai, having completed their training at the Nanking Military Academy.

They land on 10 May at Dar es Salaam Airport, where they are met by Duma Nokwe and Joseph Jack.

At the ANC's Dar es Salaam office on the 12th, Baphela, Hlaya and Metshane hold a meeting with James Hadebe, Duma Nokwe and Oliver Tambo. Nokwe asks whether they feel guerrilla warfare can ever be applied in South Africa as it was in China.

Baphela says that he is not sure about its success in South Africa, because conditions in the country are so different. China is backwards and an undeveloped country. It also has lots of mountains and forests and is exceedingly vast, while South Africa is highly developed, there are not enough forests, too few mountains, and it is not as vast as China.

Nokwe says that it's all right. They should make an attempt and see how they might succeed.[43]

*

The Supreme Court in Pretoria is again packed at 10 a.m. on 11 June when the accused in the Rivonia Trial, who have been reduced from eleven to nine, enter the dock. (As mentioned, the charges against Bob Hepple were withdrawn, after which he fled the country, while those against Kantor were dropped at the end of the state's case in March.)

Justice de Wet immediately begins reading his judgment.[44] The accused face four charges. Two concern their involvement in sabotage and their efforts to recruit and train people for guerrilla warfare. These fall under the Sabotage Act. The third, claiming that they acted in order to advance communism, contravenes the Suppression of Communism Act. The last, accusing them of accepting and distributing money to further the conspiracy, is an offence under the General Laws Amendment Act.[45]

De Wet finds Nelson Mandela, Walter Sisulu, Govan Mbeki, Denis Goldberg, Raymond Mhlaba, Elias Motsoaledi and Andrew Mlangeni guilty on all four counts, Ahmed Kathrada guilty only on the second, and he acquits Rusty Bernstein on all charges.

The four-minute judgment is received in silence. De Wet then rises and departs. As the court rises, Bernstein is immediately re-arrested and taken down to the cells on a charge of having broken his banning order by being present in Rivonia during the raid. His fellow accused file out and head down the stairs towards the cells.[46]

Sentencing comes the following day. Justice de Wet says that the offences of which the accused were found guilty were essentially treasonous, but since the state did not charge them with treason he will not impose the death penalty.

He instead sentences the guilty eight to life imprisonment.[47]

*

On the morning of Saturday 27 June, Security Branch policemen arrest Lionel Gay at his home on 13th Street, Parkhurst.[48]

*

The *Rand Daily Mail* of 3 July reports that in separate swoops in Johannesburg in the previous week, besides Lionel Gay, others arrested include Ian David Kitson, John Edward Matthews and Cyril Jones.[49]

*

On the 4th, the *Mail* reports that raids and searches conducted the day before saw 'at least 17' further people jailed under the ninety-day clause.[50]

*

Justice minister John Vorster releases a statement in Pretoria on the 5th, saying, 'Certain persons have also been detained and it is expected that the various discoveries made will possibly lead to the destruction of the Communist-inspired subversive campaign.'[51]

*

Mac Maharaj and his wife Tim are arrested on 6 July at the servants' quarters where they are staying in Pearse Street, Doornfontein.[52]

*

Then at 5 p.m. four days later, Nandha Naidoo is walking on Wills Road, close to 21 Pearse Street where he has been staying with Mac Maharaj since mid-1963, having decided to accede to the leadership's request that he report to Johannesburg.

A voice from a parked car calls out: 'Steve! Get in, we want you for questioning.' A large number of police are then involved in arresting Naidoo.[53]

*

In the middle of July, Patrick Baphela and Peter Metshane from the group trained in Nanking earlier in the year are in the company of Macdonald Masala, Siegfried Bhengu and Tennyson Makiwane on a bus exiting Dar es Salaam.

Three nights later they arrive at the home of Thomas Nkobi in Lusaka.

After a half day at Nkobi's, they transfer to a property owned by Bessie Zondi, a South African refugee.[54]

*

The ANC's National Secretariat meets in Orlando West Extension in the same month. At this stage the Secretariat consists of Gabula Mahlasela, Wilton Mkwayi, Bartholomew Hlapane and Michael Dingake, who are all present at the meeting.

Hlapane reports on the financial position of the ANC in South Africa. He describes it as critical and says there is no chance of getting funds in the future. He suggests that Dingake be sent to headquarters in Dar es Salaam to report the situation and appeal for more funds.

This proposal is endorsed.[55]

*

Bartholomew Hlapane is informed by Issy Heymann towards the end of July that he must go and see Bram Fischer at a flat numbered 82 in Berea.

Hlapane keeps the appointment and at 4 p.m. on the designated day meets Bram Fischer and Eli Weinberg in the flat.

Hlapane briefs them about the ANC's present condition. He speaks about the weakness of the National Secretariat, which is no longer in touch with any centres besides Johannesburg, and the Regional Committees which are quite unable to assist with reorganising the movement. He says the entire set-up of the organisation as it pertains to coordination between the National Secretariat, Regional Committees and Area Committees is uselessly inadequate and it seems as if nothing can be done to remedy the situation.

Fischer asks Hlapane to do everything he can to put the situation right.

Weinberg meanwhile promises to assist Hlapane in finding a new contact now that Mac Maharaj has been arrested.[56]

*

At the beginning of August a large group of trained Umkhonto we Sizwe members, including Archie Sibeko, Zolile Nqose, Leonard Nkosi, Eric Mtshali, Benjamin Ramotse and dozens of others, are reunited at Moscow Airport, where they board a plane destined for Tanganyika.

At Dar es Salaam Airport they are met by Nimrod Sijake of the ANC. The group is conveyed by truck to a residence in Dar es Salaam known as 'Mandela Camp'.

Three or so days later, Ambrose Makiwane (Tennyson Makiwane's cousin), who is in charge of Mandela Camp, informs the recruits that he has been appointed commander of a military camp that they are going to establish at a place called Kongwa, about 360 miles from Dar es Salaam and near Dodoma. They will stay in Kongwa until more trained men arrive and an attack can be launched on South Africa.

The group is then conveyed in two Tanganyikan military trucks along a rough and wet road. Along the way they see lions, zebra, wildebeest, cheetahs and other animals.

When they arrive at Kongwa, they find a site at which there are only two dilapidated buildings in which the kitchen, toilets and showers are all in need of cleaning and repair.

On the evening of their first day, the group sleeps in a courthouse in Kongwa village.

The following morning they clear the camp and move in.[57]

*

Later in August, Michael Dingake meets Duma Nokwe, James Hadebe and Tennyson Makiwane in Dar es Salaam. Dingake is there on the mission delegated to him by the ANC Secretariat the previous month.

Dingake tells them that the ANC in South Africa is weakening, the Secretariat has lost contact with other centres, and it is unable to organise political campaigns on even a small scale owing to a lack of funds.[58]

*

Peter Metshane and Siegfried Bhengu of the group trained in Nanking earlier in the year arrive by train in Ootse in the Bechuanaland protectorate, having come from Lusaka. They then walk the thirteen miles separating Ootse and Lobatse.

In Lobatse they connect with Johannes Rantau, who takes them to stay with his brother Masibe Rantau, who lives some four miles from the South African border .

At this house, Metshane and Bhengu meet Martiens Mogotsi, who then leaves to enquire about the route further on. Mogotsi heads to Gopane (inside South Africa), where he visits the house of William Senna's son Simon, who tells him to take 'Norman' and Bhengu to Johannesburg – the two are from school, and Norman will know where to go, Senna says.

A couple of days after departing, Mogotsi returns to fetch Metshane and Bhengu. He leads them across the Bechuanaland–South Africa border near the Botha gate before proceeding to Gopane.[59]

*

Peter Metshane and Siegfried Bhengu are on a bus headed for Johannesburg on a Sunday in August 1964. They get off at Roodepoort and walk to Meadowlands, where they call in on a friend of Metshane's nicknamed 'Mkoko'.

Metshane and Bhengu are then driven by Mkoko to a house in Moletsani in Soweto that is positioned right next to the railway station in the Tladi area. The house is owned by a woman known as 'Matoto'.

Shortly afterwards at Matoto's house, Metshane and Bhengu are met by Wilton Mkwayi, who says he eventually wants to have eight people who he can settle in various parts of Johannesburg to train recruits in politics and the use of explosives.[60]

*

On 1 September, Wilton Mkwayi and Bartholomew Hlapane meet in Westcliff Extension in Johannesburg. Regarding money, Mkwayi says he has sufficient cash on hand.[61]

*

Hlapane is detained by the South African Police the following day.[62]

*

By September 1964 Mnyamane Hlaya has joined Macdonald Masala and Patrick Baphela at Bessie Zondi's place in Lusaka.

During the month, Tennyson Makiwane and another man arrive to collect Masala.[63]

*

Later in September, a large group, in excess of 150, arrives at MK's Kongwa camp.[64] The group is led by Eleazor Maboya and includes Daluxolo Luthuli, Reddy Mazimba, Mack Futha and Isaac Mapoto.

*

Shortly afterwards, Ambrose Makiwane arrives at the camp with other members of his staff. They are there to conduct an inquiry into the conduct of Edwin Mkwanazi,

Elliot Zondo, Morgan Molefe and Mike Mbeya over claims that Mkwanazi, assisted by the rest, raped a Russian woman in Odessa.

Mkwanazi is given lashes and one week's imprisonment; the others are confined to the camp for two weeks.[65]

*

On another, later occasion, Ambrose Makiwane calls out the names of George Mann, Patrick Museti, Nimrod Zwane, Jefferey Mukoka, Elias Matlase and three others at Kongwa.

He finds them guilty of supporting the doctrines of Maoist China during a seminar in Odessa, and thus tarnishing the ANC's name with its Soviet allies.

As punishment, Makiwane instructs Lambert Moloi to take a piece of hosepipe and inflict twenty cuts on each man.[66]

*

On 1 October, Wilton Mkwayi is arrested at a friend's home in Orlando West, Soweto. Bartholomew Hlapane has accompanied the police to the scene of the arrest.[67]

EXTERNAL MISSION IN COMMAND

Michael Dingake, Siegfried Bhengu and Dan Tloome meet in Lobatse. Tloome tells Bhengu that since Dingake is a member of the ANC Secretariat he will take charge of the organisation within South Africa following Mkwayi's arrest.

Towards the end of October, Bhengu and Dingake leave Lobatse in the company of William Senna, who guides them across the border to Gopane Village. From there, Dingake and Bhengu travel by railway bus to Roodepoort. On the way, they converse. Bhengu says he has arranged for Dingake to meet with Josiah Jele.

When the pair disembark in Roodepoort, they travel together by taxi to Ikwezi Station. Bhengu tells Dingake that Jele is living in Mofolo. The two then part ways.

When Jele and Dingake meet, Jele says he has nobody to work with besides Hendrik Ramahadi, who is helping him distribute allowances to dependants. Jele mentions that prior to Wilton Mkwayi's arrest, Mkwayi introduced him to Siegfried Bhengu, and they spoke about Bhengu going to Lobatse to find out who was going to take over.

Dingake asks Jele to work with him because his colleagues in the Secretariat have been arrested and one has fled the country.

Jele accepts.[1]

*

Amin Cajee is part of a group that arrives in Kongwa camp on 22 October 1964.

One day during the following week the camp commander approaches the toilet, which is situated 500 metres from the main building. When he enters, 'Attention!'

is relayed throughout the camp, upon which all the troops stand to attention. The commander Ambrose Makiwane raises his hand upon which everyone is at ease.

When Makiwane exits the toilet, 'Attention!' is again relayed.

On another occasion during that first week, at about 5.30 a.m., while the recruits are doing early-morning roadwork, Makiwane follows them in a Land Rover. Cajee hears what sounds like a clink of glass from the vehicle. He sneaks a peek, and sees Makiwane with a bottle of whisky.

Later in the same week, as the recruits are sleeping at night, a bugle sounds in the camp. All the soldiers assemble. They find the commander struggling to balance on one leg. Makiwane makes a political speech and sings revolutionary songs. This lasts for nearly two hours. The men are dismissed and the best cuts of meat are taken from the store and sent up to the commander's tent.[2]

*

Mnyamane Hlaya arrives by train in Ootse and, like Bhengu and Metshane before him, walks from there to Lobatse, where he stays for two or three days with Ramatshwiritlha Mokgosi.

Johannes Rantau then arrives and takes Hlaya to Gopane, from where Martiens Mogotsi travels with him to Johannesburg by bus.[3]

When Hlaya disembarks in Roodepoort, he is met by Michael Dingake.

Later that day, Dingake and Hlaya arrive at a residence in Diepkloof. At this property Hlaya finds Macdonald Masala, whom he last saw at Bessie Zondi's house in Lusaka in September.

Henceforth Hlaya and Masala will live together there.[4]

*

At a house belonging to a comrade known as 'Skatau', Hlaya and Masala meet Siegfried Bhengu and Peter Metshane.

Bhengu suggests the four of them resume the work as leaders responsible for training others that was interrupted by Wilton Mkwayi's arrest.

The others endorse the proposal.[5]

*

Patrick Baphela is the last person left at Bessie Zondi's place in Lusaka. Tennyson Makiwane tells him Fish Keitseng will give him instructions further on in Bechuanaland.

On 26 November, Makiwane drives Baphela southwards in a Land Rover, and the two men check in at the Chandamali Government Hostel in Livingstone.

On the following day, Baphela is on a Rhodesian Railways train that crosses into Rhodesia at the Victoria Falls. At Victoria Falls Station, his luggage is inspected by a customs official. Found among his belongings is a writing pad containing notes on explosives. Baphela is arrested.[6]

*

At 2 p.m. on 21 December, Detective Sergeant Francis Smith forms part of a force of South African security policemen that arrive at 7548, Area 3, in Diepkloof.

During this raid, Macdonald Masala, Josiah Jele and the owner of the house are arrested.[7]

*

The *Rand Daily Mail* reports on 26 January 1965 that early the previous morning in Beaumont Avenue in Johannesburg's Oaklands suburb, Ilse Fischer and Pat Davidson knocked on Bram Fischer's bedroom door. When there was no reply, the two women entered, found the bed empty, but noticed it had been slept in. Next to the bed they saw a pile of letters addressed to friends and legal advisers.[8]

*

Josiah Jele meets Hendrik Ramahadi during the following month and tells him that he was arrested but was released on the 11th.[9]

*

When Michael Dingake meets Jele at Hendrik Ramahadi's house, Jele warns Dingake that the police are after him.

Upon hearing this, Dingake decides to leave the country.

Jele says he will leave with him.

Dingake and Jele take a bus from Krugersdorp to Gopane.

When they reach Gopane, they sleep at William Senna's house.

They enter Bechuanaland early the following morning in the company of William Senna and Martiens Mogotsi.[10]

*

Captain Theunis Swanepoel, Lieutenant van Rensburg and Sergeants van Niekerk and Grobbelaar arrive at 363 Dhlamini, in Soweto's Area Number Two, at 3 a.m. on 30 April 1965.

In the left front bedroom of the house, which is owned by a taxi driver, they find Mnyamane Hlaya, who gives his correct name when asked.

Various items of clothing are scattered around the room. Among them is a pair of trousers, in which Swanepoel finds two folio pieces of paper. Written on the paper are various bomb-making formulas. Swanepoel asks who the papers belong to.

Hlaya says they are his; they are notes he made during his guerrilla training in Ghana and Egypt. He is arrested and taken into custody.[11]

*

At Johannesburg Railway Station on Saturday 15 May, William Senna boards the bus going to Borakalolo via Gopane. It is not yet 7 a.m. The bus stops in Braamfontein, then Sophiatown, and then heads in the direction of Roodepoort.

Peter Metshane is waiting at Roodepoort Station with Joe Ntangala, George Mokgoro, Morgan Mbata and a young boy. A man called Nkosi Mbvomo is also there, and hands Metshane some money. Metshane gives this money to Mokgoro and Mbata to buy tickets for the bus to Gopane.

Detective Sergeant Martin Matimula is on observation duty at Roodepoort Railway Station when he sees the bus for Gopane approaching. When it comes to a halt,

Senna disembarks in order to go to the toilet. At the entrance to the bus he sees Peter Metshane, whom he recognises, but the area is now crowded with people boarding, wanting to get off, and greeting and saying farewells to others, so the two cannot speak.

Detective Constable Petrus Mohale watches passengers board the bus.

When Senna returns from the toilet he sees that Metshane has already boarded.

When the bus leaves, Senna and Metshane fall into a discussion. Metshane says he has four people with him and he will see them off to Bechuanaland.

The bus stops at Luipaardsvlei, then Koster and then Phiri. At about 12.30 p.m., between Phiri and Zeerust, Senna notices the vehicle drawing to a halt, and a group of policemen entering.

Captain Theunis Swanepoel is at the head of the police contingent. Metshane, the four recruits and Senna are then arrested and hauled off the bus.[12] With this, the whole group of MK cadres trained in China as well as the underground network responsible for border crossings between South Africa and Bechuanaland via Gopane have fallen into the hands of the security police.

*

The next regrouping takes place outside the country, with the External Mission in charge.

Tennyson Makiwane arrives at a hut in Livingstone, Zambia, where Thomas Nkobi and Michael Dingake are staying. Makiwane suggests holding their meeting immediately.

Makiwane says that the Dar es Salaam office has clarified Dingake's position; the work he must do involves establishing contacts inside South Africa, arranging for recruits to be sent out of the country for military training, and creating an effective propaganda machinery.

Makiwane says that the Lusaka office will provide Dingake with a roneo machine, a typewriter, paper and draft leaflets. He will have to work separately from the Lobatse Committee and report directly to Lusaka. He will also get a van for transport purposes.[13]

*

A larger meeting in another of the huts in the same complex in Livingstone is attended by Duma Nokwe, Tennyson Makiwane, Oliver Tambo, Michael Dingake, Fish Keitseng, Dan Tloome, Johannes Rantau, Henderson Tshepe, Moses Mabhida and Ronald Letsholonyane.

Nokwe asks Tloome for a report on the arrest of the returned soldiers.

Tloome says he received a report from Johannesburg that the organisation was controlled very badly. The soldiers had nowhere to stay and this is why they were arrested.

Nokwe asks how they got arrested.

Tloome says he was told that Metshane was arrested while on his way to Lobatse with refugees; he doesn't know the circumstances of the other arrests.

Tambo interjects that it is wrong to use trained soldiers to take people out of the country or as messengers. It is very careless, their position is very delicate and they should not have mixed with people going out. The practice should be discontinued.[14]

*

Johannes Broodryk of the South African Police goes to Overland Wholesalers on the corner of Market and Troye Streets in Johannesburg on 8 November 1965. There he finds Ms Violet Weinberg, and he arrests her under the terms of Article 215, which provides for 180 days' detention without trial (this is a new law superseding the ninety-day clause).

Broodryk takes Weinberg to his office, and then to her home in Plantation Road in Gardens suburb, where she collects some belongings.

At Pretoria Central Prison, while the matron is looking through Weinberg's personal items, Broodryk spots a key in her handbag.[15]

*

The following day a letter is written by 'Paulus' to 'Kim'.

It says Kim's morning papers probably carried the sad news of the previous day's events, which could not have come at a worse time or under worse circumstances. He continues, 'It is difficult to visualise what the consequences may be. In fact our market may be destroyed entirely though with my usual optimism I do not think that this will in fact happen.'

In the next paragraph, Paulus says, 'If Nance breaks then our entire business will probably go into liquidation – or at any rate, be put under judicial management for a long period.'

Later that day, 'Paulus' writes to 'Kim' again: 'I have now ascertained that the losses caused by this accident may be more far reaching than I anticipated.'

A sentence later he writes: 'What is disturbing however is that on the evening before the accident he was handed your latest balance sheet letter for transmission to me. This in ordinary circumstances would not be serious but two things are of importance. If there was anything arising from your statement that I should act on urgently then you must send me a duplicate immediately. Do so in any case, I shall not be able to find out for some time where he left it if it was not on his person.'[16]

*

Lieutenant Rudolf van Rensburg is doing identification service outside 215 Corlett Drive in Bramley, Johannesburg, on 11 November.

At 6 p.m. a slightly shabby looking white man with a black goatee and moustache, wearing spectacles and smoking a pipe, leaves the property. The man enters a Volkswagen registered TJ 136-212 and heads off in the direction of Oaklands.

Van Rensburg follows, all the while keeping in radio contact with other police cars. At the corner of Stella Street the police cars block the Volkswagen in.

Van Rensburg introduces himself and tells the man: 'You are the missing Abram Fischer.'

Bram Fischer denies this and says he is in fact Mr Douglas Black. He notes that the police have on previous occasions made false identifications only to later discover their mistake.

Van Rensburg repeats: You are the escaped advocate Abram Fischer.

'I am Douglas Black,' Fischer insists.

Van Rensburg contacts Johannes Broodryk over the police radio and says that they have got Fischer.[17]

*

Fischer's arrest is beaten as the lead story in the following morning's *Rand Daily Mail* by the news that in Rhodesia a government under the leadership of Ian Smith has unilaterally proclaimed independence from Britain.[18]

*

During the same month, the leaders of the ANC's External Mission visit Kongwa camp and inform the cadres there that Joe Modise has been appointed Umkhonto we Sizwe's new commander-in-chief.

Ambrose Makiwane resigns from the army soon after.[19]

*

Joe Modise addresses the cadres in Kongwa.

He refers to Ambrose Makiwane's plan, which involved sending small unarmed groups to the Transkei, where they would instruct people in guerrilla warfare, and other groups to the cities where they would offer training in sabotage; these groups would remain in contact with Lusaka and Dar es Salaam until receiving word from the External Mission, after which they would simultaneously launch rural guerrilla warfare and urban sabotage using weapons delivered along the Transkei coast.

Modise says that this plan no longer applies and that he has other ideas. He explains that these involve sending large groups to Zululand, Sekhukhuneland and the Transkei to train the local people in those areas. Only a route into South Africa remains to be found, he says.[20]

*

On 24 November, Michael Dingake receives a phone call from Tennyson Makiwane, who suggests that Oliver Tambo, Moses Kotane and the rest of the external ANC leadership are going to have an important meeting in Lusaka soon, and they would like Dingake to attend as the main contact in Bechuanaland.

Makiwane asks Dingake if he is ready to come to Lusaka.

Dingake says he is.

Makiwane asks how Dingake thinks he will make it.

Through Rhodesia.

Makiwane says he will phone later.[21]

*

On 6 December, Dingake receives a message from Tennyson Makiwane, writing under the name 'Richard'. It appears to be urgent.

On the following day, Dingake boards the Lusaka-bound train at Ramoutsa in Bechuanaland.

On the 8th, the train passes into Rhodesia. Dingake receives a transit endorsement on his passport. But then, on the approach to Figtree, some eighty miles or so from Bulawayo, two detectives, of whom one is Detective Officer Barry McKay, enter his train compartment.

When asked his identity, Dingake tells them his name.

McKay introduces himself as being from the Bulawayo CID and says he has information that Dingake is an ANC member.

Dingake says he is misinformed.

McKay nevertheless asks Dingake to come down to the station as they have a few things to check with him.

Dingake is taken by detectives from Figtree to Bulawayo Police Station, where he is led into the charge office. McKay goes ahead of Dingake and whispers something to the man at the counter. When Dingake moves forward McKay turns and says, 'Dingaka, I will see you later', and heads straight for the door.

Other policemen in the charge office then tell Dingake he is under arrest.

Dingake is handed over to the South African authorities on 7 January 1966.[22]

III

GUERRILLA WARFARE

INVASION

Bechuanaland's police commissioner sends a savingram on 24 January 1966 to the senior permanent secretary in the protectorate's Ministry of Home Affairs. It concerns a recent visit by Tennyson Makiwane to the Kasane Police District.

The commissioner writes that Makiwane expressed a desire to visit 'Gaberones' on 28 January to discuss with Home Affairs the possibility of obtaining large-scale employment for ANC 'refugees' in Bechuanaland. Makiwane admitted the visit's connection with the increasingly negative attitude of both Tanzania and Zambia towards South African refugees.

The commissioner contextualises, noting that Tanzania recently stated it could not afford to accept any more refugees, causing Zambia in response to refuse to grant refugees transit facilities to Tanzania.

Returning to the Kasane meeting, the commissioner writes: 'It is considered that Makiwane's proposed visit would serve no useful purpose, and it is recommended that he be refused permission to enter Bechuanaland.'[1]

*

Eleazor Maboya addresses Basil February, James April, James Masimini, Freddy Mninzi, Goodman Mhlawuli, James Stuart and Zolile Nqose in the Kongwa camp.

Maboya tells them to go to Morogoro, where Joe Modise will give them further instructions.

In Morogoro, Modise addresses the group and appoints 'Paul Petersen' (i.e. Basil February) its leader. Modise tells the team to infiltrate Bechuanaland and investigate possible routes through the protectorate to South Africa.[2]

*

On 1 February the *Rand Daily Mail* reports that Zambia's minister of home affairs Mainza Chona yesterday denied that Ben Turok, presently in Bechuanaland, is being refused entry to Zambia.

Chona said that Turok would not be allowed to *stay* in Zambia, because the country only accepts people fleeing from *adjacent* lands as refugees – 'others are allowed to pass in transit only'. Chona added that 'if Mr Turok can prove that he has a ticket to Britain and that the British Government will permit him entry there, we are prepared to allow him to enter Zambia in transit'.[3]

*

Tennyson Makiwane arrives in Kazungula refugee camp in northern Bechuanaland having driven from Lusaka. From the camp Makiwane collects Ben Turok, who says his goodbyes to some newfound friends.

Makiwane drives Turok to the river ferry, which takes the pair across the Zambezi River into Zambia.

They continue northwards to Lusaka. During the drive, Turok says that in the camp he spoke to forestry officials and South West Africa People's Organisation

(SWAPO) refugees who had walked there through the dense forests of northern Namibia. They said they experienced many difficulties with the Bushmen who are abjectly poor and thus easy targets for bribery by the police. The police have recruited many of them to give away any travelling refugees. The Bushmen would thus be the main obstacles for guerrillas heading south. Concerning southwards infiltration, Turok says he thinks staging posts are needed where cadres can sleep over, draw rations, be briefed on the road ahead ...

Save the report for the people in Lusaka, Makiwane suggests.[4]

*

In Morogoro, Joe Modise briefs Lawrence Phokanoka (travelling Umkhonto we Sizwe name Peter Tladi), Julius Maliba (Goodman Moloi), Justice Mpanza (Reuben Ntlabati), Theophilus Mkalipi (Victor Dhlamini) and Gladstone Mose (Jackson Mlenze).

Modise says that Phokanoka has been appointed a group commander and will lead a contingent of trained guerrillas to Sekhukhuneland in the near future. The group must form a base in Sekhukhuneland with the assistance of locally based people and then recruit people from the community to be trained as guerrillas. The training should be done by other members of the group – Phokanoka himself must not make any personal contact with the recruits. After training, the recruits must return to their normal lives until needed as guerrillas.

Maliba, who has been appointed group commander for Sibasa, is similarly briefed, as are Mpanza, who is made commander of one group headed to Zululand, Mkalipi, the commander of a second Zululand-bound group, and Mose, the Transkei group leader. (The final group, the Cape group, under Basil February's leadership, has already departed for the border area.)[5]

*

Lawrence Phokanoka and the other members of his Sekhukhuneland group, namely Sags McDonald, Reddy Mazimba, Elliot Maroga and Jack Simelane, are driven by a man named Abel Mbuli in a Land Rover from Morogoro to Lusaka later in February. Their destination is a plot in the Zambian capital owned by a South African refugee, Dr Shaik Randeree, who has a practice in the city.

One week later Chris Hani accompanies the group as it is taken by Land Rover to a place called Cindes Plot, near Livingstone. Upon arrival at this farm, they find five guerrillas already there.[6]

In Francistown in Bechuanaland on 17 February, Chris Hani disembarks from a plane that has flown in from Zambia. At immigration he produces a Tanzanian identity certificate issued to 'Chris Nkosana'.

He is, however, taken into custody and interrogated. He claims his purpose is to enquire into the facts surrounding Michael Dingake's disappearance.

The immigration officials are not convinced by his story, not least because he displays an almost complete lack of knowledge about Dingake's case.

Hani is deported to Zambia and exits on a flight to Livingstone within a few days.[7]

*

Cindes Plot is raided by Zambia's police the following month. Lambert Moloi and Steve Belle are arrested, but the rest of the MK troops escape and later return to Lusaka in a Land Rover.[8]

*

Zambia's policy of allowing refugees fleeing their native lands to settle in or transit through the country on a conditional basis is not extended to exiles who undergo military training abroad and want to return home to fight. One consequence of this is the accumulation of guerrilla fighters in Tanzania, which has led the authorities there to impose a moratorium on further refugee entries.

In 1966, Lusaka's restrictive refugee policy comes under scrutiny at pan-African level. Zambia's high commissioner in Tanzania writes to the permanent secretary in his own country's Foreign Affairs Ministry on 25 April.

He says members of the so-called 'Action Group' of the OAU Liberation Committee want to travel to Lusaka some time the following week to discuss the question of freedom fighters with the government. The background to this, he explains, is that most of the liberation movements based in Tanzania have had their recruits return from military training. They want to transit Zambia en route to their home countries, but the Liberation Committee is reluctant to provide them material support because of Lusaka's stance towards returning refugees.[9]

*

On the same day, at a plot known as Farm B on the Old Mumbwa Road about three miles out of Lusaka, Tennyson Makiwane arrives and calls Mack Futha, who is staying there, to one side.

Makiwane shows Futha a birth affidavit issued by a tribal authority in Rusape, Rhodesia. Futha looks at it. It refers to somebody with the first name Stephen – he doesn't have time to read the surname before Makiwane whisks the document away.

Makiwane says the affidavit was given to him by ZAPU (the Zimbabwe African People's Union). He rubs out the surname on the document and substitutes that of 'Hliziyo', saying that Futha will henceforth be 'Stephen Hliziyo'.[10]

*

As the year progresses, Tanzania hardens its stance towards the guerrillas in its territory. The Executive Secretariat of the OAU's Standing Committee on Defence circulates a report when the committee meets in Dar es Salaam on 12 May 1966. The report says the committee is unable to advance the necessary monies for the maintenance of Kongwa camp because most OAU member states have not yet paid their contributions for the fiscal year ending 31 May 1966.

Out of an allocation forecast for the camp of £75,000, only £46,250 has been paid to Tanzania, and consequently the 'Tanzania Government informed the Committee that, unless an amount is paid for the Camp and that the necessary funds be allocated, the government will be into a position [*sic*] to abolish this training camp'.[11]

Two days later, Zambia's high commissioner in Tanzania forwards to Lusaka his evaluation of the meeting, which he attended. He writes: 'the weight of the meeting was centred on Zambia. Members of the Committee expressed with regret Zambia's attitude towards freedom fighters. It was said by the members that freedom fighters trained in guerrilla warfare could not go to their respective countries because Zambia was not prepared to allow them [to] transit the country, this, it was said was a draw back in the National struggle.'

The commissioner says he tried to convey the grave security dangers facing the country, but with limited success. He concludes: 'The Committee through out its sitting centred its discussions on Zambia. Members held the view that the delay in intensifying the struggle in countries around Zambia was due to Zambia[']s refusal of not allowing freedom fighters to transit its country. The Committee is aware of the difficulties facing Zambia but some countries in the Committee want to impress others that [while] they are doing their best, Zambia is the stumbling block.'[12]

*

Three days later, Tennyson Makiwane and Mack Futha meet again at Farm B. Makiwane tells Futha to depart for Bechuanaland on 24 or 25 May. He says Futha will fly from Livingstone to Maun and get the first available transport from there to Francistown. The reason for not flying straight to Francistown is to escape police detention upon landing.

If asked, he should say he is going to see his mother, who will meet him at the house of a Mr Mutshekwane. His real mission, however, will be to stay in Bechuanaland for as long as it takes to establish an infiltration pipeline. He will have to establish a business in Bechuanaland as cover. Upon arrival in Maun he should contact Chief Letsholothebe and ask for accommodation. Then, in Francistown, he must see Mr Mutshekwane and say Makiwane sent him. He must then go to Mochudi and ask for Chief Lentswe's permission to stay there, but should not inform him of his mission. Instead, he should contact Basil Mokone and Ismail Matlaku and tell them he has been sent by Makiwane. Matlaku runs a transport service in Mochudi and will help Futha establish an access route from there.

Makiwane tells Futha not to contact anybody in Lobatse, and in fact to stay away from Lobatse entirely.

He adds that the completed pipeline should be able to transport personnel from the Zambian border to Francistown, and then from Francistown southwards to whichever border crossing point Futha decides on.[13]

*

On 25 May 1966, Mack Futha arrives in Maun on a flight from Livingstone. At immigration, he produces a British passport issued in the name of Stephen Hliziyo, and he completes his Declaration of Arrival form using that name. He is nonetheless taken aside for questioning by suspicious immigration officials.

He tells them his reason for travel is to see his mother in Francistown at the house of Simeon Richard Mutshekwane, the Francistown assistant town clerk.

The questioning drags on, and Futha eventually admits he has been sent to establish an infiltration route, but says that this is on behalf of ZAPU for personnel seeking entrance to Rhodesia from Zambia, via Bechuanaland.

Futha is not arrested. He is allowed to leave Maun shortly after the confession.

Three days later, however, he is again brought in for questioning, this time in Francistown by a Special Branch officer.

Futha this time admits his real identity. He also confesses that his mission was actually to organise a route to be used by trained ANC combatants in Zambia seeking passage to South Africa.[14]

*

At 2.14 p.m. on 6 September, bells summon South Africa's parliamentarians to the chamber of the House of Assembly in Cape Town. Hendrik Verwoerd makes his way to the prime minister's front bench.

Along with the members of Parliament, a messenger, Dimitri Tsafendas, enters the chamber from the lobby. He is wearing a blue uniform with green piping. He makes his way to the front bench, where he draws a sheath knife and plunges it four times into Verwoerd's heart, chest and throat.

The prime minister does not survive this time.

At a meeting seven days later, the National Party caucus votes John Vorster to be his successor.[15]

*

Joe Modise speaks to Zolile Nqose (MK name Wilson Msweli), Michael Masupye (Jimmy Mpedi), George Mothusi, Jack Tshibogo (Johannes Phalanyane), Morris Mandela (Charles Makayi), Justice Mpanza (Reuben Ntlabati) and John Mwalusi in Lusaka.

Modise appoints Masupye the leader of the group. The seven are equipped with two submachine guns, five automatic rifles, six Tokarev pistols, ammunition for all these weapons, and a first-aid kit. Modise orders them not to fire on the Bechuanaland Police unless the policemen are in the company of South African and Rhodesian policemen or soldiers.

In Livingstone, the seven are collected by Benjamin Ramotse (who skipped bail in South Africa in August 1962 after being led into Bechuanaland by Joe Modise). Ramotse drives them southwards to the border with Bechuanaland. They cross at Kazungula, with Ramotse in the cabin and the seven hidden in a secret compartment under the vehicle.

Ramotse leaves them in Kazungula and returns to Zambia.

On 26 September, a four-man contingent of the Bechuanaland Police commanded by Mr R.L. Martin encounters seven men on the Lesuma–Ngwezumba road in the Chobe district, approximately thirty miles from Kazungula. It is Michael Masupye's group. Upon being apprehended, Nqose gives his name as 'John Jones', and his colleagues variously as 'Ruben Sizwe', 'Herbert Motsese', 'James Motsipe', 'Modise Moloi', 'James Langa' and 'Charles Makayi'.[16]

*

At midnight on the evening of 29–30 September, Bechuanaland receives its independence from Britain as the Republic of Botswana.[17]

*

The incident with the Masupye group has incensed the leaders of the new nation. The office of Botswana's president Seretse Khama issues a memorandum on 4 October, following the first meeting of the cabinet, recommending that the seven be declared 'undesirable inhabitants or visitors to Botswana' and 'should thereafter be handed over to the Republic of South Africa, after undercover notice has been given to those authorities'.

Shortly afterwards, however, Khama reconsiders his decision and sends his vice-president to Zambia for consultations.

Soon thereafter, the clerk to Botswana's ruling cabinet communicates to the office of the president and the police commissioner the content of a fresh directive issued by President Khama. It is that 'as a result of advice tendered to him at the 3rd meeting of Cabinet held on the 14th October 1966' he has decided to 'vary the decision he reached as a result of advice tendered to him at the 1st meeting of Cabinet'.

Khama decided instead to deport the men to Zambia, but warned that he would issue a statement after Botswana's admission to the United Nations that if in future 'any armed guerrillas were discovered in Botswana who appeared to be dedicated to committing acts of violence against neighbouring countries, they would be severely dealt with'.[18]

*

On 15 January 1967, President Kenneth Kaunda writes to the president of the Democratic Republic of the Congo, Lieutenant General Joseph-Désiré Mobutu, outlining the results of a policy rethink in Zambia. This reconsideration is based on an acknowledgement that the country is being drawn ever deeper into the war for southern Africa, despite its efforts to stay out.

Kaunda begins: 'You are no doubt following the reports about the Portuguese activities in our North Western and Barotse Provinces. For a long time now there have been a number of violations of Zambia's territorial sovereignty through incursions by Portuguese troops who, on several occasions have destroyed villages and most recently shot some Zambian citizens near the border with Angola. At the moment, there is what amounts to a hit-and-run war.'

He continues: 'I have yet another running sore on the Southern front – the

Rhodesian and South West African minority and racialist regimes pose a continuous threat to our security. On the Eastern front I have the Mozambique problem.'
He then writes:

Our geographical location coupled with our own determination to do what we can for the freedom fighters in the liberation of their homelands from colonialism and racial oppression has placed us in a position where we must fight a war on three major fronts – West, South and East. Malawi as you know at present takes a most unhelpful attitude in terms of obligations to liberation movements and freedom in Africa. This has meant that Zambia must continue to shoulder this burden.

Kaunda accordingly suggests the following division of labour:

The crisis in Rhodesia and the development in South West Africa consequent upon the United Nations Resolution terminating South Africa's mandate over that territory demand that Zambia concentrates her future efforts in that direction. The consequences of such a policy would be that we would, for some time and until pressure on the south lessens, have less time to honour our obligations to the West and East. It is for this reason that I have sent my Foreign Minister, the Hon S.M. Kapwepwe to explain to you our proposal for future action. My proposal is that in order to maximise our future effectiveness, we should share responsibilities in the present crisis. This would mean that you would be responsible for Angola, Tanzania for Mozambique, while Zambia concentrates its attention on Rhodesia, South and South West Africa.[19]

*

On the same day, Kaunda writes the following to Julius Nyerere of Tanzania:

I am now following up our earlier discussions with a firm proposal that, while Zambia should continue her vigilance and the help she has rendered to freedom fighters in Southern Africa in general, her main preoccupation should be over Rhodesia, South West Africa and South Africa. The responsibility for Angola should be for the Congo (Kinshasa) and Mozambique should remain your major preoccupation while extending your assistance to Zambia in general. Simon, whom I have directed to discuss this proposal with President Mobutu, and Milton will give you the details of our feeling.[20]

*

Following on from this exchange of letters, the heads of the Tanzanian and Zambian security services meet at Mbeya on 28 February and agree to establish a system whereby guerrillas seeking to travel between the two countries must complete 'Recruitment Forms' stating their organisational affiliation.

These forms are then to be transmitted to the Coordinating Committee of the OAU Liberation Committee in Dar es Salaam, which will ascertain whether the applicants are bona fide freedom fighters and members of the organisations as claimed. If positive confirmation is received from the OAU, the guerrillas will be provided with travel documents and allowed to proceed.

The agreement, which crucially applies to guerrillas seeking to travel from Tanzania through Zambia as well as in the opposite direction, is ratified by Presidents Kaunda and Nyerere when submitted to them.[21] The significance of the accord is that while liberation movements had previously operated clandestinely in Zambia trying to establish routes to their home territories, now, with Lusaka's official authorisation, they can commence mass deployments of armed combatants.

*

This leaves unresolved the question of ANC infiltrations into South Africa, which lies beyond Zambia's borders. In a document distributed at the beginning of a meeting of the OAU Liberation Committee's Standing Committee on Defence in Dar es Salaam on 14 April, it is noted that 'Nothing so far has been done by the A.N.C. in the form of an armed struggle'.

The report notes that the ANC has requested a disbursement of material for the use of its personnel in East Africa (estimated at 300 militarily trained cadres), but it says that in light of the organisation's inactivity, the 'Executive Secretariat considers that since their materials are not requested for the armed struggle in South Africa, it is not in a position to recommend the issuing of most of the materials requested by the Movement'.

When the Defence Committee issues a report at the conclusion of the gathering on 18 April, the tone softens. Concerning the ANC, it is written that the meeting 'took note of the difficulties which are facing the trained personnel of this movement to infiltrate in South Africa'.

Delegates also 'took note of the negotiations that are being undertaken by the Executive Secretary with the Governments of Zambia and Botswana, in order to find a suitable solution for their situation'. The Standing Committee 'requested the Executive Secretary to submit a report of the results of these negotiations as soon as they are terminated'.

But, pending such feedback, the meeting 'further suggested that the ANC leaders be requested to integrate their trained personnel into any fighting Liberation Movements in order to fight against the common enemy of Africa and to open their way to South Africa'.[22]

*

This last suggestion is taken up. Lawrence Phokanoka, Gladstone Mose, Justice Mpanza, Theophilus Mkalipi, Julius Maliba, Tony Malume and Lennon Milane are all present in a little cottage situated on Dr Randeree's plot in Lusaka in June 1967. Oliver Tambo, who is in the company of Moses Kotane and Joe Modise, addresses them.

Tambo says they are going to be sent back to South Africa. They will be assisted by ZAPU members in entering Rhodesia. They are *not* abandoning the Botswana route, but for the time being the main route will be through Rhodesia.

Explaining the context of the shift in focus from Botswana to Rhodesia, he says that in Botswana there are no people to assist or sympathetic organisations like ZAPU. Botswana also has a shortage of water.

In Rhodesia they will operate under ZAPU command and if fighting begins they will go into combat under ZAPU leadership. A combined ANC–ZAPU group will remain in Rhodesia while the remainder of the troops proceed to South Africa.

Tambo responds to a question about sea infiltration by saying that there is no present possibility of a naval incursion, hence those who are supposed to go to the Western Cape will remain with ZAPU in Rhodesia.[23]

*

In a parallel project conceived on similar lines, during the same month Sandi Sijake is part of a group of seven under the leadership of Josiah Jele, the former colleague of Michael Dingake in the underground within South Africa, that is taken from Kongwa camp to Dar es Salaam.

Later, in southern Tanzania, the group heads for the Rovuma River, which demarcates Mozambique from Tanzania. They are in the company of Samora Machel, a commander in the Mozambican liberation movement FRELIMO.

Machel says he does not think it will be possible for them to reach South Africa, because FRELIMO has not as yet advanced to, penetrated and built structures in the areas of southern Mozambique that they will need to pass in order to reach their destination.

The infiltration proceeds nonetheless. Three members of the ANC group head to Niassa Province in Mozambique. This group includes Jele. The remaining four go to Cabo Delgado.[24]

*

In Lilanda township in Lusaka, still in June 1967, Joe Modise tells Zolile Nqose to proceed to 'Dube's Farm'.

Nqose arrives at the farm, sometimes referred to as 'Luthuli camp', which is situated about twenty miles west of Lusaka on the road to King Edward Mine. The farm's real name is 'Marydale' or 'Merrivale', but a section of it is owned by a black Rhodesian named Dube Phiri, hence the nickname.[25]

*

On 18 June, a group of nine, namely Daluxolo Luthuli, Joseph Nduli, Leonard Nkosi, Kenneth Mzathi, John Mokgotsi, Columbus Mohapi, Lucas Dolcin, Audie Moloto and Siphiwe Radebe, are taken from Kongwa to a camp in Morogoro in a Land Rover driven by Boy Otto.

At Morogoro they find a number of MK cadres already there. Daluxolo Luthuli strikes up conversation with one of them, Philemon Beyela, and asks what happened to Duncan Khoza.

Beyela says that Khoza went along with Styles Makama, Badman Ngwaxela, John Ngisi and Spy Motsila to the Mozambique area: they were clad in khaki uniform with peaked cap, and each was armed with a Russian submachine gun and Chinese grenade. Their task was to reach the Shangaan-speaking areas of South Africa via the Kruger National Park.

On the second day after Daluxolo Luthuli's group's arrival in Morogoro, Berry Nkosi shows up in a Land Rover and takes seventeen guerrillas, including Luthuli, south to Mbeya, where they find Archie Sibeko waiting.

Sibeko then drives them into Zambia.

They eventually arrive in Lilanda township on Lusaka's outskirts. There they meet a group of about twenty people, including Joe Modise and Chris Hani.

One afternoon they are taken by Berry Nkosi in a Land Rover to a plot called Kaluwe's Farm, approximately twenty-five miles east of Lusaka.

There is already a large group of cadres there, including Lawrence Phokanoka, Theophilus Mkalipi, James April, Basil February and Ralph Mzamo.[26]

*

In July, MK sends a reconnaissance team to the Zambezi River to begin locating possible crossing points into Rhodesia.[27]

*

The joint ANC–FRELIMO group in Mozambique's Niassa Province – which includes Josiah Jele and two ANC colleagues – falls into a Portuguese ambush.

They return fire, but in the skirmish the group breaks apart.

Jele flees alongside a Mozambican in search of the Tanzanian border.[28]

*

A deaf sixty-nine-year-old African man who is virtually blind in his left eye and only partially sighted in his right crosses a railway bridge over the Umvoti River north of Durban at about 10.40 a.m. on 21 July 1967.

He is struck by a goods train.

The train stops immediately and the crew calls for help.

An ambulance arrives and takes him to Stanger Hospital.

At 2.30 p.m. that day, the man, Albert Luthuli, dies.[29]

*

When interviewed by a reporter from the *Zambia Mail* at a memorial service held for Luthuli in Lusaka the following day, Oliver Tambo says there is some 'mystery' surrounding the death. He says he has been phoning Stanger since yesterday without receiving any reply.[30]

*

Oliver Tambo and Joe Modise visit Dube's Farm west of Lusaka. Tambo calls the cadres together.

Before them, Tambo praises Luthuli as a great fighter who died fighting for the rights of his people. The South African government is responsible for his death, and Luthuli's passing will go down in history because immediately after his burial the ANC's army will invade Rhodesia and South Africa.

Tambo calls on the cadres to stand and observe a silence of two minutes every day at midday for the next two weeks.[31]

*

In the final week of July, Joe Modise returns to Dube's Farm and calls Chris Hani, Freddy Mninzi, Andries Motsepe and Zolile Nqose to one side. By this time ZAPU members have joined the camp – in fact, the camp commander and deputy commander are respectively Abel Dyantyi and John Dube, both ZAPU.

Modise also calls four ZAPU members – deputy camp commander John Dube, David Madzimba (real name Jonathan Moyo), 'Makhonya' and 'Ndlela' to be part of the briefing.

Modise says he has come to divide them into sections because they are about to invade Rhodesia. They will cross the Zambezi together, but later divide into two groups with separate missions. Modise mentions in passing that there will also be a third group.

One section, Modise says, will be the 'Lupane group'. He says David Madzimba will be its commander, Andries Motsepe the deputy commander, Freddy Mninzi the political commissar, and Ndlela the chief of staff.

The second section will be the 'Tsholotsho group', which John Dube will command. Zolile Nqose will be the deputy commander, Chris Hani the political commissar, Makhonya the deputy political commissar, and Leonard Nkosi the chief of staff.

Modise then takes the leaders of the Tsholotsho group who are present (Leonard Nkosi is the only one not there) to one side. He tells them they will cross with the Lupane group and the third group, which he calls the 'Luthuli Detachment'. After entering Rhodesia, they must branch off towards Tsholotsho and establish a training camp at a suitable place; the ANC men in the group will have to assist the ZAPU men to organise and train the Rhodesian people in the area, and will then have to wait for instructions from Lusaka before launching any attack on the Rhodesian whites.

Modise clarifies: The main task at this stage is to train people rather than to fight, though if there is a clash they will have to fight to the last man.

With the leaders of the Lupane and Tsholotsho groups again assembled, Modise tells them that Basil February and James April will accompany the Tsholotsho group for part of the way and then proceed through Plumtree to Cape Town where they will prepare to receive MK guerrillas.[32]

*

Leonard Nkosi returns to Dube's Farm shortly afterwards, whereupon Chris Hani takes him aside and says Joe Modise visited while he was in Lilanda.

Hani says Nkosi has been appointed chief of staff of one of the three groups that will invade Rhodesia. According to the plan his group will stay in Rhodesia. Hani says that as well as being commander of one of the groups, John Dube will be overall commander of the entire group.

During his briefing of Nkosi, Hani takes out a map that he says Modise gave him. Hani points out the spot where they will enter Rhodesia. He also points out the Tsholotsho–Bulawayo area where their group will operate.[33]

*

Two Land Rovers make several trips on 29 July collecting combatants from Dube's Farm. The cadres reassemble in Lusaka, from where they are taken by train to Livingstone.

Lambert Moloi and Archie Sibeko meet them at Livingstone Station, and drive them in two Land Rovers to a place about fifteen to twenty miles west of Livingstone and about one and a half miles north of Chundu Island on the Zambezi River. The last five miles of the trip take them along a road that leads over the Livingstone/ Mulobezi railway line. Their destination is Drummond Park Farm, aka 'Cindes Plot', the venue where the raid by the Zambian Police on a group of MK cadres including Lawrence Phokanoka's Sekhukhuneland section occurred in March the previous year. On the property there is a reasonably good brick-built house with a zinc roof. There are also a number of small outbuildings near the house.

On their arrival they find Mongameli Tshali, the commander of the Luthuli Detachment (i.e. the third group and the section that will proceed from Rhodesia to South Africa). Tshali is there with Lawrence Phokanoka, Theophilus Mkalipi, Justice Mpanza, Julius Maliba and Gladstone Mose, who are his deputies and also the group commanders for the regions where guerrilla warfare will be launched in South Africa. Also there, and again part of the Luthuli Detachment, are Tano Mzimele, Themba Dlamini, Faldiri Mzimonke, Abraham Maloke and Graham Morodi, who are the commissars for the regions.

A number of rank-and-file soldier members of the detachment are present as well.[34]

*

At Drummond Park Farm, the troops line up in single file, and walk towards logistics officer Jacob Masondo, who hands them each two hand grenades as well as a khaki-coloured uniform made of gabardine fabric, and consisting of long slacks, a shirt, a cloth hat, a jersey, a military bag, as well as khaki-coloured boots with grooved soles. The socks are black.

They also receive a water can and rations including a pound of dates, three tins of fish, five apples, and a pound each of cheese and raisins.[35]

*

On the evening of the 31st, Joe Modise and Oliver Tambo are the only political leaders present among eighty guerrillas as a beast is slaughtered at the farm.

Modise gives them final instructions. He says they must organise recruits in their respective destinations and wait for the remainder of the guerrillas who will follow soon.

Later on the evening of the 31st, the soldiers are transported from the farm.

At 10 p.m. Lawrence Phokanoka is part of the second group to leave. He and his colleagues board the back of an open lorry driven by Joel Sibeko.

Their route takes them through Livingstone, and after exiting the town they continue driving east a further twenty-nine miles or so. For the last few miles the lorry travels through the bush – no roads. They disembark and walk for about two hours in a south-easterly direction.

Eventually they reach a place where they find the group of guerrillas who left the camp before them. They spend the night of 31 July there.

A contingent including John Dube, the overall commander of the group, is the last to leave Drummond Park Farm.

At about 7 a.m. on the morning of 1 August, they arrive at a spot in the bush about a mile from the Zambezi River. At this spot, they meet their colleagues, as well as Oliver Tambo and Joe Modise. All the troops are clad in the uniforms provided at the farm.[36]

*

On the same day, the *Rand Daily Mail* features a report from a correspondent in Salisbury, Rhodesia, to the effect that Rhodesia's security forces have commenced a new drive along the Zambezi Valley to 'tighten up terrorist loopholes'.

The report says hundreds of African nationalists are known to be on the Zambian side of the border, waiting for orders to cross.

To prevent arms smuggling, security forces are imposing heavy padlocks on vans and trucks immediately upon entry into Rhodesia, and then opening and inspecting the cargoes at the destinations. Truck drivers are forbidden to pick up passengers. On the 'danger stretch' of the Great North Road through the Zambezi Valley, civilian vehicles are being formed into convoys escorted by the army. Motorists travelling the road are asked to sign documents declaring that they will proceed straight to their destinations without stopping.

The report says Rhodesian security forces are keeping a round-the-clock watch on the Zambezi River. It concludes: 'More than 20 terrorists have crossed into Rhodesia in the last two months with modern weapons and equipment and all have been killed or captured without a major incident. The security forces say they have the situation well in hand.'[37]

*

On the evening of the 1st, the guerrillas are transported by means of a big lorry and two Land Rovers to a spot on the northern side of the Zambezi. Joe Modise and Jacob Masondo then accompany them up to the river bank. While they are there, another Land Rover arrives, carrying Oliver Tambo and Tom Nkobi.

Tambo addresses them and provides the group as a whole with details of the arrangements for the infiltration. He says it is a big day for them as it coincides with the death of Albert Luthuli. It will therefore be suitable for the group that will fight in South Africa to be known as the 'Luthuli Detachment'. He says the thirty ZAPU members (out of a total of eighty-one guerrillas involved in the operation) who will fight in Rhodesia will be known as the 'Lobengula Detachment'.

Mongameli Tshali is announced as the overall leader of the Luthuli Detachment, while Lawrence Phokanoka and Theophilus Mkalipi will be second and third in command.

Chris Hani then comes forward and calls out the names of twenty South Africans, including himself, who will remain in Rhodesia to assist the Lobengula Detachment (these men have been seconded to the aforementioned 'Lupane' and 'Tsholotsho' groups).[38]

*

On the afternoon of the following day, 2 August, the guerrillas assemble at a spot near Livingstone in sight of the Zambezi River. Tambo, wearing spectacles and dressed in dark trousers and a jersey, addresses them. He says they have a hard task ahead in which they will have to go and shed some of the blood that the enemy has been shedding for years. He also says they must fight bravely and not run away. If caught, they must not talk.[39]

At about 5 p.m. at a place just below Victoria Falls where there are high, almost vertical cliffs on both sides of the river, the crossing begins.

Ropes have been tied to trees, and to reach the river from the cliffs, the men have to abseil down the ropes. The first man to go down is Chris Hani. Tom Nkobi is on the cliff. Nkobi finds the cliff so high he can't see Hani reaching the river below.

At the bottom are two canoes, but only one is functioning. The men are rowed across, three at a time, by a man codenamed 'Boston Gagarin'.

Watching Gagarin at work, Tambo remarks within Nkobi's earshot: 'Here is a great guy.'[40]

*

In the early evening, with darkness approaching, the turn of Peter Mfene, Leonard Nkosi and Peter Sithole arrives and they depart carrying their own weapons, ammunition and food supplies.

With the ropes tied to trees at the top of the cliff, ANC and ZAPU members are positioned at various points further down the ravine to give direction to the men descending. This involves pulling on the rope as the men coming down approach, and then pushing the rope as the men progress to the next point on the descent.

As it happens, a number of the rocks on the cliff are loose, so touching them sends them crashing down. It is a matter of pure chance that none of the men in the strategic positions further down the cliff are hit by the rock missiles sent flying by their colleagues.

Nkosi, Mfene and Sithole are then rowed across the river by canoe. The stretch of water the cadres cross is about 150 feet wide and not flowing strongly.

On the Rhodesian side of the river they have to walk up the ravine, because there are no ropes or colleagues to assist. While ascending, they again notice that some of the rocks are loose.

At the top they wait for the others. The crossing takes all night, so the early crossers try to sleep, but throughout the night there are sounds of boulders crashing and the voices of comrades making their way across.[41]

*

When Daluxolo Luthuli crosses at about 10 a.m. on the 3rd, he is among the last across.

The crossing complete, the group makes camp about two miles from the river and rests there for the remainder of the day.[42]

THE WANKIE AND SIPOLILO CAMPAIGNS

Chris Hani takes aside the commander of the Lupane group, ZAPU's David Madzimba (real name Jonathan Moyo), and tells him that when the groups split, he must take one coloured man with him who will then go straight to South Africa.

Hani tells Moyo to lead this man to a railway station from where he can catch a train to South Africa.[1]

*

At about 5 p.m. on the 3rd, John Dube speaks to the group's reconnaissance team, which consists of Eric Nduna (real name Abel Jantshi), Wilson Msweli (Zolile Nqose), Alfred Mfamana, Rashidi Kawawa (Goodman Mhlawuli) and Alfred Ngwane (Joseph Nduli) of the ANC, as well as 'Nkosi' and Phiri Malama of ZAPU. Dube tells them to scout ahead within a radius of three miles to see if the area is populated or not.

Mongameli Tshali, the commander of the Luthuli Detachment, gives a compass to Zolile Nqose, who is in charge of the reconnaissance group. Nqose then leads the group southwards. After an hour he stops and instructs Nduli, Mfamana and Nkosi to go back and contact the others.

By 7 a.m. the following morning, Nduli, Mfamana and Nkosi have not returned, so Nqose leaves Rashidi Kawawa and Phiri Malama behind and goes with Eric Nduna to search for them.

After walking a few miles Nqose and Nduna encounter Joseph Nduli, who is no longer in the company of Mfamana and Nkosi, but rather with three other men from the larger ANC–ZAPU unit, namely 'Mzala', Don Maseko and Amos Ndlovu.

Nqose is told that John Dube has moved south with the remainder of the troops (Mfamana and Nkosi included) and will wait for them at Matestse River.[2]

*

On the fifth night after crossing the Zambezi, the main, roughly eighty-strong combined group under John Dube's overall command are walking in darkness when they near the road connecting Salisbury and Zambia via Wankie. The road is already relatively busy. The group crouches next to it.

When a gap in traffic occurs and there are either no cars in sight, or at least no cars for a considerable distance, the group runs across the road and into bush.

However, when they reassemble on the other side, Sekhukhuneland group commander Lawrence Phokanoka reports that he has left his rifle where they were resting. Mongameli Tshali tells him to go back and fetch it.

Graham Morodi asks Leonard Nkosi for permission to go back with Phokanoka, as they don't know what is going to happen to him.

Phokanoka says, no, he will find it.

He goes alone.

After about fifteen minutes, Phokanoka returns without the rifle and tells the commanders to march without him because by 4 a.m. they need to have reached their next destination, otherwise they will be exposed.

They leave him behind.

Two or three hours later, Phokanoka recovers his rifle and tries to catch up with his group.[3]

*

On the following night, Dube's group crosses a railway line and enters the Wankie Game Reserve. By the time they enter it is morning – still dark, but approaching sunrise – so they opt to take cover among some bushes.

When it gets light, seeing that the bushes are actually quite sparse, they proceed to another spot about a mile away.

At about 4 p.m., realising that one of the group, namely Patrick Sindili Mantayana, aliases 'Alfred Scott' and 'Mambaso', is missing, John Dube sends two people to look for him where they were in the morning.

The two do not manage to find him.[4]

*

In the Wankie Game Reserve region on 10 August, Patrick Mantayana is found – by Platoon Warrant Officer Wurayayi of the Rhodesian African Rifles (RAR), who is in the company of six privates.

Wurayayi discovers a grenade in Mantayana's pocket.

Mantayana then leads Wurayayi to a spot in the bush, about a mile away, where he points out a rifle and soldier's pack hidden under a tree.[5]

*

On the day following Mantayana's arrest, the Rhodesian Army establishes a joint operations centre at Wankie Airfield for what they dub 'Operation Nickel'.[6]

*

Two days after their entry into Wankie Game Reserve, the main group has reached roughly the middle of the park.[7] At this point, the Lupane group, under its leader, Jonathan Moyo, branches off towards the east as per the plan outlined by Joe Modise at Dube's Farm in the final week of July. They number twenty-one, but in addition they have Basil February, who is to accompany them part of the way.[8]

The other two groups – the Tsholotsho group and the Luthuli Detachment – continue southwards.[9]

Further on in the Lupane group's eastward march, Jonathan Moyo takes leave of his unit in the company of Basil February, who has a pistol in his possession.

They are now outside the game reserve. Moyo leads February to Pongoro Railway Station. When the train arrives, February runs to catch it.

Moyo returns to his group, which watches as the train pulls off.

Moyo then leads the remainder of his men on a march up to some little hills near Pongoro. They remain there the rest of the day.

After sunset they continue their eastwards march, in the direction of Inyatuwe.[10]

*

At dawn, Basil February is arrested by a black railway security guard, who takes him to Dett Police Station without conducting a body search.

This oversight proves costly when at the station February draws his pistol, wounds Corporal Tazuwinga of railway security, and escapes on a bicycle before stealing a car and heading towards Bulawayo, evading road blocks along the way.[11]

*

The members of the reconnaissance team, namely Zolile Nqose, Rashidi Kawawa, Eric Nduna, Joseph Nduli and Phiri Malama, who are still in the company of 'Mzala', Don Maseko and Amos Ndlovu, have not yet managed to reconnect with the main group. It is now 12 August.

Nqose suggests going with Kawawa and Ndlovu to look for food and water while the rest stay with Don Maseko, who is struggling.

Nqose, Kawawa and Ndlovu leave.[12]

*

Jonathan Moyo's Lupane group arrives at 5 a.m. on 13 August 1967 at a spot by the Inyatuwe River, some two and a half miles south of the Inyatuwe Railway Siding in the Wankie District.[13]

They establish camp inside a small area of dense bush next to a dry river bed. A hundred metres from them, standing tall above dry elephant grass, is a hillock with huge rocks on top, from which a panoramic view of the surrounding area can be obtained.[14]

*

At about 12.30 p.m. Patrol Officer Hopkins and an African tracker cross a dry river stream. They are at the head of a unit consisting of Rhodesian African Rifles troops and some policemen. While crossing, Hopkins is fired on from nearby bush. He runs back, shouting a warning to his colleagues who are standing exposed on the river bank. They all take cover.[15]

At headquarters, the voice of the captain of the RAR unit, Peter Hosking, sounds clearly over the two-way radio: 'There they are, the bandits.' He calls for urgent helicopter reinforcement (in addition to a Provost spotter plane that is hovering above the scene). The Rhodesian unit, which can't see the enemy, opens fire from the river bank in the direction from where Patrol Officer Hopkins was fired at.[16]

Freddie Mninzi, alias 'Comrade Rogers', the third in command in the Lupane group, lifts his head and sees a colleague manning the guerrillas' outpost twenty metres away from him get hit by an enemy bullet. Mninzi then sees the Rhodesian forces firing towards the bush from hip position.

Mninzi is pinned down by the fire. Bullets hit the sand all around him. He lies flat. Some of the guerrillas flee further into the bush, but others take up combat positions.

Then the security-force weapons go silent. Captain Hosking calls out in English: 'You should surrender!' The message is repeated in Ndebele by one of the African members of the patrol.

This call is met by a salvo of guerrilla fire. Among the guerrillas is James Masimini, who shouts that he will shoot any son-of-a-bitch that runs away. Fire back! he says.[17]

*

The first Alouette helicopter escorting the reinforcements called in by Captain Hosking lands. Out of it step Inspector Frederick Phillips, who is the officer in charge of Wankie Police Station, Detective Inspector Reeves, and two unarmed plain-clothes African detectives.

A second Alouette then brings Corporal Davison and four Rhodesian African Rifles members.[18]

Back in the bush, Freddie Mninzi, who was able to get up after the guerrillas' return fire compelled the security forces to take cover, leads Delmas Sibanyoni and James Masimini across the guerrilla positions. On the way they encounter Bothwell Tamane, alias 'Zami', single-handedly manning a post in the face of heavy Rhodesian fire. Mninzi orders Sibanyoni to support Zami, but to wait until the enemy is fifty metres away before firing.

No sooner is the order given than the enemy breaks cover, running towards the guerrillas, again firing from the hip. There are helicopters patrolling above, covering the advance. When the security forces are about fifty yards away, Mninzi orders his submachine gunners to fire. This stops the offensive in its tracks and the enemy again retreats.

Mninzi, Masimini and Tamane then set out in search of one of the guerrillas' light machine guns (LMGs). When they find one, Mninzi entrusts it to Tamane. The three men then abandon the cover of the bush and run in the direction of the hillock.

When they reach the foot of the hillock, a helicopter emerges and fires on them with 12.7-mm machine guns. This forces Mninzi, Masimini and Tamane to retreat back to the bush.[19]

Then Captain Hosking takes his turn to capture the strategically important hillock. He leads a section of his force obliquely in a south-east direction. They manage to mount the ridge. Once on top they advance abreast of each other in a line. They head southwards in the direction of the guerrillas' bush stronghold. Slightly behind the centre of this advancing line stand Inspectors Reeves and Phillips, and much further behind them are the two unarmed African detectives.

When the line nears the southern tip of the ridge it comes under heavy fire from guerrillas hidden in the gulley below.

The security forces immediately go to ground and return fire. As Captain Koroni of the RAR tries to lift his head, he is shot behind the left ear and killed at the far left of the line. Captain Davison is also shot and killed. Hosking crawls to Davison's position, finds him dead, and attempts to crawl back, but as he does so, he is shot in the rear of his thigh.[20]

Seeing a white officer pinned down between the rocks, Freddie Mninzi orders Delmas Sibanyoni and Ronnie Dube to concentrate fire on that officer. Mninzi also commands them to be ready to offer covering fire. He then takes Bothwell Tamane, James Masimini and another comrade, 'Donda', aside. He assigns them positions on the hillock from where the enemy can be expected to appear. He says that under no circumstances are they to leave those positions; the success of the group's mission depends on them.[21]

*

One of the three LMGs possessed by the guerrillas is operated by Delmas Sibanyoni. He fires from the river, offering cover for colleagues near the apex of the hillock who are trying to seize control of the ridge. Of these men trying to take the ridge, one is Ronnie Dube, who is still operating the second LMG. Dube uses it to take aim at the spotter plane. James Masimini, also on the hillock, has the third LMG.

Late that afternoon, 'Mhambi', one of the guerrillas from the hillock, returns and reports to Freddie Mninzi that both Masimini and Bothwell are injured – Masimini's arm was hit, he says, and the bone was pierced through the flesh. After the wound was dressed, Masimini continued firing with his LMG. Bothwell was meanwhile hit in the leg. Mhambi claims many 'Boer' corpses are strewn over Masimini's sector of fire.

At just that moment, fresh waves of helicopters arrive, preventing Mhambi from returning to the hillock.

Thereafter only Dube's LMG is heard firing constantly from the hillock; Masimini's sounds only intermittently. But, soon, Dube's LMG goes silent, leaving only Masimini's LMG complementing the rattle of Bothwell Tamane's submachine gun.

Nightfall at about 6 p.m. brings an end to the combat.

A group of guerrillas goes to the hillock to retrieve Donda and Masimini. They find Donda dead from a 12.7-mm bullet fired into his back.[22]

*

At around 7 p.m., in the dark, Robert Dube hears whistling from the bush. He follows it, and finds a number of colleagues around Jonathan Moyo, who tells them that three of the twenty-one-man group have been killed, and two injured.

One of the injured is James Masimini. He has lost a great deal of blood and consequently can't move his right arm.

Delmas Sibanyoni and Ronnie Dube, who were manning the group's two other LMGs, are dead. Moyo takes the three corpses (Delmas, Dube and Donda) and covers their heads with their jackets. He asks the two wounded how they are feeling.

They are not in a good state and say so. They are left behind.

Moyo takes the weapons of the dead, but leaves the two wounded with their guns. One of the weapons taken is an LMG (the other two have been destroyed in the battle), and this is given to Moyo's deputy, Andries Motsepe.

The Lupane group leaves the place under the cover of night, and rests near a little hill.[23]

*

The following day, a Rhodesian African Rifles patrol unit under Lieutenant Wardle's command is sent to the scene of the battle to conduct a sweep. They recover the three dead bodies.

They also encounter one of the wounded guerrillas, namely Joseph Bothwell Ndhlovu, who reaches for his rifle, only to be shot dead by Wardle.

The RAR men follow the tracks left by the guerrillas.

Just over a kilometre to the east, at 2 p.m., James Masimini is shot dead by a white Rhodesian soldier.[24]

*

On the same day (14 August) at Intundla Siding near the Wankie Game Reserve, Lawrence Phokanoka's campaign ends when he is arrested in a hut with a compass in his possession. He never managed to reconnect with the main group.

On the following day, the Rhodesian Police recover his arms and uniform in the nearby forest.[25]

*

Zolile Nqose, Rashidi Kawawa and Amos Ndlovu of the reconnaissance group arrive at a road and rest alongside it.

Eventually a lorry approaches. They manage to stop it.

The lorry takes them to a game camp. There they learn that they are in Botswana.[26]

*

Having abandoned his stolen car in Bulawayo, Basil February has by the 16th made his way to Figtree, where he asks a white farmer's wife for a drink. He then takes the woman and her six-year-old son hostage.

With the aid of the gardener, the wife and son manage to escape to raise the alarm.

The British South Africa Police arrive and surround the farmhouse.

February is shot dead by a section officer named Steyn.[27]

*

The Botswana Police arrive on the following day at the game camp where Zolile Nqose, Rashidi Kawawa and Amos Ndlovu are based. The three guerrillas are arrested without a fight.

Amos Ndlovu takes the police to the place where they left the other members of the group on the 12th. At the scene they find some rifles, and Don Maseko's corpse.[28]

∗

After sunset on the 17th, Jonathan Moyo's Lupane group starts marching again. Hunted by tracker teams, they are now retreating west towards Botswana. They reach an open area where there are two dead trees.

Moyo instructs a portion of the group to sleep by one tree, and the other portion at the second.

The group remains in these positions until 3 p.m. on the 18th when the RAR tracker unit commanded by Lieutenant Wardle arrives.

When one of the guerrillas crawls out of one of the trees he is challenged by a member of the security forces to surrender. The call is repeated several times in Ndebele but not answered. The patrol then opens fire.

Three men emerge with their hands up. They surface from thick bush surrounding the tree. One of these men indicates a second tree about twenty yards away.

A challenge is extended to this second group of guerrillas to surrender. It is not answered, so the security forces open fire. These shots cause a grenade to explode in the guerrilla positions. This sparks a fire that detonates the guerrillas' other grenades, creating an inferno.

The Rhodesian Security Forces find five men burnt to death at the scene of the blaze. A further two were killed by the security forces. Six of the group are captured.

Jonathan Moyo successfully manages to crawl away from the battlefield to safety, but he is now on his own; the Lupane group has effectively been destroyed as a fighting unit.[29]

∗

The southbound Luthuli Detachment and Tsholotsho group have by now consumed all the food issued to them prior to the infiltration. They cook a dove that they have managed to shoot down. They slice the dove up, cook the parts, and drink the resultant soup. There is only a small piece of dove for each man.

At sundown, as they prepare to resume their march, they listen to the Rhodesian news on a small transistor radio that they have brought with them.

They learn that there has been a second clash between the Rhodesian Security Forces and guerrillas in the Zambezi Valley. The report mentions that another guerrilla group is known to be moving south-east in the Wankie Game Reserve, headed straight for South Africa, but the security forces are on their trail.[30]

∗

At ANC headquarters in Lusaka on 19 August, James Chikerema and Oliver Tambo hold a press conference.[31]

A joint ANC–ZAPU press release is issued at the same time. It reads: 'From the thirteenth of this month, the area of Wankie has been the scene of the most daring battles ever fought between Freedom Fighters and the white oppressors' Army in

Rhodesia. Only last night the Rhodesian Regime admitted having been engaged in a six hour Battle yesterday.'

The statement notes that both the Rhodesian and South African regimes have claimed that ANC soldiers were involved in the battles. The communiqué says: 'We wish to declare here that the fighting that is presently going on in the Wankie area is indeed being carried out by a combined force of ZAPU and ANC' that entered Rhodesia 'as Comrades-in-arms on a common route, each bound to its destination'.

The declaration is signed by Chikerema and Tambo.[32]

*

Early one morning, the Luthuli and Tsholotsho groups take turns fetching water from a dam. They are now slightly outside the Wankie Game Reserve.

At about 8 a.m. John Dube instructs Chris Mampuru and Ernest Modulo to stay at the dam and shoot any game that might come to the water.

The remainder of the group walk away and take cover in some bush. No sooner are they in position than a truck appears about 75–100 metres away. The truck is moving so quietly that the guerrillas were unable to hear its approach and only became aware of it when it emerged into view. The vehicle is following the guerrilla tracks and travelling up the path that the cadres recently walked – there is thus no way, given the freshness of the tracks, that its inhabitants cannot be aware of the enemy's proximity. When the vehicle reaches the point where there is a split in the tracks it stops. This is at a distance fifty yards directly opposite from where the guerrillas are hiding.

A white officer gets out of the truck, which has about ten men in the back. Norman Duka of MK sees one of the Africans in the back manning a huge machine gun. There is also a heavy artillery piece on the truck. The officer looks around for a bit and then commands, 'Forward Jack', before getting into the truck, which pulls off slowly. However, instead of following the direction of the main force of guerrillas, the vehicle heads to the dam.

Five more trucks appear, each carrying about five men. Graham Morodi sees a carrier containing a mixed black and white team of about five Rhodesian soldiers and hears one of the white men in the carrier say: Wait, hey, they are going this side.

The vans get to the dam, where they stop. By now the ANC–ZAPU group notice aeroplanes flying overhead. Shortly thereafter they hear the sound of rifle fire. From the dam come the shouts: 'Surrender, surrender!'

There is a firefight that lasts about two minutes. Then all is quiet.

The group in the bush crawls in the opposite direction to the gunfire. Their mobility is, however, impeded by spotter planes swarming above.

Late in the afternoon, the guerrillas hear the sound of the trucks apparently leaving. The last aeroplane also disappears. Dube sends six people to the dam to see what had happened to the other two.

They cannot find the men at the dam.

The group in the bush then moves from its position towards some forest lying

about a fifteen-minute walk away. They put up for the night in the forest. Throughout the night they can hear the sound of trucks entering the area regularly. On the
next morning they move on, heading westwards before pivoting southwards.

At about 10 a.m. they cross a wire fence and re-enter the game reserve. Because
the place they enter is bushy and offers cover, they put up a kraal consisting of a
headquarters housing the commanders in the middle, and the various groups of the
unit surrounding them and facing in all directions.

They can hear dogs barking from nearby villages.[33]

*

On the morning of 22 August 1967, in the area of Siwuwu Pools, the group hears a
cock crow in the distance.

John Dube instructs two members of the group, 'Nkotheni' and 'George', to
change into their non-military clothes and search for civilians who may be able
to supply them with food.

John Dube also approaches Tennis Khumalo and asks him to fetch some water.

Later, on his way back with the water, Khumalo sees a white Land Rover.

Back at the camp, Khumalo tells the others that he saw a Jeep that he thinks
belongs to the police. He says he thinks the enemy are patrolling the area.

John Dube instructs the soldiers to remain in position for the afternoon and says
they will leave thereafter.

Nkotheni and George meanwhile return and report to John Dube at about 10 a.m.
They have food which a black cattle-ranch owner gave to them. Dube says to them
that they must go back to him and see if they can get enough food for the group as a
whole. The two depart again.

They return at midday carrying a four-gallon tin containing sour milk with
porridge. The guerrillas go up in groups to have this milk dished into their water
bottles, from which they then drink.

The guerrillas thereafter hide in their foxholes. They are divided into sections.
At the middle there is the headquarters, where a group of five, including John Dube,
Chris Hani and Leonard Nkosi, is based. The other guerrillas are deployed in a semi-
circular position facing the direction they have come (north-east). They have three
LMGs – one on the right flank, one on the left flank and a third in the middle, at the
'rear' of the crescent. In between there are other small guns.[34]

Sometime between 2 and 2.30 p.m. while food is being served to the last section,
Julius Maliba, alias 'Mancheck', the group commander of the Sibasa section, reports
at the 'headquarters'. He conveys a complaint his group has about the food. Simultaneously, members of his group in their position in the semi-circle are quarrelling
among themselves about the food situation. Other members of this Sibasa group
are trying to get some sleep. Nobody is keeping guard in this unit, which is facing
directly north-east, the direction from which any tracking unit pursuing the group
must be expected to come.

At just that moment, fire is opened on the section of the line where the groups destined for Sibasa and Cape Town are located.

They hear shouts: 'Surrender!' and 'Habanza chalita!' (you are finished).

A fragmentation grenade is tossed into the Sibasa group. Robert Baloyi and Barry Masipa die instantly and Sparks Moloi is seriously wounded from a bullet fired into his chest. Peter Mhlongo is shot through his upper arm and thighs. Charles Sishuba of the Cape group is hit just above the eye and dies immediately.

The group on the flank of the Sibasa group starts firing back and holds the enemy at bay.

In the headquarters, John Dube, Leonard Nkosi, Chris Hani and Mongameli Tshali see three planes circling overhead.[35]

Thula Bopela notices a black RAR soldier standing eighty metres to the right of the guerrillas, leaning against a tree with an ammunition belt over his shoulder, spraying bullets above the heads of his men with a Bren gun. The man, Sergeant Major C.S.M. Timitiya, pins the guerrillas down with a torrent of bullets and shouts, 'Surrender, surrender terrorist!' He is urging, directing and commanding his men all the while.

Also prominent is Lieutenant Nicholas Smith of the RAR, who is laying fire to his left and right. The bush is so thick, however, that even during the first skirmish with the Sibasa section, the Rhodesians could not be seen by the remainder of the guerrilla contingent. On the instructions of their commanders, the guerrillas keep their heads down, hold their fire, and maintain their silence.

RAR members start running in the direction of the ANC–ZAPU troops but they are firing wildly. They drop their backpacks and kneel in a long line in front of the guerrillas. They then resume their firing. But the thick bush severely limits visibility.

After some time, with little reaction from the other side, members of the RAR begin standing up. Chris Hani hears them ask: 'Where are they; can you see them?' 'Where are the terrorists?'[36]

At this point, Leonard Nkosi hears the LMG at the centre of the guerrillas' half-circle begin to fire.

Mongameli Tshali crawls to his men (of the Luthuli Detachment) on the left of the half-circle, and Hani to the Lupane group on the right. After the LMG fires, the rest of the group follow suit.

Nkosi fires over the heads of his colleagues at the enemy. However, through the bush he never actually gets to see the faces of the enemy – he just fires in the direction from which their fire is coming.

Soon, however, Nkosi hears a grenade explode and the LMG goes silent. After firing about five rounds with his submachine gun, Nkosi begins crawling to the right-hand side.

During this section of the battle, Timitiya drops his gun and falls face down on the ground. Then Smith falls to the ground clutching his chest. Bullets strike Smith's face and he spins round on his back. Even without their commanders, the RAR continue shooting.

After a while, however, RAR members start running – but in the confusion of battle and poor visibility of the bush, some start running in the direction of the guerrillas, and are fired on.

The guerrillas advance on the retreating Rhodesian troops with both flanks of the half-circle advanced, i.e. in an encircling manoeuvre.

The fire continues for a while. Then Bopela hears voices: 'They are running away.' The rate of fire diminishes, then drops to isolated shots. There is still an aeroplane flying low over them. Justice Mpanza, the leader of Bopela's group, orders that it be fired on.

As the plane comes near, John Dube fires on it with an LMG. The plane flies away.

There is a lot of confusion at this point. ANC–ZAPU guerrillas start to stand and move forward.[37]

From his position to the right of the guerrilla contingent, Lewis Nkosi sees Sparks Moloi come crawling to him groaning. He tells Nkosi he has been shot in the stomach. Nkosi supports him to the rear. By this stage the shooting has completely ceased.

Nkosi then sees Hani, Justice Mpanza, Theophilus Mkalipi and Castro Dolo come, carrying haversacks different to the standard issue given to the guerrillas.

Nkosi asks about the backpacks.

Hani says they have been taken from the security forces who have withdrawn. Hani says that one European and one Bantu of the security forces have been killed.

They all then move in a southerly direction. Jebese Makiwane helps Leonard Nkosi carry Sparks Moloi. After walking a short distance they stop and gather together.

Hani says that Barry Masipa, Charles Sishuba and Robert Baloyi have been killed, while 'Goodman Moloi' (i.e. Julius Maliba, the commander of the Sibasa group) has been wounded in the thigh. Greatwell Mabhija has an injury to the head, Peter Mfene a slight injury to the arm and Sparks Moloi is wounded in the stomach.

Peter Mfene is in possession of a Morse code radio and one walkie-talkie. Both have been captured from the enemy. Mfene is the only radio operator in the unit who can use Morse code, so he is given the radio to keep, while one of the group's other radio specialists is given the walkie-talkie.

Mfene tells his colleagues that this is not correct; the Morse code can be carried by anybody, but the walkie-talkie is useful for listening to the enemy.

He asks for and is given the walkie-talkie. Half an hour after the firing of the last shot in the battle, a signal comes across on the walkie-talkie. It is to the effect that the Rhodesian forces have planned an ambush by the dam.

The haversacks obtained from the security forces contain tinned beef, cakes, sweets, sugar, powdered soup, cold drinks and maps of the area.

The guerrillas proceed in an easterly direction. Sparks Moloi has died by this stage and is left behind. Julius Maliba has to be carried as he cannot walk.[38]

*

By 11 p.m. that evening, the group has reached a cattle post outside the game reserve.

One of the locals tells them: The enemy is around and can come at any time. If they learn that you came and we didn't report, we could be killed. You should pass quickly before they discover you have been around.

The group passes without obtaining the food they had come for. Just past the village runs the Manzamnyama (or Nata) River. A Rhodesian ambush force has established itself there.

Regardless of this, the ANC–ZAPU group sends teams out periodically to search for water along the river bed.

At some point that night, two enemy stragglers approach the position where the guerrillas are hidden. The guerrillas open fire on them.

After hearing the gunfire, a group of Rhodesian troops proceed to the dam to support the ambush team positioned there – they have erroneously interpreted the gunfire as a sign that the ambush team is in battle with the guerrillas. When they arrive at the dam, a firefight breaks out between them and the ambush team, both of whom have mistaken each other for guerrillas.

Later that evening, with all the cadres having returned from the river reconnaissance, the group's civilian radio is switched on. They hear it reported that the Rhodesian Security Forces have attacked the terrorists in fresh fighting and have killed ten.

This causes mirth among the guerrillas because they know that all their men are accounted for.

At about 8 a.m. the following morning, Peter Mfene opens the walkie-talkie taken from the previous day's battle. The group hears that the Rhodesians have had a chance to look at the dead men's bodies, and it seems as though they have killed their own men.[39]

*

Later on the 23rd, some twelve miles south-east of the previous day's battle, the guerrillas sleep in foxholes concealed by branches. Helicopters and jets are circling above.

Late in the afternoon a jet arrives and bombs a forested area about three miles ahead of the guerrillas in the direction they were heading (south-east). The bombing continues for forty-five minutes. The guerrillas' objective hitherto has been to march fifteen miles a day. If they had not been delayed by having to carry injured comrades, the bombing would have been right on target. The enemy's intelligence is manifesting an alarming increase in accuracy.

An RAR platoon consisting of between twenty-two and twenty-four men, under the command of Lieutenant William Rodney Winnal, meanwhile begins to form a base camp for the night at roughly 5 p.m. The position is just outside the Wankie Game Reserve, to the south.

At the guerrilla encampment, Harry Hadebe, who is lying in his foxhole under some mopani bushes, hears dogs barking. John Dube details Goliati Thebe and Peri Ncube to go and investigate.

While they are away, Hadebe hears shots being fired.

Thebe and Ncube return. Thebe says that he fired a shot at enemy soldiers encamped nearby.

Dube turns to the person operating the group's radio, and tells him to close it. Then Dube goes with Thebe and Ncube to take a closer look at the enemy position.

Dube leaves carrying an FN rifle and wearing a green security-force beret. Both items were acquired from the RAR following the previous day's battle.

Morris Ncube, one of the ZAPU guerrillas in the camp, hears shots being fired when the three men are gone. Then he sees Dube running back. Dube tells the group to come and assist. He says the Rhodesian forces are near and orders the soldiers to advance towards them in a line.

The detachment marches forward in a 'horn' formation, with the flanks of the line advancing ahead once again as if to encircle the enemy, with an arch of soldiers leading back to the centre or 'head'.

After Lieutenant Winnal hears sporadic firing to the right of the RAR camp, a sergeant major comes to him saying he has spotted two terrorists. Immediately afterwards heavy fire sounding like that of an automatic machine gun is opened on the camp. In addition to the fire, grenades are tossed at the camp. One of them explodes about ten paces or so from Winnal, and he gets shrapnel in his shoulder, his hip, and a little in his face. A short distance away he hears somebody shouting, 'Attack, attack, attack!'

Patrol Officer Thomas, one of two white dog handlers with the RAR platoon (Winnal and these two are the only whites in the Rhodesian group), tries to get his dog under control. Thomas is shot dead by the guerrillas while trying to do so.[40]

Chris Hani is in the vicinity of James April, Douglas Wana, Jack Simelane, Thula Bopela and Nicholas Donda as they approach the Rhodesian position. They fire short bursts at the enemy.

During the battle, the radio man on the Rhodesian side is killed while calling for helicopter support to fire on the battle scene.

Jack Simelane of MK runs after a fleeing white officer. As he does so he is shot dead by a wounded enemy soldier. Thula Bopela is involved in chasing other fleeing Rhodesian soldiers when he hears Shooter Makasi shout that Jack Simelane has been killed. Bopela hears this as he is running past a Rhodesian soldier who is trying to wriggle out of his sleeping bag in order to reach a gun. Bopela fires a short burst at the man and continues running past. Bopela says as he does so, 'That sleeping bag is mine!'

Next to Bopela is Nicholas Donda, who heads towards Simelane after hearing that he has been hit. As Donda does this he is shot in the lungs. He falls to his knees, clutching his chest. Bopela stops running, heads to Donda and when he gets there finds him breathing with difficulty. Blood is pouring from Donda's mouth. Bopela tries to lift him so as to carry him to the rear, but Donda shakes his head and waves him away. Donda tries to speak but dies before any words can come out.

The wounded enemy soldier responsible for Simelane's death is himself shot dead by the liberation army troops.[41]

Bopela runs to his section commander, Justice Mpanza, to report the news about Donda. Bopela and Mpanza then make their way to Donda and try to carry him to the rear.

While they are doing so, Luthuli Detachment commander Mongameli Tshali suddenly arrives. He tells Bopela and Mpanza that the enemy has retreated to a patch of bush 300 metres away. Tshali says: 'We cannot leave the enemy there; we must wipe them out.' He tells Mpanza, 'Bring your section, Comrade Kulak, we need your light machine-gunner.'

Bopela and Mpanza leave Donda and run with Tshali to the enemy position. They reach a point where they find Chris Hani pointing out to some fifteen ANC–ZAPU members the positions where the enemy are trying to regroup.

An open space of about seventy metres lies between the guerrillas and the enemy positions. As the liberation movement cadres crouch in position, James April, a white cloth tied round his head, breaks rank and charges across the open grass in the direction of the enemy, firing his machine gun all the while. When almost halfway across, his gun goes silent. As he struggles to obtain a fresh magazine for the weapon, one of the Rhodesian soldiers starts firing at him.

'Crawl back Comrade George, crawl back!' Tshali shouts out to April (aka 'George Driver'), whose comrades fire over his head to divert the enemy's attention and cover his retreat.

It works. April manages to crawl back to safety.

This battle, which began at dusk, doesn't last long, because as in previous engagements darkness brings an end to hostilities. The security forces withdraw from the combat area.

John Dube then orders the guerrillas to collect the haversacks that the Rhodesians have left. Leonard Nkosi collects one that is bloodstained.

Back at the foxholes where the wounded from the previous day's fight remained during the battle, Chris Hani informs the group that Jack Simelane and Nicholas Donda were killed in the engagement.[42]

*

Leaving the two radios captured in the engagement on the 22nd behind (they are worried about the Rhodesians using the radio signals to locate them), the ANC–ZAPU group immediately leaves the scene of battle and walks until about midnight when they reach a donga where they halt and rest.

John Dube suggests to the group that he lead a team to go and get drinking water from the Manzamnyama River.

Dube tells 'Mjojo' (Mongameli Tshali) to command the group in his absence. Dube then heads a group of eight whose other members are Chris Hani, Jackson Mandla, Alfred Mfamana, James April, Khanja Mlonzi, Graham Morodi and Edward Moyo. They leave their haversacks behind, but take their weapons as well as some water bottles that they have collected from the rest of the group.[43]

*

During the afternoon, Shooter Makasi, who is part of the group left behind under Tshali's command, announces while digging in the donga that he has found water.

Following this discovery, the rest of the group, who were resting on the river bed, start drinking the water and filling their bottles. They wait for Dube and the others to come back.[44]

*

The Dube-led group of eight manages to find a water source on the river bed that evening.

On their way back they get lost, so they fire into the air about three times (as per a prearranged signal, to which the main group has to respond by also firing into the air, to enable the two groups to find each other).

There is no response to the firing.

Dube and his men spend the night walking in the bush, lost, trying to find their colleagues.[45]

*

Meanwhile, back at the main group, Tshali orders Peter Sithole to fire in the air.

There is no response.

After Sithole's salvo, the group decides to shift position for security reasons. They leave the weapons and ammunition taken from the enemy as well as the haversacks belonging to Dube and companions in some long grass near the donga.[46]

Peter Mfene is part of this group. He is wearing a watch plundered from a Rhodesian soldier. Leonard Nkosi walks up to him and says: At headquarters we have no watch, as Chris [Hani] left with ours: can you give us this watch at headquarters? Headquarters can't move without a watch.

Mfene obliges.

About an hour into the march, 'Victor Dhlamini' (Theophilus Mkalipi) starts asking for 'Can Can' (Daluxolo Luthuli). Mkalipi is carrying the group's LMG and wants to be relieved.

The unit pauses and starts looking for Luthuli. They can't find him. Some cadres are sent back to the donga to have a look there. They return saying they couldn't find him.

The group puts up for the night.

They then realise that not only is Luthuli missing, but so are Thula Bopela and Leonard Nkosi.[47]

*

On the morning after this, John Dube's group of eight reach Choloza village and take cover at a spot near the Manzamnyama and Tegwani River confluence. They see helicopters above.

Then, in the evening, after sunset, Dube departs along with Chris Hani, Jackson Mandla and Alfred Mfamana, leaving James April, Khanja Mlonzi, Graham Morodi and Edward Moyo behind.

At midnight, the April–Morodi group also depart from their position. Guided by the stars, they walk until they come to the Rhodesia–Botswana border the following morning.

At about 8 a.m. they cross the border.

They are arrested in Botswana at the front of a house where they go to search for milk. A while later, a truck full of Botswana policemen arrives and leads them away.[48]

*

Having walked for two to three days since leaving the donga, grumbling begins to emerge among the rank-and-file members of the main group under Tshali's command.

Referring to the disappearance without trace of the groups (including senior commanders) over the last couple of days, the charges are: our commanders are cowards; they are now running away from the Boers; we are starving; we are going to die of hunger.

The unit's remaining commanders hold an emergency meeting. On the basis of the discussion they decide the unit must reverse course and head towards Botswana.[49]

*

On 28 August, Chris Hani, Jackson Mandla, Alfred Mfamana and John Dube arrive at a large store in Nkange, Botswana, wearing military uniforms but bearing no arms. They purchase civilian clothes from the store and change into them.

The storekeeper notifies a local councillor, who arrives and promises the four a lift to Francistown.

The Famine Relief vehicle that collects the four instead takes them to the police camp at Totome – as arranged by the councillor.

When interrogated at the camp on the following day, the four decline to give any information beyond their names. But it soon emerges from the questioning that Dube speaks fluent Kalanga, indicating Rhodesian origins. The police ask him whether he has been involved in the recent fighting in Rhodesia.

Eventually Dube agrees to lead the police to a place in the Maitengwe lands, on the border between Rhodesia and Botswana. There he points out a cache including three Russian 7.62-calibre AK machine guns, one Russian 'PPSH' submachine gun, one Russian 'RGD' hand grenade, and another hand grenade of Russian design that has in fact been manufactured in North Vietnam. He admits to the police that he and his three colleagues utilised the arms during fighting in Rhodesia.[50]

*

Jonathan Moyo has been on his own since splitting from the Lupane group on 18 August. He has severe stomach pains. He goes to a nearby kraal and asks for food.

On the following morning, he is arrested. In his possession are a Russian PPSH submachine gun, magazines for it, a Russian pistol and a Russian hand grenade.[51]

The Joint Planning Staff of the Rhodesian Army dispatches a situation report (sitrep) to the headquarters of the South African Air Force on 3 September. The report covers events in the twenty-four-hour period from 11 a.m. the previous day.

The sitrep records that Jonathan Moyo has been arrested at an unspecified place. It adds that he has been positively identified as a ZAPU leader and the sole survivor of the '24' men involved in the first action against the security forces on 13 August.[52]

*

Seretse Khama writes to President Kaunda on Tuesday 5 September. He reports that over the weekend Botswana's police arrested a further sixteen guerrillas, bringing the total apprehended to thirty-three. He estimates that there are 'still a further ten or twenty men loose in north-eastern Botswana'.

He says, 'We are not handing them over to the South African or Rhodesian authorities as we are strictly entitled to do, but are dealing with them ourselves. We are in effect saving their lives, because no-one could really believe that their isolated, small efforts can really achieve much against the organised strength and weight of the Rhodesian and South African security forces.

'This is what I find so grievous about this matter. These men stand no chance. What they are endeavouring to do is suicidal.'

He adds: 'I do hope that in *some* way you can influence matters. I know – or I believe – that you are as anxious to have these gangs gone from your country as much as I wish them away from here.'[53]

*

A sitrep from the Rhodesian Joint Planning Staff to the South African Air Force headquarters covering 7–8 September says that Operation Nickel has ended except for police action, while the Joint Operations Centre for the operation was closed at 6 a.m. on the 8th.[54]

*

The *Rand Daily Mail* on 8 September reports a British Foreign Office official as having said yesterday that, following enquiries, 'We have no evidence of South African military involvement' in Rhodesia.[55]

Before a capacity crowd at Brakpan Town Hall that evening, Prime Minister John Vorster says that South African Police members are active in Rhodesia fighting terrorists 'who originally came from South Africa and were on their way back to commit terrorism in South Africa. I want to make it very clear that we are doing this with the approval of Rhodesia.'

He says he has instructed a minister to inform the British government of this.[56]

A convoy of armoured cars enters Rhodesia at the Beit Bridge border later that evening.

Questioned by correspondents in Salisbury on the 9th, Rhodesia's leader Ian Smith says only South African Police units, not military units, are involved, and that they have been training alongside Rhodesian counterparts in areas of 'terrorist' activity, but have not participated in any fighting thus far.[57]

*

Within a couple of months, the liberation movements are involved in preparations for a fresh infiltration. Nzewu Henry Nsele of the ANC crosses into Rhodesia in November 1967 to survey a route to the Sipolilo area in the country's north-east. After penetrating about twelve miles he returns to Zambia.[58]

*

During the same month, Mathias Nyoni enters Rhodesia looking for a suitable place to establish a military base camp. Having found one, he returns to Lusaka.[59]

*

In advance of its December 1967 meeting in Dar es Salaam, the Defence Standing Committee of the OAU Liberation Committee circulates a report stating that the ANC has requested assistance to infiltrate 200 of its personnel into South Africa at a minimum cost of £5,000.[60]

On 5 December, at the conclusion of the meeting, the committee approves the infiltration of the 200, and requests that the Standing Committee on Finance makes provision for the disbursement.[61]

*

Ralph Mzamo arrives at Nkomo camp, situated about twenty-five miles south-west of Lusaka, and finds a mixed group of 112 ANC and ZAPU guerrillas already there.

Mzamo is called aside by 'Comrade Melamu' and told that in his absence a group of 100 men were selected to fight in Rhodesia. Moffat Hadebe of ZAPU will be the commander, Kenneth Mzatho of the ANC the chief of staff, Lennon Milane (ANC) the chief political officer and George Mothusi (ANC) operations chief. Mzamo himself will be chief of security, ZAPU's Patrick Sibanda will take logistics, Sparks Pooe (ANC) will lead communications, Felix Arnold Kahiya (ZAPU) personnel, and Lusceni Mpofu of ZAPU will be medical officer.[62]

*

On the evening of 18 December, Akim Ndlovu of ZAPU arrives at Nkomo camp. He reads out a list of thirty-six names that will constitute an 'Advanced Group' to lead the infiltration. Ndlovu says Ralph Mzamo will head the group.

Akim Ndlovu drives the thirty-six to Dube's Farm (aka Luthuli camp), approximately twenty miles west of Lusaka.

At the farm, Akim Ndlovu takes Mzamo aside and gives him some maps. Joe Modise is also present when this occurs. The maps date from 1942. The first map ranges from Rhodesia's border with Botswana to Kariba. The second spans Kariba to Mozambique.

On the following day, the 'Advanced Group' leaves Dube's Farm for the Zambezi.

They camp en route overnight, and on the 20th move their material to the banks of the river.[63]

*

On the banks of the Zambezi on 28 December, one end of a long thick rope is tied to a raft carrying sixty-one boxes of ammunition, ten bags with guns, and a box of explosives. The other end of the rope is fixed to a tree. The raft is then pushed into the water. A few metres from the bank, five men board the raft. As in August with the crossings for the Wankie campaign, Boston Gagarin is there, and he swims alongside the raft, pulling it with his arm.

The men on the bank, of whom Ralph Mzamo is one, slowly release the rope, thereby steadily easing the raft across the water. After a while, the raft is out of visual range. Then, however, they hear Boston Gagarin shouting: 'Hee, Dontsa, Baphel'abantu. Dontsa' ('Pull, doomed men, pull').

The overloaded boat has capsized. Mzamo orders his colleagues, 'Heyi, pull men pull. Fast, pull.'

A frogman codenamed 'Guluva' comes running from behind carrying a small boat above his head. At water's edge he jumps in the boat and proceeds in it till he is just past the raft. He then dives out of the boat and swims eastwards.

Observing the scene, Mzamo notices that there is somebody in the water being pushed by the current. Guluva drags this man back and then reaches another man. He takes them back to his small boat, one in each arm, and puts them in the boat. There is a third man in the water (out of the five who boarded the raft), who also boards the boat. The boat can only take three men, so Guluva remains in the water, pushing it to shore.

Gagarin meanwhile pushes the raft and encourages the remaining two men, who have returned to it, not to despair. On the river bank the men are pulling the rope with all they have, trying to haul the raft back.

Eventually the raft reaches shore with the men safe. The guns, explosives and ammunition have, however, not made it. They fell into the water when the raft overturned. The only materiel saved is a bag containing old Italian Beretta rifles. It only survived because it got impaled on a nail in the raft.[64]

*

On the following evening (29 December), at a spot below Kariba at the confluence of the Chewore and Zambezi rivers near the Mozambique border, the crossing of men deployed for the Sipolilo campaign commences when a rubber dinghy takes guerrillas across the river in groups of six and seven.

On the following morning they wake up on the other side of the border, and head south-east.[65]

*

In Dar es Salaam, Bifana Matthews Ngcobo approaches Matthews Zulu, and says he is very hungry.

Zulu, who is a seaman, takes Ngcobo to the galley of a ship named the *Clan Ross* on which he is a crewman. They eat there.

On the day after this, Zulu and Ngcobo meet again. This time Ngcobo says he initially came to Dar es Salaam for 'education' purposes, but is now 'looking to get home' to South Africa. He asks whether Zulu can help.

After some discussion, Zulu agrees but points out the difficulties.

An unperturbed Ngcobo says he will go to Mombasa and meet the ship there.[66]

*

Castro Dolo, Henry Majola, Greatwell Mabhija, Joel Kumano, Molefe Pitsani, Justice Mpanza, Graham Morodi and Doctor Lindwa from the Wankie campaign are being held alongside a PAC member in Gaborone Central Prison. They are therefore tantalisingly close to South Africa.

On the night of 3 February 1968, Zolile Nqose, who was leader of the reconnaissance team that lost contact with the main group early in the campaign, manages to open the cell door with a wire. Five inmates follow him, leaving Morodi, Mabhija, Pitsani and Mpanza behind. There is a platform in front of the cells. Nqose climbs on Doctor Lindwa to see if there is a policeman on top of it. He spots one warder and informs his colleagues. Upon hearing this, Majola, Kumano and the PAC man return to the cell.

Nqose, Dolo and Lindwa opt to proceed. Nqose climbs the platform, followed by Dolo. Before Lindwa can reach them, they are spotted by the warder, who turns and runs down a ladder leading from the other side of the platform to the prison yard. Nqose runs after him, followed by Dolo, while Lindwa opts to return to the cell. Nqose overtakes the warder in the yard, and prevents him from raising the alarm. A second warder appears near the main gate. Nqose charges at him, pushing him to the ground, and then proceeds to the main gate. He finds it locked, but he notices a key in the lock of a small nearby door. He tries it on the main gate and it works. He runs out, and as he does so he hears police whistles behind him.

Dolo is rearrested, despite having armed himself with an axe.[67]

*

Mabeli Tshuma is part of a group of thirty who are the last to leave Nkomo camp in Zambia in February 1968. They are driven by lorry to the Zambezi River.

On the night of 4 February they cross in a wooden boat, ten at a time. Joe Modise and Dumiso Dabengwa are with them.

On the other side they reach a hill seven miles south of the Zambezi. There they meet the groups that had previously departed from Nkomo camp. There are about 100 cadres at this hill, known to the guerrillas as 'Base One'.

On the following morning, Modise, in the company of two ZAPU colleagues, namely Abraham Nkiwane and Dumiso Dabengwa, assembles the men.

Modise says: 'Here in Rhodesia we will not start by fighting – we first have to build a lot of bases and recruit a lot of people.' He adds that after the preparatory work is complete they must convey the news to headquarters with the radio in their possession. After they have done so, they must wait for instructions to start fighting. If they cannot report back, they must begin fighting on their own initiative. 'Now we are going to fight and we are going to take Rhodesia and then we are going to take South Africa,' Modise says. 'You will cross through to South Africa and when we arrive in South Africa we will establish bases there.' In those bases they must train people, after which the revolution will commence.

After the briefing, Modise takes Felix Khayiya to one side. He gives him £1,440 and tells him to look after it. Modise then heads off with a group that includes Khayiya. They later arrive at a flat-topped mountain, where 'Base Three' will be constructed.[68]

*

On 5 February 1968 Zolile Nqose enters South Africa near Zeerust. He approaches some African-owned houses in a settlement in the Supingstadt area in the western Transvaal. There he converses with the local chief. Nqose tells him he has escaped from Gaborone jail.

The chief offers him a place to sleep.

Nqose is, however, betrayed by the community. Shortly afterwards a group of African men enter the house and handcuff him. They take him to a local police station near Zeerust where he is arrested by the South African Police.[69]

*

In Mombasa, Kenya, Bifana Matthews Ngcobo and Matthews Zulu meet again. Ngcobo takes Zulu to meet Amos Lengisi, whom he introduces as a friend who wants to join them on the trip to South Africa.

A few days later, Lengisi and Ngcobo arrive at the *Clan Ross*. Zulu locks them in the cabin until the ship is at sea.

Once the ship is on its way, Zulu transfers the two to the engine room.

On 19 February, eight days after departing Kenya, the *Clan Ross* reaches Cape Town.

When the vessel docks, Ngcobo asks Zulu to change £57 into South African currency.

Zulu complies, and is paid R30. Ngcobo then tells Zulu that when he returns to Dar es Salaam he must phone Mr Piliso and inform him that the journey was pleasant and that Ngcobo has arrived safely.

Ngcobo buys a train ticket to Durban and Amos Lengisi boards a taxi to De Aar.[70]

*

On 11 March, Ralph Mzamo is at a camp known to the guerrillas in north-east Rhodesia as 'Base Five'. Fourteen men set off from this base to find food. Led and commanded by Raymond Tichafa, the group includes Kenneth Mzathi, George

Mothusi, John Ndlovu, Happyman Marino, Simon Vera, William Nkobe, Lucky Thabethe, William Chimunye, Nasho Maseko and John Ndima.

As the fourteen approach a farm, seven advance ahead and the remainder stay behind. John Ndima is one of the seven who go forward. As they approach the farm store, another split occurs, as three go forward and four stay back. Ndima is one of the four who remain.

A long time elapses and the three who went forward have not yet returned. One of the men remaining behind says they must go and see what has happened.

This is agreed; Ndima and two others advance to the store and one holds back. When they are on a road close to the store, three motor vehicles arrive. Security-force members jump out and arrest them.[71]

*

Spotter planes begin flying in the Sipolilo area near Base Five on 12 March.[72] Then, the following day, a spotter plane flies above Base Five: twice in the morning, and then twice in the afternoon.[73]

*

David Scammell of Rhodesia's Department of Parks and Wildlife is near the Uti River in Chewore Game Reserve at about 10 a.m. on 14 March when he notices an apparently well-trodden footpath heading north–south in the direction of a prominent flat-topped hill known as Chirambakadoma, which stands among a series of yellow and reddish hills.

Scammell follows the path for several hours. He discovers a considerable foot traffic that he estimates is the result of up to forty people having marched through the area.

About ten kilometres into the march, Scammell and his African rangers encounter a torn red, white and blue label in Cyrillic (Russian) writing, as well as a button and two sugar packets.

Scammell returns to his base in Lower Hunyani and at 4 p.m. radios his findings to Sipolilo.[74]

*

A platoon consisting of members of the British South Africa Police and the E Company of the Rhodesian African Rifles is dispatched on 15 March to the area where the tracks were discovered by Scammell the previous day.

They split up to follow the trails both north and south.[75]

On the same day, the spotter plane above Base Five is even more active, and the Rhodesians start landing helicopters to the east of the base.[76]

At 9 a.m. the following day, the Rhodesian Army opens a Joint Operations Centre in Karoi.[77]

*

The guerrillas now wish to consolidate their forces, given the increased risk of being drawn into battle. At Base Five on 16 March, Moffat Hadebe says he is going to go to all the guerrilla camps in Rhodesia and order the cadres in them to reassemble at Base Five.

On that day, the spotter planes are especially active. The attack helicopters are also getting busier; during the day they are seen landing and taking off from the north, east, south and west of the base. The Rhodesians are cordoning off the area surrounding the discoveries of the past few days, so as to cut off potential guerrilla escape routes.

A group of fourteen commanded by Sidwell Mayona and including Patrick Museti, Stanley Tsotsi, Jakes Goniwe, Jumpy Brooklyn, Archion Ndhlovu, Chris Mombehuri, Chigobesintayka Tavimbo, Fredi Maphosa and Josiah Moyo prepares to leave the camp to reconnoitre a sixth base for the guerrillas.

Just before they depart, Ralph Mzamo suggests that they also try to locate the other fourteen who went missing on Monday.

The group departs under Mayona's leadership.[78]

*

At 10 a.m. on the 18th, Isaac Mapoto is at Base Five as the guerrillas prepare breakfast. One of the group's watchmen comes to report that there are further planes in the camp's airspace.

A few minutes later a burst of light-machine-gun fire is heard from the camp's northern outpost, which is being guarded by Gandi Hlekani.

Within the base, the guerrillas take up position. They are well covered by the vegetation; the enemy fire barely reaches them as it is deflected by the thick trees and the surrounding shrub.

Jet bombers screech over the guerrilla positions, but do not drop any bombs.[79]

*

At 11.15 a.m., at a spot between the Ntumbi and Maura Rivers, a clash takes place between members of the security forces and guerrillas.

An hour later, another clash occurs on the ridge just north of the Maura River. Because of weak cover, the Rhodesian ground forces withdraw, but then Provost planes assault the guerrilla positions with machine-gun fire. Following this, Canberra planes arrive and drop fragmentation bombs on the guerrilla positions.[80]

Most of the bombing misses Base Five. The sixty-odd guerrillas who are now assembled in the camp hear the firing of the heavy machine guns flown by the jets, as well as the noise of the small cannons of the helicopter gunships, but under the cover of bush they escape unscathed.[81] The Rhodesians at this stage know the general area but not the specific location where the guerrillas are based.

*

At about 1 p.m. that day a joint RAR/Rhodesian Light Infantry (RLI) group is following a trail of bootprints. The spoor leads up a high bank of the Maura River. The RLI men are commanded by Chris Pearce.

Lance Corporal Dennis Croukamp, a section commander in Pearce's unit, is on the left flank of the advancing unit. Croukamp radios Pearce and asks whether he should continue patrolling up the river, because, he says, there is a hill up ahead with a cliff on the riverside.

The response he receives is to turn right instead and come up the hill that way.

Croukamp's section follows their tracker, who is a fairly old man. They head up the small hill which is on a bend in the Maura. After walking through some Mopani trees the tracker stops and starts looking forwards, backwards and downwards in an agitated manner.

He has in fact inadvertently stepped into Base Five.

Croukamp's unit hastens to catch up with him. After an initial steep rise, the hill flattens before they reach the tracker, whom they find resting on his haunches. No sooner has Croukamp arrived and asked the tracker what he thinks than the man takes off down the hill, almost knocking Croukamp over.

A guerrilla then emerges, facing Croukamp. He and Croukamp fire on each other. The guerrilla is supported by colleagues in what develops into a shootout between them and Croukamp's section.

A lengthy battle ensues. Croukamp crawls forward and throws a grenade into Base Five while a section of the RLI contingent creeps forward, only to be met by a hail of bullets.

The RAR men then attempt a flanking manoeuvre, but are halted by a fresh round of fire that kills one of the Rhodesian men, following which the RAR force breaks up and its members flee in various directions.

Following the disintegration of the RAR section, Pearce orders Croukamp to withdraw, but he tells him to mark the target with a phosphorus grenade before retreating so that the helicopter hovering above can pinpoint the position and mark it for the fixed-wing aircraft. Croukamp crawls closer to the guerrilla base and lobs a grenade as far as possible into the camp. He then flees – with hornets pursuing him.[82]

At 3.20 p.m. Base Five is struck flush by two Vampire fighter jets and one Canberra bomber.[83]

*

Mabeli Tshuma is part of a group that arrives at Base Five from Base Four (having received instructions from a courier conveying Moffat Hadebe's orders to assemble at the former) at about 7 p.m. on the 18th. When they reach the camp, they find only eleven people there.

One of them is Moffat Hadebe. He tells them they must all proceed to Sipolilo. We can't stay here, he says; we are being tracked by the army.

Tshuma leaves the camp as part of a group of eight.[84]

*

The Joint Planning Staff of the Rhodesian Army dispatches a sitrep to Major General Hendrik van den Bergh of the South African Police on 19 March, covering the twenty-four-hour period from 11 a.m. on the 18th.

It says that after the bombing of the camp on the 18th there was an attempted follow-up by the security forces. This was repelled, with one man killed and two injured on the security-force side.

A further follow-up on the 19th 'found one dead ter and approx 50 packs, weapons and other equipment' in the camp.

A further two 'ters' were killed on the 19th.

The report says the enemy moved during the night, with their tracks leading south and south-east.[85]

*

On the 20th, South Africa's head of Military Intelligence writes to the country's defence minister.

He says that elements of the Rhodesian Light Infantry are in position by the Tsetse Fly Fence. This fact indicates that the main force of the terrorists remains within the cordon area and their chances of eluding the security forces are diminishing.

The area in question is immediately north of the Mukwishe River and west of the Angbar River. Its topography features thick bush and is not easily passable, but, the Military Intelligence chief says, it appears the security forces have the situation well under control.[86]

*

At 1.30 p.m. on the 20th, a Mr Knight proceeds to a compound on Tiripano Farm in the Mangula area. He sees two employees inside one of the huts, which has its door half open.

Knight shouts: 'Come out with your hands up.' The two employees come out. Knight then fires a shot through the door. There is no response. A few seconds later he fires another shot.

'I am coming out,' a voice calls from within the building.

The speaker, Archion Ndhlovu, comes out with hands raised. He has a wound on his arm, and he is dressed in a military uniform.[87]

*

Lieutenant Strong leads a patrol in the Zambezi Valley on the 20th in an area about fifty miles directly south of where the guerrillas had made their crossings into Rhodesia.

When the patrol proceeds up a thickly wooded, rocky ravine during the afternoon, they are fired on by a combination of automatic and non-automatic weapons. At least two grenades are thrown at them.

Lieutenant Strong deploys his troops to return fire at the guerrillas, who are concealed in the woods.

There are exactly eight guerrillas hidden – it is the group including Mabeli Tshuma that fled Base Five on the evening of the 18th. When fire is opened on them, six run away, leaving Gilbert Mpofu and Tshuma behind.

When the security forces close to within hailing distance, Mpofu calls on them not to shoot because, he says, we are not fighting. He calls out a second time, upon which the security forces fire into the air.

Lieutenant Strong then sees two Africans in military uniform stand up and shout, 'Surrender, surrender.' They are then apprehended.

An RPD light machine gun is found near the scene and an AK-47 rifle under a rock. Grenades and ammunition are also found nearby.

A helicopter then arrives, and while the two captives are being loaded onto it, the party is fired on at a distance of about fifty yards. The culprit is pursued but is not caught.[88]

*

On the Rhodesian side of the Zambezi River, Archie Sibeko is part of a patrol that disturbs a nest of hornets. Sibeko is stung so seriously that he loses consciousness. Just before he collapses, he orders his colleagues to proceed.

A medical assistant stays with Sibeko, who later revives and crosses back into Zambia. Having crossed the border, Sibeko sets off for Lusaka, leaving Benson Ntsele in charge of the forces on the Zambian side of the Zambezi.

That evening, without Sibeko's permission, Benson Ntsele crosses with some colleagues into Rhodesia.[89]

*

Isaac Mapoto is on the run from Base Four to Base Three in Rhodesia. Despite Moffat Hadebe's instructions to proceed to Sipolilo, many are fleeing towards Zambia.

On the way, Mapoto meets a group including Benson Ntsele, Mike Pooe, Duncan Khoza, Karl Chimboya, Mbhejelwa, John Moyo, Aaron Zovira and John Mrewa. They proceed with him towards Base Three.

By the morning of 21 March, Mapoto and these colleagues have managed to reach Base One. They are joined there by another group, making for a total of thirty men.

Fearing they have been spotted, they vacate the base and take up combat positions in the vicinity.

The enemy manoeuvres towards them using a signal that sounds like a bird whistling.

At about 10 a.m. Mapoto is approached by a fellow guerrilla, Comrade Mdlethshe, who points out a white soldier moving in his direction. Mapoto shoots at the man.

When the enemy return fire, Poko Benson, who is standing right behind Mapoto, is killed on the spot. Mike Pooe, also standing behind Mapoto, is likewise killed. Benson Ntsele also dies in the firefight.[90]

Mapoto manages to flee the battle. But he is now on his own. He carries his gun with him and sleeps that night in a tree.

The following morning a group of six who were involved in the previous day's engagement catch up with Mapoto and he joins them.[91]

*

The Rhodesian Joint Planning Staff sitrep covering 20–21 March 1968 mentions a 'terr hide' that was uncovered in the Mangula area on the 20th, resulting in one 'terrorist' being wounded and captured while another escaped. The report says the man captured was an ANC member and political commissar of the group; interrogation of him and another captive revealed the existence of a number of staging camps between the Zambezi and the operational areas. One of the camps, named number one, was unearthed on the 20th and tracks from it are still being followed.[92]

*

An internal South African Military Intelligence report covering the period 22–25 March says that on the 22nd a contact occurred between the security forces and some 'terrorists', in which the latter lost a man and two others were probably seriously wounded. Three AK-47s and three backpacks were recovered.

On the evening of the 22nd, the British South Africa Police killed one 'terrorist' while another escaped.

On the morning of the 23rd, a 'terrorist' in the area near Base Camp Four was killed and another escaped.

On the night of the 24th, a 'terrorist' was caught in an ambush near Camp Three, but he escaped.

On the morning of the 25th, a 'terrorist' was killed and two captured.[93]

*

Miller Nkomo, Michael Zikali and Manyali Nyati are walking through the bush along the course of a stream in a southward direction on 25 March when they are intercepted by a security-force team.

Nyati tries to run, but is shot in the stomach; Nkomo is shot in the left leg. Zikali stands still and surrenders. A member of the security-force team asks him to approach them. He does so. They ask him questions and he answers. He is asked to tell his friends to surrender. He calls out to them, and they come out and surrender.

Nyati later perishes from his wounds.[94]

*

A Rhodesian Joint Planning Staff sitrep is sent to South Africa's police commissioner. Covering 25–26 March, it discusses the interrogation of two guerrillas captured on the 25th.

The two revealed that they are defectors from Base Five. They said that a mixed unit of A, B and C platoons – in total forty-five men – were subjected to the 18 March airstrike. The two said they fled southwards as a result of army ground fire. There was no contingency plan to regroup. The two initially decided to go to Zambia, but they knew they would just be sent back. Their last meal was on 17 March and consisted only of powdered milk. Since then they have subsisted on wild fruits and water. The two estimate the morale of the guerrillas to be low. They say they last saw the detachment commander 'Hadebe' at Base Five on the 18th, but have no knowledge of the whereabouts of him or the remainder of the group.[95]

*

The Rhodesian Joint Planning Staff's sitrep for the following twenty-four hours says that contact was made with an enemy group at first light on the 27th and two enemy were killed.

The report also discusses the interrogation of another prisoner. This man said he was involved in the airstrike on the 18th and engaged the enemy that day.

The document states that it is 'generally felt that this is [the] hardcore group under Hadebe' and estimates that the group 'may either (a) make their way in group or separately towards Sipolilo (b) move north intending to regroup at established base camps (c) split up either under command or in disorder seeking food still knowing Sipolilo is final destination. SF now deployed to counter all above.'[96]

*

By 30 March, Isaac Mapoto and the group of six he connected with after fleeing Base One have marched eastwards to a point where they see the Zambezi leading through mountainous terrain. They can see Zambians on the river's north bank.

In response to the guerrillas' request, the Zambians say they are afraid to collect them because they have guns.

A Zambian police boat also comes. The guerrillas call to it, but it does not stop.

As the group set out to depart from their position, Patrick Ncube, one of their number, says he is exhausted and cannot go any further.

The rest of the men leave him behind and climb a tall mountain. Two further members of the group, Patrick Batman and Gordon Bandom, then decide to rest in the mountains.

Mapoto, Elvis Nyakonda, Solomon Mavisela and Harold Ndhlovu continue walking until they again reach the Zambezi and see some houses. Nyakonda and Mavisela go in search of food while Mapoto and Ndhlovu remain in the hills guarding the weapons. From their vantage point Mapoto and Ndhlovu see the Rhodesian Army arrive and shoot Nyakonda dead. Mapoto and Ndhlovu then flee from their position in the mountains.

On the morning of the 31st, Mapoto returns to recover his gun, but finds it has been taken. He does, however, manage to recover an AK-47 that has been left in its place and he leaves with it.[97]

*

The *Times of Zambia* on 2 April reports a joint ANC–ZAPU communiqué issued in Lusaka alleging that 'over 80' white Rhodesian troops have been killed in the latest round of fighting.

The statement claims further that South Africa's offer of reinforcements indicates the Rhodesian Army has been 'badly thrashed in the last two weeks of heavy fighting'.[98]

*

Patrick Sibanda is part of a group of ten heading in the direction of Base Four. Just before reaching the camp, they leave behind one of their number, Lucky Chawe, who is very sick.

The remaining nine get to Base Four and send a group of four, including Pilot Duba and Blackie Molife, ahead to obtain food.

At 7.30 p.m. on 2 April 1968, Pilot Duba and Blackie Molife are in a kitchen hut at a hotel compound in Makuti. They are in civilian clothing and unarmed. A Detective Sergeant Nyikadzino comes to arrest them. They offer no resistance.

When the four sent to obtain food do not return, the remaining five members of the unit split, as Chakafa and Mutero decide to go off on their own. They leave behind Patrick Sibanda, Michael Dhlodhlo and Tony Marume, who then depart themselves.

On a later date, when Dhlodhlo and Sibanda return from a hunting expedition to a position where Tony Marume is waiting for them, they find Marume with a severe wound on his side. Marume says he was thrown by a buffalo.[99]

*

At a point just east of the confluence of the Chewore and Zambezi Rivers on 3 April, George Mothusi, armed with an AK-47 rifle, walks into a prepared security-force ambush position.

On being challenged, he immediately throws his weapon down and is arrested by Sergeant Hartman of the Rhodesian Special Air Service (SAS).

When searched, a hand grenade, a booby-trap device, a magazine with a full complement of thirty rounds of ammunition and a few spare rounds of ammunition are found on him.[100]

*

A Rhodesian Joint Planning Staff sitrep sent to South Africa's police commissioner on the 3rd, and covering the previous twenty-four hours, says it is understood that the Hadebe group was 'in fact 19 terrs and on approx 30 March broke into two groups. Still no contact of Hadebe group now of nine but other group probably in contact yesterday where three terrorists killed. Total terrorists killed now 36 and captured 20.'[101]

*

Isaac Mapoto covers his AK-47 with grass and rests overnight on a hill.

He then sneaks down to the nearby village to steal food. He is spotted by locals. One tells him to go away.

Mapoto returns to the hills, but finds his rifle has been taken. He decides to return to the village again after dark.[102]

Sergeant Major Hutton arrives at a kraal settlement slightly west of Kanyemba on 4 April following information received from the local headman. He enters a hut and sees a man in camouflage overalls. Hutton calls on him to surrender.

The man, Isaac Mapoto, is unarmed and surrenders without resisting.[103]

*

The Rhodesian Joint Planning Staff's sitrep for 4–5 April reports 'two ters' captured in one incident, one in another, and a further one in a mielie field on the morning of the 5th.

The report comments 'all captured ters in a very poor physical state. Total ter eliminated now 36 killed 28 captured.'[104]

*

The sitrep covering 5–6 April notes: 'recent leaflet dropping campaign known to have been directly responsible for the surrender of the three captured ters. George Mathusi, chief of ops, states under interrogation that before he found the leaflets he had not known what to do if he saw SF but leaflet had told him what action to take and he surrendered accordingly.'[105]

*

A South African Military Intelligence overview of the period covering the 6th to the 8th reports the capture, ten miles north-west of Makuti, of 'one ter' claiming to have been present at the air attack on the 18th and on his own ever since.

Further mention is made of a man caught by locals about twelve miles north of Mangula.[106]

*

The chief of South African Military Intelligence distributes an internal communiqué on 16 April. It estimates enemy casualties since the commencement of hostilities: 48 enemy dead and 33 captured, a total of 81.

Regarding those still in the field, there are estimated to be about two guerrillas south of the operational area, five in the Mangula area under the command of 'Kahia', another five in the Mangula region under Hadebe's leadership, four deserters in Mangula, five in the valley north-west of Makuti, and twenty 'elsewhere in the operational area', making for forty-one in total on the loose.

The report says all that apparently remains of 'Operation Cauldron' is the final clearing out of the forty-or-so remaining 'terrorists' from whom no organised resistance can be expected because they are so widely dispersed in such small groups.[107]

*

In Lusaka, a meeting of Umkhonto we Sizwe's military headquarters is addressed by Joe Modise.

Pumelele Menye of the High Command can't quite believe what he is hearing. Modise is talking about sending further contingents of MK fighters into the meat grinder that Rhodesia has become. Menye expresses total disagreement with the idea.

Menye renews his objections at a subsequent meeting held between the military headquarters and Oliver Tambo.[108]

*

Johannes Phatswane is deported to Botswana from Zambia at Kazungula on 14 May. The Zambians believe him to be a citizen of Botswana.

Botswana's records, however, have Phatswane as a 'student refugee' who passed northwards from South Africa in 1964. Under interrogation, Phatswane says he is actually an ANC guerrilla trained in the communist states, but that he deserted

Umkhonto we Sizwe because he feared being murdered for refusing to join a guerrilla group that is being prepared to partake in another invasion of Rhodesia.

He objects when his questioners propose returning him to Zambia. By contrast, and to the surprise of his interrogators, when the option of entering Rhodesia is put to him, he willingly agrees.

He accordingly enters Rhodesia voluntarily on 22 May.[109]

*

On 18 June 1968, Botswana announces a six-month remission of the sentences of over thirty guerrillas captured during the Wankie campaign, including Chris Hani, Graham Morodi, Castro Dolo, James April and Justice Mpanza.[110]

*

When the meeting of the OAU Liberation Committee's Standing Committee on Defence ends on 22 June, it recommends that the Standing Committee on Finance award the full amount requested by the ANC for a fresh infiltration, namely £3,500 for purchasing medicines and drugs for the forthcoming six months, £4,000 for pre-cooked foods and preserves suitable for combat conditions, and £20,000 for transit and operational support for the guerrillas.

The Defence Committee fixes figures of £5,100 for the purchase of one truck and sixteen motorcycles, £4,200 for fuel, and £900 for 300 uniforms to support the ANC infiltration plan.[111]

*

At a further meeting of Umkhonto we Sizwe's military headquarters, Joe Modise confirms that another batch of cadres is going to be sent to Rhodesia, and that preparations must commence for their infiltration.

Upon hearing this, an appalled Pumelele Menye gets up, walks out of the camp, and for all he knows, out of the ANC. He goes to stay with a friend.[112]

*

A letter is sent by Zambia's permanent secretary of presidential affairs to his counterpart in the Foreign Affairs Ministry on 9 July. Principally focused on other matters, it concludes with the following:

although the A.N.C./Z.A.P.U. alliance has achieved good and commendable results by way of establishing routes in Rhodesia, some ANC fighters have expressed unwillingness to fight in Rhodesia rather than in South Africa. It would therefore appear that the ANC leadership may face opposition from its own men and possibly deny it the co-operation so desired from them in the revolution. This threat may cause the present alliance to be shaken and streamlining of the two groups' strategies may be necessary. At the moment the groups' top leadership continues to be one.[113]

*

Three nights later, on the banks of the Zambezi, downstream from Chirundu and in the vicinity of the Chewore River, Moses Tshuma is part of a mixed group of thirty-eight ANC and ZAPU guerrillas who are addressed by ZAPU's Abraham Nkiwane. He tells them they are to go to Melsetter to organise people there.

The group is given arms before crossing. Mkalalwa Mpata is given an AK-47 rifle, 500 rounds of ammunition, four hand grenades and some food. The cadres are all wearing khaki uniforms and steel helmets.

On 13 July the platoon crosses the Zambezi River under the command of Daniel Makoni.[114]

*

On the following day, a Sunday, Chief Mangosuthu Buthelezi attends mass at the Anglican church in Mkonyeni in the Hlabatini district of Zululand.

One of his children comes and delivers him a message, after which Buthelezi goes outside. There he sees a woman, Dorothy Nyembe, who takes him to a waiting truck.

Inside the vehicle Buthelezi finds a man sitting. The man introduces himself as Themba Dlamini and says that he has letters for Buthelezi from Moses Mabhida in Lusaka.

Buthelezi says he knew Mabhida as a one-time senior ANC leader.

After a short discussion, Dlamini asks Buthelezi whether he personally, or via an agent, could deliver a message to a Mr Yengwa in Swaziland saying Dlamini is back in the country.

Buthelezi says he doesn't want to 'get mixed up in anything like that'.

Dlamini enquires whether there is any heavy forestation in the area, or suitable places along the Zululand coast for submarine landings. Dlamini also asks whether the Buthelezi tribe in Zululand would be willing to take up arms if weapons were supplied.

Buthelezi says no, his people will not be willing to do that.[115]

*

On 18 July, the group of thirty-eight that crossed into Rhodesia on the 13th move into position in a gorge.

They are encountered by a group of security-force troops. A member of the Rhodesian military contingent calls on them to surrender.

There is no movement from the guerrillas, so battle commences.

One of the ZAPU cadres, surnamed Ncube, is part of a section of the guerrilla force that is in a cave in the gorge. Some members of his section, acting on the instruction of the section commander to join in the fighting, fire at the enemy.

Then there is an explosion in the cave. Ncube drops down to the ground. There follows aerial bombing of the guerrilla positions by an aeroplane flying overhead.

After this aerial assault there is a great deal of smoke around the cave.

When darkness comes, the guerrillas depart. Ncube, however, heads off in a separate direction.

On the morning of 21 July, Ncube has reached the tarred road connecting Kariba and Makuti. He sits on the side of the road.

Three or four vehicles pass. Eventually he sees a military vehicle approach. He flags it down. When it stops, he surrenders to the driver, police reservist Louwrens.[116]

*

The Rhodesian Army initiates a new operation codenamed 'Excess' on 27 July 1968 and opens a Joint Operations Centre in Karoi.[117]

*

At 3.30 p.m. on 30 July, the Rhodesians wrap up some unfinished business from Operation Cauldron when Detective Inspector John Fletcher of the Criminal Investigation Department, Sinoia, reaches a point downstream from Kanyemba Police Station on a bank of the Zambezi River in Mozambican territory.

There he finds John Mandiwengerayi and Rhodesia's most wanted, Moffat Hadebe. They are both lying on the bank of the river, bound hand and foot, in the custody of the Portuguese authorities. Hadebe is fully bearded and long-haired. He is wearing a red and black knitted wool jersey, a black knitted shirt with a zipper at the front, blue football shorts and a light blue vest tied round his waist. He is barefoot.

Mandiwengerayi has long hair and a small beard, and is wearing a khaki combat jacket, khaki shirt, a grey shirt of civilian pattern and blue shorts beneath civilian trousers. He too is barefoot.[118]

On the police launch travelling back to Kanyemba Station, Fletcher and Hadebe converse. Hadebe admits he entered the country in January 1968 in charge of approximately 100 men.[119]

*

By 2.30 p.m. the following day, an RLI tracking team involved in Operation Excess has reached the gulley of a dry bed of the Kamatasa River some three kilometres inside Mozambique.

The team's commander, Lieutenant Jerry Strong, hears voices. He then sees fifteen men resting in trees near an anthill on the opposite bank. He forms his men into a line to perform a sweep.

The attempted envelopment is foiled by enemy fire and the RLI unit withdraws.

Helicopter reinforcement is called in to fire on the guerrillas.

Then, under the cover of white phosphorus, Strong flanks and then attacks the guerrilla position. This time he is successful. His unit find seven men dead and one wounded in the guerrilla positions.

The tracking team pursues the remnants of the enemy contingent. In the process the RLI kill another two.

Among the nine deceased guerrillas in these engagements is Daniel Makoni, the commander of the ANC–ZAPU unit of thirty-eight men that entered Rhodesia on 13 July.[120]

*

A South African Military Intelligence digest of information received from Rhodesian sources covers the period of 1–2 August. It offers further information on the battle on the 31st. It says the interrogation of guerrillas captured that day reveals that thirty-eight terrorists crossed the Zambezi on 12 July at a point between Chikwenya Island and the Chewore River. The group planned to operate in the Mount Darwin area.

On 29 July, seven terrorists broke away from the main group, presumably on their way to Dikita Store (about a mile south of the Mozambique border and two miles east from the Musengezi River). The other thirty-one split into two groups, fifteen and sixteen strong, after a helicopter landed near them on the same day.

The report suggests that the contact leading to the capture of the prisoners was with the group of fifteen (Makoni's group).[121]

*

By early August, it is all over.

On the 5th, Detective Inspector Thomas Power of the Criminal Investigation Department, Salisbury, receives a batch of guerrillas. He warns and cautions them and then takes statements.

At 9 a.m. he takes Rudolf Aisem's statement, and at 9.50 a.m. Oscar Nyoni's.

The process continues throughout the day. This is part of a mass round-up of guerrillas who entered the country the preceding month.[122]

*

Themba Dlamini is arrested on 20 September 1968 at Dorothy Nyembe's house at K6, KwaMashu.[123]

*

Herman Stadler arrests Bifana Matthews Ngcobo three days later at Ngcobo's father's kraal in Zululand.

During the search of the premises, Stadler finds a Bible that Ngcobo has used for coding messages.[124]

*

Then at 9 a.m. on 26 September Amos Lengisi is arrested in Umtata.[125]

*

In Dar es Salaam, Sandi Sijake and Lambert Moloi are waiting to be sent to South Africa by merchant ship.

Moses Kotane arrives to inform them that the operation has been called off after the arrests of Dlamini, Ngcobo and Lengisi.

Moloi and Sijake then head back to Zambia.[126]

BY LAND, SEA AND AIR

By the end of 1968, the divisions seen in nascent form within the ANC's ranks in the middle of the year have developed into a full-blown crisis.

On 12 December, Detective Warrant Officer Michael van Niekerk proceeds to a

Johannesburg Post Office, where he confiscates an envelope addressed to Winnie Mandela. The envelope contains several documents. One is a handwritten letter signed by Lawrence Makhubu. It has been sent from Nairobi, Kenya.

In it Makhubu writes he hopes 'Cepa' has informed her about the situation in the Tanzanian and Zambian camps, and particularly 'the treacherous and adventuristic deeds in Wankie and Zambesi Valley by the Tambo Kotane Nokwe clique'.

He says he will give a rough sketch:

> In 1964 there was a clash of leadership in the army. Ambrose Makiwane and about 9/10ths fighting for A.N.C. leadership on the one hand, and Kotane and Johannes Modise fighting for Communist Party leadership on the other. Because of certain reasons, Kotane won and made Modise his Commander-in-Chief. Later a split could not be avoided because people were expected to toe the Moscow line.

An 'Assault Group' was subsequently formed by Modise with Archie Sibeko's aid, using the 'Cape boys as pawns'. Immediate victims were 'Vincent Khumalo who was stabbed and left for dead, and two Indians from Fordsburg. That same night Vincent, Patrick, Maulaoa, myself, one Indian and four other chaps were sent to detention for fourteen months.' Four months after being released, two of the four

> were again framed into a nine months' prison term. Patrick was taken to Zambia and detained in a tent in the bush after which they killed him. Mrs Moodie's son of Benoni was thrown into the Zambesi and was devoured by crocodiles. Fancy Tambo conniving to announce that [?] Selethe or Chopper, the footballer of Orlando East was stabbed to death, and Boston Blackboy, softball player from Umzimhlope was stabbed in his sleep but managed to escape.

The letter ends with a 'P.P.S.' that 'All P.A.C. and A.N.C. camps in Zambia have been closed and rank and file members and some of the leaders are back in Tanzania.'[1]

*

Chris Hani, meanwhile, is the lead signatory of a document that begins: 'The ANC in exile is in a deep crisis as a result of which a rot has set in.' The authors – 'M.T. Hani (Chris)', 'Z.R. Mbengwa (Jeqe)', 'Leonard Pitso', 'W. Hempe', 'Tamana Goboza (Mikza)', 'G.S. Mose (Mlenze)' and 'Mbali' – then accuse the movement of having created a machinery that has become an end in itself and is completely divorced from the situation at home. They argue that since Rivonia there has never been an attempt to send leaders inside the country. Instead there has been a concentration of people in offices abroad. They allege further that there are 'other departments, such as the Treasury Department which is to all intents and purposes catering for activities outside' and whose functioning is known only to a few individuals.

Furthermore, certain symptoms 'disturbing and dispiriting to genuine revolutionaries' have emerged, such as the opening of 'mysterious business enterprises which to our knowledge have never been discussed by the membership of the organisation.

For instance, in Lusaka a furniture industry is being run by the ANC. In Livingstone a bone factory, whose original purpose was to provide cover for underground work in Botswana, is now being used as a purely commercial undertaking.' Increasing numbers of MK men are being diverted to these enterprises, which is 'disturbing because the very comrade, Thabo More [i.e. Joe Modise], who is supposed to be planning, directing and leading the struggle in South Africa is fully involved in these enterprises'.

They allege that 'The Security Department is internally directed. It is doing nothing against the enemy', and that the 'tragedy of the Zimbabwe campaigns is the fact that we have been unable to analyse our operations so as to be able to assess and draw lessons'.

Individual leaders are keeping cars, they claim, and this, coupled with the allowances they receive, suggests that they are being built up as a middle class within the ANC.

A strange and alarming trend is developing whereby secret trials and executions are being carried out.

There must also be a 'full definition of the ANC-ZAPU alliance, its form and content'; a serious effort must be made to investigate ways and means of going home, and MK should be involved in this process.

'In conclusion,' they write, 'all these problems must be resolved by a conference between the ANC leadership and members of MK, and not just handpicked individuals.'[2]

*

'What the Group Feels' is another document produced around the same time. The 'group' in question are some of those who participated in the joint operations with FRELIMO in 1967.

They note: 'Frelimo comrades are achieving victory after victory because right from section to the highest commander there is that respect and understanding.' They add that when operating with FRELIMO 'we have never heard of a command of: "polish my shoes; or go wash my dish; wash my underpants; carry my knapsack" or whatever thing'.[3]

*

J.H.P. Serfontein of the *Sunday Times* reports on 26 January 1969 that earlier in the week he met Mr Setsomi Hoohla at Jan Smuts Airport.

Hoohla, a Lesotho citizen, had just flown in from Nairobi. He claimed to have spent two years in an ANC transit camp in Mbeya, Tanzania, waiting for an education scholarship. After two years he was called to Dar es Salaam and told the scholarship was ready, but he was not informed what country he would be sent to.

Hoohla claimed he used the little money the ANC gave him in the Tanzanian capital to buy a bus ticket to Nairobi, where he arrived in September the previous year. He alleged that in Nairobi he found over *eighty* other former ANC members who like him had fled from the movement's transit camps in Tanzania. Hoohla said these other men were living hand to mouth in desperate conditions. He himself is on his way home to Lesotho.[4]

*

At one of the ANC's transit camps around Lusaka, all members of the organisation based in Zambia – including all MK cadres – attend a crisis meeting. Joe Matthews, normally based in London, attends.

Oliver Tambo addresses the meeting. He is incensed by the implied attack on Moses Kotane, the ANC's treasurer, in the 'Memorandum' of Hani, Hempe et al. Tambo reminds them that Kotane is presently in a Moscow hospital recovering from a stroke.

But Tambo does also announce that a consultative conference will be held to discuss the condition of the movement.[5]

*

On 18 February 1969, the ANC headquarters in Morogoro issues a directive about the forthcoming consultative conference.

It says that the National Executive Committee's intention is for the conference to serve as the climax of a process of criticisms and proposals covering all aspects of the movement's work – only security considerations should limit the scope of the discussion.

The directive adds that all units of the ANC both inside and outside South Africa should be allowed to participate in the preliminary discussions, and members of the other components of the Congress Alliance should also be involved.[6]

*

Ben Turok meets Oliver Tambo in Dar es Salaam. He says his family will be travelling to England on an East German ship that will travel two or three miles from the coast of Pondoland and the Transkei. He offers to conduct a visual survey of the coastline to examine the possibilities for landing armed men.

Tambo readily agrees to the suggestion.

When the two men meet again, Tambo gives Turok his personal code, to which the report can be sent when complete. He tells Turok to report to Joe Slovo in London, who is in charge of the movement's work in the United Kingdom.

When Turok and his family leave Dar es Salaam on the East German cargo ship at the beginning of April 1969, they are accommodated in a cabin that can hold six people.

When the ship passes the Eastern Cape, Turok is on the captain's deck with binoculars. He has maps with him that are used by the ship. He also has a writing pad in which he compiles a daily account of what he sees.[7]

*

Speaking before a room of seventy-plus people in Morogoro on 25 April 1969, Oliver Tambo says that several developments make this conference different from its predecessors. These include the death of Albert Luthuli, the commencement of the armed struggle 'in 1967', the increased repression of the people by the fascist oppressors, and organisational problems arising from the commencement of guerrilla warfare. Of these, the last is the most vital problem facing the movement.

In the past, too much emphasis was placed on international solidarity work, he says. This is perhaps a legacy of the initial role of the ANC's External Mission. It is not that solidarity work is not necessary, but it needs to be placed in proper perspective.

Incorrect methods of work and chaotic organisation – these are the main factors hampering the movement.

The ANC must cast its eyes south and prepare to go home. There is sometimes a feeling that far too much emphasis is devoted to 'training, training, training', with the consequence that like the Zulu warrior Gumede, who was forever sharpening his spear, we might wear out our spear in the process.

Tambo says that if the conference fails to resolve these immediate problems, the struggle will be retarded for many years.[8]

*

Of the fifty-three documents submitted to the conference, 'Strategy and Tactics of the African National Congress', which is largely Joe Slovo's work, most directly addresses the questions Tambo identified as the most important for the organisation to resolve.[9]

It begins: 'The struggle of the oppressed people of South Africa is taking place within an international context of transition to the Socialist system, of the breakdown of the colonial system as a result of national liberation and socialist revolutions, and the fight for social and economic progress by the people of the whole world.' South Africa is identified as 'part of the zone in which national liberation is the chief content of the struggle'. Armed resistance is meanwhile singled out as 'the only method left open to us' in advancing that struggle.

Concerning the forms that the armed struggle might assume, Slovo writes: 'We reject the approach which sees as the catalyst for transformation only the short-cut of isolated confrontations and the creation of armed resistance centres', but at the same time he dismisses the notion that MK must 'wait for the evolvement of some sort of deep crisis in the enemy camp' serious enough to make a general insurrection possible.

Slovo acknowledges that there is a tension here. Specifically, if the 'involvement of the masses is unlikely to be the result of a sudden natural and automatic consequence of military clashes', how will the kind of mass political activity that he argues is necessary for the ultimate triumph of the armed struggle develop? Where does one begin? His answer is that 'all-round political mobilisation' must be undertaken as an accompaniment to the commencement of military activities, in a parallel, simultaneously initiated process.

Slovo flags another possible objection to the paper. This relates to his assertion that guerrilla warfare represents the 'special, and in our case only form in which the armed liberation struggle can be launched'. He notes that people have claimed that guerrilla warfare requires a 'physical environment which conforms to a special pattern' that South Africa doesn't have, such as 'thick jungle, inaccessible mountain areas, swamps, a friendly border and so on'. Against such sceptics, he maintains that guerrilla warfare 'can be, and has been, waged in every conceivable type of terrain' and that what is instead required is 'adjusting survival tactics to the sort of terrain in which operations have to be carried out'. Therefore, South Africa may not have a 'single impregnable mountain or impenetrable jungle but the country abounds in terrain which in general is certainly no less favourable for guerrilla operations than some of the terrain in which other guerrilla movements operated successfully'.[10]

The paper is adopted by the conference as the ANC's policy for advancing the revolutionary struggle within South Africa.[11]

*

The Consultative Conference sees the election of a new, streamlined National Executive Committee consisting of Tambo as president and Alfred Nzo as secretary-general, with J.B. Marks, Moses Mabhida, Moses Kotane, Joe Matthews, Tom Nkobi, Flag Boshielo and Mzwai Piliso as the structure's other members.[12]

Another major structural change is the establishment, by the new NEC, of a Presidential Council and a Revolutionary Council (RC) under Oliver Tambo's leadership.

Yusuf Dadoo is appointed vice-chairman of the RC, which is given the responsibility of focusing solely on furthering the political and military struggle within South Africa,[13] along the lines suggested by the 'Strategy and Tactics' paper.

*

When Ben Turok arrives in London, he writes up a report of his observations and hands it to Joe Slovo when they meet. The report's main recommendations are that the document should be sent on to Oliver Tambo as was agreed in Dar es Salaam, and that Turok should be allowed to undertake a full study by various methods, including stereoscopy, of the terrain on the Pondoland coast.

When handing over the document, Turok presses the second point. He asks to be given time to conduct an in-depth study of the geo-physical structure of the Eastern Cape, in order to put his report into proper perspective.

Slovo's response is non-committal.[14]

*

The ANC's headquarters in Morogoro receives a letter from the Tanzanian government in July 1969 ordering it to vacate its military cadres from Kongwa within fourteen days. The reason given is that the MK men have been there so long they constitute a security risk.

The letter threatens that if the ANC proves unable to infiltrate its cadres into South Africa within the given timeframe, Tanzania's authorities will be left with no choice but to send them to a refugee camp.[15]

*

Soon after the receipt of this order, a letter is sent to the Tanzanian authorities by the government of the Soviet Union, requesting permission to land transport planes in order to conduct an airlift of MK guerrillas out of the country.[16]

*

Umkhonto we Sizwe cadres are airlifted from Tanzania to the Soviet Union, where they are to undertake refresher courses.[17]

*

At a place called Feira Area, approximately eighty-six miles east of Lusaka, all Umkhonto we Sizwe personnel in Zambia gather in October 1969.[18]

Oliver Tambo addresses them. He says ANC members are streaming into the country from Tanzania and he does not know how they are getting there. To alleviate the pressure, the bulk of these recruits will need to go for refresher training. (This will be in addition to the groups sent from Tanzania on refresher courses.)[19]

*

At a small restaurant near Baker Street in London, *Rand Daily Mail* journalist Anthony Holiday converses with 'Tom', who asks him what he thinks of 'my article' in the issue of the *African Communist* that Holiday is holding.

'I'm not supposed to know who you are,' Holiday says.

'Tom' (really Joe Slovo) snaps his fingers and says it's impossible to maintain strict security under these conditions.[20]

*

At a follow-up meeting held late in October 1969, Slovo tells Holiday that the SACP has decided to recruit him. He says Holiday will be sent into South Africa after receiving training.

A few days later, Slovo introduces Holiday to Jack Hodgson at the latter's flat in Hampstead. The Revolutionary Council's task at this time is not to launch guerrilla warfare immediately, but instead, in the wake of the defeats in South Africa and the wider region earlier in the 1960s, to prepare the way for the resumption of armed struggle at a later date. This priority was reflected in the emphasis given in the 'Strategy and Tactics' paper to the question of the prerequisites for guerrilla warfare.

Hodgson begins training Holiday in anti-surveillance techniques, forgery, secret communication, propaganda and other methods of underground work.[21]

*

At 5.38 p.m. on 14 November 1969, a white ex-Rhodesian police officer is driving down Strand Street in Cape Town when he sees a crowd of about fifty non-whites gathered outside the railway station entrance. They are listening to a broadcast of a voice speaking in an African language. He calls the railway police.

When they arrive, they find a paper bag chained to a pole on a ledge above the entrance. The bag contains a tape recorder, from which the broadcast was made.

Then, at approximately 5.45 p.m., a charge explodes in a plastic bag outside the Standard Bank in Cape Town's Adderley Street. With the detonation, pamphlets printed on airmail paper and bearing photographs, headlines and columns of text flutter into the air. Pedestrians see that the papers have been issued by the ANC and Umkhonto we Sizwe.

By 6 p.m. the police have removed the last of the pamphlets from the scene.

The following day's *Rand Daily Mail* reports that in addition to the Cape Town blasts, Port Elizabeth saw hundreds of subversive pamphlets scattered near two non-white bus stops.[22]

*

During the following month, Anthony Holiday, Joe Slovo and Jack Hodgson meet at Hodgson's Hampstead flat.

Slovo tells Holiday that in South Africa he should not regard himself as a 'puppet' on a string, but rather as a highly valuable political agent. His first priority must always be his own safety.

Slovo says the SACP needs information on political moods and trends in South Africa, the activities of the security police, and whatever other worthwhile traffic he can find. Though you should gather intelligence on the security police, he says, you should not try to infiltrate them.

Slovo tells Holiday to focus on posting consignments of pamphlets that will be sent to him from time to time. He says that pending receipt of these materials, Holiday should obtain a mailing list by compiling the names and addresses of young black work-seekers that the *Post* newspaper has been publishing as a reader service. He should type up these names using a typewriter that he will have to purchase in South Africa and use exclusively for illegal work. Thirdly, he should be on the look-out for one or two people with whom he can form a cell. Lastly, he must produce an underground journal aimed at whites. Slovo suggests calling it *Searchlight*.

Slovo then gives Holiday £500 to cover the purchase of equipment and anything else he may need for his underground work.[23]

*

Rica Hodgson travels to the Hampstead flat that she shares with her husband. With her is Ahmed Timol, who left South Africa in 1966 aged twenty-five and settled in London, where he worked as a teacher before joining the SACP in 1969, the same year in which he attended the Party School in Moscow.

At the flat, Jack Hodgson gives Timol a prepared book, and, with the aid of a couple of blank sheets of paper, instructs him in the fabrication of coded messages.

Instruction complete, Hodgson says that the letter should be posted to 'Stephanie' (Rica Hodgson), who will ensure he gets hold of them.

Then, with a Smith clock, a fuse wire and torch batteries with wires soldered to them, Hodgson gives Timol an explanation of how to make a timing device. He also describes how, by placing gunpowder at the base of a bucket and packing the timing device and leaflets above, one can construct a bucket/leaflet bomb.

Hodgson uses two diagrams of bucket/leaflet bombs to help with the explanation.[24]

*

Alexander Moumbaris, born in Egypt, raised in Australia, employed in Britain, married to a Frenchwoman, but of Greek ancestry, has his passport stamped by immigration at Jan Smuts Airport on 30 January 1970.

He hires a Ford Cortina from the airport, and then, equipped with a snakebite kit and two cameras, heads to Durban.[25]

*

Ahmed Timol arrives at Jan Smuts Airport in February 1970. He takes a taxi to Johannesburg Railway Station, where he boards a train to Roodepoort.

Hawa Timol is cooking in her kitchen when she hears a knock at the front door. When she opens, she sees her son standing there.

'You are the reason for me coming to South Africa,' he says. 'Nobody could have stopped me from coming home.'[26]

*

At Umngazi Bungalows in Port St Johns, among the many white South Africans who are there fishing, Alexander Moumbaris tries his hand at the activity, and also takes photographs of the surrounding coastline.

Moumbaris's passport is stamped as he leaves South Africa on 22 April 1970.[27]

*

Flag Boshielo (the ANC's chief political officer and a member of both the NEC and RC), Castro Dolo, Fanele Mbali, Victor Ndaba and Bob Zulu hold a meeting in Zambia.

Boshielo tells Mbali: We need a volunteer to join us. We need somebody who can keep a secret and act with us in a small armed unit. I think five men are enough for this operation.

The other three agree with Boshielo; one says a sixth man would be unnecessary. Mbali accepts their offer.

Boshielo then says that the idea is to go home via the Zambezi River and sneak through the Caprivi Strip. We will rely on being a small group to avoid detection by the enemy. We have weapons, ammunition, food, money and a possible route. A Zambian has agreed to take us across the river in his ferry boat for a fee.

As it turns out, Fanele Mbali will not be part of the operation. A few days later, he is on a plane to Moscow on Oliver Tambo's instructions.[28]

*

In the garden of 250 Zambezi Road in Lusaka, Flag Boshielo, Castro Dolo, Victor Ndaba and Bob Zulu are doctoring themselves with herbs in a muti ritual.

Ray Alexander, who owns the property with her husband Jack Simons, is preparing to leave for an International Labour Organization conference in Bulgaria. She begs them not to depart before she has returned.[29]

*

Ahmed Timol and Salim Essop post between 400 and 500 pamphlets each, simultaneously, from Jeppe Street Post Office in Johannesburg in August 1970.[30]

*

At about 5 p.m. on 13 August, Samuel Nkosi, who is a nightwatchman for the Johannesburg City Council, is in his shack under the M1 motorway, next to the Van Brandis parking lot near Faraday Station, when an explosion occurs some seven paces away.

The detonation sends a bundle of leaflets flying into the air. Some are thrown as high as the overhead motorway. Since it is the peak of the rush hour, the area is busy. Passers-by start picking up the pamphlets, which are titled 'The African National Congress says to Vorster and his Gang: your days are coming to an end!!!'

A few minutes later another explosion occurs at the non-white entrance of Johannesburg's Park Station.

Then, at the main entrance of the *Rand Daily Mail*'s offices on Mooi Street, Joseph Sibiya, a fifty-five-year-old messenger for the South African Press Association, sees a supermarket carrier bag lying on the pavement.

He passes it by, but on returning, he sees it still there, untouched.

Sibiya informs the commissionaire.

Simon Mtatene, a nightwatchman, takes the carrier bag to the editorial offices and hands it over to J.C. Viviers, the deputy news editor, who looks inside the bag and sees it is filled with pamphlets. When he lifts up the pamphlets he sees a plastic bucket and a longish object that has various metal devices connected to it by wire. Viviers drops the whole contraption into the bag and runs out with the bag as fast as he can.

When the Flying Squad arrive, they take the carrier bag to a secluded corner of the building. Sergeant P.M. Steyn is closest to it when it explodes, sending a brilliant flash and puff of smoke into the air. Steyn is not injured, but his face, uniform, and the holster for his service revolver are blackened by powder sent flying by the bomb.

In Cape Town on the same day, a leaflet bomb explodes on the Grand Parade. Because there is no wind, the pamphlets fall straight to the ground – 'like snowflakes', in the poetic words of a *Rand Daily Mail* report the following day.

In Durban a tape recorder plays after an explosion. A warning attached to the recorder says it is booby-trapped.

This proves to be false.

There are also pamphlet bombings in Port Elizabeth and East London on that day, which is the third anniversary of the Battle of Inyatuwe, which commenced hostilities in the Wankie campaign.[31]

*

Ray Alexander's plea was not heeded. On 20 August 1970, Flag Boshielo, Castro Dolo, Victor Ndaba and Bob Zulu are killed by a South African Police contingent in an engagement in the Caprivi Strip in South West Africa (Namibia).[32]

*

Johannes P. Botha, a passport control officer at Jan Smuts Airport, stamps the travel document of Wankie campaign veteran James April on 29 December 1970. The passport is made out in the name of 'Mr Henry Dirk Marais'.

Later that day, April checks in at the Planet Hotel in Fordsburg, Johannesburg. He tells the receptionist, Alfred Kutuwela, that he has arrived from England.[33]

*

Fanele Mbali was recalled to Moscow in connection with ANC plans to launch a seaborne invasion of South Africa. It is a longstanding MK objective. Landings along the South African coastline were envisaged in *Operation Mayibuye*; they featured in Ambrose Makiwane's early plans for guerrilla warfare; and they were discussed by Oliver Tambo, Ben Turok and Joe Slovo in 1969.

The Revolutionary Council now wishes to revive the idea. Early in 1971, Yusuf Dadoo, Oliver Tambo, Moses Mabhida and Fanele Mbali meet a group of Soviet politicians, army generals and navy admirals. The meeting takes place in a boardroom in the Soviet Union.

A member of the Soviet team asks the ANC delegation what they can bring to the ongoing talks regarding a naval infiltration: is there anything new?

Dadoo stands up and says: 'Our response will come from the youngest member of our delegation, "Lammy Booi". He was trained in navigation and this operation will be his to execute if it is approved. He will address this meeting in the Russian language. We do not need him addressing us because we already know what he is going to say. There will be an English interpretation merely so we can follow the gist of what he says.'

Dadoo sits, and Fanele Mbali (aka 'Lammy Booi') stands. He addresses the meeting with the interpreter translating his Russian to English.

When Mbali finishes he receives a round of applause from the Soviets. A tall Soviet admiral stands and says: I know him. I put him through his accreditation process when he completed his navigation course in Baku three years ago. I know him and his political outlook and that he is a product of Soviet training. I am convinced he is the right choice.[34]

*

Nicholas Kombele is part of a group of four who are transported to a flat close to a railway station in Moscow in February 1971. On arrival they find a man by the name of Mbiela Dlamini already there.

On the following day, Benny Zulu, Edward Motsi and Reddy Mazimba arrive, and, the day after that, Gladstone Mose and Eric Tengwa.

Oliver Tambo and Moses Mabhida visit the ten cadres the next day. Tambo tells them that endeavours are being undertaken to send them home. They will have to take a train to Baku, where, he says, 'you will receive something'. He doesn't elaborate.

On the following day, Tambo returns. He says that they will meet other comrades at the station. The group are taken to the railway station on the same day. There they meet Fanele Mbali, who is alongside Sandi Sijake, T.T. Cholo and Jordaan Dawara, among others.

The group of twenty-four then departs for Baku.

In the Azerbaijan capital, they are taken on board a ship.[35]

*

At 6.30 a.m. on 17 February, Keith Nayager, an Indian lieutenant in the Durban Security Branch, arrives at No. 77 Road 201 in Chatsworth, Durban.

James April opens the door and gives his name as Henry Dirk Marais. He also produces a passport and an identity card, all made out to 'H.D. Marais'. He is arrested nonetheless.

On the following day, Captain Ignatius Coetzee accompanies April back to the Chatsworth house. April leads him to the bedroom. Out of a wardrobe full of clothes, April puts his hand into the right-hand pocket of a grey jacket, takes two capsules out and hands them to Coetzee.

On 25 February, Captain Coetzee takes a small amount of powder out of one of the capsules retrieved from the Chatsworth house, and dissolves it in a teaspoonful of distilled water. A brown solution results.

He places a blank piece of paper on top of a hardcover book. He next takes another book, titled *Penny Green Street*, which was seized from the house in Chatsworth. He places the double-sided page 27–28 of *Penny Green Street* on top of the blank sheet of paper that is lying on the hardcover book. Then he places a second blank sheet of paper above page 27 (therefore there are two blank sheets of paper. One is above page 27 of *Penny Green Street*, and the other is sandwiched between page 28 and the hardcover book).

With a blue ballpoint pen he writes 'Pinetown, Durban' twice on the blank sheet of paper above page 27. He then retrieves the other blank piece of paper (between page 28 and the hardcover) and swabs the brown solution onto it. At this point the words 'Pinetown, Durban', appear in pink colour.

Coetzee takes these and other documents and hands them over to Mr Venter at the Bureau of Standards in Pretoria.[36]

*

On the night of 22 October 1971, Ahmed Timol and Mohammed Essop spend an hour drinking at the Bosmont Hotel. Timol mentions that he wants to give some books to a friend. As they leave the hotel, Timol says that the friend lives in Vrededorp.

Essop drives them away in a yellow Anglia. At 11 p.m. the car is stopped in Fuel Road, at a point opposite the West Park cemetery in Coronationville.

A Sergeant Klein asks Essop to open the boot.

Essop complies.

As the boot opens, Klein sees a shoebox and a number of parcels. He asks Essop: 'What are those?'

'They are books,' Essop says.

Klein repeats the question and Essop the answer.

However, when the parcels are opened, the police unearth, inter alia, 114 complete copies of issue number 1 of the SACP's journal *Inkululeko*, 150 copies of pages 1 and 2 of the journal, fifty copies of pages 3 and 4, twenty of pages 5 and 6, and twenty-two of pages 7 and 8. There are also 447 copies of the leaflet 'The African National

Congress says to Vorster and his Gang: your days are coming to an end!!!', and twenty-eight addressed envelopes containing copies of the same leaflet.

There are various other documents; one of them is a typed piece of paper on which appears the following: 'Main Group: A. Timol, I. Moodley, M.S. Essop. Sub groups. R. Desai.'[37]

*

The *Rand Daily Mail* reports six days later that Ahmed Timol, aged thirty, died the day before as a result of a fall from a tenth-floor office at John Vorster Square Police Station, Johannesburg. The report quotes Brigadier J. Kruger as saying: 'It is true. He jumped from the 10th floor of John Vorster Square at 4 p.m. He committed suicide.'[38]

*

South Africa's intelligence service receives indications early in 1972 that something is brewing with the ANC in Somalia, though it is unclear precisely what.

A South African Military Intelligence report dated 31 January claims the ANC possesses an air base about ten miles north-west of Mogadishu. It is controlled by Russian technicians and pilots. Half a mile away stands a Russian camp.

'Eisland Kweyama' was previously the ANC camp leader, but he has been replaced by 'Robert Mwema', who regularly travels to Dar es Salaam, where he visits Andrei Komarov, the technical adviser of the Russian air force in Tanzania.

The objective of the pilots stationed there is to bombard white areas as well as strategic points within South Africa, but this action would only be launched after a revolt in South Africa commences.[39]

*

Yusuf Dadoo, Chris Hani, Moses Mabhida, Joe Slovo and Oliver Tambo arrive in 'Sironya', a suburb in Moscow, in February 1972. There they meet the guerrillas who have now returned from their naval training in Baku.

The leaders depart, after which Hani returns alone. He gives the men different maps depending on their area of origin. For example, Gladstone Mose, who was commander of the group destined for the Transkei in the Wankie campaign, receives a map of the Transkei.

A further meeting is held with the guerrillas in Moscow, at which Joe Slovo, Chris Hani and Yusuf Dadoo are present.

Slovo tells the guerrillas that their training will now cease and they must henceforth focus on the maps. He says they are going to go home by boat. The boat will offload them at Port St Johns, where they will connect with their contact. This contact will identify himself by shining a green light during the night. After receiving the signal, the cadres must gather their arms, get into the small engine-propelled rubber boats that will be provided to them, and row ashore.

They will be given radios which will be operated by 'Douglas' (Sandi Sijake) and 'Motiranka' (T.T. Cholo). They will advance in the direction of this green light, but if the light turns red they will have to retreat.

Upon arrival in Port St Johns, all the weapons they take ashore will have to be handed to the contact, as will the rubber boats and Johnson motors. It will be up to them where to go and how to organise after that, but they must not attempt to go home: 'if you attempt this sort of thing your family will be wiped out', Slovo warns. In South Africa they are to militarily train the people to destroy the government. Slovo says they will need to report to him on their progress.[40]

*

Alexander Moumbaris's passport is stamped on 9 February 1972 when he enters South Africa at Jan Smuts Airport.

From the holiday cottage where he is staying in the Isles of Shelly on Natal's South Coast between Margate and Port Shepstone, Moumbaris drives towards East London. He travels in a Volkswagen Combi that can carry around ten people but is empty for this trip apart from three bicycles.

At East London Post Office, Moumbaris meets a white colleague. The two travel to the railway station, where they collect a case that Moumbaris places in the Combi. The case contains camping equipment.

Moumbaris drives with the colleague and the equipment to a garage, where they deposit the bicycles.

Moumbaris then returns to the Isles of Shelly.[41]

*

South Africa's Security Branch head office dispatches a letter to the country's director of Military Intelligence on 17 February. The letter says that the office possesses no information regarding airfields controlled by the ANC abroad. It adds that according to unconfirmed information a group of twelve ANC terrorists were trained as MiG-21 pilots in Moscow between January 1963 and the end of 1967.

It was known that Sydney Nkala, alias Fana Ngubane, who originated in Hammarsdale, was trained as a terrorist in Odessa, but additional information that he was trained as a pilot is not in the office's possession. As for 'Robert Ntwana', allegedly in control of the airfield in Mogadishu – he is not known to them.[42]

*

During the same month, a plane leaves the Soviet Union for Somalia. There are twenty ANC cadres on board (nineteen who underwent naval training in Azerbaijan plus Chris Hani).

Waiting for them at Mogadishu Airport is a Somali officer who leads them to a waiting van. They are driven to a place in the bush outside town where they come across five tents containing Somali military personnel.

At this camp they find Moses Mabhida and Oliver Tambo, who immediately take Fanele Mbali and T.T. Cholo aside for consultations.[43]

*

One night, under cover of darkness, the cadres gather their equipment at the camp. Nicholas Kombele, T.T. Cholo and Gladstone Mose pack guns into waterproof bags, while Edward Motsi and John Melo place pistols, hand grenades, TNT, detonators and a packet of ammunition for pistols into carrier bags. There are a further six bags containing guns, two bags containing hand grenades, one bag of TNT, and one bag containing TNT and a fuse.

While they are packing, Moses Mabhida arrives. He says he has money that must be placed into the bags.

Cholo, Hani and Mbali are the first to leave. They go by car. The rest follow in two trucks. All travel from Mogadishu to Kismayo.

In Kismayo they find an engine-propelled steel boat which has a main deck with a railing around it, and painted just below the deck they see the word 'Aventura'.

They arrive at the *Aventura* in the early hours of the morning. Joe Slovo is already on the ship. When Gladstone Mose boards, he sees that food has been provided. He notices lifeboats there as well.

When they load the waterproof bags they do so 'bucket brigade' style, passing them along hand to hand.

The guerrillas spend the remainder of the night on board.

Later in the morning the *Aventura* sets off. There is a Greek crew of about thirteen manning the ship. As they depart Kismayo port, Oliver Tambo and Chris Hani bid them farewell.[44]

*

Three or four days later, as the *Aventura* approaches Mombasa in Kenya, Fanele Mbali and the ship's captain are having a discussion when they hear a loud explosion. The boat loses forward momentum and starts drifting.

The captain tells Mbali that they can still reach South Africa on the other engine but this would be risky: if anything happens to the remaining engine they might end up drifting in the Indian Ocean and have to be towed home by the first vessel that arrives, which would expose the mission. The captain also believes there is something wrong with the boat's radar system.

Mbali summons T.T. Cholo, Petrus Mthembu, Justice Mpanza and Gladstone Mose for a discussion. They decide that they must pull in to Mombasa and inform Mabhida, Tambo and Slovo about this. The rest of the group is then assembled and informed about the news.

The captain interjects, saying they ought not to go to Mombasa but rather back to Somalia, as it will take too long to effect repairs.[45]

*

Within a couple of days of the return to Somalia, the radar system is repaired and the cadres again board the *Aventura* in Kismayo.

But when they do so the Greek crew raise further concerns about the engine, and say they are afraid of going on the craft.[46]

*

Oliver Tambo visits the guerrillas in their tented bush camp near Kismayo. He says: 'We have got another crew from England. The Greeks have apparently learnt that you people are heading for Port St Johns where you will be put ashore and they have become afraid.'

Tambo adds: 'We must keep these Greeks here in the bush with us.'

A confinement area is created for the Greeks about 600 metres away. There they are guarded by Somalian soldiers, who do not allow them to leave.[47]

*

One night soon afterwards, the guerrillas again load their equipment onto the *Aventura*, with an English crew on board.

The boat sets sail early in the morning but only travels about 700 metres and is still in the waters of Kismayo when those on board hear the sound of iron clanging.

The *Aventura* is then towed back to port by a tug. The guerrillas disembark with their luggage and equipment.[48]

*

A fortnight later, Tambo arrives at the cadres' tents near Kismayo. He gathers them together and says that although the initial venture of going home by sea has come unstuck, new endeavours, either by land or by air, will be made.[49]

*

Alexander Moumbaris receives a cable in South Africa on 21 April 1972. It is from Ronnie Kasrils in London. It says: 'Regret to inform you that mother is dead. Deepest condolences.'

Two days later Moumbaris's passport is stamped as he exits the country.[50]

*

By 12 June, the cadres who were to have been part of the *Aventura* landings have relocated to a Somali government guesthouse. The Somali in charge of the property takes Petrus Mthembu aside and says he will be part of a group that will leave the next day. Later, Mthembu is transported to premises where he meets Justice Mpanza and Gladstone Mose.

On the following day, while Mpanza, Mose and Mthembu are seated together at the property, Chris Hani arrives. Hani calls Mthembu to one side and says there is a person that Mthembu will have to meet in Swaziland. He gives Mthembu a yellow tie, which he says the man will recognise him by. Hani then distributes money to the trio; Mthembu receives R600. Hani also gives him a reference book that has Mthembu's picture in it. Gladstone Mose then receives a Lesotho passport from Hani.

From Mogadishu Airport, Mpanza, Mose and Mthembu depart on an Air Somalia flight to Nairobi, and six days later they take a connecting flight from Jan Smuts Airport to Swaziland.

In Manzini, they find their way to the George Hotel.

Mthembu puts on his yellow tie and takes his copy of *Newsweek* to the George's entrance door.

A while later he returns and tells Mpanza and Mose that he met the contact.[51]

*

From the Swazi Inn Hotel on 23 June, Alexander Moumbaris, the 'contact' referred to by Petrus Mthembu, phones Avis's car rental station in Bezuidenhout Street, Johannesburg. He hires a Mercedes 220, registered TJ 353-343, and asks for it to be sent to Swaziland.[52]

*

Sandi Sijake, Nicholas Kombele and T.T. Cholo are the next to arrive by plane in Swaziland. They land at around 10 a.m. on 26 June and travel by taxi to the George Hotel.

After depositing their possessions in their rooms, they head off to the post office. Cholo has a red handkerchief in his top pocket and is carrying a copy of the *Cape Times*.[53]

Later that day, Cholo, wearing a red cloth around his neck, meets Alexander Moumbaris near the Manzini Post Office.

The two agree that the group that arrived earlier, consisting of Mose, Mpanza and Mthembu, should immediately cross the border into South Africa after receiving a fresh supply of money and clothes (the group lost their luggage in Nairobi), and that Cholo's group should follow.

Early on the morning of the 27th, Moumbaris transports Mose, Mpanza and Mthembu to Goedgegun in Swaziland. When he drops them off, Moumbaris asks if they have anything incriminating in their luggage that could bring him trouble when he crosses the border.

They say no.

Moumbaris then gives them a compass, a snakebite kit, a pair of binoculars and a map. He also gives them a pair of his shorts.

Just before departing, Moumbaris says that after they cross the border by foot, they should wait a while, then proceed to the roadway and wait for him there. He will pick them up after driving through the border with his car.

Mose, Mthembu and Mpanza are in position on a road just inside South Africa that evening. It is after dark and many cars are travelling, so every time a car comes they have to hide. This continues until just past midnight when they call it quits and opt to continue on foot to Piet Retief.

On this resumed march, Mpanza is suffering: his feet are swollen and he is freezing. Consequently the group marches very slowly.

They reach a homestead where Mpanza suggests the group has a rest.

Mose declines, saying he himself is able to continue, and 'in any event we would be splitting up further ahead; I am leaving you behind, I am going on my way'. He sets off alone and walks through the early hours of the 28th.

Approximately thirty kilometres from Piet Retief, he sees Moumbaris approaching in a Mercedes 220. Moumbaris's wife is also in the vehicle.

Moumbaris asks where the others are.

Mose says he left Mpanza and Mthembu behind.

Moumbaris says he has failed to make contact with the other group as well.

Mose enters the car and they try to find the others.[54]

On the same morning, T.T. Cholo, Sandi Sijake and Nicholas Kombele, the members of the other group mentioned by Moumbaris, are in a lorry with a black driver who takes them to a rest place where they get something to eat. They cannot swallow the food, so parched are their throats.

Later that day, in Ermelo, they buy train tickets to their respective destinations. Sijake and Kombele board the Germiston train at 6 p.m., while Cholo gets into another carriage destined for Johannesburg.

On the same day, Mose's colleagues Justice Mpanza and Petrus Mthembu travel by taxi from Piet Retief to Glencoe, and by train from Glencoe to Pietermaritzburg.[55]

By the following day, 29 June, having failed to track down the other cadres, Alexander Moumbaris drives Gladstone Mose from Piet Retief towards the Transkei.

At a place not far beyond Pietermaritzburg, where there are gum trees growing on the side of the road, Moumbaris stops and offers to lend Mose some articles from a suitcase.

Mose responds that he doesn't want to be burdened with a lot of clothes and things. He does, however, ask if Moumbaris can possibly help retrieve some of the documents and items such as passports and money that he lost in Nairobi.

Moumbaris says he will try, and if successful 'I will advise London'.

As to how the information will reach Mose, the two agree that a message will be placed in the *Daily Dispatch*, after which contact will be made via a courier fourteen days later. In a cigarette box, Moumbaris's wife writes down the message to be placed in the paper. It is: 'Mrs H. Caulincour, anyone knowing her address please write to Queenstown'. She also writes, 'If someone else *Time* magazine', which means that if the courier is somebody besides Alexander Moumbaris, that other person will be identifiable by the copy of *Time* magazine in his or her possession.

The Moumbarises drop Mose off about seven kilometres from Umzimkulu at a place where pine trees are growing beside the road.[56]

*

Just six days after crossing into South Africa, Nicholas Kombele surrenders himself at Maclear Police Station in the Cape Province.[57]

*

Alexander Moumbaris leaves South Africa on 6 July 1972 via the Kopfontein gate on the Botswana border.[58]

*

A Transvaal farmer based near the Botswana border notices that a white Mercedes-Benz is travelling regularly in the area. The driver is always the same white man, and he is usually carrying Africans.

The farmer telephones his local police station and reports what he has seen.

The police decide to keep the matter under observation.[59]

*

In Gaborone on 18 July, Pumelele Menye (long since rehabilitated and welcomed back into the MK fold) walks to a post office. He does so dressed as a priest. Fanele Mbali meanwhile heads to Gaborone Railway Station. Both are carrying copies of *Time* magazine and a plastic shopping bag from London.

Alexander Moumbaris walks up to Mbali and asks where he can buy a copy of *Time*.

'I am sorry the shops are closed,' Mbali answers.

Late in the afternoon of the following day, Mbali and Menye are in the company of Mfeketho Radebe and a fourth MK cadre known as 'Ntasarashu'. They enter a car driven by Moumbaris. After a while, Moumbaris stops, points to a hill and says, 'Continue in that direction.' He adds that at 6.30 p.m. the four men must be at a specific point on the road a couple of kilometres inside South Africa. If he is late, they must proceed on the road away from the border, with one person on lookout and the other three behind cover.[60]

Later that day, Captain Johannes van Niekerk of the South African Security Branch travels to the Kopfontein border post accompanied by Major van Rensburg, Captain Dloi and a number of others.

At 6.50 p.m., a Blue Renault, registered TJ 361-826, enters the border area from the Botswana side. When the car stops, Captain van Niekerk is in a building at the east side of the main border post terminal. He sees Alexander Moumbaris and a woman climb out of the vehicle and walk to the border control office.

Van Niekerk goes up to Moumbaris and asks who he is.

Moumbaris tells him truthfully, upon which Van Niekerk places his left hand behind Moumbaris's neck, grasps it and says he is under arrest. With his right hand, Van Niekerk, with the assistance of Dloi and others, arrests Moumbaris's wife.[61]

The apprehended couple are taken to separate buildings at the border post to be interrogated.[62]

*

At 1.30 p.m. ten days later, Major Frans Pretorius of the Security Branch travels with police colleagues to an area called Moletsi in Pietersburg district. They proceed to a hut owned by the sister of an African traditional healer. Inside they find T.T. Cholo, and Major Pretorius arrests him. When asked for his name, Cholo says 'Phuti Chacho'.[63]

*

Then, on 10 August, Detective Warrant Officer Reginald Reynolds and a team of Security Branch colleagues travel to Mandini in Natal.

At 7.30 p.m. they surround a particular house, and Reynolds goes to the back door with Detective Sergeant Nyathi. While they are taking up position, the back door flies open and Petrus Mthembu and Justice Mpanza emerge. Reynolds grabs Mthembu and Nyathi takes Mpanza.[64]

*

On 22 August 1973, Captain Johannes du Preez arrests Sandi Sijake in Elliotdale, some fifty kilometres south of Umtata.[65]

*

Pumelele Menye is arrested in Butterworth six days later.[66]

*

Justice Mpanza is taken out of Pretoria Central Prison and transported to the Compol Building in Pretorius Street, Pretoria, on 14 September.

There he is taken to the office of Lieutenant Daan Wessels, who shows him a letter of response that the police have received to a message, purportedly written by Mpanza, but which in fact the police themselves had sent to Mpanza's contact abroad.

Wessels shows Mpanza a fresh letter that the police want to send to the contact. He hands Mpanza a notepad.

For the third paragraph of the dictated letter, Wessels tells Mpanza to write: 'Box 72 still alright for letters at the same place Ghandi's shop, Main Road, Tongaat, date 28/9 – on the 28th at 1 p.m., 29th at 11 a.m. and on the 30th at 1 p.m.'[67]

*

In London on Friday 20 October, John 'Sean' Hosey receives a call in his office from Ronnie 'Reynolds', who expresses a desire to see him. Hosey asks him to come to the office.

'Reynolds', i.e. Ronnie Kasrils, visits Hosey's office on the morning of Monday the 23rd. Kasrils is carrying a brown bag. He sits down and over lunch gives Hosey further details about the mission.

From the bag, Kasrils takes two photograph frames, a plane ticket and £380 or so in cash. He gives the frames to Hosey and says that behind them there are some passbooks. He then hands over the money.

Kasrils tells Hosey that his plane ticket is for Durban, and that in Durban he must book into a hotel – the Killarney is a good one. He must then go to Tongaat, some sixty miles outside Durban. On one of three possible dates – 1 p.m. on the Saturday, 11 a.m. on the Sunday, or 1 p.m. on the Monday – he will find a man waiting there. This man will be wearing a brown jacket, a hat and spectacles. Hosey must ask, 'How far is Tongaat mill from here?' to which the man will answer, 'About two kilometres north.' At that point Hosey must hand over the passbooks.[68]

*

Sean Hosey's plane leaves England on Wednesday 25 October and arrives in Durban the following day.[69]

*

On the 28th at about midday, Detective Sergeant Billy Boy Nyathi is handed a brown corduroy jacket, a hat and spectacles by Lieutenant Daan Wessels, who tells him to put them on and go to 'Ghandi's' shop in Tongaat Shopping Centre.

At about 1 p.m., Sean Hosey walks up to a store in Tongaat and finds a man dressed in a jacket, hat and spectacles as expected.

There are a number of people around the shop, including a lot of children running about.

Billy Boy Nyathi sees a white man approach. This man asks: 'How far is the Tongaat Sugar Mill Company?'

'About two kilometres north,' Nyathi responds.

The white man asks Nyathi to follow him, and walks into the store. Inside the shop Hosey buys some cigarettes. When he steps outside he feels there are still too many people around to make the handover, so he says, 'Follow me down the street a little bit.'

After walking a while, the white man bends down as if to fasten his shoelaces. Nyathi approaches him. Hosey looks back and feels there are *still* too many people standing around.

Just when Nyathi feels as though the white man is going to speak to him, the man walks on. Then he stops again. When Nyathi catches up, the man asks him to follow him to the European toilets at the railway station.

Inside the station, the man goes to the male toilet. As Nyathi enters, the man exits the lavatories to the left and takes up position to the rear of the toilets. Nyathi follows him there. The man takes a parcel wrapped in brown paper out of his coat pocket and says 'Good luck' before walking away.[70]

'Hold it boss,' comes a voice from behind.

Hosey turns and sees four black men with guns aimed at his chest. Within moments a team of white security policemen arrive and whisk him off to Security Branch headquarters in Durban.[71]

*

On the same day in Queenstown, Gladstone Mose stands with a copy of *Time* magazine waiting for the arrival of the contact who will give him the luggage he lost in Nairobi.

Instead the police arrive and arrest him.[72]

REBUILDING THE UNDERGROUND

Kgalema Motlanthe, who is employed by the Johannesburg City Council's Commercial Department, which is responsible for the city's beer halls, travels by train to Matola on the outskirts of Lourenço Marques. His destination is a house belonging to the family of 'Makwakwa', a municipal policeman of Mozambican origin who works in the beer hall in Dube, Soweto.

At the house, Motlanthe has a conversation with Makwakwa's cousin. Motlanthe asks him to find a way to Inhambane. Motlanthe wishes to find a route through Mozambique to independent Africa, further to the north.

The cousin responds that it will be impossible to get any further than Inhambane.

Mozambicans who want to join FRELIMO usually come to South Africa, work a while in the mines, and then go via Botswana to contact the Mozambican liberation movement further to the north.[1]

*

In September 1973, Onkgopotse Abraham Tiro, Bokwe Mafuna, Randwedzi Nengwe-kulu, Tomeka Mafole and Nosi Matshoba of the South African Students' Organisation apply for refugee status in Botswana.[2]

*

At the beginning of December, Eric Molobi receives a letter from Abraham Tiro, who writes that he is in Botswana. He extends an invitation for Molobi and his wife to visit.

Shortly afterwards Eric Molobi meets his brother Frank and asks whether it will be possible to accompany him on his forthcoming trip to Botswana.

Frank Molobi says that a man called Mavuso and his wife will also be there, but that Eric can come.

Early in the morning of Saturday 22 December 1973, Eric Molobi, Frank Molobi, Mavuso and their wives depart from Meadowlands, Soweto, with Frank Molobi driving. They travel via Zeerust to Botswana, and cross legally through the Tlokweng border post. They then head to Gaborone, where they make their way to a flat in one of the government buildings in the city.

Later that afternoon, the Molobi brothers and Mavuso go to the city centre. While there, they spot Abraham Tiro.

Frank Molobi and Mavuso depart with the food that the group has purchased, leaving Eric Molobi and Tiro behind. Tiro then leads Molobi to a bookshop where he introduces him to April Zabane, an employee in the store. Zabane says he is a refugee from the Cape Province and a member of the PAC.

When the shop closes, Zabane invites Molobi and Tiro to accompany him to another friend. Zabane leads them to a house about fifty or sixty metres from Gaborone city centre. There they meet an elderly man by the name of 'Photela', who says he is an ANC member.[3]

*

At the Clermont Sporting Grounds in Durban in January 1974, Barney Dladla addresses a meeting organised by the National Union of Textile Workers and the Clermont Advisory Board.

While Dladla speaks, Raymond Nkosi walks across the field to the rostrum and beckons Bhekisisa Nxasana towards him. Nxasana moves to meet him halfway.

Nkosi tells Nxasana that it is necessary for him to meet a person who has arrived from Swaziland.

Nxasana says he is still busy; this can wait.

To this Nkosi responds that he will send Osborne Mthunywa to collect Nxasana from the reception after the meeting.

At the reception, which is held in a hall in Clermont, Raymond Nkosi arrives while tea is being drunk. He tells Nxasana that the person is now at his house.

Nkosi and Nxasana depart the hall together and encounter Osborne Mthunywa, who drives them to Nkosi's house.

Nkosi jumps out and returns shortly with Joseph Nduli, formerly of the reconnaissance group in the Wankie campaign. Nduli introduces himself by his correct name and says that the meeting will be short because he is afraid that the police might know he is there.

Nduli explains that he has been sent by the ANC and SACTU to see what conditions are like inside South Africa. The reason why he has come to Durban is to revive the ANC in accordance with the M-Plan. He says that the cell system should not be like the old one that had too many people per cell. A cell should now comprise two or three people. He suggests that Nkosi, Mthunywa and Nxasana themselves form a cell.[4]

*

On 1 February, when Abraham Tiro opens a parcel at the house where he is living in St Joseph's Roman Catholic Mission in Khale, eleven kilometres south of Gaborone, it explodes and kills him instantly.[5]

Eleven days later, Boy Mvemve, the deputy head of the ANC in Zambia, opens a parcel in the organisation's headquarters in Lusaka, which is situated in a single-storey block at the rear of a building on the main road between the central business district and a residential area. An explosion occurs, ripping a hole in the roof, shattering windows, and blowing out the doors of other offices in the 'Liberation Centre', where about seven organisations including SWAPO, COREMO, ZAPU and the MPLA also have their Lusaka headquarters.

Mvemve is killed, and Roy Kembelo, an ANC official with him when he opened the bomb, suffers serious facial and hand injuries. Max Sisulu, who was in the office at the same time, also suffers injuries.[6]

*

By a shady tree next to a football pitch at a Gaborone school five days later, diplomatic representatives from several African countries attend the burial of Abraham Tiro.[7]

Eric Molobi is present, as are ANC representatives. Bokwe Mafuna, who applied for asylum in Botswana with Tiro the previous September, introduces Molobi to Thabo Mbeki of the ANC. Mbeki says he too is a refugee and is presently staying in London. He adds that he travels throughout Africa in connection with the ANC. He asks Molobi what his political views are.

Molobi says he does not belong to any political organisation.[8]

On his return to Soweto from Botswana, Eric Molobi meets fellow students Xola Nuse, Simon Radebe and Vincent Selanto, who are members of his political discussion group. He tells them that he has just been to Botswana, where he was involved in the organisation of Tiro's funeral and had discussions with ANC members like Koos Segoale and Thabo Mbeki, as well as another man, Photela. He says he has established these men as contacts, and would like the three friends to go and meet them.[9]

*

Eric and Frank Molobi are in a flat on the second floor of a block of apartments in Gaborone on Saturday 13 April. With them are Vincent Selanto, Simon Radebe and Xola Nuse.

The lady of the house tells them that Koos is coming shortly; he has just gone to play tennis. Eric and Frank Molobi decide to go and fetch the lady's husband from the tennis courts. They return later with Koos Segoale.

During his address to the group, Segoale says he is presently working in the Department of Economics in the Botswana government, but 'they' don't know he is an ANC member. He suggests to Nuse, Radebe and Selanto that they go for military training.

They decline.

Back in Soweto, the Molobi brothers, Simon Radebe, Vincent Selanto and Xola Nuse meet in Frank Molobi's house.

Radebe and Nuse say they want to further their education; hence it will not be possible for them to partake in any political activities in the future.

On this news, the group dissolves.[10]

*

In 1974 Chris Hani enters South Africa and proceeds to Lesotho. His mission is to build ANC structures within South Africa from his base in Lesotho.[11]

*

Tim Jenkin and Stephen Lee, who have recently graduated from the University of Cape Town, arrive in London on 25 April 1974.

They decide on the spur of the moment to visit the ANC's office. They march up, knock on the door, and introduce themselves.

A person in the office types a note and hands it to them without speaking a word. It reads: 'Meet me at the pub round the corner in half an hour.'

In that pub, the man asks them what they want. They say they want to contact the ANC, and were wondering if there was any literature they could read to find out more about the organisation. Later in the conversation, the ANC man tells them, 'OK, here's some literature and if you'd like to meet some other people come back to this pub tomorrow and we'll introduce you to some other people.'[12]

*

A report in the Johannesburg *Star* on the same day claims that according to radio broadcasts from Lisbon, Portuguese troops belonging to a group calling itself the Movement of the Armed Forces have seized government buildings, taken over a radio station, and occupied the capital's centre square, Praça do Comércio. In their broadcasts, the movement promised to set up a 'national Junta of salvation' to rule Portugal.[13]

*

In September 1974, an aeroplane lands in South Africa from Europe. Out of it steps Raymond Suttner, who abandoned his studies at Oxford University in 1970 in order to contribute to the liberation struggle. He joined the SACP and received training from Ronnie Kasrils and Rusty Bernstein in counter-surveillance, invisible ink, disguises and leaflet bombs. He returned to South Africa in June 1971 and has been operating alone ever since.

Suttner walks into the airport terminal, his hands laden with books.

Lawrence Kuny is there to meet him. 'Hi Raymond. It's good to see you,' he says.

'Hello, Lawrence,' Suttner responds.

'How was business?'

'Oh good, good. Rothschild sends his regards.'

'How are the gold shares?'

'The advice from London is to sell.'

'Are you thinking of going into property instead?'

The two collect Suttner's baggage and head to the car. While Kuny drives, Suttner asks: 'What do you think of Portugal's fall in Africa?'

Kuny responds, 'It seems to indicate that everything here is going to have to change.'

'Yes, South Africa's position has changed drastically,' Suttner says, before taking pause while he stares out at the passing factories. He then turns to Kuny and says, 'Lawrence, there is no need for you to waste your life. There is much you can do.'

'What do you mean?'

'I will explain what we can do, but not now.'[14]

*

In Mozambique during the same month, the Portuguese hand over power to a FRELIMO-dominated transitional government pending the territory's receipt of full independence.[15]

*

Speaking before a town meeting in his political constituency of Nigel on 5 November 1974, Prime Minister John Vorster responds to the turn of events in the region. He says of South Africa's political critics, 'All I ask them is to give South Africa a chance of about six months. I do not ask more than that. If South Africa is given that chance they will be surprised at where the country will stand in six to twelve months' time.'

During his speech, Vorster says he is pleased to announce that reassurances have been received from Mozambique over the question of whether that country might be used as a launching pad for persons wishing to commit acts of sabotage in South Africa.

Regarding Rhodesia, he says that the police will stay there as long as there is a terrorist threat because they are there to protect the interests of South Africa and nobody else.[16]

*

One afternoon towards the end of December 1974, Lawrence Kuny follows Raymond Suttner's car to an isolated spot just outside Pietermaritzburg.

The pair transfer pamphlets from Suttner's vehicle to Kuny's, and Kuny then drives Suttner towards the city centre. Suttner is wearing a coat over his jacket and trousers. He paints nail varnish onto his fingertips. Kuny stops at a post office box. Suttner gets out and posts a small quantity of pamphlets before returning to the car.

Then Suttner takes off his coat. Without the coat he makes further deliveries at other post offices.

Suttner next removes his jacket and makes a few more deliveries.

Finally he takes off his tie before making deliveries of the last batch of pamphlets.

Kuny then drives Suttner back to the spot outside Pietermaritzburg where they left the other car.[17]

*

One Sunday morning in April 1975, Bhekisisa Nxasana is in the yard of his house when a man approaches who introduces himself as Russell Mapanga.

Moments later Jacob Zuma arrives in the company of William Khanyile. Zuma was arrested in one of Essop Suleiman's Combis in June 1963 and served ten years on Robben Island (along with the majority of political prisoners from the 1960s, including the leaders seized in the Rivonia raid), before his release in 1973.

In a bedroom in Nxasana's house the four hold a discussion. Khanyile says that he has received a message from Albert Dhlomo (an ANC member who has been a refugee in Swaziland since the mid-1960s) to the effect that the ANC is to be revived in accordance with the Mandela Plan. Khanyile says conditions in Mozambique have created fertile grounds for such a reconstitution.

Zuma elaborates, and while explaining the workings of the cell system, draws a diagram. He says after the cells are formed, recruits will have to be obtained who will be sent to Mozambique. Then, when the trainees return to South Africa, the cells will be required to protect them from the police.[18]

*

The condition of the ANC's existing army abroad is discussed in a report of the 'Commission on the State of Affairs in MK in East Africa', which was established by the Revolutionary Council on 17 April 1975 with a mandate to investigate the causes of and possible remedies for the 'deterioration of the standard of military life and discipline in the MK establishment' in East Africa, which is the region where the vast majority of MK members abroad are based.

The commission, chaired by John Motshabi, starts its work on 21 April when its three members meet the MK East Africa Command, which consists of Julius Maliba (regional commander), Julius Mokoena (political commissar), Joseph Shumo (chief of staff), Bunny Pinny (medical officer) and Morris Selabogo (chief of logistics). It continues its work until 2 May when Dingo Lamani of the commission passes away.

The commission delivers an interim report on the day of Lamani's death. It confirms that there has indeed been a marked deterioration in the standard of military life and discipline in the region, but says that this is nothing new. The picture painted by the Motshabi Commission is that the army that once fought the Wankie and Sipolilo campaigns is in urgent need of fresh blood at rank-and-file and possibly also at officer level. It says that even before the commission adjourned following Lamani's death, 'it became abundantly clear that basically most of the problems that were being investigated are well-known to the leadership' as they had been discussed in the reports of no fewer than six previous commissions of inquiry, all but one of which had been headed by Motshabi.

The report recapitulates what the factors are. One is that by now a number of cadres have families, bringing responsibilities that often clash with military commitments. Another is that 'Certain aspects of the Commission's investigation such as dishonesty (stealin [sic]) are well known. This features in the movement except that the Commission observed that in East Africa top officials encourage it or are themselves active participants.' Other possible causes of low morale include 'discrepancies in the various levels of command such as people who have records of dishonesty being promoted to leading positions – not only in MK but also in higher bodies', and also the fact that 'Regional Command was encouraging commercial private property which distracted some of the cadres from their responsibilities and duties as military men'.[19]

*

Raymond Suttner is running short of money for his underground work, so he anonymously makes an order for envelopes through the University of Natal, knowing that he will receive a discount for his bulk purchase.

The transaction is detected by the police, who head to the factory from where the envelopes were sent. They launch an investigation aimed at finding out who made the purchase.[20]

*

On a farm in Swaziland, Sylvia Gamedze is hanging out some washing when a Volkswagen car with a hump back approaches. Two men get out, and one of them asks: 'Is this the Gamedzes' place here?'

'Yes,' she says.

'Is he here?'

'Yes, he is in the fields,' she says, before going to collect her husband, Peter Gamedze. She tells him that people have arrived who are looking for him.

'Do you know them?' he asks.

She says she doesn't.

Her husband says he will come.

She returns to the two guests and tells them Gamedze is coming. When he arrives, the three men greet each other and head to the car.

After chatting for a while in the VW, the group return to the house. They sit on chairs, while Sylvia Gamedze sits on the floor mat. Her husband says to her: 'These people here come to our home. They want to send you.' He elaborates that they want to send her to Gwala in South Africa.

She asks who they are.

Albert Dhlomo says, 'I am Dhlomo from Lamontville', and, referring to his companion, adds, 'This one is Mbeki from Edendale.'

Peter Gamedze says that he knew Mbeki's father.[21]

*

On Friday 30 May, Lawrence Kuny parks his car. He looks towards the adjacent house and notices the curtains are drawn. But then he sees somebody peeping out. Shortly afterwards the door opens. It is Raymond Suttner.

The two immediately begin working in the kitchen at the back of the house. They leave the front room in darkness, creating the impression that the house is empty.

Both Kuny and Suttner are wearing gloves that have been stained with ink. Suttner types the envelopes, while Kuny collates three pages of a document and then places them in the envelopes.

By the second day, the room is full of envelopes and stamps.

At one point during this day, Suttner says he is going to see 'Les', his other contact. Before departing, he quips: 'If you're not here when I come back – I'll see you in Pretoria Central.'[22]

*

A South African Military Intelligence report concluded on 17 June 1975 claims that Oliver Tambo has written to Prince Makhosini Dlamini, the prime minister of Swaziland, requesting that the ANC be allowed to open an office, distribute propaganda and meet relatives from South Africa, in Swaziland. The report says the Swazi response to the request is not yet known.[23]

*

On the same day, Raymond Suttner goes posting envelopes in Durban, Pietermaritzburg, Pinetown and other parts of Natal. He does this in the company of University of Natal lecturer Jenny Roxburgh.

Afterwards he drops Roxburgh off and then heads home.

When he exits the car outside his home, police block the driveway and arrest him.

Roxburgh and Lawrence Kuny are detained in separate raids the following day.[24]

*

In 'Can Phumo' (the city formerly known as Lourenço Marques), a crowd in excess of 22,000 cheers when Samora Machel appears on the balcony of the City Hall for his swearing-in as president of Mozambique on 25 June 1975.

In his speech, Machel pledges to take part in 'international efforts to liberate Africa'. He also vows to maintain friendly relations with countries that 'share our ideals' and, above all, the national liberation movements that 'fought on our side'.

After Machel is finished, Joaquim Chissano leads the crowd in chants of 'Down with apartheid, down with racism, down with imperialism'. Chissano then introduces the crowd to the leaders of several guerrilla movements in attendance. First is Dr Agostinho Neto of the MPLA. Then, the leader in the fight against 'fascism and colonialism' – Oliver Tambo – followed by SWAPO's Sam Nujoma and ZAPU's Joshua Nkomo.[25]

*

During August 1975, soon after being released from Robben Island prison, Joe Gqabi appears before the so-called Main Machinery of the ANC, which consists of Martin Ramokgadi, Alois Manci and the structure's chairman, John Nkadimeng – all of them, like him, former political prisoners.[26]

*

Mosima Sexwale moves from Roma in Lesotho to Kwaluseni in Swaziland to further his studies at the latter campus of the University of Botswana, Lesotho and Swaziland (UBLS). One of the seven or so South African students he finds already studying there is Muziwakhe Ngwenya, a BSc student from Soweto. He finds Ngwenya to be highly engaged politically, and extremely hostile to the South African regime.[27]

*

At Kwaluseni in August 1975, Sexwale is informed by 'Kgotoki', a female classmate, of the presence of two ANC officials, namely Thabo Mbeki and Albert Dhlomo. Sexwale agrees to meet them and he holds a private discussion with Mbeki.[28]

*

In Soweto soon afterwards, Mosima Sexwale visits Naledi Tsiki, his friend and former neighbour. The two had initiated attempts to contact the ANC abroad in the early 1970s while Tsiki was studying at high school in Lesotho, but these were unsuccessful.

Sexwale tells Tsiki that it appears he is about to make a breakthrough in establishing contact with the ANC in Swaziland.

After this meeting, Tsiki forms a three-person underground unit, consisting of himself, Christopher Manye, and a third man.

In September, Christopher Manye then recruits Ian Deway Rwaxa into the ANC's underground.[29]

*

Kgalema Motlanthe, who in 1973 undertook the unsuccessful voyage to find a passage to the ANC via Mozambique, is now a member of another political discussion group in Soweto, alongside Siphiwe Nyanda and Stanley Nkosi.

The establishment in Swaziland of the structure headed by Thabo Mbeki and Albert Dhlomo has made possible the contact with the ANC that was previously so elusive.

In October, Nyanda meets Motlanthe and Nkosi. He tells them that during his recent visit to Swaziland he managed to contact Keith Mokoape, who is part of the ANC's Swaziland structure. Nyanda says Mokoape instructed him to form a cell. Nyanda brings Motlanthe and Nkosi into the cell.[30]

*

With the channel to Swaziland established, recruitment of a new generation of MK cadres to be sent abroad to receive training also commences. Peter and Sylvia Gamedze meet Harry Gwala in Pietermaritzburg in October. The bag in front of them contains pamphlets and stacked bundles of R10 notes.

Gwala asks Peter Gamedze if he knows of any ways into Swaziland if one doesn't have a passport.

Gamedze says that there are many ways, but one, at a place called Mahamba, is the best by far. He says that it is in an area near Hlangano in Swaziland. At that place, a man by the name of Samson Mkhize lives on the Swaziland side of the border. On the South African side there is a store, and there are steps that go over the wire fence demarcating the Swaziland–South Africa border. People on the Swazi side go over that fence all the time.[31]

*

At Stanley Mabizela's house in Swaziland on 6 November, Peter Gamedze meets Albert Dhlomo.

Gamedze hands over a letter and bag that Gwala asked him to give to Mabizela. Afterwards, Gamedze says he is going to meet the 'parcels'.

Gamedze heads to a market in Manzini. He finds Samson Mkhize's wife there. He asks her to lead the way to the house, as he is not sure of the route.

Peter and Sylvia Gamedze then leave with Mrs Mkhize in the direction of Hlangano, where they arrive at 4 p.m.

Four hours later, when there is still no sign of the youngsters, the Gamedzes and Mrs Mkhize return to Manzini.

They meet Dhlomo, who asks if the parcels arrived.

Peter Gamedze says no, they didn't.[32]

*

Anton Xaba is at his workplace when Harry Gwala arrives.

Gwala raises the issue of 'Mandla' and the other boys who were supposed to have left for Swaziland last time. They didn't arrive, Gwala says.

Gwala and Xaba then arrange that Xaba must again establish a place for the boys to sleep in Macabisa, and that they must try to make the crossing again on Thursday 13 November.

Just before dawn on 13 November at a kraal in Edendale, Anton Xaba tells Mandla Sikhosana, Madi Ntombela, Ntu Khumalo, Edgar Zondi and Philemon Mokoena that it is time.

As they leave, they find a car belonging to a man called 'Mdubane' (real name Alson Nzama). They enter his car, and Xaba tells Nzama that these are people he must take to Swaziland.

The boys enter the car, leaving Xaba behind, and travel towards the Swaziland border. When they get to a place with a gate leading across the border into Swaziland, they stop. At the gate there are policemen and four or five kraals close by.

Nzama asks the boys, 'Where are these people that you people are coming to?'

The expected couriers are not there yet, so the group waits a while.

After about two hours, Nzama says that he can't see these people, so he is going back.

On their return to Pietermaritzburg, the youngsters meet Anton Xaba between 8.30 and 9 p.m. Xaba says, 'It doesn't matter – we'll go another day if there is a way out for us to go.'[33]

*

At Alson Nzama's home, Harry Gwala takes out a map. He points to Umhloseni on it and says to Nzama: 'These boys should get off here, Nyamane River. They were just lazy to walk – they didn't want to walk on foot.' Gwala says he wants to see Nzama again the next day.

The following morning, Gwala arrives and hands Nzama R120 in R10 notes. He says the R100 is for taking the boys again and R20 is outstanding from the last trip.

Nzama then follows Gwala in his car to a place where they meet the boys. After the youngsters enter Nzama's car, Gwala leaves. This time there are six of them, only three of whom had travelled with Nzama on the 13th.

They travel on the same road towards Piet Retief as before.

On the way, Nzama speaks to one of the boys, 'Mandla', whom he knows. Nzama tells him he had better support his mother because she no longer has anybody if he is gone.

The car stops near a big house in Mahamba at approximately midday, and the six all get off.

Nzama leaves them and returns to Pietermaritzburg.[34]

*

At 2.30 a.m. on Sunday 30 November, Anton Xaba is awoken by six Special Branch members – five white and one black.

On the way to the police station, a Warrant Officer Lamprecht tells Xaba that the police intercepted a group of whom they shot two and captured four.

Lamprecht says one of the arrestees was Mandla Sikhosana, who admitted Xaba was responsible for arranging for him to exit the country to receive military training.

As the police van arrives at the station, Lamprecht warns Xaba to think very carefully what he is going to tell them about this.[35]

*

Jacob Zuma flees South Africa in December 1975 to escape the wave of arrests following the interception of the group of recruits on the border the previous month.[36]

*

Mosima Sexwale's sister Magirly meets Naledi Tsiki and tells him that the police visited her family's home and asked her brother where 'Tokyo's' friend stays. The brother said he didn't know.

Sexwale's sister warns Tsiki to be careful now.

On the following day, Selaelo Ramusi approaches Tsiki's house, but thinks better of going further when he finds policemen in position around it.

Ramusi manages to find Tsiki and tells him that there were policemen at his house.

Shortly thereafter, in Swaziland, Tsiki meets Mosima Sexwale and tells him not to go home. Tsiki also meets Keith Mokoape and Albert Dhlomo during this visit.

Tsiki returns to South Africa and meets Christopher Manye. Tsiki says he is leaving the country, and that Manye must remain and take charge of the machinery.

Early one morning shortly after this, Tsiki is on the side of a road in the East Rand, trying to hitch-hike to Swaziland.

A car stops. To Tsiki's surprise, Selaelo Ramusi is the driver.

The two travel to Swaziland.[37]

*

Ramusi and Tsiki are asleep in the bedroom of a house in Manzini when, around midnight, they are awoken by Albert Dhlomo who tells them it is time to leave.

Shortly afterwards, Dhlomo introduces them to 'Duma', who he says will take them to Mozambique. Keith Mokoape is also present during this discussion.

Bafana Duma, a veteran of the sabotage campaign in Natal in the early 1960s, drives Mokoape, Ramusi and Tsiki in a Volkswagen Beetle along the main road to the Mozambique border. About two kilometres from the Namaacha checkpoint, he stops.

While Mokoape remains in the car, Duma leads Ramusi and Tsiki about two and a half kilometres through the bush until they come to a fence that Duma says is the border (the official checkpoint lies directly to the east).

The three creep through the fence and into Mozambique. Duma tells them to wait next to a rough track road running parallel to the fence. Duma bids them farewell and returns to Swaziland.

Two or three hours later a light-coloured Land Rover stops. There are two men in the car. One of them, the passenger, is Mongameli Tshali (former Luthuli Detachment commander), who introduces himself as 'Lennox'.

The driver is wearing a FRELIMO uniform, but doesn't give his name. The Land Rover heads to Maputo (formerly 'Can Phumo') and stops at a block of flats where ordinary civilians, mostly white, live.[38]

*

Days before Christmas 1975, Mosima Sexwale is part of another group led by Bafana Duma into Mozambique. Sexwale's brother Joseph, a man named Patrick and a woman called Mavis are the other group members. They also cross illegally in the vicinity of the Namaacha border post. On the other side they find FRELIMO border guards. Duma introduces himself to them. Thereafter the recruits are taken, without Duma, in a truck to a nearby village, where they are dropped off at a house under the care of an old man.

On the afternoon following, a FRELIMO soldier and Mongameli Tshali arrive to collect the cadres. The recruits are taken to a place where Tshali sleeps in Maputo. It is next to Machava Prison.

A day later, the recruits are driven in a black-coloured official FRELIMO car to Maputo Airport. They board an East African Airways plane to Tanzania and arrive in Dar es Salaam at about 8 p.m.

A young man and Eric Mtshali, a grey-haired ANC official, meet them. The young man drives Mtshali and the recruits from the airport to an old dilapidated house in Temeke, on Dar es Salaam's southern outskirts. Mtshali introduces them to a group of about fourteen South Africans who are already there. Among the fourteen are Naledi Tsiki and Selaelo Ramusi.[39]

*

One day Mzwai Piliso and Oliver Tambo arrive at the house in Temeke. They are in the company of a third man, whom Piliso introduces as Joseph Nduli.

Piliso says that Nduli is the only individual from the Wankie campaign to have got through to South Africa (perhaps overlooking the leader of Nduli's reconnaissance group during that campaign, Zolile Nqose, and indeed James April).

Nduli becomes the commander of the camp.[40]

*

Over a lunch of fish and cooked bananas, Oliver Tambo, sporting thick, black-rimmed spectacles, speaks to the twenty-odd young cadres in Temeke.

They pepper him with questions: why don't we hear you on Radio Freedom talking about your diplomatic work; why is your image not on ANC leaflets distributed in South Africa; why can't the ANC obtain a more powerful transmitter for Radio Freedom that can bypass the state's jamming devices; why no military attacks inside South Africa; why are you still only 'acting president'?

Tambo answers all the questions. He then poses a few himself, asking them about their health, about their stay in Tanzania, and also about life back home.[41]

*

One morning in January 1976, two cars – a Fiat and a Soviet-origin vehicle – come to Temeke and take a group including Mosima Sexwale to Dar es Salaam Airport. This group is then flown in a large Aeroflot plane to Moscow.

Selaelo Ramusi and Naledi Tsiki are left behind in the Tanzanian house, but not long thereafter they are also taken from Temeke and flown to East Germany.[42]

*

Siphiwe Nyanda tells his parents in February 1976 that he plans to leave the country.

'I hope it is not what I think,' his father says.

That evening Nyanda is in Swaziland, staying at Albert Dhlomo's house. Shortly thereafter Nyanda is conveyed to Mozambique.[43]

*

Samson Lukhele receives a visitor in Mahlabatini in Natal in February 1976.

It is Jacob Zuma, back from Swaziland. Zuma says he has people who he would like Lukhele to transport. The people are in Durban.

Lukhlele says his rate will be R100 for the trip.

Zuma says 'Mtukuzi' will pay. He says he will go to Durban and when he has made all the arrangements he will come back and confirm the details.[44]

*

In the same month, Stanley Nkosi and Kgalema Motlanthe (of the cell formed by Siphiwe Nyanda) are transported blindfolded in a car near Manzini, Swaziland.

They arrive at the house of Tim Maseko, who is the principal of St Christopher's School.

Joseph Nduli, back from Tanzania, meets them there. He starts training them in the use of explosives.

A week later, with the training complete, Nduli covers two blocks of Russian-made TNT in paper that is usually used to wrap toilet soap. He takes this parcel and a piece of safety fuse one and a half inches long and places them in a large cigarette box.

He then places two detonators – one electric, one regular – in another large cigarette container.

Motlanthe and Nkosi meet Keith Mokoape later that day with these two cigarette boxes in their possession. Mokoape tells them that in South Africa a man named Joseph Moseu will have a place where they can store the explosives.[45]

*

Edna Zuma hears a knock on the door of her house in Umlazi township one afternoon.

'Enter,' she says.

Two men, Joseph Mdluli (aka 'Mtukuzi') and Jacob Zuma (no relation to her), come in and she offers them a place to sit.

Jacob Zuma is wearing glasses and a cap pulled down over his face.

Edna Zuma greets him.

Mdluli then says, 'Sit down – we have come to visit you.' After she sits, he continues: 'We have come to you – there is something we wish you to keep.'

After a back-and-forth discussion lasting a while, Mdluli asks Zuma to produce 'the thing'. It appears to Edna Zuma to be a bundle of R10 notes.

'This is the thing we wish you to keep,' Mdluli says.

Jacob Zuma then counts out R110 in R10 notes, and repeats twice over, making for three R110 bundles spread out on the table.

Mdluli then counts the money himself.

Edna Zuma asks what the money is for.

To take kids to school, Mdluli says.

When she accepts the money, they leave.[46]

*

Jacob Zuma returns to Mahlabatini and tells Samson Lukhele that Mdluli will give him everything he needs and that the people to be transported will also be provided by Mdluli.[47]

*

In Johannesburg in March 1976, Petrus Nchabeleng, once the Atteridgeville section leader of the MK Pretoria Command, meets a Mr Chetty and asks him how he might find a lawyer to defend him in the case he faces for breaching the banning order restricting him to the magisterial district of Sekhukhuneland in the northern Transvaal.

Chetty suggests going to Michael Jordan of the South African Council of Churches, who may know where to find Advocate Bowman.

Nchabeleng meets Jordan, who takes him to the house of Martin Ramokgadi.

During this visit to Johannesburg, besides talks with Ramokgadi, Nchabeleng also holds a lengthy discussion with John Nkadimeng, who is the chairman of the ANC's 'Main Machinery', consisting of former political prisoners.[48]

*

South African cabinet ministers Jimmy Kruger, Owen Horwood, Connie Mulder, Marais Steyn, Andries Treurnicht, Piet Koornhof, Punt Janson, Hilgard Muller and Hennie Smit receive copies of a pamphlet on 10 March 1976 titled 'The ANC says to Vorster and his racist regime', which claims that South Africa and its Western allies were caught out trying to recolonise Africa. It warns: 'Africa will smash you, Vorster.'[49]

The message refers to South Africa's military intervention in Angola in mid-October 1975 which aimed to bolster UNITA and the FNLA against the MPLA in the build-up to that territory's independence the following month. The invasion, however, prompted a Cuban military intervention, which in November 1975 checked the advance of the South Africans, who by March 1976 have withdrawn to the extreme south of Angola.[50]

*

Joseph 'Mtukuzi' Mdluli arrives at a taxi rank in Durban with four teenage boys on 11 March. He walks up to Samson Lukhele and says: 'Here are the people. Tell Zuma these were the only ones I was able to find.'

'No, that's all right. I will tell him,' Lukhele says, before taking the youngsters away in his Volkswagen 75 Combi, leaving Mdluli behind.

On the way, Lukhele picks up a man called Vezimuni Sibiya, whose girlfriend boards the Combi with him. The vehicle passes Pongola on the road leading to Piet Retief.

The bus reaches a bridge and stops. Lukhele tells Sibiya to take the vehicle and park it just on the other side of the bridge. While Sibiya does so, Lukhele waits with the boys.

Lukhele strikes a match three times.

There is no response.

About half an hour later Jacob Zuma appears from the bush. Zuma is in the company of Joseph Nduli, his colleague in the ANC's Swaziland-based structures.

Zuma and Lukhele greet each other, but Lukhele asks: 'Who is this person accompanying you?'

'Ngwane,' Zuma says.

Lukhele asks where he is from.

Zuma says he is from Natal, 'but he is now in Swaziland'. Zuma asks Lukhele whether he has got the boys or not.

Lukhele says yes, but only four.

Zuma says that is all right and that he must bring them. Zuma then asks Lukhele to inform Mdluli that everything is going smoothly and that he wants other recruits to be sent the following Thursday.[51]

*

That following Thursday, 18 March, Joseph Mdluli accompanies his relative, Jabulani Mdluli, and two other boys, namely Sibongiseni Vilakazi and Sipho Makhubo, by bus to town. They alight at the Durban bus rank.

While walking in the direction of the nearby Indian cemetery, Joseph Mdluli takes another boy aside and moves away.

Vilakazi, Makhubo, and the younger Mdluli continue walking without the older Mdluli in the direction of a bridge on the Indian cemetery side of the bus rank. There they meet four other boys: Sipho Chiliza, Bheki Miya, Bafana Khuzwayo and Sifiso Mapanza.

A little while later, Joseph Mdluli reappears where the boys are standing, and takes the whole group to a Volkswagen Combi parked on the road next to the cemetery. The Combi is maroon with a white roof. There are already two men inside.

Mdluli says to them before they depart that they are going to a place near the border where there will be others who will ask, 'Are you a goat?' – to which they must respond, 'Yes, I am a goat.'[52]

*

That same night, Joseph 'Mtukuzi' Mdluli goes to answer the door of his Lamontville home. He is dressed only in a raincoat and shoes.

A group of Security Branch policemen pounce and lead him away.[53]

*

The seven recruits (Jabulani Mdluli, Sibongiseni Vilakazi, Sipho Makhubo, Sipho Chiliza, Bheki Miya, Bafana Khuzwayo and Sifiso Mapanza) who crossed the border into Swaziland earlier in the evening are transferred in a white Land Rover to a single-storey house opposite a Methodist church located high on a hill at the end of a twisting dirt road, in an area called Fairview some four kilometres out from Manzini's city centre.[54]

It is about midnight on the 18th and the youngsters enter a small room. Albert Dhlomo introduces himself using his proper name.

Joseph Nduli is also there and exclaims: 'These are still young boys, their eyes are still very good, they will be able to point a gun very well to go in between the eyes or the forehead.'

Sifiso Mapanza asks out loud: 'But what kind of work is this then that we are going to do?'[55]

*

Samson Lukhele is arrested by the South African Police on 19 March.[56]

*

On the evening of the 19th, Sifiso Mapanza, Sipho Chiliza, Bheki Miya and Bafana Khuzwayo are moved from the Fairview house to another residence on Albert Dhlomo's orders.[57]

*

On 20 March, security policemen arrive at Joseph Mdluli's home in Lamontville and tell his wife Lydia that her husband has died in police custody.[58]

*

The 21st of March is Sharpeville Day in the ANC's calendar. On that day in 1976, Tim Jenkin and Stephen Lee are on the observation deck at the top floor of the Carlton Centre, Johannesburg's tallest building.

They have telescopes, and with them they observe the scene below as police cars flash their sirens and policemen scramble to clear away the pamphlets that have been spread by leaflet bombs planted by Jenkin and Lee.[59]

*

At 6 a.m. the following morning, Sipho Makhubo and Jabulani Mdluli peep round the corner of Dhlomo and Zuma's room to see if they are still asleep.

They are. Makhubo and Mdluli then go and wash. When finished, Makhubo goes again to see whether the men are still asleep.

After confirming that they still are, Makhubo, Mdluli and Sibongiseni Vilakazi head to the dining room. It is locked. Makhubo goes to another room and takes the key out of the lock. He brings the set of keys to the dining room to see if one of them will fit the door there. He finds that one does. They open the dining-room door slightly, in order to minimise noise. Makhubo exits first, then Mdluli and lastly Vilakazi.

They run until they reach a road.

At the nearest police station, the trio report their story.

The police make a visit to the Fairview house, but find nobody there. A second visit also yields nothing. However, while standing there the police see Jacob Zuma approaching and they arrest him.

Later Albert Dhlomo arrives via another road and is also arrested.[60]

Thabo Mbeki is arrested the following day on the roadside between Manzini and the Mozambique border, where he had gone to expedite the withdrawal of Makhubo, Mdluli and Vilakazi to Maputo to be interrogated by ANC security.[61]

*

On the evening of Thursday 25 March, Major Jacobus de Swardt is part of a nine-man police force – four white and five black – who have accompanied Samson Lukhele to the crossing point on the Pongola–Piet Retief road where the deliveries on 11 and 18 March took place.

After waiting for a couple of hours, they decide that it is likely nothing will happen that night so they opt to go home. They get up out of the bush and walk back towards the Combi.

As Joseph Nduli and Curnick Ndlovu (the former chairman of the MK Natal Command during the sabotage campaign) approach the bridge on the Pongola–Piet Retief road from the bush on the Swaziland side of the border, they see the lights of the Combi start moving in the direction of Pongola, upon which Nduli flashes his torch twice. The vehicle stops a few hundred yards beyond the bridge. It is now between 8 and 9 p.m.

When Major de Swardt's team reach the Combi, the black sergeant driver tells De Swardt that while they were out in the grass, a light on the Swazi side of the border appeared; it looked like a torch being carried by a person walking toward the border fence.

The group get into the Combi and travel back to the signboard next to the bridge that marks the speed limit as 50 km/h. They stop next to this signboard, off the tarmac, with park lights on.

Lukhele exits to try to make contact again. He closes the door and goes to the border fence, where he strikes a match.

When Nduli sees this he says to Ndlovu: 'Oh, it is Lukhele.'

Lukhele comes down and stands in front of Nduli, greeting him and Ndlovu. 'Why are you so late?' he asks.

'We had lost our way,' Nduli responds.

'Who is this young man accompanying you?'

'Cleopas Ndlovu.'

Lukhele returns to the Combi, and speaks to the policemen inside. From the open door on the passenger side, which is invisible to Nduli and Ndlovu, the police pour out of the vehicle.

Lieutenants Fourie and Winter reach Nduli and Ndlovu first and grab them. Their colleagues come and help. Fourie tries to bind their hands with rope, but he doesn't succeed because they resist fiercely.

Nduli cries out and struggles furiously but is overpowered. A rope is tied tightly around his neck, his hands are fixed behind his back, and a handkerchief is pushed into his mouth.

As for Ndlovu, when a black member of the police team surnamed Mngadi tries to place a rope around his neck, he manages to bite Mngadi on *his* neck.

Eventually, however, Ndlovu is outmuscled, loaded into the Combi and driven away, blindfolded.[62]

*

In arresting Joseph Nduli the police recover documents in his possession that mention the existence of a group operating in Johannesburg. One of the documents relates to Madoda Alex Nkosi.[63]

*

The Security Branch visit Stanley Nkosi's home and speak to his father.

When his father returns from the conversation he tells the family that the police told him that his son Alex has left the country. The father says they showed him a photo of Alex wearing a striped tie, indicating that the Security Branch have got a hold of his passport.[64]

*

On 22 April 1976, Stanley Nkosi is arrested by the South African Police.[65]

*

On the following day, the police arrest Nkosi's cell partner, Kgalema Motlanthe.[66] Motlanthe and Nkosi will be sentenced in 1977 to ten years' imprisonment, which they will serve on Robben Island.[67]

*

In the middle of May 1976, Selaelo Ramusi and Naledi Tsiki return to Tanzania from East Germany.

Eric Mtshali's assistant 'Jimmy' drives them to the University of Dar es Salaam campus and drops them off at a block of flats where the majority of the lecturers live.

Jimmy tells them that if anybody asks them who they are, they should say they are South African students waiting to go to Europe for further studies, but they mustn't leave the campus.

On the day of their arrival, they are met in their flat by Joe Modise and Joe Slovo, who are accompanied by Eric Mtshali.

Modise asks them how they enjoyed their training and what it involved; he says that he and Slovo are in the city to attend a meeting of the Revolutionary Council.[68]

IV

ARMED PROPAGANDA

SOWETO GENERATION

When Murphy Morobe finishes putting on his school uniform and prepares to leave his house between 6 and 6.30 a.m. on Wednesday 16 June 1976, he feels his heart racing and cold droplets of sweat trickling down his spine. Neatly tucked inside his bag is a banner reading 'Down with Afrikaans'.

Later that morning at Morris Isaacson High School in Soweto, Morobe is present during a religious assembly led by the principal, Lekgau Mathabathe, and Fanyana Mazibuko. When the prayers are over, Mathabathe and Mazibuko depart, allowing Tsietsi Mashinini, one of the students, to take over. Mashinini is chairman of an 'Action Committee' of the South African Students' Movement (SASM), which met on 13 June and endorsed a call by Mashinini for mass demonstrations to be held on the 16th against the government's decision to impose Afrikaans-medium instruction in black schools on a fifty-fifty basis with English.

After the students sing 'Senzeni Na', Mashinini leads them out of the school yard. They join up with students from other schools in the township, en route to their intended final destination, Orlando Stadium.

As the demonstrators near Orlando West Junior High, Murphy Morobe notices an old friend, Zweli Sizane, approaching through the singing, dancing, jubilant crowd. Sizane says: '*Mfowethu*, don't you think we might end up with another Sharpeville on our hands?', to which Morobe replies, '*Broer*, I hope not. But I doubt it.'[1]

Nat Serache of the *Rand Daily Mail* is looking on at what he estimates to be 10,000 students on the school's perimeter singing 'Moreno Boloka Sechaba' when four police cars, three heavy-duty vehicles and two patrol vans carrying dogs emerge at the top of the road. The convoy heads towards a hill overlooking the school. In the vehicles are about forty-eight policemen, eight white, the rest black, under the command of Johannes Kleingeld, the commanding officer of Orlando Police Station. About fifteen of them move out of their vehicles and form a line across the road. No sooner have they taken up position than another group of marchers appears to the rear of the policemen who are still on the hill.[2]

Tsietsi Mashinini and others, including Seth Mazibuko, his deputy in the Action Committee, approach the police line with their fingers raised in the peace sign. However, as they approach, a dog breaks free from a black policeman and runs into the crowd, biting a couple of protesters before being stoned to death by the now enraged students, some of whom also hurl stones at the police, who retaliate by throwing tear-gas canisters. Only one canister explodes. The students add the unexploded canisters to the stones they launch at the police. A baton and dog charge by the police follows, with the unintended consequence of bringing protesters to their flanks and even their rear. Thus threatened with encirclement, some of the police open fire with handguns.

Murphy Morobe and a fellow student, Hector Pieterson, are caught in the initial salvo of bullets. Morobe escapes unharmed, but Pieterson is killed. The scene descends into utter chaos, with people screaming and both children and policemen trying to escape, the former on foot and the latter in their vehicles, even if it means driving over pupils.

As Oupa Moloto flees he sees crowds attacking vehicles and buildings belonging to the government. Helicopters then appear above, firing teargas and live ammunition on groups of students, forcing the students to take shelter among houses. When Moloto arrives home he sees a helicopter above Morris Isaacson and police officers on the school roof. Rioting will spread overnight to Jabulani, Dube, Dobsonville, Meadowlands and White City.[3]

*

On 1 July, Elias Masinga, a SASM Soweto Regional Committee member who was present during the 16 June protests, travels on a train that enters Mozambique from South Africa through Komatipoort. When just across the border, he produces his 'Guia' (a travel document enabling people with Mozambican relatives to enter the country on family visits) at the request of a ticket inspector. But when it becomes clear that he can't speak Portuguese or Tsonga properly, he is arrested.

Masinga is taken to Maputo's Cadea Civil Prison, where he holds a discussion with Mr Gumede, another South African detainee. After explaining the circumstances of his arrest, Masinga asks that when Gumede's son next visits he be requested to convey the information to Masinga's uncle.

Gumede agrees.

Masinga writes down his uncle's name on a piece of paper and hands it over.[4]

*

L.M. Mpotokwane, the permanent secretary in Botswana president Seretse Khama's office, receives a letter on 5 July 1976 from the country's Security Branch chief. It says the police have 'no security objection' to Keith Mokoape being posted to the country as an ANC representative, as per the South African liberation movement's request.[5]

*

Martin Ramokgadi visits the house in Alexandra township belonging to his friend, Joe Tseto.

'Do you make any money with the Combi?' Ramokgadi asks.

Tseto says yes, he does.

Ramokgadi says he also wants to buy a Combi, but would like to purchase it in Tseto's name.

Tseto asks why not in his own name?

Ramokgadi says he is not working and therefore will not be able to buy a car on a hire-purchase contract. He also doesn't have a driver's licence.

Tseto asks what will happen later if Ramokgadi can't pay; what then?

Ramogkadi tells him not to worry; his wife has died and there will be money from the insurance.[6]

*

John Nkadimeng, a colleague of Ramokgadi's in the ANC's Johannesburg-based Main Machinery, leaves for Swaziland on 24 July 1976.[7]

*

Three days later, Martin Ramokgadi and Joe Tseto visit Lindsay Saker in Johannesburg's Highlands North. Ramokgadi raises his friend R1,000 for the deposit on a Combi registered TJ 367-568.[8]

*

At 10.40 p.m. that evening, a squad of Security Branch policemen take up position outside a house in Wynberg in Cape Town.

Following a knock on the door, Anthony Holiday opens.

Major van Tonder says he has information that Holiday has been 'busy with communistic activities – with terrorism in fact'.[9]

Then at 7.30 a.m. the following morning, David and Sue Rabkin are arrested at their flat in Victoria Road, Clifton.

Lieutenant Colonel J.C. Broodryk later accompanies David Rabkin to a garage at Upton Villa on Main Road in Green Point. A haul of items are confiscated there, including two duplicators, 200 cassettes, a bucket containing piping, six packets of fire crackers, two batteries, reams of blank paper, numerous envelopes, and stamped and unstamped copies of the *African Communist*.[10]

*

'Jimmy' drives Selaelo Ramusi and Naledi Tsiki to Dar es Salaam Airport.

By the afternoon, the two MK cadres are in Maputo, where Mongameli Tshali meets them at the airport in the company of the same FRELIMO driver with whom he met the pair all those months before on the Swaziland border.

The group bypasses customs and departs in a Fiat.

A while later, they arrive at their destination, a private hotel called the 'Mona Liza'.

A week later, Moses Mabhida arrives at the hotel and tells Ramusi and Tsiki that their task will be to carry out acts of sabotage. There is a mission already waiting, he says. It is to destroy one of the railway lines linking South Africa with either Rhodesia or Mozambique.

Mabhida hands them a railway timetable for Transvaal province. He cautions them that the operation must not involve any loss of human life, because the ANC's policy is not to shed innocent blood.[11]

*

In a prison in Gaborone on 9 September, Ephraim Mfalapitsa is met by two ANC officials, namely Isaac Makopo and Keith Mokoape.

The two are allowed by the Botswana authorities to depart with Mfalapitsa to house number 2067, Bontleng, which is an ANC office-cum-residence.

Six days later, Snuki Zikalala, who escaped South Africa in 1974 on a mission to contact the ANC abroad (he was acting on behalf of a larger group of activists who like him were restricted by banning orders), visits Mfalapitsa and another man at the Bontleng property.

Zikalala hands the pair aeroplane tickets and then drives them to Gaborone Airport.

The following day, Reddy Mazimba, once of the Sekhukhuneland group in the Wankie campaign, collects Mfalapitsa and his colleague from Lusaka Airport and transports them to an ANC transit house.[12]

*

Naledi Tsiki is alone in the double room he shares with Selaelo Ramusi in the Mona Liza when the phone rings. Tsiki picks up the receiver. The receptionist says there is somebody here who wants to see him.

As Tsiki arrives at the reception shortly afterwards, he is surprised to see Élias Masinga, aka 'Roller', whom he recognises as a fellow pupil from his days as a student at Morris Isaacson High School in Soweto.

Tsiki asks how Masinga knew where to find him.

Masinga says somebody told him ANC members lived there, but he never expected to find Tsiki. He says he wants to contact the ANC.

Mongameli Tshali arrives later in the day to collect Masinga.[13]

*

At approximately 7.30 a.m. on 1 October 1976, Solomon Mahlangu arrives at Pretoria's 'A' Station and finds his friend Stephen Nkosi waiting for him there. About half an hour later, Thomas Masuku, another friend, arrives. All three are wearing creased clothes. Nkosi purchases tickets to Hectorspruit in the eastern Transvaal on the group's behalf.

When the train arrives at about eight that evening, Mahlangu recognises a face peeping through one of the windows as that of Richard Chauke. On the platform the four friends greet. Chauke helps them load their bags on the train, which pulls away a few minutes later.[14]

*

By 17 October, Selaelo Ramusi and Naledi Tsiki are being accommodated at an isolated plot on Manzini's eastern outskirts, near the main road to Mozambique. There are a few cattle grazing in the area, while on the plot itself there is a tidy wooden shack consisting of one bedroom with two beds, a kitchen and a toilet. There are no taps or other sources of water.

Ramusi and Tsiki are ready to conduct reconnaissance for the sabotage operation assigned to them by Moses Mabhida. Ian Deway Rwaxa pulls in to the plot at about 2 a.m. driving a light green Peugeot. There are two passengers on board, Henry Chiliza and Simon Mohlanyaneng.

Ramusi and Tsiki enter the vehicle, which Rwaxa drives towards the border post at Mananga. Nearing dawn, at a spot where the lights of the official checkpoint are visible about two kilometres away, Rwaxa stops the car.

Mohlanyaneng gets out with Ramusi and Tsiki, whom he marches into South Africa through the bush. The trio eventually reach a green Volkswagen Passat, in which Alois Manci and a driver named 'Mandla' are waiting.

At about 6.30 a.m. Mandla stops outside Kaapmuiden Railway Station in the eastern Transvaal. Ramusi and Tsiki get out and later board a train headed northwards.

At around 9 p.m. the pair disembark at Solomondale Station and walk eastwards towards Dikgale along the road running parallel to the railway line. All the while they inspect the structure of the adjacent train tracks.

When they reach Dikgale Station, it is about 11 p.m. They loiter a while in the waiting section, observing train traffic. The only other person on the platform is a white foreman who pays them no notice.

Between midnight and 4 a.m. no passenger trains arrive.

Ramusi and Tsiki then return south. They arrive at Kaapmuiden at about 6 p.m. on 19 October, when they meet up again with Simon Mohlanyaneng, Alois Manci and Mandla, who conveys them back to the border area in the green Passat.[15]

*

Two evenings later, Moses Mabhida arrives at the wooden shack bearing a large carrier bag and cardboard box.

Ramusi and Tsiki are there. They inspect the contents with Mabhida. Inter alia, there are two Scorpion submachine guns, two each of fully loaded ten- and twenty-round magazines, and two boxes containing twenty-five rounds of ammunition each. There are also four tins that by their labelling contain innocuous items like Nestlé Cocoa milk and Milo, but which, Mabhida says, really contain a nine-volt battery and an electric detonator. Mabhida also gives Tsiki R120.

Ian Deway Rwaxa arrives at the shack at 2 a.m. with Simon Mohlanyaneng and Henry Chiliza as passengers. They pick up the MK men and drive towards the border.

With Scorpion pistols concealed on their persons while they share the responsibility of carrying the large bag containing the explosives, Ramusi and Tsiki are led by Mohlanyaneng into South Africa through the bush in the vicinity of the checkpoint at Mananga.

Alois Manci and Mandla the driver are again waiting on the other side. This time they are in a yellow Combi, in the company of a third man, Amos Lubisi.[16]

*

On the following Monday, 25 October, having spent the weekend in Alexandra, Ramusi and Tsiki disembark from the yellow Combi at a car park in Springs. They walk around casually for a while before Ramusi approaches a brown Volkswagen Beetle. He opens its boot, has a look around in it, and then writes down a number on a piece of paper before telling Tsiki to go to a nearby key cutter's shop.

Fifteen minutes later, Tsiki returns with a key.

With it, the two enter the Beetle, which they drive to the yellow Combi, in which Simon Mohlanyaneng, Alois Manci and Mandla have been waiting. From the

Combi the group load the carrier bag containing the explosives (given by Mabhida in Swaziland) into the Beetle.

After saying their farewells, Ramusi and Tsiki head northwards. A short distance from Dikgale, they stop the Beetle on the side of the road.

Just after midnight, Tsiki makes a U-turn and drives about 100 metres back in the direction of Dikgale. At this stage he and Ramusi are holding the Scorpion pistols in their hands.

On the nearby railway tracks they lay a charge.

They are in the process of plastering the main charge (known as the 'crocodile') onto the line when they notice a train, which is coming in their direction, pull in at Dikgale Station. They run to the Beetle and speed away in it.

During the getaway it starts to rain.

Then it pours.

Back in Dikgale, the downpour causes the main charge to slip off the rails.[17]

*

When George Chabalala, a railway employee, patrols a stretch of line between Munnik and Dikgale later that morning, he notices that the screws which are supposed to go into the sleeper have been removed and the sleeper itself is damaged.

Hudson Tema, another railway worker, meanwhile finds two wires sticking out from under an undamaged section of the train tracks. Tema's discovery is near to Chabalala's, some 300 metres east of the Dikgale Station.

Police investigators arrive later. One of them, Detective Sergeant Snyders, heads to the damaged concrete sleeper and takes photographs. Colonel Strydom meanwhile unearths a red cartridge together with a tin from the undamaged section of the line that Tema noticed. The tin is found to contain plastic explosives, a switch made of tin, and a detonator attached to electric wire which in turn is connected to a battery. There are also fingerprints discernible on the tin.[18]

*

Back in Swaziland, Selaelo Ramusi and Naledi Tsiki ask Moses Mabhida to be allowed to enter South Africa on a permanent basis. After the weekend they spent in Alexandra before their operation, they feel they can settle in the township. Mabhida says he can't make this decision himself, but the two cadres press their case and he eventually relents, saying he will allow them to enter South Africa where they can try to establish themselves in Alexandra.

Mabhida returns a few days later. He tells the pair that their mission in South Africa will be to develop an ANC command structure that can cover the Transvaal, while also establishing links into Natal. He mentions in passing that they should ideally extend the structure into the Orange Free State, in addition to carrying out operations themselves. Mabhida mentions the upcoming date of 16 December, and suggests they launch an attack to coincide with the anniversary.

The three discuss the mission further, during which Mabhida agrees to follow up on their request to have Mosima Sexwale join them. But he says there is a person in Mozambique right now, 'Bra T', who can join them.[19]

*

Around the beginning of November, Simon Mohlanyaneng, Norman Tshabalala and Alois Manci hold a meeting in Alexandra township with Selaelo Ramusi, Naledi Tsiki and Lele Motaung (aka 'Bra T'), who have just infiltrated from Swaziland.

Ramusi says Mabhida ordered that Mohlanyaneng be transferred to their military cell, and also that Manci must supply them with recruits whom they can begin training.

Manci says this will need to be discussed with other members of his political cell.

Ramusi continues, saying the main problem the MK men face relates to housing.

Manci says he will discuss the issue with Martin Ramokgadi, who is their man in charge of housing.

Tshabalala interjects, saying he presently lives with his disabled brother in Brakpan. Two of the military cadres could be accommodated there.[20]

*

It soon becomes clear that the infiltration of the military cell occurred before adequate arrangements could be struck between Mabhida and the Main Machinery regarding the latter's accommodation of the MK men. The matter surfaces when Naledi Tsiki and Martin Ramokgadi meet in early November.

Tsiki raises his cell's transportation problems. Ramokgadi interrupts him, saying his understanding is that the military cell has to operate under the instructions of the political structure already established in the area.

Tsiki counters by asking where he got that idea from: 'You are supposed to give us support services.'

No, Ramokgadi says, we are the political leadership in the area, and people of the military have to work under the political leadership.

Tsiki says they *do* work under political leadership; they are directly responsible to people in the Revolutionary Council who are working under the political leadership of the ANC's National Executive Committee (i.e. Moses Mabhida) – their cell is answerable to *them*. If there are any issues Ramokgadi's unit wishes to raise, Tsiki argues, they need to raise them *there*, not with his unit. His unit has to obey the orders given to them, and as far as they are concerned, Ramokgadi's unit is supposed to give them support services while they establish themselves.[21]

*

Ian Deway Rwaxa drives Elias Masinga and another ANC member in a Volkswagen Beetle from a house in Manzini to a point near the South African border. Rwaxa asks the other man to lead Masinga across the boundary on foot and join up again on the other side.

Masinga and guide cross the border fence, and in South Africa they again meet Rwaxa, who drives Masinga to Meadowlands in Soweto.

In Soweto, Masinga meets with Murphy Morobe and Billy Masetlha, two of his colleagues in the Soweto Regional Committee of SASM.

Masinga says he succeeded in the mission he was assigned. He managed to report to the ANC on their group's activities. The ANC for its part expressed an interest in working hand in hand with them.[22]

*

Following the MPLA's victory in the Angolan Civil War, it has decided to make camps available to the ANC in the country.

Ephraim Mfalapitsa, Roderick Dhlamini, Abel Maake and Isaac Maroe are among twenty-five cadres who are driven to Dar es Salaam Airport on 26 November 1976. The group includes both men and women. The men have been collected from the ANC's transit facility for male recruits in Temeke, and the women from Mzana, another transit residence in Temeke, but for female cadres.

At Dar es Salaam Airport, the twenty-five board an East African Airways flight to Angola.

In Luanda they are met by Angolan soldiers who take them from the airport in military trucks. Their destination is a camp called 'Engineering' on Luanda's outskirts. They find approximately 50 Cubans, 300 Angolan Army (FAPLA) troops, and 130 MK cadres already there.[23]

*

The ANC's representatives in Swaziland compile a document titled 'Addendum to Detailed Report. Area Q', which in part addresses the refugee situation in the country.

It estimates that while in excess of 1,500 refugees have gone to Botswana, about 150 have entered Swaziland, where they are being accommodated at a reformatory in the Malkerns Valley. The report says it is necessary to explain how the student refugees initially came to the kingdom. The first batch consisted of some youngsters from Soweto who identified themselves with the PAC and had actually been engaged in recruiting for the PAC inside South Africa.

As the stream of refugees increased, the PAC proved unable to cope, so it appealed to the Swazi government for help. Hence the establishment of the camp, to which the ANC was initially denied access. Over time, however, and following constant reports of defections from the camp, an agreement was reached whereby the PAC committed itself to hand over anybody who wished to join the ANC.

And now, the report continues, 'Veiled overtures have been made to us to interest ourselves in the students. Since these overtures are not official we have steadfastly refused to be directly involved as we have no desire to be involved in any kind of skirmish with the P.A.C. on SD. soil.'[24]

*

Ian Deway Rwaxa transports Elias Masinga, Murphy Morobe and Billy Masetlha from Soweto to the Nerston border post. It is now close to the end of November.

The three passengers get out of the car and enter Swaziland through the bush.

They meet up again with Rwaxa on the other side. He drives them to Manzini.

On the following day, Masetlha, Masinga, Morobe and Rwaxa meet Moses Mabhida, Stanley Mabizela, John Nkadimeng and Henry Chiliza from the ANC.

Masetlha briefs the ANC men on the activities within South Africa of the SASM and the Soweto Students' Representative Council (SSRC), which is the name adopted by the old Action Committee of the SASM at a meeting held early in August.

Mention is made at one point of an idea Masetlha, Masinga and Morobe have of proceeding to Mozambique for military training.

Mabhida responds that the ANC has taken a resolution that it should establish training within South Africa because its camps are overflowing – the movement wants a quicker turnaround time and accordingly has begun establishing a machinery inside South Africa. So, he asks, 'Do you want to proceed or go back?'

They opt to go back.[25]

*

Mosima Sexwale is now being housed in the wooden shack to the east of Manzini where Selaelo Ramusi and Naledi Tsiki were previously accommodated.

Moses Mabhida meets him there and says Sexwale is going to be sent to South Africa. In Alexandra he must join 'Chris' (Naledi Tsiki), 'David' (Selaelo Ramusi), 'Peter' (Lele Motaung) and 'Bafana' (Simon Mohlanyaneng). Mabhida says he wants the cell's command structure reconfigured, and that Sexwale should take over from 'Chris' as commander, 'David' should remain political commissar, and 'Peter' must stay as logistics chief.

Mabhida asks for Sexwale's input regarding the placement of 'Bafana'.

Sexwale says he doesn't know him.

Mabhida tells him to decide on how to utilise Bafana after he has entered the country.[26]

*

Sergeant Jackson Makushe is driving towards the Bordergate–Mananga checkpoint between South Africa and Swaziland on the morning of 30 November 1976. About three kilometres from the border post on the South African side he notices three people sitting on a fence on the right-hand side of the road. There is another person on the left-hand side, looking in the direction of the border post.

The four men, namely Amos Lubisi, Alois Manci, Mosima Sexwale and Selaelo Ramusi, all avert their gaze when Makushe passes.

Makushe reports this at the checkpoint to Constable Brits, who sets off with Sergeant Khoza to investigate.

At about 8 a.m. the four men are gathered together by the fence when they notice a Land Rover approaching. It stops next to them. Constable Brits, in civilian dress, and Sergeant Khoza, in uniform, emerge.

When asked where they are from, Lubisi says, 'Magudu.'

Nobody replies to the next question of what the suitcase in the group's possession contains.

When asked to open the suitcase, Manci says he doesn't have a key.

At this point, the four are ordered to enter the back of the Land Rover.[27]

*

In the back of the police van, Sexwale is seated directly behind the driver (Constable Brits), and Alois Manci directly behind the passenger (Sergeant Khoza). Manci and Sexwale have their backs to the cabin. Ramusi is sitting directly opposite Sexwale at the back of the Land Rover, and Amos Lubisi opposite Manci. The group's suitcase sits alongside a paper carrier at the centre of the floor. Ramusi is also holding a carrier bag.

The vehicle heads towards the checkpoint. Some ten or fifteen seconds into the journey, Ramusi tells his colleagues that he has a hand grenade wrapped inside some paper. He then removes some paper from his pocket and hands it over to Sexwale, who removes the wrapping and finds an already-primed grenade.

Sexwale pulls out the safety ring and leans his body to the left. He then bends forward, thereby overlooking the driver's window.

Sexwale is holding the ledge at the top of the cabin with his left hand. Sergeant Khoza can actually see his face through the window on the driver's side. Khoza tells Brits that somebody wants to speak to him.

'What do you say?' Brits replies – he can't hear Khoza over the din of the car.

Since they are very near the checkpoint, Khoza decides to keep his peace and resumes looking out of the front window.

Sexwale then throws his grenade through the open window. It is a defensive hand grenade with a delay action.

Four seconds later it explodes, seriously injuring both men. Brits applies pressure on the brakes causing the vehicle to slow.

The ANC men in the back escape, taking their bags with them.

Before the vehicle comes to a complete stop, Sergeant Khoza opens the door and falls out. Brits meanwhile collapses on to the tarred road with injuries that will leave him paralysed for life. Khoza hands his revolver to Brits and runs towards Bordergate for assistance.

On his way he sees a Combi with the registration number TJ 323-510 approaching. The driver is Norman Tshabalala, on his way to collect Lubisi, Manci, Ramusi and Sexwale.

The four ANC men continue running till they reach a bushy area. Sexwale orders Lubisi to march in front since he is from the area. Ramusi is second, Sexwale third and Manci fourth as they head back towards the Swaziland border. Having safely crossed the border fence and entered the kingdom, they manage to hitch-hike to Manzini, where they get a taxi to Fairview. There they find Henry Chiliza. When they try to tell him what happened, he says he heard the story on the radio and guessed it was them.[28]

*

G.M. Basele, the Lobatse district commissioner, writes a letter to President Seretse Khama's permanent secretary on 2 December.

Basele notes that he convened a meeting on 15 November that was attended by thirty-six refugees. He gives some details of the proceedings. One point made by the refugees was that the police were forcing them to leave Botswana and join military groupings. South African Students' Organisation representatives complained of being forced to join the ANC against their will. Others claimed the ANC was pretending to represent all refugees, which was untrue, but led to the ANC being allowed to take people away for military training. An allegation was also made that people were being hurried out of Botswana before they could complete immigration formalities or appear before the Refugee Advisory Board.

Basele notes that these complaints chime with his own experience that South African students have on occasion been collected from Lobatse Police Station by ANC representatives and sent for training before they could appear before the Refugee Advisory Board.[29]

*

On the evening of 5 December, Henry Chiliza arrives at the wooden shack east of Manzini and finds Mosima Sexwale and Selaelo Ramusi there. Chiliza says that Ian Deway Rwaxa has come.

At about midnight, Chiliza drives Ramusi, Rwaxa, Sexwale and Alois Manci in a brown Peugeot from Fairview towards the Nerston border post.

At 2 a.m., about a kilometre from the border, Chiliza stops the car, and Rwaxa, Ramusi and Sexwale get out. Rwaxa is carrying a twenty-litre tin of petrol and they are all holding pistols.

The trio then enter a forested area, and through it reach the border fence, which they cross, thereby entering South Africa. Rwaxa then leaves Ramusi and Sexwale.

A while later he returns as a passenger in a Volkswagen Passat driven by Mr Bonnie Sikhakhane. Petrol from the tin Rwaxa carried across the border is poured into the Passat, which then heads to Johannesburg.[30]

*

The Brakpan Murder and Robbery Squad raid a house in 8th Avenue, Alexandra, on the morning of 9 December. There they find Mosima Sexwale and Naledi Tsiki.

It is a false alarm. The policemen say they are looking for 'Rodger Makao', and Sexwale and Tsiki are released from Brakpan Police Station later that morning when it is concluded that they will be of no use in finding him.[31]

*

Petrus Nchabeleng, a former Robben Island prisoner who had been a section leader in MK's Pretoria Command during the sabotage campaign in the early 1960s, is at his home in Apél in Sekhukhuneland on 10 December 1976 when he sees a Combi arrive in which his old friend Martin Ramokgadi is the passenger.

When the Combi stops, two further passengers alight from the back seats.

Ramokgadi introduces them as 'Solly' and 'David', and in turn he introduces Nchabeleng to Sexwale and Ramusi as a 'comrade' from Robben Island. Ramokgadi then asks Nchabeleng how far he has progressed with arranging people for training.

Nchabeleng replies that he has found a local man while his son Elleck has recruited two friends. Nchabeleng adds he will contact another 'comrade' from Robben Island who is living in the area.

'Can we begin the training today?' asks Sexwale.

Nchabeleng says it is better to start in a few days' time when he has had a chance to see this other comrade.

Sexwale leaves a trunk containing weapons for Nchabeleng to store until then.[32]

Back in Alexandra that evening, Sexwale informs Naledi Tsiki that Selaelo Ramusi and Norman Tshabalala will be leaving shortly for Swaziland.

On the morning after this, Sexwale and Tsiki meet again. Sexwale says Tsiki will be sent somewhere in the Pietersburg area to lie low because Alexandra is getting unsafe.[33]

At around the same time that Tsiki leaves for the northern Transvaal, Joe Gqabi and Selaelo Ramusi head for Swaziland. Their mission in the kingdom is to consult the ANC abroad about the as yet unresolved issue that arose during Tsiki's conversation with Martin Ramokgadi in November, regarding how best to coordinate the activities of the movement's political and military underground structures within South Africa.[34]

*

Ian Deway Rwaxa and Henry Chiliza enter a small room in Fairview, Swaziland, on 15 December and find Selaelo Ramusi there.

Norman Tshabalala has not made the journey. Ramusi tells Rwaxa that 'Norman' has run away and they are worried that he will report to the police. He instructs Rwaxa to leave for Alexandra and warn the comrades to seek new hideouts.

Later on the 15th, Rwaxa is at the Oshoek border post. He produces a Lesotho passport, numbered B252785, made out to 'Mr Khafa Joseph Serobanyane'. It features Rwaxa's photograph, but the rest of the document is different from the travel document numbered 392381 and made out in Rwaxa's own name on which he has crossed the Swaziland–South Africa border on many occasions over the previous months.

The discrepancy is noted and Rwaxa is arrested at passport control. He is then taken to Ermelo Police Station.[35]

*

Two days later, Mosima Sexwale returns to Apél in a car driven by a certain 'Morgan'.

On the afternoon of the following day, Sexwale asks Petrus Nchabeleng about the whereabouts of the weapons.

Nchabeleng says they are with Lekgoro. He then sends his son Elleck to fetch the trunk and bring it to the river.

About fifteen minutes later, Elleck Nchabeleng appears at the nearby Oliphants River carrying a grenade and a Tokarev pistol. He tells his father and Sexwale that the 'builder' will follow with the Scorpion.

Sexwale then takes Elleck Nchabeleng and two boys, 'Molege' and 'Aaron', to a spot among some bushes on the banks of the river, and begins training them in the use of the gun and grenade.[36]

*

A couple of days later, Sexwale is transported back to Alexandra, having completed the course. At about 7 p.m. he is with Simon Mohlanyaneng at Joe Tseto's house.

Sexwale asks Tseto for a lift to Baragwanath.

Tseto agrees.

In Baragwanath, Sexwale meets Super Moloi, a representative of the SSRC. Sexwale tells Tseto he can go back to Alexandra.

Moloi and Sexwale then take a taxi to Zondi, where they meet Elias Masinga, Billy Masetlha and Murphy Morobe.

The five proceed to Dobsonville. There, in an outside room, Sexwale begins training the SSRC recruits in the assemblage and disassemblage of the Tokarev pistol.

The training continues the following evening in the same room. Sexwale takes the SSRC men through the steps for using the Scorpion pistol. He also offers them rudimentary political training. He tells them the ANC was previously an all-African organisation. He discusses the Freedom Charter, saying that with the ANC it is not a matter of 'down' with the white man, but rather of joining hands with the white man to bring about the defeat of the present government.[37]

*

Ian Deway Rwaxa is lying on the back seat of a police vehicle driven by a Lieutenant Coetzee in the direction of Krugersdorp on 30 December 1976. Rwaxa's clothes are bloodstained, his face swollen.

He is locked up overnight in a cell at Krugersdorp Police Station.[38]

Warrant Officer van Niekerk is among a group of policemen under Captain Mahoney's command that arrives at No. 142, 6th Avenue in Alexandra at approximately 3.50 the following morning.

In the bedroom at the back of the house, Van Niekerk finds Mosima Sexwale standing, dressed only in his trousers.

Asked who he is, Sexwale says 'Solomon Khumalo'. He claims that he comes from Newcastle where he owns a butchery, and that he has been in Johannesburg for three weeks.

Van Niekerk demands to see a reference book. Sexwale produces one issued to Batsoba Solomon Khumalo. Sexwale's photograph appears in the passbook.[39]

Sexwale is taken out of the house in handcuffs. One of the policemen shines a torch in his face.

From a waiting car, a voice which Sexwale recognises as Joe Tseto's says, 'That's him.'[40] Tseto, captured earlier, has been brought along by the police to perform identifications.

*

Elias Masinga, Super Moloi, Billy Masetlha and Murphy Morobe are arrested the same night at Alois Manci's house in Jabulani, Soweto.[41]

*

Petrus Nchabeleng is arrested at 11 p.m. on 2 January 1977.

He is walked to a place where fifteen Security Branch vehicles are parked. A colonel tells him they have already arrested 'Solly' – he is in one of the cars.

Nchabeleng is made to stand in front of one of the vehicles. The lights of this car are turned on so he can be identified.[42]

Naledi Tsiki is then arrested by about five policemen at Nchabeleng's household the following evening.[43]

*

On 22 January 1977, at MK's 'Engineering' camp outside Luanda, Angola, MK recruits pile into megabuses that can hold 100 people each. Led by Cuban escorts, the vehicles head southwards. En route, they see overturned trucks and roadsigns with gunshot holes pierced through them. At one stage they travel across a bridge made of planks.

After a journey lasting fifteen to seventeen hours, at about 4 p.m. they reach their destination: a wide open arid space which is empty but for a double-storey house used by Cuban guards, and a large building about twenty metres behind it that resembles a barn and has a construction attached that looks as if it was once used as a marketplace.

The venue is on the outskirts of the town of Benguela. After the recruits have finished offloading their belongings, Mzwai Piliso, who has accompanied the group, calls an assembly. His first words are 'Welcome to our new camp in Benguela.' The recruits all laugh.

After a while the realisation dawns on them that it is no joke; this is to be the site of the ANC's next Angolan camp.[44]

*

The ANC meanwhile sets out to re-establish its political and military presence within South Africa following the arrests of the Gqabi- and Sexwale-led structures at the turn of the year.

Moses Mabhida meets Siphiwe Nyanda in a country neighbouring South Africa and tells him that he is going to be sent on a mission to establish structures that will breathe life into the ANC within South Africa. These structures will then be used to sustain the revolutionary process inside the country.

Nyanda enters South Africa shortly afterwards and begins building the structures around people with whom he was in contact before his departure in February the previous year.[45]

*

The Angolan Civil War, and particularly the foreign intervention that it has generated, has brought the liberation struggle in southern Africa squarely into the global Cold War.

On 28 March 1977, Nikolai Podgorny, the chairman of the Presidium of the Supreme Soviet of the Soviet Union (effectively the country's head of state), issues a joint statement with Oliver Tambo, ZAPU's Joshua Nkomo and SWAPO's Sam Nujoma at the conclusion of a two-hour meeting between the four leaders in Lusaka.

It reads: 'The Soviet Union believes that the liquidation of the last vestiges of colonialism and racism in Southern Africa is one of the most important international tasks', and adds that 'Mr Podgorny underlined that the Soviet people will in future permanently support the just struggle of the fighters for the liberation of Southern Africa.'[46]

On the following day, Podgorny heads to Mozambique, while Tambo, Nujoma and Nkomo proceed to Angola, where in Luanda they meet Cuba's leader Fidel Castro, who is also on an African tour. Castro pledges to continue to render material support to the liberation movements.[47]

On 31 March, the South African government releases a Defence Force White Paper in the House of Assembly. It calls for a 'total national strategy' for defence, because South Africa is at war 'whether we wish to accept it or not'.

The document mentions Soviet and Cuban intervention in Angola, which it cites as a 'clear indication of Soviet imperialism which will confront Africa in the future. One can justifiably say that there is a Soviet shadow over parts of Africa.' It adds: 'The relative proximity of Soviet influence and its military aid has had its effect on terrorist activities against the northern states of South West Africa and on the internal situation of our country. The general trend of the events following the coup in Portugal in April 1974 has led to a state of decreased stability in areas to the north of South Africa.'[48]

*

In Soweto, Nicholas Molekwane meets Aitken Ramudzuli and George Molebatsi, former schoolmates of his at George Khosa Secondary School in Dobsonville between 1969 and 1971.

Molekwane says that his father is deceased and he would like the others to accompany him to the funeral in Supingstat.

They agree.

In Supingstat, following the burial, Molekwane points out the lights of Gaborone and asks his two companions if they would be willing to accompany him on a trip into Botswana.[49]

*

During May 1977 the ANC's Revolutionary Council establishes a Central Headquarters (CHQ) for MK, with Joe Modise as commander, Joe Slovo as political commissar, and Mongameli Tshali as chief of staff.

This CHQ is in turn mandated to establish Regional Headquarters (RHQ), also known as 'Machineries', which are to be located in the 'Forward Areas', which are the countries bordering South Africa. The RHQs are given specific regions in South Africa in which they will be responsible for initiating armed struggle.

Among these RHQs are the Transvaal Urban Machinery (tasked with launching armed struggle in the urban areas of the Transvaal), and the Transvaal Rural Machinery. Natal will likewise have rural and urban machineries. These Transvaal and Natal Machineries will be based in Swaziland,[50] but there will also be a machinery in Botswana which will stretch from the Transvaal/Northern Cape west of the N1 motorway, down to Cape Town.

*

When Siphiwe Nyanda leaves South Africa after completing his mission, he meets Moses Mabhida, who gives him the codename 'Gebuza'.[51]

*

Nyanda is appointed commissar (effectively deputy commander) of the Transvaal Urban Machinery.[52]

*

Towards the end of May, Solomon Mahlangu, Lucky Mahlangu (no relation) and Mondy Motloung arrive at a hotel in Maputo.

They are met there by 'Gebuza', who tells them they will now be returning to South Africa. He says that only the three of them will know each other; they will operate in different parts of the country but remain in contact. When any of them realises or sees any danger, they must contact the others.[53]

*

At around the same time in Angola, eight buses and two GAZ trucks transport some 200 MK and Angolan Army troops from Benguela to a place called Nova Catengue, situated in mountainous terrain about 100 kilometres south.

When the vehicles arrive, they find 400 to 450 cadres already there. The venue looks like an old railway camp, with used and unused railway material lying around. The cadres now gathered there begin clearing the area in preparation for its use as a military training camp.[54]

*

Aitken Ramudzuli arrives at Festus Lekaba's house in Dobsonville, Soweto, at 8 a.m. on Sunday 29 May.

He asks if Lekaba has missed him in the location over the past couple of weeks.

Lekaba says he is not certain how long it has been, but it certainly has been a long time.

It must be two weeks, Ramudzuli cuts in, because during that time he has been in Botswana, where he received a 'crash course' in 'urban guerrilla warfare'.

Lekaba asks who provided the training.

The African National Congress, Ramudzuli says.

Lekaba asks how that arose.

Ramudzuli says it is because he is an ANC member. He asks Lekaba whether he also wants to join.

Lekaba says he will consider it.

They leave the matter there and share a cup of tea before Ramudzuli leaves.[55]

*

Aitken Ramudzuli also visits Edward Huma. He says that after the burial of Nicholas Molekwane's father he went to Botswana, where he received a crash course in urban guerrilla warfare from the ANC before being placed in an intelligence section responsible for urban guerrilla warfare in South Africa.[56]

*

On 6 June 1977, an MK military parade takes place in Nova Catengue, Angola. The recruits are divided into four companies, each with a Cuban and an ANC commander.

Company 1 has 'Mthlaba Nkosi' in command, 'Titus' as political commissar and 'Karbahle' as Cuban commander. Company 2 has 'Frans Tlhapelo' as commander, 'Ché O'Gara' as political commissar and 'Fyre' as Cuban commander. Company 3 has 'Sipho Nkosi' as commander, 'Dan Peterson' as political commissar, as well as a Cuban commander, while Company 4 has 'Thom Khoza' as commander, 'Piper' as political commissar, and also a Cuban commander.

The companies each consist of two platoons. Jeff Bosigo is part of Platoon 1 of Company 1, which is commanded by 'Huitsa Mnyaka', with 'Victor' as assistant commander, 'Arkimedes' as Cuban commander, and 'Eduardo' as interpreter.

Julius Mokoena is overall camp commander. 'Thami Zulu' (real name Muziwakhe Ngwenya, whom Mosima Sexwale met at the University of Botswana, Lesotho and Swaziland in Kwaluseni in 1975) is chief of staff, and Mark Shope, the veteran trade union leader who was arrested in Northern Rhodesia in May 1963 along with the group including Chris Hani, is the camp's political commissar.

Mokoena addresses the parade. He says the camp begins 'today'.[57]

*

Solomon Mahlangu, Lucky Mahlangu and Mondy Motloung are at a house in Swaziland on 9 June. They are in the company of Selaelo Ramusi, who is Siphiwe Nyanda's immediate superior and the commander of the Transvaal Urban Machinery.

Ramusi is sitting next to a table on which, arranged in threes, are apparently innocuous containers for household cleaning aids like Omo and Punch. Also on the table are hand grenades, cartridges and detonators.

The four men work together putting the war material into the civilian-use containers.

This complete, Ramusi transports the three cadres in the direction of the Swaziland–South Africa border at Hlatikulu.[58]

*

At a Johannesburg taxi rank on the morning of 13 June 1977, Lucky Mahlangu and Mondy Motloung enter a taxi heading to Baragwanath. They put a paper bag on the seat. Solomon Mahlangu is about to get in via the right rear door when a black man wearing civilian clothes arrives and says he wants to see what is in that bag. He produces a document similar to a police appointment card.

He receives no answer to his request, so he orders Solomon to enter the taxi. Solomon obliges. The policeman starts searching the bag.

Lucky jumps out of the vehicle at this point and runs away. Almost simultaneously the policeman sees a hand grenade under the clothes he has removed from the bag. The policeman also runs away.

Motloung then takes the paper bag, puts it on the pavement, and flees the vehicle. Solomon takes the paper bag and runs after Motloung. The two run down Jeppe Street with people chasing them.[59]

Manie Steenkamp and Jan Karel Loggerenberg, both civilians, are walking down Jeppe Street at around 10 a.m. when they hear a man shouting from behind: 'Vang hulle!' (Catch them!)

Steenkamp looks back and sees two blacks about five car lengths away running in his direction. One is carrying a large paper bag. Another black man, about thirty paces behind, is chasing the two. (Lucky Mahlangu has fled in a different direction and has managed to escape.)

Loggerenberg says to Steenkamp in Afrikaans: 'Come, let's catch them.'

When one of the men runs past their position, Loggerenberg grabs him from behind by the neck. This is the one without the bag (Mondy Motloung).

Steenkamp watches as the man who has been seized puts his hand into his coat pocket and takes out an object. The object is shiny and gold and has blocks on it. The man keeps trying to bite a valve off the contraption, but Loggerenberg holds him in a position that prevents him from getting his hand to his mouth.

When Solomon Mahlangu sees Motloung being held around the neck, he puts the paper bag on the ground, and takes a Scorpion pistol and a hand grenade from it. He puts the grenade in his pocket, and retrieves a magazine from the bag. He tries to load the magazine into his firearm.

Loggerenberg looks back to see what has happened to the black man who was chasing the pair. He sees this man standing still and wonders why he is not approaching.

Steenkamp meanwhile has decided to take Mahlangu using an oblique approach. He has crept up a further car length from where Loggerenberg is, and he intends to come between two cars back onto the pavement and catch Mahlangu by surprise. As he is about to pounce, however, he sees Mahlangu cocking a pistol. Steenkamp screams to Loggerenberg, 'Los!' (Leave!) and runs away. Steenkamp and Loggerenberg both run across to the other side of Jeppe Street and take cover in a building.

Mahlangu and Motloung carry on running down Jeppe Street, in the direction of the old market – and Goch Street.[60]

At a T-junction, Motloung and Mahlangu turn left into Goch Street. Mahlangu runs until he reaches the underside of a flyway.

He looks back and sees Motloung squatting. He can also see that people are still pursuing them.

Mahlangu continues running but hears shots being fired from behind and feels pain in his right ankle. He sees that he is bleeding. Realising he can't run properly, he releases the safety catch of his firearm and cocks it as a warning to his pursuers. He fires three shots into the ground in front of him in the direction in which he is trying to escape.

Mahlangu then crosses Goch Street and starts looking for a place to hide. He enters the premises of 21 Goch Street and turns left.[61]

At 29 Goch Street, which is a warehouse for the department store John Orrs, Peter Hartogh is having tea at a table positioned about five metres from the door of an office. It is just after 10 a.m. and with him sharing the tea are Rupert Kassner, Robert Bagg and Kenneth Wolfendale. The four are friends. Wolfendale is in his twenties, Hartogh in his mid-forties, and Bagg and Kassner in their sixties.

Suddenly Mondy Motloung enters through the door carrying a Scorpion pistol and says, 'Het jy dit gesien?' Kassner makes a sudden movement and Motloung fires at him. The rest of the men dive for cover on the floor.

Bagg and Hartogh get up off the floor and run into a little adjoining room on the side. Bagg closes the door and tries to hold it shut while Hartogh, in an attempt to attract attention, breaks the window open with a curtain rod he finds standing in a corner.

When he hears no more firing from outside, Hartogh goes to the door, and with Bagg looks through a crack – the door is badly fitted and there is a bit of a jar in it.

Bagg grabs a small stick and says to Hartogh, 'Peter, he is fiddling with his gun, let's jump him.'

Hartogh opens the door and hits Motloung over the head with his curtain rod once, upon which the MK man runs out the front door. Motloung leaves the jammed pistol on the floor next to Wolfendale and takes out another Scorpion. Hartogh follows him and hits him again. Motloung stops, turns round, and fires this second pistol, hitting Hartogh in the process. Hartogh strikes him a third time. Motloung then runs around two vans parked in front of the office. Hartogh follows him, but he sees something flying through the air in his direction and ducks. The object lands under a van parked opposite the two vans and explodes. Hartogh, who is unhurt by the blast, comes round the vans and sees Robert Bagg wrestling with Motloung, battling for control of the pistol. Hartogh catches up with them and clobbers Motloung one more time with the curtain rod. At this point Motloung relinquishes control of the pistol. Every time Motloung tries to raise his head, Bagg gives him a whack with the pistol.

Eventually the pistol's magazine falls out. Bagg struggles with Motloung on the floor for possession of it. While they fight, Hartogh, who has been shot in his right breast, his left leg and his left ankle, lies writhing in pain, and shouts over and over: 'Kill the bastard.'

Hartogh meanwhile manages to crawl to the office and call the exchange. He tells them that they are being shot at. Hartogh sees Kassner motionless on the floor and Wolfendale writhing in agony. Both are bleeding. There are broken cups and chairs and tables strewn across the floor.

Hartogh walks out of the office with the phone in his hand. He starts feeling dizzy and collapses next to Motloung. Hartogh as yet has no knowledge that he has been shot. He only discovers it much later when he regains consciousness.[62]

Robert Bagg runs up to Sergeant Claassens, who has Mondy Motloung handcuffed to a police car. 'Sergeant, I think there is another one down there,' he says. 'I saw somebody run amongst the cars there.'

Solomon Mahlangu is under citizen's arrest in the car park at 21 Goch Street. He has been apprehended by a man whom he had seen approaching in the car park and had asked for help.

The police sergeant takes Mahlangu to Motloung, and the two are transported to John Vorster Square.[63]

THE ANVIL AND THE HAMMER

Sonny Singh, who attacked A.S. Kajee's office in Durban in December 1962, visits Ivan Pillay one morning in Merebank, Natal.

Singh says: 'Look, I want you to take a message to Mac, tell Mac that I'm leaving. Is there any message that he would want to pass to the outside?'

That evening, Ivan Pillay goes to a nearby flat where Mac Maharaj, released from Robben Island in December 1976, is serving a term of house arrest. He tells Maharaj he wants to see him.

Maharaj doesn't know who Pillay is, so Pillay cuts to the chase and says he has come from Sonny, who is leaving today and wants to know if Mac has any messages he wants to send.

'No, I have nothing to say.'

'Thank you very much,' Pillay says, before walking away.[1]

*

On 1 July 1977 Mac Maharaj himself leaves South Africa in the company of Petrus Nzima, who leads him into Swaziland.

Within twenty-four hours Maharaj is in Mozambique, from where he heads to London to report to Oliver Tambo.[2]

*

Shadrack Maphumulo, another veteran of the sabotage campaign in Natal, is visited by Patrick Msomi on 12 July 1977.

Msomi says he has come from Swaziland where he was given an order to convey the message that Russell Mapanga, Mdingi, and Judson Khuzwayo must be told to get out of the country. Msomi gives Maphumulo R450, which he says the ANC has provided for the transportation costs involved in getting the men concerned to Swaziland.

Maphumulo has to contact these people, Msomi says, and then get out of the country himself.[3]

*

Two days later, Shadrack Maphumulo has not yet left the country.

He is with Doris Sikhosana and Beatta Mabanda conducting interviews with harbour workers for a research project on migrant labour that is being carried out by Natal University's Institute of Applied Social Sciences.

At about 2.30 p.m., three plainclothes policemen burst in and arrest him.[4]

*

Ivan Pillay is reading a newspaper on Saturday 16 July when he sees a reference to Maphumulo's arrest. He tells his brother Joe, 'This is our man, the name here.' Although he is not certain of the name, he says, 'I think this is our man.'

Joe Pillay says: 'Okay, all right, I'm going to phone.' He calls Petrus Nzima, who confirms, 'Yes, this is the man, the man who's been arrested.'

On the same afternoon, Petrus Nzima and Joe Pillay leave for Swaziland.

The 16th of July 1977 is also the day that Nzima's wife's brother is getting married.

At the wedding, Ivan Pillay tells Nzima's wife Jabu, 'Look, you guys must go on with the wedding, your husband is not going to be here.'

She is not in the least bit understanding, but Joe Pillay and Petrus Nzima do at least manage to reach Swaziland safely.[5]

*

About two weeks later, Joe Pillay returns to Merebank. He tells his brother that the people in Swaziland and Maputo said he must return to fetch Ivan because it will only be a matter of time before the documents captured by the police lead to him.

Ivan Pillay says okay and leaves to pack his bags.

About half an hour or so later the Pillay brothers head into exile.[6]

*

The *Rand Daily Mail* reports on 29 August that Brigadier Johan Coetzee, the deputy head of the Security Police in Pretoria, yesterday declared that following an investigation dating back to the ANC-SACTU revival in Natal and the Reef in 1975 (i.e. Harry Gwala, Jacob Zuma, Russell Mapanga *et al* in Natal, the Main Machinery on the Reef), the Special Branch has arrested both the 'internal organising ring' as well as the majority of those responsible for recruiting and sending people out of the country to receive terrorist training as part of a plan aimed at launching an invasion of South Africa.

Coetzee said the project was the brainchild of the ANC and SACP, with the masterminds being London-based white members of the latter. Chief conspirator was Joe Slovo, who recently visited Luanda and other African countries, where he inspected training camps capable of instructing up to 2,000 recruits at a time. Others involved were Jack Hodgson and Ronnie Kasrils.

When approached for comment, Colonel Frans Steenkamp of the Durban Security Police admitted that some of those being sought had managed to escape to neighbouring states.[7]

*

In Langa township in the Cape, Tyrone Khumalo knocks on a door of a house.

When it opens he sees two women inside.

Khumalo says he is a friend of Aubrey's and is in trouble and needs help.

Well, Aubrey is on Robben Island, one of the women replies.

Upon hearing this, Khumalo takes fright and runs.

In Gaborone, Khumalo meets Keith Mokoape, Snuki Zikalala, 'Mike' and 'Antony'. Mokoape offers apologies, saying Aubrey is his brother and they shouldn't have sent him to that house since it may have been under police surveillance.[8]

*

Leonard Nkosi, veteran of the Wankie campaign ten years earlier, now lives in KwaMashu. After deserting his group he entered South Africa by train in December 1967. He was arrested by two policemen in KwaMashu in May the following year, after which he decided to join the force himself, rising to the rank of sergeant.

On the evening of 10 September 1977 he is in bed with his wife Doris at their home, listening to a radio broadcast of a boxing match. After turning off the lights, he puts his arms around her. Suddenly they hear a loud bang. It is part of a salvo of bullets that have been fired through their bedroom window.

When he leans over her, she feels a warm fluid. He gets out of bed and goes to another room where his father-in-law is asleep.

He collapses in that room with blood spurting from his mouth, nose and chest and dies shortly afterwards.[9]

*

On the evening of 24 September, Tyrone Khumalo and Aitken Ramudzuli are standing in a field in Botswana. A man walks up and introduces himself as Mthebe Tladise.

Khumalo shows Tladise the contents of the bag he is carrying. There is a plastic container and a thermos jar, both containing explosives, and there are hand grenades, time clocks, detonators and a Scorpion pistol.

Khumalo, Ramudzuli and Tladise are then transported to Lobatse in the company of Keith Mokoape, Snuki Zikalala and 'Eric'. The first three cross into South Africa, leaving Mokoape, Zikalala and Eric behind.

In Mafikeng late the following afternoon, Ramudzuli exits a pub called 'Mafikeng by Night' in the company of Simon Kgongoane, Sello Montshiwa and Peter Ramonye, three local acquaintances with whom he has spent the day drinking.

In the early evening, the four men, along with Tladise and Khumalo, take a taxi to Mafikeng Railway Station. After buying tickets, they climb the stairs of the bridge leading to Platform 3.

When Khumalo, Montshiwa and Tladise get to the other side of the bridge, they look down the stairs and see two railway policemen, one white and one black, on routine duty at the bottom.

Tladise is slightly ahead of Khumalo as they descend.

Khumalo is wearing blue overalls and carrying a bag strapped over his shoulders. The black policeman, Constable Mash Madi, tells him to take the bag off so he can search it. Khumalo complies and then raises both his hands, challenging Madi to search him, saying that he is a good man and that he isn't carrying any dangerous weapons. Madi body-searches Khumalo, which yields nothing. The carry bag is now lying slightly open in front of Khumalo. Madi bends forward to open it further. As he does so he feels a weapon.

At this point Khumalo thrusts his hand into the bag and simultaneously grabs Madi from above with the other hand. A struggle ensues between the two for possession of the weapon.

Tladise is the first to flee the scene. Ramudzuli also runs. Montshiwa hears someone scream, 'They have a gun, they have a gun!' after which he also runs, in his case towards the taxi rank.

Madi wins the struggle with Khumalo for possession of the pistol. He manages to get both hands round it and calls for help. Khumalo gives up the fight and runs. Madi threatens to shoot, but Khumalo ignores him. Other policemen, however, manage to block his escape. Constable Hepburn grabs Khumalo, and Hepburn and Madi cuff him.

Montshiwa manages to get into a minibus heading back to the location. On the way there, Ramudzuli and Ramonye try to stop the vehicle. The driver says they look like trouble, and speeds away.

In the township later that evening, Montshiwa heads to his girlfriend's place. On the way he spots Ramudzuli and Simon Kgongoane walking in the direction of the latter's residence.[10]

*

During the night Aitken Ramudzuli is arrested at Simon Kgongoane's house.[11]

*

Early the following morning, 26 September 1977, Lieutenant Ignatius van Niekerk of the South African Security Branch is part of a team led by Major Burger towards two rooms in the backyard of house No. 2660 in Dobsonville, Soweto.

The team enters one of the rooms and finds a single black female there. They search the room for a while but find nothing of interest.

They then go to the second backyard room, which is closed.

Major Burger knocks on the room's door and says loudly in both English and Afrikaans that they are police and that they want to enter the room and search it.

The door remains closed.

Major Burger kicks the door three times and warns that the door must be opened otherwise they will break it open.

There is silence from the room. After a while, Major Burger kicks on the door several more times.

The door suddenly flies open and two shots are fired from within the room towards the policemen.

Major Burger swerves to his right and falls below a window of the room. Lieutenant van Niekerk flees to safety, along with Constable Riekert and Constable van Heerden. As they do so a further shot is fired from the room.

Van Niekerk takes up position near the corner of the main house, about ten steps from the door from which the shots were fired. Constable van Heerden is standing next to him, and Constable Riekert is lying down beside a dog kennel a few paces away.

More shots are fired at them from the room. One of them flies just above Riekert's head.

It is about 5.20 a.m. and approaching dawn, but it is still too dark to see inside the room.

The door is open by a slit, and through that gap further shots are fired at the policemen.

Lieutenant van Niekerk then spots a large felled tree stump lying in the backyard. He tells his colleagues that he will take the stump and throw it at the door to force it open. He tells them to return fire if any shots come from the room.

Van Niekerk throws the stump at the door, and as it opens, shots are fired from inside the room. The bullets fly ten inches over the head of Van Niekerk, who fires two shots back with his service revolver. Constable van Heerden also fires a salvo with his HMK machine gun.

Thereafter there is silence from the room.

A while later, when it becomes light, Van Niekerk can see from his position that in the room there is a person on the floor next to a bed in a semi-kneeling position. Van Niekerk enters the room and finds a dead black man. Next to the man is a Makarof 9-mm pistol and behind him a Russian-manufactured 7.62-calibre Tokarev with its breech open.

Van Niekerk then searches the room. In the wardrobe are two passbooks, one of which has a photograph of the dead man and the name 'Kudugo Nicholas Molekwane'. The trail has proceeded from Aitken Ramudzuli, arrested the day before, to Nicholas Molekwane, who recruited him in May.[12]

*

And it soon extends to the leadership of the Botswana Machinery based abroad. M.C. Tibone, President Seretse Khama's permanent secretary, writes to Botswana's high commission in Lusaka on 29 September.

He notes that the ANC office in Botswana is manned by Isaac Makopo, Keith Mokoape and 'Snooky Joseph Zikalala'. He says, 'We have observed that these three men are increasingly becoming involved in the transhipment of firearms and explosives through Botswana to South Africa. We have evidence that the South Africans are aware of their involvement.'

Tibone says Gaborone's feeling 'is that Keith Mokoape and Snooky Joseph Zikalala have become careless and consequently they have been blown. It is therefore neither in the interests of the ANC nor of Botswana that these two men should continue to operate in Botswana. If we do not act promptly to have them withdrawn, South Africa may be tempted to do something ghastly against them or against us or both.' He accordingly calls on the country's diplomats in Lusaka to 'urgently request the ANC Headquarters to withdraw Keith Mokoape and Snooky Joseph Zikalala from Botswana immediately'.[13]

*

In Nova Catengue camp that evening, Thoko Mavuso, a female MK recruit, prepares to leave Nova Catengue camp with her group for some night shooting practice. They have just had supper.

Her colleagues start complaining of feeling bad after eating the fish. Some suggest the fish was not cleaned properly.

The Cuban instructors suspect they are codding and simply don't want to train, but increasing numbers of people begin complaining of symptoms of illness.[14]

Teddy 'Mwase' Williams is doing night-time grenade throwing when he feels a pain in his groin. He tells his commander that he doesn't feel okay; he feels nauseous.

The commander asks him what he thinks it is.

Williams says 'my tummy is painful and I feel like throwing out'. He tries vomiting, but nothing comes out.

'Okay, let me speak to the Cuban instructor,' the commander volunteers.

When he does, the Cuban instructor comes to Williams and releases him to see the doctor.

Doctor Mpalo gives Williams ten painkiller tablets.

Williams asks if these tablets will really help.

'No, just take two every time you feel the pain.'

Williams downs two immediately. This sends him to sleep.[15]

Back at the camp proper, Mtunzi Mthembu sees colleagues vomiting; others have diarrhoea; men and women of all ranks are relieving themselves in the open. Mthembu himself experiences cutting pains in his intestines.[16]

The Cubans were served from their own kitchens and reside in a separate facility a distance from the camp – none of them are affected. Soon more than thirty Cuban doctors arrive at Nova Catengue to help. Then camp commander Julius Mokoena commences an interrogation of the kitchen personnel with the assistance of the Cuban instructors.[17]

*

In Manzini, Swaziland, on 6 October, Selaelo Ramusi, the commander of the Transvaal Urban Machinery, briefs Bushy Molefe.

Molefe is told that his task will be to obtain a secure base and residence for himself in the KwaThema area south-west of Springs. He must also establish a place where weapons, ammunition and explosives can be delivered to him, and from where communications can be exchanged back and forth between them.[18]

Molefe meets Bafana Duma immediately afterwards. Duma gives Molefe a reference book numbered 4528142 that has been issued in the name of 'Natalio Sello Mgakane'. Duma tells him to make use of it while in South Africa.

Molefe enters South Africa through the Oshoek border post later the same day, utilising the reference book.

He returns to Swaziland on 16 October and reports to Ramusi on the outcome of his reconnaissance mission. He says that he managed to find a secure base and residence in the KwaThema area from where he can operate, and adds that he also found a secure, secret delivery place for weapons, ammunition, explosives and correspondence. He produces a sketchplan that he has drawn of the delivery place.

He then meets with Bafana Duma, still on the 16th. Molefe hands the sketchplan to Duma and explains that when the weapons are delivered they should be deposited within one of the two water drain pipes indicated on the document. They are thirty to forty metres apart, he says. In the other pipe he will leave a note containing his request for weapons.

On the following day, Molefe is back in South Africa at the corner of Thema Road and Jacob Maseko Street in KwaThema. There are two water pipes leading out of Thema Road into a field. Molefe places a piece of paper in one of the pipes. The content is a coded request for a delivery of weapons and explosives from Swaziland. After depositing it, he places a white sticker on the pipe.[19]

*

The arrangement doesn't work. On 29 October, Brigadier Jan Cronje and Lieutenant Hattingh arrive in KwaThema and head to a spot near Thema Road. There they find a variety of weapons and explosives strewn across a footpath next to a fence. The items are all scattered around a pipe from which they appear to have fallen out or been removed. Near another pipe on the same road, there are further explosives scattered around.

A number of children are playing with the weapons.

The policemen confiscate the items.[20]

*

Mac Maharaj is in Yusuf Dadoo's office in London in November 1977.

Dadoo says that at a recent RC meeting it was decided to appoint Maharaj secretary of the Internal Reconstruction Department. As secretary, he will be working under John Motshabi.

'Doc, what have you all done to me?' Maharaj asks.

'Well, if you don't do the work, who is there to do the work?' Dadoo replies. 'You'd better find a way to do the work.'[21]

*

Two trained MK cadres arrive in Francistown in Botswana during the same month and proceed to a house in the city belonging to ZAPU. One of the cadres is Thomas Hlabane, alias 'Victor', and his companion is Danger Ncube, alias 'Nkosinathi Smith'. Both are in possession of documents identifying themselves as Rhodesian nationals.[22]

*

Vuso Tshabalala crosses into South Africa from Swaziland, also in November 1977. He does so using a Swazi travel document. He has been sent by the Transvaal Urban Machinery to conduct reconnaissance on possible targets in the Pretoria-Witwatersrand-Vereeniging area.

In South Africa he heads to Soweto where he adopts the pseudonym of a Swazi student attending a school in town.[23]

*

Early in January 1978, Thandi Modise also enters South Africa from Swaziland. She similarly uses a false passport and at the checkpoint gives her name in siSwati as 'Zandile Simelane'.

She heads to Soweto, where she meets Vuso Tshabalala. Like him, she is in the township to reconnoitre possible targets in the Transvaal's urban areas.[24]

*

At a fence demarcating the boundary of a kraal in the Dibilishaba Tribal Trust Lands in Gwanda, which is in Matabeleland, Rhodesia, a unit of ZAPU's military wing, the Zimbabwe People's Revolutionary Army (ZIPRA), is ambushed by Rhodesian Security Forces on 22 January 1978. Thomas Hlabane and Danger Ncube are attached to this ZIPRA call-sign.

Danger Ncube is killed in the incident, as is Base Ncube, the ZIPRA commander in the region. Hlabane escapes alongside the remainder of the ZAPU guerrillas and eventually manages to return to Botswana.[25]

*

At 10.10 a.m. the following day, Bafana Duma unlocks his private box in the new section of the Manzini Post Office.

Moments later an explosion occurs that severs his right arm below the elbow.

A *Times of Swaziland* reporter calls Manzini's Raleigh Fitkin Memorial Hospital later that morning, and manages to speak to the doctor conducting the operation. The doctor confirms Duma will lose his right forearm.[26]

*

Thandi Modise arrives at the entrance of the OK Bazaars branch at Eloff Street, Johannesburg, towards closing time in mid-March 1978. She is wearing a maternity dress and carrying a sling bag over her shoulder. In the bag are a dozen boxes, which look like they contain matches, but which in fact consist of igniters attached to ready-made timers.

As she passes through a security checkpoint, a guard peeps into her bag, but does no more. She sighs with relief and proceeds upstairs. She then walks around the store, placing the matchboxes in assortments of clothing and jacket pockets in the men's, women's and children's departments. Then she quickly heads for the escalators to join the crowds of shoppers exiting the buildings.

She walks to a nearby park. There she waits, glancing at her watch occasionally.

Inside the store, an employee, H.A. Venter, sees smoke coming from some jackets. He also notices matchboxes positioned next to a cash till. He manages to stop the fire from spreading beyond the jackets.

Modise is still waiting in the park for signs of an explosion. Nothing seems to be happening, so she takes a taxi to Diepkloof and there listens for news.

On the following day, Modise heads to an Edgars store about a block from the OK Bazaars. She again places igniters inside clothing.

Petrus van Jaarsveld later notices some jackets 'smoking' within the store. Like Venter, he manages to extinguish the fire before it spreads.[27]

*

Keith Mokoape collects Stanley Manong and Thabo Mavuyo from Lusaka Airport and drives them to a house in Danga Road in Lusaka's Chunga township. There they find Victor Modise, Shaheed Rajie, Abe Maseke and Snuki Zikalala.

Later in the day the group are joined by Joe Modise and Joe Slovo. The meeting is being held to reconstitute MK's Botswana Machinery after the withdrawal of Mokoape and Zikalala from the country the previous year following the arrest of Aitken Ramudzuli and Tyrone Khumalo.

Under the new structure, Joe Modise, Keith Mokoape and Snuki Zikalala will exercise overall command of the structure from Lusaka. Victor Modise will be commander of the structure in Botswana itself, while Rajie will be the commissar and treasurer, Manong the chief of operations, Maseke the logistics head, and Mavuyo the man in charge of reconnaissance and infiltration.[28]

*

At a meeting of the ANC's Revolutionary Council held around April 1978, John Motshabi reads the first report of the Internal Reconstruction Department (IRD), which has been written by Mac Maharaj.

Motshabi outlines the IRD's perspective regarding the processes necessary for building underground political structures in South Africa.

He mentions that arrests have taken place in Pietermaritzburg, Pretoria, Cape Town and the Eastern Cape. He claims the approach taken to internal reconstruction by Thabo Mbeki when he was in charge of a similar project earlier in the decade, when working alongside Albert Dhlomo in Swaziland, was to take people who were very well known in the movement and entrust them with the responsibility of finding solutions to the problems of political reconstruction.

Motshabi says the IRD will, by contrast, seek during the first phase to avoid involving known political activists. The department will instead try to develop another echelon of political cadres unknown to the state.

He mentions the need to create different compartments in this internal underground. He calls these 'functional units', which will each have different responsibilities, such as propaganda distribution, trade unions, border crossings, mass work and the reception of cadres – these will all exist as separate 'functional units'.

Motshabi refers to some challenges the IRD is facing in conducting its work. He questions the training that people are undergoing, and asks where the training facilities for political work are: everybody seems to be going for military training, he complains.[29]

*

On 14 April 1978, Abel Mthembu, one of the first six to receive training in Mao's China, but since then a prolific state witness, is assassinated. He is shot three times in his head and back in Dube, Soweto.[30]

*

Selaelo Ramusi arrives with David Simelane at a hotel in Swaziland consisting of traditional Zulu huts. They find Obed Masina in one of them.

Simelane asks Masina how he is faring.

After receiving the answer, Simelane asks if Masina wants to return to South Africa. If he does, Simelane suggests, he could have better luck finding Orphan 'Hlubi' Chaphi, a Soweto-based policeman.

Masina says he would like to go back if possible.[31]

*

At about 1.30 a.m. on the morning of Sunday 25 June 1978, Detective Sergeant Orphan Chaphi arrives at his home in Rockville, which is near Moroka Police Station in Soweto. He is driving a brown Ford Granada.

Obed Masina, who was beginning to doze off on the premises of the nearby Ndondo School, is awoken by his arrival.

Chaphi stops the car, exits, and walks to the gate of his house.

As he does so, Masina emerges from the school.

When Chaphi notices Masina coming to him he pulls out his revolver. Masina staggers as if drunk.

Chaphi asks him if he is all right.

Masina says yes, he is.

Chaphi returns his revolver to its position.

Masina then brandishes a Tokarev and shoots at Chaphi, hitting him in his right arm. However, as Masina tries to fire a second shot, his gun jams.

Chaphi collapses, but retrieves his own pistol and tries to shoot back. Before Chaphi can fire any shots, Masina jumps to the other side of the Granada and tries to fix his firearm. When this fails, he flees.

Chaphi opens fire and discharges eight shots, but none strike Masina, who runs in zig-zags to avoid offering a stable target.

Mr Tshabalala, a neighbour of Sergeant Chaphi, hears the shooting. When he looks outside he sees Chaphi staggering from his house to his gate. Tshabalala goes to help. He takes the revolver and drives Chaphi to hospital in the sergeant's vehicle.

Sergeant 'Hlubi' dies at about 8 p.m. that evening.[32]

*

At a briefing in Maputo, James Mange is given the mission of returning to South Africa to reconnoitre various targets in the area of Whittlesea in the Eastern Cape.[33]

*

On 30 July 1978, Victor Modise and Stanley Manong of the MK Botswana Machinery hold a meeting with Barney Molokoane, Authu Muzorewa, Ace Phetla, John Msibi, Wilford Marwane, John Sekete, Patrick Dipholo, Dennis Ramphomane and Mooki Motsoaledi, who form a nine-man unit that will be sent into South Africa to establish routes to, and permanent bases in, the Pilanesberg and Soutpansberg mountain ranges.

Molokoane is the group commander, Muzorewa the chief of staff. Modise tells them to prepare to be infiltrated the following day. The group are staggered by the news. Molokoane says they need to transport food supplies into the country before they can undertake operations. He asks the command to provide a metal trunk containing food supplies that he and Ace Phetla can quickly transport across the border if they are to infiltrate the following day. Modise refuses to allow this. Instead he proposes that they give him the exact place where they want the trunk to be deposited, and he will arrange for a courier to deliver the food there.

The group protests but Modise is adamant. Just before Modise leaves with Manong, Molokoane provides them a sketch indicating where the group want the trunk to be placed.

At 5 p.m. the following day, Victor Modise and Thabo Mavuyo arrive in a Land Rover at a safe house in Mochudi where the nine are waiting in Stanley Manong's company. The cadres enter the vehicle, but Modise walks up to Manong with a worried look on his face. He says 'Flint' did not manage to find the place where Molokoane wanted the trunk to be placed. He asks what they should do.

Manong is left speechless for a while, but eventually suggests that they should not inform the comrades about this for fear of demoralising them. They should instead send Flint back into South Africa to try to locate the place.

Later that evening, Ephraim Mfalapitsa, who left South Africa in the wake of the Soweto uprising but has now been deployed to augment the Botswana Machinery having completed his military training, is involved in infiltrating Molokoane's group into South Africa.

Leaving Mfalapitsa behind, the nine reach the spot where Molokoane asked the food to be delivered. They find nothing there. They decide that Muzorewa and Marwane should go to the nearby village of Witkleigat the following morning to try to purchase food. The group then marches to a hilltop not far from Witkleigat, some fifty kilometres from Zeerust. They all spend the night there.[34]

*

The telephone rings at the South Africa/Botswana border post at Swartkopfontein Gate, some twelve kilometres from Witkleigat, on 1 August. Constable Solomon Sehume takes the call while Warrant Officer Albertus Smit listens in on another line.

The caller is the black owner of a café in Witkleigat, who says there are two men at his store purchasing a vast quantity of tinned food. They appear to have lots of money. He says he suspects them of being responsible for the break-in at the store on Sunday in which R700 was stolen. He says he will try to delay them until the police get there.

Officer Smit grabs his service revolver and leaves with Sehume in a police van.

On the Welgevonden Road, the policemen approach two black men dressed in civilian clothes who are carrying boxes. The two men walk past their police vehicle.

The policemen then see the shop owner a short distance behind the men, standing next to a bunch of trees. Smit drives up to the two suspects and stops the van. He orders the pair to leave the boxes.

The two men, Authu Muzorewa and Wilford Marwane, try to run away.

In Afrikaans, Smit warns: 'Stand, or I'll shoot!'

Muzorewa keeps running but Marwane stops, turns and says: 'Don't shoot.'

As Smit exits the police bakkie, he notices Muzorewa suddenly start looking for something by his side. Smit then hears his colleague Sehume shout: 'Watch out; he is looking for a firearm!'

Smit fires at Muzorewa with his service revolver, but misses, upon which both suspects flee, leaving the boxes of tinned food behind. They run down the Welgevonden Road to a settlement of houses on the outskirts of Witkleigat.

Sehume and Smit pursue them in the bakkie. They close in on Muzorewa, but he sidesteps them and runs behind a house.

As Smit climbs off the bakkie, Muzorewa fires at him again, narrowly missing the policeman's head. Smit hands his service revolver to Sehume, whom he instructs to walk to the left of the house while Smit, now unarmed, heads to the right. As Sehume approaches, Muzorewa fires two shots at him and then reaches under his shirt, from where he produces an object that Smit recognises as a hand grenade. Smit screams to Sehume: 'Pas op!' (Watch out!)

Muzorewa throws the grenade, upon which Smit screams at Sehume to fall flat. Sehume does so. The grenade flies over his head and lands to his left. It explodes but Sehume is not hurt.

Marwane surrenders and is re-taken into custody. This leaves Muzorewa at large. He climbs over a fence behind the house and runs through the veld towards the nearby hills.

Sehume and Smit jump into the bakkie in order to chase after him, but the fence at the back of the settlement prevents further pursuit.

Sehume nonetheless manages to fire at the fleeing Muzorewa, who appears to stagger as a result.

In the distance, the policemen see other men in the hills running to some bush for cover. One of these men is clearly carrying a firearm. The policemen speed back to Swartkopfontein to call for help.[35]

*

Under the command of Colonel H.A. Mouton, a South African Police counter-insurgency unit arrives in Witkleigat later that day.

Supported by a contingent of the Bophuthatswana National Guard, they pursue the fugitives inside the bushy hilltop area.

During the search, the security forces come across Barney Molokoane and John Sekete. An intense firefight ensues. Both guerrillas, however, manage to break off the engagement and flee further into the bush.

Later, blood is found at the scene of this skirmish.

There is sporadic shooting in the hills throughout the rest of the day. In the afternoon, two Frelon helicopters join the search for the men. The hunt, however, proves fruitless and the MK unit manages to complete its retreat.

When Barney Molokoane arrives back in Botswana, it is with a bullet wound in his leg.[36]

*

In Swaziland on 9 August, Stanley Mabizela informs Selaelo Ramusi that he is wanted by the Swazi Police and should therefore leave the kingdom.

Three days later, Ramusi has still not yet left and is arrested near the Diamond Village Motel in Swaziland's Ezulwini Valley. He is captured in possession of a Strakonice automatic pistol and thirty-four rounds of ammunition.

Ramusi admits to the police that he is an ANC member.

Appearing in a Swazi court on the 21st, Ramusi asks the magistrate, Paul Shilubane, not to permit his continued detention, because he is an asthma sufferer. If kept in police custody his health will deteriorate, he argues.

He is granted bail of 200 emalangeni.

As he leaves the court, the Swazi Police re-arrest him on fresh charges of illegal immigration and car stealing.

The matter returns to court the following day. Magistrate Shilubane says the police's behaviour in splitting the arms and ammunition from the immigration and car-stealing charges represents a deliberate attempt to frustrate the accused, and he orders the police to release Ramusi from custody on the bail paid the day before.

This is done, but as Ramusi leaves the court he is arrested again, this time on undisclosed charges.[37]

*

Obed Masina arrives back in Swaziland and meets David Simelane. Referring to the operation on 'Hlubi', Masina says he successfully completed the task.

Simelane says he has already received the information.

Masina proceeds nonetheless to provide further details.

During the discussion that follows, Simelane informs Masina that while he was gone, 'Dan' (Selaelo Ramusi) died after being arrested by the Swazi Police. Masina is going to take over as commander from him.[38]

*

It is, however, ultimately Siphiwe Nyanda and not Masina who will take over from Selaelo Ramusi as commander of the Transvaal Urban Machinery following Ramusi's death from an asthma attack in a Swazi jail.[39]

*

Oscar Ntombelo arrives at a flat in Lithabaneng in Maseru, Lesotho, where he reports to Chris Hani.

Ntombelo says he has been instructed to operate in the Natal Region.

Hani countermands this, saying he is short of men, so Ntombelo should remain in Lesotho for the time being.[40]

*

Thomas 'Victor' Hlabane, Leslie Dube, Mzomdala Mdhladhla, Mabala Mehlomakhulu and Salathiel Sethlapelo of MK arrive at the ZAPU residence in Francistown, Botswana, in September 1978, having hitch-hiked their way from Zambia. They are all in possession of Zambian identity documents indicating that they are Rhodesian nationals.

An ANC official named 'Tabu' arrives at the house in the company of another African. Tabu advises the ZAPU representatives that 'Victor' and his men will again join the ZAPU military group in the Tuli area and will resume the mission to infiltrate South Africa in the Beitbridge area that was terminated following the ambush of the joint MK/ZIPRA unit in January.

Elliot Sibanda, ZAPU's deputy representative in Francistown, drives Tabu and the five ANC cadres to a place called Nkala's Kraal near the 'Tuli circle' (a ten-mile 'circle' about ninety kilometres west of Beitbridge and near the Botswana border which was declared a no-go area for local cattle in the late nineteenth century in a bid to prevent the spread of rinderpest). The five then join up with a ZAPU unit in the area that is under the command of 'Sylvester'.[41]

*

South Africa undergoes a change of leadership in September 1978 when John Vorster's resignation on the 19th is followed on the 28th by the National Party caucus electing P.W. Botha, the defence minister, as prime minister.[42] Vorster is appointed state president, at this stage a merely ceremonial position.

*

Though the roster of ANC heroes has been notably enlarged by the confrontations in which MK cadres have engaged the security forces since the resumption of the armed struggle in South Africa in the mid-1970s, the organisation's leadership is concerned by the short life-span of many of its units in the country. Accordingly in October 1978 an NEC delegation led by Oliver Tambo travels to the Socialist Republic of Vietnam to imbibe the lessons of that country's revolution, which reached a successful conclusion with national reunification in 1975.

At a briefing in Ho Chi Minh City on 14 October, Tambo jots down notes of comments made by members of the local Fatherland Front Committee. The Vietnamese hosts say that in their country the period of unilateral war saw the enemy use armed violence against unarmed people. Tambo writes: 'cf RSA from our defeat in 1880 at Ulundi'. When the Vietnamese mention that in 1960 they decided to resume the armed struggle against the Americans and 'puppets', Tambo draws an arrow to the margin of the page and writes 'ANC 1961, MPLA 1961, PAIGC 1963?'[43]

Tambo again takes notes during a briefing by Major General Vũ Xuân Chiêm and Colonel Hoang-Minh Phuong of Vietnam's National Defence Ministry on 21 October.

Tambo gives a subsection of his notes the heading 'Armed prop. Str'. He writes that in Vietnam the first stage of armed struggle in a particular area would involve the revolutionaries sending an armed propaganda team into the territory in order to establish a base and start recruiting from among the masses.

The first military actions of the unit would see it execute die-hard elements of the regime, such as brutal officials, notorious policemen and informers. The point of this would be to spread the influence of the revolutionary forces in the locality, since such actions would demonstrate that the revolutionaries were strong enough to deal with the enemy. The people would know who was responsible for the actions because the unit would distribute leaflets saying so.

The chief aim of the propaganda team would not be to eliminate officials for the sake of it, but rather to plant the seeds of revolution and stimulate political activity. Each unit of this kind, which would be of platoon strength, was referred to as a 'Vietnamese armed propaganda brigade'.

It was crucial in Vietnam that the brigades kept their movements secret so as to maintain the legal position of the masses and protect above-ground political organisations. The point is re-emphasised by the Vietnamese officials time and again: the principal initial aim is to build political forces among the people – sometimes exploding a bomb will have a greater political impact than annihilating a hated enemy agent. One must be tactically flexible in pursuing the strategic aim.

Then, presuming that political structures have been created, the unarmed political units operating underground within a particular strategic hamlet would have to liaise with the armed propaganda brigade based outside the protected village. The brigade would then, by this means, tentatively establish guarded contact with the villagers.

Via this contact they could create village-based guerrilla structures that could begin attacking small enemy units.

This will initiate a stage of armed struggle where you have contested areas that the enemy control by day and the revolutionaries by night. In such areas the enemy cannot move freely with small units and will therefore have to mobilise large units. The name for such an area is a 'guerrilla zone'. In a guerrilla zone the political and military struggle develop hand in hand.

Then comes the third stage. Assuming that the revolutionary forces have developed both politically and militarily, conditions for insurrection will have matured. Insurrection consists of a combination of mass uprisings with attacks on enemy installations. Insurrection converts a 'guerrilla zone' into a 'guerrilla base', with the difference between the two being that in the latter the revolutionaries are in control day *and* night.[44]

*

The issues that provoked the Vietnam visit are again manifest two days later, on 23 October, when four black men depart Soweto by car in the direction of Warmbaths. There is a Bible on the dashboard and the driver is dressed as a Roman Catholic priest. The other three men are dressed formally, looking dignified.

At a four-way stop near Nylstroom, the car fails to stop. It is then pursued by a traffic patrol car which eventually manages to bring it to a halt.

Traffic officer Constable Isaac Nkwe emerges from the police vehicle. As he inspects the other car he notices that the registration details on the number plate do not tally with those on the licence disc.

The 'priest' gets out of the car and tells Nkwe that they are on their way to a funeral. Nkwe smells alcohol on the priest's breath, so he says he is going to arrest him.

On hearing this, the priest adopts a new tack, saying he has come to 'free the people'.

Nkwe remains unmoved, upon which the 'priest' denounces him as a 'sell out', jumps into the car, and attempts to drive away.

Another police car is dispatched to follow the vehicle.

The car is eventually stopped, and the priest – James Mange – is arrested, along with the three passengers.[45]

*

Four days after Mange's arrest, Warrant Officer Christiaan de Witt and an African constable drive to an area in the vicinity of the village of Modimola in the Bophuthatswana homeland. The village is close to Mafikeng, and near the border with Botswana.

They find three men hiding under a tree among some bushes. De Witt aims his rifle and orders them to surrender.

Two of the three raise their hands, but the third moves behind the tree and throws a grenade at De Witt, who dives for cover, causing his rifle to jam. The grenade does not explode. When De Witt has cleared his rifle he sees the three men running away.

He opens fire on the man who threw the grenade and sees him stumble. After an exchange of fire with the nearer of the two guerrillas still trying to flee, De Witt and the constable board the police bakkie and continue the pursuit. Having moved closer to the second guerrilla, De Witt gets out of the vehicle and there is another exchange of fire between the two, during which the guerrilla sinks to his knees and reaches under his clothes. De Witt fires again, after which the man falls dead on the ground.

De Witt and the constable then chase the third man. De Witt's magazine is empty. While he reloads his rifle, the man runs behind a clump of bushes.

Having reloaded, De Witt fires at and hits the man, who tries to run but falls. As the man slumps to the ground a grenade explodes in his hand, throwing his body in the air and severing his skull and other organs from his body.

Tladitsagae Molefe, the guerrilla who threw the first grenade and was subsequently shot and wounded, is captured and arrested.

This three-man unit consisted of Molefe, Cyprian Hlatshwayo and Vuyani Goniwe. They had been infiltrated into South Africa by the Botswana Machinery the day before the ambush.[46]

*

Three days after this skirmish, at a spot sixty-two miles south of South Africa's border with Rhodesia, and approximately halfway between Botswana and Mozambique from west to east, a black farm labourer approaches three men in a clump of bushes on an abandoned farm about 500 metres from the nearest cattle trail. His view is obscured by thorn trees and knee-high grass, but he can see that the men are wrapped in blankets and are asleep.

He heads to his employer Victor Miller, who is out on his cattle ranch, called Puraspan. He says armed men are on the property; they are all young and dressed in blue overalls. One of them speaks Tswana and has told the local blacks: 'Don't be scared. We are the soldiers of this place, of the Transvaal. Don't run away.'

Miller calls for help from the nearest police station, which is Mara, some fifty kilometres away. Sergeant Thinus Nel, the Mara station commander, drives four black policemen to the area. They arrive a couple of hours later and Miller accompanies the police patrol, which includes tracker dogs, into the bush.

Miller walks a few paces from Sergeant Nel, while the black policemen are about forty paces behind. Suddenly a barrage of automatic weapon fire is directed towards them from a distance of about fifty metres. Miller dives to the ground, while Sergeant Nel is wounded in an arm and a leg. Seconds later a second burst of fire is aimed at the black policemen behind them.

The black officers initiate a pursuit, but despite helicopter reinforcements being called in, the three guerrillas manage to escape. Only a cache of abandoned machine guns are discovered.

The three MK cadres involved in this incident were Ali Makhosini, Vusi Lerole and 'Bob'. They formed a reconnaissance unit that was sent into South Africa by the Botswana Machinery at the beginning of October.[47]

*

In November, following these incidents, the ANC NEC instructs MK Central Headquarters to halt all infiltrations into South Africa from Botswana.[48]

*

In Lesotho at about 2 a.m. on a Monday in November 1978, Lambert Moloi, who is Chris Hani's deputy in the country, wakes Oscar Ntombelo and tells him to get dressed and bring his provisions.

Ntombelo does as told, and when he walks out of the house shortly afterwards, he sees Moloi waiting by a small yellow Mazda lorry.

Moloi drives Ntombelo to an area called Mabatwana on the main Lithabaneng road. There they collect Temba Banzi and, a short distance further on, George Ndhlovu.

The four proceed along a terrible road in the direction of the Qacha's Nek border post. At approximately 4 p.m., Moloi stops outside a restaurant called Charlie's.

Moloi takes three holdalls from the rear of the vehicle and gives them to the men. Banzi, Ndhlovu and Ntombelo remain at the restaurant until about 10 p.m., when Banzi leads them in the direction of the border between Lesotho and the Transkei Bantustan. They proceed along a well-known route known as Paqama Path. They are each carrying a holdall.

When they reach the border about an hour later, Banzi explains the purpose of the mission: it is to smuggle explosives into the Transkei. The explosives are presently contained in large coffee tins in the holdalls, he says, adding that in South Africa they will have to locate suitable sites for arms caches in areas that will be revealed to them later.

Banzi, Ndhlovu and Ntombelo continue their journey. They walk through the night until they arrive at a bus terminal known as Mafube at approximately 4 a.m. A series of buses takes them from Matatiele to Mount Fletcher to Ketekete and finally to Ngqawi, from where they walk towards a group of huts. While Ndhlovu and Ntombelo wait outside, Banzi enters to speak to the occupants.[49]

*

Andrew Mapheto is part of a group of four, including 'Jim', 'Jonas' and 'September', who cross the Swaziland–South Africa border illegally near Malelane on the evening of 17 December.

On the South African side, a combination of trains, buses and taxis take them from Malelane to Bogenhoek to Tzaneen and finally Nkowankowa, where they disembark and begin walking in the direction of Giyani.

By this time it is after dark on the evening of the 18th. The four men are still on the outskirts of Nkowankowa when a green Al Camino stops just in front of them and puts on its bright lights before speeding away.

The four cadres flee into the bush. Jonas and September lead, with Mapheto and Jim following. September and Jonas move quickly, and this causes them to lose contact with Jim and Mapheto in the dark.

On the following morning, Jim and Mapheto are on the side of the Louis Trichardt road in Pietersburg. A small blue Datsun eventually pulls up. Its driver accepts twenty-nine rand to drive them to Sibasa. From Sibasa, Jim and Mapheto take a taxi to a settlement called Happy Homes. Once there, Jim tells Mapheto that he is going to Malamulele to see his cousin in order to get a lift to Duiwelskloof, where he will fetch the weapons. If he isn't back by 7 a.m., the others should assume he has been arrested.

By 7 a.m. on the 20th, Jim has not arrived, so Mapheto boards a taxi from Happy Homes to Malamulele. When he gets there, he asks a local for 'Maboya's' place.

He is shown where to find it.

At the house, Mapheto meets 'Maboya' and asks him where Jim is. Maboya says he doesn't know. Another person in the house tells Mapheto to get in a car. They will take him to Eric's place.

Instead they take him to the police, who arrest him.[50]

As for September (real name Glory Sedibe) and Jonas (real name George Ramudzuli), they manage to retreat to Mozambique, and in Matola on the outskirts of Maputo, they report to 'Robert Moema' (Gilbert Ramano, the commander of the Transvaal Rural Machinery) on the failure of their mission in Venda.[51]

*

This operation again highlights the saliency of the issues that induced the ANC leadership's visit to Vietnam. Besides the casualties, the most worrying aspect of the situation is the number of times MK cadres are being turned over to the police by black South Africans. Insofar as MK may have thought that it could count on the automatic loyalty of these populations, experience is teaching otherwise. This calls for the movement's existing strategic and tactical approaches, as contained in the document adopted at the Morogoro Conference, to be rethought.

A full meeting of the ANC's NEC and RC commences in Luanda, Angola, on 27 December 1978 with the aim of considering the relevance to the South African struggle of the report from the delegation that travelled to Vietnam in October.[52]

Given the emphasis placed by the Vietnamese on political mobilisation as a prerequisite for guerrilla warfare, the discussion centres on the fortunes of the Internal Reconstruction Department.

Thabo Mbeki recalls that when he was working in the RC on a similar project in the mid-1970s his structures wrote a report concerning every person they met in Swaziland. He mentions Collins Ramusi, a cabinet minister in the Lebowa homeland, as an example. Mbeki says he doesn't know what has happened to all those contacts; they were all there when he left.

Mac Maharaj, the serving secretary of the IRD, rises to respond. He says he is pleased with what Thabo says, but must tell everyone that what was given to him when he became IRD secretary was an empty folder – it didn't even have blank paper. So, he says, he would like to know: where are Thabo's reports?

After the meeting, Maharaj and Mbeki hold a discussion.

Maharaj asks where the stuff is.

Mbeki answers that it's in a trunk that he gave to Stanley Mabizela.[53]

*

Maharaj also has a conversation with Joe Slovo on the sidelines of the Luanda meeting.

Slovo implores Maharaj to *go to the camps and get people*, referring to Maharaj's repeated expressions of the difficulty of obtaining suitable personnel to operate in the political underground.

'No, I don't want those people. They are not the people I am looking for,' Maharaj says.

Slovo then offers an anecdote. He says that when he and Modise, as commanders of MK's Central Headquarters, went about selecting the first cadres to send into South Africa, they went through Angola, the Soviet Union – basically everywhere the ANC had camps. They had a batch of index cards with holes punched in them at certain points. The points corresponded to different regions of South Africa. On each of the cards was written the name of a particular recruit, where the recruit had come from, and some biographical data. These cards were all put into a box.

What they did next was go: right, now, we need guys for, say, the Transvaal. They then plunged a knitting needle into the box at the point where the cards for Transvaal had been punched, yanked the needle out, and there, on the needle, were all their cadres from the Transvaal. They then interviewed all those people and if the person impressed during questioning, they would assign them to the regional command.

'That's not the way I'm going to collect people,' says Maharaj.[54]

*

After lunch on 2 January, Oliver Tambo tells Jack Simons he is one of five people who have been elected by the meeting to serve on a Politico-Military Strategy Commission (PMSC) that Tambo will head. Its task will be to make recommendations on a number of questions related to the movement's political and military approach.

Simons says he thinks he will be more useful in Nova Catengue.

Tambo agrees that it would be wrong to cancel the visit at this stage.

Two days later, Jack Simons moves into quarters set aside for him at Nova Catengue camp. In his diary entry for the day, he writes,

> Cuban relations deteriorated. Not many Cubans in military course ended November. Students attend political classes and do guard duty. Mzwayi says the Cubs are under impression that we regard struggle as primarily political which is the case, & feel they are superfluous (one does not want to fight). Dr Peter is upset at being ignored by Cub doctor. Gwen in clinic complains of no-cooperation.[55]

*

The Botswana Machinery resumes its infiltrations of South Africa. In Lobatse a group of eight MK cadres board a Toyota. They are commanded by Authu Muzorewa, who was injured in Witkleigat in the clash at the beginning of August the previous year. Their ultimate destination is to be Ga-Rankuwa. They have in their possession a light machine gun, AK-47s, hand grenades, four defensive and two offensive hand grenades, as well as TNT. Each man is also carrying a tin of food.

On the night of 11 January they enter South Africa illegally.

Early in the morning on the 12th, Thabo Makgage, who is operating the group's LMG, asks to be allowed to relieve himself as he has a 'runny tummy'.

He leaves the LMG with Muzorewa and makes his way to the nearest road. Soon, a vehicle approaches, driven by a white man. Makgage manages to persuade it to stop.

Makgage asks the driver to be taken to the nearest police station.

The white man, who speaks Tswana, asks why.

'Look, I'm coming from Angola where I underwent training,' Makgage says. Then he produces a hand grenade, which he gives to the white man.

The car does a U-turn and heads in the direction of the police station at the Derdepoort border post, where Makgage surrenders himself.

At about 4 p.m., Major M.D. Ras is among a group of about twenty counter-insurgency policemen who follow Thabo Makgage through thick bush near the Derdepoort checkpoint.

About 800 metres into the bush, Makgage points out two men whose attention is being distracted by cattle at a farm called Klipdrift.

Major Ras takes aim with his R1 rifle and screams at the pair.

One of them turns round, weapon in hand. Ras shoots him dead. This triggers a skirmish between the policemen and the guerrilla unit. During its course, hand grenades are thrown by the MK cadres at the police. Only the descent of darkness stops the battle.

On the following morning, the security forces scour the area. They find the corpse of a man with a bullet wound under his nose. On his person is a rough map of north-western Transvaal as well as a passbook with his photograph. The name in the book is 'Patrick Opa Tawa', but it is in fact Authu Muzorewa. (Fingerprints taken later establish his authentic identity as Richard Mapetla.)[56]

*

Andrew Masondo and Mzwai Piliso monitor a Radio South Africa broadcast. While doing so, they hear John Vorster say South Africa intends to attack a 'SWAPO' camp, 'Katenga'.[57]

In his diary entry on 16 January, Jack Simons writes: 'N.C. [i.e. Nova Catengue] is now virtually a "transit" camp (perhaps because Vorster disclosed his knowledge of its whereabouts. Guard duties & essential services are maintained, with temporary units such as "special group").'[58]

*

Early in 1979, about a year after entering South Africa, Thandi Modise notices the mother of three who owns the house where she is staying in Diepkloof check in the middle of the night to see whether she (Modise) is still asleep. The woman then slips away.

Modise follows her. She spots the woman tiptoeing to a police van parked in the street outside.

Later that morning, Modise moves out of the house without giving notice. She heads to the coloured township of Eldorado Park, where she stays with friends.[59]

*

At Nova Catengue on the morning of 14 March 1979, there is a unit guarding the approaches to the camp. There is also a platoon living outside the camp. This platoon is in possession of anti-tank guns.

At about 7 a.m. Comrade Meshengu, the commander of the anti-tank platoon, is among approximately 600 cadres on their way back to the camp for breakfast after spending the night in the bush as part of the ongoing safety precautions against an attack following Vorster's speech. On their way they see two Canberra jets approaching.

There are only about eleven people in the camp at the time. These eleven are preparing breakfast. Among them are a Cuban commander and commissar.

More than 500 bombs of different types are dropped on Nova Catengue. Two South Africans and one Cuban are killed in the attack, which lasts a mere three minutes.

When the Canberras leave, the camp has been razed to the ground. Even the chickens that had been grazing there are scorched to death.

After the attack, Nova Catengue is closed down and the cadres are moved to another base in Quibaxe further to the north.[60]

*

Towards the end of March 1979 at 'Gebuza's house' (i.e. the Transvaal Urban Machinery's headquarters) in Liberdad, Maputo, Johannes Rasegatla tells Simon Mogoerane, Solly Shoke and Thabo Motaung that everything is ready for them in South Africa.

Mogoerane, Shoke and Motaung travel from Maputo to Manzini, and after two days in Swaziland enter South Africa with falsified Swazi passports.

At Johannesburg Station, the trio are met by Nicholas Hlongwane, who takes them to Soweto. The four belong to a unit known as G-5 (the fifth member committed suicide just before their departure from Angola).

They then make their way to an underground base in Soweto that Rasegatla referred to in Liberdad. In reality it is a dugout that they can crawl in and out of. They are not impressed at all. They soon discover that it leaks, and its location is known to people in the local community. They resolve to leave, but only after first conducting an operation.[61]

*

By the evening of 3 May, they are ready. Hlongwane, Mogoerane, Motaung and Shoke take a taxi from Baragwanath to Moroka, and then walk to a field from where they retrieve some weapons. The four are dressed in brown overalls and boots.

They proceed in two groups, with Mogoerane and Motaung walking about ten paces behind Shoke and Hlongwane, who arrive at the front gate of Moroka Police Station around 9.10 p.m.

Shoke and Hlongwane open fire. Constable Brian Temba, who is on guard duty at the gate and having a conversation with a Mr Tshabalala and Ms Anna Sithole, is struck at least twice by bullets. He and Tshabalala collapse into each other, while Ms Sithole, who is not struck, falls flat, taking cover.

Mogoerane follows Shoke and Hlongwane by running into the corrugated-iron building that represents the police station. When inside, they head in the direction of a room with its lights on. Mogoerane fires a shot into this room, but the bullet goes through the window on the other side. After this his gun jams.

The firing continues, and a black policeman on duty at the front desk in the charge office, Constable Edward Moreni, is shot and collapses. Ms Magagula and Mr Shongweni, who were also in the room, are struck and injured. The other policemen who were on service in the room have managed to flee behind the office and take cover in the cells.

Grenades are thrown into the enquiries office and the archive room. A grenade wrecks the archives and destroys hundreds of police dossiers.

Mogoerane is now carrying a petrol can. Outside the building, during the guerrillas' getaway, he pours petrol from the can through the window pane that was earlier pierced by his bullet. He then sets the petrol on fire with matches.

When they reach the gate they see a car that wants to enter. Mogoerane tells the people inside the vehicle to go away. The driver obliges.

Before making their final exit, the guerrillas leave propaganda pamphlets behind. One of them reads: 'Remember June 1976; Remember Mahlangu. Take up arms and fight.'

The group safely completes its retreat.[62]

*

After their success at Moroka, the group concentrates on finding a new base.

They identify a new site at a disused gold mine. The entrance shaft is three feet high, supported by pit props. It then drops downhill a bit before levelling out. This enables the cadres to get more than ten metres underground.

The men put their mattresses and other belongings inside and hide their weapons in the base, before moving in.[63]

*

Oliver Tambo delivers a presidential address to a sitting of the ANC's NEC in Tanzania on 28 May. Outlining the state of the struggle, he says: 'Comrades some years back the NEC took a decision that the process of the intensification of the struggle inside the country requires the leadership should begin to move closer to home. What is the current position?'

It is, he says, that out of the total of twenty NEC members, six are based permanently in countries bordering South Africa, five 'in departments that deal with internal work', while others participate in discussions dealing with aspects of internal work.

Considering the armed struggle, 'We must admit among ourselves that our roar is indeed very thunderous while our claws are virtually absent. To correct this situation and strike as effectively as we roar, we must, with utmost seriousness, set about the task of building up a people's army within South Africa, among the masses of our people.'

Given this priority, 'military combat within the country now, today can only have the intention of assisting in our organisational and mobilisation work. We must therefore plan for it – plan for our operations to have maximum political impact. The recent operation at the Moroka Police Station in Soweto is of the kind that I am talking about.'

As for the regional situation:

Already we have MK combatants in Zimbabwe operating with ZIPRA forces. In this regard we are pursuing the major objectives, namely, to establish a presence in Zimbabwe to enable us to be able to operate independently from Zimbabwe basing ourselves on our combatants who should have dug themselves in within Zimbabwe; secondly, we seek to open another route into our country.

This is basically a reprise of the Wankie and Sipolilo campaign objective of deploying men to Rhodesia to assist ZAPU to overthrow the Rhodesian government while simultaneously establishing transit routes through the country that cadres can later use to infiltrate South Africa.

Concerning Swaziland, 'It would seem that we have gone through the worst period … Yet it is clear that the Botha regime will continue to pressurise Swaziland if not to evict us from the country, then to make it impossible for us to work.'

Eviction from the territory through which the majority of MK infiltrations into South Africa are launched would be disastrous. Reflecting on this, Tambo says:

Our own experience points to the fact that we need Swaziland. We shall obviously remain in this position for the foreseeable future. Equally it is in our interest that imperialism should not be allowed to use Swaziland as a base of subversion and aggression against the People's Republic of Mozambique. What we are therefore confronted with comrades is a difficult, an uphill and a complex struggle for the allegiance of Swaziland to the struggle for the liberation of Southern Africa against her seduction into the ranks of the forces of counter-revolution.[64]

*

Quite how difficult, uphill and complex that struggle might be is indicated a few days later, on 8 June 1979, when Major Maphevu Dlamini, who combines the positions of Swazi prime minister and head of the Royal Swazi Defence Force (RSDF), holds a secret meeting with South African Military Intelligence officers.

Dlamini says Swaziland, South Africa and other southern African states share a common enemy. This enemy now poses a genuine threat that needs to be countered with urgency. The only effective solution lies in close cooperation, and not with the United Nations or the Organisation of African Unity. The world has belatedly begun to realise that Swaziland will not allow itself to be used as a pawn in an ideological struggle. Dlamini declares that he will not allow Swaziland to be locked in the same stranglehold as Kenneth Kaunda.

He welcomes the prospect of an exchange of information and continuous co-operation between the SADF and the RSDF in order to analyse and confront this threat.

He says he subscribes to the view that in order to cooperate effectively, the two militaries must standardise equipment and procedures and undergo a degree of joint training. Leadership, mine laying and agent handling are areas in which Swaziland would be interested in cooperation with South Africa.

He also raises the possibility of the kingdom purchasing arms from South Africa, as Swaziland is experiencing problems sourcing supplements from Britain. He calls for a workgroup or action committee to be established as quickly as possible, and recommends that good mutual connections between the two armies be established prior to a later exchange of representatives.[65]

*

Prime Minister Dlamini meets Brigadier P.J. Schalkwyk, Commandant C.J. van Niekerk and Major Ian R. Gleeson in Swaziland on 5 July 1979.

Dlamini says he is serious about cooperation. He repeats his gripe about the Swazi Army's problems in acquiring weapons and equipment. He also raises the RSDF's need for standardisation, not only in these spheres but also with regard to vehicles. These problems could be eliminated by joint procedures with South Africa. He says he would like to visit South African Military Intelligence facilities as well as oversee the training exercise that the South African Army's 81st Armoured Brigade will be conducting from 16 to 17 September.

He also mentions problems the Swazi Army is having sourcing cannons and ammunition for firing a twenty-one-gun salute on King Sobhuza's eightieth birthday celebrations on 22 July. He requests help from the SADF because the cannons from Britain will not arrive in time.

Major Gleeson offers to make an 88-mm field cannon available, as well as an instructor to train RSDF staff beforehand so they can make the shot themselves.

Dlamini accepts.[66]

*

Following King Sobhuza's birthday celebrations on 22 July, Maphevu Dlamini thanks the South African military training team for the success of the twenty-one-gun salute.

Lieutenant Colonel Dube, the second in command in the RSDF, then jocularly asks Major T.J. Vermaak, the leader of the South African training team, to transfer to the Swazi Army, for 'unity is strength'.

A Swazi civilian official present expresses his personal sorrow that cooperation between Swaziland and South Africa, which is going so well on the military level, is not being emulated in other spheres.[67]

*

The ANC's NEC meets again on 12 August, this time in Morogoro. Those assembled consider the report of the PMSC, which was established in January following the NEC/RC meeting in Luanda. Its report, also known as the 'Green Book' after the colour of its bound cover, was completed in March.[68]

In its first section, titled 'Our Strategic Line', the Green Book refers to the directives given to the PMSC in Luanda (that it offer recommendations on how a strategy based on mass mobilisation, the construction of the broadest possible front for liberation, drawing in activists from the struggle into the underground, and tailoring armed actions to meet these objectives, might best be achieved).

The document recounts that during the PMSC's deliberations, its members were influenced by the idea that consensus on a single, broad platform of common aims ought to follow rather than precede the work of political reconstruction, and that at the initial stage, 'unity of action' should instead be the goal. That said, the question of 'the more long-term aims of our national democratic revolution', and above all, of whether the ANC 'should tie itself to the ideology of Marxism-Leninism and publicly commit itself to the socialist option', was not ignored. The prevailing view was that 'direct or indirect commitment at this stage to a continuing revolution which would lead to a socialist order may unduly narrow' the 'line-up of social forces' prepared to join the envisaged national liberation front. But 'no member of the Commission had any doubts about the ultimate need to continue our revolution towards a socialist order; the issue was posed only in relation to the tactical considerations of the present stage of our struggle'.

Another discussion point was the role of armed struggle within the new strategic framework. The key question here was whether the movement envisaged the seizure of power resulting from a general all-round nationwide insurrection or from a 'protracted people's war' in which partial and general uprisings would play a vital role. The latter was generally felt to be more likely.

The authors of the Green Book note that the document contains no references to the peasantry, with mention only being made of the 'landless mass in the countryside'. The reason given for this is that insufficient attention has been paid by the movement to the questions of the existing class relations and the full extent of land hunger in rural areas. Such a survey would need to occur before any prognosis on the prospects for rural guerrilla warfare could be offered.

As an annex, the Green Book features a paper titled 'Summarised Theses on our Strategic Line', which offers further reflections on how the armed struggle will be affected by the new emphasis on 'political activity and organisation leading to the creation of a network of political revolutionary bases which will become the foundation of our People's War'. It states that given this emphasis on political reconstruction, for the foreseeable future the objective of military operations ought to be:

(a) to keep alive the perspective of People's revolutionary violence as the ultimate weapon for the seizure of power.

(b) to concentrate on armed propaganda actions, that is, armed action whose immediate purpose is to support and stimulate political activity and organisation rather than to hit at the enemy.[69]

The NEC meeting adopts the Green Book as the basic guideline for ANC work within South Africa.[70]

*

Another of the directives given to the PMSC in January was to deliver recommendations concerning the creation of a 'Central Organ' to plan, coordinate and direct all ANC activities inside South Africa.

The August 1979 NEC meeting devotes a good part of its time to considering the matter further. It decides *against* forming the Central Organ, opting instead to revamp the Revolutionary Council by creating 'Senior Organs' (SOs) based in the Forward Areas. The mission of the SOs will be to achieve greater centralisation in terms of planning, coordinating and implementing political and military work. The Organs are to be manned by NEC members resident in the respective Forward Areas, and they are to report directly to the RC.

During the early hours of 14 August, in one of the final issues considered at the NEC's Morogoro meeting, it is decided that a delegation led by Oliver Tambo should soon meet Inkatha leader Mangosuthu Buthelezi, who has repeatedly opposed the use of armed struggle as a method of resistance in South Africa.

The delegates recommend that the discussion with 'Gatsha' should be 'very frank' about his recent 'utterances and doings'.[71]

*

Montso Mokgabudi, alias 'Obadi', arrives at 'Funda', an MK base in Angola which is a finishing camp for cadres soon to be deployed to South Africa.

Mokgabudi approaches Aboobaker Ismail, the camp's chief instructor, and asks him to work with Barney Molokoane in training a special unit that can carry out select missions inside South Africa.[72]

*

The name South African Military Intelligence has given to its programme of cooperation with Swaziland is 'Operation Santa'.

At a meeting with a very senior member of the RSDF on 18 October, members of the South African Military Intelligence Directorate hand over a document containing a threat assessment.

The RSDF man tells them he will study the document and submit it to headquarters for formal approval. He adds that in the meantime he wants to warn them to be on guard against 'terrorist' infiltration from the north of Swaziland. He says the RSDF has partial information of ANC activity in the Piggs Peak plantations.[73]

*

A seventeen-man Inkatha delegation meets seven ANC members at the Exelsior Hotel in Heathrow, London, at the end of October.

In his opening remarks, Chief Mangosuthu Buthelezi says Inkatha is following the ANC tradition and he therefore wants the ANC to recognise it as a National Liberation Movement. But he also brings Inkatha's differences with the ANC to the fore. On the armed struggle, he says 'the black population of South Africa has ceased to believe that successful action on the military level will be forthcoming from the ANC'. Violence is 'emotionally and intellectually alien' to those masses, who want a return to a 'more traditional ANC stance'. Inkatha meanwhile will not be drawn into any armed conflict while peaceful change remains possible.

Buthelezi instead proposes a multi-strategy approach by the various anti-apartheid movements, in which each fights the system in its own way.[74]

*

Late on the afternoon of 31 October, while Thandi Modise is preparing supper for the family she lives with in Eldorado Park, she hears a knock on the door.

Three policemen enter the property. One of them, Seth Sols, is a coloured security officer. He is accompanied by two Indian colleagues.

The trio search Modise's flat. From it they confiscate a number of books, including one by Joe Slovo. Hidden under the sofa, they retrieve a Scorpion pistol and two passports – one for Bophuthatswana and the other for Swaziland. From a tap near the toilet, they recover a bottle containing chemical explosives and TNT.

While under interrogation later at John Vorster Square Police Station, Modise is confronted with pictures taken of her during her short stay in Mozambique in January 1978, prior to being forwarded to Swaziland and then to South Africa. The photos are kept in what the policemen refer to as their 'terror album'.[75]

*

Between 12.30 a.m. and 12.45 a.m. on the morning of 2 November, Simon Mogoerane takes up position to the rear of Orlando Police Station. He is actually inside the premises of an adjacent property belonging to the West Rand Administration Board.

His colleagues in the G-5 Unit, Solly Shoke, Thabo Motaung and Johannes

Rasegatla, simultaneously approach the front of the station. They are wearing rain-coats and are armed with AK-47s, as is Mogoerane.

From the vicinity of some trees opposite the station, Shoke, Motaung and Rase-gatla open fire at on-duty policemen standing in front of the charge office. The first officer they hit is Constable Jerry Musindane, twenty-three, who runs for about fifty metres before collapsing dead.

Constable Christopher Zibi returns fire but is struck on his side by a fusillade of bullets that nearly sever his right arm from his body.

Constable Thami Dyantyi, who was walking from office number 3 to the station's prefabricated charge office when the shooting began, is shot in the knee, causing his legs to fold. He drags himself behind the charge office, where he hides himself, though another bullet hits him in the thigh while there.

Sipho Zungu, a journalist, who was making a complaint in the charge office when the shooting commenced, is hit in the calf.

The fire returned by Constable Zibi and others causes the guerrillas to retreat behind some parked cars, from where they resume firing. During the ensuing cross-fire bullets rip into cars parked outside the station.

Mogoerane opens fire from his position at the West Rand Administration Board property. His shots are directed at police barracks housing some sixty policemen at the rear of the station.

A tall fence separates the Administration Board premises from the backyard of Orlando Police Station. Mogoerane fires until the ill-fitting dust-cover of his AK-47 falls off.

From this point, the rifle will not fire.

Mogoerane's three colleagues enter the police barracks at the station's rear, and order the policemen out of their beds. Two of the guerrillas then walk out, apparently expecting the policemen to follow. None of the policemen exit.

With his AK disabled, Mogoerane attempts to throw his six hand grenades into the police station yard to help lure the policemen out, but he struggles to throw them over the high fence. Three grenades hit the fence and bounce back before exploding. Another falls on the Orlando Old Age Home for Cripples, blowing a hole in its roof. A fifth grenade does get over the fence but explodes harmlessly on the ground.

When Shoke, Motaung and Rasegatla hear the grenade explosions, they make their getaway.[76]

*

For South Africa's security forces, an alarming signal emerges from the usual intelli-gence noise during November 1979. The signal is from the north, from Botswana and Rhodesia, which is now called Zimbabwe-Rhodesia following an agreement in March 1978 between Ian Smith and the black leaders Bishop Abel Muzorewa, Chief Jeremiah Chirau and Reverend Ndabaningi Sithole. This agreement led to elections in April 1979, which Muzorewa won. However, a Commonwealth meeting in August 1979 called for a new constitution leading to a general ceasefire and fresh elections under British supervision. Since September both the Zimbabwe-Rhodesia government and the liberation movements have been in session at a constitutional conference in Lancaster House, London.[77]

On 11 November 1979 the Northern Transvaal Command of the South African Army sends a message to military headquarters saying that a source codenamed 'Slabbie' has reported that today at Kasane, on the Botswana side of the Zambezi River, he spoke to two acquaintances who serve as guides for ANC and ZAPU guerrillas. One said they were on their way to Zambia and would return in two to three weeks with a new group that would pass from Zambia to Botswana and then to Zimbabwe-Rhodesia, before finally penetrating South Africa.[78]

*

Nine days later, a South African Military Intelligence dossier records a source reporting that seventeen ANC 'terrorists' are expected to arrive in Selibe-Phikwe with a view to infiltrating South Africa on or about 21 November 1979 in the vicinity of Martinsdrift.[79]

*

On the 22nd, a ZAPU guerrilla is interrogated in Zimbabwe-Rhodesia. He is of Matabele origin and says he was part of a group that sometimes moves with the ANC. He claims Zulu- and Xhosa-speaking MK cadres have long been in the area of Patana and east of the Tuli circle in Zimbabwe-Rhodesia.

The camps in which he resided with ANC members were near Selibe-Phikwe, at Dukwe near Francistown, and at Kabajango, from where the joint group proceeded to Zimbabwe-Rhodesia. He says some ANC 'terrorists' have moved further towards South Africa.

He mentions that he heard the MK men talk about reinforcements. He claims there are plans to infiltrate South Africa when the bush is thick during the November/December rainy season. The uniforms used by the ANC military cadres are dim green and their weapons are AKs, folding-butt AKs, hand grenades and TNT blocks.

This information is conveyed by the Rhodesians to South African Military Intelligence counterparts.[80]

*

Another South African Military Intelligence document surfaces the same day. It reports that from available information there are currently almost 200 MK terrorists in Botswana aiming to reach South Africa. Some are possibly already in the Francistown area, from where they will proceed in small groups to a division point near the South African border.

Apparently, the Botswana Defence Force is helping them, but it is not yet known whether President Khama knows or approves. Due to a lack of ongoing tactical information, the terrorists do not as yet represent acceptable targets for pre-emptive operations.[81]

*

The signals help induce a South African military intervention. On 30 November, Prime Minister P.W. Botha tells attendees at a function in Voortrekkerhoogte, Pretoria, held in honour of the outgoing chief of the South African Air Force, Lieutenant General Bob Rogers, that 'South Africa, after consultation with the government of Zimbabwe-Rhodesia, has for some time now been looking to the protection of our interests as well as our vital lines of communication such as the rail link to Beitbridge and the railway links through it'.

He adds: 'ANC terrorists, collaborating with the Patriotic Front, have set as their targets the harming of South African interests. No right thinking person can expect Zimbabwe-Rhodesia to protect these interests in the midst of her own problems.'[82]

*

In Maputo early in December 1979, Ncimbithi Lubisi, Petrus Mashigo and Naphtali Manana meet 'Paul', 'Thabo' and 'Kenny' of the Transvaal Rural Machinery.

'Paul' says they must attack Soekmekaar Police Station, because in that district people are being forcibly removed to an arid area and are not happy about it. Officers attached to the police station are assisting in the removal; hence the mission will be to stage an act of 'armed propaganda' there.

Lubisi, Mashigo and Manana enter South Africa from Swaziland on 5 December 1979 in the company of a man codenamed 'Lungile'.[83] This is one of a series of infiltrations into South Africa that MK launches through Swaziland that month.

*

Four days later, Ikanyeng Molebatsi, Benjamin Tau and Fanie Mafoko enter South Africa from Swaziland.[84]

*

Around the same time, Joseph Zakile Zulu also infiltrates South Africa from Swaziland. He has been deployed to serve as MK's commander for the urban areas of southern Natal.[85]

*

On 21 December, Wilfred Madela and Humphrey Makhubo arrive in South Africa from Swaziland. When they approach a rendezvous point at Ga-Rankuwa Shopping Centre, Benjamin Tau immediately recognises them.[86]

*

Six days later, however, Joseph Zakile Zulu, Umkhonto we Sizwe's commander for southern Natal's urban areas, walks into Security Branch offices in Loop Street, Pietermaritzburg, and surrenders.[87]

*

On the fourth day of 1980, Ncimbithi Lubisi, Petrus Mashigo, Naphtali Manana and 'Lungile' are waiting on the road from Duiwelskloof to Soekmekaar, trying to get a lift.

At about 6.30 p.m. a bakkie stops. They enter, only to hold up the driver, 'Mr Montle', at gunpoint. They then depart in the vehicle, leaving Montle behind.

At their destination, which is Soekmekaar Police Station, they get out. Mashigo and Lungile enter the station's front yard through a small gate. The only light that is on is in the charge office. Two policemen are seated on the station's porch.

As they approach this stoep, Mashigo fires two shots in the air. The two men jump up. One runs inside the station while the other flees to the left of the building and towards the backyard.

Mashigo runs towards the station and resumes firing, this time directly at the building, peppering it with bullets.

Mashigo then heads, not into the station itself, but around the left side of the building, in pursuit of the policeman who fled towards the backyard. He fires a shot over the head of the fleeing policeman.

Lungile then also runs around the building, but towards its right.

Mashigo turns to throw his grenade back towards the entrance of the station, in the direction from which he has come. As he does so, a grenade thrown by Lungile – also hurled back towards the entrance – explodes directly in front of Mashigo and injures him in both legs.

This does not prevent Mashigo from throwing his grenade. It does not explode. Only then does he notice that only the grenade's ring remains on his finger (which means that the pin remained in the grenade, and because it was not removed the device did not explode).

After this, Mashigo continues running towards the rear of the station, where he continues firing into the air.

Naphtali Manana has meanwhile remained at the gate, standing guard. He notices some vehicle lights 200–300 metres away. He fires shots into the air to scare the car away. The car's lights are then turned off, after which the driver does a U-turn and departs.

Shortly afterwards Lungile and Mashigo reunite with Manana. The trio then return to the getaway bakkie in which Lubisi has been waiting.[88]

*

Benjamin Tau, Fanie Mafoko, Wilfred Madela and Humphrey Makhubo meet in Ga-Rankuwa on 12 January. They decide to go back to Swaziland. They agree they must steal a car to facilitate the withdrawal.

Two days later, Tau is apprehended while trying to steal a car. Makhubo, who was with him, manages to escape.[89]

*

In Matola, outside Maputo, Jeremia Radebe and Grant Shezi receive instructions from Zweli Nyanda (Siphiwe Nyanda's brother) of the Natal Urban Machinery. Nyanda tells them that upon their entry into South Africa they are not to touch the buried weapons and explosives until they have contacted their link man at the Inanda Seminary on 31 January. He adds that the date for the demolition remains up to them; they will need to check the weapons and explosives every week, but further instructions will be provided by the contact.

Nyanda then gives Shezi R140 and Radebe R160 and conveys to them a final message that they must go to Umbumbulu and St Wendolins to explore that area and see if there are any bushes and forests near important urban centres.

On 23 January, Shezi and Radebe leave Matola in a green Volkswagen with a TJ registration number. The car is driven by a coloured man, Edward Lawrence. They head to Mozambique's border with Swaziland.[90]

*

Just before 1 p.m. on 25 January in Pretoria Street in Silverton, Pretoria, Mr P. Prinsloo, aged twenty-one, and his girlfriend, Miss L. Bernberg, walk past the north entrance of a branch of the Volkskas Bank. They see two men remove a couple of rifles from a bag before rushing into the bank. The men bump into a woman leaving the bank, who screams when she notices the rifles.

Danie and Margaretha Christie are also walking towards the bank's exit. The gunmen hustle them back into the building.

The people in the bank are ordered to stand; then they are told to sit; then to lie flat on the floor. Banknotes are scattered all over the floor.

One of the gunmen says his group are freedom fighters interested in 'Black Power' only, and that they don't want money. He says they have been trained in Angola.

On the bank's mezzanine level, Dina van Rooyen, a ledger clerk, hears shouting and looks down to the ground-floor level. She sees a man in overalls wearing a little cap and carrying a rifle.

Van Rooyen and other women on the upper floor are crying, but soon there is quiet on the ground floor and the women decide to escape. They flee through a doorway leading to flats attached to the building. They join the majority of the bank's staff of about sixty people in escaping through a back entrance and through windows.

This leaves about twenty-five hostages on the ground floor.[91]

Captain Christiaan de Swardt arrives at the bank at about 1.12 p.m. and finds a number of policemen already in position at various points around the property. Many civilians have gathered outside.

De Swardt climbs out of his car and runs towards the bank. He looks in through the door and at the furthest point sees a large number of white men and women with their hands on their heads. Before them is a black man with his finger on the trigger of an AK-47 strapped over his soldier.

Captain Erasmus comes to De Swardt, gives him a report, and points out another guerrilla with an AK-47, sitting on his haunches on top of a counter by a window on the left-hand side of the bank. This man's rifle is pointed at a woman sitting before him. There are also two grenades on the counter.

De Swardt notices a third man to his right, in front of whom a number of bank clerks and officials are crouching behind the counter.

De Swardt asks aloud into the building if there is anything he can do for anybody.

The man on his haunches by the window says that the woman will bring out their demands. He then tells Erasmus and De Swardt to get out. They do so.[92]

Phoebe Chatwind is the woman in question. She has bank slips on the desk in front of her and a pen in hand. The guerrilla is sitting above her on top of the table. He tells her to write that they are from the ANC. Then he tells her to say that they want Mange, that they want to be allowed to depart to Angola with Mange. Chatwind writes 'Mange'. She then writes 'Pietermaritzburg 12' after the man tells her to add this. Then 'Remember Solomon Mahlangu' – that is the next instruction. Then 'With Mange to Angola'.

The guerrilla then tells Chatwind to write down the Freedom Charter's demands. Following his dictation, she writes: '1. People shall have, people shall govern 2. All the nations shall have equal right …' This continues until '9. There shall be peace and friendship', after which she writes '10'. The man tells her that there are ten demands, but he can't remember the tenth.[93]

Captains de Swardt and Erasmus return to the entrance at about 1.30 p.m. As they do so, Chatwind is sent out, along with Mr J.S. Witmore, the bank's assistant manager.[94] Chatwind hands the note containing the demands to Captain de Swardt. On it he sees the names Mange and Mahlangu. De Swardt again asks if there is anything he can do for anybody. The guerrilla by the window again says no, but after reconsidering he asks for cigarettes for the hostages. At this stage the hostages are all sitting flat on low stools.

At 6.30 p.m. the spokesman among the guerrillas issues a demand to be given the brown bag containing hand grenades and magazines that was left outside the bank when he and his colleagues stormed the building. He says they will start shooting hostages if the demand isn't met in half an hour.

Captain de Swardt asks for more time.

The man says he will give De Swardt an hour.

De Swardt gives a report to General Mike Geldenhuys, the commissioner of police, who has flown up from Cape Town to be at the scene. Geldenhuys says the terrorists must be eliminated and gives De Swardt a code to use to alert the police sharpshooters to open fire. De Swardt is told to re-enter the bank at 7.03 p.m. and give the codeword two minutes later *if* he judges that the hostages will not be in the path of the police bullets. Geldenhuys orders the immediate area around the bank to be cleared in preparation for action.

De Swardt re-enters the bank at 7.03 p.m.

Two minutes later, six policemen in camouflage outfits and safari suits run to the bank's entrance.

Police lieutenant Charles Brazelle of the Police Special Task Force meanwhile enters a back door alongside Sergeant Hendrik Lombard. The pair creep down a basement passage and up some steps till they reach a trapdoor leading onto the ground floor. They take up position, waiting for the codeword.

Captain de Swardt gives the codeword.

Two guerrillas standing near one of the bank's entrances are immediately shot dead by sharpshooters on the mezzanine floor.

De Swardt looks to see where the man who was standing on the other side of the tellers' counter might be. This is the man who acted as chief spokesman. De Swardt can't see him. Someone screams that the third terrorist has run away.[95]

Lieutenant Brazelle and Sergeant Lombard from the Special Task Force enter the bank from the basement. As they emerge into the building, they find the third man: Brazelle sees him immediately in front, sitting on a typist's stool with his back against a wall pillar near one of the cashier's cubicles (he is facing away from them). Brazelle immediately fires three shots at the man with his Colt Calibre rifle. The shots hit the man on his lower back, and he begins to sag forward, slowly.

Sergeant Lombard is directly behind Brazelle. Lombard also fires two shots with his R1 weapon at the guerrilla's torso. Shortly afterwards Lieutenant Brazelle gives a ceasefire order. Lombard then moves along with Brazelle in the direction of the guerrilla at the counter.

As they do this, the man makes a sudden movement, and Brazelle fires another shot with his Colt. At this stage the AK-47 in the guerrilla's possession falls – but so does a hand grenade.

This F1 grenade, which has had its pin pulled out, falls to the left of the guerrilla, and close to where a hostage, Igor Grobbelaar, is laying on the ground. The grenade lands eight inches from Grobbelaar's face. Grobbelaar grabs it and throws it along the floor out of the cubicle.

Lieutenant Brazelle is about three metres from the hand grenade when it explodes. He takes two steps, but then his legs give way.

After the explosion, the guerrilla, who has now reclaimed possession of his rifle, starts firing again. Grobbelaar turns on his back and looks in the direction in which the shots are aimed. He sees a woman, Cindy Anderson, has been hit. Grobbelaar then kicks the weapon out of the guerrilla's hands and against the frame of the cashier's till. Then some policemen pull the now unarmed guerrilla out of the cubicle.

Grobbelaar then hears further gunshots.[96]

Professor Loubser performs autopsies on the bodies of the men responsible for the Silverton siege. One is identified as Fanie Mafoko, the second as Wilfred Madela, the last as Humphrey Makhubo. Mafoko was the lead spokesman and also the last of the three to be killed.[97]

*

Warrant Officer Johannes Ehlers travels from Tzaneen to White River on 29 January 1980. There he takes custody of Petrus Mashigo (of the unit that attacked Soekmekaar Police Station earlier in the month). Mashigo is in the custody of Major van Wyk. Ehlers takes Mashigo back to Security Branch offices in Tzaneen.

En route, Mashigo says they should travel along the road to Tzaneen that passes through Lydenburg, and proceed until they reach a twenty-kilometre board on the left-hand side of the road. They must then walk sixteen steps across the road and then some thirty steps in the direction of Tzaneen. There, by a shortish thick tree, they will find a place where the ground has recently been disturbed.

Later, at the mentioned place, Ehlers digs into the ground and unearths two blue trunks containing weapons.

On the following day, Detective Sergeant Johan du Plooy is part of a team that takes up position outside a rondavel with a grass roof. The hut is part of a kraal in the Oakley Reserve in the Hazyview district.

Du Plooy has a flashlight which he places on a wall so that it shines on the rondavel's door about eight metres away. Warrant Officer Potgieter moves closer to the door, keeping his back to the wall. Potgieter then knocks on the door, saying: 'Police, open up.'

There is no answer.

Potgieter knocks a second time, this time louder, and repeats: 'Police, open up.'

Ncimbithi Lubisi, a colleague of Mashigo in the Soekmekaar attack, is inside the room. A child is in there with him.

Lubisi hears the police outside the rondavel call out, 'Lubisi.' They tell him to come out.

Warrant Officer Potgieter looks through a slight gap between the door and its frame (this gap is illuminated by the flashlight) and thinks he sees movement. The child begins to scream, after which the door suddenly springs open. Potgieter calls out that the person in the room must hand himself over, adding: 'We are armed!'

Detective Sergeant du Plooy sees that Lubisi and the child have remained in the hut and that Lubisi is holding the child tightly by the arm. The child continues to scream. At one point the child escapes Lubisi's grasp and grabs the doorknob. Lubisi pulls him back.

When this happens, Du Plooy fires at the rondavel, but in the air at an angle of thirty to forty-five degrees, because Potgieter is in his line of fire. The child starts crying uncontrollably.

The police order Lubisi to come out with his hands raised and throw himself on the ground with his hands behind his back.

Lubisi lets go and the child runs out, and a few seconds later he dives out of the room himself and lies on the floor as ordered. The police pounce and place him in handcuffs.[98]

*

On 31 January, Grant Shezi and Jeremia Radebe approach Inanda Seminary, north of Durban. They are there for the meeting with the contact man to whom Zweli Nyanda referred in the briefing in Maputo.

Shezi immediately recognises Joseph Zakile Zulu, MK's Southern Natal (Urban) commander – or so he thinks. While Radebe, Shezi and Zulu greet each other, Shezi looks up and sees that they are surrounded by policemen.[99]

*

Kenneth Phiri arrives at ZAPU headquarters in Lusaka in February 1980, along with a colleague, 'Morris'. There they meet Montso Mokgabudi, alias 'Obadi', of MK. Phiri and Morris are then integrated into a group of twenty-five ZAPU military cadres.

Mokgabudi is again present when a ZAPU commander briefs the twenty-five. The ZAPU man tells them they will infiltrate Zimbabwe and proceed to Assembly Point Juliet at Zezani near Beitbridge in the Sivoka Tribal Trust Land. (Juliet is one of a number of assembly points established in Zimbabwe-Rhodesia to accommodate ZAPU and ZANU military cadres as part of a ceasefire that came into effect on 28 December after agreement was reached at the Lancaster House constitutional talks on 21 December.)

The ZAPU man adds that at Juliet they will bolster ZIPRA, because ZANLA (ZANU's military wing) at present outnumbers ZIPRA there.

Phiri and Morris are then given a separate briefing by Mokgabudi. He tells them they are joining the ZIPRA call-sign to gain experience, assess the situation in Zimbabwe, and generally reconnoitre areas that the ANC may possibly use in the future.

After these instructions, the twenty-five are taken to Livingstone, and then to a point near Kazungula, where they cross the Zambezi into Botswana.[100]

*

At Phelindaba in northern Zululand, about forty kilometres from the border with Mozambique, Nicolas Ndlovu, manager of a trading store, frees himself from a tree to which he has been bound, blindfolded.

He then walks twenty kilometres to the nearest police station.

Under questioning, Ndlovu says that 'terrorists' armed with AK-47 rifles and an RPG-7 rocket launcher, and dressed in olive-green army uniforms, dragged him and a young boy out of their rooms. They assaulted the boy and a watchman before telling everybody to inform the police of what happened. Ndlovu was then blindfolded and told he would be taken for military training in Mozambique. About one and a half kilometres from the store, however, the terrorists tied him to the tree and told him he was too useless to be trained.[101]

Lieutenant Colonel Leon Mellet, the head of the Directorate of Public Relations in the South African Police, issues a statement later the same day to the effect that the police have found weapons and ammunition caches at various places in northern Natal. Mellet says the police have established beyond doubt that ANC terrorists were responsible for the abduction. He further alleges that the MK men crossed from Mozambique and concealed arms and ammunition at several places, with the apparent intention of using them later.[102]

*

At South Africa's defence headquarters on 25 February, twenty-three representatives of the SADF meet three counterparts from the Rhodesian Army.

Brigadier L. Jacobs, director-general of combined operations in the SADF, briefs them on the elections that are in progress in Zimbabwe-Rhodesia. He says that of the fourteen assembly points, those in the west are occupied by ZIPRA, those in the east by ZANLA, and those in the south jointly by ZIPRA and ZANLA.

Jacobs predicts that if ZANU loses the election ZANLA will likely resume the war. To counter this, the Rhodesian Security Forces plan to deploy their troops during the night of 29 February in preparation for possible action, codenamed 'Operation Melba'.

Jacobs adds that after Assembly Points Juliet and Kilo have merged there will be about 200 ANC terrorists there. If ZANU rejects the election results and resorts to arms, then under the Melba plan, the attack on Juliet will be designated to the SADF. All the other assaults will be conducted by Rhodesian forces. The South African Air Force will, however, be required to assist in the attacks on the other assembly points.[103]

*

On 5 March, the *Rand Daily Mail* announces the results of Zimbabwe's independence elections. ZANU-PF has won 64 per cent of the votes cast and will have fifty-seven seats, while ZAPU will have twenty seats and Bishop Abel Muzorewa's UANC only three. ZANU will thus form Zimbabwe's first post-independence government[104] (rendering 'Operation Melba', premised on ZANU resorting to arms upon defeat at the polls, void).

*

At Lusaka Airport, Mac Maharaj disembarks from an aeroplane from Maputo. Later, at his residence, he is met by Wankie campaign veteran Shooter Makasi, who is now Oliver Tambo's main bodyguard. Makasi says he has been sent to collect Maharaj and take him straight to head office. Maharaj persuades Makasi to leave him and let him make his own way to the office.

Maharaj arrives at the office much later, wearing jeans, and without Makasi. Somebody tells him that Tambo is not there, but at a certain house.

Maharaj heads to the house, arriving just as Tambo is entering a car.

'Jump in,' says Tambo, who is unamused by Maharaj's no-show at the office.

On the road to the airport, Tambo says: 'Look, I've called you because tomorrow there's a meeting of the RC, and I'm leaving tonight.' A discussion commenced the previous day, he says, on the topic of creating a so-called '70th Region' that aims to use MK's work alongside ZAPU in Zimbabwe as a basis for establishing guerrilla warfare in the north-eastern Transvaal – places like Lebowa, Venda, Pietersburg and Seshego. The Mozambicans have given the ANC a camp in northern Mozambique close to the Tanzanian border, which could be used as a rear base.

Tambo expresses a fear that the project will degenerate into a military adventure.

He says he wants Maharaj to make sure he is at the meeting to ensure that the initiative has a proper politico-military thrust.[105]

*

On 17 March, the chief of the South African Army conveys a message to the country's military attaché in Salisbury, the capital of what is now simply Zimbabwe. The message is that the Northern Transvaal Command has received information that ANC terrorists are being deployed together with ZIPRA forces in Zimbabwe's Gokwe area where MK has 100 cadres, and also at Essexvale camp where an estimated 50 MK terrorists have been integrated with the Rhodesian Security Forces and are undergoing training. In the Tuli/Beitbridge area there are a further 175 terrorists, according to the report.[106]

*

SADF army headquarters receives another report on the same day, this time directly from the Northern Transvaal Command. It quotes a source in Zimbabwe claiming that ZAPU's Dumiso Dabengwa has acknowledged that there were 200 ANC terrorists in Assembly Point Juliet during the election period, and that 150 of them proceeded to the Hwali, Dendele and Hunga areas after the polls. Dabengwa apparently told the ANC guerrillas to stop their movements in Zimbabwe and return to Botswana.

Despite this, the 150 are still at large with ZIPRA forces in the Masera and Machekhuta Tribal Trust Lands. The report claims Dabengwa made these comments on 14 March 1980, when he spoke to the source, an ex-Rhodesian member of Zimbabwe's Special Branch.[107]

*

According to another communiqué by the North Transvaal Command's headquarters, on 1 April, it is established that 92 ANC members are still in Assembly Point Juliet. But it is predicted that this group will probably be deported to Zambia the following day, while the other 200 ANC members who were in Juliet have already departed.[108]

On 2 April, the North Transvaal headquarters confirms that the 92 were withdrawn from Juliet earlier that morning on seven trucks, and taken to Zambia via the Victoria Falls Road.[109]

*

Though *most* MK cadres may have returned to Zambia following the disbandment of Assembly Point Juliet, a group of eight, including Buti Barks (i.e. Thomas 'Victor' Hlabane, who has been involved in operations in Zimbabwe attached to the ZIPRA call-sign for a number of years), Madimetsa Ranoto, 'Ali', 'Parker', 'Roger', 'Themba', 'Vusi' and 'Sizwe', instead departs to Bulawayo, where they are accommodated by ZAPU members.[110]

Likewise, after Raymond Zulu has been demobilised from Juliet, rather than head back to Zambia, he is assisted by a ZIPRA combatant to go to Plumtree, where he finds accommodation with ZAPU sympathisers.[111]

Similarly, MK's Kenneth Phiri and 'Morris' head to Bulawayo along with ZAPU members, who assist them in finding accommodation following the demobilisation of Juliet.[112]

*

In Diepkloof in Soweto, late on the evening of 3 April 1980, Anthony Tsotsobe and Petros Jabane enter a Ford Valiant belonging to Derrick Ndlovu, who has agreed to give them a lift.[113]

Tsotsobe pulls out a pistol and demands that Ndlovu hand over the car. Ndlovu agrees, after which Tsotsobe pays him R10 and says they are borrowing his car; he will get it back in the morning. The other passengers in the vehicle are told to get out. Ndlovu is kept on board for a while, before being ordered out. With Jabane the last remaining passenger, Tsotsobe heads to a spot where Johannes Rasegatla, Solly Shoke and Nicky Hlongwane are waiting.

After their successes at Moroka and Orlando the previous year, the G-5 Unit, now reinforced by Jabane and Tsotsobe, want to hit a police station in a white area. They head to Booysens Police Station. Each man has an AK-47 and collectively they possess an RPG-7 launcher. The Valiant stops near a garage. Hlongwane gets out in order to see if there is any danger. As he climbs back into the car a police van pulls in opposite the group on the other side of the street. A policeman leaves the van and enters the station.

After this the guerrillas climb out of their car. It is just after 1 a.m. on 4 April 1980.

Tsotsobe has the RPG-7 on his shoulder. He shouts 'Fire!' before dispatching shots towards the building. The first rocket lands on the roof. The second hits the building, causing it to shake, while a third flies over the building. Tsotsobe's colleagues then spread out and open fire on the station with their AK-47s.

The policeman who exited the van had only just arrived in the station's charge office when the attack began. He looks out the window and sees the gunmen huddled at the petrol station. He returns their fire with his .38 revolver.

Dino Martins, whose house stands adjacent to the police station, awakes to the sound of automatic weapon fire as shots whistle past his house. A bullet smashes through the front door window and ricochets through the hallway. He crawls to his children's bedroom. They are crying. He quickly switches off the stoep lights. He sees that the window next to the door is broken and a bullet has knocked a large chunk of plaster out of the wall in the hall.

Leo Nikles and his friend Graham Wehr meanwhile peep round the corner of Metz and Booysens Streets and see people shooting at the police station from a golden Valiant vehicle.

About ten minutes after opening fire, the guerrillas retreat to the Valiant. As they make their exit, they toss pamphlets from the car. Some of them call for the release of Walter Sisulu.

Leo Nikles jumps into his bakkie, jumps a red light and follows the Valiant till the highway to Soweto, where Wehr catches up with him in another vehicle.

The Valiant travels at 140 kilometres per hour, but slows down at regular intervals. Fearing he will be fired on, Nikles sits on the left-hand side of his car and drives with his right hand on the steering wheel and right leg stretched across to the accelerator.

Eventually the Valiant stops completely and then starts reversing. At this point Nikles abandons the pursuit and breaks away.

The Valiant is later found abandoned in Diepkloof Zone 3, and the guerrillas manage to return safely to their base.[114]

*

An article in the *Rand Daily Mail* on 14 May refers to the incident in February when the store owner Nicolas Ndlovu was kidnapped in Phelindaba. According to the article, the trouble started when 'a few maverick Frelimo soldiers crossed into South Africa and engaged in some banditry. South Africa let out a roar of outrage and blamed the ANC.'

Though the accusations of MK involvement proved to be false, the incident was not without consequence for the South African liberation movement, because 'according to diplomatic sources, the Mozambican Government promptly ordered about 50 ANC members whose presence was not vital in Maputo to quit the city for the north of the country'.[115]

If true, this would represent probably the first instance of Mozambique acting against the ANC as a result of South African government pressure.

*

The fate met in January 1980 by the groups infiltrated to South Africa from Swaziland the previous month highlights the ongoing problem of the long-term sustainability of MK units within the country. A Revolutionary Council meeting is held on 22 May 1980 to discuss the matter. 'Our Military Perspectives and Some Special Problems' is the title of the document adopted by the meeting.

During the talks, the Silverton siege is discussed. The document notes that the RC's immediate reaction to the incident was 'one of uncertainty about the wisdom of this type of tactic. Individual reactions in our movement were generally negative and at least one public comment expressed condemnation of this action.'

A complication arose, however, because the siege quickly became perhaps the most successful operation in MK history, judged by the objectives set for the armed propaganda campaign. Over half those interviewed in a survey conducted in Soweto described the men as heroes, and three-quarters said they generally approved of the action. The document says that hostage taking should therefore not be mechanically rejected. To give one example, cadres might find themselves surrounded by police – as may have happened at Silverton.

But that leaves the larger question of whether hostage taking should be undertaken with deliberate forethought in order to compel the enemy to respond to specific demands. Would that be legitimate armed propaganda? The document is non-committal, saying it is a tricky question because of the general aversion in the West and the socialist countries to such forms of struggle.[116]

*

A possible solution to the dilemma emerges around the same time, because the special unit that Montso Mokgabudi asked Aboobaker Ismail to assist Barney Molokoane in training when the two met at Funda camp towards the end of 1979 is ready to enter the fray. The unit has the capacity to escalate the armed propaganda campaign to a level hitherto unseen without resorting to expedients such as hostage taking.

On 25 May, Mokgabudi drives Molokoane and some members of the unit, namely M.B. Salomane, 'Solly Mayona', 'Jack', 'Dick' Mtimkulu, Lati Ntshekang and Vaku Senzangakhona, in a yellow Alfa Romeo to Hlatikulu in Swaziland. There they meet Aboobaker Ismail, who is with another group, including Victor Khayiyana, David Moise, 'Mochudi' and Sipho Thobela.

These two groups are transported in the Alfa Romeo and a minibus to the Mahamba border post between Swaziland and South Africa. Khayiyana gets out and climbs over the fence. The rest follow, marching into the bush on the South African side.

First Khayiyana and then Senzangakhona depart, further into the bush. When Khayiyana returns, it is at the wheel of a Chevrolet Firenza. Mokgabudi, Mochudi, Thobela and Moise enter the vehicle, which Khayiyana drives away.

Senzangakhona returns next in a Ford Ranchero. The rest of the cadres depart with him. Just outside Piet Retief the Ranchero breaks down. The group in that vehicle wait beside the road until Khayiyana arrives in the Firenza with his group.

All the men continue in the Firenza in the direction of Bethal. Khayiyana drops off Mochudi, Moise and Thobela first; Vaku Senzangakhona and Molokoane are then taken to Molokoane's uncle's house in Bethal; Ntshekang and Jack are left at the railway station; while Solly Mayona and Dick Mtimkulu are dropped off last.

Early on the following morning, Lati Ntshekang and Jack go by train to Johannesburg, and from Commissioner Street take a taxi to Sasolburg where they disembark and head to a hostel.[117]

*

At 7 p.m. on 1 June, Barney Molokoane, Dick Mtimkulu, Lati Ntshekang and Vaku Senzangakhona are dressed in overalls, some blue, some brown, as they head to a dead letter box situated in a car scrapyard just outside Sasolburg's black township.[118]

*

Two hours later, Sipho Thobela, David Moise, Mochudi and Victor Khayiyana enter through a hole that has been cut in the fence of the SASOL 2 refinery in Secunda, 135 kilometres from Sasolburg. They are carrying limpet mines; Thobela has one, and the others two each.

After planting the mines onto fuel tanks in the complex, they run to their getaway car, the Chevrolet Firenza, and head for Swaziland.[119]

*

Lati Ntshekang, Dick Mtimkulu and Barney Molokoane meanwhile walk towards the SASOL 1 refinery in Sasolburg.

Molokoane cuts a hole in the wire fence, and the three men climb through. Mtimkulu goes to the storage tank, Ntshekang to the gas cylinders, and Molokoane to the refraction towers.

Molokoane changes plans when he sees security guards, and heads instead to the gas cylinders. After planting their magnetic mines the three leave the security area of the refinery along different routes.[120]

*

At 11.40 p.m., guards at the SASOL 1 plant notice a hole in the security fence. While they are investigating, an explosion sends flames into the night sky.

At about the same time, at the NATREF plant some four kilometres away, a black security guard, 'Robert', is patrolling on his bicycle when he also sees a hole in the security fence. When he goes to investigate he is confronted by a man wearing a black balaclava and dark jacket. The saboteur fires at him and runs.

While the man flees, a tank at the plant goes up in flames. This is some five minutes after the SASOL 1 blast.

At Secunda in the eastern Transvaal, three explosions occur at the SASOL 2 plant at 12.20 a.m. One explosion scatters drums containing a chemical, while another cuts a cable. It transpires that the chemical in the drums is non-inflammable, so no significant damage is done.[121]

*

Early in the afternoon of 2 June, two schoolboys in Springs spot a plastic explosive device at the Old Town Hall, which serves as South African headquarters of the American consortium Fluor, which is involved in building SASOL 2 and 3.

Two bombs are found. As one of them is being defused, the other slides off the rope being used to lift it from a ledge. This bomb rolls onto the street in front of the shocked spectators, but no harm is done.[122]

*

Speaking on the same day, South African police minister Louis le Grange says the Springs bombs are clearly the work of the ANC and SACP. The ANC has already admitted guilt for the sabotage at Sasolburg and Secunda, he says, and this comes as no surprise because

> For some time the police have known that terrorist insurgents have received specific orders and instructions from Joe Slovo, a South African communist, in Maputo. The placing of Joe Slovo in Mozambique is a well-considered plan of the SACP and ANC to bring him as close as possible to the Republic from where he can exercise greater control over terrorists directed against the Republic.

Le Grange further alleges that Dr Solodovnikov, the Soviet ambassador in Lusaka, plays an important role in ANC planning. He is assisted by a South African refugee,

Frene Ginwala. 'No stone will be left unturned to bring these terrorists to book and to ensure the security of the Republic and all its people,' Le Grange vows.[123]

*

In Dar es Salaam on 3 June, Oliver Tambo tells a Reuters correspondent he expects South Africa's response to the SASOL attacks to be raids on neighbouring states, even though 'there is no African country bordering on South Africa which can be said to have helped the ANC do what it is doing'.

But, 'unfortunately, no matter how little involved the countries neighbouring South Africa may be, South Africa will harass them'.[124]

*

Tambo is correct: the SASOL attack does indeed herald an intensification of the regional conflict.

On the same day as his statement, Colonel J.J. Viktor of the Security Branch tells Dirk Coetzee, a security policeman based at Middelburg Police Station, to report to Major Nick van Rensburg in Ermelo.

Major van Rensburg tells Coetzee, Warrant Officer Paul van Dyk, and Sergeants Krappies Hattingh and Chris Rorich that they must blow up two targets in Swaziland. The first is a new ANC transit house and the second a small wooden house occupied by Marwick Nkosi. Van Rensburg claims that Nkosi is involved in building false car panels with which the ANC smuggles arms and explosives into South Africa.[125]

*

At about 2.30 a.m. on 4 June, Coetzee, Hattingh, Rorich and Van Dyk return to their car after planting a bomb at Marwick Nkosi's house in Manzini. They drive a short distance and stop near a house opposite a block of flats, and Coetzee and Rorich get out. Rorich carries the explosive (a ball of dough wrapped around cordite, which is fixed to a detonator and timing device) in a big plastic carrier bag. Coetzee meanwhile brings a sandbag. Rorich places the bomb against the house's northern wall, with the sandbag on top.

Coetzee and Rorich take the cordite up a small embankment and across a neighbour's lawn. On the lawn, close to the street, they clip the battery and make their way back to the car.

The vehicle drives off in a northern direction and stops under a tree near Manzini jail. There, the security policemen unpack some beers and start drinking.

A few minutes later, sometime between 3 and 3.15 a.m., a bright white mushroom cloud shoots into the air, followed a second later by an enormous explosion.[126]

Mrs Hlubi is awoken by the ceiling falling onto her bed. She fumbles in the dark to wake a child sleeping in the house. When she gets outside, she finds a number of people walking about, confused. Blankets, sheets and clothing from the neighbouring house are scattered all over. Some are hanging from blown-up and twisted pieces of corrugated iron.[127]

At the house next door, four people – Seiso, Ali, Percy and Wanda – were asleep at the time of the explosion. Wanda's body was split in two, the lower torso remaining in the debris scattered at the property, the other half thrown into a neighbour's house.

The simultaneous explosion at Nkosi's house reduced it to bits and pieces, killing a grandchild instantly while two others required hospitalisation. Nkosi's daughter, one of the injured, was badly lacerated and the bones on her left arm and right leg were left completely without flesh. Nkosi himself is unharmed.

On the 5th, Stanley Mabizela writes to John Nkadimeng communicating these details. He says 'I must point out that the question of the security of our people has become a real dilemma for us. The SA system is teeming all over the place. We as yet do not know what the ultimate reaction is going to be. We are no more sleeping in our houses – and with the collapsed transport system in the area we have to rely on our SD 10s – its sad; really sad!!'[128]

*

Jack, Victor Khayiyana, Solly Mayona, Mochudi, David Moise, Barney Molokoane, Dick Mtimkulu, Lati Ntshekang, M.B. Salomane, Sipho Thobela and Vaku Senzangakhona assemble at the headquarters of the MK Special Operations Unit in Matola, Mozambique, to report back to their superiors on how the squad's virgin voyage into South Africa went.

Aboobaker Ismail, Montso Mokgabudi and Joe Slovo – the three commanders of the unit, which is also known as the Solomon Mahlangu Unit – are present.

After hearing all the reports, Slovo expresses his satisfaction with the results of the exercise viewed as a whole.[129]

*

A picket staged outside the South African embassy in London on 11 June 1980 marks the beginning of a new 'Free Mandela' campaign. On the same day, a BBC radio report says that a message from Nelson Mandela has been smuggled out of Robben Island prison. Its contents are said to have been released to coincide with the campaign's start.[130]

The document is actually from a group of Robben Island prisoners, not just Mandela, and it was smuggled out of South Africa by Mac Maharaj when he left the country in 1977. It offers a statement of where the prisoners felt the struggle was at the time, and more importantly, where it might be headed.

In the document, the prisoners declare: 'Apartheid is the rule of the gun and the hangman. The Hippo [a South African armoured vehicle], the FN rifle and the gallows are its true symbols ... In the midst of the present crisis, while our people count the dead and nurse the injured, they ask themselves: what lies ahead?'

The first condition for victory in the struggle is identified as black unity: 'Every effort to divide the blacks, to woo and pit one black group against another, must be vigorously repulsed. Our people – African, coloured, Indian and democratic whites – must be united into a single massive and solid wall of resistance, of united mass action.'

They then laud their Soweto-era counterparts: 'We salute all of you – the living, the injured and the dead. For you have dared to rise up against the tyrant's might.'

Looking forward, they predict that those 'who live by the gun shall perish by the gun. Between the anvil of united mass action and the hammer of the armed struggle we shall crush apartheid and white minority racist rule.'[131]

In the years between the drafting and the publication of the statement, ANC strategic thinking has been dominated by the question of how best to harness these two forms of struggle in service of the revolution. It has proven to be by no means a straightforward issue to resolve. It will continue to be the key strategic question into the new decade.

BATTLEFIELD SOUTHERN AFRICA

At an ANC NEC Working Committee meeting on 11 July 1980, a minute taker jots down 'Meetings of President with President Machel and Mugabe and PM Dlamini'. Concerning Oliver Tambo's meeting with the Swazi premier, the secretary writes that Dlamini 'expressed fears on security of Govt of Q [Swaziland] because of MK presence – Panicky situation – Swazis have done enough'.[1]

*

In August, Dirk Coetzee arrives at a forty-four-hectare farm located some seven kilometres out of Erasmia on the Schurveberg road. The farm's southern border is the Hennops River. On the plot itself there is an old farmhouse with an outbuilding that has a garage and two servants' quarters.

On the farm there are a number of animals including chickens, geese, ducks, turkeys, a cow, goats and a dog or two. There is also a garden with a few mielie plants, some pumpkin and sweet-potato creepers, tomatoes, green beans and onions. A number of black men are living there.

This farm's name is 'Vlakplaas'.

Coetzee reports there as the new commander of Section C1 of the Security Branch, which is headquartered at the farm. The black men are 'askaris', former guerrillas who have been 'turned' and now work for the Security Police. They will henceforth operate under Coetzee's command.[2]

*

The 'panicky situation' in Swaziland leads the kingdom's police to try to clamp down on the transit of refugees through the territory. On the morning of 9 September, Petrus Nzima, Moses Mabhida and Stanley Mabizela pay a visit to Timothy Mthethwa, Swaziland's police commissioner. They are there to convince him to permit the forwarding of South African refugees to Mozambique.

Mthethwa tells them that all he is doing is applying the laws of the land. He knows they are constantly violating the agreement reached a few years back between Oliver Tambo and former prime minister Maphevu Dlamini that they would only use Swaziland to retreat to Mozambique and not to infiltrate South Africa. He tells them to look elsewhere for relief.

Later that morning the three ANC representatives are in the office of Swaziland's deputy prime minister (DPM), which is the ministry in the kingdom that deals with refugee affairs. The permanent secretary in the DPM's office, Mr Shabangu, meets them. After hearing what they have to say, he phones Mthethwa.

Mthethwa says that the ANC is not being truthful, and that they can take their personnel through Swaziland to Mozambique as they always have. Shabangu informs the ANC troika that they are free to move their cadres to Mozambique.[3]

But the police do not deliver on the pledge. The ANC representatives mention this at a follow-up meeting with Permanent Secretary Shabangu on the 18th. He says he is very surprised to hear it, and offers to write a blanket permit granting ANC personnel and supporters unhampered movement throughout Swaziland. He is reluctant to create a letter containing such sensitive information, but he nonetheless asks his assistant secretary, Mr Khumalo, to draft and type one. The ANC representatives leave with it.

The ANC men are back in the DPM's office later in the day, however, after Police Commissioner Mthethwa refuses to budge. This time Shabangu says that only the DPM himself can resolve the matter. He arranges a meeting between the ANC and the DPM for the 22nd.[4]

*

On 22 September, a document titled 'Guidelines for the development of our political machineries in TX' is delivered to the ANC NEC's Working Committee (TX is a code for South Africa). It comes two days after a Revolutionary Council Headquarters (RC HQ) meeting held to discuss the matter.

The document states that the 'pressing question is one of restructuring and expanding our strength at home to a higher level. This higher phase can be described as the creation of locally based leadership committee's [sic] which we call Area Political Committee's [sic] (APC's).' The area to be covered by each APC is to be 'decided by the RC HQ after receiving recommendations from the Senior Organ'. Wherever possible, MK machineries are to be created in the same areas. The document emphasises that the MK units in question will maintain their own command structures, which will remain subject to the authority of the Forward Area Machineries.

Given this, the question arises of how politico-military coordination between these parallel structures operating in the same areas will be achieved. The meeting felt the answer was that MK structures in those areas should be expected to accept guidance from the APCs regarding the targets that would best assist the priority of political mobilisation if attacked. Meanwhile the APCs would be expected to deliver on requests for assistance made by the MK cells. A so-called 'liaison machinery' would be established to facilitate communication between the two structures.

The creation of the APCs is to commence with immediate effect, with the understanding that 'by September 1981 RC HQ will take full stock of progress made to date in order to prepare the ground to initiate the next stage at the end of 1981'. This 'next stage' will involve the 'linking up of APC's on a wider regional or other basis'.[5]

*

In Swaziland on 22 September, the meeting between the DPM and the ANC representatives takes place. The DPM says that because of his absence he is not sure why the police are acting as they are. Perhaps, he suggests, it is a security matter affecting but not due to the ANC. He promises to approach his colleagues and phone back.

He nevertheless cautions that while he is aware of the existence of certain agreements between the ANC and Swaziland, the kingdom's vulnerability must be borne in mind. He suggests the ANC might also have made mistakes somewhere and somehow, and advises them to check whether the fault might somehow be on their part.

The DPM's inability to resolve the issue suggests the problem emanates from above his rank. This is Moses Mabhida's conclusion. He writes to 'Comrade Mkhize or Secretary General' the following day about the ANC's deteriorating position.

He warns: 'the forces of reaction are definitely on the offensive. Our feeling is that the P.M. has been convinced by the Police Chief that our presence in Q is a definite threat to the security of this country. The motive is clear – to drive us out of Q.'[6]

*

On 14 October, Nicholas Hlongwane orders Anthony Tsotsobe and Petros Jabane, who were part of the G-5 Unit which attacked Booysens Police Station, to plant explosives on the railway line near Dube Station.

Later that evening, in the vicinity of the station, Tsotsobe places ten charges of TNT at various points under and next to the line. He pairs each of these to electric timers and batteries.

Two of the ten explosives detonate early in the morning of the 15th.[7]

*

Anthony Tsotsobe queues for tickets at the Eyethu cinema complex in Soweto on 20 November. He spots somebody who trained with him in MK's Angolan camps. The person also notices Tsotsobe, but the two do not speak.

When Tsotsobe departs the theatre after the film, he is arrested.[8]

At 4 a.m. the following morning, members of the South African Police knock on the door of a house in Chiawelo, Soweto.

This awakens Jacob Mabuza and his wife, Joyce, who goes to the door. As the door opens, about half a dozen policemen rush past her, brandishing torches and guns.

A firefight breaks out between the policemen and a friend of one of Mrs Mabuza's sons. This friend is being accommodated in one of the bedrooms. A section of the police contingent hustle Jacob and Joyce Mabuza, four of their five children, and two uncles out of the property. This leaves the fifth child, Henry Mabuza, aged eight, who is holed up in the same room as the man engaging the police.

The policemen break open the window of that bedroom, and spray it with bullets. The man continues to fire back.

During this shootout, heavy-calibre bullets and shotgun pellets extensively damage the walls and roof of the house and rip open furniture.

Then, about ten minutes into the skirmish, a Russian hand grenade explodes.

A short while later a second explosion occurs in the room in which the wanted man is based. When the police enter, they see that the child has been shot in the head. He is taken to Baragwanath Hospital with a bullet lodged in his brain (he will survive).

They also find the dead body of the man who engaged them in the shootout. It is Petros Jabane.[9]

*

Towards the end of 1980 the South African security forces devise a plan for a simultaneous attack on ANC properties in Swaziland and Mozambique. The former is charged to the security police, the latter to SADF special forces.

To carry out the Swaziland attack, Colonel J.J. Viktor and Dirk Coetzee go to the Oshoek border post, where they meet up with Lieutenant Chris Deetlefs and Warrant Officers Chris Rorich and Paul van Dyk. Colonel Viktor then departs to a spot located in a wattle brush at the Red Hill turn-off, three and a half kilometres from the border post.

Coetzee, Deetlefs, Rorich and Van Dyk later enter Swaziland in a van, crossing illegally through the bush. In the vehicle is a metal box with a hole drilled into its side, containing half a kilogram of plastic explosives.

Later that evening, they stop about half a kilometre beyond the Manzini Showgrounds, near a store called Manhattan. The four security policemen go behind the store to look for a certain vehicle in the parking lot, but they do not find it, so they withdraw to the nearby Mozambique Restaurant.

They return to the parking lot periodically, to check whether the car has arrived. Well past midnight, they give up, and head back to Colonel Viktor.

In the early hours of the morning, Viktor and Coetzee head to Komatipoort. Viktor says he wants to find out how the raid on Matola has gone.

It transpires that the Mozambican leg has also had to be called off.[10]

*

Brand Fourie and three South African colleagues meet a three-person Mozambican delegation headed by minister of state for security affairs Jacinto Veloso, in Paris, France, on 5 December 1980.

Fourie, who is South Africa's director-general of foreign affairs, says that for his government the major element breeding suspicion is the problem of the

ANC. Veloso can say the ANC is there but not operating, but that does not allay suspicions.

Veloso responds that the Mozambique government does not support the ANC, though it *does* give full political support to the achievement of equal rights for all people. The thought arises, Veloso ventures, as to whether the ANC might be accommodated politically inside South Africa? He hurriedly qualifies this, saying it is just a thought. But he says that if P.W. Botha continues in the reformist direction he is taking, the ANC will have no justification for acting against South Africa from outside. Indeed it will have no justification for styling itself a 'liberation movement' at all.

Fourie states in response that Pretoria fears the situation with the ANC in Mozambique developing over time into one akin to that with SWAPO in Angola, whereby it will become an 'irritant' and action could be taken.[11]

*

The South African security forces have long identified Joe Slovo as the prime orchestrator of the ANC's military campaign.

A South African National Intelligence report compiled on 9 December 1980 states that Slovo lives in Maputo at Julius Nyerere Street 744, Apartment 12, Direito. This is a right-hand apartment on the 11th floor of a complex adjacent to the present Portuguese consulate, and directly opposite the old South African consulate. A guard from the Mozambican Army has recently been placed at the building. Joe Slovo and Ruth First's parking bay is 11D and is located in the basement of the complex.

Regarding Slovo's routine, every Sunday morning he plays tennis at the Polana Hotel, and he also frequents the Naval Club in Maputo. On an irregular basis he visits the ANC office in an apartment block on Rua Ke Kossuenda and Avenue Armando Rivane about 500 metres from his apartment. Slovo also regularly visits Muthembu Street 288, Rua Sanao, a house used by ANC troops. He also sometimes visits Armando Tivane Street, Maputo, where ANC and PLO members live together. Finally, he is a regular visitor at 'Terro Nest or Robbie's house – Operational Sabotage Headquarters'.[12]

*

Sometime between 11.30 p.m. and midnight on 29 January 1981, Dick Mtimkulu, the watchman on duty at the headquarters of the MK Special Operations Unit in Matola, comes back and alerts four colleagues that there are a lot of soldiers outside.

Mtimkulu then goes upstairs and wakes Montso Mokgabudi, the unit's commander, who is sleeping on the upper floor with Solly Mayona, Mochudi and Sipho Thobela. Mtimkulu, Mokgabudi and Lati Ntshekang (who had been sleeping on the bottom floor) go outside while Thobela tries to get back to sleep.

As the three men reach the gate, they see black soldiers dressed in Mozambican Army uniforms. One of these soldiers orders them to kneel down. The cadres obey, upon which the soldier giving the orders confiscates Mokgabudi's pistol and watch.

This soldier also tells the group to take off their shoes. They do this as well. He then tells them to proceed to the white wall. Again, they conform. When next to the wall they are slashed around the sides of their faces and ears with what feel like razor blades or knives, causing them to cry out.

Sipho Thobela gets up and looks out the window. He sees his comrades lined up as if by a firing squad. He goes to fetch his AK.

From the house's balcony, Thobela opens fire on the men in the yard, upon which they start shooting at the captives as well as back at the house. The first captive they hit is Montso Mokgabudi, the commander. Ntshekang tries to take cover by lying down next to him. Other members of the attacking force, who remained at the rear of the property while their colleagues went to knock at the front, open fire and throw grenades at the house's windows.

Authentic Mozambican Army troops, located 500 yards to the rear of the property, are alerted by the noise. A party of them proceed to the house and open fire over the back wall. This counter-attack compels raiders positioned at the rear of the house to withdraw to their vehicles.

Sipho Thobela escapes the house via the roof, and climbs across a tree. As he does so, he sees the body of a white soldier, Sergeant Robert Hutchinson, aged twenty-four, who is one of two fatalities suffered by the assault team. The other is Sergeant Ian Sutill, thirty-two. Both are ex-Rhodesians.[13]

*

Elsewhere in Matola at roughly the same time, there is another attack by South African Special Forces, this time on a residence of the MK Natal Machinery. Mduduzi Guma (aka 'Inkululeko') and Lancelot Hadebe are killed instantly when an upstairs bedroom is struck by a rocket. Another man, Krishna Rabilal, staggers from the room badly wounded, only to be mowed down at close range by the attackers.[14]

*

At a third ANC property in Matola, belonging to SACTU, William Khanyile (a protégé of Harry Gwala in the Natal trade union movement) lies dead after being killed by a rocket that was fired through the wall of the bedroom in which he was sleeping.[15]

*

The short soldier who ordered the cadres to kneel down during the attack on the Special Operations headquarters comes to Lati Ntshekang and kicks him. Ntshekang immediately gets up, only for the soldier to order him to lie face down. He takes Ntshekang's hands and ties them behind his back. Ntshekang is led to a military truck.

On the way there, Ntshekang sees Special Operations headquarters burning. One of the enemy soldiers, 'Keith', asks Ntshekang a series of questions. First he asks if 'Obadi' (Montso Mokgabudi) was in the house.

Ntshekang says yes.

Keith then asks if 'Vaku and Victor' (of the SASOL raid) were there.

Ntshekang says they are in Swaziland.

Keith asks if 'Chief' (Joe Slovo) was in the house.

'No he was not.'

'Who are you?'

'Ghost.'

Ntshekang boards the truck and is driven to a place in the bush where he is quizzed further.[16]

*

Montso Mokgabudi staggers away from the scene of the attack on the Special Operations Unit. His guts have been ripped open. He is taken to hospital, where he will survive for a week before succumbing to his wounds.[17]

*

In Lusaka on 28 February, ANC treasurer-general Thomas Nkobi signs off on a message that he sends under the letterhead of the movement's secretary-general's office.

The correspondence is to the secretary of the office of Botswana president Seretse Khama. It begins that the ANC 'have been made to understand that two of our cadres Elliot Mazibuko and Sipho Khumalo are presently in Botswana and have been detained at the request of our representative there'.

The pair left Zambia on 14 February 'illegally without passports. The manner in which they managed to leave Lusaka airport without passports is still under investigation here.' Khumalo was 'doing rather sensitive work for the organisation. At the time of his departure he was being investigated for conduct prejudicial to the ANC and conduct which violated the Criminal Code of the Republic of Zambia.' Nkobi says that the aim of sending the letter is to request Botswana's cooperation 'in the return of the two cadres to enable us to complete our investigation and thus clear the name of our organisation'.[18]

*

Elliot 'Piper' Mazibuko, formerly a commissar in one of MK's companies at Nova Catengue, is deported from Botswana to Lusaka, along with 'Oshkosh'.[19]

*

Ephraim Mfalapitsa of the MK Machinery in Botswana is involved in the interrogation of three ANC members suspected of spying, of whom one is 'Piper'.

During questioning, Piper says he was recruited by the South African Police in 1977 and underwent spy training in Hammanskraal.

Mfalapitsa is also present during a brutal interrogation of 'Oshkosh'.[20]

*

A team from the ANC's Counter-Intelligence Section visits Mac Maharaj in Lusaka. One of them says they found tapes in Piper's possession and asks if Maharaj can listen to them, to verify if they are authentic – if it is he who is delivering the talks and lectures recorded on them.

Maharaj listens to the tapes and recognises his own voice. 'Good God!' he says,

'This is what I was running [for] these five graduates from Lenin School. Who did you find it with?'

With Piper, one of the security men repeats.

Maharaj replies: 'Well, Piper was in that course. That means that Piper was recording unknown to me. That means he was taking it to hand over to the South African security.'[21]

*

In Matola early in May 1981, Jerry Mosololi and Sydney Molefe are briefed by the Transvaal Urban Machinery's commander Siphiwe Nyanda, who tells them their mission will involve infiltrating South Africa and executing acts of sabotage in the Soweto area.

Nyanda, Mosololi and Molefe are then joined by 'Keith' and 'Lake' in a car driven by 'Dunkin' to the Mozambique–Swaziland border.[22]

*

Back at the Transvaal Urban Machinery's premises in Liberdad, Maputo, Moses Mbatha and Suzman Mokoena walk into a room where they find Johannes Rasegatla and Thabo Motaung waiting.

Motaung asks Mbatha if he knows the Mabopane area.

Mbatha says he does not.

Motaung then explains how they will find the place he is talking about. He says that as they enter Mabopane district they will see a huge police station on the right-hand side, opposite which is a bus shelter known as Transkei. There are another two or three bus stops there. On one of the bus stops – not the Transkei stop, but one in its vicinity – they must write on a seat the time and date when the contact person must visit them.

Rasegatla says they will receive further instructions in Swaziland.[23]

*

At the bus station in Mabopane later in May, Suzman Mokoena finds Thabo Motaung waiting at one of the stops.

Motaung subsequently holds a meeting with Mokoena and Moses Mbatha before taking them to Ga-Rankuwa Station. Waiting for them at the station are Siduma Theophilus Dlodlo (alias 'Viva Zenge'), Solly Shoke ('Jabu') of the G-5 Unit that attacked the Moroka, Orlando and Booysens Police Stations, and a third man, 'Budis'. Motaung says that Jabu will be the unit's commander, Viva the commissar, while Mbatha, 'Budis' and 'Kid' will be unit members. This unit will be known as G-7.

Motaung says that seeing that the five have undergone the survival course, they must find somewhere to locate themselves in the mountains surrounding Ga-Rankuwa. They must construct a base there. Motaung suggests a place near Medunsa University.[24]

*

In the early hours of 25 May 1981, after spending one day in Soweto, Jerry Mosololi and Sydney Molefe perform the mission assigned to them in Matola by Siphiwe Nyanda. They place charges on the lines connecting New Canada with Mzimhlophe

Johnnic/PictureNET Africa

Dead and wounded protesters outside Sharpeville Police Station after the anti-pass protest of 21 March 1960

AP Photo/PictureNET Africa

Albert Luthuli publicly burns his pass after the Sharpeville massacre

(*Right*) A policeman uses his torch to inspect the wreckage at Fordsburg Post Office following the explosion there on the evening of 16 December 1961. Lying at his feet is the inside half of the office's main door. The hands of the clock on the wall point to 10:22 as the exact time of the explosion

(*Bottom left*) MK's first casualty: The body of Petrus Molefe lies covered with newspapers outside the gate of the Dube municipal offices on the night of 16 December 1961

(*Bottom right*) A photo from the *New Age* newspaper on 28 December 1961 shows what is left of one of the notices pasted on lampposts and walls in Johannesburg on the night of 16 December 1961 announcing the formation of 'UMKONTO WE SIZWE'

Rand Daily Mail

New Age, 28 December 1961

Spark, Historical Papers Research Archive, University of the Witwatersrand

Nelson Mandela's tour of the army camps and headquarters of the Algerian Front de Libération Nationale (FLN) in Morocco in March 1962. Mandela receiving a briefing at the headquarters of the Armée de Libération Nationale (ALN), the FLN's military wing. On the right in the background is Robert Resha

Wikimedia Commons

Mandela (left) looks on during a display by the ALN of an artillery piece. Ahmed Ben Bella is standing with arms clasped

Pan African News Wire

Mandela in sunglasses behind Ahmed Ben Bella. To Ben Bella's left in spectacles is the leader of the liberation movement in Guinea-Bissau, Amilcar Cabral, and to Cabral's left is Houari Boumediene

The first group of MK recruits to complete sabotage training in Ethiopia, photographed upon the completion of their thirteen-week course in 1962. (Back row, standing, from left to right): 'Zoni', Maxwell Mayekiso, John Tami, Jack Ndzuzo, Alfred Jantjies, Ernest Malgaz, Gandi Hlekani. (Middle row, squatting) Philemon Beyela, Isaac Rani, 'Matthews', 'Sondele', Macdonald Masala, Nganzile Nkaba. (Front row, sitting) Henry Fazzie, Jakes Goniwe, 'Bangu', Matthews Makhalima, Alfred Khonza, James Chirwa

hotograph taken by Ebrahim Ismail Ebrahim on 2 November 1962, in his capacity as a *New Age* urnalist, of his handiwork the night before as part of a sabotage squad led by Billy Nair that upended pylon in Montclair

The Star, 28 October 1962

The house of Jonas Matlou in Lobatse, Bechuanaland, venue of the ANC's consultative meeting held on the weekend of 27–28 October 1962, where the organisation endorses the armed struggle as its official policy

Star, 28 October 1962

Some of the forty delegates at the Lobatse Conference gather in the backyard of Jonas Matlou's house to discuss a point

Rica Hodgson, Jack Hodgson and Michael Harmel upon their arrival in Lobatse on 1 May 1963 having fled house arrest in South Africa

J.B. Marks and Joe Slovo in Francistown on 20 June 1963. Slovo is on his way to present 'Operation Mayibuye', the MK National High Command's blueprint for guerrilla warfare, to Oliver Tambo, the leader of the ANC's External Mission

The front of the smallholding in Travallyn, Krugersdorp, where Raymond Mhlaba and Govan Mbeki took up residence in the first week of July 1963

Cottage in Mountain View, Johannesburg, where Denis Goldberg went to live, also at the beginning of July 1963

Liliesleaf Farm in Rivonia, with the main farmhouse at the front and the outbuildings behind it

Captured in disguise during the Rivonia raid, 11 July 1963: Walter Sisulu, Govan Mbeki, Ahmed Kathrada

Raymond Mhlaba, Denis Goldberg, Rusty Bernstein

Bob Hepple

Arthur Goldreich, Harold Wolpe and Ismail Bhana in Francistown Jail, where they are being held under protective custody

(*Left*) Wilton Mkwayi, MK commander in the Second National High Command that was established after the Rivonia raid

(*Right*) Bram Fischer, who went underground in 1965 to try to revive the liberation movement's clandestine structures within South Africa

ANTI APARTHEID NEWS

NOVEMBER 1967   PRICE 6d

First pictures of the guerillas

OAU backs freedom fighters

THE NEWS that South African para-military forces were going to the aid of white Rhodesians coincided last month with an announcement from the Organisation of African Unity setting up a new military committee to aid African freedom-fighters.

The committee was the outcome of a remarkably effective meeting of the OAU – effective despite grim auguries.

In the 18 months since the last conference in Addis Ababa, fratricide spread through Nigeria, the Arab member states were clobbered by Israel and white racism remained buoyant in the south. And, set against the wretched backdrop of the Congo, the extravagant hospitality of President Mobutu only added to the gloom.

Yet against all the odds this fourth assembly of the Organisation of African Unity was sober, workmanlike and effective. Most encouraging of all, perhaps, the delegates decisively reaffirmed their support for the armed struggle against Smith, Vorster and Salazar.

African National Congress representative in London Joe Matthews was a member of the joint ANC–ZAPU delegation to Kinshasa. We asked him for his impressions.

"A most important step forward was the decision to create a committee of military men to co-ordinate aid for the armed struggle in the south", he said. Broadly, the OAU decided to set up a 17-nation commission of military experts as an adjunct to the existing Liberation Committee. It is expected

THESE ARE THE FIRST PICTURES OF THE ANC–ZAPU FREEDOM FIGHTERS TRAINING IN CENTRAL AFRICA

In the aftermath of the Wankie Campaign, the November 1967 issue of *Anti Apartheid* News releases the first authorised photos of ANC and ZAPU guerrillas training in central Africa

Oliver Tambo (with his spectacles on the table in front of him) at the opening of the Morogoro Conference in April 1969

THE AFRICAN
NATIONAL CONGRESS
SAYS TO VORSTER
AND HIS GANG:

YOUR DAYS ARE COMING TO AN END!!

Sergeant P.M. Steyn, cap in hand, has part of his uniform and service revolver holster blackened while his colleagues run to safety as an explosive device in a supermarket carrier goes off a few feet from the main entrance of the *Rand Daily Mail* in Mooi Street on 13 August 1970

Photo from the front cover of *Die Transvaler* on the morning of 14 August 1970 of a man holding one of dozens of pamphlets that were sprayed by bucket bombs at noon the previous day

Mondy Motloung (left) and Solomon Mahlangu (right) were captured at Goch Street on 13 June 1977 in the first incident of urban guerrilla warfare in South Africa since the sabotage campaign in the early sixties

The gutted charge office at Moroka Police Station after the G-5 Unit's attack on the station on 3 May 1979

Some of the scores of policemen who rushed to the Volkskas Bank in Silverton, Pretoria, after customers and tellers were taken hostage there on the afternoon of 25 January 1980

Fanie Mafoko, one of the hostage-takers in the Silverton siege, lies dead behind the bank's counter after the police storm the building

The bodies of Mafoko's colleagues Wilfred Madela and Humphrey Makhubo on the floor along with their weapons as the police prepare to move one of them to the government mortuary

The aftermath of the G-5 Unit's attack on Booysens Police Station on 4 April 1980, their first in a 'white' area. The broken windows are from AK-47 rifle fire and the roof damage from the first use of the RPG-7 rocket launcher in the armed struggle

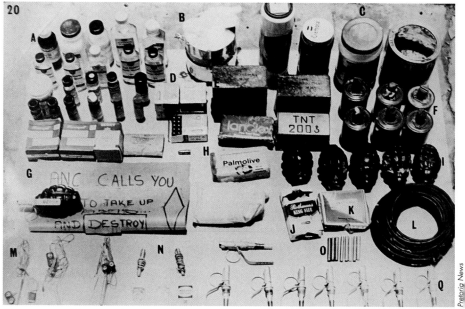

Weapons on exhibit at a political trial of an MK cadre in June 1977

Sergeant Hendrik van Niekerk holds a replica of a limpet mine and a detonator

Chrizelle Wentzel with a rocket launcher that was an exhibit at the 'Silverton siege trial'. The projectile on the launcher is a dummy

Arms cache of weapons including AK-47s and rocket-propelled grenades that were used during the attack on Wonderboom Police Station on Boxing Day 1981

The aftermath of the MK Special Operations Unit's attack on SASOL facilities on 1 June 1980. A foam-spraying fire engine battles to put out one of the worst blazes in the country's history

A tower of smoke from one of the bombed SASOL plants

The South African security forces exact revenge by attacking the headquarters of the Special Operations Unit in Matola, Mozambique, on the evening of 29–30 January 1981

The damaged servant's quarters at the home of a senior officer at Voortrekkerhoogte after a rocket attack by the MK Special Operations Unit on 12 August 1981

ACTU House, where William Khanyile was killed in one of the three attacks during the Matola Raid

Church Street, Pretoria, 20 May 1983

Thami Zulu (extreme left) and Ronnie Kasrils (centre) in Luanda, Angola, n.d.

ME NEWS

Visuanathan Pillay — alias Ivan.

Shadrack Ndaba — alias Paul Dikeledi.

Collingwood August — alias Maphumulo.

B A Mhlambo — alias Solly.

Zondi Roller Molape — alias Clement alias Selby.

Sidumo Theophilus Dlodlo — alias Viva.

Siphiwe Nyanda — alias Gebhuza.

Boniface Mziwakhe Ngwenya — alias Thami Zulu.

Letoshle Glory Sedibe — alias September.

Michael Modise.

D. P. Motsoaledi — alias Castus.

Mduduzi Cecil Sithole — alias Trevor Vilakazi.

Ephraim Ndondo Thusi — alias Mike Ngozi.

Keith Mokoape.

Nelson Hlongwane — alias Nsizwo.

Wilson Welile Twala — alias Chief.

Reavell Rhodes Nkondo — alias Ricky.

'Wanted' photo of MK cadres, released by the Swaziland police during the second Battle of Swaziland in December 1984

Edward Lawrence

Ebrahim Ismail Ebrahim

Robert Dumisa

South African Defence Force personnel sweeping the main road between Volksrust and Brereten for landmines on 11 June 1986, following explosions on nearby dirt roads the previous day in which five people were injured

The exterior of Magoo's Bar on Durban's Marine Parade, following a car bomb there on 14 June 1986

Robert McBride

Ashley Kriel

Robbie Waterwitch and Coline Williams of the Ashley Kriel Unit

From left to right, Sheikh Nazeem Mohammed, Archbishop Desmond Tutu, Cape Town mayor Gordon Oliver and the Reverend Allan Boesak lead a march of thousands from St George's Cathedral to Cape Town City Hall on 13 September 1989 to support peaceful change in South Africa

Raymond Mhlaba accompanied by guards in khaki uniforms 'symbolic' of MK as he does a lap of honour at Soccer City, during a rally on 28 October 1989 held to celebrate the recent release of eight long-term political prisoners including Mhlaba

An ANC supporter holding a child and an imitation rifle at the 28 October 1989 rally. The stadium would fill up for what was to become the largest opposition rally in South African history up until then

Shirley Gunn and Chris Hani, holding Haroon Gunn-Salie, at a rally at Langa Sports Stadium in Cape Town on 16 December 1991, marking the 30th anniversary of the formation of MK

Joe Modise (left) and Siphiwe Nyanda (right) carrying the coffin at Chris Hani's funeral on 19 April 1993. Behind them are other senior MK officers

Nelson Mandela taking the presidential oath of office during his inauguration on 10 May 1994. Chief Justice Michael Corbett administers the oath while outgoing first couple F.W. and Marike de Klerk look on

and Mlamlankunzi Stations. The Mzimhlophe detonation does not succeed because the charges fall off the line, but Mosololi himself electronically detonates the other explosion at 2.32 a.m.

The *Rand Daily Mail* reports the following day that the ANC has claimed responsibility for the Johannesburg bomb. The article adds that it was one of a series of actions the previous day that appeared to be aimed at disrupting South Africa's celebrations of twenty years as a republic. Rail traffic on the Durban–South Coast line was disrupted after a bomb explosion near Lamontville Station in the morning, and in central Durban the police confiscated an unexploded leaflet bomb containing some 1,500 pamphlets purportedly produced by the ANC, calling on people to reject republic festival activities.

Likewise, in Umtata, thousands of anonymous pamphlets were scattered, calling on Transkeians to boycott work and buses for three days in protest against the 'white Republic of South Africa'.

There was also a grenade attack on a police station in Fort Jackson, eleven kilometres from East London, while a police vehicle carrying three people including the head of the Ciskei intelligence services, Brigadier Charles Sebe, was attacked shortly afterwards in the nearby Ciskean town, Mdantsane.[25]

*

In the vicinity of the mountains near Medunsa University in Ga-Rankuwa, Theophilus Dlodlo, Suzman Mokoena, Budis and Moses Mbatha of the G-7 Unit are in Thabo Motaung's company.

Motaung departs in a vehicle and returns a while later with Solly Shoke. In the car are zinc plates, picks and shovels.

With these instruments, the group dig a rectangular hole sixty to seventy centimetres deep ('Rectangle One'). They then dig another rectangle around this first one ('Rectangle Two'). In doing so, they establish a sixty-centimetre 'wall' around the first hole.

They then dig a tunnel leading to the two holes.

The inner hole is then dug deeper till it is just over two metres in depth.

The reason for building the 'wall' is so that poles can be balanced on top of it to hold in place the zinc plates that will form the base's 'roof'. Soil is then planted on top of the roof as camouflage.

Jabu, Viva, Mbatha, Kid and Budis move in.[26]

*

Marion Sparg, Arnold Geyer and Damian de Lange are three South African journalists who make up a unit calling itself the 'South African Liberation Support Cadre'.

Between 4 and 6 a.m. on 1 June they proceed to a house in Ivy Road in Johannesburg's Norwood suburb and petrol-bomb the property. They do the same at Oxford Galleries at 240 Oxford Road. They also try to petrol-bomb President Place on Jan Smuts Avenue, but are not successful in this last instance.

All the targets in question contain offices belonging to the Progressive Federal Party (PFP), the liberal parliamentary opposition party.

Within days, Geyer leaves South Africa and heads to London.

Sparg and De Lange exit on 26 June, crossing into Botswana illegally before hitch-hiking to Gaborone in search of the ANC.[27]

*

Following the incident with Piper and Oshkosh earlier in the year, the ANC is convinced that there is a much wider spy network within its ranks, and is in the process of trying to root it out.

Around 28 July 1981, Joe Mamasela and his adopted brother, Chief Montampede (aka 'Monde') are driven between Selibe-Phikwe and Gaborone in a convoy of two cars containing ANC personnel.

In Gaborone, Mamasela and Monde are split up. Mamasela is taken to Okavango Flats.

Towards the evening, Mamasela insists on being taken to see Monde because Monde is supposed to get back to South Africa and needs money for transport.

Elias Masinga, formerly of SASM's Soweto Regional Committee, is one of the ANC men. He takes Mamasela to a house numbered 404 in Gaborone's Broadhurst suburb.

Inside that property, Mamasela sees 'Iotola', an MK cadre. He also sees Monde, who seems dazed. The clothes he is wearing are too large for him, and are different from what he was wearing in Selibe-Phikwe. Mamasela also notices signs of panic on Monde's face.

Mamasela asks what is happening.

Masinga says that Mamasela should not talk to Monde any longer, as it is against the protocol of conspiracy. (Monde is being held on suspicion of being an informer.)

On the following day, Mamasela is driven from Gaborone to Selibe-Phikwe to fetch his clothing and money. There Mamasela meets his girlfriend Priscilla. He manages to tell her that he and his brother have been kidnapped; he doesn't know what has happened to his brother, but they have been kidnapped.

She says she will phone the police.

Later, the police raid the property at the Okavango Flats, and arrest all the residents there, including Mamasela.

At the police station, while under interrogation, Mamasela is told by a policeman that a corpse matching the description of his brother has been picked up in Lobatse, and his remains are in the government mortuary. The policeman suggests Mamasela goes to identify the corpse.

At the mortuary, Monde's body is so charred that Mamasela can identify him only by a ring on his finger.

Mamasela is released at about midnight, and heads back to South Africa with the corpse in the back of a bakkie. The border is closed, but Mamasela is allowed in. On the South African side, he is arrested by the police.

On the following day, members of the South African Security Branch arrive. They start working on him, trying to induce him to work for them. One of them tells Mamasela to look at what the ANC has done: they were supposed to liberate him; now they are killing people, burning them alive.[28]

*

When driving out of his residence in Eves Crescent in Salisbury's Ashdown Park suburb on the evening of 31 July, Joe Gqabi is shot dead.

His secretary arrives at the house at 12.15 a.m. There are eighteen spent cartridges in the driveway and a .22-calibre Beretta pistol fitted with a silencer is near his body in the car.[29]

*

Sidney Sibepe, Vuyisile Matroos, Johannes Mnisi and 'Vicks' are met by Philemon Malefo on the South African side of the republic's border with Swaziland on 8 August. Malefo drives them to Mamelodi, outside Pretoria.

The next day, Malefo again drives the four, this time to Erasmia, south-west of Pretoria, where they find Barney Molokoane waiting to give them instructions. It is a Special Operations Unit mission. He tells them that those charged with carrying out the reconnaissance have done their work and now they have to perform the operation.[30]

*

On the evening of 12 August, at a spot between the Indian areas of Erasmia and Laudium, some four kilometres from the SADF's Voortrekkerhoogte military base in Verwoerdburg (between Pretoria and Johannesburg), Vuyisile Matroos, Johannes Mnisi, Barney Molokoane, Sidney Sibepe and Vicks set up a GRAD-P rocket launcher. Near them is Philemon Malefo in a Ranchero motor car.

At 10.30 p.m., Lieutenant van Dyk is at the Voortrekkerhoogte base writing a situation report, when he hears a large explosion outside. He immediately calls the guards at the gate and asks what happened.

A guard responds that there was a great explosion somewhere.

No sooner has he said this than a second explosion occurs.

The guard tells him that this second blast exploded on the other side of the street.

Ten minutes later a third, fourth and fifth shot fall – all from the west.

By this time a crowd has begun to gather on the hill from which Molokoane, Mnisi, Sibepe, Matroos and Vicks have finished firing their rockets and now wish to withdraw. Some of the spectators mistakenly believe that the explosions are part of a SADF military demonstration.

As the crowd accumulates, the guerrillas agree that Philemon Malefo should exit alone to prevent the vehicle from being identified. Malefo accordingly leaves.

Without a getaway car, Molokoane and Mnisi head towards Laudium to find one.

At about 11.25 p.m. seventeen-year-old Zahied Patel steps out of his home to park his father's car. He is approached by two black men. When they ask him for a lift, he refuses.

Mnisi and Molokoane ignore him, open the door and get inside.

Patel says that he is not in a position to give them a lift.

Molokoane shoots Patel and leaves him injured at the side of the car. As Molokoane and Mnisi prepare to make off with it, Patel flees towards his house.

Mnisi and Molokoane soon realise that Patel has left with the car keys, so they abandon the vehicle and run in the direction where Vicks, Matroos and Sibepe are waiting. As they flee, local residents, having heard the gunshots, emerge from their homes. Some start firing in the direction of the cadres.

Vicks, Matroos and Sibepe provide covering fire, and Sibepe throws a grenade. The group manages to escape.[31]

The damage at Voortekkerhoogte is limited to the destruction of the servant's quarters at the home of a senior officer.[32]

*

At 24 Danga Road in Chunga, Lusaka, a meeting of the MK Operations Department takes place on 19 August. It is chaired by Joe Modise, with Keith Mokoape, Charles Motaung and Ephraim Mfalapitsa attending.

Modise says the RC has decided that he will take control of the Botswana Forward Area in the wake of the destruction of the Botswana Machinery following the arrest of 'Roller' (Elias Masinga) and others.

Modise says it has been decided that the area in South Africa from Beitbridge to Mafikeng will be developed as an operational area. In the future, Botswana will be used as a springboard for these operations. This will occur without the permission of the Botswana government, which in any case would not be able to prevent it.

These actions will involve a change in the ANC's existing strategy, Modise says. The order is that they must now proceed to guerrilla warfare proper. The Botswana dimension of this project will be known as 'Operation P', and it will involve reactivating contacts last used in 1979.

Modise says he has already selected twenty cadres in Angola who have undergone special training in bush tactics and survival. They have been issued with fake passports by Johnny Sexwale in Luanda.

He then produces a topographical map of the Transvaal/Botswana border area. He explains that underground bases have to be established in Botswana along the border. They should be about forty kilometres from the border and fifteen to twenty kilometres from each other. He tells them to start with three, and then they must build another three before moving on to construct a headquarters and a hospital.

Later in the briefing, Modise tells Mokoape and Mfalapitsa that they must accompany the first group because they know the Sikwane area from where operations will begin. Within a month they must be finished with the construction of the first three bases and the reconnaissance of the terrain. The chief of staff and commander of this special unit are expected any time from Angola. 'Sponi' will be commander and 'Kroestjoff' the chief of staff.[33]

*

On 20 September, Nat Serache, formerly a journalist at the *Rand Daily Mail*, in which capacity he witnessed the shootings outside Orlando West Junior High on 16 June before fleeing the country and receiving military training in Tanzania, drives Ephraim Mfalapitsa to a house in Mochudi in which they find 'Kroestjoff' and 'Sponi' waiting. The two board the vehicle, which heads in a south-easterly direction to Sikwane. From there the car follows a dirt road running parallel with the South Africa/Botswana border. This takes them past Mathubudikwane and Malolwane and on to the Bonakallo area about twenty kilometres further west.

There they offload everything. Mfalapitsa suggests to Serache that they meet again on Saturday 26 September at 1 p.m. so that Mfalapitsa can collect more equipment and report back on progress.

Mfalapitsa, Sponi and Kroestjoff hand their passports to Serache, who departs. The former three then carry their weapons deeper into the bush. While there, Mfalapitsa tells Kroestjoff and Sponi to wait while he looks for a place to spend the night. Mfalapitsa moves in a northerly direction and finds a spot. But he cannot find Kroestjoff and Sponi when he returns, so he spends the night alone.

The following morning, Mfalapitsa manages to find the two, and tries to lead them to the place where he spent the night with the equipment. But he is unable to find it, so he asks them to wait while he searches again.

Mfalapitsa walks for a while, unsuccessfully trying to find the base. During his wanderings, details of the interrogations he was involved in conducting earlier in the year flash before his mind: some of the detainees were his friends, yet he assisted in their torture, and helped kill one of them. He starts walking purposefully in the direction of Derdepoort and spends that night in the bush near Mathubudikwane.

On the following day he walks into the Derdepoort border post and surrenders to the security police. He tells them he has come to South Africa because it is the land of his birth, but he is not interested in joining either side of the conflict. He wants to go home.

The officer taking his statement says that having been in a military structure in which Joe Modise, the chief of the armed forces of MK, was the head, they are hardly going to just debrief him and let him go.[34]

*

Simon Mogoerane and Nicholas Hlongwane enter South Africa in late September/ early October 1981.

At Pretoria Station they meet Thabo Motaung, who leads them to Hammanskraal, north of Pretoria. There Motaung points out an island on the Apies River. He tells his colleagues they can start building a base there.[35]

*

In Maputo on 11 October, Aboobaker Ismail meets Rogerio Chamusso. Joe Slovo and 'Christie' are also present at this meeting. Chamusso has scars on one of his knees, caused by splinters during the Matola raid.

Ismail and Slovo are there to discuss targets that the Special Operations Unit would like to assault. In front of them is a map. On it is the town of Evander in the eastern Transvaal. Chamusso knows the area, having been employed as a driver at the nearby SASOL complex in Secunda during the June 1980 attack. He was wrongly imprisoned and tortured on suspicion of being involved in the raid; his treatment led him to flee the country to join the ANC.

With Christie translating, Slovo also explains how one gets to Transalloys.

Finally, Slovo tells Chamusso that he must see 'George' in Swaziland.[36]

*

In Evander in the early evening of 21 October, Chamusso cuts a V-shape in the security fence outside the town's main electricity substation. The station is completely deserted at the time. Within the building, he places a limpet mine on one of the five transformers.

At 8.45 p.m. the mine explodes in an enormous blast that can be heard fifteen kilometres away.

Near midnight that evening, Chamusso is hidden on a conveyer belt that carries coal from a mine to the inside of the in-construction SASOL 3 complex in Secunda. Within the complex he heads to a water treatment plant and places a mine there. The aim is to cause an explosion that will lead to the evacuation of the plant and thus avoid civilian casualties when the principal blast occurs at a reactor in one of the main plants. He heads to one of the main plants and places a mine on a reactor there.

When the first mine explodes just after midnight, causing slight damage to a water pipeline, Chamusso leaves the complex as company employees are herded out. The second mine is scheduled to explode fifteen minutes later.

Policemen arrive promptly at the scene, however, and manage to locate and defuse the mine before it can detonate.[37]

Between 6.30 and 7 p.m. on 23 October, Chamusso walks to the fence of the ESKOM substation at the Transalloys plant near Clewer in the district of Witbank. He cuts the fence and enters. He places a limpet mine on a transformer before heading back to his getaway car.

The mine explodes later that evening, damaging the transformer in the plant. A lightning diverter is also struck, and two radiators lose a lot of oil.

At 3.20 the following morning, Detective Warrant Officer Johannes Dietricksen is manning a roadblock at the Loskop Dam T-junction on the road from Groblersdal to Bronkhorstspruit when he notices a Datsun Stanza that was approaching from Bronkhorstspruit do a U-turn a few hundred metres away.

Dietricksen gets in his police vehicle and, accompanied by Lieutenant Senekal, drives in pursuit of the car. The road is well lit, so they can keep eye contact with the vehicle ahead.

After a pursuit of three to four kilometres, the Datsun's lights disappear from the policemen's view before suddenly reappearing, flung into the air.

They arrive at the scene and see the Datsun has overturned on the side of the road. With the aid of a flashlight they search the car. There are no people inside but they see a firearm, which Dietricksen hooks out. It is a Makarov 9-mm pistol containing eight rounds of ammunition.

Meanwhile, in the front door Dietricksen finds a driver's licence with a photo of its owner. The name on the licence is 'Rogerio Chamusso'.[38]

*

At about 8 a.m. on the morning of 27 October, Captain Urban Strydom of the South African Police leads a group of policemen to a smallholding called Keerom about ten kilometres outside Middelburg on the road to Steelpoort.

He instructs his men to go inside the huts and make inquiries. Strydom himself walks around the huts, and comes across a black man. Strydom tells the man not to run away, but to come towards him. He says there will be no problems, and asks the man to identify himself.

He says he is Rogerio Chamusso.

Strydom tells him not to say anything further. They will talk to him later.[39]

Strydom has a photograph that he uses to confirm that this is the man they are looking for. It is. Chamusso is in very poor physical condition having been on the run since the 24th.[40]

*

Philemon Malefo, too, is in police custody. He is there for questioning in connection with being the owner of a Ranchero matching the description of one spotted in Laudium during the Voortrekkerhoogte attack.

Malefo confesses. He says he was present during that attack, as well as one on 21 July at the Impala electrical substation on the Pretoria–Bapsfontein road outside Elardus Park in Pretoria.

In cooperation with the investigative team, Malefo telephones Johannes Mnisi, who was part of the Special Operations Unit involved in the Voortrekkerhoogte attack. During the conversation – to which the police are listening in – Malefo and Mnisi arrange to meet at the Oshoek border post.[41]

*

At Pretoria Railway Station on 11 November, Jerry Mosololi, Sydney Molefe and 'Bruce' find Nicholas Hlongwane and Thabo Motaung waiting.

It is early in the morning, so they spend some time at the nearby Pretoria Zoo. From the zoo, Hlongwane takes Mosololi and Molefe to an OK Bazaars to buy food. But when Hlongwane and Mosololi exit the shop, they realise that Molefe has disappeared. They search for a while but cannot find him.

Back at a taxi rank, which is on the same road as the zoo, Motaung says, after hearing their report, that they should walk and he will carry on looking for 'Pindela' later. Hlongwane leads the group to a place at the taxi rank from where they get a ride to Hammanskraal.

When they alight in Hammanskraal, they make their way to an island on the Apies River. There they find Simon Mogoerane digging a hole. They join him in the task. When they are finished, they put poles and posts on top of the hole to keep zinc plates in place. They then disguise the surface by placing soil and shrubs over it as camouflage. The group, known as the G-6 Unit, moves into this, their new underground base.[42]

*

The Transvaal Urban Machinery's other unit inside South Africa, the G-7 Unit with its base in the mountains near Medunsa University, gathers in Ga-Rankuwa early in the evening of 12 November.

From the base later that night, Madoda Mbatha, 'Budis' and Theophilus Dlodlo set off, leaving Solly Shoke and Suzman Mokoena behind. It is raining, so the three are wearing raincoats. They head to Medunsa Station, where they board a train to Rosslyn at about 8.30 p.m.

At Rosslyn Station, the trio proceed by foot to the nearby power station. Mbatha and Dlodlo both have Makarov pistols, while Budis carries two offensive and two defensive hand grenades. By now the downpour has stopped.

In a large paper carrier there are four limpet mines, pincers, four blocks of TNT and four fuses. They reach a place where there is a bridge over a stream. Budis keeps watch while Mbatha and Dlodlo go under the bridge. Next to the stream the two attach the TNT to limpet mines with sellotape.

Mbatha and Dlodlo then walk alongside the stream, out of sight of any onlookers who might be on the bridge. Mbatha carries the pincers and has two limpet mines tied to his waist.

Mbatha crouches and starts walking on his hands and knees until he reaches a wire fence. With the pincers he makes a U-shaped incision in the fence, opens it upwards, and he and Dlodlo enter.

Mbatha fixes one of his limpet mines onto the transformer nearest to the opening (it is a magnetic mine that clips onto the metallic transformers). Dlodlo goes to another transformer and places a limpet mine there.

They both remove the safety pins from their mines. Mbatha waits for Dlodlo to return to him, and the two exit the station. Outside they find the rest of their equipment, including a piece of TNT that they conclude must have fallen off one of the mines as they were entering the premises. It is too late to do anything about it. They take all the equipment and flee with it.

After climbing off at Medunsa railway station, the three men walk towards the base. While doing so they hear an explosion. They look in the direction of Rosslyn and see flames.[43]

*

In the final week of November, at a place about a kilometre from the Oshoek border post, Johannes Mnisi emerges from a field alone, and proceeds to the road connecting Oshoek and Carolina.

Instead of Philemon Malefo, whom Mnisi was expecting, policemen suddenly emerge from the bush. Enjoying the advantage of complete surprise, they arrest Mnisi without encountering any resistance.

S.J. Visser, the division head of the Security Branch in the eastern Transvaal, is present. He finds in Mnisi's possession an A4-size sheet of see-through plastic on which there appear certain notes made in pen.[44]

*

Zweli Nyanda of the Natal Urban Machinery tells an ANC inquiry into an incident on the Swaziland–Mozambique border that when he and five other MK cadres encountered RSDF soldiers when returning to the kingdom, the Swazi soldiers fired in the air to indicate they were serious in calling on them to halt, upon which Nyanda fired twice into the air, causing them to become so frightened that they ran away, injuring themselves in the process.[45]

*

While in detention, Johannes Mnisi phones a number in Swaziland. With the police listening in, he asks 'George', one of his instructors, to collect him in South Africa.

George calls back shortly afterwards. He expresses reluctance to enter South Africa itself, and suggests meeting just inside Swaziland on the evening of 7 December.

This is agreed.[46]

*

A group of about twenty-five MK cadres crosses into Swaziland from Mozambique near the Namaacha border post on 1 December 1981.

They are spotted by two patrolling Swazi soldiers. This time there are no calls to halt, no warning shots. Instead the soldiers rush immediately to call for reinforcements.

At about 11 p.m. a contingent of RSDF troops arrive in the area and open fire without warning on the ANC guerrillas, who are waiting for transport at the time.

Petros Mkhanya, Mandla Nicosi and Henry Tatane of MK are wounded in this ambush. They are among five ANC men taken prisoner.

Mkhanya, Nicosi and Tatane are taken to the Good Shepherd Mission Hospital in Siteki where they are kept under armed guard.

When they recover they are charged and slapped with R200 fines.[47]

*

On the evening of 7 December, Johannes Mnisi is in a car with two policemen, Major Frederik Nel and Detective Warrant Officer Phillipus Selepe. The vehicle heads in the direction of the Oshoek border post.

At Oshoek they meet up with Colonels Bert Wandrag and J.J. Viktor, Captain Schalk Visser (divisional commander of the Security Branch in Middelburg), Brigadier

Schoon, and some members of the police's Special Task Force who are operating under the command of Captain M.B. Strydom.

Later, with the senior officers (Wandrag, Viktor, Schoon and Visser) remaining at the border post, the Special Task Force members enter Swaziland illegally and proceed to a spot on a gravel road about a kilometre inside the kingdom.

The seven or so members of the Task Force are deployed by Captain Strydom to positions on the terrain.

Gert Visser takes up a position a bit behind the Task Force members. It is dark, so all he can see are the silhouettes of his colleagues, who are either lying or kneeling down before him.

A while later Adriaan Dercksen, one of the Task Force men lying on the grass, sees a blue Citi Golf arrive. It drives past him and stops about twenty metres in front. The lights of the vehicle are then switched off.

Dercksen is to the rear right-hand side of the vehicle. He gets himself into a readiness position and then, along with his colleagues, starts moving towards the car.

Douglas Hope takes up position concealed within some grass. He is facing the driver directly. Suddenly he hears a loud shout from the vehicle. Gert Visser, who remained behind when the others advanced, discerns what he takes to be the sound of a weapon being cocked in the car.

Task Force members open fire on the vehicle. Visser sees red flames issue from the policemen's tracer bullets. Hope then hears a whistling sound, after which the vehicle catches fire. Two MK members, 'George' and 'Brown', are killed in this incident.

The Task Force members return to Oshoek, where they report their success to Frederik Nel.[48]

*

In Swaziland on 10 December, Police Commissioner Titus Msibi, Deputy Commissioner E. Hilary, Secretary A. Dlamini, Lieutenant Colonel Dube, Lieutenant Colonel J. Nzimandze and Captain S. Dlamini meet South African counterparts Major General Earp of Army Special Operations, Brigadier du Preez from the Security Branch, and Colonels de Bruyn and Saaiman from the Directorate of Military Intelligence.

Msibi welcomes all present and tells them the discussions are occurring at South Africa's request. The two countries share a common enemy, he says. He reminds everyone that Swaziland's minister of foreign affairs was recently in Cape Town, where he was briefed about the ANC.

Msibi says Swaziland's politicians believe that Swazi voters may put pressure on them if the kingdom's security forces do not act. He states that the Swazi Security Council has convinced the government that ANC members in the kingdom must be detained in a refugee camp under armed guard.

Swaziland is willing to make an agreement with South Africa to cope with the ANC, Msibi says. The kingdom has a task force that it can utilise for that goal. He asks South Africa also to raise a task force for possible joint actions. Swaziland and

South Africa are brothers and neighbours, he declares, adding that King Sobhuza will consent to joint South African–Swazi actions against the ANC.

General Earp responds. He says South Africa's security forces have an interest in advancing peace and stability in Swaziland. They are both under pressure from their governments to control the ANC threat. There are methods whereby South Africa can support Swaziland; for example, ANC elements released by the Swazi security forces can be intercepted outside Swaziland in Mozambique. There are many other proposals that can be discussed later. But in the nearer term, cooperation will need to be placed on a more formal basis. The two countries' respective armies will require permission from higher authorities to do this, but after such consent has been obtained, further steps can be taken. Actions by various police and army elements from low to high level can then be established under such an accord. Earp says that after an initial informal agreement is in place, a formal agreement can follow.[49]

*

On 14 December 1981, Jerry Mosololi, Simon Mogoerane and Sydney Molefe set off from the G-6 Unit's base on the Apies River in Hammanskraal to conduct the group's first attack. (Molefe has rejoined the group having reported to Swaziland after he went missing in November.)

Under Mogoerane's command, they head to the Capital Park electricity substation. They place five limpet mines there before returning to base.

The explosions are successful.[50]

*

At the Transvaal Urban Machinery's other base in the mountains of Ga-Rankuwa, Solly Shoke arrives in mid-December. He says that he couldn't find 'Abe' (Thabo Motaung) at the usual meeting place.[51]

*

The ANC's representatives in Swaziland complete a document titled 'Report Compiled in Q on the 24-12-81'.

It says that earlier in the month, Stanley Mabizela and Petrus Nzima were informed by Swaziland's deputy prime minister that the kingdom had recalled its ambassadors to Nairobi and Maputo in order to brief them in detail about the ANC's activities. This was so they could then inform Presidents Kaunda, Moi and Machel about what was going on and why.

What was brewing was an effort to expel ANC members from the country. A list of the first people to be arrested had been compiled by Swazi Police top brass with South African assistance, and it was sent to the prime minister. Arrests were to have commenced on 9 December. What saved the ANC was that when the matter was taken to King Sobhuza, he expressed outrage that such a document could be agreed without consulting Oliver Tambo. Sobhuza pointed out that the Swazis had just shot some of the ANC's cadres, and that more had been killed by the 'Boers' in Swaziland on previous occasions. He demanded to know what steps had been taken to deal with those acts. The question was rhetorical, for Sobhuza immediately picked up his royal blanket and left.

The representatives then discuss more general aspects affecting the movement's position in the kingdom. They note that the organisation has not always helped its own cause. They mention the king's jubilee celebrations held earlier in the year, during which the ANC was specifically requested by the Swazi government not to create any incidents. They point out that 'despite warnings from Q to respect the celebrations of the jubilee', as well as having been informed that security would be tightened, the Senior Organ in Maputo 'ignored these warnings and allowed for movement leading to embarrassment on the part of the representative mission in Q'. And the last batch of guerrillas sent from Maputo during the celebrations, which greatly disturbed the Swazis, 'was uncalled for. The Ncwala ceremony was being prepared for and security was being tightened. Yet our comrades in Maputo pushed an unussual [sic] big batch of cadres.'

This is part of a broader problem whereby 'Even cadres who are irresponsible; people who can ignore orders' are 'quickly' allowed by Maputo to come and operate in Swaziland. It appears that 'the Senior Organ tends to listen more sympathetically to cadres than to factual advice given by us'.[52]

*

On Boxing Day 1981, the G-6 Unit launches another attack. Jerry Mosololi, Sydney Molefe and Nicholas Hlongwane leave the base and walk to a motor rest place near the Hammanskraal taxi rank, which they reach at about 8.30 p.m. Between them they have five AK-47s and a rocket launcher.

Half an hour or so later, Simon Mogoerane and 'Bruce' arrive in a Ford Valiant and Mosololi, Molefe and Hlongwane get in. Mogoerane drives to Wonderboom Police Station and stops the vehicle in the parking lot in front.

There are two policemen on a bench outside the station. Before they know what is happening, Molefe and Mogoerane open fire on them with their AKs. One of the policemen, Constable D.M. Nkosi, is killed.

Hlongwane and Mosololi proceed to the charge office, and Hlongwane throws a grenade into it.

Meanwhile, Bruce opens fire on the station with the rocket launcher.

Mogoerane runs to the vehicle entrance section at the rear of the premises to keep watch for any incomers.

Molefe meanwhile enters the charge office, but sees there is nobody there, so he tells his colleagues to retreat.

Besides the fatality to Constable Nkosi, four policemen, including two whites, are wounded in this attack.

Later, at the junction of a gravel and tar road, Mosololi, Molefe and Mogoerane get out of the Valiant, while Hlongwane and Bruce proceed further in order to burn the vehicle.[53]

*

Jerry Mosololi and Bruce are inside the G-6 Unit's underground hideout in Hammanskraal, while Sydney Molefe is outside under a tree. Nicholas Hlongwane is washing his clothes in the Apies River some 400 metres away. Simon Mogoerane is at some nearby shops. It is approximately 11 a.m. on 28 December.

While sitting by the tree, Molefe sees a man standing in front of the base. He spots another man standing a further distance away. Molefe approaches the nearer man, who runs away.

Molefe goes to Mosololi and Bruce and says that the base has been spotted and that they have to remove the weapons and hide them.

Mosololi responds that while Molefe and Bruce remove the weapons he will go and alert 'Commandant Ntziswa' (i.e. Hlongwane), because he is busy washing.

A while later Mosololi returns with Hlongwane. All the weapons have by now been removed from the dugout and only kitbags remain. Mosololi and Hlongwane take the kitbags and hide them away.

When the two cadres return, Mosololi enters the dugout alone. While inside he hears a shot go off outside, accompanied by what sounds like the hasty footsteps of somebody running away. A moment later he hears the voice of somebody at the surface of the base saying he wants to come in.

Mosololi says he will come out, and tells them not to enter and not to shoot. He gets out of the hole and sees a large number of policemen waiting.

The policemen seize Mosololi and start searching him. They take his money and his reference book and handcuff him.

Constable van Wyk asks Mosololi what he wants here.

Mosololi does not reply, so Van Wyk punches him in the mouth.

The police repeatedly ask him where the weapons are.

Mosololi eventually indicates the direction in which the others who took the weapons went. The police manage to confiscate the weapons.

While this is happening, Simon Mogoerane returns to the base from the shops. He is carrying some food that he has just purchased.

He is set upon by the police and arrested.

Nicholas Hlongwane, Sydney Molefe and Bruce, however, complete their escape.[54]

∗

Madoda Mbatha and Suzman Mokoena leave the G-7 Unit's mountain hideout in Ga-Rankuwa on the third day of 1982. They move because Thabo Motaung has still not been found, and the unit accordingly judges the base to be unsafe.

They travel to Mamelodi and arrive at house number 5548 in Section C. Mbatha and Mokoena move their belongings to a room in the house's backyard.[55]

∗

The senior staff officer of South African Military Intelligence's liaison project with Swaziland, 'Operation Santa', meets with Lieutenant Colonel Ndzimandze, the chief of staff of the RSDF, on 28 January 1982.

Ndzimandze reports growing anxiety in Swaziland among certain political, military and police leaders regarding the presence and activities of the ANC. He mentions that earlier in the month a document was delivered to Pretoria by Swaziland's minister of foreign affairs containing an official request for assistance in efforts to eliminate the ANC in Swaziland, as well as to protect the kingdom against possible ANC reprisals.[56]

*

Thabo Motaung and Solly Shoke meet Madoda Mbatha and Suzman Mokoena in the hideout in Mamelodi at the beginning of February.

Motaung says the reason for his absence was that there were roadblocks so he had to lie low for a while. He mentions another unit in Hammanskraal, commanded by Simon Mogoerane, that he was also responsible for. He says Mogoerane was arrested along with Jerry Mosololi, but three other members of that group managed to escape.[57]

*

At 8 p.m. on 15 February, Congress of South African Students (COSAS) members Zondisile Musi, Fanyana Nhlapo, Itumeleng Matabane and Bimbo Madikela are waiting by the road near Leratong Hospital in Kagiso.

A minivan arrives with two people inside. The driver is a man with a scar on his face, and Musi knows the passenger as a friend of his elder brother. The two men are actually Joe Mamasela (the driver) and Ephraim Mfalapitsa, both once connected with the ANC's Botswana structures. The COSAS members climb in and Mamasela drives them away.

At an isolated spot, Mfalapitsa and the COSAS members disembark, leaving Mamasela behind. Mfalapitsa walks the COSAS four through a forest until they arrive at mining premises near Kagiso cemetery. They proceed to an old pump room, which Mfalapitsa enters first, with the others following. Mfalapitsa then closes the door and says he is in a hurry. They all sit down. Mfalapitsa takes an offensive and a defensive hand grenade as well as a pistol out of his pocket and places them on the floor. He then demonstrates how to connect the detonator to the grenade and pull the detonator. Having done this, Mfalapitsa says he is coming back; he is going to fetch some equipment from the Combi.

When he exits the pump room, Mfalapitsa makes sure to lock it from outside. Instead of heading to Mamasela (who has driven off), he runs to a spot where Chris Rorich (the Security Branch's explosives expert), Abraham Grobbelaar, Warrant Officer van Tonder and Lieutenant Jan Coetzee (who has taken over from Dirk Coetzee as commander of Vlakplaas) are looking on.

Inside the pump installation, Zondisile Musi looks at the box Mfalapitsa has left behind and wonders what is inside it. The answer is one kilogram of plastic explosive, known as PE4. While Musi contemplates the question, Rorich turns a detonator, causing the box to explode, killing Nhlapo, Matabane and Madikela.

Musi survives. At about 8 a.m. the following morning the police arrive at the installation and find him. He tries to open his eyes, but can't.[58]

*

A letter undersigned by Prime Minister Mabandla Fred Dlamini is sent to P.W. Botha from Swaziland's Government House on 17 February 1982.

It begins, 'I have the honour to refer to your letter of 12 February', and mentions various discussions between the foreign ministers of the two countries. These talks resulted in agreement that 'international terrorism, in all its manifestations, poses a real threat to international peace and security and that our respective Governments should take steps to protect our respective states and nationals against this threat'.

In the letter on the 12th, Dlamini recalls, Botha proposed an agreement between the two countries to combat 'terrorism, insurgency and subversion' individually and jointly, and to call on each other where possible for assistance to this end. This was Article 1 of a formal agreement that Botha was proposing by means of the letter.

The second article called for each contracting party to preserve the other's territorial integrity and to refrain from using force to settle disputes.

Article 3 called for neither party to allow their territory to be used for hostile acts against the other.

The next article called for neither to allow foreign military bases or units within their countries – except as stipulated by the UN Charter, and only after due notification with the other.

Should Swaziland agree with the provisions, Botha wrote, 'this letter and your affirmative reply thereto shall constitute an Agreement between our two Governments'.

Prince Mabandla writes that, with King Sobhuza II's authorisation, 'I have the honour to inform you, Mr Prime Minister, that the Government of the Kingdom of Swaziland agree to the abovementioned provisions and regard your letter and this reply as constituting an agreement between our two governments'.[59]

*

In mid-March 1982, Christopher Mnisi (the brother of Johannes Mnisi, and who, like him, is an MK cadre who was captured by the police) is with Isaac Moyema in Tonga, an area between the South Africa–Mozambique border post at Komatipoort and the South Africa–Swaziland border post at Mananga. They are in the company of a security policeman surnamed Vermeulen on observation duty, trying to spot possible MK cadres.

In the evening the three set up camp in the bush.

On the following morning, back on a farm where askaris are accommodated, Mnisi asks Vermeulen for R200. He says he wants to get married.

Mnisi heads off with the money to Mamelodi. He gives it to a friend, Freddie Shongwe, who uses it to drive him and his brother Johannes to Swaziland.

In Mbabane, the Mnisi brothers meet Siphiwe Nyanda. They report to him on their experiences in enemy hands.[60]

*

On 23 April 1982 Madoda Mbatha of the G-7 Unit is arrested in Mamelodi, Section C, number 5548. Police recover a Makarov pistol and hand grenades from his room.

On May Day, Lati Ntshekang (formerly of the Special Operations Unit, but later captured in the Matola raid) travels to Stinkwater in Hammanskraal. He does so in a Combi containing a number of security police members, including the commander for the operation, Major Frederik Nel. Also in the vehicle is Madoda Mbatha.

At a spot in Stinkwater, on the approach to a shop, the police drop off Ntshekang and Mbatha. Mbatha's feet have been placed in gypsum (plaster) and a microphone has been concealed on his body. Ntshekang and Mbatha walk towards the shop and reach a corner where two roads adjoin. Mbatha sees a man who he recognises as Thabo Motaung coming out of the shop in the company of Solly Shoke.

Mbatha tries to communicate with Major Nel over the radio, but the device malfunctions.

Motaung and Shoke notice Mbatha, who lifts his hand in a motion indicating to them to wait. Shoke puts both his arms forward with fingers meeting, indicating that they should meet up at the spot where the two roads adjoin. Mbatha and Ntshekang turn around while Motaung and Shoke walk to them at the corner of the street.

Motaung comes closest, with Shoke standing in a passage a few metres away.

Mbatha sits. Ntshekang sits in front of him.

When Motaung is about five steps away he greets Mbatha and says he was at Mbatha's place and assumed he had been arrested. He asks what happened.

Mbatha says, 'Man, it is bad,' and pointing to his legs adds: 'Here I got injured.'

While Mbatha and Motaung converse, Ntshekang hears the sound of an oncoming vehicle and takes it as his cue to pull out his service pistol and point it at Motaung. Ntshekang tells him to walk in the direction of the vehicle; he is under arrest.

Shoke flees from his position, making a U-turn and running deeper into the township.

Motaung walks towards Ntshekang, who steps backwards. Motaung continues moving forwards, upon which Ntshekang fires two shots in quick succession. One of the bullets strikes Motaung in the chest.

The wounded Motaung is arrested. Captain Nel puts him in the Combi where Mbatha identifies him as 'Abie'.

Shoke meanwhile sees policemen who seem to be closing in on him. He jumps fences and moves further until he reaches open country outside Stinkwater. He then notices some police vans that have joined the chase. He also hears helicopters. Just as he thinks there is no way out, he notices a donga and drops into it. He then creeps along it. His clothes are torn and covered in mud, but he manages to get to a village five miles away where people hide him for the night.[61]

*

Within a couple of months of the signing of the secret South Africa–Swaziland security agreement, the ANC notices a tangible hardening in the kingdom's attitude towards the movement's cadres.

On the night of 3 June 1982 Ronnie Kasrils meets Petrus Nzima in Swaziland to discuss the increasing harassment of undercover ANC operatives by the Swazi Police.[62]

On the following day, Nzima is driving with his wife Jabu near Mbabane when a bomb destroys their car, killing them both.[63]

*

The solid, covert relations between South Africa and Swaziland receive a public manifestation on 14 June when the former's minister of cooperation and development, Dr Piet Koornhof, informs the KwaZulu legislative assembly of the South African government's intention to cede the Ingwavuma region of KwaZulu and most of the KaNgwane homeland to Swaziland.

Mangosuthu Buthelezi, the KwaZulu chief minister, warns Koornhof in his response that the cession of Ingwavuma will severely damage Zulu–Afrikaner relations as well as cause bad blood between Zulus and Swazis.

Speaking on the night of the announcement, KaNgwane's chief minister Enos Mabuza also expresses opposition to the move.[64]

The ANC conveys its response just over a month later on 15 July when it releases a statement titled 'Memorandum to the Government of Swaziland on the Agreement between Swaziland and the Pretoria regime on Ka-Ngwane and Ngwavuma', from Lusaka.

In it the ANC asserts that the agreement has already 'generated intense animosities between Swazi and Swazi and between Swazi and Zulu, involving millions of African people'. They remind the Swazi authorities that the ANC has consistently fought South African attempts to annex Botswana, Lesotho and Swaziland. It would thus be 'highly regrettable' if Swaziland undermined this 'by joining hands with the apartheid regime in carrying out a policy which aims at transforming South Africa into a white man's country by declaring the African people aliens in the country of their birth'.

The ANC promises that South Africa and Swaziland 'can and will, in future, solve any territorial disputes between them peacefully and amicably'. At that later stage, Swaziland would be 'perfectly within its rights to raise any territorial questions with the government of a liberated South Africa, should there be such questions'.[65]

*

The ANC holds a meeting at a property in Matsapha in Swaziland to discuss its longer-term response to the land deal.[66]

The ANC's plan to reverse the transfer of Ingwavuma receives the codename 'Crow', and KaNgwane, 'Sparrow'.[67]

The Natal Regional Military Command also meets to discuss these developments. In attendance are members of the Northern Natal Military Command, which is a substructure of the Natal Machinery.

296 | JULY 1982

Spread out on a table is a map of the whole of Natal. Zweli Nyanda, the chief of staff of the Natal Command, stands up periodically to pace around and gather his thoughts.

From time to time he breaks off from his contemplation to talk to the man sitting opposite him at the table, who is the political commissar of the Northern Natal Command. Nyanda peppers him with questions about his time spent in the Ingwavuma area as a political operative over the past couple of years.[68]

The increased pressure on the ANC in countries neighbouring South Africa meanwhile re-emphasises the need to shift the pattern of armed struggle from cross-border raids to a campaign based within South Africa. Zweli Nyanda is also involved in a discussion with Charles Ndaba and Rayman Lalla in 1982 concerning the possibilities of creating underground structures in the greater Durban area, using the Alan Taylor Residence of the University of Natal as a kind of headquarters.

Ndaba and Nyanda are both former medical students at the University of Natal. During the conversation, Nyanda opines that perhaps 'it's time the medical students stopped dissecting butterflies and get involved in political activities'.[69]

*

The situation in Swaziland also forms the basis of a discussion between Temba Banzi and Oscar Ntombelo in Maseru.

Banzi instructs Ntombelo to carry out a task in the Bergville area of Natal. It is necessary to establish a new route to Natal, he says, because the path through Swaziland is no longer viable due to the recently adopted aggressive attitude by the authorities there.

If Swaziland does not change its attitude, Banzi says, the ANC hierarchy will airlift its trained men and material from Swaziland to Lesotho, which will then become the main springboard for incursions into Natal and the Cape.[70]

*

But Lesotho is not immune from the pressures experienced elsewhere. On 2 August, Lesotho Radio reports that the homes of Temba Banzi and Chris Hani have been attacked in Maseru. Banzi's wife was injured in the first attack. In the other, the roof was blown off Hani's house, but nobody was injured.[71]

*

The ANC's Representative Mission in Swaziland completes a 'Report on political cases faced by our cadres in Swaziland (supplementary report)' on 7 August. It discusses the impact of the kingdom's tightened security measures on ANC underground activity in and through the territory.

The representatives begin by noting that since April they have had to deal with increasing cases of cadres arrested for possession of 'arms of war' in Swaziland. They point out that according to Swazi arms laws, possession of, say, a Makarov pistol, its magazine and ammunition for it are three separate offences. Hence there are heavy fines for people caught in possession of such articles of war.

The representatives mention that there have been regular police raids of ANC premises in search of arms during the period covered by the report.

But as with the report they compiled on Christmas Eve the previous year, they again criticise certain aspects of the ANC's own practices, which, they allege, have unnecessarily exacerbated the problems. For example, on two occasions the Swazi Police forewarned the ANC of imminent raids, saying that they had to conduct the searches because the 'Boers' threatened unilateral action unless they did. The Swazis then divulged that it seemed as though the South Africans obtained the information about the hideouts from women who had been allowed to visit ANC residences by MK cadres – and even to take photographs there.

The representatives mention that neighbours in the places where the movement has residences also tend to submit reports to the police about activities going on there: they note that 'we tend to have a lot of traffic to and from our residences on a daily basis', and this only creates suspicion.

The document features a tally of the financial penalties incurred by the ANC in Swaziland between April and August 1982. The totals were R1,778.32 in fines, R1,880 for bail, R75 in legal fees and R47.72 in sundry expenses, making for a total of R3,781.04.[72]

*

On the following day, 8 August, Oscar Ntombelo travels with a colleague, 'Njongwe', through the Paqama Path in the vicinity of the Qacha's Nek border post between South Africa and Lesotho. They walk along the path in the direction of the Mafube Mission in the Eastern Cape.

At about 4 a.m. on the 9th, Ntombelo, who is wearing a corduroy cap, blue bomber jacket, fawn-coloured jeans and black shoes, is travelling alone, and is stopped at a roadblock. He is walking on the side of the main Lesotho–Transkei road near Qacha's Nek.

His singling out is wholly coincidental. The policemen were manning the road-block waiting for the next car, when they noticed him walking past and decided to stop him. During questioning, the fact he is a Zulu-speaker aroused suspicion, so they decided to arrest him.

Only later at the police station do they discover quite who is in their hands. In the process they acquire a wealth of intelligence about ANC activities in Lesotho.[73]

*

By now Lesotho is firmly in South Africa's cross hairs. On 7 October 1982, Alfred Nzo and two other ANC members meet Lesotho government officials in Maseru. They are told that the security of ANC members in the country can no longer be guaranteed, and therefore if members of the organisation don't leave the country voluntarily, they will be removed.[74]

*

Christopher Mnisi and David Simelane meet in Maputo. Mnisi's brother knows Warrant Officer Phillipus Selepe from the December 1981 operation in which MK members 'George' and 'Brown' were killed. Christopher Mnisi and Simelane discuss Selepe. Simelane says he has to be killed, because he is stopping the liberation army from freeing the country.[75]

*

Christopher Mnisi is in Mamelodi at the home of his friend, Freddie Shongwe, on 7 November. At about 8 p.m. Mnisi and another man, Jerry Magubane, leave the property in a car driven by Shongwe.

The car stops in another part of Mamelodi. Mnisi gets out and walks several streets until he reaches a plot in Section A214 of the township. At this house, he requests a toilet. He is shown where to find it in the yard.

Warrant Officer Selepe is meanwhile walking home in the dark from the residence of a family friend, Auntie Miema. Selepe, who is carrying a paper bag, opens the gate to his house.

'Selepe!' Mnisi calls.

Selepe responds while closing the gate.

Mnisi fires at Selepe at close range and then runs off to the getaway car, which promptly flees the scene.[76]

When Julia Selepe comes out of the house to investigate the noise, there is still gunsmoke in the air. When she reaches the gate, her husband is already dead.[77]

*

On 22 November, the SADF's Northern Transvaal Command sends the Military Intelligence Division's headquarters in Pretoria copies of documents that have recently come into the possession of the Royal Swazi Defence Force. The papers were intercepted en route to Durban.[78]

The perennial problem of political reconstruction comes up in one of the documents. In it, this longstanding concern is accompanied by an additional worry that the ANC is now caught in a race against time in solving it, given Pretoria's more aggressive regional stance. The paper refers to a special seminar in Maputo attended by four senior ANC officials and eighteen cadres stationed either in Swaziland or Maputo. The seminar ran for four days. According to the document, the delegates

> unanimously agreed that the revolutionary armed struggle was not taking root
> and we are in danger of being outmanouvered by the Racists and the Imperialists.
> (The CIA has announced that in five years time it hopes to succeed in throwing
> out ANC personnel from the Frontline States). Swaziland has steped [sic] up its
> harassment of the Anc and it is only a matter of time before they kick us out. And
> Swaziland has had the strongest Anc organisation.

Delegates argued that though MK had proven its ability to strike at the enemy, 'because we are "fishes out of water", when the enemy began to strike back, we suffered too many casualties'. They agreed that the ANC undoubtedly possesses strong popular support, but felt 'it does not matter how much support we have, if we continue to lead the struggle by remote control, we will be doomed'.

The remedies advocated are for 80 per cent of resources to be allocated to building political and military units at home and only 20 per cent to special operations; for leadership to be built up within South Africa at sector level; and for 'the best cadres from the NEC, RC, SO and the implementation committees be sent home to form this sector leadership together with leading cadres from the established cells. This is nothing but the APC that we discussed earlier.'[79] (This refers to the document of September 1980, according to which the area committees were supposed to have been linked up on a regional basis by the end of 1981. In fact, little progress has been made towards their establishment on even a local level with the end of 1982 approaching.)

*

The ANC's Representative Mission in Swaziland sends a letter to the organisation's Lusaka headquarters three days later. It concerns the ongoing conflict between the Swazi Police and the ANC underground.

It says that between 10.30 a.m. and midday that day, comrades K.B. Baartman, E. Vundla and P.M. Maduna visited Swazi Security Branch offices. Present on the Swazi side were P.A. Mamba, 'Vilakazi' and 'Msibi' from the police. The problems raised by the Swazis related to the fact that MK's cadres were not exactly submitting meekly to the kingdom's crackdown.

The police officers complained that on various occasions their men had received death threats from MK cadres, to the extent that they now wondered whether the ANC had changed its policies. Certain members of the police now feared for their lives.

The Swazis mentioned three cadres in police custody, in Manzini and Mbabane, who had threatened policemen. They named another cadre who was threatening to kill policemen when released.

They accused MK members of despising the police, judging by how they insult them in various ways – and sometimes in front of members of the public. Some ANC guerrillas had even stopped police cars to swear at members of the force who had dealt with them at one time or another.

The policemen raised the issue of the ANC's use of stolen cars, saying it blemished the organisation's name and reduced its status to that of criminals and thieves.

They brought up the tendency for MK men deported from the kingdom to show up again in the country within days, mentioning 'Zweli and Tebokgo Kgope and a Shiyumhlaba, who return to Swaziland every now and then despite warning', while Zweli remains 'ever armed and ready to shoot at the police'.

The three ANC representatives responded that there had been no change in the movement's policy and that they had nothing against Swaziland or anybody else besides apartheid South Africa. They did, however, apologise.

The officers expressed thanks for the apology.[80]

*

In 1978, former SADF corporal and South African national sword-fighting champion Rodney Wilkinson used his degree in building science to obtain employment at the in-construction Koeberg nuclear power station after the nearby commune in which he had been living ran out of money. With the encouragement of his girlfriend Heather Gray, he later stole a set of Koeberg's building plans and took them to Zimbabwe on a trip in which he successfully managed to contact the ANC.

Now in 1982, Wilkinson and Gray dig up four limpet mines packed with incendiary charges on the side of a road in a remote area of the Karoo desert. The couple place the mines in wine box decanters and drive back to Cape Town with the boxes concealed in their Renault 5. When they arrive home in Claremont, they cache the devices in holes dug in their garden.

From there Wilkinson smuggles the mines one by one to his workplace. On each occasion he gets the mine past security at the Koeberg plant by concealing it in a hidden compartment in the Renault.

Once inside, he takes the mines to the prefabricated building in which he has an office and hides them in his desk drawer.[81]

*

Phyllis Naidoo opens the curtains at her residence in Maseru on the evening of 8 December in order to allow the moonlight to illuminate the room. At about midnight she falls asleep.

Soon afterwards she hears what sound like explosions and jumps to the floor. The sound hurts her ears so much that she has to cover her head with a pillow. From her window she sees flares blazing across the skyline. One strikes a flat about four blocks away.

The explosions continue for a while.[82]

The ANC issues a statement signed by Alfred Nzo on 10 December detailing the magnitude of what happened in Maseru. It reads: 'At Hahoohlo at the residence of one of our people, comrade Mathabatha's home was completely destroyed. The explosion also killed a cow. A woman neighbour was shot dead when she peered out through the window.'

Also affected were Juena Flats, 'where the SADF were looking for Comrade Chris's wife'. The raiders forced their way into a neighbouring flat belonging to Mr Jerry Peko. There they found 'Matumo Ralebitso, daughter of Lesotho's former ambassador to Mozambique. In panic she threw herself out of the window and died.' Another fatality at the flats was a man who put up a fight but died when he attempted to escape through a window.

At Florida, a government house was bombed and four ANC members were killed.

At Upper Thamae, two houses belonging to Comrade Lehlohonolo (Lambert) Moloi were destroyed. In one house two people were burnt to death and a third was shot dead. In a house next to Moloi's they shot eight people dead and burnt a car.

At Lekhaloaneng, two houses were bombed. In one house three people died – all of them Lesotho nationals – while in another house three ANC members were killed.

Chris Hani's house in Lithabaneng was completely destroyed.

At a house near Motaung's towards Qoaling four corpses were found.

At Mohlalalitoe five people were killed but they have not yet been identified.

'Our information is that a total of 40 people were murdered: 10 Lesotho nationals (women and 3 Children) and 30 ANC refugees.'[83]

*

On the morning of 17 December, Rodney Wilkinson sets the fuses on the limpet mines stored in his office desk to a twenty-four-hour delay. He then leaves the pre-fabricated building on foot, with the four mines hidden in his overalls.

Access to the clean area around the reactors is through an airlock where people seeking entry must strip and don protective clothing. But there are also pipe tunnels leading into the area that have plastic diaphragms to keep the air clean. Wilkinson pushes the mines through these diaphragms and then passes through the airlock in his protective clothing, before collecting the mines on the other side. He then makes his way to the two reactor heads in the Reactor One containment building. These reactors are made of 110 tons of steel.

On his way to plant the second mine, Wilkinson spots a guard eyeing him suspiciously. Wilkinson can feel beads of sweat on his own forehead. He makes a detour and places the mine at a concentration of cables under the second control room.

Of his four mines, two are planted on a pair of reactor heads, one on a section of the containment building, and one at the concentration of electric cabling under the main control room.

Later that morning, Wilkinson attends a farewell party held in his honour by fellow engineers at the plant. In the afternoon he flies to Johannesburg and is then driven by car, with a bicycle on board, to a point near the Swaziland border. After being dropped off he rides the bicycle illegally into Swaziland en route to report back to the Special Operations Unit.[84]

*

In Komatipoort on the same day, South Africa's foreign minister Roelof 'Pik' Botha meets two Mozambican counterparts: the security minister Jacinto Veloso, and Sergio Viera, a long-time confidant of President Samora Machel.

The Mozambicans put forward three principles. The first is that Mozambique wants to 'promote peaceful coexistence with all countries, regardless of their systems'. Secondly, Maputo seeks 'good relations with all our neighbours, regardless of their systems'. Finally, Mozambique demands – 'and we shall do the same – total respect for the sovereignty of each country and its territorial integrity. We don't interfere in any country.'[85]

*

In Soweto, still on 17 December, Beverley Hlapane opens the front door of her house, only to find a man dressed in green pointing an AK-47 at her. The man demands to know where her father and mother are.

He brushes past her to the room where her parents are, and opens fire with the AK. Bartholomew Hlapane and his wife Matilda are killed, while their fourteen-year-old daughter Brenda is shot in the neck, paralysing her for life.[86]

*

At 3.23 p.m. on the 18th, at the Koeberg 1 and 2 site just under thirty kilometres north of Cape Town, one of the Westinghouse reactors in the auxiliary containment building is destroyed by a limpet mine.

At 8.36 p.m. a limpet mine explodes on a second reactor in the containment building.

Nearly three hours later, at 11.25 p.m., when the facility is swarming with security personnel, a third explosion occurs.

And finally the fourth detonation comes at 2.53 a.m. on the 19th.[87]

*

The ANC issues a statement from Dar es Salaam claiming the Koeberg attacks as a 'salute to our fallen heroes' – a reference to the Maseru raid.[88]

The planning for the Koeberg attacks preceded the Maseru raid. They were therefore not a response to the events in Lesotho. It is in December 1982 that Aboobaker Ismail and Joe Slovo begin discussing the Special Operations Unit's next major project, and they decide they want it to be a direct attack on South African security-force personnel.[89]

*

Thamsanqa Hadebe is alongside 'Vusi', Gabriel Ngwenya and Sithabiso Mahlobo in a car driven by Edward Lawrence of MK's Natal Machinery on the first Friday of February 1983. Lawrence leads them to a house in Manzini where he tells them to prepare themselves for their mission to South Africa.

Early the following morning, Lawrence returns alongside Zweli Nyanda, who tells them that after crossing the border they must board a train from Piet Retief to Durban. Vusi and Mahlobo will have to get off at Pietermaritzburg, and Ngwenya and Hadebe at Durban, where they must find themselves a secure house. They are warned not to drink alcohol and to be on the lookout for South African Police members. To Ngwenya and Hadebe, Nyanda says that the first part of their mission will be to sabotage the power line in the Dove's Road area. After this they must maintain a low profile at the safe house and await further instructions.

Each of the four men are given R200, blue overalls, a pistol and two hand grenades (one offensive, one defensive). Four pistols are laid out on the ground in front of them, from which they can choose. Hadebe takes a Luger.

Following the briefing, Nyanda drives the group in a Toyota Cressida to the border area. They arrive at sunset and he lets them off some four kilometres from the border fence. He wishes them strength and returns to Manzini.

A courier helps the group over the border, and they walk a further kilometre along a gravel road until they reach a spot from where they manage to hail a taxi to Piet Retief railway station. When they arrive at the station at 6 a.m. the courier departs.

At 1 p.m., when the train to Durban departs, the four are on board, but in two different compartments. In their section, Ngwenya and Hadebe purchase beer – in violation of Nyanda's explicit orders – from a black woman. They start drinking heavily.

Ngwenya is later woken by the conductor in Pietermaritzburg. He is still drunk. Contrary to his orders to head to Durban, he gets out at Pietermaritzburg and goes to Sobantu Village.

Hadebe has also lost consciousness. He wakes up to find himself still on the train but in handcuffs, with South African Police members in civilian clothes searching him.

Ngwenya is arrested in Sobantu Village the following Monday, 7 February.

At about 10 a.m. that day, Mathanzima Bhungane is at his home in Edendale, Pietermaritzburg, when a friend, Siphiwe Mguduso, arrives and asks him to come to the Lay Ecumenical Centre.

On their way there, they encounter Duma Gqubule, who is in the company of another man, whom Gqubule introduces as 'Jabu' (it is Sithabiso Mahlobo).

The four proceed together to the Lay Ecumenical Centre, which lies a few metres away.[90]

*

A South African Military Intelligence report compiled in February 1983 notes that Chris Hani has left Maseru for Maputo, and that his father, who lives in Mafeteng, also wants to go, but is awaiting his son's return so that he can sell the house.[91]

Hani soon returns to Lesotho, and in Maseru towards the end of the month meets Lizo Bright Ngqungwana. Hani tells him he has been appointed MK commander for the Western Cape.[92]

*

Following on from his discussions with Joe Slovo about an attack on enemy personnel, Aboobaker Ismail meets Johannes Mnisi and Freddie Shongwe in Swaziland. Ismail tells Shongwe to go with Ezekial Maseko and reconnoitre targets within South Africa. He identifies Voortrekkerhoogte as a target that Special Operations would like to hit again. He mentions other possible targets like the South African Air Force's headquarters in Church Street.

Ismail then shows Shongwe the weapon that the ANC would like to use for the operation. It is a forty-kilogram explosive device with a trigger mechanism activated by radio.[93]

*

Aboobaker Ismail meanwhile is the subject of a conversation inside South Africa between his brother Mohamed and Mohammed Shaik. The two are friends. Mohamed Ismail mentions that his brother, alias 'Rachid', is involved with MK.

Shaik tells Ismail he would like to be recruited into MK himself.

A while later in Swaziland, the two meet Aboobaker Ismail, who quizzes Shaik about his political background, disposition and allegiances. He warns Shaik about the implications of joining MK and how damaging it would be if he were ever caught.

Shaik is adamant: he wants to join.

On the basis of the interview he is recruited into MK. Shaik and Mohamed Ismail are then formed into a unit by Aboobaker Ismail. The three discuss a possible name for the cell. Aboobaker Ismail suggests 'Dolphin', in honour of Montso Mokgabudi, the Special Operations Unit's former commander, who had operated under the pseudonym 'Dolphin Ngake'.

His proposal meets no objections, so the 'Dolphin Unit' is born.

Aboobaker Ismail then explains to them the ANC's operational guidelines. He says the nature of the operations they will be involved in will require them to purchase a motor vehicle to which a dead letter box can be fitted. He tells them to bring a car on their next trip, so that a dead letter box can be added to it.[94]

*

Ben Martins drives Sithabiso Mahlobo to Commercial Road in Pietermaritzburg on 21 April.[95]

Mahlobo goes to the buildings of the old Supreme Court of the Natal Provincial Division, opposite the Old City Hall. He walks to the wall of the court facing Commercial Road. On the right-hand side of the steps, he places a bomb.

At about 7.15 p.m. it explodes, shattering the doors and windows of the Supreme Court building. A nightwatchman is injured.[96]

Four days later, Mahlobo is driven from Natal to the Lesotho border by 'Comrade Zola', a doctor at Umtata Hospital. At an official checkpoint, Mahlobo declares that his reason for travel is that he is looking for accommodation at Roma University.

It works, and on the other side of the border Comrade Zola drops him off at Maseru's Airport Hotel.

After being flown to Maputo, Mahlobo completes a document titled 'Year of United Action Report' on 4 May. It is an account of his experiences while operating inside South Africa.

He recounts that his mission was to reconnoitre a base that could service a unit operating in the Pietermaritzburg/Estcourt area. He says he went to both areas and each has sites that could be used. He says that in his judgement Pietermaritzburg's location and infrastructure makes it better suited, because

almost all the secondary roads branch off from the main roads to the cities and towns, thus giving an advantage of having a base in or not far from the outlying rural areas where even the main force of worker comes from. The area suitable for a base would be in the mountain range shadowing the Nxamalala area. It is covered by both natural bush and planted forests. This area has 3 roads leading to it and all branch off from the main road, 2 from Bulwer and one from Howick.

As for Estcourt, where he spent a week, he reports that the terrain is good but the people 'are not yet conscientised to the level of harbouring the guerrillas unless you have a good legend'.[97]

*

South Africa's minister of constitutional development Chris Heunis holds a press conference on 5 May in which he speaks about the Constitution Bill released by the government earlier in the day.

The seventy-one-page draft bill calls for the creation of three separate parliamentary chambers for whites, Coloureds and Indians respectively, the idea being that each group will decide on matters that concern their own affairs, while issues of overlapping concern will be a joint responsibility. The decision on what constitutes a group issue and what represents a common concern is to be made by the incumbent of the executive presidency that will be established if the constitution is approved. No matter will be discussed in any chamber until the president has decided whether it is a general or an exclusive affair, and he can change his mind about classifications at any time. A crucial aspect of the constitution is therefore how the president will be elected. Under the draft bill, he will be voted into power by an electoral college comprising fifty members from the white assembly, twenty-five from the coloured chamber, and thirteen from the Asian house. This will effectively preserve white domination under the new dispensation.

The bill excludes black Africans from parliamentary representation. This issue dominates the press conference. In response to one question, Heunis strongly denies that blacks are being excluded from constitutional development, government consultations or decisions about their own group interests; he says they have been denied parliamentary representation because their constitutional development has taken a different path (a reference to the homelands and urban township councils). He says in a later response to a further inquiry: 'My philosophy is that they will not be included for the reasons I have enumerated and because I believe the inclusion of blacks will destroy the constitution – as it did elsewhere.'

Heunis adds that the bill still needs to be approved by Parliament and then by the white population in a referendum. The method for testing Indian and coloured people has not yet been decided, he says.[98]

*

The United Press International news agency reports on 9 May that Pik Botha and Mozambique's Joaquim Chissano met in Komatipoort four days previously. No details of the talks were revealed at the time, the article says, but there have been reports that South Africa is prepared to cease its support for Mozambican opposition group RENAMO 'in exchange for the transfer of black nationalist guerrillas of the African National Congress from their sanctuaries in Maputo to northern Mozambique. But the reports have not been confirmed.'[99]

*

Hélène Passtoors, aged forty, who was born in the Netherlands but is now employed in the linguistics department of Maputo's Eduardo Mondlane University, drives out of Swaziland on 19 May in a cream-coloured Colt Gallant. In South Africa she heads to Mamelodi, where she parks the car.[100]

*

On the same day, Freddie Shongwe arrives at the house of a friend, Jerry Shabangu, and asks if Shabangu knows where he can find a stolen car.

Shabangu gives him an address.

On the 20th, Shongwe returns to Shabangu and says he couldn't get a stolen car, but he has found a vehicle that he could use if the engine numbers are removed. Shongwe says he would like to use this 'straight' car for a 'big job' he has on for later in the day. He asks Shabangu whether it would be possible to keep the car in his garage, as he doesn't want anybody to see it.

Shongwe then takes Shabangu to the house of Ezekial Maseko. As they arrive there they see Maseko's Combi outside. Shabangu also sees that behind the house is a 'white' Colt Gallant with Swaziland 'SD' registration plates.

Shongwe tells Shabangu that he has come from Swaziland with friends.

Shabangu asks who his friends are.

Shongwe tells him not to worry about it.[101]

*

Anna Maseko sees her husband, Ezekial Maseko, in the company of Freddie Shongwe at the Maseko family home. The two are under the bonnet of a cream-coloured Gallant working with a grinder.

Shortly after 3 p.m. the two men depart in two vehicles. Shongwe drives the Gallant and Maseko the Combi.[102]

*

Ezekial Maseko parks the Combi in the vicinity of Schubart Street in central Pretoria and proceeds on foot to the northern kerb of Church Street, where he takes up position. The Colt Gallant is parked on the opposite side of the road in front of the Nedbank Plaza. Freddie Shongwe is still inside it.[103]

*

At 4.28 p.m. that day, Friday 20 May, Arnold Kirkby is finishing an article at his desk in the offices of the *Pretoria News*, situated some two blocks from Church Street, when an almighty blast occurs nearby, causing the large plate-glass window next to his desk to reverberate.

Kirkby leaves the offices and joins a policeman in running to Church Street. When he gets there he sees a black plume of smoke issuing from a car outside the Nedbank Square building, which houses the South African Air Force's headquarters. The bomb has made a huge crater in the ground.

On the other side of the street is the Poynton building, which houses the SADF Directorate of Military Intelligence. Almost all the shops on both sides of the street are destroyed, as are three floors of the Nedbank building. Worst hit is the Golden Egg Restaurant on the ground floor of the Nedbank building. Mangled bodies lie in the street and in the restaurant. The *Star*'s Pretoria correspondent sees a young soldier, his face charred and his eyes blinded by the explosion, rocking back and forth. A girl, lying alongside two bodies, looks blankly at the destruction, crying for her mother, while another woman, her face bleeding from the blast, points a finger to the sky and groans in pain.

The smoke creates an eerie haze around Church Street. There is a nauseating smell accompanied by cries from people trapped inside the Golden Egg Restaurant.

When the bomb exploded prematurely, Freddie Shongwe's body was hurled some distance from the Colt Gallant and was crushed against a lamp post. Ezekial Maseko suffered critical injuries to the lower half of his body. He is taken to hospital only to be pronounced dead upon arrival.[104]

*

At a press conference in Nairobi the following day, Oliver Tambo says: 'Never again, never again are our people going to be doing all the bleeding, never again.'

He announces an escalation of the armed struggle, saying that from now on the ANC will extend its sabotage from buildings, railways, and bridges to 'attacking the enemy forces, and that is what we are going to be doing'.

He is asked if that means Church Street is a foretaste of things to come.

'Absolutely, yes, indeed.'[105]

*

The retaliation is quick in coming.

Just before 7.30 a.m. on the 23rd, South African Air Force planes fly low over the Bay of Maputo.

At Rua Ingineira Pinto Texeira, they plough rockets into an orange grove next to an old Portuguese villa. The shrapnel from the explosions wounds a girl. Just behind the building is the state-run Soinopal grapefruit and jam factory. Rockets strafe the outer walls of the factory crèche and blow two holes out of the foot of the breeze-block walls surrounding the property's grounds.

Further on, a whitewashed Spanish-style house has its living room devastated by a rocket fired from the planes. At a property just beyond this house, two children who went to look when they heard the planes approaching are hit by shrapnel splinters.

At the Transvaal Urban Machinery's former headquarters in Liberdad, rockets fall in a garden but do little damage to the building itself, whose walls are decorated with faded slogans such as 'At this hour of destiny your country and your people need you' (the slogan is embellished by a drawing of a Soviet-type assault rifle), 'The future is yours' and 'Umkhonto We Sizwe – the People's Army'.[106]

*

In an article appearing in the *New York Times* on 30 May, the paper's correspondent Alan Cowell writes: 'Mozambique could be ruined by South Africa, and that appears to be the reason that its leaders have sought to disperse concentrations of African National Congress personnel in its capital and have moved some of them to the northern province of Nampula.'[107]

*

Eugene de Kock, a security policeman with counter-insurgency experience in Rhodesia and South West Africa, receives a telex report on 1 June 1983 that he is to be transferred to Section C1 of the Security Branch – 'Vlakplaas'.[108]

*

A report in the *New York Times* on 6 June features extracts from an interview conducted the previous day by the paper's correspondent Joseph Lelyveld with General Constand Viljoen, chief of the SADF.

Viljoen explains the rationale behind South Africa's regional strategy. He says that if the SADF were to succeed in shutting MK out of neighbouring countries, 'They will be able to have single incidents but they will not be able to sustain a high intensity of operations for a long time'.

Asked whether the ANC would be stopped dead in their tracks if that occurred, Viljoen said:

> I think so. Oh yes. I wouldn't say 'dead in their tracks' but they would just not be able to operate. If we deny them bases in all our neighbouring states, either through the cooperation of the states themselves, which we hope will be possible, or by means of military action against their bases, then they have only two ways to come in, by air or by sea. It makes it almost impossible for them.[109]

*

Facing pressure on its traditional infiltration routes, the ANC explores other fronts.

Madimetsa Ranoto (one of those who headed to Bulawayo following the disbandment of Assembly Point Juliet in 1980) enters South Africa from Zimbabwe on the evening of 9 June at the head of a group including three others: Philemon Morake, 'Thabo' and 'James'.

On the following morning, a South African Police counter-insurgency unit notices a hole that has been cut in the border fence with Zimbabwe, some sixty kilometres east of Messina.

Late that afternoon, three SAP members make contact with Ranoto's group in the Limpopo River area. A shootout ensues, during which the four guerrillas flee in different directions. The police recover a great amount of war material from the scene.

On the 11th, Ranoto and Morake manage to find each other. As they lost all their equipment during the clash they decide to go and seek food among the local population.

While doing so, however, they are arrested by locals, who hand them over to the police. They are taken to Sibasa for interrogation, during which it is established that they are trained ANC members and that they entered the country from Zimbabwe. The news is a revelation for South African Military Intelligence; it is the first confirmed case they have of an infiltration launched through Zimbabwe.[110]

*

A report arrives on 14 June 1983 at the headquarters of the SADF's Special Forces at Voortrekkerhoogte. It is based on an account by a source whose observations stretch over the past six months. The source alleges that the ANC is developing a base in Mozambique's Nampula province, and that the camp is located twelve kilometres north-west of a small centre called Mecuburi, which in turn lies north-west of the town of Nampula.

The camp is on an old farm called Impirima, previously owned by Portuguese rancher Helio Cardoso, an associate of Pendray Souza, a former commercial farmer. There is only one road leading to this farm. It is a dirt road, as are all other roads in the area.

The camp was started in June 1982. It has no special fencing around it, only normal cattle fences. Its size is 600 hectares.[111]

*

Towards the end of June 1983, Sithabiso Mahlobo arrives at the ANC's camp in Nampula, where David Jiba Bhengu is in charge. Mahlobo hands Bhengu a letter from the Senior Organ in Maputo. In it is an instruction for Bhengu to assist Mahlobo in selecting four people to be infiltrated into South Africa. Bhengu is to join them as the fifth man.

Bhengu allows Mahlobo to look through the camp and select people for the mission. After Mahlobo has selected some potential candidates, Bhengu provides further information about them. Mahlobo then departs for Maputo.[112]

*

Julius Mokoena, MK's chief of staff in Angola, is summoned to a meeting with the commander of the Angolan Army (FAPLA) in the Malange region.

The FAPLA commander requests help from MK in fighting UNITA in the area. He says their assistance is needed because most FAPLA combatants are engaged in fighting the SADF in the south.

On 18 July, Uriah Mokeba, the ANC's chief representative in Angola, writes a letter to the organisation's International Department. He notes that the ANC's training base in Malange has become an enemy target, because UNITA has sent groups of 'bandits' to sabotage and destabilise the surrounding area. The bandits have thus far captured a village near the camp and have unsuccessfully tried to raid an MK logistics store. 'In view of this prevailing situation,' Mokeba writes, 'we have come into agreement with the Angolan Defence Force – FAPLA [–] that we will patrol an area near our camp.'

A joint FAPLA/MK brigade is therefore established, to which the ANC contributes 450 cadres.

The unit's overall commander is to be FAPLA's Senior Lieutenant Sebastiao, while Julius Mokoena will be chief of staff, and Chris Hani will represent the ANC leadership and MK's military headquarters on the command structure.[113]

*

Outside the Rocklands Civic Centre in Mitchell's Plain in the Western Cape on Saturday 20 August, two men are seated inside a car with Transkei number plates. The men possess two-way radios and are among a number of plainclothes policemen in the vicinity. Watching through binoculars, they take the registration details of the cars and buses that start arriving at the venue from the early morning.

The Civic Centre is packed later that afternoon, with people sitting on the rafters and occupying every ledge. Diplomatic representatives from foreign embassies are also there, along with international television and newspaper crews.

Adjacent to the hall is a marquee in which the proceedings are being relayed by video (thereby avoiding violating a ban on outdoor meetings).

The occasion is the founding of the United Democratic Front (UDF), an umbrella organisation seeking to bind local and national groups into an anti-apartheid coalition. Its immediate focus is to oppose the new constitution.

Reverend Allan Boesak, the president of the World Alliance of Reformed Churches, addresses the gathering. He says the UDF rejects the government's constitutional reform proposals, because they enshrine the 'heresy' of racism and wilfully exclude 80 per cent of the population. He argues that under the proposed constitution, racism 'will be modernised and streamlined, and in its new multi-coloured cloak it will be less conspicuous and less offensive to some. Nevertheless, it will still be there.'

That system cannot be modified or streamlined; it must be eradicated. 'We want all our rights, we want them here, and we want them now,' he says.[114]

*

Meanwhile the situation in Angola deteriorates.

Uriah Mokeba writes another letter to the head of the ANC's International Affairs Department on 22 August. This time he warns that 'the situation in the province of Malange is really critical. Most of our people have been withdrawn from the North to assist in manning the security in the Province. Both comrades Joe Modise and Chris Hani are at the scene with units of MK assisting in combing the area which is to a very large extent infested with bandits.' But, he adds, 'We have been told, that our units, in the meantime, are in control of the situation. We shall keep in touch.'[115]

*

On the sixth floor of Johannesburg's fifty-storey Carlton Centre building, Mohammed Shaik of MK's 'Dolphin Unit' approaches a row of five offices belonging to the 'embassy' of the 'independent' Ciskei Bantustan.

It is about 5.30 p.m. on 26 August 1983. He places a limpet mine containing about a kilogram of plastic explosives in a wastepaper bin outside the entrance of the consulate offices.

At 6.50 p.m. the mine detonates, leaving a three-centimetre depression in the building's concrete floor. Only one man, Samuel Mahlangu, a passer-by on the street below, suffers injuries from glass sent flying by the explosion. Four office workers who were on the sixth floor at the time of the blast escape injury.[116]

PLANNING FOR PEOPLE'S WAR

The ANC's fear of being cut off from the Forward Areas before it has established politico-military structures within South Africa forms the backdrop to the editorial in the September 1983 issue of the organisation's official journal *Sechaba*.

Noting that the Morogoro Conference established the Revolutionary Council to guide the struggle inside South Africa, it says the ANC has agreed a new organisational structure to replace the RC, consisting of a 'Politico-Military Council (PMC) with its sub-departments, and the External Co-ordinating Council (ECC) with its sub-committees. By definition the latter will co-ordinate our external work.'

The designers of the new organisational structure considered whether the movement's existing priorities were correct, whether resources were being concentrated where most needed, and whether existing structures were effective and efficient enough in implementing policy.

The editorial reflects: 'There is a sense of urgency in this because, though historically time is on our side, strategically it is not. This is how urgent the ANC views our struggle.'[1]

*

Three bomb blasts occur in Warmbaths on 10 October.

Stanley Mabizela claims ANC responsibility for them in an interview on Tanzanian radio the same day.

A week later, on 17 October, a South African task force raids Mozambique, and Magnus Malan, South Africa's defence minister, issues a statement afterwards claiming that the 'planning office' responsible for the Warmbaths attack was destroyed in the operation.

'The Mozambique government has been specially warned to get rid of the ANC,' he says, but it is 'obviously not prepared to heed these warnings'.[2]

*

About 2,000 people are present at Pietermaritzburg City Hall on 27 October 1983 to hear Prime Minister P.W. Botha speak about the forthcoming referendum for a new constitution.

Warrant Officer Botha of the South African Police's Reaction Unit is standing at the front of the Capital Towers Hotel, about 100 metres away. He is in civilian clothes.

Thembinkosi Ngcobo gets off at a bus stop near the Red Cross building in Pietermaritz Street, carrying a parcel wrapped in newspaper. He walks up the lane between the NBS building and the Capitol Towers building. When he gets to Commercial Road, he sees a crowd of people at City Hall, so he turns and walks back down Commercial Road to Pietermaritz Street. When he reaches a spot opposite the steps leading into Capital Towers, Warrant Officer Botha approaches him, having become suspicious about his movements and the parcel he is carrying. It is about 9.15 p.m.

Botha asks what is in the parcel.

Ngcobo does not reply.

Botha then opens a corner of the parcel and sees it contains a TG-50 demolition mine. He asks what time the bomb is set to explode. Ngcobo again does not reply. Botha grabs the parcel, asks a traffic officer to detain Ngcobo, and places the parcel on the pavement some distance away. He then contacts the demolition squad by radio.

Warrant Officer Cary is on duty inside City Hall when he receives the call. He runs out into Commercial Road. On the pavement near Capital Park Hotel he sees a parcel partly wrapped in newspaper. Cary notices the mine has been primed with an electric detonator connected to a time delay switch. He cuts off the detonator's wires with a pocket knife and removes the detonator.[3]

*

In an editorial on 2 November 1983, the *Cape Times* encourages its (white) readers to vote in today's constitutional referendum. To fail to do so would be an 'evasion of moral responsibility'.

As for the choices at hand, the editors say that while they would not presume to dictate to readers how they should vote, 'our considered judgement of the constitution has been made plain', and it is that the document is 'fatally flawed':

> Instead of moving away from the philosophy of Verwoerdian apartheid, the Botha constitution entrenches it by excluding Africans from political rights in the South African Parliament. Apartheid is further entrenched by the institution of three separate chambers, dividing Coloured people, Indians and whites on racial lines, and requiring the retention of the Group Areas Act.

The constitution also concentrates real power in the white chamber and gives the president sweeping powers, thereby entrenching authoritarian Nationalist rule buttressed by the military. It is therefore clear that a successful 'Yes' will be a vote to refuse South African citizenship rights to Africans, by force if necessary, and to go into laager against black South Africa, the rest of Africa and, if needs be, the rest of the world. Those who are persuaded that success for Mr Botha in today's referendum will promote reform are wrong. Mr Botha does not believe that blacks should be recognized as citizens and represented in Parliament. This fundamental Nationalist principle is not negotiable, now or in the future, as Mr Botha has repeatedly reaffirmed. To imagine otherwise is wishful thinking.[4]

*

Two days later, the Johannesburg *Star* reports the results of the referendum. Out of 2,062,469 votes cast, 1,360,223 (65.95 per cent) voted 'Yes', and 691,577 (33.53 per cent) 'No', thereby ratifying the constitution.[5]

*

The ANC's new Politico-Military Council distributes a discussion document titled 'Planning for People's War' to all the movement's structures in November 1983.[6] The paper echoes the sentiment articulated in *Sechaba* two months previously about historical and strategic time moving in opposite directions in the struggle.

Concerning strategy, the document refers to the Green Book and asks: 'has the situation been so transformed and have we fulfilled enough of our objectives to move on to a new phase? In other words can we now move with greater purpose and begin to take concrete steps towards people[']s war?' The answer given is that in the narrow sense, the objective of creating political revolutionary bases has not been met: 'The policy of creating APC's has been an almost complete failure.'

Historically, however, 'The ANC and its allies stand virtually unchallenged (in the eyes of the overwhelming majority of the oppressed) as the guide of our revolution. The mass receptivity to violence as the only real answer is becoming more and more evident.'

And 'of equal importance is the dramatic advance which has been made in the past few years in growth of mass organisations both at the regional and National level', culminating in 'the creation of the U.D.F. which also represents 1 to 1½ million organised people'.

In answer to the question 'what does all this add up to in relation to our strategy in the coming period[?]', the document states that, firstly, the developments emphasise the need for the internal underground to keep pace with the growth of mass organisations, and, secondly, that while armed propaganda actions ought to be increased in their sophistication and frequency,

we cannot continue to confine ourselves to armed propaganda. If we do, then the promise which armed propaganda held out that it is merely the first phase in the struggle for the violent overthrow of the regime will sound less and less convincing and the credibility of our strategy of armed struggle will begin to fade, leading to political demoralisation both within our ranks and among the people.

Guerrilla zones must therefore be prepared with immediate effect, and they must have the potential to be developed over time into centres of guerrilla warfare. In the first stage of this process, 'commando units' must be infiltrated into the country to train and command local groups, while there should also be an internally based leadership assigned to coordinate political and military activity.[7]

*

Colonel Cronje of the South African Security Branch tells Eugene de Kock, Frederik Pienaar, Chris Rorich, Paul van Dyk and James van Zweel, who are in the company of the askaris Jeff Bosigo, Joe Mamasela and Almond Nofamela, that Mr Nyanda, Mr McFadden and Mr Lawrence are very active in Swaziland and are creating great problems in the northern Natal area.

This group has to be wiped out, Cronje says. *They must be wiped out* – he repeats this phrase over and again during the briefing.[8]

*

In Maputo, Henry Chiliza briefs Sithabiso Mahlobo and David Jiba Bhengu and tells them to prepare to be forwarded to Swaziland and then South Africa. He hands them each a handgun, two grenades and a false passport. Bhengu's passport is made out to 'Thomas Masiza'.

On 14 November, Bhengu and Mahlobo proceed to Swaziland.

The following day, the two are met by 'Ralph' (Edward Lawrence), 'Douglas' (Zweli Nyanda) and 'Magabula', who are in the company of 'Thami Zulu' (Muziwakhe Ngwenya) who has now been deployed to serve as overall commander of the Natal Machinery.

After the men have greeted each other, Mahlobo and Bhengu are left sitting together in one room reading newspapers, while the commanders gather in an adjacent room, which appears to be a sitting room. The commanders' meeting takes the whole day.

On the 16th the commanders convene again and at midday call Mahlobo in for a briefing. About half an hour later Bhengu is also called in.

With the two cadres and four commanders all assembled, Lawrence begins by telling Bhengu to enter South Africa with Mahlobo, who has fixed and arranged everything. Mahlobo will introduce Bhengu to the people with whom he will work. The region in which Bhengu will operate will be between Durban and Pietermaritzburg. He will be the commander, and after Mahlobo has introduced him to the contacts and shown him the base, Mahlobo will have to return to Swaziland. Mahlobo has to be back by 17 December, Lawrence adds. After the 17th four reinforcements will arrive and start working with Bhengu.[9]

*

On 19 November, at a kraal settlement in the KwaShange area outside Edendale, some twenty kilometres from Pietermaritzburg, Mgqutshwa Radebe sees 'Jabulani' (i.e. Sithabiso Mahlobo), whom he knows, approaching in the company of another man, whom Mahlobo introduces to Radebe as 'Masiza' (it is David Bhengu).

Radebe allows the two men to stay at his kraal for the day.[10]

*

After lunch on Sunday 20 November, Mahlobo tells Bhengu he is going to go and look for other accommodation, because the place where they are is not safe; too many people know him there.

At about 3 p.m. Mgqutshwa Radebe returns home from church. When he arrives he bumps into Mahlobo, who says he is off to Vulisaka store.

About an hour later, fulfilling Mahlobo's forebodings, Captain Ranier A. du Rand and a mixed contingent of three black and a larger number of white policemen arrive in KwaShange.

One of the white policemen walks up to Radebe and says they are police.

A black policeman asks Radebe where his visitors are.

Radebe says 'Jabulani' has gone to Vulisaka store.

The white policeman orders Radebe to accompany two policemen in trying to find 'Jabulani'.

Radebe departs with two of the black cops. When they return a while later, without finding Mahlobo, they see some of the police contingent driving away with David Bhengu.

Just after 7 p.m., Warrant Officer Thomas O'Connell arrives at the KwaShange settlement in the company of Detective Warrant Officer Zondi, and Detective Sergeants Duma and Gumede. Zondi and Gumede take statements in the kitchen while O'Connell and Duma do the same in an outside room separate from the house.

At approximately 8.30 p.m. Sithabiso Mahlobo returns. He goes to the door of the outside room and finds it locked, upon which he heads to the kitchen. As he enters, Zondi and Gumede point their service pistols at him and order him not to move, bringing to an end after only a couple of days an operation the Natal Machinery has spent the best part of 1983 preparing.[11]

*

Just after midnight on the morning of 22 November, Eugene de Kock and Warrant Officers Pienaar and Van Zweel finally see a sign of life outside a prefabricated house in Mbabane, Swaziland: a vehicle has appeared at the premises since their last drive-past. The house itself remains dark.

The three policemen head to a hotel where they awaken Colonel Cronje and brief him on developments.

Together with the other assembled members of the force (Chris Rorich, Paul van Dyk, Jeff Bosigo and Almond Nofamela), they head off in three vehicles to the prefab house. They are all equipped with guns fitted with silencers.

Once there, De Kock moves into position by the rear of the property and removes the pin from his stun grenade. No sooner has he done this than he notices his colleagues are still in the cars.

With a live grenade in his hand, he opts to proceed. He breaks open a window with the butt of his AK-47 and hears somebody rolling off a bed. He then throws the grenade into the house. The grenade has a double action, causing two explosions.

By this time his colleagues have begun to take up positions. Van Dyk moves past De Kock, breaks open a window, and throws a stun grenade through it. Van Zweel and Cronje proceed to the house's back door, where Cronje repeatedly pounds a machete into the lock and handle section. Seeing the difficulty Cronje is having, De Kock runs to assist him. De Kock breaks his toe trying to kick the door open, but the door finally opens.

Cronje and Pienaar enter, and find that the lights have been switched on inside the house. De Kock sees a black man running from room to room and down the passage before being shot in the legs. The man struggles to the bathroom and locks the door.

Colonel Cronje then kicks down the kitchen door and sees somebody running down the passage towards a bedroom. Cronje and Pienaar both chase and shoot at the man, with Pienaar killing him.

The opening salvo of bullets has struck the house's heating system, causing the entire house to fill with steam.

De Kock sees the shadow of a figure fleeing the house in an easterly direction. He poises to fire, but cannot be sure that it is not Bosigo or Nofamela, so he hesitates.

Paul van Dyk, who has remained outside the house, uses his torch to try to illuminate the man. He sees him running away from the house in a curved direction. Van Dyk notices that the person is naked. Van Dyk shoots at him but misses.

This leaves the man who ran into the bathroom earlier. De Kock enters the room into which he initially threw the stun grenade. He sees a trail of blood on the floor leading to the bathroom. De Kock tries and fails to break the lock on the bathroom door.

De Kock asks a colleague whether he knows if the person in the bathroom is dead.

The colleague says the man has only been shot.

De Kock exits the house and approaches the bathroom window from the outside. Just as he is about to throw a grenade through it, the man bursts out of the window, almost taking the frame with him.

De Kock fires at the man, who falls to the ground but stands up again. De Kock sees that Jeff Bosigo would be in the line of fire so doesn't resume firing immediately. When the man starts running again, De Kock fires three or four shots at his back causing the man to fall about a metre and a half from the gate. Pienaar then comes from the right and fires two shots with his Perchet (a British gun with an integrated silencer system) at the man's head.

The man killed by Pienaar in the passage leading to the bedroom was Keith McFadden; the man dead by the gate, Zweli Nyanda.[12]

*

On the morning after the operation, Warrant Officer Pienaar phones a counterpart in the Swazi Police. His Swazi contact tells him that the man who ran from the house naked was Edward Lawrence, who managed to reach a police station to report the attack.[13]

*

Edward Lawrence testifies to an ANC commission of inquiry into the attack.

Asked how he survived, Lawrence says he managed to run away.

Questioned about the circumstances of the escape, he says he fled in his boots.

Asked where his boots were, he replies that he happened to be asleep in his boots.

This idea that he went to sleep naked but for his boots is initially not believed, but eventually somebody suggests that it could possibly have happened that way.

Lawrence is allowed to rejoin the Natal Machinery.[14]

*

The year 1983 closes with MK still engaged in counter-insurgency operations against UNITA in Angola. In December, from Cacuso, just over sixty kilometres west of Malange, Norman Phiri leads a unit of ten cadres to Kangandala, twenty-eight kilometres south-east of Malange. At Kangandala, they find forty MK cadres already there. Phiri is made commander of a platoon of about twenty men.

On 16 December, Kangandala hosts the customary ceremony commemorating MK's formation. The ceremony is accompanied by a gun salute.

Following the ceremony, cadres continue firing their guns in the air. Thereafter, again without authorisation, some members of the unit go into Kangandala town to drink.[15]

*

Mongameli Tshali arrives at Kangandala shortly afterwards to listen to the grievances of the troops.

From there he proceeds to Musafa, where two MK platoons are stationed in defence of a base. Tshali speaks with the MK platoon commander and learns that there has also been a problem in Musafa with random firing under false pretexts.[16]

*

Just before dawn on 20 December, a group of Mozambican negotiators arrive in Mbabane.[17]

Four hours later, South African foreign minister Pik Botha lands at Matsapha Airport in a chartered plane. He is met by Swaziland's foreign minister and other government officials.

The delegates all head to the Royal Guest House in Manzana, seventeen kilometres south of Mbabane. Also present at the meeting are the following Swazi officials: the prime minister, now Prince Bhekimpi; minister of foreign affairs Mr R.V. Dlamini; police commissioner Titus Msibi; and Defence Force chief Mangomeni Ndzimandze.

On that afternoon, Lisbon Radio quotes Samora Machel, speaking on the sidelines of a meeting of Portuguese-speaking nations, saying: 'South Africa will not oblige us to recognise apartheid nor to murder the ANC', but the talks in Swaziland could help enable us to 'live with each other, because we are both extremely uncomfortable with each other right now'. Machel said he hoped the discussions would lead to a non-aggression pact under which 'nobody attacks anybody', after which good commercial relations could be established.[18]

∗

Towards the end of December 1983, Julius Mokoena, MK's regional commander in Angola, visits Kangandala to give audience to the grievances of the fifty-odd cadres there.

He asks all those who wish to leave Angola to step to one side.

Virtually all the troops indicate that they want to leave Angola.[19]

∗

Alfred Nzo writes to the Secretariat of the ANC's Politico-Military Council on 23 December concerning the ANC's apparently ever-worsening relations with Swaziland.

'What might be the causes for this development?' he asks.

One answer could be pressure from the South African government, but Nzo says: 'can we ascribe our deteriorating situation in Swaziland only to this form of activity by the racist regime?' He suggests that to do so would be to 'deliberately blind ourselves to a problem which manifests itself as a critical breakdown of revolutionary discipline within our ranks'.

The picture Nzo says he has obtained from a number of verbal and written reports by the organisation's own structures is of 'some of our cadres who supposedly are operating underground but are constantly found in public places such as hotels, bars and other drinking places where in their drunken state some have on instances provoked brawls against local citizens threatening to use and in some cases actually using fire arms that are meant for use against our racist enemy in South Africa'.

Yet more disturbing are reports that 'some of our commanding personnel get involved in this form of hooliganism'. He mentions by name a commander of one of the Swaziland-based Machineries who recently 'used his authority to order some of our comrades who are supposedly living underground to punish a Swazi National who had picked a quarrel with one of our members'. This commander actually led this group to the Swazi subject's shop where the MK contingent opened fire. 'Fortunately nobody was injured, but the Swazi man's car was riddled with bullets. Of course the Swazi law enforcement authorities conducted a search after this incident which resulted in the arrest of one or more of our comrades.'

Nzo asks:

as a result of this deteriorating situation, where else except in Swaziland have we had to defend so many of our people appearing in courts of law charged with one crime or other[?] This has meant that a considerable amount of funds destined for work inside the country have had to be used for legal defence. Some of our financial resources are just wasted in bars and this has imposed considerable hardships on those of our people who have been entrusted with custody of our funds.[20]

*

On Boxing Day 1983, about seventeen MK members take part, alongside members of the Angolan Army (FAPLA), and an Angolan militia known as 'LCB' ('Lucha Contra Bandidos' – 'Struggle against the Bandits'), in an operation across the Kwanza River in Angola's Malange province. The aim is to attack a UNITA base.

When crossing the river, the unit is ambushed by UNITA, causing the FAPLA and LCB contingents to break up and flee. The MK section suffers five fatalities.[21]

*

From MK's garrison in Musafa, a group of ANC cadres joins FAPLA troops in travelling towards the scene of the ambush in six large Russian trucks called Urals.

A couple of hours later, in pitch dark, they arrive at the ambush point in the bush near the Kwanza River. About five kilometres away there is a large hill at the top of which lies the UNITA base that was to have been the focus of the Boxing Day attack.

'Beki' is one of the survivors of the ambush. He has a bullet wound in his foot. He leads the MK/FAPLA force to a position where they encounter two bodies in a state of extreme decay. The troops postpone the search for the night, which they spend in a nearby evacuated village.

When daylight arrives, they comb the area properly. Amidst terrible heat, they find maggots crawling over the corpses of the dead. The MK/FAPLA men carry five more bodies in military canvas bags to the waiting Urals.

The search continues, and the team comes across two wounded soldiers, still alive, hiding under some small bushes. Joseph Makhura, a member of the search team, recognises one of them as 'Jeff', an MK medical officer. The other survivor is a FAPLA soldier. Jeff has medical equipment with him and his head has been bandaged. He is holding an F1 defensive hand grenade. He has been shot in the stomach and his right leg is broken. He struggles to communicate with Makhura but eventually manages to say that he could hear them moving in the night but didn't have the strength to cry out.

Makhura is holding Jeff half an hour later when the wounded man dies. Makhura carries him to one of the Urals and lays him down on top of the bodies piled inside.[22]

*

Oliver Tambo and Alfred Nzo meet with Samora Machel and Mozambique's minister of security, Mariano Matsinhe, for two and a half hours in Maputo in January 1984.

Machel says that the ongoing talks with South Africa are a bilateral affair between sovereign states.

He also offers the ANC some advice. He says they should no longer try to be a liberation movement like FRELIMO. They are not fighting for independence – South Africa is already an independent state. Instead, the ANC should fight for political, democratic and human rights. The ANC made a big mistake, Machel claims, in trying to pose as a communist party. They developed links too close with the SACP – to the point that they now appear to be a tool of the Soviet Union. FRELIMO never spoke about 'Marxism' in its struggle; it was only after independence that they started making such declarations.[23]

*

An ANC NEC delegation led by Oliver Tambo arrives on 12 January 1984 at the MK training centre in Caculama, Angola. Chris Hani, Joe Nhlanhla and Lambert Moloi then travel the eighty kilometres or so from the centre to Kangandala.

When they arrive, they are mobbed by cadres expressing grievances and issuing demands about a number of matters including the war with UNITA, the lack of manpower devoted to the armed struggle in South Africa itself, the activities of the security apparatus, and the need for Oliver Tambo to come and address them in person. The men are wielding AK-47s. Some say they will not surrender the rifles till their demands are met.

Hani asks them to stop their random firing into the air. He also appeals to them to wait for feedback while he briefs the NEC about their grievances.

The air shots in Kangandala stop for a day after Hani's departure. But they resume the day after that.[24]

*

Mariano Matsinhe, Mozambique's security minister, holds a follow-up meeting in Maputo with ANC representatives including Oliver Tambo.

Matsinhe informs them that the implication of the talks with South Africa is that the ANC will not be allowed to engage in any form of underground activity against South Africa from Mozambican soil. Second, the ANC presence in the country will be reduced to a diplomatic mission. Lastly, Joe Slovo will have to leave.

Tambo proposes that the ANC delegation be allowed to return to Mozambique shortly with the response of its NEC.

Matsinhe agrees to this.[25]

*

The ANC's NEC and PMC hold a joint meeting after which they draw up a document titled 'Decisions and suggestions from NEC/PMC meeting of 25th Jan 84'. It consists of a list of numbered points.

It begins by recommending that the ANC must consult with regional countries like Tanzania, Zambia, Zimbabwe, Lesotho and Botswana – 'We need to know the thinking of these countries.'

'2. ANC cannot rescind its decision to engage in armed struggle.'

'3. We must indicate to Mozambique … that this decision is tantamount to saying to us we must stop the armed struggle.'

'4. We must find out from the Mozambican comrades the implications of their decision that they will allow us only Diplomatic presence in Mozambique.'

'5. Without the armed struggle, our struggle is dead. ANC will not be a party to the destruction of the ANC.'

Further on, point 12 says: 'ANC must be angry and aggressive. We must give Mozambique the benefit of our overall analysis of the situation and show that if the present trend in Mozambique continues it will represent capitulation to imperialism.'

'15' recommends that the ANC turns its diplomatic mission in Maputo into an underground one while still carrying on overt political and diplomatic activities.

'16. The African National Congress should undertake operations inside South Africa without consideration of the borders. The self imposed restrictions should be considered non-existent.'

'41. ANC must go underground everywhere. JS is not the only one who is likely to be expelled.'

In all, 77 points are made.[26]

*

The fifty-odd soldiers in Kangandala head to Cacuso in January 1984. The soldiers they meet in Cacuso, who are also about fifty strong, join them in firing shots into the air.

This group in Cacuso is further swelled by other units that arrive from Musafa. Then, at the beginning of February 1984, the cadres proceed from Cacuso to Viana transit camp, close to Luanda. Upon their arrival, a commander in the Viana camp asks them to disarm because the Angolans don't want to deal with an MK revolt on the doorstep of their capital.

Some men disarm upon hearing this, but many refuse.[27]

*

Julius Mokoena, the MK commander in Angola, arrives in Viana on Sunday 5 February in the company of Edwin Mabitse, who is the regional commissar, and 'Comrade Captain' the regional chief of security.

The cadres are told to prepare for a meeting with the regional leadership on Tuesday.[28]

*

On the afternoon of Monday 6 February there is a general meeting of cadres at Viana.

The meeting, which takes place in the open, is joined by a group of MK men who have travelled from a facility called the 'Plot', also near Luanda.

One of the men from the 'Plot', Mwezi Twala, addresses the crowd. By his estimate there are about a thousand people there. He tells them that any intensification of the armed struggle requires the election of a new leadership. He says they can't simply be sent back to fight – the operations must be properly planned and executed.

After supper, the meeting continues in the camp's main hall. It runs on until midnight. Then a 'Committee of Ten' is elected to present the grievances of the cadres to the leadership at the following day's talks. The people on the committee are Ephraim Nkondo, Omry Makgoale, Simon Botha, Sipho Mathebula, Moses Thema, Grace Mofokeng, Kate Mhlongo, Jabu Mofolo, Bongani Matwa and Mwezi Twala.

Before the meeting breaks up, a secretary notes the chief demands that have been made.

First and foremost is a call for a national consultative conference to be convened to discuss the movement's direction; second is a request for the leadership to reconsider whether fighting in the Angolan Civil War is in the movement's best interests; third is a demand that the ANC disband the Security Department and investigate abuses perpetrated by it.

The Committee of Ten then meets to formulate a Plan of Action for the meeting.[29]

*

At around 2 a.m. on the morning of the 7th, David Makhubedu is in the kitchen of Viana camp preparing fat cakes for breakfast when he notices armoured personnel carriers (APCs) approaching in the distance. He goes with two or three others to alert the rest of the cadres.[30]

The APCs belong to FAPLA. Luthando Dyasop is asleep in a bivouac just outside the camp when he is awoken by the combat bell clanging 'Gang, gang, gang, gang'. He gets up in the bivouac and hears gunfire. He takes his rocket launcher, his shells and an AK-47 containing 500 to 600 rounds of ammunition, and runs to a trench located on the camp's perimeter. When he jumps into it he finds four men already there.

Because people fled in time to a network of trenches surrounding Viana, the Angolans besieging the base are themselves encircled when they arrive at the camp.

As the Angolans enter, they shoot dead one of the MK men, 'Babsy'.

From his trench, which is separated from the camp by a parapet wall, Luthando Dyasop sees the APCs dropping Angolan soldiers off.

One of the armoured cars is a mere twenty or twenty-five metres from the trench. All the Angolan soldiers have their backs to the hiding MK men. It is still dark, so the Angolans are as yet not aware of their presence.

At dawn, some Angolan soldiers enter Viana and see there is nobody inside.

The driver of the APC near Dyasop opens the vehicle's hatch and climbs on top, still with his back to the trench. After a while, his attention wanders and he starts looking round. Then he spots the trench.

The Angolan immediately jumps inside the vehicle, opens the side door and calls out to the commander, who responds by rushing to the trench, saying in Portuguese that they must come out of the trench or he will kill them now.

One of Dyasop's companions says: 'Tell us why.'

Upon hearing this, the commander takes out a grenade and fixes to throw it. At this point Dyasop aims his rocket launcher at the APC and opens fire. Dyasop's colleagues in the trench also open fire, but well above the heads of the Angolans, who nonetheless run in disarray as a result.

The exchange disrupts the commander. When he releases the grenade it lands and explodes three or four metres from the trench.

The driver of the APC meanwhile tries to turn the vehicle around. In response Dyasop uses the remainder of his shells to unleash further rocket fire on the vehicle.

The driver of the armoured car is killed by the barrage.

Dyasop and his colleagues flee from their trench and run deeper into the bush. Some of the Angolan forces pursue them, firing on the MK men. The bullets fly past Dyasop and his companions.

The MK cadres manage to reach a trench where they join some of their colleagues. This is one of the trenches around the camp, to which many of the MK men fled when the Angolan soldiers arrived. Now the ANC guerrillas in these trenches begin returning fire on the pursuing Angolans.

The Angolans finally realise they are encircled. They see MK cadres in the various trenches with their guns trained on them.

'No, no, no, comrades, comrades, please don't shoot,' the Angolans say.

Shortly thereafter, Vusi Shange, aka 'Callaghan Chama', one of the guerrilla commanders, calls out 'Cease fire' from one of the firing positions, before climbing out of a trench to request peace.[31]

*

Following negotiations between the Committee of Ten and Colonel Antonio dos Santos Franca (who is the commander of the regiment that tried to take the camp and national chief of staff of the Angolan Army), the MK cadres all surrender their arms to the Angolans.[32]

*

Chris Hani, Andrew Masondo, Joe Modise and two members of the OAU Liberation Committee arrive at Viana in the company of an Angolan Army contingent.

All camp members are called to a meeting in the camp's main hall. As Hani addresses them, Masondo sits at a panel table in front staring wide-eyed and open-mouthed at those assembled.

Hani denounces the mutiny and its demands as an adventure by disgruntled elements. He says the ANC is an organisation of the South African people, while the mutineers are not even a drop in the ocean. The ANC can do without them. Hani calls on all those still committed to serve the ANC to move out of the hall.

The hall empties completely.

As the guerrillas exit, one of them, 'Mpho', hovers at the door and asks where they are all going. Another cadre pulls him outside.

A short while later they are all ordered to re-enter the hall.

Hani resumes and expresses relief that they are all still MK cadres. He says he will report the good news to the leadership in Lusaka.[33]

*

An intelligence report distributed on 10 February 1984 by the Natal headquarters of the SADF makes reference to Ntunja Mngomezulu, a candidate for the leadership of the Mngomezulu tribe in the Ingwavuma area.

Since 10 April 1973, the report says, he has been in exile in Swaziland, where he regularly attends ANC gatherings in Siteki. His followers have already established a weapons cache in a place in Swaziland called Ndivane, north of Nsoko and near Magugo. If the Mngomezulu and the ANC can successfully reach an agreement to assist each other in obtaining a leadership position for Ntunja in Ingwavuma, it could lead to friction between them and Chief Buthelezi's Inkatha.[34]

*

In Swaziland, Rayman Lalla, the head of Military Intelligence in the MK Natal Machinery, meets Thami Zulu, who was appointed the Natal Machinery's overall commander in 1983.

Zulu tells Lalla that a Special Operations Unit is to be established within the Machinery. He says the project was originally to have been commanded by Zweli Nyanda, but his assassination delayed implementation.[35]

*

Another project Zweli Nyanda was involved in aimed at turning Ingwavuma into an MK operational area. The Natal Machinery also pursues this initiative after his death.

When Msongomane Nyawo travels to Swaziland in February 1984, he visits a rondavel belonging to his uncle, Jameson Mngomezulu, one of the Mngomezulu clan exiled in the kingdom. There are two other men present at this meeting, namely Robert Dumisa and Norbert Buthelezi.

In the hut, Mngomezulu shows Nyawo a cache of arms, including an AK-47, a machine gun and some hand grenades.[36]

*

With the diplomatic wind in his sails given the imminent peace agreement with Mozambique, P.W. Botha offers to release Nelson Mandela on condition that the ANC leader lives in one of the homelands after his release.

Mandela rejects the offer. On 11 March, his lawyer Ismail Ayob tells the press: 'He will not stay in a homeland under any circumstances. If he is banished there, he would return to Johannesburg immediately.' Ayob adds that two years previously Mandela rejected a similar offer.[37]

*

Brendan Boyle of United Press International is among 1,200 people sweltering in ninety-degree heat on the banks of the Crocodile River between Mozambique and South Africa on 16 March.

Also present are Cuban, Soviet and American diplomats, as well as South African and Mozambican troops. A white railway coach stands on the exact spot marking the border. After about eighty minutes of talks inside the carriage, Samora Machel, clad in a marshal's uniform, emerges alongside P.W. Botha, wearing a pin-striped suit. The two leaders proceed to a wooden canopy located on a parade ground that consists of red earth carved out of the shrub and bush on the river's bank. There they sign the eleven-page 'Accord of Nkomati', a non-aggression pact between the two countries.[38]

*

A *New York Times* report claims that according to both Mozambican and ANC officials in Maputo, at least twelve homes of ANC activists in the city were raided on 24 March, including the residence of Joe Slovo.

According to the ANC officials cited, no documents were seized, but four people were detained. Some weapons were confiscated, including a handgun issued to Slovo, who was not at home at the time.[39]

*

Joe Slovo is busy appointing a 'Co-ordinating Committee' tasked with overseeing ANC political and military work in Swaziland following the Nkomati Accord.

The committee's chairman is to be Ronnie Kasrils, and its secretary and treasurer Ebrahim Ismail Ebrahim. Like Kasrils, Ebrahim was a member of MK's Natal structures during the sabotage campaign. Siphiwe Nyanda is to represent the Transvaal military structures on the committee, while the representative of the Natal military structures is to be Thami Zulu.[40]

*

Ronnie Kasrils knocks on the door of a house in Mbabane.

The door is opened by Ebrahim Ismail Ebrahim, who says, 'I thought you had left today.'

Kasrils enters. He reports on the situation in Mozambique and the consequent tasks of the Co-ordinating Committee. He says that there is a threat of imminent deportation of MK cadres to Lusaka. He says many of them will instead infiltrate Swaziland. The influx will involve in excess of two hundred cadres.

Kasrils and Ebrahim then discuss the implications of this for the Swaziland structures.

Following the discussion, they arrange to meet Siphiwe Nyanda and Thami Zulu.[41]

*

In March 1984, during the crisis in relations with Mozambique, Marion Sparg (formerly of the 'South African Liberation Support Cadre' which sabotaged the PFP offices in June 1981) has a meeting with the ANC's Reg September in Lusaka.

Two years earlier, Sparg completed a six-month course of military training at MK's camp in Caxito, Angola. In 1984 she is working as an editor at the *Voice of*

Women, the journal of the ANC Women's Section. September asks her if she would be willing to join MK. When she responds positively, he arranges for her to meet Chris Hani.[42]

*

By the beginning of April, the exodus from Mozambique to Swaziland has begun.

On the evening of 2 April, Swaziland's police commissioner Titus Msibi tells a *Times of Swaziland* reporter that ten people are being held for questioning following a dawn raid at Mobeni Flats in Matsapha over the weekend.

He says most entered from Mozambique: 'There may be one or two ANC members, but we are still sorting them out.'[43]

*

On the morning of 3 April, an orange Datsun 120Y is parked near the dock entrance at Durban's Victoria Embankment. Though it is positioned adjacent to open ground on the bay side of the road, a Department of Internal Affairs building, a Customs and Excise house, and the Citizen Force's navy headquarters are in the vicinity.

At 7.30 a.m., at the peak of the morning rush hour, a massive charge of TNT and plastic explosives concealed in the car's boot explodes, flinging the Datsun some twenty metres into the air. Three pedestrians are walking next to the vehicle at the time, namely Erica Green and Mr and Mrs Rangasami, an Indian couple. Their bodies are hurled into the air and land in nearby trees. Mr Rangasami dies instantly, his wife and Mrs Green minutes later.

Shrapnel from the Datsun flies into a passing minibus, causing it to veer into the path of another vehicle, causing a crash that results in both drivers being injured.

The blast opens a three-foot crater in the road and shatters windows on buildings up to 500 metres along the esplanade. Of the government buildings, only Internal Affairs is affected, its windows shattered.[44]

This marks the debut of the Natal Machinery's Special Operations Unit.[45]

*

In Maputo on 7 April, Chris Hani writes to MK's chief of operations in Lusaka.

He begins: 'We are all well though it is clear that very soon all of us will have to clear out of this place. It is just a matter of a few weeks or even days for that matter. We shall have to demonstrate that this accord has not destroyed our capacity to act against the enemy both politically and militarily.'

He notes that 'the car bomb was our operation (Natal Command). The target was a bus carrying officers and it was hit. It is a lie that the casualties were mere civilians.' This is perhaps a reference to the minibus hit by shrapnel as a result of the explosion. He admits, though, that civilians were struck by the fragments.

In another letter on the same day, this time to 'Bra Simon', Hani writes that everyone is well, but pressure is 'piling': everybody is expected to get out. He mentions that of ten people suggested by the ANC for its diplomatic mission in Mozambique, four were rejected, presumably because of suspicions they were 'military, security and

NEC'. Jacob Zuma, who has been the head of the ANC's Senior Organ in Maputo, has been accepted as chief representative, Hani says.[46]

*

The influx of MK cadres from Mozambique makes April 1984 a month of confrontations between them and the Swaziland authorities.

The trigger comes on the 10th. On that day, Mr Owusu, United Nations High Commissioner for Refugees in Swaziland, tells a *Times of Swaziland* reporter that a Swazi government official has informed him that a group of at least fifteen ANC members captured near the Mozambican border over the past few weeks have escaped from police custody in Simunye.[47]

That evening, Capital Radio in the Transkei reports that Swaziland has ordered all ANC members out of the country.[48]

Later that night, a man enters the 701 Bar in Mbabane. He heads to where a couple are sitting, and demands that the woman goes with him. Her male companion offers no resistance and leaves. She, however, flatly refuses to go with the man.

The man points his gun in the air and starts firing. This sends the patrons running for cover. Plainclothes policemen outside the premises quickly rush in and overpower the armed man. Under interrogation, it is discovered that he is an MK cadre.

Then at 2.30 a.m. on the 11th, while another pub in Mbabane is closing, a man comes running in and tells an employee there is a man outside with a revolver.

Shortly afterwards gunfire is heard from outside.

The employee blows his whistle to alert the security guards.

With the help of some members of the police force, the guards manage to arrest the man. Under questioning he also admits to being an MK member.[49]

Later on the 11th, a mixed group of thirty men from Swaziland's Special Branch and Police Mobile Unit head to the road leading to the golf course in Jubilee Village about a mile beyond Mbabane's Eveni suburb. They are on their way to raid a house.

A section of the group calls out to a young man wearing a white shirt and black trousers. The man responds by dashing into the nearby bush. Some of the security-force members give chase. The man then runs inside the house that the remaining members of the police contingent are poised to raid.

A group of men emerge from the house wielding machine guns. Some of them execute somersaults in a show of military bravura.

The Swazi security forces open fire. The guerrillas shoot back.

After a while, seven of the guerrillas, Kenneth Mebeke, Eric Matyobani, Themba Msibi, Thabo Mokoena, Michael Mabuza, Raymond Kekoenyetsoe and Samuel Menyoke, come out with their hands raised. But while they surrender, another eight rush out of the house and into the river adjoining Mbabane Golf Course. Eyewitnesses see that the fleeing men appear to be carrying small bags as they dash down a hill.

A group of policemen then sweep the woods near the house in a search for the fugitives.[50]

*

Pedestrians come across the bullet-riddled corpse of a man on the side of the road between Siphunga and Sidvokodvo in Swaziland.

The *Swazi Observer* reports on the 14th that the man has been identified as twenty-one-year-old Zakhele Shongwe, an ANC member believed to have been killed by unidentified gunmen on the night of the 11th.[51]

In the early hours of the 14th, Swazi Police squads head to a house in Manzini's Zakhele township. They surround the property and call on the men inside to come out.

At about 6.30 a.m., some five hours later, eleven guerrillas surrender by coming out through the kitchen door. They are carrying bags. When the policemen attempt to search their haversacks, however, some refuse to allow them to be inspected.

A stand-off ensues, during which a twelfth man, who has remained concealed from the policemen until that point, bolts out and opens fire. In the process he kills one of the policemen, Inspector Jabulane Dlamini, at very close range.

Swazi Police members arrive at the home of Bafana Duma later that morning. They collect him and take him to a police station.

When he arrives there he is confronted with the accusation that the ANC appears now to have ordered its soldiers to kill Swazis.

Duma denies this.

After lunch the police take Duma to the scene of the morning's fatal shooting.

That afternoon, when a team of Swazi police encircle a house in Dalriach, Mbabane, and four men emerge to surrender, nothing is left to chance.

A policeman asks the four if there are any people left inside. One of them says there is somebody inside. Another guerrilla calls on the colleague to come out.

After a while the remaining man appears and surrenders.

The police search the house and recover four AK-47s, six hand grenades, and a variety of other explosives.

On the following day the Swazi Police round up and detain known ANC members in the kingdom.[52]

*

A combined Swazi Police/Army unit goes to a house in Manzini's Old Ngwane Park on the 19th. When they get there, gunfire and grenades are directed at them from the house. They return fire and a shootout ensues.

After a while, the Swazis take the decision to bomb the house in order to flush out the guerrillas. The bomb rips open a hole in the roof.

Following the bombing, two heavily armed young men are spotted peering out of the hole in the roof. They open fire, apparently at random. The police return fire, killing the pair.

There are further guerrillas in the building. Sporadic gunfire continues between them and the police. At about 10 p.m. the gunfire dies down.

The remaining three guerrillas voluntarily give themselves up in the early hours of the following morning. As the police enter the house they find that one of the dead has had his head blown off.[53]

*

Vuxumuzi Nyawo, whose brother Msongomane travelled to Swaziland in February 1984, is at his home in Nhlalavane in Ingwavuma when a visitor arrives. Vuxumuzi recognises the man from an earlier visit that he himself made to Jameson Mngomezulu's rondavel in Swaziland. It is Robert Dumisa, who says he has been sent by Nyawo's uncle.

Dumisa and Nyawo later converse. Dumisa says he will explain in time why he is there, but in the meantime he needs to be taken to a particular spot the following morning.

In the morning, Nyawo and Dumisa head off in the company of a third man, Bernard Mngomezulu. They arrive at their destination, a nondescript spot in the bush.

There, Dumisa starts walking along cattle tracks. After a while he stops. Apparently he has found what he is looking for. He merely points at something. He does not dig it out or open it. He just points at it and leaves.[54]

*

At around the same time, MK cadre Wilfred Maphumulo enters South Africa illegally from Swaziland. He also makes his way to the Nhlalavane area of Ingwavuma.[55]

*

Dissent meanwhile continues to simmer in the ANC's Angolan camps. On 13 May, at the MK camp in Pango, a group of armed guerrillas attempt to disarm the guards keeping watch of the armoury. One of them refuses to surrender his weapon and is shot and injured by the attackers.

With the armoury's weapons, the mutineers manage to obtain control of Pango, but the camp commander and other forces loyal to the camp administration manage to escape before the takeover is complete.

At the ANC's Quatro camp, also in northern Angola, an assembly bell rings out in the dark. Wonga Bottoman, a guard there, is part of a platoon called by the on-duty officer to assemble at the Admin Block. There the platoon gathers, facing the interview room.

Dexter Mbona, one of the camp's recording officers, comes out dangling a folding-butt AK assault rifle. The on-duty officer orders the platoon to attention and delivers a roll-call report.

Mbona then marches to face the platoon. He says a mutiny is taking place in Pango, and all who support it must step aside.

When nobody steps aside, Mbona expresses relief. He adds that as a security centre containing enemy agents, Quatro is a likely target of the mutineers. They must therefore barricade the camp, and all access points hitherto qualified as inaccessible must be re-classified as vulnerable.

Fighting continues through the night for control of Pango. On the loyalist side,

Zenzile Pungule (the camp commissar), Wilson Sithole (a staff commissar), Duke Maseko, Cromwell Qwabe and a security guard will lose their lives.[56]

*

Within a week, Julius Mokoena has assembled a crack loyalist force and has encircled Pango camp.

The direct assault commences at 5 a.m. on 18 May and ends by dusk. A number of mutineers are captured, but some fifteen rebels manage to break through the cordon and escape into the open bush.[57]

Seven captured mutineers, namely James Nkabinde, Ronald Msomi, Bullet Mbumbulu, Thembile Hobo, Mahero, Wandile Ondala and Stopper, are publicly executed by firing squad shortly thereafter and their bodies are buried in a mass grave in Pango camp.[58]

*

On the night of 20 May, Clarence Payi, Sipho Xulu and George Martins are driven by Dennis Hadebe to a house in the Georgetown area of Pietermaritzburg.

Martins walks up to the house. The door is opened by Benjamin Langa, an acquaintance. While the two men converse, Xulu and Payi walk up. Xulu fires a shot from a Makarov into Langa's chest, while Payi shoots Langa in the head with his Luger.

Both cadres fire another shot each. These bullets lodge in a wall of the building.[59]

*

Sipho Xulu and Clarence Payi are arrested on 7 June.

It emerges that the assassination of Langa was ultimately attributable to Edward Lawrence because, retrieved from under Xulu's mattress is a document titled 'Report May 15–31', which is signed, 'Clarence Payi D699 Kwa Mashu (Sihle). Sipho Machina Xulu, 441 Khwezi St, Sobantu, Pietermaritzburg (Pat)'.

Part of the report reads: 'Mission executed – Ben Langa eliminated on May 20 – reason – Leonard [a pseudonym for Edward Lawrence] informed us on the day we left that Ben is the guy who handed two comrades to the Boers. Also that he operated fully for the enemy, D.C.O. Youth and other various people confirmed through litigation.'[60]

*

The fifteen or so fugitives from the battle for Pango camp have, since breaking out of the encirclement on the 18th, spent many days marching through the bush. They eventually reach Angola's Uige province, where they opt to seek refuge at one of the Soviet establishments in the region.

When they reach one such camp, they surrender their arms to the Soviet and Angolan authorities within.

A while later the mutineers are woken from their sleep by ANC personnel, who tie them hand and foot, and then, with whips, lashes and kicks, lead them to a convoy of military vehicles into which they are thrown.[61]

*

The year 1984 has seen MK's strength dissipated by the clampdown in Mozambique, the struggle with the Swazi authorities and the fratricide in Angola. Each in its own way is a manifestation of the problem of 'strategic time' which has so worried the movement during this period.

The ANC NEC issues a call on 26 June for all members of the movement to prepare for a national consultative conference. The call identifies three areas of particular concern that will need to be addressed. They are (a) assessing the situation within South Africa and internationally; (b) considering measures to strengthen the ANC and consolidate its gains; and (c) defeating enemy manoeuvres and charting the way forward.[62]

*

The Battle of Swaziland in April resulted in over eighty ANC members being detained. On 19 July David Matse, Swaziland's justice minister, announces that the last of them will be released.

In the trials already conducted of those apprehended during the round-up, Matse says, 'there was no conclusive evidence against the men because their arrests and the discovery of arms were effected in very difficult circumstances when the police were in combat. Hence since their trials began there have been several acquittals.' Meanwhile, the evidence against the remaining accused is also 'generally inconclusive', hence their release.

The remaining forty-odd ANC captives are flown to Tanzania two days later.[63]

*

In Durban's Wentworth suburb, Gordon Webster asks his friend Robert McBride, 'What kind of law is it that makes my mother less human than me?' (He is referring to the elections scheduled for a week's time for the Tricameral Parliament, which was established following P.W. Botha's win in the November 1983 referendum. Classified as a coloured, Webster could vote in the elections for the coloured chamber, but as an African, his mother would not be allowed to participate.)

At another meeting later in August, Webster says he is going into exile to join the ANC and asks McBride to come with him.

McBride says he feels he can't.

Webster does not push the matter. Instead he promises to send McBride a message from abroad.[64]

*

A dispatch from the Inter Press Service news agency on 23 August states that the United Democratic Front

> today claimed a 'major success' in its campaign for a boycott of elections to South Africa's new racially-segregated Parliament. Poll returns released today showed that only between 25 and 30 percent of registered voters cast ballots in yesterday's elections to the 'colored' (mixed-race) chamber of the three-chambered body.

South African Internal Affairs Minister F.W. de Klerk today described the poll turnout as 'disappointing' but attributed this to 'intimidation'.[65]

*

Robert Dumisa arrives at Jameson Mngomezulu's rondavel in Swaziland five days later.

Dumisa says he heard while operating in South Africa that the presence of his unit in Ingwavuma is now known, including the precise location of their base. He adds that Msongomane Nyawo also instructed the unit to kill one of his brother's enemies, Tindla Mngomezulu, who is a relative of Chief Ntunja Mngomezulu. They refused, Dumisa says, based on the ANC's policy and aims in the region.

By 1 September, Dumisa is back in Ingwavuma. Accompanied by 'Tonkie', another member of his unit, he pays a visit to Tindla Mngomezulu's kraal.

With Tonkie keeping watch outside, Dumisa and Tindla converse.

Tindla says he is glad to see Dumisa. He says he has wanted to see them since learning about their presence in the region. He learnt they were in the area after some of the people that they had trained told him so. His informants also warned him of the plan to assassinate him. He says he is prepared to help the unit where they need help. He could have reported them to the enemy but he didn't because he heard they were soldiers of liberation – ANC members.

Dumisa responds that his unit are not roving bands or hired assassins. Their objectives are national. Their job is to weld people together. As for personal quarrels, these endanger their aims. The ANC will always try to settle such feuds peacefully, by showing each side the fruitlessness of the quarrel and explaining how they endanger national work.

They drink on that. Tindla buys Tonkie and Dumisa five bottles of beer.

In his diary entry for the day, Dumisa writes: 'I had a very delicious supper. We drunk with our contact.'[66]

V

PEOPLE'S WAR

TOWNSHIP REBELLION

On the morning of Monday 3 September 1984, with the new constitution having come into effect at midnight, chief justice Pierre Rabie swears P.W. Botha in as acting state president pending the election of a permanent incumbent when the incoming Tricameral Parliament meets on the 5th.[1]

The papers that morning contain alarming news from the Vaal Triangle townships (Sharpeville, Boipatong, Sebokeng, Evaton, Bophelong and Tembisa) to the south of Johannesburg. The *Star* reports that in Sharpeville, where there is an ongoing school boycott, youths went on the rampage the previous night, gutting houses, bottle stores and cars.

The *Sowetan* adds that meetings were held throughout the weekend in the Vaal townships, resulting in a decision by residents and students for a stay-away on the 3rd against the imposition of higher rentals (with the increases, Sebokeng, the township in the Vaal with the lowest rents at R50 a month, would have rates higher than the highest charged in Soweto, at R48 a month). The *Sowetan* notes that hundreds of police are expected to be out in force in the Vaal area today.[2]

*

A riot-proof police van and two armoured personnel carriers snake their way through the streets of Sharpeville three days later. In the van are South Africa's minister of law and order Louis le Grange, interior minister F.W. de Klerk, education minister Gerrit Viljoen, and defence minister Magnus Malan. They look out at burnt shops and houses through the steel mesh protecting the vehicle's windows.

After seeing Sharpeville, the ministers are flown by helicopter to Sebokeng and Evaton, where they are driven through the streets by bus. As the convoy approaches a group of youths in Sebokeng, it turns down a side street so as to avoid any confrontation.

In a report appearing in the Associated Press the following day, Le Grange is quoted saying he doesn't wish to make any categorical statements yet, but he is not convinced that the 15 per cent rent increases are the real reason for the rioting: 'There are individuals and other forces and organizations very clearly behind what is happening in the Vaal Triangle,' but 'more than that I would not like to comment at this stage.'

De Klerk says he felt 'shocked as we drove through and saw the havoc'.[3]

*

At the Transvaal Province Congress of the National Party on 5 October, Louis le Grange comes off the fence regarding what he feels lies behind the violence.

He alleges that over 90 per cent of UDF officials are former ANC members, and that when its actions in the republic are judged against its 'objectives, affiliations, public actions, pronouncements', then 'one can reach no other conclusion but that the United Democratic Front is pursuing the same revolutionary goals as the banned

ANC and South African Communist Party, and is actively promoting a climate of revolution'.[4]

Five days later, Albertina Sisulu, now one of the UDF's presidents, issues a response on the organisation's behalf when she tells a press conference that the conflict in the townships springs from 'people's alienation', while the government has 'lost control', with its accusations against the UDF being an 'attempt to divert attention from its own bankruptcy and inability to govern'.

Trevor Manuel, the UDF's acting general secretary, also addresses the briefing, saying: 'Let them ban the UDF. What they are facing here is the will of the people, and that cannot be banned.'[5]

*

Oliver Tambo appears on the ANC's broadcast station Radio Freedom on 17 October. He discusses the ongoing unrest and says he thinks a position has been reached where the 'apartheid policy is going to become unworkable and the country is going to become increasingly ungovernable'.

The show's announcer says later in the broadcast: 'Botha's guns and batons are failing. This is being demonstrated every day in the streets of Soweto, Sharpeville, Sebokeng, William's Town and other areas.'[6]

This idea gains traction within the organisation. Tambo returns to Radio Freedom's flagship 19:30 GMT broadcast three days later, this time reading an NEC statement. 'All revolutions are about power,' he says. 'Ours is no exception. The slogan of "Power to the People" means one thing and one thing only: It means we seek to destroy the power of apartheid and replace it with popular power, with a government whose authority resides with the will of all our people.'[7]

The notion that the state's authority is crumbling and can realistically be replaced by people's power is soon disproven, however. Louis le Grange issues a press statement on the evening of 22 October barring reporters and photographers from Sebokeng until daybreak. In the statement he explains that over the past few months revolutionary elements have created a situation of unrest in several black residential areas, and 'In the Vaal Triangle alone, damage runs into millions of rands. The Government has therefore decided that this lawlessness must be curbed with all available means, and that law and order must be restored effectively.'

At 3 a.m. a long convoy of Casspirs carrying a mixed force of 7,000 policemen and soldiers enters Sebokeng. The security forces then go door to door through 19,500 homes in Sebokeng and parts of Evaton. At each house two policemen stand on either side of the front door, while colleagues dressed in a mix of camouflage, standard issue uniforms and plain clothes surround the premises. They knock until the inhabitants open, then at least eight policemen enter and search the property.

Later that day the press are escorted through Sebokeng in SAP Casspirs. They see SADF troops standing metres apart on all roads as well as manning roadblocks at intersections. Houses that have been searched and cleared bear red stickers reading

'I'm your friend – trust me' and 'Co-operation for peace and security'. Individual residents have also been given these red stickers to enable them to move freely through the township.

At 3.20 p.m., with the work in Sebokeng done, the operation, known as 'Palmiet' in Afrikaans ('Bullrush' in English) is extended to Sharpeville and Boipatong. Rain and mud hamper progress, but by 7 p.m. the sweep in those areas is completed.[8]

On the morning after the operation, police spokesman Lieutenant Henry Beck tells the media that Sebokeng, Sharpeville and Boipatong are 'very quiet' and no incidents have been reported there.[9]

But the picture that morning remains far from sanguine from the state's perspective. The police report that rioting broke out the previous day in townships to the east and west of Johannesburg as well as in the Eastern Cape. Meanwhile, despite the police's claim that the Vaal Triangle is quiet, Edgar Posselt, spokesman for the Department of Education and Training, notes that 'there were no pupils at the schools' in Sharpeville, Evaton and Boipatong, and only 'very poor attendance' in Sebokeng, where 147 learners in the whole township appeared for class.

Responding to scepticism about whether Palmiet could really be described a success, Leon Mellet, Ministry of Law and Order spokesman, tells the media: 'Can it be expected that immediately, the following morning, everything returns to normal? Let's give it a couple days.'[10]

But normality hasn't returned by then, and on 31 October the police are back in Sebokeng, Sharpeville, Boipatong and Bophelong, setting up roadblocks and patrols to break up crowds of youths.[11]

The implication of this from the government's perspective is that its authority in the townships no longer extends much further than the immediate reach of its security forces. Withdraw them and see the system collapse. At the same time, the opposition lacks the strength to seize power. Though in embryonic form, there are signs of a stalemate in these developments. But these are as yet early stages; it will take a while, and a great many drives by both sides to break the deadlock, before the lesson and its momentous consequences are fully absorbed.

*

In Lusaka on 26 October, when Associated Press reporter James F. Smith asks Alfred Nzo and Thabo Mbeki about the accusations that the ANC instigated the revolt, Nzo offers a qualified

> Yes, in these uprisings that are taking place, yes, certainly the ANC has got its hand. Naturally, as the leader of the people's effort for their own liberation. One thing the ANC, over the years of its existence, can be said to be guilty of is its ability to make the people conscious of their own oppression, and show them that it is necessary for them to do something about their own oppression. If they say it is the ANC because of that history, we plead guilty.

Mbeki replies in a similarly circumspect manner, saying: 'Of course the people will respond if you provoke them like that, if you shoot at them', for 'such is the determination to be free. The people will fight back with whatever they have. And of course the ANC is continuously saying, "let's fight them with what we have"', but 'we're not going and standing around saying, "now is the time to throw stones". The secretary-general of the ANC is not in Sebokeng, when the police come there, to tell people to pick up a stone.'[12]

*

Robert Dumisa meanwhile confides to his diary on 28 October that there are 'many recruits who are having doubts' about his Ingwavuma unit, with scepticism 'ranging from being hired assassins, boer agents deceiving them to find out where they don't [sic] have guns, to our capability to beat the boers in real combat'.

One old woman, 'Ma Cwele', asked openly 'whether are we not going to leave them behind when the war becomes fierce so that the boers will kill them we having a nice time in Swaziland [sic]'. Dumisa writes: 'No we answered we'll better die here than leaving them in the lurch. Really people are expecting much from us. It is up to us to prove our worth. To enhance the confidence people are already having to erase doubts in their minds about the myth of the invincibility of the whiteman + SADF.'

On the 5th, while members of Dumisa's unit are on their way to Swaziland, they pass some Swazi soldiers either asleep or pretending to be asleep about a metre from the path they are walking.

Two days later, the group meets Thami Zulu in Swaziland. He suggests they shift operations from Ingwavuma to the Ubombo area because of the strategic significance of Ingwavuma; secondly, to confuse the enemy as to where they are coming from, since it is customary for MK to infiltrate through Golela rather than Ingwavuma; and thirdly to prepare the passage of people and material further south.

On the unit's way back to Ingwavuma, they pass a drunken Swazi soldier who blurts out that he knows they are ANC and that they have come from the mountains. The cadres manage to pass, but then later see traces of boots near their base.

Dumisa writes in his diary on 10 November that the unit's commissar told him that SADF troops have been seen patrolling the river and the road in the vicinity of the base, while others are observing from Salamfene. Yet more are making their way down the mountain.

Dumisa notes that given this ominous turn of events, 'Recon, must be done' to determine enemy whereabouts and 'avoid confrontation or detection since our organisation is not up to the required standard. People must help us with information + tip-offs. The enemy must be kept speculating.'

But the situation deteriorates. On 13 November Dumisa writes that two days before, Jameson Mngomezulu's young daughter Busisiwe 'surprised us all when she came alone from Swaziland to report the arrest of [her] father ... This action to come and report without being told to do so shows a mature thinking. Asked by the soldiers where the guerrillas were, she told them that only one man lives with [her] father and [that she] did not know where he was. She denied our presence. We emulate her. She is around 10 years old.'

But the writing is on the wall. Dumisa confesses: 'This arrest is going to give us serious problems.'[13]

*

At about 9.30 p.m. on 7 December, Superintendent Petros Shiba, deputy chief of Swaziland's security police, leaves a party at the kingdom's police headquarters.

Shiba enters the driver's seat of a car, and another officer sits in the passenger seat. Suddenly shots are fired at Shiba. He manages to shoot back, into the dark, at the assailant, before falling onto the legs of the officer in the passenger seat, who then runs for cover.

Senior policemen rush to the scene from the police mess. They count eight bullets that have pierced the front of the car. Three have struck Shiba in the chest, one in the stomach; one hit the bonnet and three others the driver's seat.

An officer finds traces of blood where he thinks the killer might have been hit by Shiba's return fire. The blood indicates the suspect must be seriously wounded.[14]

*

By December the net has closed on Robert Dumisa's unit. In Mackobeni, Ingwavuma, on the 11th, policemen arrest Vuxumuzi Nyawo while he is resting in a room at his mother's house. Later the same day, Norbert Buthelezi, a member of the unit, is arrested near a shopping centre.[15]

Two days later, in the Isihlangwini area, James Marupeng and Robert Dumisa himself are confronted by policemen in the Ubombo Mountains.

Marupeng removes a hand grenade from his pocket as the police approach. He attempts to remove the safety pin, but doesn't make it in time and the police over-power him.[16]

Dumisa resists the white officer who tries to apprehend him. During the subsequent struggle, Dumisa tries to incite the black policemen present to kill their white superiors and release him.

It is to no avail. Dumisa is arrested.[17]

*

A contingent of Swazi policemen on the hunt for Superintendent Shiba's killer deploy outside a house in Esicelwini in Manzini on Sunday 16 December.

A shootout follows. A man passing the house is caught in the crossfire and killed instantly. Sandile Khumalo, aged twelve, is also caught up in the skirmish and starts running around the firing line in panic and confusion before being hit. He will die of his wounds.

The suspect in the house manages to escape and heads to a nearby river. He jumps into the water, but when he sticks his head out in order to breathe, he is shot dead.

When his body is recovered, the police find that his left hand has been seriously injured in a prior incident – consistent with their profile of Superintendent Shiba's likely killer.

This is Swazi police commissioner Majaji Simelane's interpretation the following day when he tells the media that the man killed was 'Andreas Ngcobo', alias 'Solly'. Simelane says: 'we have now fully established that he is the man who killed Shiba with the same AK-47 rifle he was carrying on Sunday'. Simelane alleges further that Ngcobo was also linked to the murder of Inspector Jabulane Dlamini, the policeman killed during the shootout between the police and ANC members on 14 April 1984.[18]

*

Commissioner Simelane releases a further statement on the 20th saying that at least twenty-three MK guerrillas have gone to ground in violation of the kingdom's laws.

He calls on them to either surrender or be treated as common criminals and deported to their country of origin when found and convicted. He names those he wants 'to come out from their hiding places and report themselves to the police with immediate effect' as '1. Sidumo Theophilus Dlodlo alias Victor alias Sipho Victor Simelane. 2. Siphiwe Nyanda alias Gebhuza alias Tebogo Kgope. 3. Thami Zulu alias Mandla John Kunene. 4. Lefosho Glory Sedibe alias September'.

He continues until '21. Keith Mokoape. 22. Michael Modise alias Fanie. 23. Cliff Mashinini'.[19]

Simelane's statement that the ANC men must either surrender or be arrested and deported to South Africa sparks a miniature rerun of April's battle of Swaziland.

In one incident, the Swazi Police's paramilitary unit raid a house in Dalriach, Mbabane. As they do so, Thami Zulu drives up in a white Golf. Noticing them, he tries to escape. The police open fire and hit the car but Zulu manages to get away. He abandons the Golf at a house in Sandla.[20]

On 27 December, the Swazi Police intercept a car travelling between Manzini and Luyengo. They open fire and a shootout lasting fifteen minutes ensues. Two inhabitants of the car are arrested but the third escapes.[21]

Then at dawn on 30 December, a group of Swazi paramilitary policemen proceed to a flat on the fourth floor of Parklane Court in Allister Miller Street, Mbabane, where a party is under way.

With the police poised to raid, somebody exits the flat to go downstairs. The man, 'Jabu', is arrested. 'Gebuza' leaves the flat to investigate when his colleague fails to return. But he sees the police and opts to hide away from the flat, as do most of the partygoers.

The police arrive at the apartment and knock on the door for a couple of minutes. When there is no response, they break down the door, only to find the flat empty apart from a man who has locked himself inside with a woman.

They see the man climbing through a window. He tries to open the window of another flat, but realises the police will catch him before he can, so he decides to jump. This man, 'Mateio', breaks both his legs as a consequence of the four-floor fall. The police arrest him and rush him to hospital.

Gebuza meanwhile waits until he thinks the police have gone before returning to the flat. But when he enters he finds some police still there.

He manages to escape, but the police corner him in a nearby flat. Once again Gebuza manages to elude them, this time by climbing onto a roof.[22]

Matters come to a head when Commissioner Simelane informs a press conference on 3 January 1985 that three jailed ANC men were freed after a police station in Mbabane was raided early the previous day by what Simelane claims were MK cadres armed with AK-47s. He reiterates his force's determination to capture all the ANC men still at large, but, backing down slightly, says his men will then 'deport them to a country of their choice'.[23]

Speaking to journalists in Lusaka on the same day, Alfred Nzo refers to the 'strange disappearance' of the ANC men from the Mbabane prison and says the organisation is 'gravely concerned', because four ANC cadres were handed over to South Africa by Swaziland the previous year. He appeals to the OAU to 'intercede with the government of Swaziland to ensure that no opponent of the apartheid regime is handed over to Pretoria and that all ANC members in the hands of Swazi Police are accounted for and their security guaranteed'.[24]

*

At a meeting in Swaziland, Ivan Pillay, who fled to the kingdom along with his brother Joe in 1977, says to Yunis Shaik: 'Listen, I have to surrender your unit, you're considered mature to a certain level. Ebrahim Ismail Ebrahim is now going to take command of your unit and I wish you lots of luck.' Pillay gives Shaik a handshake and a hug, and then walks away.

Ebrahim then enters the room and tells Shaik, 'This is what you're going to have to do and it starts today. You start your preparation to return me into the country. I'm going to be the first guinea pig.' He means that he is being sent into South Africa to test whether conditions are ripe for the infiltration at a later stage of larger numbers of senior members of the movement – a step the ANC has been discussing since the late 1970s.

Ebrahim then gives Shaik a list of 'dos and don'ts', including: 'Don't tell your mother about this operation; take your entire work now into a new level; start disengaging with girlfriends and everybody.'[25]

*

Jacob Mofokeng, who is in his mid-thirties, is home alone in Lamontville, Natal, when he is visited by a man he knows as 'Kawe' and another man he doesn't know, who Kawe introduces as 'Tallman'. Mofokeng and 'Tallman' then go to a house owned by Mapiki Dlomo.

In Dlomo's bedroom, with the door safely closed, 'Tallman' (real name Lulamile

Xate) says he has heard that they are interested in joining Umkhonto we Sizwe and that he is here to confirm this.

When the two men confirm that they are, Xate says that MK is an illegal underground organisation in South Africa, and that they shouldn't talk openly about it because they will only be endangering themselves – MK is an ANC regiment at war with South Africa.

Xate then asks Dlomo for a blank piece of paper. On it he makes drawings of limpet mines, electrical time delays and detonators. He says he is making the drawings in order to give them knowledge of explosives and their mechanisms. He adds that he will train them until the person actually responsible for their training arrives. In the meantime he has been asked to go around recruiting and training people so that when the boys from outside arrive the recruits inside will have had some training.[26]

*

Lord Bethell, a Conservative Party member of the European Parliament, interviews the now sixty-six-year-old Nelson Mandela in Pollsmoor Prison on Monday 21 January 1985.

Mandela says:

> The armed struggle was forced on us by the government, and if they want us to give it up, the ball is in their court. They must legalise us, treat us like a political party and negotiate with us. Until they do, we will have to live with the armed struggle. It is useless simply to carry on talking. The government has tightened the screws too far. Of course, if there were to be talks along these lines, we in the ANC would declare a truce.

Mandela refers to his rejection of P.W. Botha's offer in March 1984 to release him provided he lived in one of the Bantustans after being freed: 'My place is in South Africa and my home is in Johannesburg. If I were released I would never obey any restriction.'[27]

Extracts from the interview appear in Britain's *Mail on Sunday* on 27 January.

*

When President Botha addresses Parliament on 31 January, he offers revised terms for Mandela's release. He says the government is 'willing to consider' freeing Mandela '*in the Republic of South Africa*' (dropping the demand that he return to one of the homelands), if he pledges he 'will not make himself guilty of planning, instigating or committing acts of violence for the furtherance of political objectives, but will conduct himself in such a way that he will not again have to be arrested'.[28]

So 'the choice is his. All that is requested from him now is that he should unconditionally reject violence as a political instrument, a norm which is respected in all civilised countries of the world.'[29]

*

Ebrahim Ismail Ebrahim illegally enters South Africa from Swaziland in the vicinity of the Nerston border post in late January/early February 1985.

Yunis Shaik is waiting in a car. Shaik sees a flash from the forest, after which Ebrahim emerges and gets into the vehicle. Shaik drives him towards Durban. On the way Ebrahim puts on a false beard and glasses, adopting the guise of 'Salim Areff'.

They arrive at their destination, Highpoint Flats, West Road, at Overport in Durban, which becomes Ebrahim's residence.[30]

*

In a Soweto amphitheatre before an estimated 8,000 people on 10 February, Nelson Mandela's twenty-two-year-old daughter Zinzi is hoisted for ten minutes on the shoulders of the dancing, singing crowd.

She is there to convey her father's response to Botha's release offer. She reads: 'I cannot sell my birthright, nor am I prepared to sell the birthright of the people to be free.' Then, referring to President Botha directly, she reads: 'Let him guarantee free political activity so that the people may decide who will govern them ... Let *him* renounce violence. Let *him* say that he will dismantle apartheid.'[31]

*

Nat Serache is at home in Jinja in Gaborone on the night of 12–13 February in the company of another man, 'Moadira', when they notice men approaching the house at around 1 a.m. Serache and Moadira slip out the back door, thus narrowly escaping death when a bomb wrecks the house.[32]

*

Nine days later, on 22 February, Pik Botha and Botswana's foreign minister, G.K.T. Chiepe, meet in Pretoria at the head of delegations respectively seven and ten persons strong.

Following the security pacts with Mozambique and Swaziland, South Africa is seeking a similar success in Botswana, whether through a bilateral agreement with the government or via the methods that nearly cost Serache and Moadira their lives. Botha says the meeting's main purpose is to find agreement on the serious issue of the infiltration into South Africa of ANC and PAC terrorists. It seems that the two countries are not making satisfactory progress on the matter.

Chiepe disagrees that no progress has been made since the last meeting on 30 October; it has been slow, she concedes, but certain problems have been solved. For example, Botswana does not allow trained terrorists to enter its territory, and is also prepared to provide information on people caught with weapons of war. Furthermore, though there are indications of increased ANC activity in Botswana, the country is doing more about it than before. In the past few months, she points out, it has refused twenty-five people entry and deported seventeen, even though no direct evidence of terrorist activity existed in their cases. She says she is under the impression South Africa wants Botswana to sign an agreement. That is not necessary, because the two countries are good neighbours and not at war.

Botha responds that he can see that Botswana would be in a difficult political position were it to sign a pact with South Africa. He says he has abandoned the idea of an Nkomati-type agreement with the country, because results on the ground are more important.[33]

*

The following day, Minister Chiepe is present when Oliver Tambo and Thabo Mbeki meet President Masire, S. Hirschfeldt (the commissioner of Botswana's police), A. Hirschfeldt (head of the Security Branch) and Major General Merafe (the army chief).

Masire says Botswana has decided that all ANC military cadres in the country must be removed. This includes commanders, and only bona fide refugees concerned with the agricultural project in Mogoditsane will be allowed to stay.

When he gets to respond, Tambo requests that the previous ANC representative, Isaac Makopo, be allowed back into Botswana to continue his tasks. He also asks that an ANC military representative be granted entry to the country.

Masire rejects both requests.

Tambo then promises to withdraw all MK cadres.[34]

*

In February/March 1985, Quentin Michels, a UDF area committee coordinator in Bonteheuwel in the Western Cape, meets a friend, Ismael Moss, who works for the South African Committee for Higher Education (SACHED).

Moss tells Michels that if he is as dissatisfied as he says with the political situation under the Tricameral Parliament, there is an alternative. Moss does not elaborate.

When the two men meet again, Moss is more expansive on the matter. He advises Michels to go to Botswana. He hands over money and an envelope containing a letter. Michels reads the letter. It tells him to purchase an air ticket to Gaborone before the end of May.[35]

*

An eleven-man Swazi delegation headed by M.M.P. Mnisi, the minister of foreign affairs, meets Andrew Masondo and Jacob Zuma of the ANC, as well as Brigadier Hashim Mbita and Jose Sebastiao of the OAU Liberation Committee, in Swaziland on 8 March. It is a clear-the-air meeting following the renewed hostilities between the ANC and Swaziland in December–January.

Mnisi begins by welcoming all present. Mbita responds with thanks, after which Mnisi asks the press to leave the conference room. Mnisi then hands over two copies of the *Rand Daily Mail* to Brigadier Mbita. The articles feature various recent South African accusations against Botswana and Botswana's responses. While Mbita reads, police commissioner Majaji Simelane circulates a document titled 'ANC activities in the Kingdom of SD after the Nkomati Accord signed by the Government of Mozambique and SA'.

Mnisi says he is showing these documents to illustrate how unfortunate Swaziland is. If those articles were about Swaziland everybody would be up in arms in criticism. When countries like Botswana say they will not allow their territory to be used as a springboard for attacks on neighbours, nobody says anything. But let Swaziland do the same, and she gets criticised, heavily.

In the case of Benjamin Langa, the Boers accused Swaziland of continuing to harbour guerrillas. In the evidence given in that trial, it was said the decision to assassinate him was taken in Mbabane.

Also, in practice it seems all ANC actions in South Africa originate in or are fed through Swaziland in one way or another.

A while later Mnisi says, turning to Brigadier Mbita, that in January three ANC cadres were taken from a police station in Mbabane. Immediately after this raid – by ANC cadres – Swaziland was again blamed. But as this meeting is taking place his delegation is aware that the three are safe, well, and not in South African hands as claimed. Nobody has seen it necessary to clear Swaziland's name. They are seen as traitors in the eyes of the world.

Mnisi gets increasingly emotional during his delivery, his eyes welling up before he breaks down and becomes unable to continue.

Resuming the meeting after lunch, Z.L. Mkhonta, the permanent secretary of the Ministry of Foreign Affairs, says he wants to know from the ANC delegation the exact whereabouts of the three taken from the police station.

Zuma says he doesn't know.

Mkhonta turns to Mbita and asks him the same.

Mbita says he doesn't know either.

After the talks, a short meeting takes place between the ANC delegates and Brigadier Mbita at the hotel where they are all staying. Mbita says it is clear the Swazis have a lot of information. He feels the ANC needs to do something to catch up with the situation. A statement correcting the facts needs to be issued and immediately afterwards they can arrange a meeting with the Swazis. There does, however, appear to be a delay in reporting with the ANC and in coordinating reports. Mbita adds that he has observed this at other meetings when ANC members will raise some points but when he meets other ANC members they are not aware of what has taken place during those meetings. He feels this element showed itself again in the meeting with the Swazis. The information the Swazis have could be damaging to the ANC.[36]

*

In April 1985 Mduduzi Sithole, aliases 'Trevor Vilakazi' and 'Belgium', one of the twenty-three on the wanted list issued by Majaji Simelane in December, arrives in South Africa.

During the month, near Folweni in Natal, Sithole trains, among others, Audway Msomi, Thuso Tshika, Sipho Stanley Bhila, Sibusiso Mazibuko and Zinto Cele in the use of the AK-47 and explosives.[37]

*

Lizo Bright Ngqungwana, appointed MK's Western Cape commander by Chris Hani in February 1983, marches into South Africa from Botswana in the vicinity of the Ramatlabama border post on the night of 3 May 1985. He sleeps in the veld, and on the following morning a comrade arrives in a vehicle that takes him to Bloemfontein. From there Ngqungwana boards a plane to Cape Town. He is collected from D.F. Malan Airport and driven to Gugulethu, where he makes contact with a comrade codenamed 'Speedo'.

On the same day, Quentin Michels moves in the opposite direction, arriving at Gaborone Airport having flown from the Cape. He stands around for a few minutes before a car arrives. In the vehicle are Ismael Moss, who recommended he come to Botswana, and Ivor Adams, whom Michels does not know.

At a motel in the city Adams quizzes Michels about his activities, his biography, and the organisations in South Africa that he works for.

Adams then departs and Moss gives Michels a bundle of ANC journals to read, but suggests that Michels rest instead of reading them then, because he is evidently tired from travelling.

Adams returns to the motel the following day. He gives Michels the instruction to return to the Western Cape and recruit three other people into a cell that must not number more than four people. That cell will need to obtain a safe house, Adams says. The goal behind this is that if they get weapons one day, the arms will need to be stored somewhere. They must then procure additional safe houses in order to temporarily host people sought by the police.

On his return from Gaborone, Michels approaches his friends Ashley Forbes and Pieter Jacobs and recruits them into an ANC cell under his command.[38]

*

At 10 a.m. on 14 May, behind a block of flats near Northside Primary School in Gaborone's Extension 9, Rodgers Nkadimeng, who is involved in infiltrating MK cadres from South Africa to Botswana, enters his Datsun Skyline sedan.

As he turns the key in the ignition, a car bomb explodes, destroying the vehicle and killing him, as well as causing extensive damage to the block of flats and houses in the immediate vicinity.[39]

*

The consultative conference that the ANC announced in June 1984 is now on the horizon.

In his capacity as ANC chief representative in Maputo, Jacob Zuma (who, following the Nkomati Accord was allowed to remain in Mozambique as head of the ANC's diplomatic mission in the country) forwards a letter to the conference's National Preparatory Committee (NPC).

Zuma writes that the letter is from a military unit 'presently based in our region', and that '[s]ome of them are those who were involved in the Ingwavuma episode'.[40]

The document itself, from 'Unit U', begins: 'Historically the ANC has rightfully won the vanguard position in the South African liberation struggle.' But 'the point in question now is to ask ourselves as to whether the ANC and her gallant army MK, has at the present and the recent past of (about 8–9 yrs back) or even more, done justice to the armed struggle of our people at home. The response of Unit U engaged in deliberation and discussion is that the ANC as a vanguard has done very little indeed.'

So, 'what are and were the problems? How can we solve them?'

Unit U felt the 'first and foremost problem is our failure to escalate the military sphere of our struggle so as to match the tremendous achievements already scored in the political sphere'.

The 'key problem to the whole issue', they argue, 'has been and is still with the incompetence of those in command'. Therefore 'It is high time, now and later to remove such people and we must be frank about it.'

Speaking more specifically, they then say: 'In short from practical experience we have lost hope that the commander of this army [Joe Modise], mkhonto we Sizwe[,] can or will ever beyond any reasonable doubt provide the green light from the army to march forward and engage the enemy in all fronts.'[41]

*

The office of Uriah Mokeba, the ANC's chief representative in Angola, also sends a document to the National Preparatory Committee. Titled 'Report of the Regional Preparatory Committee – Angola Region', it summarises the feedback received from MK units based in Angola.

Mokeba notes in a covering letter that 'There was and still is to a certain extent a trend which wants to interpret the call for the National Conference as a direct result of the mutiny – as a victory for the mutineers.'

Accordingly:

> We would like to bring to the attention of the N.P.C – the existence of a definite core which is conscious and deliberately and persistently striving to frustrate the objectives of the National Conference. It is striving to create a rift between the general membership and the leadership of the Movement. The main areas of distortion are: the situation in the front – paint a very bleak and gloomy future of the state of affairs at the front and about armed struggle in general. The conclusion leadership has failed. 2 Period – during 1979–1984 the beatings and accidental death of comrades, the logistics and health situation, the training process – the eastern campaign etc. For them this was the most horrible period in the history of MK – the conclusion again – the leadership has failed. They came out to openly demand the release of the mutineers. The security Organ is the main target here.

The main task now is to defeat this core politically. Concerning the prevalence of the trend, Mokeba says it is there in different degrees in all ANC sections in Angola except one.[42] He is possibly referring to Caculama camp, where trainees who have just arrived from South Africa are accommodated, and which accordingly has a different political profile.[43]

*

On 28 May 1985, on the first floor of the Nedbank East City Building at End Street in Hillbrow, Mohammed Shaik of MK's 'Dolphin Unit' approaches the offices of the SADF's Transvaal Medical Command. He is carrying a shoebox containing two limpet mines that have been attached together. He places the box on the floor outside a lift that provides access to the medical inspection office.

At about 2.45 p.m. an army officer comes to the office of Mrs Agnes Matthews, the building's caretaker, and asks to use her phone. He tells her not to be scared, but he has seen a mysterious box in the passage on the first floor. He asks somebody over the phone to come and check the box.

Matthews tells her security guard to go to all the offices and tell the occupants to exit the building.

At 2.49 p.m., just as the security guard has finished the task, Matthews hears a blast, and sees glass and shoes land on the forecourt in front of her office. Then she sees people screaming and being led away.

In all, sixteen people are injured and ten offices demolished in this explosion.[44]

*

Ebrahim Ismail Ebrahim is meanwhile seeking to leave South Africa in order to report to the National Consultative Conference on his mission inside the country.

On 6 June, Hélène Passtoors, who couriered the car used in the 1983 Church Street bomb blast, is accompanied by two colleagues in trying to help Ebrahim escape illegally in the Amsterdam/Nerston border area. The attempt fails.

They try again on the 11th and again fail.[45]

*

Before 1 a.m. on 14 June, at a house in Gaborone neighbouring the ANC office at house 2067/8 Bontleng, Mrs Sefako fears something is amiss when she hears strange sounds outside. She peeps through the window and sees the street laden with soldiers. She opens the door to get a better view, upon which one of the troops threatens to kill her if she moves an inch forward.

Back inside the house she hears the soldiers arguing among themselves about which property to bomb.

Mrs Sefako's granddaughter Keitumetse, aged eight, is asleep in a room in the house when she is awoken by the sound of automatic machine guns and grenades. It sounds to her as if their house is being targeted. The other people in the room rush out, leaving Keitumetse and her eleven-year-old uncle Thatayaone Mabophiwa behind.

She scrambles for safety under the bed. Thatayaone meanwhile manages to scale a window, but realises Keitumetse has been left behind, so he decides to return and rescue her. Before he can act, however, a white man in black uniform enters the room. Thatayaone opts to hide instead.

All Keitumetse can see from her position under the bed is a pair of boots.

When the man leaves, Thatayaone comes and takes Keitumetse away.

At the ANC office next door, there were no occupants at the time of the attack. The only living thing was an aggressive guard dog which the assailants quickly shot dead when it interfered with their mission.[46]

*

At around the same time, at House 15717 in Broadhurst, Gaborone, a team of about twenty white Afrikaans-speaking men storm the premises and shoot their way into a back room, where they corner George and Lindie Phahle, South African refugees who arrived in Botswana in December 1976. They fire fifty rounds into walls, beds and cupboards. The couple are struck repeatedly, causing their death.

Joseph Malaza, also a tenant at the house, takes cover in a wardrobe. He is shot and killed by a bullet fired through the closed door.

Levi Phahle, George's brother, survives by rolling under a bed. From his position he hears the attackers shooting, laughing and swearing. One asks: 'Are they all dead? Have we finished off all the fucking kaffirs?'

The dead bodies are kicked around before being photographed.[47]

*

The lock on the back door of Duke Mashobane's house in Nomatata suburb in Gaborone is blasted off, after which Mashobane's six-year-old nephew Peter Mofoka runs from his bedroom, only to be killed as six bullets are fired into him.

Mashobane himself is sprayed with multiple rounds of gunfire from point-blank range. His wife Rose is allowed to escape. 'We're not interested in women, only terrorists,' one of the attackers says.[48]

*

In Tlokweng, a home and studio inhabited by Thami Mynele, an exiled South African artist, is attacked shortly after 1 a.m. as tear gas is thrown inside. Mynele is shot in the back and killed as he tries to flee.[49]

*

Eugenia Kobole and Gladys Kelapi, two Batswana women, are killed when the servants' quarters they inhabit are destroyed by explosives. The blast tosses two arms, three legs and chunks of flesh about the yard. Some body parts are later found hanging from trees and a head is discovered lodged in a window at the back of the main house.[50]

*

Uriel Abrahamse is awoken by the sound of the interspersed gunshots and explosions. His home is close to the National Stadium in Gaborone. He gets dressed and stands up. Then everything goes quiet, so he lies back on his bed, fully clothed, and falls asleep.

At about 5 a.m. his Muslim housemates awaken him when they return from early morning prayer at the mosque. One says that a white refugee in Extension 9 has been killed.

Still fully dressed, Abrahamse walks to a house he previously lived in that is located on the way to the mosque. He arrives there at the same time as a Botswana Defence Force truck, which stops, leaving a cloud of dust in its wake. A group of about six Botswana soldiers then deploy in prone position.

'What are you doing?' Abrahamse asks.

'Can't you see this house has been attacked?'

'Yes, four hours ago. Whoever did it won't be hanging around for you to find them.'

At that point some ANC colleagues arrive. One of them explains that Abrahamse is angry because he used to live there.[51]

Later that morning, the University of Botswana publishes the results of its Science exams. Only one student received a first-class mark. It was one of two exam scripts in any discipline in the whole university which achieved that distinction. The student was Michael Hamlyn, aged twenty-four, killed earlier that morning in the attack on the house in Extension 9.[52]

*

Acting on orders to avenge the Gaborone raid, Phumezo Nxiweni takes a walk on Durban's Lower Marine Parade on the afternoon of 14 June.[53]

Just after 8 p.m., Dave McGarry is having coffee among forty-odd other patrons inside the X-L Restaurant on South Beach Walk on the Lower Marine Parade when a huge explosion occurs outside, sending glass flying. The force of the blast lifts McGarry off his seat while another man is thrown right over his table.[54]

When Mr Sotiris Spetsiotis, the owner of the restaurant, arrives at the scene, he finds the road blocked by police. He asks for permission to go through police lines, identifying himself as the owner.

He finds that the north-eastern side of the restaurant has been blown up. The windows are smashed; chairs and tables lie skew. The side of the building has collapsed, including half of a pillar that once stretched to the roof. There is an electrical wire laying on the ground and the electrical lights leading outside have all fallen. The electricity as a whole is on, but some of the lights have been cut off.[55]

*

'Comrade Chairman, Members of the National Executive Committee, Fellow Delegates, we meet two days after Pretoria's assassination squads invaded the Republic of Botswana and murdered South Africans, among them members of the ANC, as well as citizens of Botswana and foreign nationals – men, women and children.' So begins Oliver Tambo's opening address to the ANC's Second National Consultative Conference, held in Kabwe, Zambia.[56]

Further in his address, Tambo reads what he introduces as being a message from Nelson Mandela and other leaders in jail.[57] Signed by Mandela on behalf of ANC leaders in Robben Island and Pollsmoor prisons, it begins: 'We were most delighted to hear that the ANC will soon have another Conference. We sincerely hope that such an occasion will constitute yet another milestone in our history.' The prisoners say that 'the positions taken by Oliver Tambo on various issues and also stressed by Joe

Slovo inspired us tremendously. Both drew attention to issues which, in our opinion, are very timely.'[58]

*

On the conference's second day, the National Preparatory Committee submits its report. The document is based on feedback received from units in the ANC's regions on some of the key questions facing the movement.

Regarding feedback related to matters concerning 'People's War (Armed Struggle)', the report notes that 'Several units make the point' that

> Our present tactics seem to be aimed at registering our presence rather than serious military conflict, consequently we have failed to expand and draw in the masses who have become spectators: our actions encourage mass passivity. Failure to follow up gives the enemy time to regroup and counter-attack. There is still no organised ANC or MK presence inside the country.

Many charged that 'Rather than remedy this situation, our MHQ go in for ill-advised plans instead of building up our forces inside the country'.

A related critique, also raised frequently, was that

> Rear bases are untenable for our struggle, therefore the commanding personnel should go into the country. Commanding from the rear has caused a time lag between events and our response and encouraged negligence and faulty preparations. Decisions to this effect have been taken and await implementation.[59]

*

During the conference's plenary session on the 17th, preliminary comments are allowed from the floor.

A group of delegates from Angola sits in the corner making constant criticisms of the leadership. Their criticisms specifically relate to the manner whereby delegates who they claim have not been elected have nevertheless somehow managed to obtain credentials to attend the conference. The group repeatedly tries to raise the matter of how delegates received accreditation.

Every time they do so, they are met by a choir of boos from the other delegates. One member of this critical group is Jabulani Nxumalo, aka 'Comrade Mzala'. He rises to ask why MK is suffering so many casualties inside the country. He later asks how much money is being directed into South Africa as opposed to being spent outside.[60]

*

After the plenary meeting the conference breaks into specialised commissions.

Chris Hani and Pallo Jordan chair the Commission on Strategy and Tactics. During the session a number of points are raised from the floor. There is a debate on how the movement views the relationship between insurrection and people's war, and the place of partial and full insurrection in the struggle; a warning is given not to play with insurrection; a criticism is made of the tendency to classify the Bantustans as 'rural' by definition (ignoring forms of urbanisation that have been taking place);

another call is for greater emphasis to be placed on mobilising opposition within the Bantustans, including the utilisation of patriotic chiefs.

Following the contributions, Joe Slovo sums up the discussion and notes the value of a number of the individual contributions from the floor.[61]

*

The Strategy and Tactics Commission sets up a drafting committee consisting of Pallo Jordan (chair), Simon Makana, Mac Maharaj and Joe Slovo, among others, to draw up a formal Strategy and Tactics document on the commission's behalf that can be circulated within the movement at a later date.

Though unable to deliver a full Strategy and Tactics document at the time, the commission does manage to deliver a draft document for the conference's consideration.

A number of recommendations are made, including some concerning the Bantustans and bringing the workers into the struggle in greater numbers. The final recommendation reads:

> We can no longer allow our armed activities to be determined solely by the risk of civilian casualties. The time has come when those who stand in solid support of the race tyranny and who are its direct or indirect instruments, must themselves begin to feel the agony of our counter-blows. It is becoming more necessary than ever for whites to make it clear on which side of the battle lines they stand.[62]

*

The Commission on Internal Mass Mobilisation meanwhile issues its completed report to the conference. It recommends the establishment of Area Political Committees (first proposed in September 1980 but unimplemented since then) inside South Africa in order to ensure the presence of an all-round political and military leadership in all areas of the country.

It further recommends that 'The ANC should be present in all public organisations. Operatives manning the PMC's should now and again go inside the country to get first hand information on the situation.'[63]

*

On 17 June, at Durban's Louis Botha Airport, Hélène Passtoors arrives on a flight from Johannesburg. She is met by Ebrahim Ismail Ebrahim. From the airport the two head to the Blue Waters Hotel.

In a room there, they discuss 'Operation Mango', a plan to smuggle Ebrahim out of the country illegally via a route passing from Nelspruit to Komatipoort and then into Swaziland.

At the hotel Ebrahim also gives Passtoors a coded report to send through to 'ANC Khumalo' (i.e. Ronnie Kasrils) when she returns to Johannesburg.[64]

*

Detective Sergeant Pitout is on observation duty on the afternoon of 22 June. He is keeping track of Hélène Passtoors' movements.

He sees her pick up a man, Klaas de Jonge, and drive him to a place in Halfway

House (halfway between Johannesburg and Pretoria). The two stand for a while looking about, and then they leave.

They return to the same spot at around 8.30 p.m. in a car driven this time by De Jonge. They spend some time standing round a sand heap. At 11.55 p.m., after they have left, Pitout proceeds to the sand heap and finds that it is in fact a well-camouflaged arms cache.

Klaas de Jonge is arrested the following day while en route to Botswana. A two-page written route description and one-page sketch showing how to flee South Africa illegally are found in a secret compartment of his car.[65]

*

At a press conference held in Lusaka on 25 June, a journalist asks Oliver Tambo: 'There have been reports in the run-up to conference, some allegedly well-sourced, which say that ANC Conference might reconsider the movement's hesitancy in the past about hitting militarily what are termed soft targets. Did the Conference arrive at any closer definition of what it would regard as a legitimate military target?'

Tambo replies:

> I will summarise the position taken by Conference in these terms: that the struggle must be intensified at all costs. Over the past nine to ten months at least – at the very least – there have been many soft targets hit by the enemy. Nearly 500 people have now died in that period. That works out at about 50 a month, massacred, shot down, killed secretly. All those were very, *very* soft targets. But they belong to this sphere of intensification of the struggle because when people were killed they did not run away, they kept on – at all costs, and went back into battle at all costs. In the process some innocent people were killed, some white some black. What we have seen in the Eastern Cape and places like that is what escalation means for everybody. The distinction between 'soft' and 'hard' is going to disappear in an intensified confrontation, in an escalating conflict.[66]

*

On the evening of June 25th, three MK cadres, Mzwandile Vena, 'Jabulani' and 'Dick', blow up the Transkei Development Corporation's fuel depot in Umtata.

On the same night, two other members of the unit, 'Mpilo' (real name Mzizi Maqhekeza) and 'Monwabisi', sabotage Umtata electrical power station.

Jabulani and Dick then go without Vena to demolish the drain-water pipeline of Transkei's Department of Agriculture and Forestry.

For several days the Transkeian capital is left wholly without electricity.[67]

*

On the 26th, Ebrahim Ismail Ebrahim has a conversation with Yunis Shaik's brother Moe (not Mohammed Shaik of the Dolphin Unit).

Ebrahim says they are under surveillance, but the ANC has made a decision that he should escape. Shaik's unit must serve as the decoy to enable him to escape.[68]

*

Hélène Passtoors is arrested two days later on the corner of Pritchard and Von Wielligh Streets in Johannesburg.[69]

*

At about 10 p.m. on 29 June, Yunis Shaik receives a phone call from his brother Moe.

In a code that they as brothers developed in their youth, Moe tells Yunis that he can see security personnel all around the building (Highpoint Flats in Overport), and that he can't leave his apartment. A raid is imminent, he says; they have to get Ebrahim Ismail Ebrahim to safety.

Highpoint Flats consists of two buildings that are quite close to each other. Moe Shaik is in one building, Ebrahim in the other. Yunis throws on some clothes and manages to get to Ebrahim's flat and move him to a safe house. When there, Ebrahim moves into the basement.

Yunis then heads to Moe's flat but finds him already under arrest.[70]

*

Yunis Shaik is not kept in detention. Early the following month, he has a private discussion with Pravin Gordhan at a meeting of the Housing Action Committee.

'I can't sustain the commander [Ebrahim Ismail Ebrahim] any more, I've got to defend my unit,' Shaik says. 'Our unit has suffered this hit. I need to surrender this man.'

Gordhan interrupts: 'Don't say any more. You ought not to even assume I'm in the ANC.' He tells Shaik to just leave the man at the Roadhouse on Umgeni Road near the Queensborough Mosque.

Shaik does so, and Gordhan's network manages to get Ebrahim Ismail Ebrahim out of the country.[71]

*

Vijay Ramlakan arrives at Unit 2 Shopping Centre in Bayview, in Durban's Chatsworth suburb, driving a white Toyota Cressida.

Raymond Sakloo, like Ramlakan an activist in the Natal Indian Congress, jumps in the passenger seat and notices there is a black man in the back wearing Ray-Ban sunglasses and a hat.

Ramlakan says he knows about Sakloo's plan to petrol-bomb the home of a member of the House of Delegates (the Indian chamber of the Tricameral Parliament), as one of his operatives in Chatsworth informed him of this.

Ramlakan then introduces the man in the back seat as 'Lincoln' (it is Lulamile Xate, who recruited Jacob Mofokeng and Mapiki Dlomo into MK earlier in the year).

Ramlakan urges Sakloo to stop his plans regarding that attack, as he has better methods. He says he is a member of the underground structure of the ANC, Umkhonto we Sizwe, and that 'Lincoln' is internal commander of MK's Natal Region. He says that he wants to recruit more Indians into the MK underground. For security reasons, he adds, members of the underground do not operate with their real names. Ramlakan suggests that Sakloo choose a codename.

'Revaleno Singh, alias Rev,' Sakloo suggests.

Ramlakan raises no objections and produces a cardboard box on which is written, '1. How do I feel about the ANC 2. What do I feel about the underground structure of the ANC, Umkhonto we Sizwe. 3. What do I think about socialism, Marxism and communism. 4. What targets I prefer that MK must take on.'

He tells Sakloo to write his answers on another page and return it next week.[72]

*

By this time the township rebellion has brought government structures in black urban areas to the point of collapse.

Writing in the *Christian Science Monitor* of 19 July 1985, South African journalist Patrick Laurence reports that the Centre for Applied Social Sciences in Durban estimates that by the end of June at least 240 local government councillors in South Africa's black areas had resigned.

Consequently, fewer than six black councils are operative in the entire country. Laurence says the resignations are the consequence of a sustained campaign of violence from militants against councillors, in which upwards of 300 black councillors have been attacked in various forms, mainly arson-related.[73]

*

In Pretoria the following day, at a press conference restricted to South African journalists, President P.W. Botha says 'violence and lawlessness' in the townships have 'increased and become more severe and more cruel'.

These actions 'take the form of incitement, intimidation, arson, inhuman forms of assault and even murder' and 'can no longer be tolerated'. He says he is therefore imposing a state of emergency to be applied in thirty-six districts nationwide (mainly the Rand and the Eastern Cape).[74]

*

Two days after Botha's declaration, the ANC releases a statement from its Lusaka headquarters predicting that the state of emergency will only increase levels of violence. The statement prophesies further that 'This struggle will also spread to the white areas of our country regardless of enemy efforts to confine it to black townships.'

Claude Robinson of the Inter Press Service contacts David Ndaba, an ANC representative at the United Nations on the 23rd to inquire about what that phrase actually means. Ndaba tells him that in keeping with views expressed by Oliver Tambo, it means 'white areas cannot be immune when our people are dying by the hundreds'.[75]

TAKING THE WAR TO WHITE AREAS

On Sunday 4 August at Road 901 in Chatsworth, Durban, Raymond Sakloo, Derrick Naidoo, Lenny Naidu and David Maduray get out of a car driven by Richard Naidoo, who then proceeds with the vehicle down Road 602 before parking on the corner of Roads 602 and 615.

Sakloo and Derrick Naidoo walk down 602. They are dressed neatly as if returning from church. Derrick Naidoo carries a limpet mine (which is camouflaged by grass taped over it with cellophane) on top of a Bible in his left hand. Lenny Naidu and David Maduray walk ten paces behind in tracksuits. They are bouncing a white ball.

About five metres before they reach the house of Amichand Rajbansi, leader of the National People's Party (which won the majority of votes in the elections for the Indian House of Delegates in the Tricameral Parliament), Derrick Naidoo pulls the pin from the detonator. A policeman is on duty at the gate at Rajbansi's house. When Sakloo and Derrick Naidoo reach the plastered fence that demarcates the beginning of Rajbansi's property, the white ball is thrown at them from behind.

'Please pass the ball,' comes a cry.

Sakloo and Derrick Naidoo both turn, upon which Sakloo takes the mine from the Bible and places it down on the grass between the sidewalk and the plastered fence. He covers the mine with grass when placing it down. He then takes the ball and throws it back to Lenny Naidu.

They turn around again, and continue down 602 till the corner with 615, where they all jump in the car in which Richard Naidoo is waiting for them.

At about 10.35 p.m. Amichand Rajbansi is in his study when he hears a loud blast that shatters a window in the room. Further investigation by him reveals that the window in the dining room has also been damaged. Rajbansi assumes a grenade was thrown at the house, but the policeman outside the house says he did not see anybody.

Capital Radio reports the following morning that Amichand Rajbansi's house has been bombed.

Upon hearing this, Raymond Sakloo telephones Vijay Ramlakan, who offers him congratulations, saying the guys are very happy. Sakloo and Ramlakan agree to meet the following Wednesday.[1]

*

Thami Zulu meets Jacob Zuma in Mozambique to discuss the establishment of a new politico-military structure for Natal in line with the recommendations of the Kabwe Conference. Zuma gives him the go-ahead to draw up a plan.

Thami Zulu then meets with Edward Lawrence, Sue Rabkin and Terence Tyron in Maputo. Using koki pens they start drawing an organisational chart: who would report to whom, what units would be necessary, how they would coordinate, and so on.

On this chart, they make provisions for what they call 'area mobilisation' within Natal, i.e. mobilising Indian and African communities on a separate basis.

The final structure of the chart is roughly as follows. At the top comes the 'Headquarters' – whether the Politico-Military Council or some other entity – which would integrate political and military functions and would be based abroad. Its members would have certain areas of specific responsibility such as mass mobilisation, propaganda, military, communications, logistics and intelligence.

This Headquarters would establish subordinate structures in the 'Forward Areas' neighbouring South Africa (for Natal this would be Swaziland).

Then, on the bottom row, which deals with the extension of the structure into South Africa, the arrangement is that people would first be tested politically in the mass organisations. If they impressed there they would be recruited into the underground, where they would begin with tasks like propaganda distribution. If they worked well in the political underground, they would be brought into three-person military combat structures. Each combat structure would have a commander who would report to a regional committee, which would have a single line of communication out to Swaziland.[2]

The operation is codenamed 'Butterfly' in honour of Zweli Nyanda, who used the term when discussing a very similar project with Charles Ndaba and Rayman Lalla in 1982.[3]

*

Herbert Beukes, South Africa's ambassador in Washington, tells the press on 13 August that P.W. Botha will make a 'fundamental statement' in two days' time 'on some of the most crucial and fundamental issues in South Africa'. Referring to the governments of Britain, the United States and West Germany, with whose diplomats South African counterparts held a meeting in Vienna the previous week, Beukes says he feels that 'on the basis of what we believe President Botha might be announcing ... they would find that helpful in maintaining their relationships with South Africa.'[4]

With expectations thus raised, when President Botha addresses the National Party's Natal Provincial Congress in Durban's City Hall on 15 August, most of the 120 journalists present are from foreign news organisations.[5]

Botha proceeds to rain on his own parade. Noting that appeals have been made both internally and externally for Nelson Mandela's release, he says Mandela must first renounce violence. On constitutional reform, he says most South Africans 'will not accept the principle of one-man, one-vote in a unitary system', because 'such an arrangement would lead to domination of one over the others and it would lead to chaos'. He doesn't even favour the creation of a fourth chamber of the Tricameral Parliament for blacks.

In a speech that will quickly become notorious for what is not said in it, Botha does commit to abolish the pass laws and grant South African citizenship to blacks both in the urban areas and in the six homelands yet to be granted independence.

In his peroration Botha says: 'The implementation of the principles I have stated today can have far-reaching effects on us all. I believe that we are today crossing the Rubicon. There can be no turning back.'[6]

But the 'Rubicon speech' is not what the world was expecting. The *Star* reports on the 17th that several diplomats and foreign journalists have confirmed that foreign minister Pik Botha had beforehand given them details of certain reforms which did not appear in the speech.[7]

*

During Operation Palmiet, when the security forces concentrated their strength in the Vaal Triangle, rioting emerged elsewhere, and when they withdrew, it returned where they had been. As a response to the township rebellion, this 'firefighting' approach proved ineffective because it created an impossible situation for those representatives of the councils who had to live permanently in such places. The result was the collapse of most of the township councils by early 1985.

The government responded by imposing a state of emergency in the affected regions – in effect an unprecedented concentration of force. But this only sees the established pattern of the insurrection repeat itself on a grander scale.

At 9 a.m. on 28 August in Gugulethu in the Western Cape (which has not been affected by the emergency), approximately 3,000 youthful protesters march down Klipfontein Road, which leads to the coloured township of Athlone. Along the way they set two cars alight and defy policemen who fire teargas to prevent them getting to their intended destination of Athlone Stadium, which is to be the marshalling point for a planned march to Pollsmoor Prison, where Nelson Mandela, Walter Sisulu, Raymond Mhlaba, Andrew Mlangeni and Ahmed Kathrada have been held since 1982.

When they reach Gugulethu Police Station, three Casspir armoured vehicles deploy in their path and fire teargas at them, after which policemen wielding sjamboks chase them back towards Gugulethu.

At 9.50 a.m. at a spot further down Klipfontein Road directly opposite Athlone Stadium, a large cohort of local and foreign photographers look on as a group of about six hundred are told by a policeman on a loudhailer to disperse. The demonstrators carry on swaying and singing, and those at the front hold hands. The policeman calls on his men to form a line on the road. Six minutes later he shouts 'Maak skoon' after which the policemen charge into the crowd with sjamboks.

By that evening, all entrances to Gugulethu and Nyanga are blocked off by the police, while Casspirs within these townships spray teargas to disperse groups of protesters. In Khayelitsha, a few kilometres away, various acts of arson are reported through the night.

This, Cape Town's first riot since 1976, effectively brings the national insurrection to the Western Cape.[8]

*

About two weeks later, Niklo Pedro travels from Mossel Bay to Kraaifontein in Cape Town. He arrives to a scene that seems to him to resemble a war zone, with barricades and fires everywhere.

He goes straight to Bonteheuwel, where he calls on the home of a friend, Ashley Kriel. He discovers that Kriel has gone into hiding because the police are looking for him.[9]

*

At President Kaunda's private game lodge in Mfuwe, Zambia, on 13 September, Gavin Relly and Zach de Beer of Anglo American, Tony Bloom of Premier Group Holdings, Tertius Myburgh (editor of the *Sunday Times*), Harold Pakendorf (editor of *Die Vaderland*), J. de L. Peter Sordor (director of the South African Foundation) and Hugh Murray (editor of *Leadership South Africa*) meet Oliver Tambo, Pallo Jordan, Mac Maharaj, Chris Hani, Thabo Mbeki and James Stuart. The discussion centres on negotiations.

In an ANC summary of the meeting that is compiled for the movement's own records the following day, it is written that the ANC's present stance on the matter, as expressed at Mfuwe, is that 'we have not reached the stage where we can even talk about talks. The Botha regime has to take concrete steps in order to create the atmosphere where even talk about talks can be entertained.'

The concrete steps include the release of Nelson Mandela and all political prisoners, lifting the state of emergency, releasing all detainees, halting political trials, removing police and troops from black townships and 'ghettoes', lifting the ban on the ANC, and removing laws that would prevent the movement from organising the masses freely.[10]

*

Audway Msomi meets Thuso Tshika and Bafo Nguqu, the other members of his cell.

Msomi conveys a message from 'Comrade Belgium' (Mduduzi Sithole, who trained Msomi and Tshika near Folweni in April) that they must carry out an operation in solidarity with the workers fighting for living wages. Their targets are retailers OK Bazaars and Game, where there is an ongoing dispute between the retained workers and management.

Tshika, Nguqu and Msomi head to Durban's West Street on 27 September. Tshika proceeds to place a limpet mine inside Game Discount World, a three-floored department store on West Street between Field and Grey Streets.

Nguqu meanwhile plants another mine inside the OK Bazaars, which is situated almost opposite the Game store and on the corner of West and Field Streets.

Tshika returns to Msomi and says he has carried out his instruction.

At 5.08 p.m., just after closing time, OK Bazaars staff are still in the store when a blast from the basement rips through the crockery department, causing the building to shake.

About seven minutes later, David Fingland, the manager of the Game store, is in his office on the level above the third shopping floor when he hears a loud bang from a floor below. He immediately leaves his office to investigate, and is met on the way down by John Gibson, the store's sales manager. When they get to the first floor, they look down the escalators and see dust settling on the ground floor in the crockery department on the west side of the store. Tableware, plates, cups, saucers and glasses have been broken, while the metal fixtures used to display the merchandise have also been damaged. Structural damage from the attack is, however, limited to one window pane.[11]

*

By October, 'Operation Butterfly' has reached the implementation stage.

Linda Moni leaves Pango Camp in Angola, and is flown from Luanda to Mozambique.

In Maputo, he meets 'Sihle Khumalo' (real name Sibusiso Ndlanzi) and 'Master'.

The three are then joined by Edward Lawrence of the Natal Machinery, who tells them that they must go to South Africa and execute the task set by the National Conference of the ANC, namely establishing area political-military committees. They must also provide people with military training. First, however, they must go to Swaziland.[12]

*

At Lyford Cay in Nassau in the Bahamas on 20 October a new initiative to find a negotiated solution to the South African conflict commences when the assembled leaders of the Commonwealth agree an 'Accord on Southern Africa'.

It calls on South Africa to declare openly that apartheid will be dismantled; that the state of emergency will be ended; that Nelson Mandela will immediately and unconditionally be released along with all other political prisoners; that the ANC and other political parties will be unbanned; that a process of dialogue across colour, political and religious lines will be initiated with a view to establishing a non-racial, representative government within the context of 'a suspension of violence on all sides'; and that the ensuing dialogue will be one 'involving the true representatives of the majority black population of South Africa'.

'To this end,' the leaders declare, 'we have decided to establish a small group of eminent Commonwealth persons to encourage through all practicable ways the evolution of that necessary process of political dialogue.'[13]

*

Three days later, Thami Zulu arrives at a Manzini residence where he finds five people: Linda Moni, Sibusiso Ndlanzi, 'Master', the man who drove these three from the Mozambican border, and Sibongiseni Dhlomo.

Master, Moni and the driver leave the room so that Zulu, Ndlanzi and Dhlomo can converse. About an hour later Zulu returns and tells Master, Moni and the driver to go to the car, as they will now proceed to the border.

Moni and Master are transported a while later by the driver to the area of the border in the vicinity of Jozini. When there, Sibusiso Ndlanzi emerges from the bush and enters the car, which then proceeds to a spot just inside South Africa. The driver exits, walks ahead alone, and returns about fifteen minutes later. He tells his colleagues to follow him and marches Moni, Master and Ndlanzi through the bush until they reach a vehicle in which Vijay Ramlakan and Sibongiseni Dhlomo are waiting. Ramlakan and Dhlomo take turns driving the group to their destination in Durban, the Alan Taylor Residence of the University of Natal in Wentworth.

At this residence the group are met by Lulamile Xate, who introduces himself as 'Mr X' and allocates them a room on the premises.[14]

*

On the following evening, Zinto Cele, another one of Mduduzi Sithole's April 1985 trainees, places an armed SZ-6 demolition charge on the steps to the entrance of Grosvenor Girls' High School on Durban's Bluff. His colleagues Mandinkosi Dimande and Sibusiso Mazibuko are standing nearby.

The charge explodes as Cele switches it on. The premature explosion kills Cele and Dimande, who was about three metres away. Their mutilated bodies are left lying in the vicinity of the blast. Mazibuko, who was about ten metres further away, is thrown onto open ground by the explosion, but survives and manages to run away.

Some two hours later, Lulamile Xate arrives at Vijay Ramlakan's house with Mazibuko, who has severe lacerations on his face and a burst eardrum. Xate tells Ramlakan to treat the wounded man and ensure he leaves the country if possible.

While Mazibuko recuperates, Ramlakan questions him on what happened. Mazibuko says he was involved in an explosion at Grosvenor Girls' School which was targeted because it is being used by the government as a polling station.[15]

*

During November 1985, Robert McBride meets Gordon Webster, who has returned from his training abroad. Webster gives McBride information about the ANC. While doing so, Webster repeatedly probes his friend about his feelings regarding the organisation.

This time he is successful in recruiting McBride. Webster brings him into his MK Special Operations Unit cell.[16]

*

Mzondelele Nondula and Jabulani Mbuli are part of a group of twelve MK cadres who are briefed in Zimbabwe in November 1985 by Julius Maliba, aka 'Mancheck' (formerly Sibasa group leader during the Wankie campaign and now chairman of the ANC's Forward Area Machinery, which after the Kabwe Conference is called the 'Zimbabwe Regional Politico-Military Committee').

In line with the recommendation by the conference's Strategy and Tactics Commission that whites must be made to feel the impact of MK's armed actions to a greater extent, Maliba says that the areas next to the border, specifically Soutpansberg, will be their group's operational zone. The white community there is organised into rural commando structures. That farming community is regarded by the regime as its first echelon of defence in the sense that the population there is encouraged – even sponsored – by the government to stay there as militarily trained personnel safeguarding the border area. Therefore they are legitimate targets.

The group of twelve are transported southwards to the Limpopo River and stay overnight on the Zimbabwean side of the border. They divide into two groups of six, one unit commanded by 'Agrippa', the other by 'Chilies'. Each individual is equipped with a landmine and a rifle. The landmines, brown in colour, are round, about 25 centimetres in height, and weigh about six kilograms.

From their position, which is concealed by bush, the twelve can see a patrol vehicle doing its rounds on the South African side of the border. Along with the Jeep-style truck, the patrol also consists of footsoldiers led by tracker dogs.[17]

*

At about 9 p.m. the following evening, Agrippa's group crosses the Limpopo. Once in South Africa, the six continue travelling south so as to bypass the route of the border patrols. They spend their first night in the republic concealed in the bush.

At 7 p.m. on the following evening, they retrace their steps northwards to the border patrol route in order to lay their landmines. Agrippa tells them that after placing one mine they must move to the next site. The mines should not be cluttered, he says; this will make them more difficult to detect.

The group plant their six mines on the patrol road and on approaches to it. In each case, Agrippa accompanies the person responsible for planting the mine while two other members of the group stand to the side and the final two members of the group stand elsewhere.[18]

Chilies' group is also on the patrol road. Chilies himself plants a mine. The group then heads to a curve in the patrol road, where there is a farm nearby. Chilies digs a hole and plants the second mine.

Chilies then accompanies 'Solly', 'Terence', 'Tabane' and 'Mwumeleni' in turn to plant the remaining four mines at spots on the patrol road and its approaches. In each case Chilies orders his companion to dig a hole in which he then plants the mine. After planting their six mines the group crosses back to Zimbabwe.[19]

*

At about 8.20 a.m. on 26 November, Elijah Mokgamatha is driving a Nissan diesel truck, which belongs to the cement delivery company Petermix. Attached to the vehicle is a semi-trailer. Mokgamatha has a passenger, Edward Meluba, sitting next to him. The truck is travelling in the direction of a farm in the Weipe area of Messina district.

Mokgamatha misses his turn-off, so he does a U-turn. On the way back he hears a blow and goes into shock, as a result of which he temporarily cannot see anything. The truck has just detonated a landmine. The vehicle itself is seriously damaged by the explosion.

About half an hour later, Gert de Villiers drives his Toyota bakkie eastwards along the so-called 'sisal fence road' running parallel to the South Africa–Zimbabwe border. De Villiers has a dog on board.

Suddenly he hears a tremendous thud. He climbs out and sees that the rear part of his bakkie has been thrown thirty metres into the bush.[20]

*

In Lusaka the following day, the ANC completes a policy paper titled 'A Submission on the Question of Negotiations'.

It offers an expansion on the views expressed about negotiations at the Mfuwe Lodge meeting just over two months before. It says talks are not harmful if viewed as another terrain of struggle rather than a means of drawing the struggle to a close. The example of Namibia is cited as a warning that the enemy may press for talks in order to employ them as a means to buy time and force a downscaling of the struggle. 'We must therefore approach talks as a means of winning at the conference table or consolidating what we have won on the battlefield. In other words we will enter into talks as a means of pursuing our political objectives employing other means, and to supplement our conventional means.'

If and when talks commence, 'Our first task will be to prevent the other side from emasculating us by surrounding and bracketing us with an array of dubious political forces within an "anti-apartheid spectrum"'.

The preconditions for talks outlined in the document remain essentially the same as those articulated at Mfuwe. They are: the unconditional release of all political prisoners; the lifting of the state of emergency; the withdrawal of the security forces from the townships followed by their return to barracks; the cessation of political trials; and, finally, the repeal of laws proscribing freedom of assembly, speech and the press.

The document urges that when the ANC reaches the negotiating table it should do so with its own set of concrete proposals in hand. It is emphasised that the demands of the Freedom Charter will not be enough, and that without more specific proposals, the organisation will be forced to react to the enemy's initiatives. Therefore the NEC must set up a constitutional think-tank.[21]

*

Two vans arrive at the home of Matthew Simelane at house 17 in Zinoni township in Bethal. Three men emerge from each of the vehicles. One of them is Barney Molokoane, Simelane's nephew. Other individuals in the group are Victor Khayiyana, Vincent Sekete and Vaku Senzangakhona. Simelane recognises them all, having hosted them and other members of MK's Special Operations Unit in Bethal and Swaziland on previous occasions.[22]

*

At about 1 a.m. on 28 November 1985, about half a dozen 122-mm rockets are fired at the SASOL 2 and 3 oil-from-coal complex in Secunda in the eastern Transvaal. Though the rockets land on the grounds of the complex, they do not damage the installations themselves.

Shortly afterwards, Warrant Officer Cornelius J. Botha is staking out a back road near Piet Retief, to the north of the Houtkop border post with Swaziland, as part of an operation to track down the saboteurs. A bakkie with three men inside drives by. Botha gives chase and forces the bakkie off the road while under fire. In the ensuing gun battle, the three guerrillas abandon the bakkie and flee into a dense bluegum plantation lying nearby.

Botha calls for armed reinforcements by radio and SADF troops in the area are deployed. A pursuit of about eight kilometres follows. At first light, the guerrillas are cornered on open ground on a beef farm about 800 metres from the border. A shootout lasting almost two hours then occurs. In the process the security forces kill Barney Molokoane, Vincent Sekete and Victor Khayiyana, the three Special Operations cadres in the bakkie, who had conducted the attack on the SASOL complex earlier that morning. No security forces are killed, but three army members received injuries in the pursuit.[23]

*

Sibongiseni Dhlomo travels to Ingwavuma in November 1985. From the border area he collects three ANC members, namely 'Sandile', Terence Tyron and Andrew Zondo, who have been sent to reinforce Operation Butterfly.

Dhlomo brings them to Durban.[24]

*

The December 1985 issue of the ANC's journal *Sechaba* reproduces a leaflet titled 'Take the Struggle to the White Areas!' which it says was recently distributed inside South Africa.

The document reads that over the past year 'we have confronted the evil system of apartheid on a scale unheard of in the history of our struggle'. This has thrown 'Botha and his clique into confusion' and now the regime is doing all it can 'to confine our struggle to the Black areas and protect the comfort of Whites'. Therefore the '*time has come* to take the war to the White areas. White South Africa cannot be at peace while the Black townships are in flames.'

The document aims to flesh out what this potent slogan might practically entail. The definition offered is restrained. The document suggests it may mean strengthening labour organisations and spreading united action to the workplace; it may involve expanding consumer boycotts nationwide; organising well-planned demonstrations in white suburbs and business districts; conducting acts of sabotage at workplaces; attacking military structures in white areas; and acquiring weapons for internal units from arms dumps and armouries.[25]

*

On an early December evening at the home of Mapiki Dlomo in Lamontville, recently infiltrated MK cadre Andrew Zondo tells Jacob Mofokeng to organise some cloth, as they are going somewhere that night.

Zondo, aged nineteen, is there to provide Dlomo and Mofokeng with the kind of training in the use of actual weapons that Lulamile Xate referred to when he briefed the pair earlier in the year.

The three later walk in the direction of the local Anglican church. At about 10 p.m. they arrive at a place near the church which is concealed by bush and tall grass and illuminated slightly by a high electricity post in an open area close by. Zondo places a hand into the bush and withdraws a bag from which he takes an AK-47. He then begins instructing Mofokeng and Dlomo in dismantling, reassembling and using the cloth to clean the rifle.[26]

*

Eugene de Kock and a unit of six men are in the company of a young coloured man, Elvis Macaskill, in Hoohlo township in Maseru at about 1 a.m. on 20 December.

Macaskill, a local resident, briefs them, saying Joe and Jacqui Quin have left the party early, but the others are still inside.

De Kock instructs Macaskill to lead Anton Adamson and another member of the group to Joe Quin's house (some two kilometres away). De Kock himself then proceeds with the other three men of the unit to the main target house.

As they approach the main house, a mere 300 metres from the South African border, De Kock's group sees a man leave the premises to look for something in a car. When the raiding group are approximately twenty metres from the car, the man notices the approaching group. De Kock fires two shots at him.

Then, while two members of the security-force team stay outside keeping watch, De Kock and Willie Nortjé storm the target house. Inside they shoot dead six people.

Later on, back at the getaway vehicle, one of the two who went to the Quin residence says that they struggled to capture Joe alive, so they shot him. He adds that Joe's wife grabbed one of the guns by the silencer, so he killed her too.

A few minutes later, the glass panel of the front door of a woman's apartment is cracked open. A man edges through, feet first. He has two bullet holes in his side and is bleeding heavily from the mouth and stomach. The man asks for painkillers.

The woman phones for an ambulance but can't get through. She heads off to the hospital. By the time she has managed to arrange an ambulance, the man, Leon Meyer, aka 'Joe Quin', who was an MK commander in Lesotho, is dead.

When police enter the Quin household, they find a one-year-old baby girl unharmed.

Altogether nine bodies are recovered from these attacks. At the main target house, seven people, Mr Vivian Matthee, Mr Joseph Monwabisi aka 'Mayoli', Ms Nomkhosi Mini, Mr Mankahelang Mohatle, Mr Lulamile Dantile aka 'Morris Seabelo', Ms Midian Zulu, and one citizen of Lesotho, have been killed. Morris Seabelo was an MK commander in Angola, and Joseph Mayoli his chief of staff.[27]

*

At around 9.30 p.m. that evening Lulamile Xate meets Andrew Zondo at Mapiki Dlomo's Lamontville house. Xate says there were ANC people killed in Maseru. They have to avenge the killing. The reprisal must be undertaken on Saturday (the following day), Sunday or Monday.[28]

Also that evening, Xate visits Audway Msomi and says the regime has raided Maseru. They must retaliate to show them there is no point looking for MK abroad, because it is inside the country.[29]

*

On the following day, Thuso Tshika and Audway Msomi arrive in Durban's Pine Street. A while later a Volkswagen Combi with white occupants enters Pine from Free Street. The vehicle proceeds to the corner of Pine and Albert Streets and parks there. The occupants leave the vehicle.

Msomi tells Tshika to make sure he gets out of the way quickly once he has pulled the pin out. Tshika proceeds to the Volkswagen and attaches an SPM limpet mine to it.

Five minutes later, the mine explodes.[30]

*

That same Saturday, Andrew Zondo walks to the Sanlam Centre in Amanzimtoti.

Inside the centre, he goes to 'Toti Restaurant' where he has a bun and juice. While eating, he sees people reading a newspaper that features a picture of a woman shot dead along with her husband in Lesotho, thereby orphaning a nine-month-old baby.

On leaving the restaurant, at the end of the passage, Zondo sees a travel agency. He associates South African Airways with the government. There is nothing else in the vicinity which is a government target, let alone a military target. He also sees a dustbin that is suitable for his purposes. He then buys a newspaper – and reads more details regarding the carnage in Maseru.[31]

*

A police wiretap on Vijay Ramlakan's phone monitors a conversation between 'Comrade Braso' and 'George Fakude'.

From follow-up investigations of previous phone calls from Ramlakan's house, the police know that this means Rayman Lalla is talking to Sibusiso Ndlanzi.[32]

*

On the morning of Monday 23 December, Andrew Zondo and Jacob Mofokeng travel by taxis from Lamontville to Merebank to Isipingo to Makhutha and finally to Amanzimtoti, from where they walk to the shopping centre. Zondo is carrying a sports bag.

At 9.30 a.m. inside the centre, they rest outside Toti Restaurant.

'Is that the bin you were talking about?' Mofokeng asks.

'No,' says Zondo, 'it's not the one, but go in yourself, buy some buns and juice, and come back with the things and I'll show you the dust bin.' Zondo asks Mofokeng to also buy a T-shirt. He gives him a R50 note and waits in the passage.

Zondo is standing near a bin when Mofokeng returns. Zondo asks him to put the food on top of the dustbin. The two then share the cakes, quarter bread, orange juice and milk that Mofokeng has purchased. Zondo finishes first and tells Mofokeng that he will have to finish eating on the way home.

Zondo collects all the waste paper left over from the meal and puts it into the sports bag. A moment later he retrieves the waste paper from the bag and drops it into the bin through a side opening. When the paper hits the side of the bin, a knock is audible, as the bundle now consists of more than paper and plastic.

Zondo then tells Mofokeng they must leave – slowly.

Once they are beyond the passage they quicken their pace.

By 10.45 a.m., the area around the bin has become crowded, because the passage is near an ice-cream shop where a Father Christmas is having a display. Then nineteen-year-old Sean Gordon hears an ear-splitting blast and sees a flash. At least a dozen shops are devastated by the explosion, which shatters windows up to thirty metres away, propelling thousands of lethal shards of glass. Screaming people run in all directions.

Later, scores of the wounded, some unconscious, others in tears, are carried out of the mall with blood seeping through their clothes. The dead are laid out on a lawn outside the building before hundreds of mute onlookers. The police draw a wide cordon around the incident and are approached continually by parents begging to be allowed through to search for their children.

Back in Lamontville that afternoon, Zondo listens to Capital Radio and hears that five people were killed. They are Willem van Wyk, aged two, Corneo Smit, eight, Sharon Bothma, sixteen, Anna Scheurer, forty, and Irma Bensisni, forty-eight. All are white. In addition, seventeen white men and boys, twenty-eight white women and girls, one black woman and two black men are injured.[33]

*

At about 10.30 p.m. that evening, a large group of security and railway policemen surround house number 2, Narbada Road, Merewent, a residential home near the Mobil Oil refinery in Durban.

Major Andrew Taylor is on the back lawn as Lieutenants Colin Robertshaw and Hendrik Botha knock on the property's rear door, which is the point of entry to the house.

The door is opened by a woman, Sandy Afrika. Robertshaw and Botha introduce themselves and say they would like to search the house. She accedes.

The door leads to the kitchen and the first person they find is Richard Naidoo, the driver during the attack on Amichand Rajbansi's house. In the lounge they see another man, who introduces himself as 'Kwazi Sithole'.

Robertshaw then asks Afrika where her husband is.

When she tells him, Robertshaw makes his way to the upstairs bedroom where he finds three people: Vijay Ramlakan (Afrika's husband), Sibusiso Ndlanzi (who introduces himself as 'George Fakude'), and a woman, Phila Ndwandwe.

They are all arrested.[34] Hence a process not directly related to the Amanzimtoti bombing has led to the demise of Operation Butterfly on the evening of the blast.

*

At Vlakplaas early in 1986, Eugene de Kock instructs Riaan Bellingan to go to Cape Town, where he will operate for a while under the command of the Security Branch.

Bellingan travels to Cape Town with Joe Coetzer and the askaris Johannes Mbelo and Eric Maluleka, who are alongside an older askari, now going under the title 'Captain Moss'. It is actually Gladstone Mose, co-signator of the Hani Memorandum and the group leader of the Transkei section of the Luthuli Detachment during the Wankie campaign.[35]

*

On 3 January 1986 South Africa's Foreign Ministry issues a statement confirming that following a build-up of guerrillas inside Lesotho, vehicles at checkpoints between the two countries have, from New Year's Day, been subject to searches for weapons and hidden passengers.[36]

*

Gordon Webster arrives with a colleague, Nazeem Cassiem, at a workshop called Factorama in Durban's industrial district of Wentworth on 9 January 1986. The workshop belongs to Robert McBride's father.

Webster requests that Robert McBride drive them to Rossdown Road.

McBride does so, and leaves Webster and Cassiem at the home of Webster's brother, which is in Rossdown Road, Wentworth.[37]

At 9.15 p.m. that evening, Sergeant Vincent Zimmerman is parking his car in Durban's Yellowwood Park suburb when he hears an explosion. He drives in the direction of the blast.

Ten minutes later he is at Jacobs substation on the corner of Chamberlain Road in Wentworth. The area is cordoned off and a fire engine is on standby.

Zimmerman enters the station through the front gate, followed by Mervyn Dunn of the Durban electricity department and Detective Constable Roelof van der Merwe.

At the first transformer, Zimmerman shines a torch that illuminates a large jagged hole in the scorched metal.

'Colonel, it's a limpet,' Zimmerman says to Colonel Robert Welman, who has joined them.

'Yes, I've seen it before.'

Welman moves to the second transformer, while Zimmerman goes to the third.

'This one looks clean,' Zimmerman says after shining his light on the grey metal. He gives the torch to Welman and leaves for the front gate.

At the gate, Zimmerman passes Sergeant Dudley Booyens, who has a patrol dog on a leash. Suddenly there is a blast from the substation and its force throws Zimmerman and Booyens to the ground.

As Booyens staggers to his feet he sees three figures emerge, running and screaming. Colonel Welman staggers past Booyens, his clothes blazing. Booyens lunges at him and throws him to the ground, rolling him on the grass to extinguish the flames. Mervyn Dunn meanwhile races through the fire and makes his way to the grass verge where he throws himself to the ground and rolls round repeatedly.

Detective Constable van der Merwe also runs towards Zimmerman, but he starts running round in circles, inadvertently fanning the flames. Zimmerman yells at him, before grabbing him and throwing him to the ground. Zimmerman scrapes together some sand and heaps it on the residual flames on Van der Merwe's clothes.

Colonel Welman will later perish from his injuries.[38]

*

In Cape Town, Jimmy Mbane and Eric Maluleka are in the company of Captain William Liebenberg, Riaan Bellingan and Colonel Peters.

Liebenberg says there is a group of four trained ANC men who have been destabilising things. He reels off their MK names and hands over photographs of their faces. The photographs have the names of the men on the back. One of them is 'Mandela'.

Liebenberg tasks Mbane and Maluleka with infiltrating the group and finding out what they can about them. He says that the four can be found in Khayelitsha, and adds that they must first of all go to the chief in the area and ask for his permission. The chief will then take them to the four.[39]

*

At a press conference in Pretoria on 17 January, Neil van Heerden, the head of the Africa desk of South Africa's Department of Foreign Affairs, says that at that morning's meeting at the Union Buildings it was made 'very clear' to the Lesotho delegation that the 'pervasive' ANC presence in their country and consequent violence in South Africa was the 'root cause' of the border crisis.

He adds that it was also clearly communicated that Lesotho would need to address South Africa's security concerns before the situation could return to normal.

Van Heerden is asked if this means Pretoria is seeking a commitment from Maseru to 'eliminate' the ANC.

'Yes, in effect,' he replies, 'that is the bottom line.'

Three days later, South Africa's pressure, applied since the beginning of the year, helps engineer a coup. The Associated Press reports that Lesotho's '[a]rmed forces ousted Prime Minister Leabua Jonathan and installed their commander, Maj. Gen. Justin Lekhanya, as head of a ruling military council today' in a putsch that sparked 'wild rejoicing' as '[t]housands poured into Kingsway, Maseru's main street, chanting, ululating and waving bamboo fronds'.

Pretoria soon gets its quid pro quo. On the 25th, United Press International announces that South Africa has lifted its twenty-five-day blockade of Lesotho a few hours after the landlocked nation's freshly installed junta expelled the first 60 of an envisaged eventual total of 140 ANC members from its territory.[40]

*

Faced with a mass expulsion of cadres, the ANC opts, as it did at the time of the Nkomati Accord, to forward some combatants into South Africa.

Tony Yengeni is collected by a car in Lesotho with a man and woman inside. Yengeni boards and is driven in the direction of South Africa. Just before the border, Yengeni gets out alone, jumps the border fence, and meets the two on the other side. They then drive on the N1 highway towards Cape Town.

In Beaufort West they encounter a huge roadblock. All three are asked to get out of the vehicle and put their hands on the car.

They oblige.

They are questioned about where they are from and where they are going to. They are body-searched and the car is searched. Nothing is found (indeed, there is nothing to find because for security reasons Yengeni made a point of not carrying weapons on him during his infiltration).

The trio reach Cape Town in the evening, and Yengeni stays in KTC squatter camp.[41]

*

Lizo Bright Ngqungwana, MK's Western Cape commander, also arrives in Cape Town from Lesotho in January 1986.[42]

*

In Khayelitsha, the askaris Jimmy Mbane and Eric Maluleka meet Chief Yamile, the leader of a squatter camp. They show him that they have weapons, specifically an AK-47 and hand grenades, and they claim to be from exile.

He agrees to find them a place to stay.

A couple of days later, Chief Yamile meets Mbane and Maluleka again. Yamile says that some boy from exile has a problem with his AK.

Mbane asks him to bring the man.

Chief Yamile leaves and returns with the man, 'Chris Rastaman', to Mbane. 'Rastaman' says the problem is that the AK-47 is having trouble firing automatically and can only discharge single shots.

Mbane asks him where he got his training.

Locally, he says. The people who trained him gave him the AK-47.[43]

*

A few days later, Jimmy Mbane and Eric Maluleka are seated when 'Chris Rastaman' calls them aside. He tells them there is a Combi that travels daily from Montana to the police stations in Gugulethu and Manenberg. The vehicle is usually full of senior police officers.

Mbane says in response that they must reconnoitre that place first thing tomorrow morning.

On that following morning, the Combi traverses the same route as usual, and is full of officers.

After the morning's recce mission, Mbane telephones William Liebenberg and Riaan Bellingan and alerts them to what is brewing.[44]

*

On 18 February, Marion Sparg (who has joined the Special Operations Unit since her conversation with Reg September in March 1984 about joining MK) enters South Africa from Lesotho in the company of a man called Stephen Marais.

When stopped at roadblocks, they pose as a couple on holiday. Hidden in the door panels of their hired car are eight limpet mines and detonators.

The following day, in East London, Sparg places two limpet mines in the toilet at Cambridge Road Police Station.

Both explode.[45]

*

In Botswana a woman named Pamela holds a conversation with Obed Masina (the assassin of Detective Sergeant Orphan 'Hlubi' Chaphi in June 1978) and Frans Masango. She says that the 'army commissar' (Chris Hani) has given the instruction that the two men must return to South Africa and revive the assassination unit.

Carrying a landmine, hand grenades, AKs and a couple of pistols between them, Masango and Masina jump the fence near the Ramatlabama border post and enter South Africa. They then take public transport to Mamelodi.

In Mabopane, at a school known as 'TCE', they split up, with Masango departing in possession of the weapons.[46]

*

Johannes Mbelo is part of a police group positioned at the top of NY 2 Street in Gugulethu on the morning of 3 March.

About five streets away, Riaan Bellingan is in another police vehicle. Both are part of a number of vehicles stationed in strategic positions around the crossing in Gugulethu that Jimmy Mbane, Eric Maluleka and Chris Rastaman reconnoitred a few days previously. In all, there are about twenty armed policemen in various ambush positions.

The police van does its daily rounds carrying policemen from Montana to Gugulethu Police Station. But this time there is a difference. The van is packed with heavily armed policemen prepared to ambush any ambushers.

But there is no ambush. The bus reaches the intersection, crosses the bridge and heads to Gugulethu. Bellingan then receives a radioed message that the police bus has crossed the intersection without incident. Johannes Mbelo's group receives a message shortly afterwards that it can disperse.

Bellingan is in a Datsun driven by Sergeant Andrich Grobbelaar. Captain Charles Brazelle is in the passenger seat and Bellingan in the back. Following the issue of the call to disperse, they cross the NY 1 in the direction of Gugulethu Police Station.[47]

*

In the same area of Gugulethu that morning, Jimmy Mbane is driving a Nissan E20 minibus with eight passengers. They are on their way to conduct the ambush.

Eric Maluleka, the other askari, is one of them. The other seven are bona fide MK cadres. While driving, Mbane recognises a minivan that he knows belongs to the Vlakplaas unit.

Mbane stops and lets Eric Maluleka and one other passenger out. He tells them to go and fetch the AK-47s.

Mbane then continues with the van for a further 200–250 metres, where he drops another three off and gives them pistols and hand grenades.

He proceeds further and drops off another man.

This leaves three people in the vehicle: Mbane, Chris Rastaman and a third man. All are equipped with AK-47s.[48]

*

After leaving its ambush position following the call to disperse, the police Combi carrying Constable Johannes Mbelo approaches the intersection of NY 3 and NY 1. Mbelo sees men on the right-hand side.

He warns the other police vehicles over the radio: 'It seems as if these men are already here at this intersection.'

Bellingan's Datsun receives the message and heads back to the intersection. When they get there they see people wearing long coats. They turn right onto the NY 3. A short while later Bellingan spots Eric Maluleka standing on the left-hand side of the road and tells Grobbelaar to stop.

Bellingan asks Maluleka what is going on.

'Sergeant, watch out, they are in the area. I tried to keep some of the weapons and they are lying behind a bush.'

After conversing with Maluleka, Bellingan gets back in the Datsun, which makes a U-turn and travels back towards the NY 3/NY 1 intersection. When they get there they see black men on the road in front of them. The Datsun stops on the left-hand side.

Bellingan is in the process of getting out of the Datsun when he hears an explosion, followed by a number of shots. He holds his R1 rifle in front of him as he gets out. As he does so, however, his rifle is hit by a bullet and he falls into the back seat of the car. At that moment two shots come flying through the front windscreen. His eye starts bleeding slightly.

Bellingan gets out of the vehicle a second time and kneels beside it before trying to open fire. He is only able to discharge one shot, as his gun can't reload after being hit. Bellingan then runs towards the crossing.

As he does so he approaches the Nissan E20 being driven by Jimmy Mbane, which has returned to the intersection. Mbane stops, and as part of a prearranged plan, opens the door, jumps out, and runs to the back of the vehicle.

Somebody shouts, 'Shoot the tall man!' – referring to Mbane.

Bellingan responds in Afrikaans: 'Don't shoot the tall man. He is one of us.'

Mbane runs across the road and stops there.

He sees Bellingan open the passenger door. Mbane hears another shot, but can't tell from whom. He looks and sees Chris Rastaman falling on the other side of the tar road.[49]

*

In Johannesburg later that day, police commissioner-general Johan Coetzee releases a statement saying that following the receipt of information that the ANC was planning an attack on a police vehicle in Cape Town, precautionary measures were taken, with the result that 'At 7.20 am, near the Gugulethu police station, after the police had stopped a vehicle with black occupants, a skirmish between the police and ANC terrorists ensued, during which a grenade was hurled at the Police and they were fired on. In the clash seven ANC terrorists were killed.'[50]

*

At about 9 a.m. on the day after the ambush of the Gugulethu Seven, Marion Sparg applies for a gun licence at John Vorster Square Police Station in central Johannesburg. She then makes a detour to the stairway between the second and third floors, and places a limpet mine there.[51]

At midday the mine explodes, shattering windows up to the fourth floor, blowing a fifteen-foot hole in a wall, and scattering glass and rubble over a wide area.

Two people inside the building, both officers from the motor-vehicle theft unit, are injured, as well as two pedestrians who were walking outside the building.[52]

*

South Africa's state of emergency is lifted on 7 March 1986, three days after a speech in which P.W. Botha claimed that there had been a discernible drop in levels of violence in the country.[53]

*

On the same day, 7 March, policemen arrive at Marion Sparg's apartment. One of the officers says they have come to arrest her in connection with the bombing of police stations.

They search the premises and find three limpet mines.

While the search is in progress, Sparg casually says they have probably come about the Hillbrow bomb.

An alarmed policeman asks her where she placed that bomb.

She says inside a plastic bag in the toilets.

A team is sent to Hillbrow Police Station, where they perform a controlled detonation.[54]

*

On Friday 14 March, Frans Masango and Obed Masina wait in the yard of house number 18765 in Mamelodi East. The yard is covered with corrugated iron, broken bottles and empty tins, there to provide the house's security-obsessed occupant with an audible early warning of any intruders outside. There are also burglar bars on all the windows.

Close to midnight they hear a car arriving. It parks next to the house's door. Constable Senki Vuma gets out and enters the premises.

Masango watches Vuma through a small window that has burglar bars but no glass. Masango sees Vuma moving from the kitchen to the bedroom and then back to the fridge, which he opens before coming to the room whose window Masango is looking through. Vuma is carrying a bottle and a glass. He sits down.

Masango fires at Vuma through the window with an AK-47. Vuma hits a wall and falls on the floor. Masango fires till the whole room is so filled with pink smoke that he can no longer see his target.[55]

*

Moe Shaik is released from detention on 22 March 1986.[56]

Shortly afterwards he meets up with a security policeman who was present during the many rounds of severe torture that he received while incarcerated.

The man hands him a folder and says: 'Take this file; you've got two hours.'

Shaik has the police intelligence file photocopied and returns the folder containing it a couple of hours later. Shaik tells the policeman that he has copied the document.

That's okay, the man says.

If Shaik's informant is genuine then this would represent a significant penetration by the ANC of the Security Branch. Shaik later shows the copy to Billy Nair, formerly of the Natal Regional Command during the sabotage campaign. Shaik asks, 'What do you think?'

Nair says: 'Look, there's only one way out here. You've got to get to London, you've got to take this file to London and you've got to show them and if they confirm this then you're on to something. If not it could be a set-up.'[57]

*

Joseph Makhura, Neo Potsane, Justice Bizana and 'Rufus' enter South Africa from Botswana in March/April 1986. Their mission is to support Obed Masina and Frans Masango's assassination unit.[58]

*

The Transvaal Implementation Machinery meets in Swaziland (this machinery is a structure to coordinate the activities of the ANC's political and military, rural and urban structures for the Transvaal).

In attendance are Paul Dikeledi, who heads the Machinery, as well as Vusimusi Sindane, Acton Maseko and Glory Sedibe (alias 'September'). Since participating as a member of the Transvaal Rural Machinery in the failed mission to Venda in December 1978, Sedibe has filled a number of senior roles in MK Transvaal structures, including head of the Rural Machinery and head of Military Intelligence.[59]

Dikeledi has received an order from ANC headquarters in Lusaka that the Swaziland Regional Politico-Military Committee (RPMC) and the Transvaal and Natal Implementation Machineries (which are subordinate to the Swaziland RPMC) must commence landmine warfare.

Dikeledi takes Sedibe aside. He suggests that Sedibe's structure (responsible for rural operations in the Transvaal) commences military operations in compliance with the directive.[60]

Following this meeting, Acton Maseko meets Simon Dladla and tells him to identify potential targets for mine warfare on white farms in the eastern Transvaal.

Dladla and Maseko enter South Africa shortly afterwards to reconnoitre the Breyten and Volksrust areas.[61]

*

On 18 April, in the vicinity of Crossroads township, MK Western Cape commander Lizo Bright Ngqungwana gives Quentin Michels two bags containing altogether seven limpet mines and twelve hand grenades.

Ngqungwana instructs Michels to go and identify hideouts to be used to accommodate Michels himself and to store the weapons.

Michels takes the equipment home.[62]

*

At about 7 p.m. that evening, Phumzile Mayapi and Ndibulele Ndzamela exit a vehicle parked outside the Wild Coast Casino hotel in Bizana in the Transkei. They are under orders from Mzizi Maqhekeza, who participated in the operation on Umtata's electrical power station on 25 June the previous year, to attack the casino to make MK's presence in the area known to the local population.

Mayapi and Ndzamela enter the casino foyer, each with a limpet mine and a pistol concealed on their persons. Ndzamela heads to the men's toilets in Pebbles Restaurant. He places his mine under a sewerage pipe attached to one of the toilets. He returns to Mayapi and tells him where he placed the mine. Mayapi then proceeds to place his mine on top of Ndzamela's. When he returns, the two head for their getaway vehicle.[63]

At 9.45 p.m., Yaseen Khan enters the casino and is walking near Pebbles Restaurant when he hears a loud explosion from behind. He turns and sees a man who looks to be in his thirties covered in blood. Realising that a bomb has exploded, Khan flees the building. Don Fisher, meanwhile, is one of many who abandon their cash in the one-arm bandit machines and their chips on the gambling tables and flee for the exit. In the foyer he sees a bloodied white woman and a black boy staggering out of Pebbles Restaurant. There is another unconscious man who is being treated by a doctor.

Not all patrons have followed him. In an extraordinary exhibit of human behaviour, many, seemingly mesmerised, continue playing on the machines even after repeated calls to evacuate the building are issued over the casino's loudspeakers. It takes a while for security personnel to prise them away from the machines and seal off the premises.

In this attack two people lose their lives, namely Thomas Hudson, in his fifties, and twelve-year-old Bhekinkosi Ntakana, the wounded boy seen by Fisher.[64]

*

At midday two days later, Quentin Michels arrives at Cecil Esau's home in Cape Town's Wynberg suburb. Michels hands over the two bags given to him by Lizo Bright Ngqungwana containing the limpet mines and hand grenades and tells Esau to give them to Ashley Forbes.[65]

*

At approximately 8 a.m. on 21 April, on a dirt road between the towns of Chrissies-meer and Breyten some 110 miles east of Johannesburg, Ben Ndluli is driving a taxi with two passengers inside when an explosion suddenly occurs under the vehicle.

Ndluli is badly lacerated and Jan Moshuloane, one of the passengers, has part of a leg blown away.

About three hours later at the farm Vlakfontein, a few kilometres from the scene of the first incident, Simon Makwanazi is driving a tractor about 100 metres from a farmhouse when his vehicle detonates a landmine. Makwanazi receives injuries to his right leg, face and an eye, and two passengers in an attached trailer, Piet Sibanyoni and his son Stoel Sibanyoni, are seriously injured.[66]

*

On the evening of 22–23 April, Lizo Bright Ngqungwana is asleep in a three-roomed hut – two at the front, one at the back – in Crossroads. With him in the bed are his girlfriend and their seven-week-old child.

At around 2 a.m. Ngqungwana sees car lights flickering through the window. The lights silhouette the frame of a person standing outside the house. Ngqungwana stands and watches.

Sergeant Riaan Bellingan, still on his secondment to the Security Branch in Cape Town, is part of a team of fourteen security policemen who then storm the premises. As they do so they train their torches on Ngqungwana, who is now sitting on the bed with his hand under a pillow.

The police hear a click as Ngqungwana opens the safety pin of his Makarov, but they arrest him before he can make any further moves. They retrieve the Makarov from him.

At dawn, Ngqungwana is taken to Gugulethu Police Station in Loop Street.

During an extremely violent interrogation he is repeatedly accused of being MK's Western Cape commander and consistently denies it.

Eventually, Ngqungwana is shown a picture of himself from the police's 'terror album', an earlier version of which had been shown to Thandi Modise during her interrogation. It proves the tipping point in the questioning.

He is asked again when he came in.

He says June last year.

At 7 p.m. that evening, Quentin Michels is arrested at his home and brought out to a waiting police van. Ngqungwana, who is in the vehicle, is asked to confirm if it is Michels.[67]

*

Shirley Gunn, who was recruited into MK in 1984 by Leon Meyer (killed in the Maseru raid in December), enters Botswana hidden under a load of cabbages before being transported to a safe house.

A while later, in this hideout, she meets an ANC contact whose first question is 'Who are you following?'

'I am not following anyone. I am here for military training. Take me where I must be.'

Momentarily taken aback by the insubordination, the man composes himself and says: 'You know where you have to start. You must write your biography.'

She does so, hands him the document, and then he leaves.

A couple of days later he returns and escorts her to another ANC safe house.[68]

*

Sergeant Richard Nxumalo and Detective Constable Dorasamy are driving along a deserted dirt road in Natal's Edendale district on the evening of 27 April.

They see a Ford Granada, registered NP 86602, parked on the other side of the road. They see the backs of two men, who are standing by the boot, which is open.

Nxumalo orders Dorasamy to pull up. Upon seeing the police, one of the men, Gordon Webster, closes the boot.

Asked to open it, Webster says he doesn't have the key.

Dorasamy radios to check if the Granada is stolen, while Nxumalo inspects the vehicle using the police car's headlamps for illumination.

Lying on the ground by the boot he notices a brown leather bag and sees it contains several clips of ammunition.

Nxumalo draws his revolver and tells Webster and his colleague, Bheki Ngubane, to lie on the ground, face down.

As Dorasamy radios for help, Webster and Ngubane make a run for it in separate directions. Webster runs towards a barbed-wire fence while Ngubane flees across the road.

Webster's spectacles fall and he stumbles. Nxumalo orders him to stop. Webster ignores the call, after which Nxumalo fires several shots. Three of them hit Webster – two on his body, one on his right hand. Webster continues running for a while before crashing into the fence, falling over it, and tumbling on the other side.

Webster hears several more shots fired at Bheki Ngubane, who falls dead on the gravel verge on the edge of the dirt road.

Webster is taken to the second floor of Edendale Hospital's intensive care unit, where he is placed in a bed directly opposite the door.[69]

*

On 29 April, Robert McBride's father Derrick sees his son reading a newspaper in the takeaway attached to the family's Factorama workshop in Wentworth.

Robert McBride mentions 'Steve Mkhize', who according to the report was injured by the police in an incident related to the ANC, during which somebody died. He says Steve Mkhize is somebody he knows.[70]

*

On 2 May, Robert McBride visits Antonio du Preez, a twenty-two-year-old political activist in the Wentworth area.

McBride says a friend of his has been shot and is in hospital. The latest he has heard is that somebody is trying to kill him. The friend has undergone an operation and is in the intensive care unit. McBride says he wants to save his friend and would like Du Preez to help.[71]

*

At about 4.20 p.m. two days later, Derrick McBride is present alongside Matthew le Cordier, Antonio du Preez, Greta Apelgren and Welcome Khumalo at the Factorama workshop. Robert McBride addresses the group. There is a piece of cardboard on the wall featuring a hand-drawn street map.

'There is no need to make an introduction, we know all of us for what purpose or reason we are all here,' Robert McBride says. He points to the map and says, 'This is the Edendale Hospital.'[72]

*

After cutting a hole in the perimeter fence at Edendale Hospital that evening, Robert McBride takes an AK-47 and a doctor's coat from a bag. He puts the coat on and places the AK under his arm. He tells Le Cordier to enlarge the hole while he and his father are in the hospital.

Antonio du Preez and Le Cordier then each take an AK-47 and wait by the bakkie that the group arrived in (Apelgren and Khumalo are elsewhere with orders to create an incident that will divert the police). Derrick McBride enters the gap in the fence first, followed by his son.

When the McBrides enter the hospital building Robert looks at his watch. It is 8.30 p.m.

As they approach the second floor via the stairs, Robert McBride sends his father to scout the route ahead. He tells him to turn left once he is in the ward and then left in the corridor. The bed is directly opposite the door of the ward.

Derrick McBride follows the instructions, but sees many civilians as well as some black policemen, so he retraces his steps. He returns to his son at the top of the stairs and says, 'Abort. Civilians.' They make to withdraw, but then Robert McBride says he wants to see who these civilians are.

Constable Edward Ngcobo is leaving Ward 2R when he sees two men approaching. The older is dressed in grey trousers and a grey jacket, the younger in a doctor's coat. As soon as they catch Ngcobo's eye they about-face and walk in the direction they came.

Ngcobo meets up with police colleagues and tells them the way those guys turned round was suspicious. He says he is going to see where they have gone.

Ngcobo has a pistol in his possession as he approaches the McBrides.

Realising he is being followed, Robert McBride takes his AK, which is half extended out of his coat, slips it off safety and onto automatic, and fires in front of him. Derrick McBride looks behind and sees the policeman running away to the right of the corridor.

From his bed, Gordon Webster hears the fire from the AK. He also hears a single shot from a pistol.

Robert McBride is about one or two steps down the stairway when he turns and says to his father, referring to the policeman: 'He's gone. Stay here and see that he doesn't come back.'[73]

*

The door bursts open in Gordon Webster's ward.

'Humphrey, Humphrey!' Robert McBride says, looking at bed number 4 which stands directly opposite the door. It is empty.

Gordon Webster, who has been moved, has a white policeman next to him who draws a revolver and shoots at McBride, who turns round and returns the fire, striking the policeman in the arm. The policeman runs into an adjacent room. The policeman fires another shot through the closed door.

Now McBride sees Webster and approaches his bed. He tells Webster to stand up. Webster can't. McBride pulls the drip and transfusion from the apparatus on which it is fixed. McBride asks a nurse conveying linen to give him the trolley.

The nurse is hysterical – screaming, shouting and holding her head.

'Keep quiet, keep quiet, keep quiet,' McBride repeats.

There is a basket on the trolley, and McBride lifts Webster and puts him on the basket. Webster takes the AK-47 from McBride. This enables McBride to push the trolley with both hands.

As he pushes the trolley through the door of the ward and into the passage, there are scenes of chaos, with people running in all directions screaming. Webster fires a salvo into the ceiling.

McBride tells him: 'Stop! Let's get out of here.'

When they reach the stairs and try to go downstairs, the basket slides off the end of the trolley and Webster falls out. McBride picks him up and returns him to the trolley. Further down, Webster falls again, and has to crawl down the last couple of stairs himself. At the bottom, McBride puts Webster on another trolley and places the AK-47 on the lower level. With the help of his father he wheels Webster to the fence.

Matthew le Cordier and Antonio du Preez see the McBrides pushing a man on a trolley towards them. Robert McBride calls out to Le Cordier to come help carry 'Steve' off the trolley and put him on the back of the bakkie.

Le Cordier notices that Gordon Wester is holding an AK-47 and that he has some plaster on his stomach with a small piece of pipe sticking out.

With the trolley remaining on the other side of the fence, Le Cordier helps pull Webster through.

Robert McBride drives with his father in the front, while Du Preez and Le Cordier are in the back with Webster, who is naked on this freezing winter night. Du Preez and Le Cordier give Webster their jackets.

Word has somehow spread. As the bakkie makes off, there are people shouting their approval in the surrounding areas. Nurses are shouting 'Viva ANC!' and 'Amandla!' from the hospital. Others in the hospital give the men a round of applause.[74]

*

At Factorama, Robert McBride enters the workshop first. He places a mattress on the floor and lies Webster on it. Webster is feeling extremely cold, so McBride puts a tracksuit on him and gives him a massage.

A nurse, Pam Cele, comes to assist Webster. She is assisted by Webster's brother, Trevor, in helping him recover.[75]

*

On Friday 9 May, Robert McBride and Greta Apelgren get in the front of an ash-grey Ford bakkie, registered NPS 20454, while Gordon Webster and his girlfriend climb into an attached caravan.

The group spends the night in Van Reenen, and the following day they cross into Botswana, with Webster and his girlfriend hidden in the caravan.[76]

*

The ANC's NEC convenes just before the middle of 1986. On the agenda is the matter of what progress has been made in implementing the Kabwe Conference's recommendation that senior members be sent into the country to provide leadership of the mass movement. This is not the first follow-up since the conference, and again there is little progress to report.

During the tea break, Mac Maharaj and Joe Slovo converse.

'Look JS, you know that I think the problem here is that – and everybody is saying that this is the usual thing – you know the problem here is this: we are not making headway because this is a sensitive task.'

'Ja, ja.'

'No, I am thinking differently.'

Maharaj expands, but Slovo is evidently not wholly persuaded.[77]

Maharaj then goes to Chris Hani.

'Chris, the problem is simple. This is a 30-odd person National Executive. How to take this decision is really the problem, how to implement it.'

'What are you saying?'

'I am saying, let's adopt it, move a resolution empowering the president to be in charge of that area of the work and not to disclose details before us.'

'I think you are right,' Hani says.

Maharaj and Hani then walk over to Jacob Zuma. They have a discussion with him. Then all three proceed to Oliver Tambo.

Tambo says, 'Okay chaps, when we resume the meeting after tea break, will you re-raise the matter? Although we have just concluded that agenda item I will re-open it.'

The meeting reassembles. Chris Hani stands up and proposes that there should be an operation involving sending the leaders of the movement – including members of the NEC – home, and that Oliver Tambo should be in sole charge of the project.[78]

*

The meeting adopts a resolution establishing a special committee comprising Tambo and Joe Slovo to take charge of the mission of sending senior members of the movement into the country. Tambo and Slovo are empowered to conduct the work without reporting to the NEC unless they wish to do so.

'Are you people aware of the powers that you are giving me?' Tambo asks those congregated.

Somebody responds, 'Yes, we're giving you these powers because of the highly secret nature of this operation.'

'I want the meeting to be very clear, I don't want anybody to come to me and say that you gave the president powers which you did not understand.' Tambo then starts jabbing his finger randomly at people in the room: 'You, it means I can send you and you have no reason to refuse my orders and I can put restrictions where you are not to tell a single other member what you are doing.'

Mac Maharaj interjects: 'Look this is a very sensitive task and I think it should be left to volunteers: nobody should feel pressured ...'

'No, no way,' Tambo says.[79]

∗

On 16 May, the Commonwealth Eminent Persons Group (EPG), consisting of its co-chairmen, Malcolm Fraser of Australia and Olusegun Obasanjo of Nigeria, along with members Lord Barber, Nita Barrow, John Malecela, Swaran Singh and Edward Scott, is allowed by the South African government (which agreed in December 1985 to cooperate with the peace initiative that the Commonwealth had launched two months previously) to visit Nelson Mandela in Pollsmoor Prison.

The EPG discuss with Mandela a paper that they have developed, titled 'A Possible Negotiating Concept'. It details actions that might be taken to ensure negotiations and break the cycle of violence. Specifically, it calls on the government to end martial law in the townships, release Mandela and other political prisoners, and unban the ANC, which for its part is urged to suspend its armed struggle.

Mandela tells them he has no problem accepting the document as a starting point, but he emphasises that he is responding as an individual. He says it is important to have the ANC's reaction, and he adds that in order for him to arrive at a more considered view, arrangements must be made for him to consult with his colleagues in Pollsmoor and on Robben Island, as well as with other influential figures within South Africa. The ANC in Lusaka would want to take these internal views into account.

On the following day the EPG fly to Lusaka where they meet Oliver Tambo.

Tambo also says he can't give a considered response to the document until he has had a chance to consult within the movement, but he adds that in so far as it is in line with the principles and requirements of the Nassau Accord, his initial feeling is that it will command the ANC's support.

At the very end of the meeting Tambo says that he and his colleagues will require about ten days for consultations before giving a firm answer.[80]

∗

In Gaborone's Mogoditshane suburb two days later, when a Batswana student leaves his house for a jog at about 6 a.m., he notices six helicopters circling overhead.

One remains above and drops pamphlets. They are addressed to Botswana Defence Force soldiers. They read: 'We have no fight with you. For your own safety, please do not interfere. Our only objective is to eliminate these ANC gangsters.'

Five helicopters land, two of them about 500 metres from a complex of houses.

A number of heavily armed troops disembark and march to a compound which they spray with bullets before retreating to the helicopters.

The Inter Press Service announces later in the day that the attack in Botswana was accompanied by others in Zambia and Zimbabwe. It says that in Harare an ANC office was bombed and the house of a refugee razed, and that a South African government statement is claiming that a property belonging to the ANC's Department of Information and Publicity in Makena, some nine miles south-west of Lusaka, was also hit.

President Kenneth Kaunda is quoted saying that the planes actually hit a refugee camp on Lusaka's southern outskirts, killing a Namibian refugee and a Zambian civilian, and wounding eight to ten others.[81]

*

The Commonwealth Eminent Persons Group meets with members of the South African government's Cabinet Constitutional Committee, which includes Louis le Grange and F.W. de Klerk, on the same day as the raids in Zambia, Zimbabwe and Botswana.

Chris Heunis, the minister of constitutional development and planning, says that in any negotiating situation there will be many negotiating parties, but the South African government can't be treated as just another negotiator. It represents the state and it would have to endorse any proposals issuing from talks.

The government would also be guided by the president's pronouncements on conditions for talks. Heunis proceeds to enumerate them: central is the creation of an atmosphere of non-violence, and an essential aspect thereof is a renunciation of violence, especially by the ANC. The state president specifically used the phrase 'suspension of violence' in his first letter to the Commonwealth group, Heunis reminds the EPG. This has to be interpreted – not in a temporary sense – but as a public commitment to reject violence as a means of obtaining political goals.

Heunis says there will have to be a visible reduction in violence before the government can respond to the negotiating concept. The government has proved its commitment to political reforms, he says; now the onus is on the other side.[82]

These preconditions cannot be reconciled with the ANC's as stated in its 'Submission on the Question of Negotiations' (27 November 1985), and the events of 19 May throughout the region scupper the EPG initiative.

*

Pieter Jacobs meets an acquaintance, Donovan Jergens, in Cape Town on 21 May and asks him to assist in getting to Queenstown the following day. Jergens agrees and they decide to meet at Landsdowne Railway Station.

On the 22nd, Jergens and Jacobs meet at the station as arranged. From there Jergens drives to Wetton Circle, where they pick up Ashley Forbes, who like Jacobs is seeking to leave the country to escape the wave of arrests following the capture of Lizo Bright Ngqungwana and the leader of their cell, Quentin Michels, in April.

Forbes is in the company of another man named Mark Henry. Jergens then transports Forbes, Henry and Jacobs to Queenstown.[83]

*

In Mamelodi, Frans Masango reads a pamphlet issued in the name of the main opposition party in KaNgwane. It apparently originates from one of the Bantustan's key politicians, David Lukhele.

The pamphlet states, among other things, that KaNgwane ought to be incorporated into Swaziland. It also endorses the continued detention of youths in the area till the incorporation is achieved.

Masango shows this document to other members of his underground unit (Joseph Makhura, Obed Masina, Neo Potsane, Justice Bizana and 'Rufus'). He suggests they do something about it.[84]

*

In Lusaka, MK cadre Fani Basil Msibi is briefed by Thami Zulu about the situation in Natal.

Zulu says basically all activities at present are concentrated in the southern part of the province, while the ANC is doing nothing to impact on the struggles waged by the people in the north. He briefs Msibi to return to northern Natal to achieve the political objective of increasing ANC activity there. First go to the area, Zulu says, and provide a thorough analysis of it politically, militarily and socio-economically.[85]

*

In May 1986, Mtheteleli Titana, Bongani Jonas and two other MK members illegally enter South Africa from Botswana to reinforce the ANC's Western Cape military structure.[86]

During the following month, Mxolisi Petane likewise enters South Africa to augment MK in the Western Cape. Petane has been deployed to serve as the regional structure's political commissar. He settles in KTC squatter camp.[87]

*

General Johan van der Merwe, the head of South Africa's Security Branch, attends a meeting at which General Ignatius Coetzee, Brigadier Schoon, and Colonels Eugene de Kock and Lodewyk de Jager are present. They discuss the 'September Machinery', responsible for rural operations including the landmine attack in Breyten on 21 April, under the Swaziland-based Transvaal Implementation Machinery.

Van der Merwe says he agrees, under the circumstances they have described, that it is both necessary and advisable that Glory Sedibe and as many other members as possible of the September Machinery be eliminated.

In the early hours of 4–5 June, a five-vehicle convoy containing South African security-force men travels the twenty kilometres between the KwaLoseni Hotel and an underground safe house in Fountains, Mbabane.

About 500 metres from the house, the vehicles stop. Willem Coetzee, Eugene de Kock, Anton Pretorius, Lodewyk de Jager, Paul van Dyk and Douw Willemse are walked by an agent codenamed 'SWT180' to the house. According to the agent's information, the house is used by the September Machinery. The policemen take up position by a wall close to the front door while 'SWT180', who is a courier for the September Machinery, knocks.

Someone speaks from inside the house, and then a key turns in the lock. As soon as the door is open, De Kock and De Jager storm in, followed by Van Dyk.

De Kock fires immediately on Sipho Dlamini, the man who opened the door, killing him instantly. There are no lights in the house, so for illumination the raiders use the torches attached to their firearms.

From one of the bedrooms, a woman tries to run past them into the lounge. De Jager fires and kills her. She is Busi Majola, alias 'Mzala'.

'Pantsu' is then also mortally wounded.

With the raid complete, 'SWT180' enters the house and performs identifications of the dead while Colonel Pretorius takes photos of the deceased and their weapons.[88]

*

Neo Potsane and Obed Masina head in an Audi to house 10509 in Mamelodi East on 6 June. Potsane has an AK-47, while Masina carries a pistol and a grenade.

They wait in the car for about fifteen minutes, because there are a lot of people at the house. At about 7 p.m., when most of the people are gone, Potsane knocks on the door.

David Lukhele opens and asks if he can help.

Potsane says he has been sent by a man in Mamelodi East.

Lukhele replies that he first wants to listen to the news. He nonetheless invites Potsane, who is dressed in a brown polo neck and blue jacket, to enter. Potsane steps inside. Lukhele's wife is in the room, along with another woman named Elizabeth Dludlu.

Just before Potsane reaches the stool in the corner, he pulls the AK-47 out from his jacket, turns round and shoots David Lukhele, who has a one-year-old child standing next to him. Lukhele falls. Potsane carries on firing. In the course of the shooting, Elizabeth Dludlu, who is sitting on a bench near the door, jumps up and falls on David Lukhele, only to be hit herself.

Potsane walks out of the front door. He meets with Obed Masina and they flee in the getaway car.[89]

*

On the following day, Robert McBride and Greta Apelgren arrive at the Oasis Motel in Gaborone in their grey Ford bakkie.

One evening while they are there, Aboobaker Ismail arrives and has a private discussion with McBride in a bedroom. Before talking, Ismail sweeps the room for bugging devices and turns on the air conditioner.

McBride outlines the reconnaissance previously conducted by Gordon Webster for a possible attack on the SADF Natal Command's military base on Durban's

Marine Parade. McBride says he has conducted further reconnaissance himself, but the problem is that under all scenarios civilians will be hurt.

Ismail reminds McBride that at the Kabwe Conference the movement endorsed a change of policy, and that it would not be as cautious as before in going after security-force personnel. Injuries to civilians are a secondary consideration at this stage; the main consideration is to hunt security personnel whether they are on or off duty. The only qualification is that there should be absolutely no chance of children being killed.

After the meeting, McBride returns to Greta Apelgren. He tells her that he and Ismail discussed carrying out a car bomb attack in the Durban area on the weekend before 16 June.[90]

*

Simon Dladla enters South Africa on 8 June 1986 in a beige Datsun registered SD 314.

Two days later, he and Acton Maseko plant a mine on the dirt road near Bloemhof farm in the Volksrust district, where the south-east of the Transvaal and north-western Natal meet.

They return to Swaziland in the Datsun to report to the Transvaal Implementation Machinery.

At about 7.20 a.m. the same day, 10 June, eighteen-year-old Martin Coetzer is on his way to school in a bakkie when, about a metre from the gate to his parents' farm, there is an explosion under the vehicle.

He is thrown in the air by the impact. Both his legs, his right arm and his jaw are broken, and he also suffers a skull fracture.

Then, at about 10.15 a.m., farmworkers Elias Shabangu (aged twenty-three) and Lucas Lushaba (twenty-five) are driving a tractor on a dirt road on another plot in the area when they detonate a landmine, causing them chest and leg injuries.[91]

*

Before a joint sitting of the three segregated houses of the South African Parliament on 12 June, four days before the tenth anniversary of the Soweto uprising, President Botha says: 'The government has intelligence regarding plans which have been made by radical and revolutionary elements for the coming days, which pose real dangers for all population groups in the country.'

He adds: 'Because I am of the opinion that the ordinary laws of the land are inadequate to enable the government to ensure the security of the public and to maintain public order, I have decided to declare a national state of emergency.' He acknowledges that his re-imposition of martial law is likely to 'elicit strong criticism and even punitive measures from the outside world' – a reference to the possibility of sanctions.[92]

*

Robert McBride and Greta Apelgren return to Wentworth from Botswana on the 13th, and go to the Apelgren family home. Penelope Apelgren, Greta's sister, tells McBride that a new state of emergency has been imposed nationwide. She says, shaking while speaking, that many people have been arrested including her sister Jeanette and brother Eric. When Jeanette was detained, she continues, the police entered the house brandishing firearms and pointing them at people. When they saw Diakonia Council of Churches pictures on the wall they said, 'We feel like shooting everyone in this house.'

McBride himself reads newspaper reports that many people have already been killed in the first hours of the emergency.[93]

*

At 7 p.m. the following day, 14 June, the one-year anniversary of the Gaborone raid, Robert McBride shows up at the house of Matthew le Cordier, who says he is not ready.

McBride tells him not to worry; he can come in the clothes he is wearing.[94]

Just before reaching Magoo's Bar on Durban's Marine Parade that evening, McBride flashes the lights of the blue Ford Cortina he is driving.

After he does so, Greta Apelgren drives a greenish-brown Mazda out of a parking space. McBride parks the Cortina in the vacated spot. Matthew le Cordier is in the passenger seat.

There are fifty kilograms of explosives in the boot. A limpet mine has been placed at their centre to set them off. A cord that is concealed under a blanket leads through the armrest into the boot.

McBride pulls the black cord. At its end is a round metal pin. He shows it to Le Cordier and says the cord leads to the limpet mine in the boot. McBride pulls the pin out. He and Le Cordier wait for two minutes and then leave the car, walking slowly.

At the next turnoff both men get into Apelgren's Mazda, which is waiting there for them.

The Cortina has been parked just outside one of Durban's most popular nightspots. On the adjacent block there is Magoo's Bar, the Why Not Bar, Garfunkel's Restaurant, the Parade Hotel and the Easy Beat Bar at the Empress Hotel. All are packed with Saturday-night revellers.

Just under fifteen minutes later, Russell Davidson, the owner of the Parade Hotel, exits the Why Not Bar and walks into the hotel's foyer. He buys two cold drinks and puts them down on the counter. He is standing next to his manageress. Suddenly he sees a white light. He grabs the manageress and pulls her down to the ground. The light turns yellow, and then orange. For a moment there is complete silence.

Rita Edson, who is walking her dog along the street, sees a blinding flash and the ground shakes under her. She looks to the entrance of Garfunkel's. Two people stagger out, one a white man with blood all over his shirt and the other an Indian woman with numerous cuts on her face. There is glass everywhere.

Three women, namely Angelique Pattinden, Michelle Gerrard and Julie van der Linde, are killed by the blast.[95]

*

Simon Dladla drives a green BMW registered SD 026 legally through an official South Africa–Swaziland border post on 19 June, while Michael Roller Molapo, aka 'Clement', and Acton Maseko, equipped with hand grenades, limpet mines, AK-47 rifles, an RPG launcher and rockets, jump the border fence. Dladla picks them up on the other side and transports them further into the country.

On the evening of 22 June, Dladla and Maseko are travelling back to Swaziland from Johannesburg in the same BMW. In the vehicle are two other MK cadres.

The vehicle is stopped at a roadblock in Edenvale. The police constable who arrives at the car notices a strange-looking object in Maseko's overalls.

Maseko refuses to allow himself to be searched when asked by a policeman. A struggle ensues. The policemen prevail. A hand grenade and Makarov pistol are found in Maseko's possession.

All four men in the vehicle are arrested.[96]

*

Shortly after midnight on 5 July, six men of the East Rand Administration Board are patrolling in Vosloorus township when a white Cressida with three men inside drives past. Michael Molapo, aka 'Clement', infiltrated on 19 June in Simon Dladla and Acton Maseko's company, opens fire on them from the car with an AK-47. Two policemen are killed and three wounded.

Ninety minutes later, in the Ncala Section of Katlehong in Germiston, the Cressida passes a group of board officials standing beside their official vehicles. Molapo again opens fire, killing three and wounding nine.

At 4 a.m. a police patrol in Katlehong spots the Cressida and gives chase. A gun battle ensues, in which two of the men in the Cressida are killed. Molapo, however, is not one of them. He manages to escape.[97]

*

In July 1986 in the Western Cape, Niklo Pedro, Ashley Kriel's friend, recruits Clement Baatjies into a cell referred to as the 'Mobile Unit'.

Then, on 16 July, Pedro recruits Anwa Dramat into the MK underground.[98]

*

At 6 a.m. the following morning, Robert McBride gets up in the sitting room of a house in the Alra Park section of Nigel, south-east of Johannesburg, belonging to his brother, Leslie. He opens the door, only to shut it when he sees a policeman facing him.

Greta Apelgren peers through the curtains. Dawn is breaking. There are uniformed policemen in the yard, in the road and on the rooftops.

'Open up, police!' comes the call from outside.

Robert McBride opens the front door and sees a police captain standing there with a rifle trained directly at him. He and Greta Apelgren are arrested.

Matthew le Cordier is arrested at his home two days later.[99]

*

On the following day, 20 July, Michael 'Clement' Molapo's killing spree continues when he shoots a black policeman dead and wounds a black female informer in Katlehong's Ncala Section.[100]

*

Mxolisi Petane, the political commissar of MK's Western Cape Machinery, parks a stolen car in the disabled bay near the entrance of the Dion shopping centre in Parow on 25 July.

When Petane departs, he makes sure that the vehicle's windows are open, and that on the back seat, clearly visible to passers-by, is a landmine which he has placed alongside two gas cylinders. Petane also leaves an open coffee tin inside the vehicle. He starts a fire in the tin by embedding a flashlight filament in a quantity of potassium chlorate. The aim of the operation is to announce MK's presence in the Western Cape region rather than to cause any great damage.

At around 4 p.m. Anton van den Berg, a civilian, sees smoke emanating from the car. From one of the vehicle's open windows he withdraws a coffee tin and finds that besides the flashlight filament and the potassium, it also contains TNT and a hand grenade. He closes the tin with its lid which Petane left on a seat in the car.

Van den Berg then heads off to contact the police.[101]

*

The following day, Michael 'Clement' Molapo is shot dead by South African policemen. An AK-47, a missile launcher and ammunition are found in his possession.[102]

*

On 13 August 1986, Eugene de Kock tells the askari Almond Nofamela he has information that a highly placed ANC official by the name of 'September' has been arrested by the Swazi Police and is in custody there. It has been arranged that they will kidnap him and bring him to South Africa. He tells Nofamela to go and get one of his false passports.

Later that day, De Kock and Nofamela are joined by Lieutenant Paul van Dyk and two askaris, Warrant Officer Johannes Koole and Aubrey Mngade, and they travel to Swaziland. They have firearms concealed in various parts of the vehicle.

Later that evening, the Vlakplaas group meet security policemen Christo Deetlefs and Frederik Pienaar at a hotel in Swaziland. Deetlefs tells the group that as part of a routine visit to Swaziland that day, he visited the head office of the Swazi Police. He spoke with the head of police and the police commissioner and learnt that the Swazi Police apprehended Glory Sedibe the day before. Sedibe was part of a group that had illegally entered Swaziland, and is being held at Mankanyane Police Station prior to being deported to Zambia shortly.[103]

Around midnight, the South African policemen travel to the outskirts of Manzini. When they reach Mankanyane Police Station they park their vehicles on high ground overlooking the western side of the station. The cars are some eighty to ninety metres from the station entrance. De Kock then leads the three askaris (Koole, Nofamela and Mngade) down to the station. Following them is Paul van Dyk, and behind him are the other white members.

De Kock tries to open the door to the charge office but finds it locked. He can see a dim light reflecting out of the corridor beyond the charge office. The policemen also notice that the window of one of the offices is not sealed properly. De Kock takes his close combat knife and puts it in the seal as a wedge to open the catch.

De Kock enters through the window, followed by Nofamela. As De Kock reaches the corridor, he bumps into a young police officer who aims a G3 assault rifle at him. The barrel is about a metre from De Kock, who in turn aims his pistol, fitted with a silencer, at the man.

De Kock notices that the Swazi policeman's rifle is still on safety, giving De Kock a decisive advantage in the event of a shootout. De Kock uses this advantage to persuade the man to put his gun down. He then cuts the station's telephone wires and asks the Swazi policeman where his colleagues are.

The Swazi policeman calls out, and an older, senior Swazi policeman arrives from the charge office.

De Kock walks down the corridor after the young Swazi police officer. He is carrying the policeman's G3 rifle.

'September!' De Kock shouts.

A voice answers from a cell.

De Kock asks the older Swazi policeman for the keys. He hands them over and De Kock opens the cell. He sees three men, one of whom is well built and over six foot tall.

'Are you September?' De Kock asks.

'Yes,' says the man.

De Kock turns to the other inmates and asks what they are there for. When they say stock theft, he chases them out, saying, 'Go.'

When Frederik Pienaar enters the cell he says triumphantly: 'Yes, Glory, you thought I would not find you but now today the Boere have you.'

Van Dyk orders Sedibe to lie down on the floor. Sedibe does so. Van Dyk then calls Koole, who helps him drag Sedibe out of the cell. The two Swazi policemen are then locked inside the cell.

Outside the building, Sedibe manages to free himself momentarily from the clutches of Van Dyk and Koole. In the ensuing scuffle a tie or scarf is placed round Sedibe's neck, after which Van Dyk hits him on the lower part of his body. Other members of the group come to help Van Dyk and Koole. Eventually Sedibe is overpowered by four men. In the process, Sedibe receives injuries including deep scratches on his nose.

Sedibe is loaded into one of the vehicles, which then depart, with Van Dyk driving. De Kock and Nofamela are in the back with Sedibe. As they drive away, De Kock interrogates Sedibe about ANC activities in Mozambique, while periodically beating him on the stomach and chest.

Sedibe says he was alone in Mozambique.

'September, I don't believe you,' De Kock says, giving specific names and places. Sedibe continues to maintain that he was alone at those times.

As the interrogation and beatings continue, however, he admits to an increasing number of details put to him by De Kock.[104]

*

A couple of days later, a bakkie with a canopy arrives at a police safe house near Piet Retief. There are a number of corpses in the vehicle following an ambush earlier that evening near the Nerston border post. The attack was undertaken by a security police unit including Eugene de Kock, Christo Deetlefs, Eugene Fourie and Frans Labuschagne. Among the dead is the source – an ANC courier turned informer who had outlived his usefulness to the Security Branch. He was driving the bakkie at the time of the attack.

Glory Sedibe (who was not the source of the information leading to the attack) is brought from his holding cell to identify the bodies. He manages to identify two.[105]

*

Thuso Tshika, who escaped South Africa during the arrests following the demise of Operation Butterfly, has a meeting in Swaziland with Edward Lawrence and Charles Ndaba of MK's Natal Machinery.

He accepts their order to deploy to the Newcastle area in Natal in order to support Fani Basil Msibi.

When Tshika enters South Africa on 27 August near a place called Mfene in the Lothair district near Ermelo, he is met by Msibi, who drives him to Newcastle.[106]

*

On the evening of 13 September 1986, Frans 'Ting-Ting' Masango drives Neo Potsane and Joseph Makhura of the MK assassination unit past a petrol station in Soshanguve.

A car emerges from the garage forecourt and drives behind them. Masango keeps an eye through the rear-view mirror at the vehicle's headlights. Soon four other cars join the convoy.

Masango pulls aside to allow them to pass, but they decline the offer. Masango says: 'We're being followed.'

When the car reaches the Winterveld area, Masango turns right onto a dirt road. He says: 'If it is the police, they'll have to move soon before we're too deep into the houses where they might lose us if we run for it.'

No sooner has he said this than the car immediately behind accelerates and pulls up alongside his. Masango looks to his right and sees the three passengers in the vehicle pointing R4 rifles at his car. He brakes.

'Stop the car. Out! Stand there,' says the policeman closest to the car.

Masango stops. The vehicle is quickly surrounded by plainclothes policemen.

Masango, Potsane and Makhura are pushed to the ground and fixed in position by the soles of the officers' boots.[107]

*

When Ndandi Mpontshana arrives at Musk Mkhwamubi's kraal in the KwaMbuzi area of Ingwavuma, he finds Mkhwamubi there alongside Moloyi Ngwenya. Mpontshana and Ngwenya, who are nephews of Mkhwamubi, have been deployed to the area as MK cadres.

Mpontshana is excited. He expects positive news regarding the mission he gave them to plant a landmine in the Maputa area (of Ingwavuma). He asks how things went.

When he hears, he rounds on Ngwenya and says, 'You, Moloyi, do not want to work. Why did you not do what I told you?' He refers to a landmine which is concealed in an upturned pot at the kraal. 'You left here with this thing and you went over there and then you brought it back. Why?'

Mpontshana decides to handle the matter himself. On 28 September, he arrives at a kraal in KwaMbuzi belonging to Musk Mkhwamubi's brother, Khahla. Mpontshana is holding two bags, one of which is a carrier containing liquor.

Mpontshana says there's something he want to discuss with Khahla. He wants Khahla to accompany him somewhere.

Khahla asks where they are going.

Mpontshana says he will see when they get there.

There is light rain and thick mist at about 3.20 a.m. the following morning when Themba Mpembe travels in his Ford F100 truck on the road to Mamfene. Because of the mist, he decides he can't go any further, so he pulls in to a gate at the Jozini Experimental Farm in order to do a U-turn. On his way back out, while he negotiates a bend, an explosion throws the Ford off the road and blows open the driver's door, hurling Mpembe out of the truck in the process.

Khahla Mkhwamubi and Ndandi Mpontshana are asleep in thick bush a distance away when this happens. Mkhwamubi asks: 'Did you hear an explosion?'

Mpontshana remains quiet for a while, but then says: 'Yes, I heard it. Get up, let's go, let's go.' When Mpontshana stands up he says: 'Yes, it's that thing we planted there that exploded.'[108]

On the following day, 30 September, Gerhardus Schoon is part of a police team sent to the farm to investigate the landmine blast. While combing the surrounding area they discover some AK-47 cartridges. They follow footprints heading away from the point of discovery. The trail leads to a spot on the Ilambongwenya River in KwaMbuzi, a few kilometres from the kraals of the Mkhwamubi clan.

There they find two men and a shootout ensues. In the process, the men, Ndandi Mpontshana and Moloyi Ngwenya, are killed.[109]

*

Fani Msibi and Thuso Tshika of MK's northern Natal unit are in the company of a third man, Thembi Nkosi, when they take position across the road from Osizweni Police Station outside Newcastle on the evening of 10 October. Msibi and Tshika each have an AK-47 and three F1 hand grenades.

Inside the station, Constable Timothy Hlubi of the KwaZulu Police is in the charge office giving instructions to Constable Msibi, who then departs the room in the company of Constable S.T. Ndwandwe. The constables enter a police van parked in front of the station at about 7 p.m.

While Thembi Nkosi stays behind as lookout, Thuso Tshika and Fani Msibi cross the road and open fire on the police vehicle. Constable Ndwandwe is struck on his hip and on his left knee.

From the charge office, Constable Hlubi hears a series of gunshots, some apparently from the front and others the side of the station. Fani Msibi also throws a grenade into the police station.

Retaliatory fire is opened on the attackers from the station. One of the bullets hits Thembi Nkosi, who afterwards runs towards his colleagues.

The police fire forces Tshika and Msibi to retreat. The guerrillas flee in separate directions. Tshika and Msibi's paths later reconverge, but they don't find Nkosi.[110]

*

After the attack an intensive police hunt for the perpetrators is launched.

During its course, Fani Msibi withdraws to Swaziland and meets Thami Zulu. The two discuss a couple of targets in the Newcastle area that Msibi wants to attack.

One is Newcastle Magistrate's Court. He says this is because there are a number of trade union leaders who are presently being tried there.

Zulu raises no objections.

Msibi then says he also wants to attack the Wimpy Bar in Newcastle.

Zulu asks why. He enquires about civilian casualties.

Msibi says the attack will limit the pressure on his structure in northern Natal, because all the Special Branch people tasked with pursuing his unit use that Wimpy. The attack will kill some of them. Secondly, Wimpy has placed advertisements in the *Citizen* newspaper saying it supports the police force.

Offered the rationale, Thami Zulu approves the operation.

On his return to Newcastle, Msibi meets Thuso Tshika, who then meets Basil Sithole at a bus stop in Osizweni on 1 November. Tshika tells him to undertake an operation in town, by the Game Centre, and plant a limpet mine there.

Tshika also meets Thembi Nkosi and instructs him to undertake an operation on Newcastle Magistrate's Court.[111]

*

Two women, Melodie Temple and May van der Walt, are walking out of the Game Centre in Newcastle at about 2.42 p.m. on 11 November when they hear a huge blast from behind.

Within the complex, Maria Brown, the manageress of the Wimpy Bar, ushers twenty or so uninjured customers out of the emergency exit at the building's rear.

When she returns she sees that glass from windows in the centre has burst and roofing sheets have fallen off. Two women, one black and one white, are slightly injured from the blast.

At the Newcastle Magistrate's Court, some 500 metres from the Game Centre, Abel Nkosi is about to give testimony in a theft case at 3.10 p.m. when an explosion rocks the building, after which there is dust everywhere and people begin stampeding towards the door.

Nkosi suffers spinal injuries after being trampled by people racing to the exits. Among the others wounded are Constable Vusi Nene, who at the time of the explosion was sitting on the dustbin outside the 'B' Court in which Tshika had placed the mine. Nene will have to have his legs amputated above the knees, while Student Constable Johannes Simelane suffers injuries in the right leg and chest, and Sipho Khumalo has a fractured fibia and tibia.[112]

*

The search for saboteurs in the area intensifies following these bombings. The police throw a dragnet round Newcastle and initiate a huge manhunt.

By 13 November they are ready to act. A group of policemen meet at the Special Branch's office in Newcastle in the early hours of the morning. Some are dressed in camouflage, others in civilian dress. After a briefing by Colonel Burger, they break into two groups under the command of Captains Davidson and Strydom.

The two groups depart at about 3.45 a.m. in a Casspir armoured vehicle. Fifteen minutes later they arrive at their destination, house 1749 in the Madadeni area. Captain Strydom's group heads to the front of the house, while Captain Davidson's team approaches the rear.

At the back of the house there are two temporary buildings made of zinc. Sergeant van Dyk and Constable Yates go to one of them, kick down the door and throw in a shock grenade. They discover, however, that the structure is only a storeroom, so they head to the other zinc structure.

Sergeant van Dyk kicks down the door. Thuso Tshika, who is hiding in this room, is seized, dragged out and ordered to lie flat with his face on the ground.[113]

Fani Msibi is not in South Africa at the time and so escapes arrest.

*

Mxolisi Petane, the political commissar of the MK Western Cape Machinery, flees from four policemen at KTC squatter camp near Cape Town on 27 November.

While attempting to elude them, he throws a hand grenade. It wounds some of the policemen, but they eventually catch up with him and arrest him.[114]

*

Towards the end of 1986, Tony Yengeni meets Jenny Schreiner, daughter of Denys Schreiner, the deputy vice-chancellor of the University of Natal. From this point the two begin working together in the MK Western Cape structure.[115]

*

At 11 p.m. on 11 December, Swiss couple Corinne Bischoff and Danny Schneider arrive at their home near Mbabane Golf Club after a shopping trip to Johannesburg. They go straight to sleep.

At about 2 a.m. the glass on their front door is shattered and the lock broken by a powerful blast. Five men in overalls – two are Portuguese-speakers and two Afrikaners – enter their bedroom bearing machine guns. They threaten to shoot, and pull the couple out of bed.[116]

*

At around the same time, at Tembelihle in Mbabane, teargas canisters are thrown into the house inhabited by the Nyoni family. Armed men enter the premises and seize Danger Nyoni. The men leave but return shortly afterwards and shoot Nyoni's fifteen-year-old son Dumisani dead as he attempts to jump through a window.[117]

*

At Mbabane's Kuvehlela Flats, also at 2 a.m., Grace Cele is asleep in her bedroom when awoken by a deafening sound. Shortly afterwards, three men – two black, one white – storm the bedroom, abduct her and lead her to a white Toyota Cressida which then drives off into the night.[118]

*

Shadrack Maphumulo, who has been in Swaziland for just over five years having fled a banning order restricting him to the Inanda area of Natal following his arrest in 1977, is awoken at his apartment on the third floor of Matsapha's Magevini Flats by a loud bang, which is followed by the entrance of four men – two black, two white – brandishing guns.

The door leading to the bedrooms is locked, but the attackers blast it open. They first enter the children's bedroom, where they order the children to be quiet. One of the black men stands over the children while the other three proceed to Maphumulo's bedroom. They find this door locked too so they shoot through it. One of the bullets hits Maphumulo in the stomach.

The attackers enter, pick him up, carry him out and drive him away at high speed in a Toyota Corolla with a South African number plate.

This attack is also at 2 a.m. on 12 December.[119]

*

Corinne Bischoff and Danny Schneider are handcuffed in a car heading towards Bhunya, which is a junction on the road from Mbabane to the Nerston border post. Near Bhunya, they see that the car is at the head of what appears to be a four-vehicle convoy.

As they approach the border gate, one of the captors tells his colleagues to get their weapons ready, as they will have to shoot their way into the republic if stopped.

After crossing to the South African side without incident, people from all the cars are gathered into a van. Besides Schneider and Bischoff, there is an elderly woman, a man who continually moves his hands because his handcuffs are making him uncomfortable, and the dead body of a man who was shot in the stomach.[120]

*

South African Military Intelligence compiles a report at 3 p.m. on 12 December saying that the following are the available details: firstly, Grace Cele is a prominent ANC and SACP member who was deployed to Swaziland to advance the ANC/SACP's revolutionary objectives. She was a member of the Transvaal Implementation Group and an important courier/contact person between ANC structures in Maputo/Swaziland and underground ANC agents in the Transvaal.

Shadrack Maphumulo was involved in the so-called Natal Implementation Group. He was sent to the kingdom as the ANC's acting representative in April 1984.

Danny Schneider is a Swiss citizen who lives and works in Swaziland. He was part of an ANC network in the kingdom involved in establishing infiltration routes from Mozambique via Swaziland to South Africa. Schneider gave overnight housing to ANC terrorists in transit to or from South Africa through Swaziland. Nothing is known about Schneider's companion.[121]

*

The cross-border raids have been accompanied by a mass round-up of activists within South Africa. In a nationally televised speech that evening, President Botha seeks to justify the repression. He says the ANC has 'plans to incite revolution in South Africa before, on and after the 16th of December by way of extensive acts of sabotage and mass actions'.

It is furthermore clear, he says, 'that the ANC is now striving to divide our black communities and to incite them against the whites, and to encourage the committing of acts of violence against whites, even if these were to include large-scale bloodshed'.[122]

*

Cross-border operations continue in the run-up to the 16th.

At 10 p.m. on the evening of 15 December at the Umgugu rest camp in Mbabane's Pine Valley, two men knock on the door of a house.

Ebrahim Ismail Ebrahim is inside watching television with his gardener Dumisani Zwane. He asks Zwane to go and find out who it is.

Zwane opens the door and finds two black men clad in overalls. One of them addresses him in Shangaan.

Zwane says in siSwati that he doesn't speak Shangaan.

The other man then says in poor siSwati that they need help; they need spanners to fix their car, which has broken down along the road.

Zwane returns to Ebrahim, who he calls 'Roynie', and says that some people want to borrow a wheel spanner.

Ebrahim goes to the door and sees two men. One of them tells him that they have had a breakdown.

Ebrahim goes with his keys to his own car, which is parked outside the house. Just as he is about to open the boot, the two men produce firearms.

'If you make a noise or shout, we will kill you,' one says.

'Who are you?' asks Ebrahim.

They say they are South African policemen.

The two men escort Ebrahim back to the house, where they also hold up Zwane. Ebrahim's hands are tied behind his back and he is dragged to his bedroom and ordered to sit down. Zwane is told to lie face down and threatened with being shot if he continues to look at them.

Later that evening Ebrahim is smuggled into South Africa.[123]

*

The crackdown also continues within South Africa, but when security policemen arrive to detain Moe and Yunis Shaik following Ebrahim Ismail Ebrahim's arrest, they find the two brothers are not at home, as if tipped off, which they have been, by their source in the police.[124]

*

Ashley Forbes and Pieter Jacobs return to South Africa in December 1986 having completed their military training abroad. They head to Port Elizabeth, where they stay at the Griffin Hotel under the aliases 'P. Philander' and 'K. Samuels'.

Shortly afterwards, Niklo Pedro receives a phone call from Jacobs, who says they have returned from Angola and need accommodation in Mossel Bay.

Pedro journeys to meet Forbes and Jacobs shortly thereafter. He arranges a tent in which they can sleep at Diaz Beach.

Forbes and Pedro converse on the beach. Forbes asks Pedro whether he is willing to serve in their command cell as a contact person with the subordinate cells.

Pedro agrees.

On 23 December, Forbes and Jacobs arrive in Cape Town, where they stay in the Kensington Hotel under the 'Philander' and 'Samuels' aliases.[125]

*

Mthetheleli Mncube is part of a group of five commanded by 'Agrippa' that enters South Africa on Christmas Eve 1986. (Agrippa was the head of one of the six-man units that commenced the landmine campaign in the northern Transvaal in November 1985, and Mncube was a member of the other unit.)

Dressed in blue overalls, they cross the Limpopo under cover of darkness. They then cross a tar road, before reaching a farm where they sleep overnight.

After sunrise on Christmas Day, Mncube keeps watch while his colleagues sleep. When he hears the sound of an approaching vehicle he alerts the others.

Agrippa tells the group to get combat ready and be prepared for all contingencies. The men take up position with their AK-47s.

Mncube is the first to catch sight of the vehicle. It is a Land Rover with an open top. There are six or seven children on board, some in the back and others in the cabin. There is also a black man to the rear of the vehicle.

Mncube tells Agrippa they are civilians.

Agrippa tells his men not to shoot but to stand still.

The black man on the back of the vehicle spots the MK men and alerts the driver, after which the Land Rover stops. The distance between the bakkie and the guerrillas is a mere fifteen metres.

The driver of the vehicle opens fire on the MK men.

Agrippa orders his men to retreat.[126]

*

The South African Army's 902 Special Service Company Reaction Unit is deployed later on Christmas Day under the command of Major Petrus Oosthuizen.

At Newark farm, prints from five pairs of boots headed southwards are pointed out to Oosthuizen. The unit follows the tracks.

On Boxing Day, the reaction unit continues its hunt. The spoor of the five men is followed up to two large rocks.

A section of the company searches the rocks. A.Z. Eloff, a member of the search team, becomes aware of a man lying behind him, flat on his stomach, in a cleft between the rocks. All Eloff can see is the man's head and one shoulder.

Eloff commands the man to come out, show his hands, and give himself up.

At first the man does not react.

Mthetheleli Mncube is in a nearby position alongside a comrade, 'Peter', looking on at the rocks.

A helicopter lurking overhead shoots at the rocks, supplemented by fire from the ground forces. Two shots from Corporal Willie Mhlari kill the man hiding between the rocks.

Mncube and Peter decide to flee. The helicopter spots them and starts firing in their direction.

A.Z. Eloff joins the pursuit of Mncube and Peter, but receives a radio message from Major Oosthuizen to return to the original contact scene.

The helicopter pursuing Mncube and Peter also ceases the pursuit.

Mncube tells Peter to run one way while he runs the other, so that if the helicopter returns, one or other of them can get back to Zimbabwe.

Eloff arrives at the original contact scene and joins a search under way there. They spot two men wearing blue overalls and carrying AK-47s, huddled together under the rocks.

Eloff tells them to come out, show their hands and give themselves up. They do not react. One of them retrieves a hand grenade from behind his back and lifts it up, upon which Eloff shoots them both dead.[127]

*

Eloff then resumes the pursuit of Mncube and Peter. At a certain point he sees that the trail splits. The tracking team decides to follow one of them.

Mncube has run himself to exhaustion. He can't see any ground forces, but a helicopter has picked up his trail and followed him. At a position about two kilometres from the large rocks, he gives up and sits down.

At 5 p.m. the ground forces catch up with him. Eloff makes Mncube take off all his clothes bar his underpants and marches him back to the initial contact point by the rocks, where he is handed over to Major Oosthuizen.

Mncube is blindfolded and led a short distance. The blindfold is then removed. Mncube sees the corpses of three of his colleagues. He is asked to identify them. He does so.

It is now about 7 p.m. Three men dressed in civilian clothes arrive in a white bakkie. When they disembark, Mncube sees that they are carrying pistols. Mncube is blindfolded again and thrown into the bakkie, landing on his head. The bodies of the three dead men are then thrown on top of him. They are already decomposing, and Mncube tries hard to avoid inhaling air.

The vehicle starts moving and after a while it stops. Mncube is taken off the bakkie and thrown onto another one. All the while he remains blindfolded with his hands bound.

This second bakkie moves away quickly and at some stage it stops, Mncube does not know where, and the blindfold is ripped from his face. He sees two white men in civilian dress and notices that the scene is somewhere deep in the bush. But he also sees that an AK-47 has been left lying in the back compartment of the vehicle.

The two white men return to the bakkie and put the blindfold back on Mncube. The vehicle starts up again. After a short distance, Mncube manages to break the ropes binding his hands and picks up the AK.

With it he opens fire on the cabin and the bakkie comes to a standstill. Mncube leaps off and runs away. He jumps a fence and continues running through the night, but he has no idea where he is going.[128]

*

At 6.30 a.m. on 27 December, two farmers, John Rall and a Mr Schneider, are travelling in a Toyota light delivery vehicle when Rall hears banging on the roof.

Rall looks through the back window and sees his farmworkers jumping off the vehicle. The foreman tracker, who is still in the bakkie, points forward at something on the road ahead.

Rall looks ahead and sees a small donga next to the road that runs under a game fence. He sees a man lying on his stomach in the donga and aiming a rifle in his direction.

Rall shouts at Schneider to stop the vehicle. Before it comes to a complete halt, Rall jumps off and lifts his hand, upon which the foreman tracker gives him his R1 rifle. Rall takes it and runs to the front of the bakkie.

The man by the road ahead is struggling to cock his rifle – it has jammed.

Rall shoots him dead.

The black man killed is 'Peter', the fifth member of the unit of which Mncube had been a part.[129]

*

By 3 January 1987, Mthetheleli Mncube can no longer walk properly. His feet are full of thorns, one of his knees is giving him problems and he is exhausted after a week without food. He has shorts on, and so-called rampantjanas on his feet ('shoes' consisting of a piece of leather tied onto the foot by rags). His body is full of scratch marks.

He leaves his temporary hiding place and starts walking. Near some houses he finds an old blanket. He puts it on and walks to a tarred road.

On his way there he sees a woman with two children exiting a farm gate. He approaches them and asks for water.

The woman promises to get some. Mncube waits by the gate.

About twenty minutes later, they still haven't returned, so Mncube starts moving again. He has only moved a small distance when he feels he must rest because he is so weak. While he is resting, a police van passes him in the direction of the farm. A while later the police vehicle returns from the farm. Erasmus, a white policeman, and Siphuma, a black counterpart, approach Mncube. The former speaks while the latter interprets.

Mncube is arrested and taken into the van, which heads back to the farm. There they find the woman and two children that Mncube earlier asked for water. They are in the company of the farmer's wife. When the children are asked if this is the person that asked for the water, the girl says yes.[130]

*

Tim Jenkin, formerly a colleague of Stephen Lee in the ANC propaganda unit operating in South Africa in the 1970s, arrives by plane in Lusaka.

In the Zambian capital he meets Mac Maharaj, who is working on the presidential project approved by the National Executive Committee the previous year that is aimed at infiltrating senior leaders of the movement into South Africa. Maharaj says he has heard that Jenkin is involved in experiments with computer communication, and expresses an interest in how the work is progressing.[131]

*

At his home in Eersterus, a township near Pretoria, a coloured man, Keith McKenzie, receives a call from Lester Dumakude of the MK Special Operations Unit.

Dumakude requests McKenzie's presence at a meeting in Botswana.

The call is being recorded by the South African Police.[132]

*

Security Branch chief Johan van der Merwe is briefed soon after by Brigadier Loots, who tells him that Johannes Mnisi, aka 'Victor', Ernest Lekoto Pule, aka 'Oupa', and Lester Dumakude, aka 'Chris', are important MK operatives. They head the arms smuggling and terrorist infiltration activities of the ANC between South Africa and

Botswana. Mnisi is also directly responsible for acts of terror in South Africa, including the Church Street bomb. An agent, Keith McKenzie, has said the weapons and explosives he is involved in smuggling into South Africa are usually obtained from Mnisi, Dumakude and/or Pule.

Loots says it now appears that McKenzie has received an instruction from MK to smuggle weapons and explosives into South Africa during the Easter weekend. For the upcoming mission, McKenzie will use his Combi, which is equipped by the ANC with a hidden compartment for arms smuggling. This creates an opportunity to use the Combi to eliminate Mnisi, Dumakude and/or Pule.

Van der Merwe gives Brigadier Loots permission to proceed on the proviso that the SADF will control the operation inside Botswana and that deaths of civilians will be prevented.[133]

*

About ten kilometres from the Diepgesit mine near Josefsdal in the eastern Transvaal, Dick Mkhonto and Ndumiso Mkhonto plant a mine. They choose a spot about one mile down a dirt road that heads from Josefsdal to a small village.

They then return to Swaziland where they report to Theophilus Dlodlo, alias 'Viva', a member of the Transvaal Urban Machinery's unit in Ga-Rankuwa in the early 1980s, but now chief of operations of an MK landmine warfare project code-named 'Kletshwayo'.

At 3.30 p.m. on 28 March, an open van travelling on the dirt road in Josefsdal triggers the landmine, killing two black women and two black men, and injuring another black man.[134]

*

Moe Shaik's mole in the Security Branch gives him a security police file on Aboobaker Ismail. One of the documents in the file refers to source 'NP395' who has infiltrated the Botswana Machinery.

Reference is made to an incident in which NP395 obtained a glass that 'Rachid' (Aboobaker Ismail) had touched, from which fingerprints were subsequently taken. There is also mention of a plan to lure Rachid into a Combi rigged with explosives, which are then to be detonated.[135]

*

Aboobaker Ismail phones London from Botswana. When nobody answers, he leaves a message providing a return number.

On the following morning, he receives a call from Helena Dolny, who is Joe Slovo's second wife following the assassination of Ruth First by a parcel bomb in August 1982. While discussing the matter Ismail had wanted to raise, Dolny suddenly says: 'Oh just hold on, Joe wants to talk to you.'

Joe Slovo comes on the line and asks Ismail, whom he calls 'Rachid', if he remembers an incident he once described to Slovo where he met someone in a Gaborone Hotel and drank juice or something like that.

'Yes, what about it?'

'Well there's some information, but all we know is that there's someone, an enemy agent, and this person met with you and the glass that you drank from, etc., this person preserved and took back across the border because they're trying to get fingerprints and things off that.'

Ismail tries to remember but draws blanks.

'Just think about this because only you know because you related this incident to me,' Slovo says.

After the conversation Ismail lies on his bed trying to recall the incident.[136]

*

Keith McKenzie or 'NP395', the man involved in the incident Ismail was trying to recall, arrives in Gaborone on Saturday 4 April.

Ismail *did* remember. After being heavily plied with drink by members of the MK Logistics Unit, McKenzie is taken by them into Zambia, where they arrive on the morning of the 5th.[137] McKenzie will eventually be sent to the ANC's detention camp in northern Angola, officially called the Morris Seabelo Rehabilitation Centre (for Lulamile Dantile, killed in the December 1985 Maseru raid), but alternatively known as 'Camp 32' or 'Quatro'.

*

In a residential area of Gaborone on 9 April, an SADF Special Forces operative spots the minibus he has been seeking for a number of days. It is the van that South African Intelligence believe Johannes Mnisi, Ernest Pule, Lester Dumakude and/or Aboobaker Ismail will be using over the Easter period. By means of a remote controlled device, the operative detonates explosives that Brigadier Loots's team have attached to the vehicle.[138]

On the following day, London's *Guardian* reports that the Gaborone explosion yesterday killed a thirty-year-old welfare worker, her seven-year-old son and an infant girl staying in their house. The minibus used in the explosion was registered in South Africa in the name of a married woman living in the coloured township of Eersterus.

Approached for comment the night before, the woman said her husband sometimes used the vehicle to run a taxi service to Botswana. He went to Botswana on Saturday (4 April) but she has not heard from him since.[139]

The McKenzie affair represents perhaps the first major operational victory for MK following their penetration of the Security Branch through Moe Shaik's mole. The codename given by the ANC to this counter-intelligence project is 'Operation Bible'.

*

From Lusaka, Operation Kletshwayo commander Theophilus 'Viva' Dlodlo phones his wife Felicia Azande Dlodlo in Swaziland.

He says the ANC is intending to clear out quite a number of its operatives from Swaziland, where it seems the movement can't even trust its own cadres. While the organisation does this there is going to be a lot of movement of people from there to Lusaka. He mentions that the ANC wants him to come to Swaziland to find a few things out and question some individuals about all the assassinations of ANC members that have been taking place.

By about 20 April Dlodlo is in Swaziland, where he meets his wife. He tells her he is on a very dangerous mission. He would prefer it if he wasn't seen coming to her place all the time, more so because they have a very young child whom he doesn't want to endanger.[140]

*

On 22 April, Joe Slovo says in an interview on a Lusaka radio station that he has quit his post in MK to reduce his workload.[141]

*

Ashley Forbes drives Pieter Jacobs and Niklo Pedro to a house in Rangerslot in Mitchell's Plain the following evening. The house belongs to Mr Nissan, whom they believe to be a policeman.

Jacobs and Pedro exit the car. Jacobs heads to one of the house's windows, while Pedro goes to a car standing next to the house. Pedro sees that the lights at the far side of the property are on. He punctures the car's tyres. Jacobs meanwhile breaks the window with a stone and throws a hand grenade inside.

On the same evening, Anwa Dramat, wearing rubber gloves and a balaclava, jumps over the locked front gate of the home of Constable Jones at 115 Bonteheuwel Avenue with a grenade in his hand. About halfway between the gate and the house, he throws the grenade through the window immediately to the right of the door, which he runs towards in order to avoid shrapnel.

After the explosion, Dramat exits the premises and dumps the grenade pin during the escape.[142]

*

Mrs Elizabeth Elias receives a telephone call from a woman who says she has two male friends who urgently need a place to stay.

Elias says her partner is still fixing the place.

The woman stresses the urgency of the situation.

'Okay,' Elias says, but she recommends that the lady first has a look at the property to make sure it will be fine.

The lady arrives at Elias's place, which is 4 Dunster Road in Athlone, with one of the men, Ashley Forbes, who introduces himself as 'Faizul Abrahams'. When Elias shows Forbes the place, he says: 'No, it's all right.'[143]

*

A general election is held in South Africa on 6 May 1987. According to the provisional results released the following day, the National Party is projected to increase its parliamentary representation from 127 to 132 seats, the Conservative Party from 16 to 22 seats, and the Progressive Federal Party to decline from 26 to 19.[144]

Therefore, in the first major gauge of white opinion since the imposition of the nationwide state of emergency, President Botha has emerged with increased support, with the new official opposition taking the position that he has not gone far enough in suppressing resistance.

In an interview broadcast on state-run television that evening, Botha declares that he interprets the election result as a mandate to crack down on extra-parliamentary protest:

> there is a tendency in South Africa to organise extra-parliamentary organizations to bring about change and there is a tendency to finance those organisations from sources not originally South African. I must warn against this. The government cannot allow it. The outside world must now have a clear picture that they cannot dictate to South Africa. South Africa wants to solve its own problems and South Africans believe in moderate reform. Any reform, any change, must be brought about by parliamentary means and by negotiations with other leaders in South Africa who reject violence.[145]

Oliver Tambo responds to the election outcome the following day. Speaking on the sidelines of a World Council of Churches meeting in Lusaka, he tells reporters that the results 'blew the whistle to intensify the armed struggle', because the white electorate have essentially said 'it is all right for thousands of children to be detained and tortured, and that it is even illegal for their parents to protest against that'. Furthermore, 'the results are also saying that it is all right to attack peaceful neighbouring countries, as if the cause of South Africa's problems is outside its borders'.

He adds: 'It is all moving in the direction we had feared, towards heightened levels of conflict, not only inside South Africa, but throughout the whole region.'[146]

SEASON OF VIOLENCE

While addressing Sergeant McQueen, Sergeant Roman and Warrant Officer Edward Stoffels on 16 May, Captain William Liebenberg produces a photo of Pieter Jacobs. He says they are pursuing this suspect who is active in terrorist activity, and that he will be at Klipfontein Road in Athlone. McQueen, Roman and Stoffels depart from the meeting and proceed to Athlone with the photo in their possession.

Later that day, in a passage running alongside Klipfontein Road, Stoffels sits 'reading' a newspaper (he actually has a photo of Jacobs inside the paper) when a woman gives him a signal, indicating that Pieter Jacobs is across the road. Jacobs is indeed sitting there, also reading a newspaper.

Stoffels gives Roman and McQueen a nod. At 9.57 a.m., the three policemen walk up to Jacobs, who denies he is Pieter Jacobs when asked – he claims he is 'David

Samuels'. He is arrested all the same and taken to Manenberg Police Station. There he is handed over to Warrant Officer Johannes Nel.

Lieutenant Liebenberg and Warrant Officers Nel and Jeffrey Benzien proceed to Dunster Road in Athlone later that day as part of a police team of six or seven men. Pieter Jacobs is accompanying them. When they reach house number 4, they head to a free-standing garage situated on the property. It is about 2.15 p.m.

The policemen take up position by the front door. Liebenberg holds Jacobs in front of him. Benzien is directly behind, armed with a 9-mm Beretta sidearm as well as a Beretta shotgun. Liebenberg also has a key in his possession, and uses it to unlock the door, which opens outwards. When entering, he holds Jacobs half in front of him.

Liebenberg then looks to the left and says: 'Hello Ashley.' Benzien enters next and points his gun leftwards. There are two beds parallel to each other. Ashley Forbes is on the one to the left, nearest to the windows. His toes are sticking out of the bed.

Liebenberg warns him not to make any sudden movements.[1]

*

Joseph Koetle and William Mabele drive in separate cars from Soweto to central Johannesburg early on the morning of 20 May. Koetle is driving a Volkswagen Golf and stops it near the junction of Fox and Main Streets, close to the rear entrance to Johannesburg Magistrate's Court. Koetle gets out, enters Mabele's car, and is driven back to Soweto. Before they part, Koetle tells Mabele to watch the news that night.

Just after midday, Koetle is back in central Johannesburg, and at about 12.10 p.m. he connects a battery to a bomb located in the boot of the Golf. He then proceeds to plant a mini limpet mine near the car.

Some fifteen minutes later, Koetle is in a café close to the scene when the limpet mine explodes. He leaves the café and sees policemen cordon off the area and move towards the scene of the explosion.

He waits for his moment. Then he activates the car bomb by means of a remote-controlled device, killing four policemen and wounding several more.

When Mabele watches the television news that evening from a neighbouring country, he sees a report about the bombing and recognises the Golf.[2]

*

Siphiwe Nyanda, who is working with Theophilus Dlodlo in Swaziland, is recalled to Lusaka on 21 May 1987.[3] That evening, Dlodlo speaks with his wife, Felicia, at their home.

He says he needs her help. He has information from various sources that 'September', who was allegedly abducted last year while he was away, is in Swaziland. He asks if she remembers what he looks like.

She says she does.

He says he has just received information that September is in a certain hotel. He doesn't know with whom.

The couple leave and head to a hotel close to Swaziland's Houses of Parliament. Dlodlo parks the car underneath a tree and tells his wife to please proceed but to make sure nobody sees him.

As she approaches the hotel entrance she notices a number of South African–registered cars. Inside the hotel, there are quite a number of people, but she can't see Glory Sedibe.

She asks an employee if the hotel perhaps has a pool room. The man says it does, and leads her there.

Inside the room she spots Sedibe playing pool in the company of ten or so white men with South African accents. She quickly walks out.

On her way out she sees a black female MK member. When the two make eye contact the other woman assumes an expression of fright.

Back at the car, she confirms that she saw September playing pool in the company of about ten white men.

That's fine, her husband says.

She says she also saw something else: she saw 'Maniki'. She asks whether he knows why Maniki might be there.

He says he doesn't know. Maybe entertainment, maybe a similar assignment, he doesn't know. He hasn't given her any instructions to be there to the best of his knowledge.

Just before they leave, Maniki approaches the car and says: 'Hey you guys, do you know that September is in there playing snooker with the Boers?'

Dlodlo and his wife leave the hotel. After a while spent in silence in the car, he remarks: 'These people have come to kill us. I know that.'

She asks what he is going to do.

He apologises for putting her in danger, but says he just needed someone he could trust to confirm that September was really there. He says he should take her home. He doesn't want her to be involved. It is a very, *very* dangerous mission.[4]

*

On 22 May, after a brief appearance at a party in Thembelihle, Mbabane, Theophilus Dlodlo departs.

He gets into the driver's seat of a cream-coloured Ford Laser. Mildred Msomi is in the passenger seat, and Tutu Nkwanyane (a South African student studying at the University of Swaziland), Lungile Zwane, Candy Ntshontsho and 'Shezi' are in the back.

The car heads to town. When it reaches Dalriach South at about 11 p.m., it approaches the bottom of a hill. At this point the passengers notice a car approaching from behind at high speed with its lights on full beam.

As the Laser slows to negotiate a curve in the road, the other vehicle moves to overtake. This other vehicle, which they can now see is a dark van, pulls up alongside them with the side door wide open. Dlodlo hears a voice that he recognises as an

ANC colleague's saying, 'Viva, Viva, stop, what are you doing, we need to talk to you, there is something very urgent I need to tell you!'

The van makes to stop, upon which Dlodlo also slows the Ford down. Both he and Shezi reach for their guns. Then the occupants of the other vehicle emerge from it, brandishing firearms.

A strange sound, 'Ggrrrrrrr' – that of guns fitted with silencers – issues from these men.

Lungile Zwane lowers herself in the back seat when she sees what is happening. A bullet grazes her face, shattering one eye and seriously injuring the other. She loses consciousness.

The next thing she remembers is going to a nearby house with Candy Ntshontsho.

In the Ford Laser, Theophilus Dlodlo, Tutu Nkwanyane and Mildred Msomi lie dead.[5]

*

At 7.30 p.m. on 24 May, Sheila Nyanda – Siphiwe Nyanda's wife – hears a knock on the door of her house in Mbabane.

She opens, only to be confronted by a white man armed with a submachine gun fitted with a silencer. He tells her not to make any noise. Behind him is another white male.

'André', the man in front, leads her back into the house and says: 'We know you are Sheila Priscilla, Gebuza's wife.' He asks who is in the house.

Nobody else, she says.

After the house is searched by the men, Nyanda is taken blindfolded from the house to her white BMW 3 series, which is parked in a carport.

Later in the day she is smuggled over the border into South Africa.[6]

*

Siphiwe Nyanda is called to Oliver Tambo's office in Lusaka.

Tambo says that Nyanda is going to be part of a mission, a very sensitive mission known only to a few people. It will be to establish an ANC leadership core within South Africa (this is the presidential project approved by the NEC the previous year; it has been codenamed 'Operation Vula'). Nyanda will be working with Joe Slovo, and will have to see Mac Maharaj and Slovo, who will brief him.

Nyanda then meets Slovo and Maharaj. Slovo says Maharaj will deal with the details of the mission, but in the meantime Nyanda will have to stay in Lusaka while preparing. His preparation will also involve going to East Germany on an intelligence course.[7]

*

Simon Makana, the secretary of the ANC's Department of Political Education, compiles a letter on 4 June 1987 titled 'Suggestions from the units', which is based on certain grievances contained in recent feedback received from MK cadres based in Lusaka.

The top point made by the units, Makana writes, is for 'Cadres en route for home not to be made to stay too long in Lusaka. In the process, there is a possibility of them losing their skills and specialisation.'

Second was a call for 'Mhq to pay them regular visits. They would also greatly appreciate visits from the leadership. Especially to be addressed by cde President.'

Among the other suggestions are for more political work to be done in border areas in order to assist with infiltrations; and for more attention to be paid to long-standing grievances over welfare aspects including food supply, clothing, living conditions, recreation facilities and the need for household items.[8]

*

After a long delay, Siphiwe Nyanda steps through the glass door of 'Arrivals' at Amsterdam's Schiphol Airport. He is met by Conny Braam, a leader of the Dutch Anti-Apartheid Movement, who asks him what happened.

Saying nothing, he brandishes his Ghanaian passport.

The following morning, Braam and Nyanda are walking side by side in the dunes of the Dutch seaside town of Castricum. Braam has a hiking map and is apparently searching for routes, but her mind is elsewhere. Suddenly she suggests to Nyanda a black businessman – young, ambitious, up-and-coming, sporting Western dress, part of the international corps of well-dressed men in suit-and-tie? Many South African hotels now welcome them, she says.

Nyanda nods approvingly.

Or, she continues, a young man, snazzy jacket, wet-look hairstyle, a disco regular? She snaps her fingers, swings her hips, and pouts her lips. She sees out of the corner of her eye that Nyanda is smiling – for the first time since his arrival. She corrects herself: 'Not the disco – the shebeen.'

Nyanda starts laughing.

Braam pursues the theme: 'The type that's not interested in politics, a trendy kid who's good with the girls, with his Walkman headphones.'

Nyanda shakes his head, repeating slowly, '*Walkman headphones?*'

He walks closer to Braam, slaps her on the shoulder and says that's not such a bad idea at all.[9]

*

On 12 June 1987, Shirley Gunn is infiltrated back into South Africa after completing her military training in Angola. She heads to the Western Cape.[10]

*

A group of eight MK cadres are ambushed on 25 June while on patrol in the vicinity of MK's camp in Caculama, Angola.

Two are killed and four escape, while two are captured and led on a forced march towards UNITA headquarters in south-eastern Angola. The two captives are Michael Mkona, aged thirty-two, and Mthunzi Mnguni, twenty-five. Documents found in their possession indicate Mkona is a commander and Mnguni a commissar in MK.[11]

*

Damian de Lange (like Marion Sparg formerly part of the 'South African Liberation Support Cadre') enters South Africa from Botswana near Makopong on 1 July 1987. He infiltrates in the company of Ian Robertson, who left South Africa to join the ANC in Zambia in 1978 after being radicalised by events that occurred while he was studying at Wits University between 1974 and 1977, including the death of Joseph Mdluli and the Soweto uprising.

De Lange is the commander and Robertson the political commissar of a special MK unit tasked with settling in the country on a permanent basis to execute ANC orders.[12]

On the following day, Rodney Toka and his immediate commander, Mishack 'Mensday' Maponya, enter South Africa, also from Botswana.

They are also to establish a permanent internal structure. In their case they will operate out of Pretoria's satellite townships.[13]

*

Uriel Abrahamse, now based in Luanda as the ANC's regional treasurer in Angola, is present when a man arrives in July 1987 to brief the movement's structures in the capital.

The man lives on the ANC's farm near Malange. He says the farm is in the vicinity of the route used by UNITA to ferry supplies from Zaire to UNITA headquarters in south-eastern Angola.

The man tells them that he was out with a group of ANC comrades hunting when they were ambushed by UNITA bandits. What was unusual, he says, is that when the MK group retreated after the contact, they saw a long column of men, numbering in the hundreds, marching with parcels on their heads. The UNITA ambush was not planned, and was apparently aimed merely to scare the comrades away from the columns of people.[14]

*

South Africa's hit squads continue their operations in Swaziland. At Matsapha Airport on 9 July, Eliza Tsinini welcomes Paul Dikeledi and Cassius Make, who have just arrived on a Lesotho Airways flight from Mozambique. The three get into a Colt Gallant with 'Maza Taxi' imprinted on its doors, and are driven away by Sipho Gamedze, the taxi driver.

As the taxi takes a turn to the University of Swaziland, a white BMW with Transvaal number plates tags behind. As the taxi passes the Usushwana Bridge near the entrance to the Swazi king's royal palace, the BMW flashes its lights. When the Colt stops, the BMW's occupants rush out and spray the taxi with gunfire, killing Tsinini, Dikeledi and Make instantly, but sparing Gamedze.

These slayings occur in broad daylight.[15]

*

Six days later, Captain William Liebenberg tells Warrant Officer Jeffrey Benzien and Sergeant Abels to go to 8 Albermarle Road in Athlone. Liebenberg tells them to perform surveillance and determine if the trained ANC terrorist Ashley Kriel is in the house or one of the adjacent properties.

While he is reconnoitring the area, the house looks quiet to Benzien, but then he thinks he sees movement from the property. He tells Abels to knock on the back door of the house.

After a couple of minutes of Abels knocking, Ashley Kriel opens, carrying a towel and jersey. Within the bundle he has an automatic pistol.

Benzien tries to pin Kriel down and a tussle commences, during which Benzien manages to seize the bundle. Benzien then takes handcuffs from his pocket and tells Abels to handcuff Kriel. Abels manages to handcuff Kriel's left wrist while Benzien sits on Kriel's back.

Kriel tries to crawl back into the house. As the three men fight they alternate from struggling on their knees to wrestling on the ground. During the scuffle, Kriel's firearm, which is in Benzien's right hand, goes off. Kriel is killed by a bullet fired into his back at point-blank range.[16]

*

Kriel's death serves as the cue for an increase of activity by MK in the Western Cape. Tony Yengeni meets with Jenny Schreiner, his fellow operative in the Regional Command, and says they should detonate an explosive at Castle Court in Cape Town's Tennant Street, where married members of the SADF are accommodated in a block of flats.

On 20 July, Yengeni and Schreiner jointly load six gas cylinders filled with liquid petroleum gas into a Toyota Corolla sedan. Yengeni attaches two 158 mini limpet mines and one SPM limpet mine fitted with a fuse and a detonator onto the gas cylinders.

Schreiner drives the car to Castle Court and stops in a parking bay on the corner of Caledon and Tennant Streets. She pulls the safety pin from the SPM, then departs the scene.

At 8.40 p.m. the vehicle explodes. Stephen Day, who lives in a flat in Castle Court with his wife, looks out of the shattered apartment window, and he sees a huge ball of flame. Only the twisted, blackened chassis of the Toyota remains. Two other cars are badly damaged. Many windows in the complex have shattered, leaving glass everywhere.

On the evening of the 21st, Yengeni and Schreiner meet again. Yengeni says that Cape Town's D.F. Malan Airport is their next target. He gives her two SPM limpet mines fitted with fuses and detonators, and tells her to place them inside the airport terminal buildings.

Just after midnight on the evening of 21–22 July, a member of the public notices a suspicious-looking parcel in the toilets at the airport. The person calls for help, but before the package can be examined it explodes, causing extensive damage to the building.

A second SPM mine is discovered nearby by members of the South African Police's bomb disposal unit. It is taken out of the building and destroyed by police explosives experts.[17]

*

The *Cape Times* reports on 25 July that it has recently received letters from a group calling itself the 'Basil February MK Squad', claiming responsibility for recent bomb attacks in the Cape Peninsula. In the letters, the group vowed to continue to 'answer racist violence with people's revolutionary violence, until the black, green and gold flag flies over the Union buildings in Pretoria'. The article says the security police are investigating the claims.[18]

The London *Times* reports two days later that in a further letter to a Cape Town newspaper, the Basil February MK Squad has declared that by its actions it is 'honouring our late commander and leader Comrade Cassius Make, Ashley Kriel and all other heroes and martyrs of our struggle'.[19]

*

In Cape Town Shirley Gunn meets Aneez Salie, a colleague in the MK underground. They decide to combine their units. In a further tribute to the recently slain MK man they decide to call the merged structure the Ashley Kriel Unit.[20]

*

Heinrich Grosskop, in his early twenties, is the son of a well-known university professor from a prominent Afrikaans family. Grosskop left South Africa in January 1986 to join the ANC in exile, the tipping point coming when a speech delivered by Louis le Grange late in 1985, in which he cited the fact that the police were killing an average of six people a day as evidence that they had the situation 'under control', was met with public indifference.

Grosskop drives a Valiant motor car from Lyndon to Johannesburg. He is wearing a thick, grey, padded jacket under a white medical/laboratory-type coat. There are three time switches made from alarm clocks in the front of the car. It is about 9 a.m. on the morning of 30 July.

Around forty-five minutes later, he parks the Valiant in a space in Quartz Street. With the car idling, he lashes the steering wheel securely. As he does so, he sees in the rear-view mirror a soldier on sentry duty talking to a young woman at the SADF's Wits Command headquarters. The man seems to look in Grosskop's direction, but gives no sign of suspecting anything. Grosskop then moves a lever in each of the time switches. Within the next ten seconds he exits the car, locks it, and starts walking in the direction of the nearby Sterland cinema complex.

At the end of the ten seconds, one of the time switches – the one controlling the electricity supply to the van's motor – begins working, thereby increasing the engine's speed and moving the gear selector. Grosskop hears the Valiant's engine revving fast and loudly. This is just before he reaches the cinema complex.

The vehicle then explodes, sending glass flying as far as some properties in front of Grosskop, in what is the biggest bomb yet exploded in the armed struggle. It leaves sixty-seven people wounded, none fatally. He runs through the cinema complex and is soon joined by other people running in the same direction.

About a block from the explosion, Grosskop removes his white overcoat and puts it into a rubbish bin. He stops running and walks to where a motorcycle is parked. By now he can hear sirens all over the city.

He drives the motorcycle to Lyndon, where he collects some belongings and departs again with the bike to Botswana, which he enters via Ramatlabama.

He then makes his way to a prearranged rendezvous spot, where he meets a MK Special Operations Unit support group. On 31 July Grosskop travels to Lusaka, where he is debriefed by the MK Special Operations Unit and Military Headquarters.[21]

*

Moses Nchangasi meets Gordon Webster, his immediate commander in MK. Webster says they are going to capture a judge, a major, a captain and other officers and hold them as hostages for the release of Robert McBride and others facing the death sentence.[22]

*

In August, Mzwandile Vena is driven by Jenny Schreiner from Botswana to Cape Town. He has been deployed as Lizo Bright Ngqungwana's successor as MK Western Cape commander. Vena settles in the Landsdowne area.[23]

*

During the same month, Susan Westcott, a British citizen through a marriage of convenience under the surname Donnelly, and who was born in Swaziland in 1964, enters South Africa having undergone military training in Angola earlier in the year.

At Johannesburg Zoo, she meets Damian de Lange. She reflects to herself that with his disguise he now looks like Lenin.

She joins the unit, based in Broederstroom, in which De Lange is commander and Ian Robertson the commissar. Westcott becomes the unit's communications officer.[24]

*

At midday on 15 August, Detective Constable Rosewell Ngwane, who is on duty at Tele Bridge border post between the Transkei and Lesotho, sees a beige-coloured Toyota Corolla registered CB281754 pull in. Two coloured women get out and enter the office. After their passports are stamped, some policemen accompany them outside in order to search the vehicle.

At just that time Warrant Officer Vuyile Gcaba arrives at the station in an official police vehicle. He hands an elderly lady and young man over to Ngwane, saying that he met them along the road and that they were dropped off by the Toyota earlier. Gcaba suspects the group were engaged in an illegal border crossing.

The young man – Niklo Pedro – gives his name as 'Denver Pedro', and the elderly lady as 'Yasmina Pandy'.

At about 1 p.m. Constable Ngwane phones the Security Branch office in Aliwal North, as Pandy earlier told Gcaba that she and Pedro had come from Aliwal North.

Captain William de Lange heads from Aliwal North to Tele Bridge following the call. On his arrival at the border post, Constable Ngwane points the four coloured suspects out to him. Two are in the yard and two in the office of a fenced-off area at the checkpoint.

Captain de Lange takes Pedro out of the office and asks him what his name is. 'Pedro,' comes the answer.

De Lange asks if it is 'Jerome Pedro'.

Pedro responds affirmatively.

De Lange asks if he is from Cape Town.

Pedro says yes.

De Lange asks if he knows Ashley Forbes.

Pedro says he does.[25]

*

Two days later, Warrant Officer Jeffrey Benzien is accompanied to a house by two explosives experts, other members of the South African Police's Reaction Unit, and personnel from the Dog Unit.

With the rest of the team in position around the house offering protection, Benzien enters the property and proceeds to one of the bedrooms.

Anwa Dramat is in the bedroom asleep. He wakes to find Benzien holding a pistol to his face.[26]

*

Tony Yengeni is driving in Rondebosch on the evening of 16 September with a passenger codenamed 'Bonono' next to him.

When he reaches the courts of the Western Province Tennis Club, situated right next to the University of Cape Town, he stops the car. On his watch it says the time is 8 p.m. He waits a short while before getting out of the vehicle and walking to a nearby phone booth. While standing next to the booth, Yengeni speaks to Bonono, who has remained in the car.

Two white men pass by. Yengeni and Bonono ignore them and carry on talking. Then Yengeni sees out of the corner of his eye two men approaching. The next thing he knows, a gun is being pointed at his forehead by Jeffrey Benzien, who says: 'Tony Yengeni, you're under arrest.' Sergeant Riaan Bellingan and Captain William Liebenberg arrive shortly afterwards.[27]

Mzwandile Vena is arrested the same evening in the Lansdowne area.

At 3.40 the following morning, Jenny Schreiner is arrested in her flat at 5 Marie Court in Wellingon Avenue in Cape Town's Wynberg suburb.[28]

*

Later on the 17th, Moses Nchangasi climbs over a border fence separating Botswana and Bophuthatswana, in the company of Gordon Webster, on their mission to take hostages to force the release of Robert McBride. Webster has had his hair permed and silicone has been pumped into his face, giving him fuller features and a more pronounced jaw.

In Bophuthatswana they are met by a courier who has come in a large saloon car with his wife and children serving as cover.

The courier tells them the area is crawling with soldiers.

Webster and Nchangasi enter the car nonetheless.

Almost immediately, on the outskirts of the town of Mabaalstad, they see a road-block. The driver successfully manages to take evasive action and head along another route. But on this alternative route, at a spot ten or fifteen kilometres from the border, they encounter a Casspir obstructing the road. They have no choice but to stop.

It seems as though there has been a serious penetration of the ANC's structures in Botswana. One of the soldiers tells them: 'We've been waiting two weeks, where've you been?'[29]

*

At 5 p.m. that day, when Isaiah Siyali arrives at Milnerton Police Station, he finds his white commanding officer in the company of about fifteen askaris. The captured Tony Yengeni is also present.

The commanding officer briefs them on a plan to arrest Bongani Jonas, a member of MK in the Western Cape. He says that Siyali, Yengeni and 'David' (one of the askaris) will take a civilian motor vehicle to the meeting place. Other members of the team (i.e. the white Security Branch officers and the remainder of the askaris) will be following and will keep in radio contact. The meeting will be at 7 p.m.

Siyali, Yengeni and David depart from Milnerton Station in a light blue Fiat at 6.15 p.m. David drives, Yengeni is in the passenger seat with his hands and feet bound, and Siyali sits in the back. They head in the direction of Athlone. The other police-men and askaris follow at a considerable distance.

While driving on the main road near Athlone, they see a black Mercedes with three people inside approaching from the opposite direction. David turns to Yengeni and asks if this is Bongani Jonas. Yengeni nods, so David turns the car around. They try to alert the commanding officer in the car following them of this change of dir-ection, but the radio malfunctions.

This leaves the Fiat alone in pursuit of the black Mercedes, which enters the N2 in the direction of Somerset West. David follows. Then, after passing the Gugulethu turnoff, David accelerates until he is alongside Jonas (with the Mercedes being in the left lane).

David shouts at Siyali to shoot the driver, Bongani Jonas, who is now about two metres away. Siyali withdraws his service pistol, winds down the window, and aims his gun. Siyali fires a shot – but in the air – at which point Jonas becomes aware of their presence for the first time. David rebukes Siyali for not having shot the Mercedes itself. David withdraws his service pistol and opens fire.

A car chase begins. At one stage they leave the N2, only to return. Then Jonas crosses the middle of the road and travels for a while in the direction of Somerset West *against* the flow of traffic. David pursues him. Then Jonas stops at the side of the highway, and he and one other male passenger get out of the car and flee into the nearby bushes.

David stops behind the Mercedes and runs after them. Siyali stays with Yengeni in the car.

A female passenger in the Mercedes remains in that car.

David catches up with Jonas, who puts his hands up. Jonas can see that David has the gun pointed at his genitals, finger on trigger. Jonas jumps to one side and is shot through the left thigh. When he tries to get up he discovers he can only walk on one leg.

Back on the N2, Siyali sees David emerge from the bush with Jonas in hand. He can see that Jonas has been shot in the leg. As David drags Jonas through the bushes, the MK man is screaming and evidently in immense pain.

Jonas, Yengeni and the female passenger in the Mercedes are taken to Security Branch headquarters in Culemborg for questioning.[30]

*

Gary Kruser arrives at Cine 400 cinema in Athlone on the evening of 21 September. He is there for a meeting with Bongani Jonas.

The place is saturated with police vehicles, however, and he is arrested.[31]

*

Speaking late on the night of 6 October, Adriaan Vlok, who is Louis le Grange's successor as law and order minister, feels sufficiently emboldened to declare victory in the Western Cape. He claims his men have smashed the ANC's Cape regional network following fifteen months of investigation.

The Inter Press Service reports on the 7th that since May forty-nine people connected to the spate of sabotage and guerrilla attacks in the province have been arrested.[32]

*

Also in October 1987, MK dispatches two companies totalling 200 men to the area between Angola's Uige, Cuanza Norte and Bengo provinces. The operational zone for this 'Northern Front' contrasts with the 'Eastern Front' campaign of 1983–84, which centred on Malange.[33]

In another difference from the earlier campaign, this time the unit is exclusively MK, with no FAPLA admixture, as the Angolan army is heavily committed in the south alongside Cuban troops trying to repel an SADF invasion.

MK's objective on the Northern Front is to protect the transport links connecting the ANC's camp network in the area against attacks by UNITA.

Following the arrival of the MK troops, peasants flock back to villages such as Mdlaza, Quibna and Tona Angola, from which they had fled following UNITA gains.

Ronnie Kasrils' son Andrew, who a few years previously underwent military training in Caculama, is now working in a Luanda print shop. One day he joins a convoy travelling the route between the ANC's Angolan bases. When they enter villages in the operational area, they are cheered and clapped by locals. These villages are administered by MK cadres. Kasrils recognises some of them from his time in Caculama.

When the convoy returns to Luanda, it is with Angolan civilians in tow. These villagers are carrying wares such as sugar cane which they hope to sell in the capital.[34]

*

At a ceremony in Lusaka marking his seventieth birthday on 27 October, Oliver Tambo announces that Chris Hani will become the new MK chief of staff, replacing Joe Slovo, and that Steve Tshwete will be the new army commissar.[35]

*

On 5 November, South Africa's justice minister Kobie Coetsee issues a press statement from Pretoria in which he announces that Govan Mbeki will be released later that day. He warns journalists that though they can record and quote statements made by Mbeki at his post-release press conference, he remains a listed communist and the ban will resume immediately thereafter.[36]

In an interview published by the *Sunday Star* three days later, Stoffel van der Merwe, the deputy minister of information and constitutional development, makes it clear that the government views the process as a trial run for the release of further political prisoners. He says 'the future of Mandela and others are, to some extent, in Mr Mbeki's hands'.[37]

*

In Lusaka on 23 February 1988, Steve Tshwete, in his new capacity as MK commissar, delivers a speech titled 'Politics and the Army' at the opening of an ANC Department of Political Education workshop.

Echoing a warning given by Simon Makana the previous year, he informs those gathered that 'in the rear, around our transit areas one discerns visible demoralisation and disgruntlement and even a loss of interest in the very life-line of the army – politics'. By contrast, morale is high in the Angolan training camps resisting UNITA encroachments (a notable difference from the operations in Angola in 1983–84).

What, then, is the problem among the cadres in the transit areas? For Tshwete, 'Certainly the cause lies not in a lack of political work.' Rather, 'When you talk to them and question their political lethargy, they will retort that "an army marches on its stomach".'

This is 'probably true', he says, and 'those of us who go to the transit areas quite often will discover that the logistics section is not at the job as it should [be]'. This needs to improve.

Tshwete raises a related point: 'One other problem about which almost all the cadres feel strongly is one of their prolonged stay in these transit areas.' At the present time, MK is 'contending with a series of applications in which cadres are requesting to opt out of the army for academic studies elsewhere'.[38]

*

The day after Tshwete's speech, President P.W. Botha signs an emergency order authorising Adriaan Vlok to place special curbs on individuals and organisations at his discretion.

Vlok immediately bans seventeen organisations (of which the largest are the UDF and the Congress of South African Trade Unions) from engaging in political activities without his express approval – the organisations are therefore not being banned outright, only restricted.

On 25 February, black paper is draped as a sign of mourning at Khotso House, the headquarters of many of the restricted organisations (including the UDF), as Anglican archbishop Desmond Tutu and Reverend Frank Chikane hold a press conference.

The churches were not affected by Vlok's measures, but Chikane says, 'I would not be surprised if they act against the church.' Tutu meanwhile says he hopes the people will still be willing to try non-violent strategies, 'but we have nothing to show for our non-violent approaches. If violence erupts, what will be surprising is that it has taken so long.'[39]

*

On 29 February, Damian de Lange of the Broederstroom cell presses a button on a radio transmitter, just as a South African Air Force bus conveying personnel from Dunnotar near Johannesburg to Waterkloof in Pretoria passes Fifth Avenue in Benoni. De Lange is standing nearby keeping the intersection under observation.

Pressing the button detonates home-made explosives that have been placed next to shrapnel and two limpet mines in a refuse bag. The bag has been placed on a pavement, about a metre from the bus as it passes.

The explosion only strikes a part of one of the limpet mines, however, and does not detonate the mine's explosive charge.

At 6.05 a.m. the following morning, De Lange again looks on as the Air Force bus approaches the intersection of Pretoria Road and Fifth Avenue. This time the bag containing the explosive device is placed next to a lamp post near a vibacrete wall that leads on to houses.

Using an improved detonator, De Lange again presses a button on a remote radio transmitter. The explosion occurs when the bus, packed with eighteen members of the military, is four metres from the lamp post.

Though nobody is injured, the bus is hit by shrapnel and damage worth R88,936 is caused to it and surrounding homes and businesses.[40]

*

In Atteridgeville outside Pretoria in March 1988, Mishack 'Mensday' Maponya converses with Rodney Toka. They are part of the unit infiltrated into South Africa from Botswana one day after the Broederstroom cell in July the previous year.

Maponya discusses a target that they need to attack, saying the policemen in question are notorious for petrol-bombing the houses of comrades in Atteridgeville and its vicinity. He says approval for the attack has been sought and obtained from Naledi Molefe, the unit's external commander based in Botswana.

Rodney Toka then speaks with MK operatives George Mathe and Ernest Ramadite. He gives them the location of the target and instructs them to assault it.[41]

*

Mohammed Shaik of the Dolphin Unit parks close to the entrance of the Krugersdorp Magistrate's Court on 17 March. The front of the court is occupied by the South African Police. Shaik enters the court complex and heads to the toilets.[42]

At 8.35 a.m., a bomb consisting of at least twenty-five kilograms of explosives detonates in the boot of a Nissan Skyline parked outside the court. The explosion rips the body of security policeman Simon Manabalala apart. Also killed are Frans Modalise, a labourer in the government mortuary, and Mr Papetsana Rampa, who like Manabalala and Modalise was on the pavement at the time.

Hours later, a second bomb, consisting of two mini limpet mines, is defused by police explosives experts in a ground-floor lavatory inside the court building.[43]

*

The following day, Francis Pitsi, Ernest Ramadite and George Mathe head to a tavern at 3 Mariana Street in Atteridgeville. As they walk past it, they see that there are ten or twelve people scattered in clusters in the yard. Closest to them, at a distance of four or five metres, is a table where four policemen are seated.

The MK men walk past and then gather. Pitsi, the commander, says that the grenade isn't suitable for the operation because of the way in which the policemen are spread out in the yard. He suggests they use the Makarov and the AK.

They then put on brown overalls, but while they are doing so, somebody passes them in the direction of the tavern. This causes the MK men to accelerate their plans and rush to the target in order to get there before the man.

Pitsi has the AK-47. At the tavern, from a distance of about five metres, he opens fire on the nearest table, at which there are now only three off-duty policemen, namely Barney Mope, Andrew Mphahlele and Nelson Phenyane. All three are killed by the salvo.

George Mathe, who has the Makarov, also begins shooting, but he accidentally fires a bullet through Pitsi's right side.

Pitsi, Ramadite and Mathe retreat from Mariana to Manaka Street.

Later, between 7 and 8 p.m. Mensday Maponya checks on them in Manaka Street to see if everybody is all right and to find out how things went.[44]

*

At about 1 a.m. on 28 March an SADF unit raids a house in Phiring in Gaborone's Broadhurst area. Four people are killed, three of them women. The fourth fatality is a man known to the Botswana authorities as Charles Mokoena, a registered South

African refugee, but to the South African security forces as Solomon Molefi, aka 'Paul Naledi', MK's regional commander in Botswana[45] (and it is indeed the same 'Naledi Molefe' who was the Botswana-based external commander of the Mensday Maponya–led unit operating in Atteridgeville).[46]

*

Mensday Maponya is driven by Peter Maluleka through central Pretoria in the early evening of 15 April. Maluleka stops on the corner of Beatrix and Church Streets. Maponya gets out and then Maluleka drives on towards Van der Walt Street.

At around 7.30 p.m., when Maponya is a few metres in front of the Sterland cinema complex on the corner of Beatrix and Pretorius Streets, a bomb explodes in his hands, killing him instantly. Though a car in the street is destroyed by the explosion and a woman receives slight injuries, no other damage is done. The cinema itself is left wholly undamaged.

When he hears the blast, Peter Maluleka immediately drives back towards Beatrix Street. When he gets to the scene he finds it crowded with people. He then proceeds in the direction of Church Street, and he parks in front of Van Aswegen Store. There are already a number of police personnel in that area as well.

Maluleka places a limpet mine on the verge of the pavement by the store.

At about 7.45 p.m. Maluleka's mine explodes, causing some windows to break in Van Aswegen and a few other properties in the vicinity, but no fatalities result.[47]

*

Hugh Lugg walks into a police station and hands himself over to the Security Branch on the morning of 8 May. He tells them of his activities as part of a group based at a nearby smallholding. He says he is the unit's intelligence officer.

Lugg is allowed to return to the smallholding, where he waits among his colleagues, who are oblivious to his treachery.

The police raid the smallholding in Broederstroom later that day. In the process they capture Damian de Lange, Ian Robertson and Susan Westcott, and recover a huge quantity of explosives, mines and weapons, along with two-way radio equipment and, in a new addition to the usual MK arsenal, a SAM-7 anti-aircraft missile.[48]

*

Francis Pitsi addresses Ernest Ramadite and George Mathe, the two members of his cell. He orders them to launch an attack in Pretoria. He tells Ramadite to place a limpet mine at the Juicy Lucy restaurant in the vicinity of Vermeulen and Andries Streets. He says the surrounding area houses offices of the Ministries of Finance and Trade and Industry, as well as premises used by the SADF.

He tells Mathe to place his mine at any isolated spot around Pretoria. The purpose of the blasts, he says, is to undermine the security of the regime and make the ANC's presence felt.

Mathe travels with Ramadite from Atteridgeville into central Pretoria on 26 May. The two part at a taxi rank.

At 12.53 p.m., a bomb explodes near the engine compartment of a white Renault parked outside a block of flats in Proes Street, about 100 metres from the corner of Proes and Potgieter Streets.

Just over twenty minutes later, four female librarians from the Pretoria City Council library are standing outside the Juicy Lucy restaurant on the corner of Andries and Vermeulen Streets, waiting to cross the road.

An explosion suddenly occurs, from a bomb in a concrete flower pot positioned on the street corner. It explodes in the face of one of the librarians, who runs back in the direction of the Juicy Lucy holding onto her arm. She is assisted by one of her colleagues, who is also injured. They leave a trail of blood in their wake.

They are turned away from the restaurant, because it is being evacuated.[49]

*

On the corner of Simmons and Pritchard Streets in Johannesburg's central business district the following day, municipal workers are tossing rubbish bins onto the back of one of the city council's garbage trucks. This causes a limpet mine in one of the bins to detonate in an explosion heard far and wide. The bin handler is not injured, but the driver suffers slight injuries on one arm and his face is scratched.

At 4.30 p.m. on the day after this, a limpet mine explodes on the staircase leading from the main concourse to Platform 16 at Johannesburg Railway Station. Mrs Priscille Atjesi receives shrapnel wounds to her legs, and has to be taken to hospital.[50]

*

John Battersby interviews Chris Hani and Steve Tshwete in Lusaka on 3 June. As chief of staff and army commissar, Hani and Tshwete are respectively numbers two and three in the MK hierarchy following the October 1987 reshuffle.

Hani says MK's key objective in 1988 is to cause the collapse of the municipal elections scheduled for October. He says the ANC views them 'as one gigantic step by the regime to restore what our people destroyed three years ago' when 'in the place of this puppet system our people were experimenting with new people's administration. Street committees, people's organs of power, people's courts.' But then 'the regime came in, deployed its troops, deployed the police and went out of its way to systematically try to destroy what the people had achieved'. Now the government wants to 'bring back the traitors and instal them and strengthen the position of the regime in the townships'. The ANC is therefore 'committed to aborting the municipal elections in October. And it is going to use both political and military methods to stop that.'

Battersby asks whether the recent Johannesburg and Pretoria blasts represent what is meant by 'armed propaganda'.

Hani's comments are notable for the hardening they show of the movement's interpretation of the slogan of taking the struggle to white areas when compared to the first formulations of it that appeared in 1985. He says of the bombs that 'they were to tell the whites that we are able to creep and crawl next to you. That be careful, and this is not just a threat, we are growing and we shall be able to do something big within your areas.'

Battersby asks about white civilian casualties.

'The death of white civilians is regretted too. I don't think we have any interest in the death of white civilians. But white South Africans, for a long time, have been complacent.' There must be 'soul-searching' among them, Hani says; they should ask, 'How long are they going to sacrifice loss of limb to maintain a system that deprives the overwhelming majority of the right to vote, of the right to a proper house, to proper medical attention, right to proper education?'

He adds: 'Before we turned to revolutionary violence we have turned so many cheeks.'

Tshwete interjects: 'We continued to turn our cheek even after we adopted armed struggle', but 'in the meantime the so-called white civilians in our country have been expressing complicity in this crime of genocide against our people. When they crossed the borders into Lesotho in 1982, massacred women and children and even innocent Lesotho citizens, an opinion poll was held after the raid and over 90 per cent of the white population said: "well done boys".'

Hani says apartheid 'guarantees a happy life for them, a sweet life. And part of our campaign is to prevent that sweet life.' He ends on a conciliatory note, however:

> We are saying to the whites: fellow countrymen. Let us join together and save our country from this madman [P.W. Botha] so that it remains a prosperous country. There is place for all of us. It is a big country. We accept that you are fellow South Africans who must rule this country together. We are not asking for the monopoly of ruling South Africa as blacks. It is not a racial struggle. We are not saying 'power to the ANC' but 'power to the people of South Africa'. We are not advocating a one-party state. We are advocates of parliamentary democracy. But not fascist and racist parties.[51]

*

The government's attention is also fixed on the October polls. Early in June, P.W. Botha takes Adriaan Vlok aside after a meeting of the State Security Council (a body whose function is to advise the government on all matters concerning national security), in which the cabinet was informed that the South African Council of Churches (SACC) and its affiliates are doing everything in their power to disrupt the municipal elections.

Playing on the Sotho name of the SACC's headquarters, Botha says Khotso House is no longer a house of peace, it is a house of danger. He suggests doing something about it. The pair discuss banning the SACC, but conclude that banning churches is not feasible.

The briefing that day followed others at previous meetings in which information, supposedly sourced from informants and interrogations, was advanced of MK cadres using Khotso House as a hideout, a storage depot, and a funding and communications channel.

Botha tells Vlok at the end of their discussion that this situation cannot continue whereby ANC terrorists use Khotso House as a base for operations against innocent South Africans and nobody does anything about it. Referring to the SACC he says: 'I have tried everything to get them to other insights, nothing helped. We cannot act against the people. You must make that building unusable – don't let them use that building.' He adds that they must at the same time ensure that no civilians are killed.

Vlok returns to Pretoria and briefs Johan van der Merwe, the chief of the Security Branch, about the president's order.[52]

*

Frederik Pienaar tells Eugene de Kock on 8 June that he has information that a group of armed MK members is expected to enter the country from Swaziland, and De Kock is going to have to deal with them. The terrorists will cross the border illegally in the vicinity of the Houtkop border post, and they will then follow the road to Piet Retief, from where they will proceed to Durban. Pienaar mentions that their source is of such a nature that they can plant one of their own agents as the driver.

Later that day, Pienaar, De Kock and Captain Gladstone Mose are at a spot near the border with Swaziland that is readily identifiable because it is right next to a large bluegum tree.

That evening, Pienaar, De Kock, Marthinus Ras, Flip Theron, Jury Hayes and Gerrie Barnard take up positions near the bluegum tree.

A Toyota Corolla approaches from the direction of Houtkop. It has its lights dimmed and the left indicator light on. Gladstone Mose, the driver, stops, climbs out and runs around the front. Eugene de Kock primes to storm the Corolla from its left-hand side. One of his colleagues is pointing a high-intensity hand-held search-light at the vehicle, which reveals that its windows have completely misted up from the inside.

Three or four seconds later, the left rear window starts to unwind. De Kock takes this as his cue to open fire on the left front door with his Uzi 9-mm-calibre sub-machine gun. His colleagues then fire on the back door on the left-hand side and also on the rear window. De Kock fires about twelve shots before ordering his colleagues to cease fire.

As he walks towards the car, the right back door opens and a woman falls out. She displays some signs of life; it appears as though she is trying to speak.

'Shoot her,' De Kock tells Ras, who complies.

In the left front of the car lies a black woman, at the left back door an Indian man, and in the middle of the back seat another black woman – all dead.

The dead Indian man is Lenny Naidu, who attacked Amichand Rajbansi's house in August 1985. The black women are Lindiwe Mthembu, June-Rose Cotoza and Makhosie Nyoka, members of an MK reconnaissance group.

When Frederik Pienaar searches the car a slight problem emerges. There are no weapons in the vehicle or on the persons of the deceased. After a discussion by the policemen about what to do, Lieutenant Ras tells Eugene de Kock he has a pistol and hand grenade. Ras places Lenny Naidu's hand around the pistol and fires two shots. He then gives two hand grenades to Pienaar, who deposits them in the group's carry bags.[53]

*

Flip Theron receives a phone call four days later. He tells the woman on the other side of the line that her information led to a successful operation.

The woman tells him there is another infiltration planned for that night.[54]

*

Members of the Security Branch offices at Middelburg, Witbank and Ermelo arrive in waves in Piet Retief during the course of the day.

Eugene de Kock, Christo Deetlefs and Frederik Pienaar have a conversation. De Kock suggests that a second shooting incident in such a short space of time would make it clear to the enemy that there has been a security breach, and the commander on the other side (who they believe to be Charles Ndaba of the MK Natal Machinery) would probably lose control of his network and not be allowed by his superiors to infiltrate people again.

De Kock therefore suggests sending a second group into Swaziland so that after the terrorists have been sent across the border, the commander and his companions can be killed as well.[55]

*

Johan Tait, Marthinus Ras, Cornelius Botha and Paul van Dyk are on the Swazi side of the border on the evening of the 12th. They are positioned by the road leading to the place where the MK men are expected to cross into South Africa. In keeping with De Kock's expanded plan, they are there to ambush the commanders who will send the men on their way.

A vehicle stops about 100–150 metres away. The four security-force members hear the sound of the boot being opened, of rifles being cocked, and of footsteps heading in the direction of the border.

The policemen wait a while, and then move towards the empty vehicle. The road makes a slight embankment. Behind it, at a distance of fifteen or twenty metres from the vehicle, they take up ambush positions and wait.

After a while they hear two people returning from the border. Van Dyk opens fire on the pair as they start entering the vehicle. His colleagues follow suit.

Botha moves closer to the vehicle after the policemen have ceased fire. Next to the car is a dead man with a Makarov in his possession.

The other man has apparently managed to escape (they presume it is Charles Ndaba because the dead man is not Ndaba). Botha shoots the car's petrol tank and Ras sets it alight with matches.[56]

*

Detective Sergeant Manzini drives a Nissan E20 van on the Houtkop–Piet Retief road. As he approaches the bluegum tree, he puts on the left indicator but then he drives a further eighty metres beyond the tree before stopping. Manzini then jumps out and runs round the vehicle.

Driving beyond the tree was not part of the plan. Eugene de Kock runs towards the vehicle. When he is about a metre away, the left front door opens and a man climbs out with an AK-47. De Kock opens fire with his Uzi 9-mm. With the third or fourth shot the man begins to fall.

From the periphery of his field of vision on the right side, De Kock notices the barrel of an AK-47 pointing at him from the back seat of the car, but at this stage some members of his Vlakplaas unit have taken up position diagonally behind him and open up on the minibus. Then the other security policemen form a line behind the minibus and fire through its back window.

De Kock gives a ceasefire signal. Four black men, Jabulani Sibisi, Joseph Mthembu, Sifiso Nxumalo and Nkosi Thenjekwayo, are killed in this incident. This time each was carrying an AK-47.[57]

*

Rodney Toka, Francis Pitsi, George Mathe and other members of the MK unit in Atteridgeville are arrested on the following day.[58]

*

Ayanda Dlodlo, a female MK military intelligence operative who is also head of the section of the Natal Machinery responsible for the infiltration of cadres, returns to Swaziland having been away in Angola during the period when the two ambushes occurred on 8 and 12 June.

She arranges a meeting with her second-in-command, Phila Ndwandwe, who, since being arrested at Vijay Ramlakan's house on 23 December 1985, subsequently managed to flee the country and receive military training in Angola prior to her present deployment in Swaziland.

Dlodlo asks what happened to 'Umakhosi' (Makhosie Nyoka).

Ndwandwe says she was sent on a reconnaissance mission (on 8 June) and was expected to report back information about the level of safety of that route. This was so that the second, larger team could safely be dispatched. However, when Umakhosi failed to return with word about the safety of the route, they assumed the route was clear and safe, so they sent the second team (on 12 June).[59]

*

As Eugene de Kock suspected, following the June ambushes, the ANC launches an investigation into those in the Natal Machinery responsible for armed infiltrations.

This affects the greater part of the Machinery. In the process, virtually the entire Natal Command is withdrawn to Lusaka.[60]

The source who provided Flip Theron the information that led to the two ambushes is arrested by the ANC in Swaziland some two weeks after 12 June, during this process. She is also sent back to Lusaka for questioning.[61]

*

Ayanda Dlodlo is summoned to meet Oliver Tambo. The ANC president expresses unhappiness at the timing of the missions, saying that from 15 May onwards it would have been too risky to have cadres entering the country because the South African security forces would be on high alert with the 16 June anniversary on the way.[62]

*

Lester Dumakude, one of those targeted in the McKenzie affair the previous year, is now commander of the MK Special Operations Unit. He drives Harold Matshididi in a BMW from Zone 5 in Diepkloof, Soweto, to central Johannesburg on the afternoon of Saturday 2 July. Aggie Shoke and Itumeleng Dube, the two remaining cell members, follow close by in a van. The two vehicles stop by the off-ramp on Harrow Road.

After agreeing that they will meet up in Hillbrow after the mission, Dumakude and Matshididi return to the BMW. Dumakude again drives, and he and Matshididi head to Upper Meyer Street, which runs adjacent to Ellis Park rugby stadium.

Dumakude drops Matshididi off and parks the car opposite a house a few metres ahead. He sets the explosive, and then walks towards Matshididi. The two then proceed on foot in the direction of Hillbrow.[63]

At 5.17 p.m., Roger Haggerty is among the first wave of Transvaal supporters to exit Ellis Park following their team's victory over Free State. He is close to the BMW left by Dumakude, which is about fifty metres from the stadium's north-east turnstiles, when there is a massive blast. He feels like he has been hit by a car and is thrown to the ground with injuries that will result in him having a leg amputated.

Peter Soal, a member of Parliament for the Progressive Federal Party, is in a minibus driven by a friend some thirty metres from the BMW when the blast occurs, causing the bus's door to bend and its windscreen to crack, while a chunk of metal from the destroyed vehicle flies over the roof and lands next to the bus. Christina Mosomane, aged seventeen, sees fragments of the BMW flying towards her home at number 4 Upper Meyer Street. She closes her eyes and dives to the floor. When she opens her eyes she sees that the room is on fire.

The Ellis Park bomb blast kills two men, Clive Clucas and Lenus Maree, and leaves at least thirty-five others injured.[64]

*

Mac Maharaj sleeps overnight on a bench in the transit lounge of Nairobi's Jomo Kenyatta International Airport. In the morning, he boards the only Royal Swazi Airways flight of the day from Kenya to Mbabane.

Siphiwe Nyanda boards the same flight a bit later and sits a seat in front of Maharaj. Nyanda's face is disguised: he has had special teeth put in that have changed the shape of his mouth.

After take-off, the aeroplane heads first to Dar es Salaam, and then to Mbabane. During the flight, Nyanda is served by one of his best friends. She doesn't notice him under his disguise.

When the plane lands in Swaziland, Nyanda walks past a local security policeman that he knows from the past. Again, this old acquaintance suspects nothing.[65]

*

Ivan Pillay drives Totsie Memela, who works in reconnaissance in the ANC under-ground, from Mbabane to Ezulwini in Swaziland. On the way they stop for an old man standing next to the road. The man gets into the back seat and starts talking to Pillay when the journey resumes. Memela recognises the voice and has to fight the temptation to look back.

The vehicle arrives at a chalet in Ezulwini, opposite the Ephesus-Emlalatini Development Centre, a correspondence school.

They enter the chalet, and Memela can at last have a closer look at the 'old man'. It looks vaguely like Mac Maharaj. The look combined with the timbre of his voice convinces her it *is* Mac Maharaj, but she doesn't say anything.[66]

*

An askari walks down Wanderers Street in Johannesburg at lunchtime on 20 July. He spots a policeman who he knows inside a parked vehicle. He walks up to the car, gets in, and sits alongside the four policemen. The policeman that he recognised then steps out of the car, saying he is going to buy food.

The askari looks out the window of the police car and happens to see a man he knows well from Angola. He tells the policemen to get him, and the officers exit the vehicle and proceed to a clothing store in the street into which the man has stepped.

The fourth policeman comes out of the shop having purchased the food, and runs to the car when he notices his colleagues are gone. After being told by the askari where they went, he drives to the clothing store.

The three policemen then emerge from the store. In their custody is Douglas Mathambo, who is in the country as part of a mission to reconnoitre targets and build structures in the West Rand area. Mathambo was in the store checking out lumber jackets that were on sale.

When Mathambo enters the vehicle he immediately recognises the askari, whom he last saw when undergoing training in exile.

The askari greets Mathambo, who remains silent as the vehicle departs. The askari calls him 'Johnson' and asks how he is doing.

Mathambo (alias Johnson Maputo from his days at Caculama camp in Angola in 1985) denies that he is Johnson.

'Do you still remember me?' the askari asks.

'No,' says Mathambo.[67]

*

Edward Lawrence of the Natal Machinery appears before an ANC panel of inquest on 26 July. He is asked to talk about his 'wife'.

Lawrence says she was the first enemy agent he was sure of.

He is asked how many times she went to South Africa and for what purposes.

Lawrence says he was never in a position to monitor her movements. She went to South Africa about four times, as far as he knows, and she never wanted to reveal the purposes behind her visits. She also refused to submit her Lesotho passport when asked, because it reflected her trips to South Africa and could have led to her being questioned and discovered to be an enemy agent.

After about an hour and a half spent covering the same terrain, everybody is tired, so they adjourn for the day.

When Lawrence is awoken the following morning, he complains of stomach pains. He says he wants to vomit.

A doctor is called, and when he arrives he certifies Lawrence dead. The doctor informs the panel of inquest that Lawrence may have taken poison.[68]

*

Three days later, on 30 July, Alfas Ndlovu plants a limpet mine in a Wimpy Bar in Benoni, about a kilometre from Benoni Police Station.

Just before noon, Albert Clementson is sitting with his fiancée and daughter at a table inside the restaurant, where there are about seventy people. He has just ordered a late breakfast.

Suddenly, there is an explosion. The top of the Clementsons' table disappears and debris flies across the building.

Warrant Officer Chris Craucamp, who is just outside the Wimpy at the time, sees a man running from the restaurant with his hair alight. Then other people start running out. They are all bleeding.

This Wimpy Bar bombing results in one fatality, a woman named Mary-Ann Serrano.[69]

*

Thami Zulu is brought in for questioning by ANC security in August 1988 as part of what has become a general inquiry into the Natal Command as a whole, not just those directly involved with infiltrations.

Believing now that Edward Lawrence and his wife were spies, the interrogators focus their questions on whether Zulu was a third person working for the South African security forces.[70]

*

Totsie Memela, Ivan Pillay, Mac Maharaj and Siphiwe Nyanda meet in Swaziland. They discuss the recent arrest in Natal of the people who were supposed to pick them up after crossing the border.

Maharaj says: 'We do it now. We go in now before they start talking. By the time they are broken we should be inside the country.'[71]

*

On his farm, Korea, in the Bridegwater area of the northern Transvaal, Dawid Swanepoel looks through his binoculars between 3 and 4 p.m. on 3 August 1988 and sees South African Police members in an armoured vehicle a kilometre away open fire on a group of black men. The guerrillas fire an RPG rocket in return, but it misses the policemen.

Swanepoel next sees five of the guerrillas fall in a hail of bullets and a cloud of dust. The police bullets detonate grenades in the guerrillas' possession.

A sixth guerrilla escapes, though badly wounded.[72]

*

On 5 August, following three days of talks in Geneva, Switzerland, negotiators representing Angola, Cuba and South Africa sign an agreement aimed at ending the fighting in which they have been embroiled in southern Angola (which provided the broader context for MK's campaign in the north of the country).

The resulting 'Protocol of Geneva' commits the signatories to recommend to the United Nations (UN) secretary-general that 1 November 1988 be set as the date to start implementing Security Council Resolution 435, which will lead to free and fair elections in Namibia and independence for the country.

The protocol consists of ten clauses. The last calls on the parties to act in accordance with two principles. The first is 'non-interference in the internal affairs of states', and the second advocates 'the acceptance of the responsibility of states not to allow their territory to be used for acts of war, aggression, or violence against other states'.[73]

The words are vague, but their implications for the future of MK's camps in Angola are not.

*

Jacob Rapholo is commander of a group of seven heavily armed MK cadres who infiltrate South Africa from Botswana two days later. They make their way through Ellisras district and stop in the bush at a place called Beauty. There they establish a temporary base on a farm next to the Palala River, about ten kilometres from Tom Burke. As with the group ambushed on the 3rd, this position is close to the Botswana border.

At 4 p.m. the following day, with darkness descending, Rapholo listens to the news on a portable radio. The dispatch is led by a report that Botswana's presidential jet has been struck by a missile in Angola while on its way to a summit in Luanda following the signing of the Geneva Protocol.

While listening to the news, Rapholo hears a group of people approaching. He orders his men to be on the lookout. Then he hears a voice say, in Afrikaans, 'They are here.'

Rapholo orders his men to shoot. In the ensuing skirmish the guerrillas employ grenades to neutralise the enemy fire. The security forces in turn toss grenades back at the MK cadres.

The disarray caused by the grenades in both ranks brings the fighting to a stop. Rapholo orders his men to cease fire. One of his men, James Kgwatlha, aka 'Benson', lies dead. Rapholo and the MK unit's commissar, Mike Mokoena, also have slight injuries caused by shrapnel.

On the security-force side, Constable M.N. Claassen is dead.

The surviving guerrillas manage to escape to Botswana under the cover of darkness. Mokoena loses contact with them but makes his own way across the border.[74]

These two incidents in close succession in August 1988 indicate how difficult infiltration across the Botswana border has become by this time.

*

The incidents also emphasise the importance of the ANC's longstanding commitment to shift its command and control structures to within South Africa's borders.

At about 2 p.m. on 8 August, Ivan Pillay walks Mac Maharaj and Siphiwe Nyanda from Swaziland into South Africa, thereby initiating 'Operation Vula', the project involving the infiltration of senior ANC leaders into the country, which has been discussed since the 1970s and was approved in 1986. Siphiwe Nyanda kneels and kisses South African soil. The group proceeds to a stretch of tar road about forty kilometres from Piet Retief, where Totsie Memela is waiting. Nyanda and Maharaj are wearing overalls as if farmworkers. Maharaj is also sporting a Copperhead cap to conceal his straight hair. Hidden on their persons are arms as well as falsified identity papers.

There are many people around, mainly women who are there to buy old clothes from an auction organised by a local farmer.

A car driven by an expatriate Irishman pulls up, and Maharaj and Nyanda enter. They give their guns to Pillay and Memela, who stay behind as the vehicle pulls off.

On the evening of the same day, the vehicle arrives in Johannesburg. The Irishman asks where Maharaj and Nyanda want to be dropped off.

They say the Carlton Hotel.

'But where's the house you're going to?'

'Don't worry comrade, thank you very much, just drop us at the Carlton Centre,' Maharaj replies.[75]

*

Having been briefed earlier in August by Johan van der Merwe regarding President P.W. Botha's order that Khotso House be rendered unusable, towards the end of the month Willem Schoon, the head of the security police's covert operations section, meets Vlakplaas commander Eugene de Kock. Schoon tells De Kock to contact members of the Security Branch in Johannesburg – Brigadier Erasmus will then make the necessary arrangements.

On the evening of 30 August, less than a week later, Brigadier Gerrit Erasmus drives a short distance from his house to a property in Honeydew, Johannesburg. There he finds a group of white Vlakplaas troops, headed by Eugene de Kock. They are equipped with daggers, leather batons and coats. Between them the group have eight rucksacks packed with heavy explosives.

Erasmus tells them the operation is directed against members of the terrorist movements who are using Khotso House. He wishes them luck and then departs.

The Vlakplaas operatives get into two vehicles which head in the direction of De Villiers Street in central Johannesburg. They arrive at about midnight. After exiting the vehicles they walk in formation towards Khotso House.[76]

*

At about 1.20 a.m., the rucksacks containing the explosives, which have been left by the Vlakplaas team at the dividing wall between two lift shafts in the basement of Khotso House, are activated by electronic time switches.[77]

At Chiltern House, which is a block of flats next to Khotso House, residents are awoken by a huge explosion which rips doors from hinges, shatters mirrors and hurls people from their beds. At Khotso House itself, the foyer floor collapses into the basement and a large section of the front façade is blasted open, tossing rubble into the street, where two female passers-by are in shock after the clothing is torn from their bodies by the force of the detonation.

In all twenty-three people are injured, including a security guard who fell into the gaping hole created by the foyer's collapse. There are no fatalities.

Adriaan Vlok that night issues a statement of condolence to the injured and says the police are conducting an intensive investigation to find the culprits.

When dawn arrives, it can be seen that what was Khotso House is now a pile of rubble flooded by water from burst pipes. The building is unusable, so the mission has achieved all the objectives set for it by President Botha.[78]

*

The now well-honed askari system displays its worth once more on 21 September. At 7.50 a.m. three former MK cadres are dropped off by their white handler at the Black Chain Shopping Centre outside Baragwanath Hospital in Soweto.

The askaris are all in civilian dress and none are armed. They walk in the direction of the taxi rank. Then one of them says, looking leftwards: 'There is a terrorist. Man, there is Metsing.'

Simon Modise, alias 'Metsing', the commander of an MK unit operating in Soweto, is standing about twenty paces to the left. He notices the askari and starts running. One of the askaris starts chasing Modise while the other two run to the car.

The South African Police captain who has remained in the car sees two of his men come running back.

'Captain, we've found a terrorist there,' one of them says.

He asks who it is.

'Metsing,' they say.

The police car drives round the shopping centre and the passengers spot Modise, who is wearing brown trousers, a maroon shirt and a white cloth cap.

Modise looks back at the police car and takes off his cap before holding it to his chest. The vehicle catches up with him and one of the askaris shouts: 'Metsing, stand! If you don't stand still you are going to be shot.'

Instead, Metsing runs faster.

The askari calls a second time, upon which Modise runs into another street in Diepkloof.

Just when Modise is about to enter the yard of a house, one of the askaris, Jimmy Mbane (from the ambush of the Gugulethu Seven), opens fire and Modise falls into the yard.

People from the neighbourhood start gathering at the scene. With the crowd swelling, the policemen abort their plan to arrest Modise there and then. They head to Protea Police Station instead to file a report.

They return to the scene afterwards but find that Modise has already been removed. He is later arrested, however, and hospitalised because of his wounds.[79]

*

Adriaan Vlok was premature with his boast in October 1987 of having crushed the armed underground in the Western Cape. Just before eight o'clock on the evening of 28 September 1988, Sidney Hendricks, Vanessa November and Coline Williams of the Ashley Kriel Unit, which is headed by Shirley Gunn and Aneez Salie, arrive at the Bonteheuwel Rent Office.

The area is poorly lit and thus largely dark. Williams primes a brown limpet mine. The mine is inside an empty milk carton at the office's front door.

At about 8 p.m. a homeless man, Nurudien Bartlett, picks up the carton, but then drops it, causing the mine to explode. The blast shatters windows and tears off roof tiles in the rent office. Bartlett himself is later found lying outside the building having suffered extensive burns. He has lost his eyesight, two fingers, and his hearing on one side.[80]

By now, all attention is focused on October, the month of the municipal elections. On the day after the blast, a spokesman for Adriaan Vlok discusses the police's plans to thwart the ANC's attempts to cause the failure of the elections. He says: 'All police leave has been cancelled and we have taken a host of other steps, some of which are visible and some of which we cannot disclose.'[81]

*

In October, Major Andrew Taylor drives Jakobus Forster and Brigadier Steyn from Port Natal to Swaziland. They stop at a house in the vicinity of the Onverwacht border post, where Brigadier Steyn gets out.

Warrant Officer Lawrence Wassermann and Major Salmon du Preez travel to the border area on the same day, driving a Toyota van and an Isuzu bakkie.

They are accompanied by two former MK operatives. These askaris creep through the border fence and join up with Wassermann and Du Preez on the other side. The askaris then drive the Isuzu to Manzini.

Later that afternoon, Phila Ndwandwe, who since Thami Zulu's arrest has been appointed acting head of the Natal Machinery (thus becoming the most senior female frontline commander in MK's history), is driven by a comrade, Richard Jones, to Manzini's George Hotel.

When she arrives at the George, Ndwandwe sees two other 'comrades' in a vehicle parked nearby. She is pleased to see them, and walks up and begins conversing with them in an animated manner.

She then returns to Jones to fetch her purse from the dashboard.

Jones has no petrol in the car and so asks for money.

She opens her purse and gives him ten rand. Then, looking at him through the passenger window, she says she will see him later.

Looking on are Andrew Taylor, Hendrik Botha and Jakobus Forster. They are in a car parked behind the police's Isuzu bakkie, which has the two askaris inside. The Isuzu in turn is parked behind the Toyota which has Lawrence Wassermann and Salmon du Preez inside.

It is about 6 p.m. Ndwandwe enters the Isuzu. She sits between the two men. When the Isuzu heads off in the direction of Big Bend it is followed by the Toyota, with Taylor trailing further behind. The Toyota soon overtakes the Isuzu.

At a turnoff about fifteen kilometres outside Manzini, the Toyota hems in the driver's side and Taylor's car the passenger side of the Isuzu.

The driver of the Isuzu gets out, after which a number of policemen from the two other cars enter the vehicle. They take Ndwandwe and put her in the Toyota.[82]

*

Later that evening, the security officers are back at the police house near the Onver-wacht border post where Brigadier Steyn has been waiting for them.

Hendrik Botha interrogates Ndwandwe.

Wholly unresponsive at first, she begins to answer some questions over time. She tells them that a limpet mine explosion at Pinetown Post Office on 12 August, as well other incidents, were the work of units operating under Phumezo Nxiweni's command.

Throughout the questioning, Botha searches for signs Ndwandwe might be will-ing to cooperate as an informer.

None are forthcoming, so he asks her directly.

She flatly refuses.

The following morning, she is transported to a safe house on a farm called Elandskop near Pietermaritzburg.[83]

At Elandskop, when it becomes clear that she is unwilling to become an agent, Botha hands her over to other members of the Security Branch who execute and bury her on the farm.[84]

*

Speaking at the Cape Congress of the National Party on 5 October, Adriaan Vlok announces that the police possess 'confidential information that a number of terrorists have infiltrated the country' to sabotage the forthcoming municipal elections, and he announces a R5,000 bounty for information leading to their arrest.[85]

As promised by Chris Hani and Steve Tshwete earlier in the year, the elections are the focus of a major campaign by MK to cause their collapse. In September, twenty-nine limpet mine explosions were recorded in South Africa – a monthly record for MK.[86]

On the same day as Vlok's speech to the National Party congress, there are explosions at the magistrate's courts in Wynberg near Alexandra and in Stellenbosch in the Western Cape, with no injuries resulting. These are the third and fourth limpet mine blasts in South Africa during October.[87]

Six people are injured – one critically – the following afternoon when a limpet mine explodes in a rubbish bin outside the Tembisa municipal offices.[88]

A series of blasts in Tembisa and Duduza on the East Rand, as well as Bishop Lavis in the Cape on the long Kruger Day weekend (7–10 October) leave nine dead and twelve injured, including four policemen hurt at the South African Police barracks in Tembisa on the morning of the 10th.[89]

Six security-force members guarding a hostel in Katlehong are injured on the evening of the 12th when a gunman opens fire on them with an AK-47, while a few hours later three black men are injured by a limpet mine explosion in a telephone booth at Dunnotar Post Office.[90]

On the 21st, Adriaan Vlok announces that the police have arrested fifty armed terrorists since the beginning of September.

On the following day, as Vlok officiates at the opening of a police station in Crossroads in the Western Cape, Riot Unit members spot a man carrying a black bag approaching at a distance of approximately 150 metres. A warrant officer stops him and a sergeant searches the bag. The sergeant uncovers a primed limpet mine. At the man's house in Crossroads later that day, ANC literature is found by the police.[91]

On Monday the 24th, a car bomb explodes in Witbank on the corner of Delville and Botha streets at 8.14 a.m. This rush-hour blast occurs within metres of an office block housing South African Police and security-force personnel, and it kills Elias Masina and Samuel Matsuko, both civilians, while injuring over forty others in what is the nineteenth explosion of the month.[92]

A bomb placed under a stairwell at the Eland Building in Kerk Street in Potchefstroom's central business district explodes at 7 a.m. the following morning. The security police have offices in the building, and one of two officers at work at the time is slightly injured by flying glass. The building will have to be declared unsafe.[93]

*

On 26 October, the day after the Potchefstroom blast, the Associated Press reports the outcome of South Africa's municipal elections.

In the black townships, it says turnout was generally below 10 per cent, but the government's view is that when advance votes are taken into account, the total black turnout will exceed the 21 per cent recorded in the 1983 local elections, making the process a qualified success from Pretoria's perspective.[94]

But the ANC also claims victory in a reaction conveyed on Radio Freedom the following evening. 'Compatriots,' it begins, '26th October has come and gone. But the day will remain another milestone in our struggle against apartheid and white minority domination. No matter how much the regime tries to convince the world that it has received a mandate from the black people to go ahead with its apartheid reforms, no matter what percentage the regime claims as its support within the black community, one thing became clear out of the fraudulent elections yesterday. It is that more than 80 per cent of the insignificant number of involuntarily registered voters refused to [vote] yesterday.'[95]

*

Sergeant Casper van der Westhuizen is with Hendrik Botha and Salmon du Preez in a car on the way to Durban's Kings Park Stadium on the afternoon of 4 November. Botha tells Van der Westhuizen that the person they are going to arrest is a very dangerous ANC terrorist and that after they capture him they are going to eliminate him.

Later that evening at a safe house in Verulam, Botha, Du Preez and Van der Westhuizen have in their custody Phumezo Nxiweni, the man they were looking for.

Under questioning he confirms some of the information provided by Phila Ndwandwe, but offers no new information. After being held in custody for about two days Nxiweni is executed on the farm.[96]

*

On the evening of 18 November, Hendrik Botha and Salmon du Preez wait alongside Lawrence Wassermann at the Avoca Bridge between Durban and KwaMashu. They spot three men, Sibusiso Ndlovu, Amanzi Filakazi and Elias Matjale, approaching.

The policemen arrest the three and confiscate a bag containing three SPM limpet mines and detonators from them. The captives are then driven in the police van to the safe house in Verulam where Phumezo Nxiweni was executed.

Later that evening at Phoenix Railway Station, Andrew Taylor remains in a van with Ndlovu, Filakazi and Matjale, while Botha, Du Preez and Wassermann get out and prepare the limpet mines retrieved earlier in the evening at Avoca Bridge. The three policemen then return to the van, haul the captives out, remove their handcuffs, and drag them to a place near the railway line.

Botha asks them to kneel down and show where they would have placed the limpet mines.

Each of the three policemen stands behind one of the captives. Botha gives a nod, upon which he and his colleagues fire one shot each from their Scorpion pistols into the back of the head of the man in front.[97]

*

In New York City on 22 December, Angola, Cuba and South Africa sign a final Tripartite Agreement. The accord calls on the parties to request the United Nations secretary-general to seek authority from the UN Security Council to commence the implementation of Resolution 435 on the (now delayed) date of 1 April 1989.

Echoing the Geneva Protocol, the signatories also pledge that:

> Consistent with their obligations under the Charter of the United Nations, the Parties shall refrain from the threat or use of force, and shall ensure that their respective territories are not used by any state, organization, or person in connection with any acts of war, aggression, or violence, against the territorial integrity, inviolability of borders, or independence of any state of southwestern Africa.[98]

This marks the end for MK in Angola.

This is confirmed by Oliver Tambo at Lusaka's Inter-Continental Hotel on 8 January 1989. Flanked by the Reverend Jesse Jackson from America, Tambo says ANC fighters will pull out of Angola in order to facilitate efforts to achieve Namibian independence.

He says the move is meant to deny South Africa and her allies the opportunity to use the presence of ANC facilities in the country as an excuse for stalling. He vows that the withdrawal will be conducted in such a way that the struggle is not interrupted.

Tambo pledges that the ANC will do 'everything in our power to facilitate this process, recognising the fact that the agreements signed in New York constitute an advance of great strategic significance for our region'.[99]

*

At 4 p.m. two days later, Shirley Gunn, who is eight months' pregnant with the child of Aneez Salie, her co-commander in the Ashley Kriel Unit, listens to a radio broadcast in which a Major Jaap Joubert reads a statement from Pretoria on Adriaan Vlok's behalf, in which he announces that the police are seeking her in connection with being involved in the Khotso House bombing.[100]

*

It meanwhile transpires that Pretoria has chosen to interpret the October elections as a mandate from the black community to continue with its reform programme. This becomes clear on 18 January, when Chris Heunis, South Africa's minister for constitutional affairs, holds a press conference following a meeting the same day with over sixty representatives of the black urban councils elected in the municipal polls.

They release a joint statement declaring that the councilmen agreed to establish a forum that would 'represent black people outside the self-governing territories, which can eventually participate as a component together with other components, in the broad national process of negotiations' envisaged by the National Party, leading to a new constitution for South Africa.

Crucially, however, having homeland leaders and township councillors represent blacks in these negotiations would effectively exclude the ANC from the reform process.

Heunis hails the initiative as evidence that 'the evolutionary movement is gaining tremendous momentum against the radicals'.[101]

Other observers are not so sure. The Inter Press Service reminds its readers when reporting the news that the proposed spokesmen for urban blacks were elected in a poll marked by less than 20 per cent participation. An equally underwhelmed *Natal Mercury* predicts that the forum will be rejected by blacks, as will any other initiative that fails to respect two basic conditions: firstly, blacks must have faith in those speaking for them; and, secondly, they must have confidence that the resulting talks will lead to the end of apartheid.[102]

The articles therefore agree that the constitutional reform programme is likely to suffer the same fate as its predecessor earlier in the decade, raising the spectre of continued political stalemate and an indefinite prolongation of emergency rule – if President Botha remains in power.

*

But on 18 January, the same day as Heunis's meeting with the councillors, P.W. Botha is hospitalised following a mild stroke at his home.[103]

INTERREGNUM

On 3 February the National Party chooses F.W. de Klerk its new leader. P.W. Botha will remain as state president for the time being, but he resigns his leadership of the National Party.[1]

*

F.W. de Klerk makes his first major statement as National Party chief when addressing the Tricameral Parliament on 8 February.

'I want to state unequivocally,' he says, 'that the National Party is against domination of any one group by others. White domination, in so far as it still exists, must go.'

But he also affirms his commitment to 'group rights', saying: 'a strong emphasis on group rights, alongside individual rights, is based on the reality of South Africa and not on an ideological obsession or racial prejudice'.[2]

At a press conference in Cape Town on the evening of the 8th, De Klerk stresses his belief that 'typical one-man-one-vote leads to majority rule', which 'would be catastrophic for South Africa'.[3]

Oliver Tambo responds the following day from Lusaka, saying De Klerk's reform pledge 'does not mean anything'.

Noting the reaffirmation in the pledge of P.W. Botha's rejection of a one-person-one-vote system, Tambo contends 'we are back to square one, because if you do not accept the system, then, the white domination stays in place'.[4]

*

But once-stable international currents are beginning to shift. At a press briefing in Moscow on 14 March 1989, a journalist asks the Soviet Foreign Ministry spokesman, Gennady Gerasimov, about Soviet support for armed struggle in South Africa.

'What armed struggle? How can one support something which doesn't exist?' comes the acerbic response.[5]

The following day, at a roundtable in Moscow organised by the Novosti press agency, Yuri Yukalov, head of the Soviet Foreign Ministry's Department of African Countries, says in more measured tones: 'We would prefer a political settlement and want apartheid to be dealt with by political means.' He warns that 'any solution through military means will be shortlived'.

He stresses: 'We do not want to emphasize the need to enlarge the armed struggle. South Africa should not be destroyed. It should also be spoken to not only through threats or pounding our fist on the table. There should be dialogue.'[6]

*

Speaking the same day in London following a meeting with British prime minister Margaret Thatcher, South African foreign minister Pik Botha tells reporters that the apparent shift in Soviet policy is of great significance.

'The season of employing violence is over, it's gone,' he says. In the new international climate, 'terrorism is not going to be used any more to achieve political objectives, and the organisations that embark on this might as well pack up. They are in for a surprise.'

A journalist points out that the ANC feels otherwise.

'The season is out, whether they like it or not, and there is no way you can continue along a certain course when the tide has turned and the tide *has* turned. Moscow is not interested in using these tools any longer to further its interests in various regions of the world.'

Regarding Nelson Mandela, Botha says:

> Make no mistake, the South African government fully realises that Mr Mandela inside prison or in restricted living conditions is doing us far more damage. The problem is how to do it, that his release is not accompanied by an upsurge in violence that leads to bloodshed and the re-arrest of Mr Mandela and other people. The issue is not whether he ought to be released – I think we have already decided he ought to be released. The position is how to do it in such a way that there is no risk.[7]

*

At the British Houses of Parliament the following day, Prime Minister Margaret Thatcher says she told Pik Botha when she met him yesterday that Nelson Mandela must be released.

Speaking for her government, she says that if this were to happen,

We believe then the atmosphere would change completely and it would be possible to get negotiations started between the government of South Africa and black South Africans and the Coloured people of South Africa. I think that a number of people in South Africa in very high places take the same view. They have not yet been able to bring it about. But I remain optimistic that before very long they will be able to do so, because it is vital that voluntary negotiations get started.[8]

＊

In Harare on 22 March, at a one-day meeting of the OAU Ad-Hoc Committee on Southern Africa, Oliver Tambo makes a move on the ANC's behalf in response to these developments.

Citing United Nations Security Council Resolution 435, which served as the framework for the resolution of the Namibian conflict, and lacing his observations with a thinly veiled swipe at Margaret Thatcher's recent manoeuvring, he urges the OAU to adopt 'a strategy that would involve a kind of Resolution 435 for South Africa. This would enable Africa to take the initiative and not respond to strategies of those who have defended South Africa at every turn.'[9]

＊

Quatro detention camp detainees Charlton Mavundla and Pat Hlongwane are among sixty-nine passengers (some Angolan army troops, others MK cadres) who are flown on a military charter plane from Luanda to Uganda at midnight on 28 March 1989. This is part of the great withdrawal of MK cadres from Angola.

It is still dark when they arrive in Uganda. They land on an airstrip that seems far from any town. As they exit the plane they are met by Chris Hani and a welcoming contingent of Ugandan military forces. They are then taken to a camp.[10]

＊

At an ANC-run farm in the Makeni area forty-two kilometres north of Lusaka on 15 April, Sadhan Naidoo, the farm's manager, and Mthunzi Ningiza, a mechanic, are shot dead by a gang of men who steal some household goods including TV sets and stereo players before speeding away in a Toyota Land Cruiser.

At the funeral service for Naidoo and Ningiza at Lusaka's Hindu Hall on 22 April, Oliver Tambo reveals to the five hundred mourners assembled that the killers are suspected to have been ANC members. He says 'we must blame ourselves that we keep enemies and tolerate them. Zambians are also victims of these killings.'

Zambia's *Daily Mail* confirms the following Monday that the suspected assailant is believed to be an ANC member who has been captured and is being held by ANC security officers.[11]

＊

Joe Modise instructs a group of about twenty-five MK cadres to go to South Africa and attack a military base near Mafikeng. The group heads from Zambia to Zimbabwe and then crosses into Botswana near Francistown.

On the night of 2 May, three Land Cruisers transport the men southwards. Then, after the border fence has been cut, the vehicles enter South Africa at a point between Lobatse and Mafikeng. In their cargo the guerrillas have five mortars and 270 shells. They head to the Klippan military radar station in Slurry, fifteen miles from Mafikeng.

They arrive at the station sometime between 2.30 and 3.30 a.m. on the morning of 3 May. The Cruisers then deploy in the vicinity of the station. Some six mortar shells are fired at the compound from distances in excess of 1,000 yards. A number of shells explode within the compound. Some living quarters are struck, but no casualties result. In terms of the numbers of men involved, this is probably the largest ever single operation carried out by MK on South African soil.

After firing their shells, the group departs in the direction of Botswana, planting landmines to cover their retreat. One of the mines is detonated by the SADF pursuit patrol. An ANC guerrilla is captured during the chase.[12]

*

An article in the *Washington Post* on 10 May features extracts from an interview that the paper's correspondent William Claiborne recently conducted with Thabo Mbeki and John Nkadimeng.

Mbeki said: 'The time has come to challenge the state of emergency more forcefully – not to take the emergency as an act of God that there is nothing we can do about.'

Referring to a recent prison hunger strike that led Adriaan Vlok to order the release of 800 political detainees, Mbeki said it offered evidence of growing black resentment against the restrictions: 'The fact that the emergency hasn't been lifted says something. It hasn't broken the spirit of people opposed to apartheid.'

The UDF would be expected, he continued, to coordinate this new defiance campaign from underground until matters reached the stage where the emergency decrees would become unenforceable due to the sheer number of people who would have to be detained to quash it.

Nkadimeng meanwhile observed: 'The people have already unbanned the ANC, in effect. They speak about the ANC openly. They hoist the ANC flag at funerals. Why shouldn't they defy other restrictions?'[13]

*

On 18 May, a Soviet Iluyshin 62 Aeroflot aircraft leaves Luanda with 135 ANC members among those on board.

As the plane enters Tanzanian airspace, two men, one white, the other black, stand up in the aisles. The white man, Bradley Richard Stacey, brandishes what he says is a hand grenade and orders that the flight be diverted to South Africa because one of the passengers on board is 'a Russian communist wanted in South Africa'.

A Soviet security man shoots Stacey in the chest, wounding him seriously.

The other would-be hijacker surrenders.

At 2.46 p.m. local time, the plane lands at the end of the runway of the old Dar es Salaam Airport. There are policemen and soldiers waiting for it.

Witnesses on the tarmac see Stacey being taken from the plane by stretcher. He is then flown by military helicopter to Muhimbili Medical Center in Dar es Salaam and placed under heavy armed guard. The second hijacker is arrested by the Tanzanian Police.

The hijackers were both disillusioned with the ANC. Stacey, who is in his late twenties, had left South Africa in March 1986 with the police seeking him in connection with an act of arson at Natal University where he was a student. He became disillusioned with the ANC because of its involvement in the Angolan Civil War, and particularly the approximately eighty lives lost by MK during the 1987–88 Northern Front campaign against UNITA.[14]

*

On 25 May 1989, following the incident the previous month in which Sadhan Naidoo and Mthunzi Ningiza were killed, ANC spokesman Tom Sebina informs *Times of Zambia* reporter Fanwell Zulu about the commencement of a process aimed at disarming ANC cadres in Zambia. These measures are not meant to leave the ANC and its members 'naked and defenceless', he says, but rather to ensure that discipline prevails within the movement's ranks.

'It is not an easy job, but it has to be done and it is being done,' Sebina adds.[15]

But attacks on ANC properties and personnel in Lusaka increase as this attempted disarmament proceeds. Between 10 p.m. and midnight on 18 June an explosion occurs at Alfa House in Emmasdale suburb, where some ANC members are staying. No casualties result.

Half an hour later a bomb explodes at a petrol station in Matero township. A security guard is injured.

Then, at about 6.30 a.m. on the 19th, an explosion occurs in the alley joining Nkwazi Road between Chachacha Road and Freedom Way. This incident occurs during the morning rush hour. Commuters see pieces of flesh and bone being thrown through the air. The bomb's reverberations rip open the roof of an outlet belonging to Associated Wholesalers, and also damage the walled fences of nearby commercial enterprises. A man's blackened torso and his feet, severed at the ankles, are found at a rubbish heap near the scene of the explosion. One other person is injured in this attack.

Then, at about 11 p.m. on the 21st a bomb rips through the ANC's Lusaka offices. A man in his mid-twenties loses both legs as a result.[16]

*

Speaking in London the following day (22 June) ANC member Aziz Pahad tells the media that the organisation's NEC gathered on the 8th after all its members had met with COSATU and UDF representatives who had been allowed to leave South Africa.

Pahad says the NEC meeting drew up a discussion document centred on the issues of whether the organisation should negotiate with Pretoria, and if so, on what terms, under which preconditions, how the negotiating body should be composed, whether to cease armed hostilities, whether a transitional government should be formed, and what the role of the international community would be.

This document, he says, is now being circulated inside and outside South Africa. 'We will initiate discussions throughout the entire country to elaborate what are the aims of negotiations.'[17]

*

Stoffel van der Merwe, South Africa's information minister, tells a press conference on 28 June that the National Party congress in Pretoria the following day will adopt a platform for the forthcoming parliamentary elections envisioning a direct vote for blacks in national affairs within five years.

But the proposals remain within the framework of the principle of 'group rights' espoused by De Klerk in February. Under the platform, while the Group Areas Act will remain on the books, in cases where people are found living in a zone designated for another race there will be a system of 'assistance and negotiation' to 'solve the problem without legal intervention'. There would also be a dual education system comprising racially segregated 'public schools' and multiracial 'private schools', both funded by the government. For political purposes there would be 'a shift from the present race-defined groups to culturally defined groups', and it would be for the people in the groups, and not the government, to decide who can join. A Bill of Rights would be established and, finally, a new Constitution would be negotiated with 'recognised leaders of all groups committed to the pursuit of peaceful solutions'.

In order to prevent the white minority being dominated by the black majority, Van der Merwe adds, government officials will contemplate the formation of a body like the United Nations Security Council, in which the major powers have a veto on some issues, but not all.[18]

*

Addressing the opening session of a conference held in Lusaka on 30 June, Oliver Tambo describes the five-year reform programme as a 'shocking insult'. The conference is attended by 20 senior ANC officials and 115 white South Africans belonging to a body called the Five Freedoms Forum. The meeting is being held to discuss the possible shape of a post-apartheid society.

'Apartheid must be destroyed now, not after five years,' Tambo says. The reform programme unveiled yesterday offers 'no meaningful alternative'.

Helen Suzman, former PFP leader and a member of the Forum, asks Tambo later at this meeting whether the ANC would suspend its armed struggle for a period of two years if Pretoria met its basic demands.

Tambo replies the ANC would be prepared to suspend its armed struggle if

Pretoria met five basic conditions. These are: lifting the ban on the ANC and other political organisations; removing South African troops and armed police from the townships; scrapping the detention laws; releasing Nelson Mandela and other political prisoners; and lifting the state of emergency.[19]

When saying farewells following the conference, Helen Suzman's final words to Steve Tshwete are: 'No damn bombs between now and September!' (September 1989 is the scheduled date for South Africa's next general election.)[20]

*

On 5 July in the president's office at Tuynhuys, the early Cape Dutch home that is situated alongside the Houses of Parliament in Cape Town, Nelson Mandela sits in the middle vehicle of a five-car convoy.

The vehicles enter the premises.

An elevator later takes Mandela from the underground parking area to the ground floor. The doors open out to a wood-panelled lobby. In the room are justice minister Kobie Coetsee and Niel Barnard, the head of the National Intelligence Service, along with a host of prison officials.

A while later the door to the adjoining office opens. Mandela enters and President P.W. Botha walks from the other side, smiling broadly with hands outstretched. They meet halfway and pose for a picture shaking hands.

Everybody leaves except for General Willemse, Kobie Coetsee and Niel Barnard, who join Botha and Mandela at the long table for tea.

Mandela begins by saying he recently read an article in an Afrikaans magazine about the occupation of a town in the Free State during the 1914 Afrikaner Rebellion. He says that he sees parallels between that struggle and that of black South Africans. They get to talking about the rebellion.

After about half an hour the discussion winds up, and Mandela chances raising a substantive issue. He asks Botha to unconditionally release all political prisoners, including himself.

Botha says he is afraid he can't do that.

Mandela asks him to release Walter Sisulu on compassionate grounds.

Botha asks Niel Barnard to look into it.

Botha rises, shakes Mandela's hand and says it has been a pleasure.

Mandela thanks him and heads to the door.[21]

*

On 23 July 1989, Coline Williams, aged twenty-three, and Robbie Waterwitch, twenty, of the Ashley Kriel Unit are killed while planting a bomb inside a public toilet across the street from Athlone Magistrate's Court in Klipfontein Road.

About half an hour later at 9.45 p.m., an explosion at a temporary satellite police station in Mitchell's Plain causes light damage.

A third bomb blast occurs at Somerset West Magistrate's Court at 11.23 p.m.

Then, at Bellville Magistrate's Court, a policeman spots a man about to plant a mini limpet mine. The man flees, and police bomb disposal experts arrive later to defuse the device.

The magistrate's courts targeted were to be used the following morning for the nomination of candidates for the general elections, which are to take place on 6 September. Speaking the day after the blasts, Colonel Nik Heynes informs the press that the police are investigating the possibility that the incidents form part of a 'campaign of terror' that the ANC has launched ahead of the elections.[22]

*

At a news conference two days later, Saki Macozoma of the South African Council of Churches says non-whites requiring medical care will seek treatment at four white hospitals in the Transvaal and four in Natal beginning on 2 August.[23]

*

Prakash Napier walks in to his family home and bumps into his brother Shan, who hasn't seen him for five months.

'It is nice to see you back, where were you?' Shan asks.

'No, I was in Cape Town.'

'You know, we were really worried about you,' Shan says.[24]

*

On 2 August, the Associated Press reports that in Johannesburg and Durban that day, scores of black and Indian patients, backed by throngs of protesters, sought treatment at whites-only hospitals. The patients were granted entry and hospital officials told the media they would not turn anyone away who appeared to be in genuine need of medical care.

This is the commencement of the new defiance campaign led by the UDF from the underground that Thabo Mbeki and John Nkadimeng advocated in the *Washington Post* in May. The Associated Press report quotes Dr Aslam Dasoo, a Johannesburg general doctor, saying: 'As of today, the mass democratic movement considers all health facilities in South Africa open.' He adds: 'The government doesn't seem to be able to end apartheid, so we are going to end it for them.'[25]

*

At St Mark's Catholic Church in Bonteheuwel three days later, 5,000 people attend the funeral service for Coline Williams and Robbie Waterwitch. Also present are dozens of policemen carrying automatic weapons and teargas canisters strapped to their belts. A police helicopter hovers above.

The coffins of the deceased are draped in ANC colours as they are carried through the crowd. One attendee, sporting a keffiyeh, waves a green, gold and black flag.

'One must not be surprised that in the end, young people begin to think that to plant bombs is the only way to bring change,' Reverend Allan Boesak says at the service. 'It is our duty to make sure that this election will be the last election where our people are excluded.'

Archbishop Desmond Tutu says, 'Thank you, Coline. Thank you, Robbie. Thanks especially to you young people in your dedication to justice and peace, caring and humanity.'

At the traditional post-funeral meal, which is held in a public hall at the church, police fire teargas and remove the ANC flags from the coffins. Demonstrators quickly replace the flags and link arms to prevent the removal of another flag in the hall. The flags are nonetheless all removed.

During the burial at Maitland Cemetery, however, additional ANC flags are smuggled past the police and placed on the coffins just prior to burial.[26]

*

On the same day as the funeral in Bonteheuwel, eight armed men storm the house of Ms Vinus Choobe in Lusaka, and abduct her boyfriend, Sipho Mbeje, at gunpoint.

Speaking four days later, Iheukumere Duru, acting representative of the United Nations High Commission for Refugees (UNHCR) in Zambia, names Mbeje as one of four men, along with Richard Sikhosana, Norman Phakati and David Lephoto, who had left the ANC and asked the UN to resettle them in other countries, only for them to be arrested by ANC security on 4–5 August, with the two detained on the 4th being apprehended 500 metres from UNHCR offices. Duru calls on the ANC to return the four.

Zambia's director for refugees, Musyani Simumba, echoes the appeal the following day.[27]

When quizzed by reporters at a meeting of the Frontline States in Lusaka later on the 10th, Thabo Mbeki confirms that the four men were picked up by ANC security. He says they were detained on suspicion of involvement in the recent bombings of ANC properties in the Zambian capital.[28]

South Africa's *Citizen* newspaper the following day quotes Sipho Mbeje's aunt saying her nephew is being held with thirty-two other ex-ANC members in Lusaka where they are being beaten, with the real reason for their detention being that they disagree with the movement's policies. A *Washington Times* report three days later alleges that in Sweden twelve further ANC members have defected from the organisation.[29]

The latter report appears under the headline 'Tambo and ANC appear to be ailing', referring in part to the ANC president's non-appearance at the Frontline States meeting on the 10th.

Speaking to a *Times of Zambia* reporter in Lusaka on the day of the appearance of the *Washington Times* article, Thabo Mbeki denies a BBC report that Oliver Tambo is in London receiving medical treatment for a stroke: 'The ANC president did not suffer any stroke,' Mbeki says. 'He is in London to see his family where his wife works.'

Asked why Tambo missed the Frontline States meeting, Mbeki answers that Tambo had been asked to 'take a rest for a while' and 'doctors have advised him not to work too much because too much work may have its consequences. He was told to keep away from meetings.'[30]

*

Seated at a desk in his office at Tuynhuys that evening, 14 August, President Botha makes a televised address to the nation in Afrikaans. The broadcast follows a three-hour emergency cabinet meeting in Cape Town which discussed F.W. de Klerk's plans to hold talks with President Kenneth Kaunda later in the month.

In his address, Botha says he can no longer continue as head of state after not being consulted about the plans for the meeting between De Klerk and Kaunda.

'The ANC is enjoying the protection of President Kaunda and is planning insurgency activities against South Africa from Lusaka,' he charges. 'It is evident to me that after all these years of my best efforts for the National Party, and for the government of this country, as well as the security of our country, I am being ignored by ministers serving in my cabinet. I consequently have no choice other than to announce my resignation.'

He says he asked the cabinet what reason he should give to the public for his abrupt departure. 'They replied I could use my health as an excuse. To this I replied that I am not prepared to leave on a lie.'

In Pretoria the following day, F.W. de Klerk is sworn in as acting president for an interim period till the September elections.[31]

*

The ANC hands Sipho Mbeje, Norman Phakati, Richard Sikhosana and David Lephoto to Zambian authorities on 18 August.[32]

*

In a report appearing in the *New York Times* that same Friday, it is reported that anti-apartheid activists yesterday declared that their organisations, banned during a crackdown on dissent in February the previous year, will resume operating on Sunday 'openly and without the shackles of unjust restrictions'.

Quoted is Archbishop Desmond Tutu, one of the organisers of the Sunday demonstration. He said they would not ask the government for permission to hold the meeting.[33]

*

On Sunday 20 August, a three-hour service at Cape Town's St George's Cathedral is attended by 5,000 people.

'We have won a very great victory,' Desmond Tutu says. 'We are saying to the world that if we don't get to the beaches we will have been stopped by dogs from being on God's beaches. We are saying this is God's sea. This is our country and we are claiming what is ours.'

Murphy Morobe, now a UDF spokesman, tells the service, 'There have been many battles. Some of these battles we have lost, but when you look at what is happening on the beaches, within our schools and what is happening here in Cape Town, we can truly say that we are winning.'[34]

*

With Egyptian president Hosni Mubarak chairing, the OAU's Ad-Hoc Committee on Southern Africa meets in Harare the following day. President Kaunda submits a twenty-four-point document to the meeting. It has been drafted by the ANC.[35]

In the document the ANC vows that 'we shall continue to do everything in our power to help intensify the liberation struggle and international pressure against the system of apartheid until this system is ended'.

It notes, however, that 'a conjuncture of circumstances exists which, if there is a demonstrable readiness on the part of the Pretoria regime to engage in negotiations genuinely and seriously, could create the possibility to end apartheid through negotiations. Such an eventuality would be an expression of the long-standing preference of the majority of the people of South Africa to arrive at a political settlement.'

Section III of the document, titled 'Climate for Negotiations', sets out the ANC's terms. It says the government must, 'at the very least',

19.1 Release all political prisoners and detainees unconditionally and refrain from imposing any restrictions on them;
19.2 Lift all bans and restrictions on all proscribed and restricted organisations and persons;
19.3 Remove all troops from the townships;
19.4 End the state of emergency and repeal all legislation, such as, and including the Internal Security Act, designed to circumscribe political activity; and,
19.5 Cease all political trials and political executions.

Upon 'the creation of this climate, the process of negotiations should commence along the following lines':

21.1 Discussions should take place between the liberation movement and the South African regime to achieve the suspension of hostilities by both sides by agreeing to a mutually binding ceasefire.
21.2 Negotiations should then proceed to establish the basis for the adoption of a new Constitution by agreeing on, among others, the Principles enunciated above.
21.3 Having agreed on these principles, the parties should then negotiate the necessary mechanism for drawing up the new Constitution.
21.4 The parties shall define and agree on the role to be played by the international community in ensuring a succesful transition to a democratic order.
21.5 The parties shall agree on the formation of an interim government to supervise the process of the drawing up and adoption of a new constitution; govern and administer the country, as well as effect the transition to a democratic order including the holding of elections.
21.6 After the adoption of the new Constitution, all armed hostilities will be deemed to have formally terminated.
21.7 For its part the international community would lift sanctions that have been imposed against apartheid South Africa.

The OAU meeting adopts the document as the 'Declaration of the Ad-Hoc Committee on Southern Africa on the Question of Southern Africa'. In time it will be better known as the 'Harare Declaration'.[36] Its adoption marks the realisation of Oliver Tambo's call earlier in the year for a Resolution 435 for South Africa, in what will prove to be the last great effort of his tenure as ANC leader.

*

On 28 August, F.W. de Klerk and Kenneth Kaunda meet at Victoria Falls.

The event is an anti-climax. At a joint press conference held after the talks, De Klerk says, while Kuanda looks on silently, 'There was a lot of speculation as to whether we would have discussions on the so-called ANC proposals.' But, he says, 'It didn't come up, it wasn't discussed, it wasn't on the agenda at all.'[37]

*

Alfred Nzo confirms two days later that Oliver Tambo has been in a London hospital for more than two weeks having suffered a brain spasm. He is comfortable, in good spirits and progressing well.[38]

*

In South Africa's general election on 6 September, the National Party wins 93 seats, the Conservative Party 39 and the Democratic Party 33.[39] (In the previous election, the National Party won 123 seats, the Conservatives 22, and liberal/moderate parties 21.)[40]

*

St George's Cathedral in Cape Town, situated just a few dozen metres from Parliament, is packed again on 13 September.

In the streets outside, there is a crowd perhaps 20,000 strong consisting of heavily bearded Muslim men wearing keffiyehs, black militants with T-shirts bearing UDF and ANC insignia, others in shirts with the image of the AC Milan footballer Ruud Gullit, Indian ladies in saris, coloured schoolgirls in blue uniforms with thick red lipstick and heavy earrings, prosperous-looking men in dark suits, and other young upwardly mobile whites in aerobic gear.

The riot police are not present.

In the cathedral, a Muslim cleric, a rabbi, a Catholic priest and an Anglican minister speak. After the service, Cape Town's mayor Gordon Oliver and some of his city councilmen walk arm in arm with Archbishop Desmond Tutu and Sheik Nazeem Mohammed, the president of the Muslim Judicial Council, in the direction of Cape Town's City Hall. When two black, green and yellow flags are unfurled by somebody in the large crowd following them, a loud cheer breaks out.

From the balcony of City Hall, Jay Naidoo, the general secretary of COSATU, speaks about 'liberation from the shackles of apartheid' and 'the people's wrath'.

Allan Boesak addresses the crowd next. 'Mr de Klerk says the march is OK so long as we keep within the confines of the law.' But 'what law? We have defied the law! Mr de Klerk says he wants to talk ... about what? Until this is a free and open and non-racial society, the protest will continue.' He concludes: 'Today we march on City Hall. Tomorrow we march on Parliament to claim our full rights. And you, *you, you* the people, shall make it happen!'

Archbishop Tutu, wearing purple robes and a gold chain, refers to a statement by President de Klerk declaring an intent to initiate discussions on how to incorporate everybody into a new South Africa: 'We want to say to Mr de Klerk: we have already won. Mr de Klerk, if you know what is good for you, join us! Join us in the struggle for a new South Africa!'[41]

*

In a statement broadcast nationally on 10 October 1989, F.W. de Klerk says 'most South Africans are tired of confrontation', before announcing the release of Walter Sisulu, Andrew Mlangeni, Raymond Mhlaba, Ahmed Kathrada, Elias Motsoaledi, Wilton Mkwayi and the trade unionist Oscar Mpetha, pending the conclusion of prison formalities.

Nelson Mandela, De Klerk says, is fully aware of the steps that have been announced, but his own release is 'not on the agenda now'.[42]

*

The South African Police deliver Walter Sisulu to Orlando West at 5.25 a.m. five days later.

'It's good to be home,' he tells the assembled press corps. 'Let me see my wife.'

Upon his release, Ahmed Kathrada meets Prakash Napier and Yusuf Akhalwaya, who have been assigned to his house as bodyguards.

On the evening of the 15th, Sisulu appears with Kathrada, Mhlaba, Mkwayi, Mlangeni, Motsoaledi and Mpetha. Behind them is a large gold, black and green banner.

Sisulu informs the press that he and his colleagues are appearing as ANC leaders; therefore the event represents the organisation's first press conference inside South Africa since being banned.[43]

*

London's *Financial Times* reports on Monday 23 October that the South African government has approved the staging of the ANC's first rally in the country for twenty-nine years the following Saturday. The rally is to be addressed by the seven newly released prisoners.

The article notes that the ANC 'appears to have suspended its guerrilla campaign against Pretoria, although its officials have yet to spell this out'. The correspondent, Michael Holman, bases this surmise on the fact that there have been 'no reported violent incidents linked to the ANC's military wing, Umkhonto we Sizwe, for nearly two months'.[44]

*

On 25 October, the day before Transkei's Independence Day, South Africa's military attaché in the homeland compiles a memorandum in which he warns his colleagues, 'Die pot begin kook in Transkei.'

He mentions a meeting held that morning in which harsh words were exchanged. The initial idea was that President Ndamasa would announce in a speech on Independence Day that the ANC is being unbanned in the homeland. However, when given the prescribed speech by General Bantu Holomisa (who took power in a bloodless coup in 1987), the president insisted that the measure must first be discussed with the police and the security services.

The police, the army and the security services all raised objections on the grounds that if the move were taken, the territory would develop into an ANC stronghold equipped with cells that would be used to launch operations against South Africa, leading to South African reprisals that would be seriously detrimental to the country. The attaché says that on the basis of those arguments, General Holomisa agreed to hold back the announcement in order to have some time to think about it.

Later in the meeting, according to the attaché, Transkei's minister of finance, G.S.K. Nota, proclaimed that the homeland was headed for financial disaster because South Africa was in the process of turning off the fiscal taps.

Holomisa 'snarled' at him to shut up.

At another point in the meeting, President Ndamasa expressed unhappiness at the ANC being allowed to make the reburial in the Transkei of Sabata Dalindyebo (a chief loyal to the ANC who had died in exile) a political demonstration.[45]

Despite the objections raised at the meeting, the ANC is de facto unbanned in the homeland by this time. On the 26th, Holomisa attends an ANC rally in Umtata as part of a 70,000 crowd who are addressed by the seven leaders released by De Klerk earlier in the month.[46]

*

Prakash Napier leaves his home on Saturday 28 October and heads to Soccer City, the newly built football stadium on Soweto's outskirts.

Later that day, a crowd of 80,000 gathers in the stadium.

Two dozen goose-stepping soldiers in khaki caps and military uniforms lead Ahmed Kathrada, Raymond Mhlaba, Wilton Mkwayi, Andrew Mlangeni, Elias Motsoaledi, Oscar Mpetha and Walter Sisulu onto the pitch. Prakash Napier walks by Kathrada's side.

Christopher Wren of the *New York Times* looks on as the honour guard of uniformed men, marching briskly and, he notes, out of step, lead the released prisoners on a lap of honour. A rally spokesman announces that the escorts are 'symbolic' of Umkhonto we Sizwe.

When the lap is complete, the escorts lead the seven onto a platform dominated by giant flags of the ANC and the SACP. These flank a fifteen-metre-high banner reading 'The ANC Leads! The ANC Lives!'

Murphy Morobe reads a speech from the stage on Oliver Tambo's behalf. 'This is a joyful day for all of us,' Morobe says. 'We meet to celebrate a victory that belongs to all the people of our country.' He says of the whites: 'They are part of our heritage.

In the end, they too must learn to celebrate freedom and not oppression.' Tambo-through-Morobe then offers De Klerk a place among South Africa's peacemakers, but warns that if De Klerk chooses to preserve apartheid 'he will disappear with the criminal system he has sought to defend'.

Walter Sisulu delivers the keynote address. He makes it clear that there is no question of the ANC unilaterally abandoning the armed struggle. However, if De Klerk creates the right climate by releasing political prisoners and detainees unconditionally, unbanning all political organisations, removing troops from the townships, ending the state of emergency, and ceasing political trials and executions, the ANC would be willing to discuss a suspension of hostilities by *both* sides.[47]

*

Dr Ralph Mgijima, the head of the ANC's Health Department, is at his Lusaka home late one afternoon in November 1989 when security men deliver Thami Zulu, an old friend, to his door. Mgijima is shocked by Zulu's condition and general weakness.

The two converse. Zulu tells Mgijima that his condition deteriorated rapidly when he was kept in an isolation cell. He had to lie all day on a mattress on the floor.

On the morning of the fifth day after his release to Mgijima, Thami Zulu's breathing becomes extremely laboured and he is rushed to Lusaka's University Training Hospital, where he dies shortly afterwards.[48]

*

A meeting of the ANC NEC's National Working Committee begins in Lusaka at 9 a.m. on 21 November.

Joe Modise says they will need to get the latest on TZ (Thami Zulu). A post-mortem will show the actual cause of death. He says the case is going to be problematic because the South African Council of Churches have become involved. The NEC must have a report about TZ because from the very beginning there was no clarity on his involvement in spying activities. Modise hails TZ as one of the movement's most outstanding cadres: he rose and excelled, he was called to the front and his introduction immediately brought a rise in activity. Modise demands to know what was found against him.

Mzwai Piliso of the ANC's Department of Intelligence and Security (often referred to as 'Mbokodo') is under fire because the deterioration of Thami Zulu's health occurred while he was in the hands of the ANC security department. Piliso says the important thing is to conduct a post-mortem. The board has started work in 'Sun City' (the detention centre where Zulu had been held). He adds that he went to see TZ personally, and he raised the issues in the doctor's report.

Chris Hani demands an ANC commission of inquiry. This is no longer an internal matter, he says. The parents have become involved, the press has carried letters, *Africa Confidential* has information about his detention. Hani recounts that after Zulu's release to Comrade Ralph, he took the first opportunity to visit him. He says Military Headquarters had never been given an opportunity to visit TZ. Hani found

TZ alone, looking over sixty, emaciated, gaunt, eyes protruding. Zulu told him: 'Chris, I am dying … since February.' Hani says TZ was in security's hands; they knew his issue was explosive. He asks why the loss of weight was detected so late: why did it take security so long to notice that the comrade was so gravely ill?[49]

*

Eugene de Kock and Glory Sedibe are in a luxurious hotel room in Vienna, Austria, where they have to keep each other awake because they are awaiting a phone call that must be answered.

To help stay awake, they converse. De Kock asks how much information Sedibe really gave the security police.

Sedibe says approximately 10 per cent.

De Kock asks why so little.

Sedibe answers that it was enough to keep him alive. In any case, they already had much of the information. He only had to confirm it.

Later during their two-week stay in Vienna, and having received the call from a member of South African Military Intelligence's Directorate of Covert Collection (DCC), De Kock and Sedibe meet the DCC man, who is accompanied by a very prominent member of the ANC's Department of National Intelligence and Security ('Mbokodo'). Sedibe knows the man well and is there to convince him to work for South African Military Intelligence.

At one point the Mbokodo man gets to talking with De Kock privately about Thami Zulu. He recalls an occasion in which he and other ANC members wanted to shoot Mr Deetlefs, Mr Labuschagne and four other members of the South African Security Branch at the Royal Swazi Hotel while they were playing golf. Thami Zulu was sent to fetch the weapons. When Zulu returned he didn't have the weapons and said he couldn't find them. It was after this incident that he was recalled and arrested.

The Mbokodo officer asks De Kock whether 'Boniface' (Thami Zulu) was an agent. De Kock says no.

The ANC man says his organisation then made a terrible mistake in that particular case. He asks whether Edward Lawrence was an agent.

De Kock says Lawrence was not a source; he was a very effective operative.

Then they made a terrible mistake with him as well, the Mbokodo man replies.[50]

*

On 3 December 1989, President de Klerk, his cabinet and some fifty advisers board two Hercules transport planes at Waterkloof military airport. At 7 p.m. they arrive at D'Nyala Game Reserve near Ellisras in the northern Transvaal.

The meeting begins the next day. During the discussions, defence minister Magnus Malan speaks out against adding the SACP to the list of organisations to be unbanned.[51]

Much debate follows as the meeting continues into the 5th, but eventually sufficient consensus is reached for justice minister Kobie Coetsee to feel able to say: 'Fasten your seatbelts, we are going places.'[52]

*

On 11 December, Jacob Rapholo (the commander of the failed infiltration into South Africa near Ellisras on 7 August the previous year) and Charles Seakamela arrive at a property in the Nelspruit area. They leave a container there that has two AK-47s and some hand grenades inside.[53]

*

At around 7 p.m. that evening, Shan Napier says to his brother Prakash at the family home: 'Okay, just lend me the car, I just want to go somewhere and come back quickly.'

Shan leaves in Prakash's Mazda. He returns slightly after 8 p.m.

Prakash takes the keys from him and says: 'It's late. I've got to go somewhere'.

'Okay, no problem,' Shan replies.

Prakash looks at the time and repeats: 'It's late. I've got to go.'

At Hillbrow Police Station later that evening, Prakash Napier is in the company of Jameel Chand and Yusuf Akhalwaya, his colleagues in MK's Ahmed Timol Unit, of which Napier is commander and Chand political commissar.

Akhalwaya walks fifty yards ahead while Napier remains at the police station with two limpet mines. Chand stands on lookout a further fifty metres behind. By the time Napier has planted the first mine, the detonator on the second has begun counting down.

From the police station, the group then walk to Park railway station, where they plant their second mine. But then they see a goods train approaching, and, mistaking it for a passenger train (bringing with it the possibility of unwanted civilian casualties), they run to remove the second limpet mine from the spot where they have planted it. This consumes more time with the mine still counting down.

Shortly afterwards, just north of Park Station, some fifteen metres from an empty steam locomotive, Akhalwaya and Napier begin replanting the second mine, while Chand is again on the lookout, this time on some stairs about fifty metres away.

It is approximately 11.25 p.m. The mine explodes, shattering windows and spraying glass over a wide area. Akhalwaya suffers fatal burns, and the explosion severs Napier's head and one of his legs from his body. Human remains are tossed up to sixty metres from the scene.

Chand is thrown off his feet by the blast, but lives. While he is lying on the ground with a Soviet gun in his hands, soldiers rush past him to the scene of the explosion. None of them notice him and he walks away. After a couple of hours he realises he needs to get rid of the gun. He deposits it in a rubbish bin.[54]

*

Two days later, on 13 December, Nelson Mandela meets F.W. de Klerk in the president's office in Tuynhuys, where the meeting with P.W. Botha occurred in July. Also present are Kobie Coetsee, General Willemse, Niel Barnard, Mike Louw and Eddie Roux.

Mandela says that he totally rejects the concept of group rights as entailed in

De Klerk's five-year plan: 'This is going to discredit the whole effort by the National Party to help bring about democracy in this country.'

'If you don't want the concept of group rights, I will remove it,' De Klerk replies simply.[55]

*

On Christmas Eve, Jacob Rapholo and Charles Seakamela arrive in Johannesburg. They spend a couple of days on the Rand looking for ANC members who might be able to assist them in accessing the arms cache they left in Nelspruit on the 11th.

On Boxing Day, having failed, they travel back to the northern Transvaal.

When they reach Zebediela on their way back to their hideout further north, Rapholo heads to a motel, from where he phones Mozambique to request more money and a vehicle. When he fails to get through, he tries to contact Zambia. He is again unsuccessful, leaving the two cadres effectively cut off from either internal or external support.[56]

*

Speaking in Lusaka at the ANC's anniversary celebrations on 8 January 1990, Chris Hani responds to the recent rumours that MK has suspended its armed struggle to facilitate the peace process. He tells reporters that the lull in MK attacks in 1989 was instead due to logistical problems. The ANC was forced to close its military bases in Angola and relocate to Tanzania and Uganda, he says, but now 'we have completed the process of re-establishment and re-organisation'. He adds that another complicating factor was the manner in which, over the past couple of years, the movement had been infiltrated by askaris. But now 'we have learned our lessons and know how to operate'.[57]

Reporting on the 8 January celebrations in the London *Independent* the following day, John Carlin argues that there exists a 'fiction' that the ANC and the South African government share an interest in propagating. This is the myth of what the one refers to as 'terrorism' and the other as its 'armed struggle'. In reality the phenomenon 'barely exists beyond the minds of those who employ these terms'.

Carlin contends that the ANC's statements that it seeks to intensify the armed struggle belie the fact that

> There is not a great deal to intensify. Planned attacks on police, military or government personnel by the ANC's military wing, Umkhonto we Sizwe, were unheard of in 1989. Hazy reports of attempted sabotage operations occasionally appeared in the inside pages of the local press. Most frequent were limpet mine blasts, usually late at night in remote corners of cities. But not one civilian was reported killed or wounded during the year as a consequence of ANC military action – a fact which places in context the police claim that 144 'terrorist' incidents took place in the first eight months.[58]

*

On 15 January 1990, a group of foreign diplomats, ANC leaders including acting president Alfred Nzo, and senior Zambian government officials are waiting for an aeroplane to land at Lusaka Airport. It is a steamy, tropical day, and rain pounds the runway.

The dignitaries take cover in the airport terminal, leaving a hardy group of young ANC comrades on the tarmac. These youths chant: 'Viva the South African Communist Party!' 'Viva Umkhonto we Sizwe!'

Among those in the terminal is Chris Hani. He tells reporters: 'De Klerk has not done anything; this is our victory. And all forms of struggle now have got to be escalated.'

When Zambia Airways flight ATR 42 touches down at 4 p.m., Andrew Mlangeni, Ahmed Kathrada, Elias Motsoaledi, Wilton Mkwayi, Raymond Mhlaba, Oscar Mpetha, Walter Sisulu, Govan Mbeki and Harry Gwala step out. The journalists surge forward while the security men struggle to maintain order.[59]

*

On the same day, Jacob Rapholo is standing outside a house in a village near Moria in the northern Transvaal. A Combi stops at a nearby shop.

Rapholo walks up to the vehicle and says: 'Hello, how are you?'

One of the two people in the vehicle is the owner of the shop and of the house outside which Rapholo was standing, which is where he and Charles Seakamela have stayed during their deployment into the country.

He greets Rapholo in return.

'I am asking for a key,' Rapholo says.

The man gives him one.

Rapholo asks: 'Where is Willie?' He is referring to 'Willie Mandisi', Charles Seakamela's *nom de guerre*.

'No, he was here yesterday, he was here Saturday.'

Rapholo takes the key and heads back to the house. When he opens the door he finds a number of policemen dressed in camouflage uniform waiting for him. When he tries to retreat, the policemen open fire. Rapholo is shot in the leg and falls, and the police overpower him.

The police try to initiate an impromptu interrogation but Rapholo says: 'No, I can't give you any information until you take me to Pietersburg hospital.' Otherwise, he says, he will not cooperate and they must rather kill him.

'Okay, let's take him to hospital,' the commander says.

In Pietersburg Provincial Hospital, Rapholo learns that Charles Seakamela was earlier shot dead by the police.[60]

*

A meeting of the ANC NEC takes place in Lusaka's Mulungushi International Conference Centre on 18 January. Alfred Nzo contributes some introductory remarks. It is an open session, so journalists are still in the hall, as is President Kaunda.

There is a text full of statements for public consumption that is supposed to be read at this open session, while another speech exists which is intended for the closed session when the media are gone. Nzo starts reading the document intended for the *closed* session.

He raises the question of whether, in the event of the ANC being unbanned, it should call it a day as far as the armed struggle is concerned and 'operate solely as a legal movement', or whether it should 'continue to maintain some underground units' in South Africa. He tells the audience that the Harare Declaration called for first a mutual suspension of, and then a negotiated end to, hostilities. Nzo says, 'While this has not happened, the armed struggle must continue.'

But then, before a stunned international press corps, he adds: 'Looking at the situation realistically, we must admit that we do not have the capacity within our country to intensify the armed struggle in any meaningful way.' He continues, 'It may therefore be that the main military task that we should pay attention to is precisely the building up of that capacity within the country ... [to] both be able to fight effectively should the need arise, and to have sizeable forces at the moment when a new South African Army is formed.'[61]

*

Following the NEC's meeting, there is an event held for all ANC members stationed in the Lusaka area. This includes representatives from the contingent of MK cadres who have been marooned in the capital city for a number of years, and whose grievances Simon Makana and Steve Tshwete were warning of as far back as 1987–88 (and from whose ranks ANC security suspects that the bombings of the organisation's own properties in Lusaka the previous year are ultimately attributable). They are part of about 1,000 people packed into a hall in the Mulungushi Centre.[62]

When Raymond Mhlaba walks on to the stage, the MK cadres start cheering loudly. Some call out to him: 'Commander!'

When the meeting is opened to questions, they take over. One asks: 'Please, we know there is work to be done inside the country, but Comrade Mhlaba we need you out there because we don't have a commander.'

Another asks if the leadership can explain why so many cadres are dying before they get into the country.

There are questions about problems in the Forward Areas and others about logistical failures.

Somebody veers off topic with an allegation about the acting president and young girls, vowing to manually castrate Nzo if he comes near his house.

Then, somebody stands, points to the platform, and says of the existing leadership of the ANC External Mission, 'If you leaders want to represent us there is one thing to do, all of you: resign now', upon which the hall erupts in cheers of approval.

Somebody stands to try to offer a defence of the leadership, but is drowned out by cries of 'Shut up!' and 'Sit down!'[63]

From the stage, Harry Gwala joins the condemnatory chorus, saying that the MK that exists is nothing compared to the old MK. It is politically bankrupt. Cadres are given military crash courses but they have no political perspective. The leadership is stopping young cadres who want to return to South Africa.

This induces Joe Modise, the implied target of many of the attacks, to rise to defend himself.[64]

Walter Sisulu, visibly shocked by the turn of events, says the ANC will work towards negotiations while simultaneously intensifying the armed struggle to maintain pressure on the regime.

Following Sisulu's contribution the atmosphere in the room moderates somewhat.[65]

VI

ENDGAME

HOMECOMING

Towards the end of F.W. de Klerk's address opening South Africa's Parliament on 2 February 1990, he reminds his audience: 'I committed the government during my inauguration to giving active attention to the most important obstacles in the way of negotiation.' He continues:

> Today I am able to announce far-reaching decisions in this connection. The steps that have been decided, are the following: the prohibition of the African National Congress, the Pan Africanist Congress, the South African Communist Party and a number of subsidiary organisations is being rescinded; people serving prison sentences merely because they were members of one of these organisations or because they committed an offence which was merely an offence because a pro-hibition on one of the organisations was in force, will be identified and released. Prisoners who have been sentenced for other offences such as murder, terrorism or arson are not affected by this.

He says the decision followed consultation with senior officials, including members of the security community, who said it posed no threat to public safety.

The agenda is now open for negotiations leading to a democratic constitution, De Klerk says, adding that

> in this connection Mr Nelson Mandela could play an important part. The govern-ment has noted that he has declared himself to be willing to make a constructive contribution to the peaceful political process in South Africa. I wish to put it plainly that the government has taken a firm decision to release Mr Mandela uncon-ditionally. I am serious about bringing this matter to finality without delay. The government will take a decision soon on the date of his release. Unfortunately, a further short passage of time is unavoidable.[1]

∗

In Lusaka the following day, Pallo Jordan reads the ANC's response on Oliver Tam-bo's behalf. In it he says 'the notion of the ANC unilaterally abandoning the armed struggle is out of the question', and he reiterates the movement's stance, as outlined in the Harare Declaration, that 'any ceasing of hostilities will have to be negotiated and will arise out of a mutually binding cease-fire'.

Though he acknowledges that President de Klerk 'has gone a long way towards creating a climate conducive to negotiations', he says the ANC is 'gravely concerned that the Pretoria regime has taken the decision that some political prisoners will not be released, that the State of Emergency is not lifted and that the practice of deten-tion without trial will continue'.[2]

∗

Ronnie Kasrils checks in to the Sandton Holiday Inn in Johannesburg on Friday 9 February.

At midday he proceeds to a post office from where he makes a phone call to London. He tells Tim Jenkin, who is on the other side of the line, that he is okay for the meeting.

Kasrils stays overnight at the Holiday Inn.

At 9 a.m. the following morning, he arrives at a Wimpy restaurant, only to find that it has closed down. He cases the surrounding area for an hour, before returning to the restaurant. He stands there for a while before moving off.

As he is walking up the road, a car approaches. Inside is Mac Maharaj. Kasrils gets in and they drive away.

'Well where were you last night?' Maharaj says, breaking a long, frosty silence.

'Well here I am now. That's the meeting place, why is it closed down?'

They eventually reach a house owned by a Canadian couple in Twelfth Street, Parkhurst. In the yard of the property stands a cottage. There, Maharaj and Kasrils find Siphiwe Nyanda.

Maharaj begins proceedings, taking Kasrils to task for not having indicated where he stayed the previous night.

Nyanda gives Kasrils a tap on the foot under the table, indicating that he must bite his lip.

Kasrils refrains from responding.

They proceed to the real agenda of the meeting. Maharaj says he is standing down because Joe Slovo in Lusaka is not paying enough attention to the needs of Operation Vula. Maharaj tells Kasrils that he must take over.

'Mac, you can't do that. There's no way I can take over like that,' Kasrils says. 'You ought to be committed to your duty and at least see it out for a period that I can find my feet and see how things go.'[3]

*

At 4.16 p.m. the following day, marshals of the mass democratic movement struggle to hold back a crowd outside Victor Verster Prison when Nelson Mandela emerges hand in hand with his wife Winnie.

When the couple reach the prison gate, Nelson Mandela thrusts both fists in the air. He and his wife then leave the grounds and get into a Japanese car which departs, only to collide with a van near the prison gates. Neither car is seriously damaged, and the vehicle transporting the Mandelas then heads in the direction of Cape Town as part of a cavalcade led by three traffic policemen on motorcycles.[4]

Nelson Mandela appears on the podium at Cape Town's Grand Parade at about 7.45 p.m. that evening. By then, windows of businesses around the Parade and the nearby Golden Acre shopping centre have been broken and shops have been looted by restless sections of a crowd that expected Mandela to begin speaking at 5 p.m. In the police response to the disorder, over a hundred people suffered birdshot wounds and four were killed by gunfire. The crowd is tightly packed, and ambulances struggle to get through to those needing treatment for exhaustion or who have fallen unconscious.

Mandela stands a moment, nodding slightly to the crowd. Then he raises his right hand for quiet.[5]

During his address he says:

Our resort to the armed struggle in 1960 with the formation of the military wing of the ANC, Umkhonto we Sizwe, was a purely defensive action against the violence of apartheid. The factors which necessitated the armed struggle still exist today. We have no option but to continue. We express the hope that a climate conducive to a negotiated settlement would be created soon, so that there may no longer be the need for the armed struggle.

He compliments F.W. de Klerk as 'a man of integrity', but laces this with the veiled warning that the sitting president 'is acutely aware of the dangers of a public figure not honouring his undertaking'.

He then exhorts the audience: 'We have waited too long for our freedom. We can no longer wait. Now is the time to intensify the struggle on all fronts. To relax our efforts now would be a mistake which generations to come will not be able to forgive.'[6]

The next day Mandela holds a press conference in Johannesburg. In a similarly militant vein to the previous day he says 'the nationalisation of mines is a fundamental policy of the ANC. I believe the ANC is quite correct in this attitude.'

When reporting Mandela's comments later that afternoon, the Associated Press notes the response of a powerful constituency which henceforth will have to be reckoned with. It says that following the statement gold prices fell 4 per cent on the Johannesburg Stock Exchange, while the financial rand, a special currency used to encourage foreign investment, dropped 10 per cent.[7]

*

In a statement to journalists in Pretoria the following morning, 13 February, Herman Stadler, the South African Police's chief of public relations, says Natal has 'exploded' since Sunday (the day of Mandela's release), with the police 'snowed under' by the volume of reports they have received about violence in townships around Durban and Pietermaritzburg. When reporting his comments, the Natal Witness estimates that over fifty people have been killed in the province during the forty-eight-hour period.[8]

Regarding the causes of the violence, Jack Buchner, chief of police in the Kwa-Zulu homeland, tells reporters on the 13th that the killings were triggered by the murder of two Inkatha members by a UDF mob on the Saturday, sparking violence between supporters of the two organisations, which has left thousands homeless.[9]

*

Former Quatro camp detainees Luvo Mbengo, Amos Maxongo, Bandile Ketelo, Zamuxolo Tshona and Ronnie Masango stage a press conference in Nairobi, Kenya, on 10 April. They are accompanied by Selinah Mlangeni, Maxongo's pregnant partner.

Tshona mentions two operations he was involved in where, he alleges, he smuggled drugs and diamonds and stole luxury vehicles for MK officers. 'Certain members of Umkhonto were getting fat from the blood and sweat of the cadres,' he claims.

Mbengo removes his shirt to reveal discoloured, shrivelled scars. He says they are from hot plastic or burning plastic bags dripped on him by security members who themselves were awaiting execution.

Maxongo says their main concern now is to return to South Africa and establish the truth of their claims: 'These elements, who have committed all these crimes within the ANC, should not be allowed a chance to be at the leadership positions of our people in South Africa. Our fear is that, given a chance, they would still continue to do all of these things.'

Reporting on the briefing in a *Times* of London article the following day, Margaret Heinlen writes that the men said they illegally crossed the Tanzanian border into Kenya in February, leaving behind ten other members who also fled the ANC's ranks in December. She adds that several of the other ten are known to have attempted to re-enter South Africa through Malawi, but their present whereabouts have not been established.[10]

*

When Nelson Mandela arrives at Umtata Airport in the Transkei on 21 April, a *Sunday Times* reporter notes that included in the local reception committee is Phumzile Mayapi, who was responsible, along with Ndibulele Ndzamela, for the Wild Coast casino bombing on 18 April 1986.

An article containing this information appears in the paper the following day. In it the journalist notes that Mayapi's liberty is a consequence of a decree issued by the Transkei Military Council around the time of Mandela's release, under which he and Ndzamela were freed from death row.[11]

One of Mandela's bodyguards during his trip to the Transkei is Mzwandile Vena, formerly of the MK Western Cape structure until his arrest in September 1987. Vena was subsequently extradited to the Transkei to stand trial for offences there, including his role in the attack that caused the week-long blackout in the homeland in June 1985. In February 1990 he too was released, on R2,000 bail.[12]

*

The other group of ten mentioned in Margaret Heinlen's report includes Mwezi Twala, Vusi Shange, Diliza Mthembu, David Makhubedu, Luthando Dyasop, Sipho Phungulwa, Motyatyambo Mzimeli and Patheka Sodo, many of whom played prominent roles in the mutiny in 1984. They arrive in Johannesburg from Tanzania on the afternoon of 24 April, having initially been repatriated from Malawi.[13]

*

Three days later, a chartered Zambian jet arrives at Cape Town's D.F. Malan Airport. Out of it step seven ANC members including Alfred Nzo, Thabo Mbeki, Joe Modise, Ruth Mompati and Joe Slovo.

On the tarmac, Slovo quips to reporters, 'Well, as I was saying before I was so rudely interrupted 27 years ago!'

Nzo reads a statement on the group's behalf. It outlines the ANC's agenda at the 'talks about talks' set to commence next Wednesday. 'Our main task here,' he says, will be to explore together with the delegates of the apartheid regime 'the possibility of removing certain obstacles to enable a negotiations process to take place which will lead to the establishment of a non-racial democracy in our country.'[14]

*

The talks take place from 2 to 4 May in Cape Town, after which Nelson Mandela and F.W. de Klerk address the media. At the meeting they agreed a joint communiqué, better known as the Groote Schuur Minute, committing the signatories to pursue 'a peaceful process of negotiations'.

Mandela says the day was the 'realisation of a dream', and he promises to 'honour every word' of the document. He adds: 'we are going to look very hard and earnestly into the whole question of armed struggle and take appropriate decisions'.

The journalists repeatedly ask him to elaborate.

At one point De Klerk intervenes and says, 'He's already dealt with that.'[15]

*

At a flat in Berea that evening, Mac Maharaj and Joe Slovo meet. Maharaj reads through the text of the joint communiqué. For him it confirms the objections to Slovo's leadership of Operation Vula that induced his resignation earlier in the year (subsequently retracted following a meeting with Nelson Mandela).

'Slovo, what did you do?' Maharaj asks.

'What do you mean?'

'In all this statement you have not said one word about the safety and security of your illegal cadres living in the country.' Maharaj says the statement takes into account those who are in prison and those who are in exile, but ignores the illegals and the people who are in the underground – be it political or military – inside the country. 'This was the time when you should have inserted that into the Groote Schuur record. You should have told De Klerk without disclosures, you know we are committing ourselves to negotiations, you know that the movement has got people that it has infiltrated over the years living here illegally, I won't disclose how many or who they are, but I do want you to give an undertaking that their safety will be assured.'

'I assumed that it's there,' says Slovo.

'Slovo, were you involved in the drafting?'

'Yes, Thabo and I were involved in the drafting.'

'And you didn't think of this? You are making a fatal mistake, not from the point of view of the progress of the country but from the point of view of whether the movement stands by its cadres.'

Slovo moves to defend himself.

'No, let's read it,' Maharaj says.

Slovo reads the document. He says they are covered.

'We're not covered,' Maharaj retorts.

'It's implied.'

'Bullshit, show me; where's the implication here? De Klerk is not going to protect us by implication. Show me where you've put it.'

A personalised and heated exchange ensues, Maharaj redoubles on his basic point: 'Joe, you were in that delegation as the man who knows the army, the MK and the underground [and who] knows of this mission. It was your job to advise our delegation and Madiba that we need this phrase stuck in and you didn't do it.'[16]

*

On 16 May, after being released from South African Police custody in Johannesburg earlier in the day, the group of ex-MK cadres repatriated from Malawi addresses the media.[17]

In the Transkei, Mfanelo Matshaya, another MK cadre who has been released from custody in the homeland, watches footage from the press conference on television in the company of some colleagues. They see and hear the criticisms made by the group of the ANC, its leadership and the MK command structure.[18]

*

The SACP holds a two-day conference in Tongaat, Natal, on 19–20 May 1990. Siphiwe Nyanda and Mac Maharaj from Operation Vula attend.

Nyanda informs those present that the ANC is going to sign an agreement with the government to suspend armed operations. However, the likes of the AWB (the Afrikaner Weerstandsbeweging), Inkatha and others will not be bound by it. He offers his personal view that even in the event of an agreement with the regime, the ANC must retain the capacity to defend itself against attacks from these other forces.[19]

*

In a forty-five-minute speech in Cape Town on 7 June, President de Klerk announces that at midnight the following evening the nationwide state of emergency will lapse everywhere but Natal, where due to a 'factual state of emergency' the police will not be able to maintain law and order with the ordinary laws of the land.

De Klerk expresses hope that the measure will remove one stumbling block in the way of negotiations, but claims the step has nothing to do with pressure from any quarter or any desire on his part to make political capital.[20]

*

Sipho Phungulwa and Luthando Dyasop of the group released from police custody on 16 May visit the ANC office in Umtata in the Transkei on 13 June.

When the pair leave the office, they see two men. One of them is Mfanelo Matshaya (who watched their post-release press conference); the other is Ndibulele Ndzamela (released with Phumzile Mayapi from death row in February for his role in the Wild

Coast casino bombing). They have been tracking Phungulwa and Dyasop since their arrival in Umtata. They suspect them of working with the enemy.

Phungulwa and Dyasop enter a taxi which drives off, followed by two vehicles. In a beige Peugeot 504 Ndzamela drives Matshaya, while two colleagues, Pumlani Kubukeli and Akga Thia, are in the other car.

When the taxi reaches the 'back location' of Khangaliswe township, it stops, and Dyasop and Phungulwa disembark. There are a number of people walking about.

Matshaya gets out of the Peugeot and approaches Phungulwa. Sensing the threat, Phungulwa throws a jersey over Matshaya's face. Matshaya opens fire, hitting and killing Phungulwa with a bullet from a Scorpion pistol. But he misses Dyasop, who escapes into the crowd.

Matshaya fires into the air to scare people off, before entering the Peugeot, which then speeds away.[21]

*

In Natal, meanwhile, conflict flares up again despite the re-imposed state of emergency.

On 16 June, three buses from Nxamalala are stoned as they travel through neighbouring Inadi on their way to attend a 'Soweto Day' rally in Pietermaritzburg. Four people are injured as a result.

Later at Wadley Stadium in Pietermaritzburg, Harry Gwala shares a stage with Bernard Kouchner, France's health minister, who announces the donation of over six tons of medical supplies by his government to the 'people of Natal' injured in the regional conflict.

From Pietermaritzburg, Gwala heads to another rally at Umlazi Stadium where he delivers a speech in which he tells the 10,000 gathered: 'When we negotiate, we negotiate with an AK-47.'[22]

On the following day, two Inkatha supporters are shot dead in Nxamalala. That evening, Inkatha followers mobilise in neighbouring Esibomveni, Bhongonono and Inadi, effectively throwing a cordon around Nxamalala. In response, men and boys take to the streets of Nxamalala in preparation for battle.[23]

Elsewhere in Natal, it is Inkatha supporters who feel under siege. Timothy Zondi, the organisation's chairman in Greytown, tells the *Natal Witness* that people in Enhlalakahle are 'trapped' following a series of attacks with AK-47s by ANC supporters on Inkatha followers seeking to leave the township for Greytown. Zondi claims non-aligned residents of Enhlalakahle are being intimidated in order to get them to join the ANC. Solomon Mzolo, the ANC representative for Greytown, denies this, and accuses Inkatha supporters of provoking ANC followers.[24]

*

Shirley Gunn is visiting a guest farm outside Victoria West in the remote Karoo on 25 June. She is with her mother, sister and sixteen-month-old son.

Suddenly a number of vans arrive and security policemen emerge from them.

They arrest her on the trumped-up charges of her involvement in the Khotso House bombing. She refuses to be parted from her son, who is still being breastfed, and is therefore taken along with him to Cape Town. She will be held for sixty-four days before eventually being released on the comparatively minor charge of possession of a Makarov pistol.[25]

*

Chris Hani gives a media briefing on 26 June after spending a week in the Transkei addressing numerous rallies and visiting family. He says he believes in a peaceful solution, but adds that negotiations will not nullify the struggle – including armed struggle – which will continue till a mutually binding ceasefire can be agreed by both sides. He also states his hope that the ANC will emerge from the 6 August talks with the government equipped with a concrete position regarding the armed struggle.[26]

*

'I feel very disappointed that the right-wing feels that I am only worth R20,000,' Hani quips on 6 July in answer to a question at a Cape Town press conference asking how he feels about being identified by far-right groups as an assassination target.[27]

*

On the same day, at a private meeting in Cape Town, Hani addresses representatives from a number of underground MK units. He debriefs them on the pending talks between the ANC and the government, and tells them to carry on with their underground activities in the meantime.

After attending Hani's briefing, Fumanikile Booi heads off to Khayelitsha, where he meets up with the other members of his unit, namely 'Lincoln', 'Wiseman' and 'Mabuya'. Booi tells them they will need to proceed immediately to NY 47, because Chris is going to sleep in Gugulethu tonight.

In a white Toyota Corolla the group heads out of Khayelitsha towards Nyanga East. Wiseman drives, Mabuya is in the passenger seat, with Lincoln and Booi in the back seats. When entering Nyanga East they approach a stadium and see a parked police riot patrol van. It is now roughly 1.20 a.m. on 7 July.

In the police vehicle are Sergeant N.J. Els and Constable G. Beeselaar. As the Toyota passes the van, the van's lights are off. When the Toyota reaches a T-junction further on, the police vehicle's headlights are turned on and it starts moving.

There are other vehicles on the road at the same time, so it is not clear to the men in the Toyota if they are being followed. However, as a precaution, Booi instructs Wiseman to turn left into Turf Street. They proceed through some back streets but the police van follows them. They then return to the main road, Ems Drive, that they had left earlier.

When the Toyota passes a school with big trees that stands opposite a dark area with no houses, the police van moves to overtake. When alongside the Toyota, Sergeant Els, the passenger, indicates to them with his torch to get off the road.

Booi orders Wiseman to stop the car and tells the others to sit tight until it is possible to see what is going to happen. The van stops slightly across the front of the Toyota, blocking it from escaping. Booi opens his window.

Sergeant Els gets out of the van carrying a pistol in his right hand. He is clad in camouflage uniform. Constable Beeselaar meanwhile exits from the driver's side.

Booi opens fire with his AK-47, hitting Els in the chest, killing him instantly. Beeselaar returns fire, only for Booi to open fire on the van and unleash twenty-three bullets, many of which go straight through the bodywork and out the other side. The vehicle protects Beeselaar from being hit, and he runs off.[28]

*

Later the same day, 7 July, Hendrik Botha receives a phone call from Lieutenant Salmon du Preez, who says an MK terrorist has been arrested and is in detention at C.R. Swart Square Police Station in Durban.

Botha arrives at the station and meets Du Preez. The two walk together to the Security Branch offices at the station. In those offices they find Vusi Ninela, an askari, who says excitedly that he has arrested Charles Ndaba aka 'MK Zwelake' (formerly of the Natal Machinery) himself.[29]

*

Later that day, Botha and Du Preez are with Lawrence Wassermann and Casper van der Westhuizen in a Volkswagen Combi near the Greyville Racecourse in Durban. Charles Ndaba, who has accompanied them to the scene, gets out. It is between 1.30 and 2.30 p.m.

Ndaba walks about 100 metres to a street adjacent to the racecourse. Botha and Van der Westhuizen follow him on foot and see Ndaba enter a blue Toyota Corolla. Botha radios the position of the Toyota to Du Preez and Wassermann.

Shortly afterwards, the police van stops on the same road, but some distance behind the Corolla.

About fifteen minutes after entering the Toyota, Ndaba touches his head, upon which Botha radios to Du Preez and Wassermann that the signal has been given.

Botha approaches the Toyota's right-hand side. The window is open. He puts his handgun through the window and points it at the stomach of the man in the driver's seat. In that seat is Mbuso Tshabalala, commander of Ndaba's underground unit.

'Sit still,' Botha says.[30]

*

Hendrik Botha and Johannes Steyn meet Johan van der Merwe, who is now police commissioner, four days later. After being briefed by the two, Van der Merwe says the Department of Foreign Affairs and the state president must be informed of the identity and the objectives of the people involved in Operation Vula. He recommends delaying action against the Vula structures until the week beginning 16 July in order to provide time for both domestic and foreign intelligence services to be informed. They will need to be prepared for the revelations, he says, because the detentions will have a very definite effect on the negotiation process.[31]

*

The following day, 12 July, Siphiwe Nyanda and Rayman Lalla meet at No. 48, the Knoll, in Durban's Kenville suburb.

Nyanda says, 'there is a problem like this. This man [referring to Charles Ndaba] has disappeared and we don't know what is happening and so prepare. I'm going to have to remove you from this place.'

Nyanda leaves the house alone and enters a white Toyota Cressida registered ND268230. As he does so, he is being watched by Lawrence Wassermann and Salmon du Preez in a Nissan sedan.

When the Toyota departs, the Nissan follows. When Nyanda reaches Umgeni Road just outside the Knoll, he begins to suspect the Nissan behind him.

From this point onwards, Du Preez and Wassermann note increasingly erratic behaviour from the Toyota; things like signalling left but not turning left, then indicating right and again not following through. They know that he knows he is being followed. By now a second police car has joined the pursuit of the Cressida.

When Nyanda turns right into Brickhill Road the Nissan blocks his progress. Wassermann and Du Preez alight from the vehicle, with guns at the ready. The arrest is performed without incident.

Nyanda is blindfolded and his arms are tied behind his back as he is driven to the Knoll.

'Who is there in this house we come to? No. 48 The Knoll,' a policeman says. 'Who is in here?'

'No, there's only one person, Rayman Lalla,' Nyanda says.

'What is there in the house?'

There is nothing, Nyanda responds.

At the house the police knock on the door. Lalla opens and is arrested. During the search of the premises the police find weapons and a computer.[32]

*

John Mndebele, Nicolas Zwane and Silos Nkonyane meet Chris Hani at the ANC's headquarters at Shell House in Johannesburg.

They say that in their area of Wesselton (Ermelo's satellite township), the Inkatha Freedom Party, assisted by the South African Police and the Black Cat and Black Chain gangs, are terrorising, killing and harassing members of the community in general, and in particular members of the ANC and UDF.

After hearing what they have to say, Hani advises them to go back to Wesselton and set up self-defence units in order to arm themselves, protect ANC members and structures, and defend the community at large. 'Do what is necessary to quell the violence,' he says.

When Mndebele, Zwane and Nkonyane return to Ermelo they meet their local leader, Jabi Mkhwanazi.[33]

*

At around the same time in Secunda, Eric Valla introduces MK cadre Mzwandile Gushu to J.J. Mabena, the ANC chairperson in that area. Gushu says he wishes to assist in 'normalising' the situation in the Ermelo, Piet Retief and Secunda areas.

Shortly afterwards, Valla takes Gushu to Nelspruit and introduces him to Jabi Mkhwanazi, the aforementioned leader of the ANC in Wesselton/Ermelo. Mkhwanazi tries to put Gushu through a refresher course, but it soon becomes clear that the pupil has nothing to learn from the master about the operation of the weapons.[34]

*

When Nelson Mandela returns to South Africa from a six-week global tour on Tuesday 17 July there is a rush of people at the airport. Walter Sisulu manages to get a word in, telling Mandela he has got to see Mac.

At 7 a.m. the following morning, Maharaj and Mandela finally meet.

Maharaj conveys information about the arrests of Charles Ndaba and Mbuso Tshabalala, as well as the observation and surveillance that is being carried out around him.

Mandela picks up the phone and calls F.W. de Klerk.

'I've got to meet you,' Mandela says.[35]

*

At the University of the Transkei later that day, Chris Hani addresses about 3,000 students. He says the ANC might have to 'seize power' if the regime is unprepared to share or shift control. 'The struggle still goes on,' he declares. 'We are still deploying our cadres inside South Africa and that's no secret.' He adds that negotiations in the true sense have not yet begun because the removal of certain obstacles is still at issue.[36]

Hani adds that the ANC is strengthening all its strategies including the armed struggle, because it is important that when it negotiates it does so from a position of political and military strength.[37]

*

F.W. de Klerk tells the media that in his forthcoming meeting with Mandela he intends raising the matter of Hani's speech, which 'militated against the words and the spirit of the Groote Schuur Minute'.[38]

*

In Umtata on 20 July, Chris Hani is dressed in MK's camouflage uniform and brandishes an AK-47 rifle, accompanied by bodyguards waving AK-47s, in front of a crowd of ANC supporters toting imitation AKs.

He responds to De Klerk, saying he has no regrets about his statement, while he expresses hope that the comments will not be used by the regime as a 'red herring' in the next round of talks. He says he understands the Groote Schuur Minute, which nowhere says the ANC must abandon the armed struggle. 'I said we must prepare ourselves and Umkhonto we Sizwe in such a way that if this government decides to go back and push back the present momentum, then Umkhonto we Sizwe is duty bound to mobilise itself and continue with operations.'[39]

*

Adriaan Vlok phones Nelson Mandela on Saturday the 21st and warns that the following day's papers will publish allegations about a Communist Party conspiracy to stage an armed insurrection in South Africa.[40]

The *Sunday Star* is one of a number of papers to lead with the story. It reports that up to forty MK insurgents, '[a]ll said to be members or supporters of the SA Communist Party', have been detained in the Transvaal, Natal and other areas in connection with alleged plans for an insurrection.

Unnamed security sources claimed the unit was so secret that not even MK's conventional command structure knew of it. Peet Bothma, a spokesman for Adriaan Vlok, said the arrests followed a spike in violence in June. Another anonymous security police source said SACP members are believed to be largely responsible for the upturn in violence following the lifting of the state of emergency.[41]

*

Mac Maharaj departs the ANC's head office in Sauer Street on Wednesday 25 July and heads to a house in Mayfair owned by Mohammed Valli Moosa.

When he pulls up in front of Moosa's house he is arrested by policemen, who retrieve from him a document in his handwriting referring to an NEC draft resolution advocating the suspension of armed actions by MK.[42]

*

Revelations about Operation Vula, fuelled by police leaks, continue to seep into the press.

Beeld newspaper reports on the day after Maharaj's arrest that the security police possess some 2,000 pages of evidence culled from the computer system of the group arrested in the recent raids.

The data tells a story of machinations within MK by a group of communists known privately as the President's Committee. Some of them were on the ANC's NEC and were quietly preparing a wholesale uprising against the state in the event that talks with the government failed – *and they were convinced that the talks would fail.*

To this end they sought to construct an extensive underground network with hubs in Durban, Johannesburg and Cape Town, and senior ANC/SACP members – who have received amnesty for the length of the negotiations – infiltrated South Africa and spent many months establishing the clandestine structures.

The computer system was used as a channel of communication and information between the interior hubs, but it was also used to liaise with accomplices in London, Lusaka and Moscow.

A costly blunder gifted the system to the police. It came when a computer and a paper containing access codes for it were found during a raid on a so-called 'safe 'house' in Durban. The information unearthed there was followed up day and night, leading to the subsequent arrests.[43]

*

In their determination to use the revelations to implicate the SACP in a conspiracy against the negotiation process, the police overplay their hand.

Nelson Mandela briefs Joe Slovo on allegations made by President de Klerk at the meeting between the two leaders.

Slovo hears Mandela out, but then responds: 'No, this is not true. They have distorted the documents they found. Those documents make it clear that the Communist Party agrees with negotiations and they also compliment Mr de Klerk for having had the courage to come out openly and to call for a change of the political system.'

Slovo hands Mandela a copy of the documents so he can see for himself.[44]

This is enough ammunition for the ANC to launch a fightback. Nelson Mandela briefs foreign ambassadors to South Africa on the 28th. He says Joe Slovo will take part in the talks with the government whether De Klerk likes it or not. He accuses the police of trying to drive a wedge between the ANC and the communists.[45]

Then on 29 July, Patti Waldmeir of the *Financial Times* is in a half-full Soccer City Stadium as Nelson Mandela addresses a rally marking the SACP's relaunch inside South Africa.

'The ANC is not a communist party,' he says, 'and as a national liberation movement has no mandate to espouse Marxist ideology.' However, referring to the allegations of the past week or so about communist machinations, he says that to suggest 'these outstanding sons and daughters of our people harbour ideas of unilateral military action against the peace process is an insult manufactured by the enemies of democracy'.

Joe Slovo, who is on stage with Mandela, speaks next. 'We know', he says, 'who is behind the poisonous offensive which has been launched in the last few days. The peace process has many enemies, and some of them surround De Klerk himself ... they feed him on a diet of the most ghastly lies and distortions about our party.' These are:

> Lie No 1: That I was at a meeting in Tongaat on the 19th and 20th May. Their own records will show that I left for Lusaka on the 14th May, and returned for the business conference at the Carlton on the 21st.

> Lie No 2: At this Tongaat meeting, which I did not attend, I was supposed to have said that whatever agreement was signed between the government and the ANC relating to a cease-fire would not apply to the SACP. I have never said anything of the sort, at any meeting anywhere. I go further, I have been shown a copy of the Tongaat minutes and I challenge anyone to demonstrate that the meeting adopted a position that the SACP would not be bound by a cease-fire. This is an outright

and deliberate distortion. [The Tongaat Conference minutes refer to a 'Comrade Joe', but this was in fact Siphiwe Nyanda, and what he actually said has been discussed earlier.]

Lie No 3: In an attempt to link us with the Red Plot they talk about Operation Vula as an SACP project and about SACP arms dumps. They know perfectly well that Operation Vula was an ANC underground ... project, including the preparation of arms caches under the direct control of the President of the ANC, dating from 1987. Not one mention is made in the minutes of the Tongaat meeting about the delivery of weaponry.

Chris Hani is part of the show of unity. He tells the crowd: 'Slovo does not want violence. He wants peace. We must not allow the party to be isolated, because that is what they want.'[46]

*

With the talks scheduled for 6 August on the horizon, both sides share an interest in defusing the crisis.

On 1 August Nelson Mandela reads a statement to the media saying he was mistaken in 'inferring De Klerk was demanding the exclusion of South African Communist Party general secretary Joe Slovo from the peace negotiations'.

Mandela says: 'The ANC National Executive Committee will do whatever we can to ensure that steps are taken to guarantee strict adherence to the Groote Schuur Minute.' He says he understands De Klerk's concerns, and these will be discussed at the forthcoming meeting.

This is good enough for President de Klerk, who tells the media the following day that he welcomes 'the fact that Mandela again unconditionally committed the ANC, Umkhonto we Sizwe and the SACP to honour the agreements of the Minute and undertook to take specific steps in this regard'. In light of Mandela's statement, 'the government has decided to go ahead' with the 6 August talks 'at which the above-mentioned problems would be discussed further'.[47]

*

At around 11 p.m. on 6 August, following their meeting, De Klerk and Mandela hold a nationally televised joint press conference at the Union Buildings in Pretoria.

Mandela is flanked by senior ANC leaders including Joe Slovo and Joe Modise. At the talks the ANC made a concession on the armed struggle that the government would have been prepared for, given the intelligence acquired during the suppression of Operation Vula.

The first question comes from Clarence Keyter of the SABC, who asks Mandela: 'What action will you be taking, and what steps will you be introducing, to ensure that the announcement of tonight will be adhered to at grassroots?'

'Well, firstly, there will be no infiltration of men and arms into South Africa,' Mandela answers, 'and any related activity to military action will be suspended. And, of course, we hope to be able to communicate with our people and to inform them of what we have decided.'

Later, Gordon Bates of *Journal le Geneve* asks the leaders where they think they made the greatest concessions in terms of their previous positions.

'Well,' Mandela says, 'as far as the ANC [is concerned], that is very clear what concessions we have made. We have declared for the suspension, in favour of the suspension of armed action with immediate effect. You will notice that, on previous occasions, we have said that the ANC will be prepared to consider the suspension of hostilities only if the government first removes the obstacles to negotiation. But we came to this meeting already having decided that we will declare a cease-fire with immediate effect. So, we have made a very significant concession.'[48]

The document ensuing from this meeting, in which the ANC's agreement to suspend the armed struggle is contained, is called the Pretoria Minute.

*

Speaking at the annual conference of the National General Council of the Congress of South African Students in Umtata on 12 August, Chris Hani says that the suspension of the armed struggle merely means MK members will remain in their 'trenches' waiting for orders from the ANC. He says that in the meantime military *training* will intensify, and MK's overall numbers will increase.[49]

At the launch of the ANC Women's League at Currie's Fountain in Durban on the same day, ANC Natal Midlands convenor Harry Gwala tells the 10,000 crowd that the suspension of the armed struggle is a 'big test' for the government. He says the ANC leadership has effectively told the regime: 'If you say the armed struggle is hindering negotiations, let us test how sincere you are about this. We are going to suspend military action.' He then adds to loud applause: 'But when we are attacked in the townships you will see what we are going to do.'[50]

*

During the furore over Operation Vula, mention was made by government sources of the increase in violence in the country during June.

The ANC and Inkatha release a statement at the conclusion of four hours of exploratory talks on 19 September. The joint communiqué says their 'historic' meeting was the first of its kind since 1979, and during its course each endeavoured to understand the other's stance on the violence wracking the country.[51]

Two days later, Radio Freedom in its 19h00 GMT broadcast from Addis Ababa announces that on 18 September the ANC NEC began a three-day extended meeting attended by representatives of COSATU, the UDF, and various regional and interim ANC leaders. The gathering was 'convened as a matter of urgency to review the ANC strategic and tactical perspectives in view of the current wave of violence'.

While the government has postulated an Operation Vula angle to the violence, the September NEC meeting advances an alternative, ANC narrative regarding the causes of the conflict. The Radio Freedom announcer says that the feeling of the meeting was that while the government is

> evidently committed to political change in South Africa, it is becoming clear that it would prefer the change to occur on terms most favourable to it. In pursuance of that objective, the government has adopted a two-track policy which on the one hand accepts the need to negotiate the settlement of our country's problems when, on the other hand, devising strategies to weaken the ANC and other democratic formations. The government has consequently adopted a laissez-faire attitude to the violence in Natal and in the Transvaal with the hope that it can generate a climate of insecurity, fear and terror and thus make ... the majority of our people amenable to an authoritarian regime.[52]

When Nelson Mandela and Chris Hani hold a press conference in Umtata on 30 September, they take up this theme.

Hani says allegations of a 'hidden force' deliberately seeking to derail negotiations will be discussed at Mandela's forthcoming special meeting with the government. The ANC is convinced such a force exists, Hani says, though he notes that he believes the ANC and the government together can find a solution.

Mandela adds that it is interesting that the violence has flared up again a day after De Klerk's return from the United States. This confirms, he says, that the lull in violence during De Klerk's absence was created to provide 'space' for his visit.[53]

*

Meanwhile the war on the ground with Inkatha continues, with MK members involved in the fighting. Sipho Motaung meets Sibisi Nhlanhla in Edendale in Natal on 30 October, and asks him to participate in a mission against Lolo Lombo, an IFP Midlands leader.

On the following day at Henley Dam outside Edendale, Motaung and Nhlanhla are together in a red Volkswagen Golf when their commander, 'Mandla', gives them each a 9-mm handgun and orders them to kill Lombo.

A while later a Combi arrives with two men inside, namely Johannes Sithole and Philemon Dlamini. Motaung and Nhlanhla transfer to the Combi, which Sithole drives to Burger Street in Pietermaritzburg.

Motaung and Nhlanhla exit and walk towards the Joshua Doore store, which they enter and see Lolo Lombo. Nhlanhla fires a shot at him from point-blank range, killing him, before fleeing alongside Motaung.

Sithole sees Nhlanhla and Motaung running back. He then hears further gunshots being directed at the MK men. Motaung and Nhlanhla manage to reach the vehicle safely. 'You should leave this place as soon as possible,' one of the two says to Sithole, who does not need to be asked twice.

In Alexandra Road, however, the Combi is blocked in and Dlamini, Motaung, Nhlanhla and Sithole are arrested and taken to the nearby police station.[54]

*

The early months of 1990 have seen the Transkei develop into the kind of strong-hold for the ANC that President Ndamasa and the homeland's security services feared when they warned the meeting on 25 October 1989 that such a development could expose the territory to South African reprisals.

Marthinus Ras books in to a holiday resort in the Eastern Cape on 20 November 1990.

There he bumps into his Security Branch colleagues Snor Vermeulen and Lionel Snyman. They are equally surprised to see him. The three have a short discussion.

On the following day in East London, Ras meets Willem Nortje, who mentions that they have brought weapons for a coup in the Transkei.[55]

*

On the evening of 21–22 November, Ras, Nortje, Snyman and Vermeulen are joined by Eugene de Kock and Jan Nieuwoudt in a security police safe house listening to the radio for news from the Transkei.

At 3 a.m. at the Transkei Defence Force's (TDF) Ncise military base (some ten kilometres from Umtata on the main road to Engcobo), about twenty-five men launch a mortar attack. The rockets fall on the south side of the road, where the base hosting recruits for 1 Transkei Battalion is located. Rockets are also directed at the guard house of the 'Air Wing', positioned on the north side of the road.

Then a voice booms over a loudhailer. It is that of Colonel Craig Duli. (Duli assisted the coup led by General Bantu Holomisa which overthrew George Matanzima in 1987. He then served as Holomisa's second in command in the TDF before resigning in 1989 following a disagreement.) Duli says he has taken over the government and the soldiers must respond to his commands.

After about forty-five minutes the bombardment of the base ends.

At 6.55 a.m. Bantu Holomisa receives a phone call at his home from a reporter who works for the SABC. She asks him about an alleged state coup.

Holomisa says he knows nothing about any state coup.

Just after 7 a.m. Holomisa's adjutant Captain Mbulelo Xaba is in the company of two other TDF officers when he shows up for work at the Botha Sigcau building in Umtata's city centre. When he tries to open his office door, he is fired on by Colonel Duli, who is in the company of Boetie Davis, a former bodyguard of one-time Trans-keian president Kaiser Matanzima (who after his retirement in 1986 was succeeded by his younger brother George).

Xaba survives, but is taken captive and interrogated. When he reveals his identity, Duli asks him for keys to Holomisa's office, which is on the eleventh floor of the building.

At 8.05 a.m. a call is made by the South African ambassador's protector, Warrant Officer Bambeni, to Holomisa's office. Captain Xaba answers. Bambeni asks if there is a problem. Xaba says there is a small one (he is speaking with the barrel of a gun pointed at his temple).

Ten minutes later, Duli calls the South African ambassador. He says he has acquired minor injuries and asks for South African support for the coup.

As the morning progresses, Holomisa loyalists in the TDF manage to seal off the streets surrounding the Botha Sigcau building. They also attack it from below with automatic weapon fire and grenades.

At 3 p.m. Holomisa receives a call from Colonel Madikiza saying Duli has been taken prisoner and is being interrogated.

Holomisa asks if Duli has 'sung' and said who sent and/or supported him.

Madikiza says he was not involved in the interrogation but he heard that Duli made mention of one Captain Fourie.

Later on the 22nd, Holomisa appears in army camouflage in front of 18,000 people at Transkei's Independence Stadium. He is flanked by senior TDF and police members. Captain Mbulelo Xaba is there. So is Ezra Sigwela, the ANC's regional chairman. Holomisa proceeds to recount the events of the attempted coup and its suppression.[56]

*

A SAPA dispatch on Tuesday 18 December 1990 reports David Ntombela, an Inkatha leader in Natal's Vulindlela region, stating that the plans announced by the ANC over the weekend to spread self-defence committees to the townships are 'no more than a thin disguise for Umkhonto we Sizwe to rebuild its underground terror structures'.

Ntombela recalls that in October, Harry Gwala, in his capacity as the ANC's Natal Midlands chairman, raised the possibility of setting up self-defence units in the Pietermaritzburg area in cooperation with local COSATU branches.

Ntombela says that viewed in the light of what happened next in the Midlands, IFP Natal members can only view the plans announced to roll such structures out nationwide with 'considerable alarm'.[57]

*

On 12 February 1991, a government/ANC working group reaches an agreement at Cape Town's D.F. Malan Airport. Known as the D.F. Malan Accord, it seeks in part to obtain clarity on certain questions left ambiguous by the wording of some clauses in the Pretoria Minute of 6 August which saw the ANC suspend its armed struggle.

Regarding what the suspension of 'armed actions' and 'related activities' entails, the document says that the ANC will stop the infiltration of arms and men into South Africa, *as well as* the military training of cadres inside the country; it affirms that there will be no armed attacks and no creation of underground structures inside South Africa.

It does, however, add that 'the population at large has a right to express its views through peaceful demonstrations'. And in its final clause it recommends that the working group established by the Pretoria Minute to resolve all questions arising from the suspension of the armed struggle should now 'give attention to further matters that may arise from the implementation of this agreement [i.e. the D.F. Malan Accord], such as proposed defence units'.[58]

The battle of interpretation continues despite this attempt to gain clarity. The agreement is made public on 15 February, after being ratified by the South African cabinet and the ANC's NEC.[59]

Early that evening Pallo Jordan and Mathews Phosa address a news conference on the ANC's behalf. Jordan says that in the accord, the government has acknowledged the use of mass action as a form of legitimate political activity, while the ANC for its part has undertaken not to embark on any *new* underground military activity.

The briefing is opened to questions.

In answer to one inquiry, Jordan emphasises that in the document the government has accepted the validity of the principle of self-defence.

Phosa says, in response to another question about the ANC surrendering arms: 'We made it clear that we are not going to surrender weapons, now and even in the future. Those structures, arms, and men, are to remain where they are.'[60]

*

Thabo Mbeki and Cyril Ramaphosa represent the ANC at a bilateral meeting between the organisation's negotiating commission and counterparts from a similar structure within the National Party.

During his presentation, Mbeki mentions '1999' and says perhaps they might need to look at some sharing of power in one way or another for a certain period of time till then to assist in the process of transition.

'Oh, you mean sunset clauses,' offers Barend du Plessis from the National Party side.

'Yes,' Mbeki says.[61]

*

Following the D.F. Malan Accord, the ANC presses forward with efforts to develop self-defence units. The movement releases a thirty-one-page booklet titled *For the Sake of our Lives – Guidelines for the Creation of People's Defence Units* on the afternoon of 16 April 1991.

In reporting the news, SAPA says the document was first circulated to all ANC regions for discussion in November 1990. Initially drawn up by a joint ANC–COSATU committee in consultation with the ANC Youth League, it envisages that a township defence force of 2,000 volunteers will be sufficient to police a community of 20,000 residents. It adds that while the townships served as the model on which the concept was formulated, self-defence committees would also need to be established in rural areas, squatter camps and, possibly, industrial zones.[62]

*

Just under seven months after the failure of the state's attempt in November 1990 to shut down the ANC's use of the Transkei, on 10 June 1991 a vehicle containing Mzwandile Vena (among those released in the homeland in 1990), Mike Hala and

S. Mantyi is stopped by police in the Harding area of southern Natal. They have just entered the province from the Transkei.

Three AK-47 rifles, two Stetchkin pistols and a 9-mm pistol – each with loaded magazines – are found in their possession, as well as a Beretta fitted with a silencer, two F1 hand grenades and one RGD hand grenade.[63]

Two days later an article appears in the *Citizen* based on information extended to the paper's Tony Stirling by the security forces. The report alleges that the ANC has established bases in Lusikisiki and Port St Johns in the Transkei at a cost of R250,000, in a development that is causing extreme alarm in government circles. It is further claimed that over a hundred members of the Transkei Defence Force have been trained by the ANC in the Lusikisiki base, while more were recently recruited by Chris Hani following a visit to the TDF's Maluti base. Stirling alleges that the relationship between MK and the TDF is such that MK is being allowed to use the TDF's special forces to store weapons.[64]

General Bantu Holomisa releases a statement the same day denying the claims. He attributes the allegations to 'a certain group' of holdovers from the P.W. Botha era that 'has a vested interest in ruining the negotiation process'.[65]

*

Nevertheless, on 1 July, from Gamalakhe township, which is close to Port Shepstone which neighbours the Transkei, Bobbie Matabata phones Joel Makhanya, who lives in Umkomaas on Natal's south coast. Matabata is with two colleagues, and asks Makhanya to collect the group.

Makhanya boards his Ford three-litre and heads south. When he arrives in Gamalakhe, he proceeds to a house belonging to one 'Comrade Bam'. There he finds Bobbie Matabata with Mlungesi Majosi and another comrade, 'Dumaklaba'. The group's aim is to smuggle arms into Natal. They have two bags of weapons, including AK-47s, Stetchkins, ammunition and hand grenades.

After the bags have been loaded into the Ford, the men see a white-coloured police vehicle doing its rounds in the area. Matabata tells them to stand guard.

The police car moves away, so the four enter the Ford and head towards Pietermaritzburg. Along the way they notice that the same police car they saw in the township is now following them. They are stopped by this police vehicle on the road between Hibberdene and Port Shepstone.

Sergeant Fanie Groenewald walks up and asks Makhanya to open the boot. Makhanya does so. Groenewald finds nothing but a cylinder head there.

Groenewald then moves to the front door.

Makhanya is in the process of closing the boot when he hears a gunshot and sees Groenewald step backwards. Matabata orders Makhanya to get in and drive off. Makhanya does so.

After a while, police cars appear on the road behind them. They encounter a roadblock, but Makhanya does not stop. The police fire at them but the vehicle gets away.

As they approach Mtwalume, however, the car is hit by a bullet that disables it. Makhanya, Dumaklaba and Bobbie Matabata exit and flee in the direction of nearby sugar cane fields lying just beyond a river.

Mlungesi Majosi gets out of the vehicle last. He has a gun in his possession. He aims to provide covering fire for his colleagues. A firefight ensues between him and the police.

Majosi himself then also flees into the fields, but is arrested there.

Matabata is shot by the police and arrested. His wounds are serious; he will have both legs amputated.

Dumaklaba is shot dead by a police helicopter called in to assist in the chase.

Makhanya hides under a bridge and is not found. He eventually manages to escape and flees to the Transkei.[66]

*

The ANC holds a conference in Durban in the first week of July 1991, in which Nelson Mandela is elected ANC president. In his closing address to the conference, Mandela says:

> On Friday I attended a session of the MK commission. It became very clear to me after listening to the speakers that the problems of MK cannot be properly addressed in a one-day commission. A separate conference of MK cadres attended by leading members of the NEC is necessary if justice is to be done to their complaints.[67]

The conference also passed a resolution advocating the formation of township-based self-defence units. Speaking on the subject to reporters in Durban on 7 July, Chris Hani cautions that 'we need to ensure there are good command and control structures, to prevent them from degenerating into vigilantes and lynch mobs'.[68]

*

In Wesselton informal settlement outside Ermelo, Mzwandile Gushu, as part of his mission to 'stabilise' the Ermelo, Piet Retief and Secunda area, walks up to a convenience store at about 7 p.m. There he sees Jwi Zwane, a member of the IFP-aligned vigilante group known as the Black Cats. Zwane is standing alongside another person whom Gushu does not know.

Gushu enters the shop, then exits. He returns a while later with an AK-47.

Zwane is still standing there with the other man.

Gushu approaches the pair but walks slightly past before swivelling and opening fire.

Zwane is killed by the salvo.

The other man, Happy Mhlongo, is also hit, but manages to escape and run to a corner house and then to a shack at the back of the property.

Gushu pursues him and opens fire on the shack. Mhlongo and two other people inside, Eric Nkosi and Sibusiso Nkosi, are injured, but not fatally.[69]

*

Parks Mankahlana is present at an ANC negotiating forum meeting held at the Rand Hotel, which is just in front of the organisation's headquarters at Shell House, Johannesburg.

Joel Netshitenzhe delivers a presentation on the issue of 'sunset clauses'. It is the first time the idea has been raised formally at an ANC meeting.

After Netshitenzhe's talk, Thabo Mbeki, who is chairing, expands on the topic.

During the ensuing discussions, Mac Maharaj rises to criticise the concept. He does so cuttingly.

Netshitenzhe defends his position, in the process taking a swipe at Maharaj, saying the reason why a lot of them advocate compromises like sunset clauses is because they know they have to fight a strong regime, which is also why they don't resign when they are under pressure.

The atmosphere is tense. Nkosazana Dlamini-Zuma speaks on the matter. She observes that if there is a sunset clause then there must also be a sunrise clause.

Jacob Zuma summarises the arguments made for and against the proposal. The predominant feeling is against sunset clauses.[70]

*

In its 19–25 July 1991 edition, the *Weekly Mail* claims it has obtained copies of Security Branch documents indicating that there have been extensive discussions between Inkatha president Mangosuthu Buthelezi and Major Louis Botha, a senior Durban policeman, about how the ANC might be prevented from eroding Inkatha support in Natal.

According to the documents, Buthelezi was concerned about Inkatha's declining membership figures in Natal following Nelson Mandela's release. The report alleges that at least R250,000 was paid by the security police into an Inkatha-owned bank account for the purpose of organising rallies and other anti-ANC activities shortly after Mandela's release.[71]

'Inkathagate' offers grist for the ANC's view that it is a 'hidden force' within the state apparatus that is ultimately responsible for the violence.

*

The MK conference that Nelson Mandela called for in Durban in July opens on 9 August at the University of Venda in Thohoyandou.

In his opening address Mandela says he wants to see MK restructured in a way that enables its cadres to join the armed forces of a democratic South Africa. He also refers to the recent disclosures of clandestine government funding to political groups, and says they 'demonstrate in the clearest possible terms the pressing need for an interim government of national unity to preside over the entire transition from apartheid to democracy'.[72]

On the same day, Chris Hani delivers a behind-closed-doors speech to the 500 conference delegates. He discusses the state of the army abroad following the relocation from Angola to Tanzania and Uganda in 1989. He says:

From the very beginning MK encountered serious logistics, accommodation and transport problems in these countries. Most of our vehicles were left behind in Angola and those we could ship out were not very serviceable and there was also the problem of spare parts. We were also faced with a problem of medical supplies and drugs.

In a place like Tanzania, MK had to adjust to a process where the running of a camp and its security was shouldered by the Tanzanian People's Defence Force. Our transfer from Angola to the two countries seriously affected the morale of our troops, especially in Tanzania, due to a number of reasons. The fact of our nearness to populated villages increased the number of AWOLS. This was followed by growing desertions either to Mazimbu or Dakawa or even to Zambia and South Africa. As many of our cadres were undeployed, the feeling of idleness contributed to the general decline of morale.

The situation in Uganda was generally favourable and continues to improve. I believe it is not an exaggeration to point out that the morale of the army in Zambia continues to decline. In most cases in Zambia, we have comrades who have been waiting for deployment long before the legalisation of the ANC. We also have a category of comrades who retreated to Zambia either from the Forward Areas or from inside the country. Even with the comrades in Zambia, the basic question of nondeployment contributed to their low morale. In the Forward Areas, the problems had not been so serious. If there were any, comrades were able to solve them.

Regarding talks with the government, Hani observes that 'the reality exists, that short of a major disaster in the negotiation process, the transition is very likely to be relatively peaceful', and

If the negotiations, therefore, lead to a peaceful transfer of power from the minority to the majority, it would have definite implications in the way we organise our new army. It would mean we inherit a fully fledged SA Defence Force, Transkei Defence Force, Venda Defence Force, Bophuthatswana Defence Force, Ciskei Defence Force et al.[73]

The conference reflects a high degree of confidence within the ANC that, whatever concerns they may have about the activities of the 'hidden' or 'third' force, the negotiations will probably see a generally peaceful transition to majority rule. In another closed-session address, Joe Modise expands on the issue raised by Mandela of the restructuring that MK must undergo in preparation for its inclusion in a new national army:

Steps have been taken to train our men in ground, air and naval forces. It is important that we institute training in those areas in which we lag. In other words, it means that the conversion of our guerrilla detachments into a modern army should play a pivotal role if the liberation movement is to be present in the future South African defence apparatus. That is why the building of an officers' corps is a task which we cannot delay.

He says Tanzania and Uganda are already involved in training MK cadres, and similar agreements will be finalised with three other countries.[74]

*

On the morning of 14 September 1991, about 2,000 IFP supporters wearing red headbands assemble outside Johannesburg's Carlton Hotel, whistling, chanting and blowing trumpets. They are also wielding an assortment of wooden and iron sticks (some with sharpened ends), knobkerries, spears, shields and bricks. Media observers see others clearly brandishing firearms.

IFP weapons fall high on the agenda of talks taking place inside the hotel, where delegates from a number of organisations including the IFP, the ANC and the NP are discussing a draft document outlining a code of conduct for political parties and organisations in the country.

The document, which will become known as the National Peace Accord, is signed that afternoon following two last-minute compromises. In the first, the word 'dangerous' is dropped from a statement forbidding the carrying of weapons at public gatherings, processions or meetings (a definition broad enough to prohibit the full array of weapons earlier exhibited by the IFP followers outside the hotel). Secondly, as a quid pro quo for Inkatha, the statement in the draft that 'No private armies shall be formed' is extended in the final version to read 'No private armies shall be allowed or formed'.[75] The original wording left loopholes for claims about no 'new' military activity being initiated, and for arguments about existing structures only being used to assist community efforts at 'self-defence'. The IFP intends the reworded statement to mean that MK should be disbanded and its hidden arms caches neutralised.

But the ANC views MK as a people's army, not a private army, and at a three-way press conference held with F.W. de Klerk and Mangosuthu Buthelezi at the Carlton just after the signing ceremony, Nelson Mandela declares that MK will not be dissolved 'now or in the future'.[76]

Freek Robinson interviews F.W. de Klerk on SABC television's Agenda programme the following day and reminds him that ANC arms caches have as yet not been exposed.

De Klerk says: 'in more than one discussion in the days before the peace summit this issue was firmly addressed between me, my ministers and the ANC. I obtained certain promises which made it possible to sign the peace accord. I do not want to discuss it further. I am waiting for certain answers and certain feedback.'[77]

Mangosuthu Buthelezi is not reassured. An independent South African radio station interviews him the day after this. He says he has no reason to be enthusiastic about the prospects for peace following the signing of the accord, for 'how can one talk about peace when there are caches of arms hidden all over the country?'[78]

TRANSITION

MK proceeds with the objective identified at its August conference of building up its conventional military capabilities.

Inter Press Service correspondent Gavin Evans interviews Mosima Sexwale and Bantu Holomisa in Johannesburg on 17 October.

Sexwale says: 'We will be going to New Delhi for two weeks at the invitation of the Indian government. We are taking definite proposals with regard to training and will also inspect a number of facilities. We will look at their ground forces, air force and navy and see what they can offer.'

In Evans's article, which appears on the same day as the interview, he writes that he was told by the two that the trip was being arranged by Alain Guenon, a French-man. Evans notes that Guenon

> is alleged to have close links with the South African Defence Force (SADF) military intelligence. He also has made several propaganda films for the SADF. Guenon arranged their April visit to Paris, where the ANC met with French arms manu-facturers, senior military officials and the minister of industries, Roger Fouroux, to discuss French future arms sales to South Africa and the training of ANC mili-tary cadres. Acting as a consultant with the French military industrial company, SAGEM, Guenon set up the visit to discuss the possibilities of re-establishing French military links with a post-apartheid South Africa.

Evans writes that he asked why, given Guenon's background, the ANC was working with him. Sexwale answered that Guenon was a South African representative of several French companies, some of whom insisted on being represented by him during the visit to France.

Holomisa expressed no qualms at the link.[1]

*

Despite the commitment to transform MK into a conventional force, many of its cadres remain engaged in the war against Inkatha.

Mzwandile Gushu meets Sithule Hleza, chairperson of the ANC Youth League, in Piet Retief, at the latter's house.

Hleza says that life is bad there. The mayor, Mr Msibi, is Inkatha. Askaris, Inkatha members trained at Mpuzwa camp, are staying at the mayor's house. They are bring-ing chaos to Piet Retief, killing ANC and SACP members – civic members as well. Hleza suggests that Gushu should kill him.[2]

On 12 December, Gushu and Hleza are outside an under-construction house near a bottle store in Thandakukhanya township near Piet Retief. Soon afterwards, a van parks in front of the bottle store. Alpheus Msibi, the township mayor, gets out and enters the shop.

Msibi re-emerges from the shop shortly afterwards in the company of a second man and the pair enter the van. Another man emerges from the store and puts books inside the vehicle.

Gushu and Hleza approach. Gushu opens fire on the van as Msibi tries to start it. Msibi exits and throws himself under the vehicle. Gushu runs to the other side and opens fire under the van.

In the process Gushu becomes aware of a fourth man, Themba Mlangeni (Msibi's bodyguard), who has emerged from the shop holding the cashier's till that contains the store's takings for the day. Fearing Mlangeni is concealing a weapon, Gushu fires at him and drops to the ground, taking cover. Mlangeni falls. Gushu again fires at Alpheus Msibi (who is still under the car), before telling Hleza to take the till and search Msibi.

Gushu and Hleza flee on foot, leaving Mlangeni dead and Msibi wounded, though not fatally.[3]

*

Nelson Mandela calls F.W. de Klerk on the evening of 18 December to express concern about two paragraphs in the so-called Declaration of Intent (the 'intent' being that all signatories to the document thereby commit themselves to establish a constitution for South Africa that will provide for a united, non-racial, non-sexist, multiparty democracy under the rule of law).

For Mandela, there are no problems with any of that; his worry centres on the fact that according to the document, which is to be signed at the imminent Convention for a Democratic South Africa (CODESA), all the parties but one are to pledge themselves to be 'bound by the agreements of CODESA and in good faith to take all such steps as are within our power and authority to realise their implementation', while the final signatory, the South African government, is only to be bound 'by agreements we reach together with other participants in CODESA'.

Mandela asks De Klerk to commit himself to the principle of 'sufficient consensus' as the basis for decision-making at the convention.

De Klerk assures Mandela that he is approaching the talks in good faith.[4]

*

South Africa's multiparty constitutional negotiations commence two days later, when the first CODESA meeting occurs. In his address, Mandela tells the three hundred or so delegates that the ANC is prepared to discuss 'the question of control of all armed formations in the country, including Umkhonto we Sizwe'.

F.W. de Klerk speaks after him. He expresses his willingness to move expeditiously to dissolve the white Parliament and replace it with a more representative one, but says there are three preconditions that must be met.

Firstly, a mandate has to be obtained from the white population by means of a referendum.

Secondly, such constitutional changes will require legal ratification from the existing Parliament.

Lastly, the ANC must terminate its armed struggle.

He charges the ANC with failing to live up to September's peace accord as it has failed to make a full disclosure about its arms caches. Despite repeated assurances to the contrary, it has failed to live up to its side of the bargain. 'An organisation which remains committed to armed struggle cannot be trusted completely when it also commits itself to peacefully negotiated solutions,' he says. 'The choice is between peace through negotiation or a power struggle through violence. The ANC now has to make that choice.'

Following De Klerk's speech, the Declaration of Intent is signed, but then the convention announcer says Nelson Mandela wants to speak again.

From the podium, Mandela states: 'I am gravely concerned about the behaviour of Mr De Klerk today. He has launched an attack on the African National Congress and in doing so he has been less than frank. Even the head of an illegitimate, discredited minority regime as his has certain moral standards to uphold.'

Mandela expresses an opinion that he says he first conveyed to De Klerk before the signing of the National Peace Accord, that by calling on the ANC to disclose its arms caches

> you are asking us to commit suicide, because when your Government is not prepared to intervene and stop the violence, when the perception amongst our people is that it is the element in the security forces that are killing our people, when our people are demanding to be armed – what political organisation could hand over its weapons to the same man who is regarded by the people as killing innocent people?

This is met with stormy applause from the ANC delegates.[5]

*

When the ANC issues a press statement on the occasion of its eightieth anniversary on 8 January 1992, it focuses on the bigger picture emerging from the CODESA meeting when, referring to the Declaration of Intent, it says

> Given a commitment on the part of all parties to realise the democratic constitutional principles adopted by CODESA, the process of transition can be accomplished within a reasonably short period. The ANC will strive for the setting up of an interim government in the first half of this year, and elections for a constituent assembly to be held by December 1992.[6]

*

In Potchefstroom on the evening of 19 February, the results of a by-election held after the death of Louis le Grange are read out. Andries Beyers of the Conservative Party wins 9,746 votes and Theuns Kruger of the National Party 7,606, marking a dramatic swing from the 1,583 majority gained by Le Grange for the National Party in the 1989 general election.

Conservative Party leader Andries Treurnicht is present when the results are announced. He tells the crowd afterwards that De Klerk's government no longer represents the white nation and thus can no longer speak on its behalf in negotiations.[7]

In Parliament the following afternoon, F.W. de Klerk uses the result as his opportunity to seek the mandate from the white community that he has always vowed he would try to obtain. He announces he will hold a referendum for white voters before the end of March to determine from them who they think their best representatives are in the ongoing talks. He says if he loses the referendum, he will dissolve the government and hold a general election.[8]

*

Jeff Radebe, the ANC's chairman in southern Natal, briefs Chris Hani about the conflict with Inkatha in his region.

Hani advises him to get involved in the establishment of self-defence units in his area.[9]

At ANC headquarters in Johannesburg in March 1992, Radebe approaches Edwin Dlamini, MK's head of ordinance in Maputo. Radebe says he wants to talk about something secret.[10]

When the two meet in private, Radebe raises the hardware requirements of the ANC in southern Natal. He says he has learnt about the operations taking place involving the entry of arms into the country and their distribution to civilians, and he wants to make sure that such operations are properly authorised. All operations should have proper authorisation, he says, and when such authorisation is given, all such operations must fall within the domain and guidance of the regional MK command structures.[11]

*

Edwin Dlamini next meets Aboobaker Ismail, alias 'Rachid', now the overall head of MK's Ordinance Department.

After being briefed by Dlamini about the request from southern Natal for arms, Ismail says that nothing is needed inside South Africa; they have all the material they need. He also reminds Dlamini that Joe Modise has instructed that no arms be brought into the country in violation of agreements reached with the South African government.[12]

*

After weeks of campaigning by both sides, white South Africans go to the polls on 17 March to vote in the referendum. They are required to vote yes or no to the question: 'Do you support continuation of the reform process which the State President began on February 2, 1990 and which is aimed at a new constitution through negotiation?'[13]

By the afternoon of 18 March, with the results no longer in doubt, hundreds of spectators join journalists in the gardens of Tuynhuys, while more look on from windows in the Parliament buildings. F.W. de Klerk, who is flanked by members of his cabinet and other allies, including Democratic Party leader Zach de Beer, emerges onto the sunlit steps to whistles and chants of 'F.W., F.W.' and 'Yes, yes, yes'.

After the opening prayer, there is applause, after which De Klerk speaks and says, 'it was a big day for our land'. He argues that 'today will be [remembered] as one of the most fundamental turning points in the history of South Africa. Today we have closed the book of apartheid. That chapter is over.'[14]

On the following day, the *Star* gives the results. 1,924,186 white voters (68.6 per cent of the total) answered 'Yes' and 875,619 (31.2 per cent) 'No'.[15]

*

The ANC is meanwhile involved in an important policy shift of its own. On 20 March Nelson Mandela addresses businessmen and diplomats at a breakfast in Cape Town.

He tells them the ANC 'has no ideological attachment to nationalisation'. He says, 'we have to be realistic. As long as nationalisation remains our official policy, it is not going to be possible to get the cooperation of big business and foreign investors.'

This was brought home to him clearly at a World Economic Forum summit meeting in Switzerland recently. Concerning the attitude that potential foreign investors displayed towards the prospect of nationalisation in South Africa, he says: 'I could cut their hostility with a knife.'[16]

*

Despite Aboobaker Ismail's objections, which, as he said, were based on commitments given by the ANC, most explicitly in the D.F. Malan Accord, the project of smuggling arms from abroad into Natal's southern regions proceeds.

Jeff Radebe meets with Sipho Sithole, MK's chief of staff in southern Natal. He says Sithole has been identified as a person who needs to be involved in the operational aspect of creating self-defence units. He will need to set up that structure.

Sithole asks what precisely he will be required to do.

Radebe says arms will be coming into the country that will be distributed to the SDUs. He gives Sithole a set of keys and explains that they are for the cars that will be bringing material into southern Natal. Radebe says Sithole will be responsible for setting up the structures that will ensure that the weapons get to the trouble spots where the people are under attack.[17]

*

Jeff Radebe and Sipho Sithole then meet Edwin Dlamini (MK's head of ordinance in Maputo) and Derrick Ngobese in a Durban office.

Radebe introduces Sithole and Ngobese to Dlamini as the men who constitute the MK Regional Command in southern Natal. Dlamini knows them both from exile.

Radebe says the Regional Command will coordinate with Dlamini regarding the transportation of ordinance. He says further that he is prepared to send people over to Maputo, but what Dlamini must know is that all people going to Mozambique will be under Radebe's command, and nobody will ever be on that side except on his orders. Radebe says he wants everything to be straight.[18]

*

Paulos Nkonyane and Mzwandile Gushu take up position outside some shops in Wesselton township on 12 April 1992. Nkonyane waits in an alley holding an AK-47 while Gushu stands on a corner.

Chris Ngwenya, an IFP Youth League official, is their target. Ngwenya is walking towards Nkonyane and Gushu alongside Lindiwe Nkosi, an IFP Women's League member, and Ms Thembisile Nkambule.

Gushu opens fire, after which Nkonyane also takes up position and starts firing as well.

Ngwenya does not fall immediately. He first makes to run away, and manages to move about five metres before dropping dead. Lindiwe Nkosi is also killed in this incident but Nkambule manages to escape.[19]

*

On 20 April, ANC official Gill Marcus confirms that Chris Hani is no longer MK chief of staff, and that Siphiwe Nyanda will be acting chief of staff for the time being. She says Hani has resigned due to his workload as SACP general secretary.[20]

*

By this time, some of the fears that Chris Hani expressed at the ANC conference in July 1991 have materialised concerning problems that might arise if issues relating to the command and control of the self-defence units were not properly resolved.

Writing for the Inter Press Service on 29 May, Eddie Koch reports the case of Colbert King, who was a leader of the South African Metalworkers' Union before being gunned down outside Kwamasiza Hostel in Sebokeng earlier in the month.

Initially people postulated a security force or Inkatha angle, but it soon became clear that King was killed by the self-defence unit operating out of his hostel. Koch writes that the matter became the subject of high-level talks clouded in 'political intrigue and secrecy' at the ANC's headquarters in Johannesburg, but it would now appear that the heart of the dispute lay in the union's demands that SDU members firstly accept the political leadership of the local shop stewards committee and, secondly, account for money that went missing after the SDU imposed a levy on the hostel residents. The SDU rejected the demands, sparking the conflict that led to King's death and an attack on the home of another Iscor shop steward.[21]

On 6 June another article appears in the Inter Press Service, this time by Philippa Garson. She reports on conflict that has emerged between SDUs for control of two ANC-aligned hostels in Sebokeng.

The rivals are said to be some 200 MK members returned from exile who support Ernest Sotsu. They are allegedly ranged against leaders of local ANC and civics structures. The conflict apparently began earlier in 1992 when an MK initiative to coordinate existing SDUs in the Vaal area met with resistance from established defence units. Sotsu told Garson: 'These new units [i.e. the ones organised around the civics structures] boycotted this initiative. MK was prepared to give skills. But they rejected the MK cadres. We called them to meetings and they didn't come.'[22]

*

Baleni Lerabane, fifty-eight, is at her home in a squatter camp in Boipatong on the evening of Wednesday 17 June 1992 when a group of men kick the door open and say that they want somebody from the ANC. She says there is nobody there from the ANC, but the group slit her throat regardless and strip her down to her underwear in full view of her daughter.

Benjamin Mosoetsa and his brother are shot dead in their dwelling nearby. In a street in the vicinity, a mother is stabbed to death along with her nine-month-old child; a woman in full-term pregnancy is dead a few streets away; the corpse of a one-year-old child lies on the next block.

In all, thirty-nine people are slaughtered in Boipatong that evening.[23]

*

When Nelson Mandela addresses a rally of thousands on a dusty football pitch in Evaton four days later, he says 'the negotiation process is completely in tatters'.

Some rally posters read 'Mandela – give us permission to kill our enemies', while the crowd periodically chants, 'We want arms.'

Mandela tells them: 'I instructed Ramaphosa that he and his delegation will not have any further discussions with the regime.'[24]

Cyril Ramaphosa elaborates when reading an ANC NEC statement at a press conference in Johannesburg two evenings later. He says the present crisis owes to the government's determination 'to block any advance to democracy. It pursues a strategy which embraces negotiations, together with systematic covert actions, including murder, involving its security forces and surrogates.' This is what led to the Boipatong massacre, 'one of the most chilling instances of the consequences' of the policy. The regime must now agree to the 'creation of a democratically elected and sovereign constituent assembly to draft and adopt a new constitution; and the establishment of an interim government of national unity which is the only way all South Africans will recognise that the country shall have moved decisively to end white minority rule'. (The ANC had called in its 8 January statement for an interim government to be in place by the middle of the year and for elections to be held for a constituent assembly by the end of the year.)

The government should also call off its clandestine war, Ramaphosa says. This should include, inter alia, terminating covert operations; confining special forces and detachments consisting of foreign nationals to barracks; prosecuting security-force personnel involved in the violence; ensuring repression in the homelands is ended; phasing out hostels and converting them into family units; banning the carrying of dangerous weapons – including so-called 'cultural weapons' – in public; and launching a commission of inquiry into the Boipatong massacre.

Until these demands are met, he says, 'the ANC has no option but to break off bilateral and CODESA negotiations'.[25]

*

On 27 June, before a crowd of 10,000 in Kliptown, Soweto, that consists mostly of young men, some carrying axes and machetes, Nelson Mandela declares that 'mass mobilisation for democracy is now the number one priority for the ANC', and 'those who say there can be no alternative to negotiations do not want to expose the regime'.

He warns that if the government fails to meet the ANC's demands (enunciated by Ramaphosa on the 23rd), he will personally lead a protest campaign 'of unprecedented dimensions', though he does say that if the demands are met he will re-enter talks 'without hesitation'.[26]

*

Lucky Mbokane meets Mzwandile Gushu and tells him a message has been received that at the Giwi Breyten Construction Compound they are training members of the IFP and the Black Chain. They are being trained by the owners and there are guns there.

On the evening of 6 July, Mbokane has a .38 revolver and Mzwandile Gushu an AK-47 as two black security guards lie flat on the ground in front of them at the Giwi Breyten compound.

Gushu tells Mbokane and another colleague, Mlungisi Gombela, who has joined them for the mission, to tie the guards' hands. Gushu aims his AK at the guards while Mbokane and Gombela fulfil the order.

Once the two men are bound, a car approaches. A white man is driving the car and another is in the passenger seat.

The car stops and Gushu obligingly opens the compound gate for them. But the two men, sensing something isn't quite right, refuse to leave the car. Suddenly the vehicle reverses and the white men spring out. One of them fires into the air.

Gushu runs from the gate into the compound yard where he has concealed his AK. He collects his rifle, and returns fire on the white men. In the process he kills one of them, David de Bruyn, and injures the other, Wynand Fourie. As he makes to exit the yard again, Gushu notices De Bruyn lying motionless in front of the car. While Gushu passes him, Fourie opens fire, inducing Gushu to take cover behind the car. Gushu and Fourie then trade shots with each other. Gushu is struck in the leg and falls, while Fourie flees.

Gushu's leg injury is serious enough for him to require hospitalisation. He is arrested in hospital on 17 July while receiving treatment for his wounds.[27]

*

On 7 September Cyril Ramaphosa is at the head of a crowd of 70,000 that marches to a razor-wire barrier a few kilometres outside King William's Town. Hundreds of troops on the other side of the Ciskei 'border' cock semi-automatic rifles while soldiers on nearby buildings move machine guns into position. The march is part of the ANC's mass action campaign to drive De Klerk to agree to establish an interim government.

While Ramaphosa begins talks with a group of officials representing the 'National Peace Secretariat' (established as part of the National Peace Accord), Ronnie Kasrils leads a large portion of the crowd away from the main group. Chanting 'Down with Gqozo', they proceed towards Bisho Stadium, about 100 yards inside the Ciskei. The perimeter of the stadium is also ringed with razor wire, but on the far side there is a large gap in the fence. Kasrils leads groups of demonstrators through the gap and onto some open grass. Ahead of them is Bisho's central business district, which they hope to occupy and hold a 'people's assembly' to demand political freedom in the territory.

Seconds later they come across a long line of soldiers kneeling in concealed positions. The soldiers open fire without warning, killing twenty-nine people.[28]

*

The events prove to be a watershed.

Two evenings later F.W. de Klerk calls for urgent talks with Nelson Mandela, warning that reform efforts cannot continue until the bloodshed ceases.

At a press conference the following day, Cyril Ramaphosa says the ANC is 'prepared to participate in a summit' with a delegation led by De Klerk.[29]

The summit takes place at the World Trade Centre near Jan Smuts Airport in Kempton Park on 26 September. At the meeting, Mandela and De Klerk sign a 'Record of Understanding'. Afterwards, the two leaders hold a joint press conference.

'The channels of communication are open again,' De Klerk announces, adding 'we have focused, as was the intention, on violence and violence-related issues, and the "Record of Understanding" deals with three important aspects in that regard. It deals with problems surrounding hostels, it deals with problems surrounding the display of dangerous weapons, and it deals with mass action and violence-related problems arising from mass action.'

Mandela meanwhile says: 'practically, implementation has been agreed upon to ensure that a proclamation will be issued to prohibit the carrying and display of dangerous weapons at all public occasions'. He adds that 'on the issue of hostels, the government undertook amongst other things, to fence identified hostels by 15th November 1992'.[30]

But the 'violence-related issues' discussed at the meeting do not include private armies, hidden arms caches or any of the other established negotiations codewords for MK.

Chief Mangosuthu Buthelezi of KwaZulu, President Lucas Mangope of Bophuthatswana and Brigadier Oupa Gqozo of the Ciskei take this as a sign that the government is pursuing a bilateral agreement with the ANC over their heads. The three leaders issue a statement on 29 September after a trilateral meeting in Mmabatho. In the statement they reject the 'Record of Understanding' and charge that De Klerk and Mandela have taken decisions affecting their interests without involving them.[31]

*

'Negotiations: What room for compromise?' is the title of a paper by Joe Slovo which appears in the third issue of 1992 of the SACP journal, the *African Communist*. It appears alongside a cluster of articles focusing on the events in Bisho and their aftermath.

Slovo begins bluntly: 'Sooner or later we will be back at the negotiating table.'

He reminds his readers why there are negotiations at all. It is because the ANC realised towards the end of the 1980s that 'the apartheid power bloc was no longer able to continue ruling the old way and was genuinely seeking some break with the past. At the same time, we were clearly *not dealing with a defeated enemy* and an early revolutionary seizure of power by the liberation movement could not be realistically posed.' With this balance of forces there 'was certainly never a prospect of forcing the regime's unconditional surrender across the table'.

This raises the question of what the ANC's objectives in the negotiations ought to be. Slovo's suggestion is that the goal is an outcome 'which will result in the liberation movement occupying significantly more favourable heights from which to advance'.

Slovo suggests the following as 'bottom-lines' required for such a subsequent advance. Firstly, a constitution adopted by a democratically elected sovereign constitution-making body (CMB); a CMB bound solely by adherence to CODESA's Declaration of Intent and any other *general* statements of democratic principle that the key actors may feel it necessary to adopt; the creation of effective structures to ensure free and fair elections; the setting of acceptable time frames and deadlock-breaking mechanisms to guide the process; the dissolution of the Tricameral Parliament upon the election of the CMB; and ensuring that the legislation that establishes the CMB must not lead to its authority being usurped by a body like CODESA.

What, then, of the movement's myriad other deeply held positions that are not essential for advancing the objectives outlined above? Slovo argues that they represent the room for compromise indicated in the article's subtitle.

He recommends four areas in which greater flexibility would help break the current negotiations impasse. Firstly, sunset clauses covering the period immediately after the adoption of the constitution. Secondly, reaching a bilateral understanding with the National Party prior to the establishment of the CMB regarding the boundaries, powers and functions of regions in the new dispensation. Thirdly, the ANC indicating clearly that as part of a government of national unity it would support a general amnesty 'in which those seeking to benefit will disclose in full those activities for which they require an amnesty'. Finally, honouring existing contracts and/or providing for retirement compensation for present members of the civil service.[32]

*

Before a joint sitting of the Tricameral Parliament in Cape Town on 12 October, F.W. de Klerk says: 'Out of the negotiating process of the past years a general consensus has crystallised already in respect of several important elements of a transitional dispensation.'

Among them are the following. The first is that 'there should not be a constitutional hiatus at any time. Constitutional continuity means that the current constitution will be replaced by a comprehensive transitional constitution to be adopted by this Parliament.'

Second, the 'transitional Constitution will provide for the election, in a constitutional and orderly way by all South African citizens, of a Parliament which will also have the task of drawing up the final constitution'.

Thirdly, in due course, 'governmental responsibility will be taken over from the present government by a multi-party government of national unity in which all significant political parties who so desire will participate'.

He continues until reaching the final, seventh point, which is that under the envisaged transition

> Parliament naturally will have the authority to amend or replace the transitional constitution, but special majorities for the acceptance of constitutional provisions will be stipulated by the transitional constitution. In the coming constitutional negotiations attention will be given as well to the unambiguous formulation of principles which will be binding on the transitional parliament in its constitution making task in respect of a final constitution.[33]

*

At a meeting on 25 November 1992, the ANC's NEC adopts a paper titled 'Negotiations: A Strategic Perspective'. In it, the NEC concedes that the 'regime still commands vast state and other military resources' and 'continues to enjoy the support of powerful economic forces'. Therefore, 'objectively, counter-revolutionary violence and the growing potential of long-term counter-revolutionary instability acts as a resource for the regime'.

The paper lists the ANC's own strengths. These are the support it commands from a majority of the population, its ability to generate large-scale mass action, and its ability to mobilise the international community.

But 'the liberation movement suffers many organisational weaknesses'. Above all, it 'does not command significant military and financial resources' and 'is unable to militarily defeat the counter-revolutionary movement or adequately defend the people'.

Given this strategic balance, the ANC possesses three options: the first is 'resumption of the armed struggle and the perspective of revolutionary seizure of power'; the second is 'mass action and international pressure, within the broad context of negotiations, until … we secure a negotiated surrender from regime'; and the third is 'a negotiations process combined with mass action and international pressure which takes into account the need to combat counter-revolutionary forces and at the same time uses phases in the transition to qualitatively change the balance of forces in order to secure a thorough-going democratic transformation'.

Taking into account all of the above, the last of these options is identified as 'the most viable and preferable', though it is stressed that the ANC 'should guard against being captive to a given approach'.[34] Therefore a negotiated settlement is once again the ANC's number-one priority, reversing the position taken earlier in the year.

*

At a press conference in Pretoria the day after the adoption of 'Negotiations: A Strategic Perspective' by the ANC, F.W. de Klerk announces a timetable whereby an interim constitution will be in place by September 1993 and non-racial elections will be held by April 1994. He describes this schedule as 'Ambitious but attainable'.

De Klerk says he wants 'checks and balances' introduced into the constitution-making process. Such checks would include provision for minority or regional representation in central government, for the protection of property rights, and for independent security forces.

'All these must be part and parcel of the constitutional principles, to which the constitution-making body will be bound,' De Klerk says. They must then be enshrined in the final constitution '*in addition* to the concept of power sharing, and *not as an alternative* to power sharing'.[35]

If the ANC can live with this, and various policy commitments given by the organisation during 1992 suggest that they can (albeit with sunset clauses applied to some concessions), then they and the National Party have basically agreed the framework of a transitional period leading to democratic elections in April 1994 and beyond. This is not to say that they agree on the details of issues such as minority representation and the powers of the provinces – there is much hard bargaining to come. But they are in broad agreement about what needs to happen by when, and no matter how sharp their exchanges may become as they jockey for position in the negotiation of specifics, from this point onwards they will in fact be allies in defending the agreement against its opponents.

*

But there are plenty of sharp exchanges to come. Two days after De Klerk's statement at the press conference, the *Sunday Times* reveals that the ANC has dispatched more than a thousand 'raw recruits' to receive military training in Uganda over the past couple of months.

Edith Bulbring, the article's author, writes that according to sources some 320 ANC members from across South Africa arrived in Johannesburg in the first week of September. They spent a night in Hillbrow's Johannesburger Hotel at a cost of R30,000. They were then flown to Uganda on two Air Zimbabwe charters at a cost of more than R200,000.

Then, in the final week of October, more than 640 recruits arrived from across the country. After undergoing a briefing at a Kwandebele holiday resort they left on four chartered flights for Entebbe. The operation allegedly cost more than R1 million in charter flights and hotel accommodation.

In Uganda, the report claims, the new MK cadres are to receive six months' basic training before being sent out of Africa for specialised training.

Bulbring quotes the reaction of the NP's constitutional development minister Roelf Meyer: 'This can't continue once you have a transitional government. One party can't go on with its own separate so-called army. That is totally unacceptable.'[36]

*

MK cadres who have returned from exile stage a public protest in Johannesburg on 27 December. They make demands to be provided with accommodation and rations.[37]

On 5 January 1993, Nelson Mandela jots down in his notebook: 'need urgent meeting of MK cadres'.[38]

*

A car registered RBM533T passes through Golela border post at about 5 p.m. on 1 February 1993. There are two men inside, Mandlenkosi Makhoba and Derrick Ngobese. There are bags on the back seat. A uniformed border policemen walks to the vehicle's boot and asks the driver to open it.

Ngobese agrees but says he is in a hurry. He opens the boot, which contains tools and a five-litre oil can. The policeman and his colleague rummage under these items and then lift the mat. This reveals a panel plate.

One of the policemen asks why the paint on the panel isn't the same as in the rest of the car. The policemen force the panel open with crowbars and find thirteen Stechkin 9 x 18-mm pistols with twenty-six magazines; nine Makarov 9 x 18-mm pistols with eighteen magazines; two RPG 7 rocket launchers; six PG 7 rockets; six PG primary loads; thirty-one F1 hand grenades; forty UZRG detonators for hand grenades; and 2,800 AK-47 bullets – a huge haul.

The policemen point their guns at Ngobese and Makhoba and tell them that they are under arrest. The two men are taken to a room in the station to be interrogated.[39]

*

These arrests lead to the unravelling of MK's southern Natal structure.

At about 2 p.m. on 3 February, Sipho Sithole, the chief of staff in the regional MK command, is at the ANC office in Durban's Umgeni Road when he looks outside the window and sees policemen and police cars.

The phone rings. Sithole picks up the receiver.

'Mandla,' says a voice on the other side of the line, at which point the policemen storm the room, handcuff Sithole, and leave the office with him.[40]

*

Under the title 'Arms Caught at Golela', Nelson Mandela makes the following entry in his personal notebook:

this incident ought not to cause the hysteria that has come from the Govt. The leadership of the ANC and of our armed wing are not involved. It is the first time in more than 3 years that an incident of this nature has occurred. Only a systematic smuggling of arms into the country ought to cause the panic which has gripped the NP. For all the things this Govt has done to our people we ought not to be talking to them at all.[41]

*

After conducting an internal investigation into the matter, on 2 March 1993 the ANC publishes a strictly confidential document titled 'Brief Summary of Findings of Inquiry into Golela Incident'. The report is undersigned by Siphiwe Nyanda and is based on interviews conducted with the persons arrested in connection with the incident.

The inquiry has unearthed evidence of systematic arms smuggling implicating senior leaders of the movement. The document notes that it became clear from the interviews that at least five trips had been taken to Maputo (referring to the link between the Southern Natal Command and Edwin Dlamini, MK's ordinance chief in the Mozambican capital) to smuggle weapons into the country. These numbers

> suggest that the comrades relied on a good infrastructure and had access to resources. They therefore could not have been acting on their own. The movement has denied the involvement by its top structures. We therefore must treat this report with the utmost confidentiality and circumspection because it has serious implications if it is handled otherwise.[42]

*

Janusz Waluś, a Polish-born right-winger who is a member of both the Conservative Party and the AWB, sets out in a red Ford Laser from his flat in Muckleneuk in Pretoria on 10 April 1993. He arrives at the Stan Schmidt Centre in Illovo, Johannesburg, but he finds the centre closed, as it is the Saturday of the Easter weekend, so he heads to Corlett Drive, where he enters a gun exchange. He emerges from the shop with twenty-five rounds of 9-mm subsonic bullets.

Waluś then drives to Hakea Crescent in Dawn Park near Boksburg, where he pulls in outside a house. From this vantage point he sees Chris Hani leaving a property alone. Hani gets into a Toyota sedan and drives off.

Waluś follows the Toyota to a local mini-market where he observes Hani purchasing a newspaper.

Hani and Waluś take separate routes back to Dawn Park.

At about 10.20 a.m. Retha Harmse is driving in Dawn Park when she realises she has left her shopping bags at home, so she turns back to fetch them. In her rear-view mirror she sees a red Ford pull up in the street behind a Toyota.

Inside the Ford, Waluś puts on gloves, and places his Z88 pistol in the belt of his trousers, behind his back.

Harmse sees a tall thin man with blond hair get out of the Ford. The man is brandishing a gun. She stops her car.

'Mr Hani,' Waluś calls as Hani moves away from the Toyota. When Hani turns, Waluś fires into his body. As Hani falls, Waluś fires again.

Harmse reverses her car to see what the blond man is shooting at. She notices that there is a man lying on the ground. The tall white man walks up to the prone man and fires twice into his head at point-blank range.[43]

*

The funeral ceremony for Chris Hani is held at Soccer City Stadium in Soweto on 19 April. Mandela addresses the gathering, saying:

> It is our unceasing struggles – in the prisons, in mass campaigns, through the armed struggle – that has brought the regime to the negotiating table. And those negotiations are themselves a site of struggle. It is not a question of armed struggle or negotiations. *Armed struggle brought about negotiations.* It is precisely because negotiations will force them to relinquish power that certain elements are resorting to the cowardly tactics of assassinations. This government is illegitimate, unrepresentative, corrupt and unfit to govern. We want the immediate installation of a transitional executive council with one purpose: to ensure that free and fair elections are held in the shortest possible time. This TEC must put in place multi-party control of such areas as the security forces, the budget, foreign relations, local government.[44]

These are tough words, but during and after Hani's funeral there is a historic first, as MK and SADF troops cooperate in keeping order.[45]

*

On 2 May another funeral is held at Soccer City, this time for Oliver Tambo.

With about 5,000 mourners in attendance, the coffin arrives just before 10 a.m. It is followed by family members and ANC officials, including Nelson Mandela. Between 150 and 200 MK soldiers are present in starch-pressed uniforms during the service.

At a Johannesburg intersection following the ceremony, half a dozen MK soldiers in full battle dress help direct the traffic. Alongside them is a white traffic officer. Behind these traffic marshals are three armoured vehicles and twenty riot policemen, keeping watch.[46]

*

Laurens Mbatha, the regional commander of MK in the Northern Cape, is in the ANC Youth League's office in Kimberley between 8 and 8.30 a.m. on 25 May.

He meets Sipho Mbaqa and asks for a hand grenade.

Mbaqa provides him with an F1.

Mbatha heads from the office to a vehicle in which some colleagues are waiting. He gets in and drives to a bus stop, where they pick up Walter Smiles, another member of the Regional Command. The vehicle proceeds to an area in the city centre that is a commercial hub for the local Indian community.

Mbatha stops the vehicle and exits it holding a white bag. Inside the bag is another bag wrapped in newspaper. Walter Smiles also gets out, and the vehicle drives away without them.

There is a march in progress in the area. The procession has been organised by the ANC Youth League and COSAS. It is heading towards the Trust Bank building, where the 'Consulate of the Republic of Bophuthatswana' is located.

Mbatha and Smiles join the march. Mbatha says to his colleague that as soon as they reach the Trust Bank building, after the last memorandum has been submitted and the marchers start moving away, Smiles must throw his hand grenade right into the sliding door.

After walking a short distance further, Mbatha breaks from Smiles and heads to the front of the procession.

At the Trust Bank building, while the last memorandum is being submitted, a squabble breaks out between a group of marchers. One of the senior march organisers comes to the front and asks them to calm down.

The doors of the building are still open, but people have begun to head home, so Walter Smiles takes it as his moment. He removes the pin from the F1 and tosses the grenade towards the door. Just as the explosive leaves his hand he sees a security guard emerge in the doorway. The grenade hits the guard on the forehead, before falling to the ground and rolling to a corner where a man named Ezekiel Mokone is standing. It explodes and kills Mokone.

Chaos follows, with people running in all directions. Members and leaders of COSAS and the ANC Youth League are also injured in the blast.[47]

*

When MK chief of staff Siphiwe Nyanda arrives in the Namibian capital Windhoek for a southern African defence and security meeting on 13 June, he tells reporters that the ANC will contribute more than 13,000 trained personnel to a future defence force.

He rejects the notion put to him by a questioner that MK recruits should only be integrated if they meet certain standards: 'The SADF must overcome their notion that they have a monopoly on standards,' he says. 'We want people in a future army who can defend democracy.'

He says good progress has been made since talks started with the SADF in April in Simon's Town over the future of the defence force. He could now easily imagine the SADF and MK serving together in a unified, depoliticised defence force.[48]

*

At the World Trade Centre in Kempton Park, while talks between the NP, ANC and other negotiators are taking place, a cry goes up at 8 a.m. on Friday 25 June. It is from AWB members positioned outside the perimeter fence.

Some 2,000 of them then surge forward, led by their leader Eugène Terre'Blanche. The police manning the main gate step aside for the AWB men, who are armed. Having thus entered the compound, Terre'Blanche leads the AWB members across 200 metres of open field to the main building.

At around 9 a.m. Terre'Blanche orders one of the AWB's armoured vehicles to drive into the large glass doors at the main entrance. The vehicle smashes through, opening a wide breach through which hundreds pour in. As riot policemen look on in confusion, the main negotiating chamber is overrun by men in black and khaki uniforms.

Delegates of the various parties to the negotiations take refuge in a small office. Among them are Joe Slovo, Roelf Meyer and Cyril Ramaphosa. The policemen standing guard at the door tell them to lie on the floor if they hear shots.

Eugène Terre'Blanche, Constand Viljoen (the retired SADF chief and present leader of the Afrikaner Volksfront) and Ferdi Hartzenberg (Conservative Party leader) walk through the breach opened up by the armoured vehicles and stride up to speak to government officials.[49]

In a report published the following Monday in the *Christian Science Monitor*, John Battersby observes that if the storming of the World Trade Centre was aimed at halting the momentum of the talks, it failed. Shortly after the incident, MK and SADF generals struck a deal on the formation of a peacekeeping force. The force will consist of between 7,000 and 12,000 men; it will primarily consist of the SADF, the South African Police and MK, but members of other liberation movements and the homeland military forces will also participate. The deal is expected to be endorsed by negotiators before the end of the week.[50]

*

In front of some 2,500 IFP supporters in Thokoza on 11 August, Mangosuthu Buthelezi says, 'as president of the IFP, I direct that every member and supporter of my party, the Inkatha Freedom Party, translates the letters I-F-P into the slogan "I'm for peace"'.

He adds, however, that the reason why there is no peace is the continued existence of MK, to whose 'evil activities' the government is turning a blind eye. He says he is 'bitterly opposed' to the inclusion of MK in a multiparty peacekeeping force. 'Nowhere in the world has an ill-trained, underdeveloped and wrongly-motivated liberation army ever been able to act as an honourable peacekeeping force.'

He adds: 'I warn that the handing over of responsibility by the South African government to such a peacekeeping force will only exacerbate the circumstances in which endemic violence is now flourishing in South Africa.'

Later he says: 'I call again for the disbandment of MK, and I warn the South African government, and I warn the whole world at large, that the absorption of MK into the South African Defence Force, and the absorption of MK into a so-called multi-party peacekeeping force is a total prescription for disaster.'[51]

*

An Agence France-Presse report on 24 August states that former MK soldiers have formed a security company to protect industries in Johannesburg's northern suburbs.

In the dispatch, Acton Maseko of the landmine campaign in the eastern Transvaal in 1986 says the company will employ 200 former cadres who have been unemployed since returning to South Africa from 1990 onwards. The company will patrol the Kew, Marlboro and Wynberg industrial zones. Maseko says mounting crime has driven at least fifty businesses away from those areas, and it is in the interests of Alexandra township residents that industries remain.

The plan has broad support, according to the article. Brigadier Frans Malherbe of the South African Police is quoted saying: 'It is the best thing that could have happened to Alexandra. It will be a community effort in which everyone, regardless of political affiliation, will participate.'[52]

*

MK holds another conference in Kangwane, beginning on 3 September 1993.

'It has been particularly painful,' Nelson Mandela says from the podium, to see 'that so many of you who sacrificed your childhood and youth, left the comfort of your families and made a commitment to sacrifice your lives for our country's freedom, should find yourselves back in South Africa unemployed and without support or the means to sustain yourself.'

He says 'the welfare of our combatants and that of our returned exiles in general is directly linked to a commitment on the part of the ANC to recognise the incredible sacrifices and commitment to liberation by generations of our people who found their way into the ranks of the ANC and MK'.

In fulfilment of that commitment,

> I want to state unequivocally that the ANC is committed to ensuring that any future democratic government will be committed to providing the necessary means to address this issue. But we are not simply waiting for that. It gives me great personal pleasure, to inform you today, that the ANC has managed to raise an amount which we have allocated to MK, and with which we hope to start the process of catering for your needs.[53]

At a closed session of the conference, Joe Modise reads a report compiled by MK headquarters. He tells the three hundred or so delegates, 'We enter the transition with our heads held high and look to the future with confidence.'

He notes that 'Negotiations are almost complete on the kinds of steps we want taken by all parties in both the transition and beyond. The agreements are of such a nature that we have compromised nothing.'[54]

VICTORY

On 7 September 1993, agreement is struck on the establishment of a Transitional Executive Council (TEC). The TEC is envisaged as having seven sub-councils covering law and order, defence, intelligence, finance, regional and local government, foreign affairs and the status of women.[1]

*

The white chamber of the Tricameral Parliament passes a bill by 211 votes to 36 on 23 September allowing for the formation of the TEC.

After the counting of votes, Conservative Party members walk out in protest. They are joined by parliamentarians who have recently defected to the IFP. Conservative Party leader Ferdi Hartzenberg declares that the 'Afrikaner volk' will interpret the bill as a declaration of war.[2]

*

Siphiwe Nyanda announces at a news conference in Johannesburg on 13 December that in three days' time MK will celebrate its last anniversary before becoming part of a combined defence force after the 27 April elections.

He says that at the 16 December ceremony some fallen cadres, including Chris Hani, will be given the Chief Albert Luthuli Medal for Valour.[3]

*

When Nelson Mandela steps out of a car dressed in camouflaged fatigues, a military cap and stiff army boots on 16 December 1993, the crowd at Orlando Stadium breaks out in tumultuous applause. They are there for MK's farewell parade.[4]

Mandela's speech begins:

> Master of ceremonies, ladies and gentlemen, comrades and friends, I am overwhelmed by the great feeling of glory and pride which permeates the air in this stadium today. Those of us who stand at the helm of your organisation, the ANC, and our popular army, Umkhonto we Sizwe, are moved to the highest possible level of satisfaction in the near conclusion of a mission we set ourselves to accomplish, this day, 32 years ago. A mission which shall find its historic emblazonment in the establishment of a genuinely free and democratic South Africa come 27th April 1994.
>
> It is right and proper that, as we celebrate what is perhaps the last national occasion of MK as a liberation army, we should pause to salute the entire officer corps of MK, the numerous commanders and commissars here gathered, the complex of martyred heroes and heroines, the maimed and disabled veterans of the liberation struggle, as well as those of us who are still fit and willing to join the new national defence force which is to be established in the coming period. I elect this moment to ask you to rise up in solemn remembrance to all our fallen comrades who remained loyal to their assigned tasks up to the very last. As you

stand erect, in recognition of the unparalleled heroism, dedication and commitment of our erstwhile comrades, I ask of you a pledge to remember them to our
people and to posterity. Immortalise their memory through good deeds and the
force of example in your contribution towards a future of hope and justice for all.
I have no doubt in my mind that what we ask of you today cannot be any less
than what that greatest of South African leaders, O.R. Tambo, and that matchless
commander, Chris Hani, would have asked you to do. Let us observe a moment
of silence in memory of our gallant heroes and heroines.[5]

One of the forty-four people given a medal for his service to the struggle is Mthetheleli
Mncube. After the ceremony he tells the Johannesburg Star's Justice Malala, 'There is
joy and tears at the same time. It's like divorce for me. There are so many people here
I have not seen before in the country, people I met outside. Now here they are and I
will probably never see them again. But at the same time I am looking forward to the
new army and am optimistic that it will be a people's army.'[6]

*

On the same day, in Isandlwana in Natal, Zulu king Goodwill Zwelithini urges a crowd
of 10,000 to 'let the valour and the honour that led to the defeat of the British in this
place in 1879 rise up to claim Zulu warriors'. He says: 'Resist, I command you, resist,
I implore you. We will not be ruled by a constitution we spurn. We will not be sub-
jugated by a political party which wants to destroy us simply because it wants to rule.'

Meanwhile, some fifty kilometres from Isandlwana, General Constand Viljoen
speaks at the historic scene of the Battle of Blood River. He says 'the darkest hour
of the darkest night' has descended on the Afrikaner people. That nation must now
draw lessons from Blood River, when the Voortrekkers called on God to defend them,
swearing a sacred vow to honour him if they were spared.

Viljoen offers a renewed pledge to the Almighty: 'If you give us victory over the
darkness which now faces us, we will renew and affirm that vow.'[7]

*

In a news bulletin on Capital Radio, which is based in Umtata, it is reported on
4 January 1994 that Siphiwe Nyanda has set March as the target date for the creation
of a Multi-Party Peacekeeping Force.

Nyanda says the force will replace the South African Police, and specifically its
Internal Stability Unit, in dealing with political violence. It will consist of about
10,000 men who will be selected from recruits gathered at assembly points.[8]

*

On 24 January 1994 The Times of London reports that South Africa's election campaign is kicking into high gear. The paper's correspondent, Inigo Gilmore, writes of
the opening by the National Party of an office in the heart of Soweto, and the remarkable fact that its representative is former MK cadre and Robben Island prisoner
Vronda Banda.

After being released in 1990 – shortly after Mandela – Banda spent a further couple of years with the ANC, but by his own account grew increasingly disillusioned with the lack of benefits and jobs offered by the organisation.

But there were further reasons for his defection. Banda told Gilmore the National Party alone possesses the necessary political and economic 'expertise' to run the country. Unlike the ANC, they 'know how to govern'.

Gilmore notes Banda's views have not gone unnoticed by his former comrades, some of whom claim he has gone mad. The previous weekend Banda appeared on television to defend himself against another former MK guerrilla.

Banda said he still had friends in the ANC, and expressed confidence that others would come round when they realised, comparing the National Party to the ANC, that 'it is better to sleep with the devil you know than the devil you don't'.[9]

*

On 24 January, over 3,600 troops, including contingents from the SADF, MK and the armed forces of Ciskei, Venda and the Transkei, begin training at a military base outside Bloemfontein called De Brug. The troops will complete six weeks of training before being deployed to mainly black areas to curb violence in the build-up to the elections.[10]

*

When Nelson Mandela tells a rally in Rustenberg six days later that President Mangope of Bophuthatswana does not have long to 'lead', he is surprised by the ecstasy of the crowd's response – and alarmed. Sensing that he might perhaps have been misheard, he clarifies that he said 'lead', the Bophuthatswana leader does not have long to 'lead'.[11]

*

A convoy of vehicles, one carrying Mandela, approaches Thaba Nchu on 6 February 1994. Thaba Nchu is officially part of Bophuthatswana, but is encased completely by the Orange Free State. As the cars approach a checkpoint, the ANC bodyguards take up position and draw their handguns, but jump back into their vehicles when the homeland's policemen do not respond.[12]

Referring to the incident at a rally later in the day, Mandela says: 'They were very lucky they did not prevent us because I had made it clear to my men whether Lucas Mangope liked it or not, we will go through. We do not need to ask for permission from Mangope to move around our country.'[13]

*

The *Sunday Times* that day records that a mere two weeks after its formation, the National Peacekeeping Force, due for deployment around the country in five weeks' time, is in chaos.

The newspaper's Chris Barron reports that leading instructors informed him of a collapse of discipline, mass desertions and widespread drunkenness among the 3,500 volunteers at De Brug.

Nine SADF officers seconded to the force have gone 'on strike', and are refusing to have anything to do with the force. Meanwhile more than 100 statements have been submitted by SADF volunteers who want to return to their units. Some 60 to 80 per cent of police volunteers have already left, and a further 40 per cent of those from the homeland military forces have gone home as well.

The troops 'do pretty much as they like', an SADF officer said. 'If a guy threatens someone or disobeys a command, there's nothing we can do. They can say what they like to you, but if you try to punish anyone and something happens, you're in trouble.'

The worst incident came last Saturday night when some 600 MK cadres, many of whom were drunk, allegedly began toyi-toying and singing 'One settler, one bullet' and 'Down with F.W.' They demanded one dead SADF and one dead SAP member before sunrise. At least two SADF instructors were assaulted, while terrified members of other groups armed themselves with tent pegs and poles in case of being attacked. Many refused to sleep in their tents that night, heading instead for the bush.

An SADF instructor told Barron: 'At this stage, the SADF is carrying MK. While we're still in training, this is okay. But once the force is deployed, it's going to be a no-go situation. When the SADF and police are withdrawn and we're left to sort out the problems, there's going to be serious shit.'[14]

Speaking on the following day, the National Peacekeeping Force's commander Gabriel Ramushwana admits there are problems within the force and it may not be ready in time for the elections.[15]

*

A SAPA dispatch at 3.33 p.m. on 10 March 1994 reports that 200 Bophuthatswana homeland policemen have demonstrated outside the South African embassy in Mmabatho, and have handed over a memorandum calling for the incorporation of the homeland into South Africa, full payment of their pension fund contributions, and the opportunity to participate in the April elections.[16]

*

A further SAPA report at 4 p.m. that day quotes President de Klerk as having stated that the TEC must take 'far reaching decisions and use its powers' to stabilise Bophuthatswana.[17]

*

Later that afternoon, Ontlametse Menyatsoe is at his home in Seweding in Bophuthatswana when he hears the sound of people shouting outside.

He goes to see what is happening. When he opens the door he sees people running around the streets, singing ANC songs, raising their hands, proclaiming the fall of Mangope's government, and saying Mega City is on fire.

Menyatsoe looks in the direction of Mega City shopping centre and sees a huge plume of smoke rising from the building.[18]

*

SAPA reports at 8.23 p.m. that President Lucas Mangope has fled Mmabatho.[19]

*

At 9.45 a.m. on the 11th, another SAPA report states that AWB general Steven Meninger has said that his organisation has between 4,000 and 5,000 members in Mmabatho.[20]

*

At 12.36 p.m. SAPA reports Johannesburg *Star* photographer Ken Oosterbroek saying 'The Bophuthatswana Defence Force is running a large group of right-wingers out of Mmabatho.'[21]

*

On the afternoon of the 11th, Peter de Ionno of the *Sunday Times* arrives at a stop street near the headquarters of the Bophuthatswana Police Force, where a blue Mercedes-Benz has come to a halt. As he and others reach the vehicle they see three white men on the ground alongside the vehicle. They are clad in AWB uniforms. There are several policemen around the vehicle. One of the AWB men lying alongside the vehicle appears to De Ionno to be dead.

De Ionno tries to communicate with the other two. One is lying on the ground, face down, and the other against the rear wheel of the vehicle. De Ionno asks an officer of the Bophuthatswana Defence Force at the scene what is going to happen to the men.

The officer says an ambulance has been called.

A while later, a man dressed in the green fatigues that constitute the uniform of the Bophuthatswana Police approaches the scene. This policeman, Ontlametse Menyatsoe, asks the three AWB men where they are from.

One of the AWB men says they are from Naaboomspruit.

'What are you doing here and who called you?'

'Go and ask your state president.'

One of the AWB men says: 'We want an ambulance.'

Menyatsoe asks: 'Why didn't you bring your ambulance here?' As he says this he sees one of the wounded men move his hand underneath his body. Menyatsoe then opens fire on them at point-blank range with his R4 rifle.

He then heads back to the yard of the police headquarters.[22]

*

Following a strike by civil servants in the Ciskei homeland to demand full pension payouts ahead of the April elections, and with signs of a mutiny under way in his police and armed forces, Ciskei's leader Brigadier Oupa Gqozo resigns on 22 March and asks the TEC to appoint an interim administration.

When the news arrives at ANC headquarters, Joe Slovo says: 'Two down and one to go,' meaning that with Mangope and Gqozo 'down', KwaZulu, which is ruled by Inkatha, remains the last homeland holding out against the 27 April elections.[23]

*

On the evening of Sunday 27 March, Gary Kruser receives a call from Commissioner Gadu, who tells him that the following day's march is going to be used as a decoy to attack Shell House, the ANC's headquarters.

Gadu mentions that the police have been called to assist with the protection of Shell House, and says that Nelson Mandela at some stage phoned President de Klerk to inform him of the news.[24]

*

At 7.45 a.m. the following morning, Captain Wilken, the South African Police's liaison officer for the area encompassing Shell House, phones Humphrey Ndlovu, the IFP's West Rand chairman.

'Humphrey! Good morning and how are you?'

'Hi,' Ndlovu answers. 'I'm looking for you. I wanted to page you but I'm on my way to the office.'

'Humphrey, listen, we have big problems this morning, man.'

'Where?'

'You know, in Alexandra, at the hostels. People are throwing stones to the vehicles. They are shooting, shooting at the policemen who have got big chaos in town. I wonder, can you make contact with the people at the hostels, man, to tell them to discipline and come into town? Either discipline, or we're going to have big problems today.'

'I see.'

'You know really, we want to give our full support, but the people seem to me, they're getting out of hand now, man. We need your support, but from your side Humphrey as well, you must try your utmost to calm the people down and tell them they must not loot the places or throw stones, etc.'

'That is true.'

'Otherwise we're gonna have chaos in town this morning.'[25]

*

Just before 8 a.m., Gary Kruser is driving through Hillbrow and Joubert Park on the way to Shell House when he sees people fleeing from armed groups of marchers. He also notices marchers assembled in groups of about fifty each, armed with 'traditional weapons' such as pangas, assegais and knobkerries.

Noting the direction in which the people are running, he deduces they must be fleeing from Lancet Hall, about two streets south of Shell House. Kruser decides to go to Jeppe Street, where Lancet Hall is located. When on Jeppe Street he sees an ambulance parked close to Lancet Hall's eastern entrance.

He walks up to the ambulance and sees medical people treating two injured persons.

Inside Shell House, the ANC's twenty-two-storey headquarters on the corner of King George and Plein Streets, Kruser pops in to Commissioner Gadu's office. He finds Gadu on the phone trying to contact the police.

When Gadu is finished, Kruser briefs him on what he saw on the way to work. They then discuss the information that has been made available to them by their respective intelligence organs.

Gadu instructs Kruser to try to find members of the ANC intelligence department, arm them, and then deploy them together with the rest of the security members.[26]

*

At 3.03 p.m. Eastern Time in the United States, Gene Randall, the Cable News Network (CNN) anchor says 'We begin today in South Africa, where the key players in the country's complex political scene have agreed to meet for a four-way summit later this week. At issue – the bloodshed that threatens to upset South Africa's first all-race elections. The announcement follows a weekend of deadly political violence that claimed at least 55 lives in Natal and at least 18 others today in Johannesburg. CNN's Mike Hanna has the story.'

The report begins with a voiceover by Hanna: 'From the start of the day, violence is in the air.' An image is shown of some Zulu women ululating while marching in the streets.

'Thousands of Zulus take to the streets of downtown Johannesburg,' Hanna says, 'marching in support of their king and his call to boycott the April elections – registering, too, their angry opposition to Nelson Mandela and his African National Congress.'

There is then a caption of Humphrey Ndlovu, the IFP West Rand chairman, telling a crowd: 'If they try sideline us, South Africa will be a catastrophe! We are going to destroy – no one will go to the polls on the 27th!'

Hanna resumes: 'Then, from at least three points on surrounding buildings – a volley of shots sent to the supporters of the Zulu king.'

There is then an image shown of gunfire and whistling.

'Police take cover,' Hanna says, 'unsure of the snipers' location as some of the many armed Zulus in the crowd *return* fire at random. The gun battle continues for more than twenty minutes as any lingering hopes [of a] peaceful movement towards democracy disappear in the streets of the country's largest city.'[27]

*

But after the Shell House massacre, the TEC tightens the noose around Buthelezi and Inkatha. Three days after the shootings, President de Klerk declares a state of emergency in Natal.[28] Then on 7 April, a large convoy of tanks carrying about 600 mainly white reservists arrives in the northern Natal town of Eshowe.

On the same day, the National Peacekeeping Force is deployed for the first time as its troops are sent to townships near Johannesburg. A BBC correspondent sees forty of the distinctive light-blue vehicles of the force move into townships on the East Rand.[29]

*

In Pretoria on the same day, the Joint Military Co-ordinating Council (JMCC), which is overseeing the birth of the new South African National Defence Force, holds its first press conference, with its co-chairmen Siphiwe Nyanda and Wessels Kritzinger (operations chief of staff in the SADF) presiding.

They release a press statement outlining the processes to be followed in integrating the forces of MK, the SADF and the homeland armies of the Transkei, Bophuthatswana, Venda and the Ciskei. It says that in the initial stages, three assembly points at existing SADF bases in Wallmannstal to the north of Pretoria and in Bourke's Luck and Hoedspruit in the eastern Transvaal will be established for MK troops. The former will host 8,000 cadres, Bourke's Luck 2,500 and Hoedspruit 1,500. An advance party of 400 military instructors has already reported to Wallmannstal. The soldiers in these assembly points will undergo evaluation tests and six months of training before being integrated into the new force. Other camps will be established in the Cape and possibly Natal.

The conference is opened up to questions. Nyanda says there are over 20,000 MK troops, but he only expects about 16,000 of them to show up for integration. He adds that there are thousands of cadres abroad in Uganda and Tanzania. Since the three initial assembly points lack the carrying capacity to accommodate them, they will stay abroad until after the elections, and will be recalled when the camps are ready.[30]

*

On the following day, 8 April, the troops in northern Natal gear up in preparation for deployment to townships and rural villages in the region.

On the 9th they begin fanning out around Eshowe.[31]

*

Just prior to an IFP rally in Durban on Sunday 17 April, Kenyan professor Washington J. Okumu takes Mangosuthu Buthelezi aside. He hands Buthelezi a handwritten message and tells him that F.W. de Klerk is now quite prepared to accept this. If Buthelezi agrees, Okumu will go and see Nelson Mandela in Cape Town.

Buthelezi reads the document and says he is sure he can live with it, but he must first check with his colleagues at a central committee meeting that night.

Okumu advises Buthelezi to be prepared to fly to Pretoria later that evening, because Mandela will be flying there as well, and the three leaders could then sign the document in the capital.[32]

*

The following day in Thokoza township, ANC activists endeavour to string a 'Vote Mandela' banner between a pine tree and lamp on Khumalo Street. A National Peacekeeping Force vehicle stands between them and the Mshaya'zafe hostel.

Shots ring out and everybody scatters.

The peacekeepers' vehicle moves up the street.

Photographers follow the armoured personnel carrier, using it as cover. But the vehicle starts accelerating, leaving them exposed, so they branch off to houses on the street, and take cover there.

An SDU member toting an AK-47 appears, and the journalists follow him as he weaves his way through alleys winding between houses. They emerge at a disused petrol station in Khumalo Street. There they see a barrier of armoured vehicles standing between the forecourt and Mshaya'zafe hostel.

The SDU member disappears into the crowd, after which the photographers move towards the troops, who let them pass through their lines. The reporters move on to the garage forecourt's precast concrete wall. The garage wall is some twenty metres from the hostel's outer wall, which is pitted with bullet holes, while the hostel's windows are also barricaded with plywood and iron sheeting.

Dozens of soldiers are in position along the forecourt wall. The photographers, along with a couple of television cameramen, lie parallel to them. Greg Marinovich, one of the photographers, approaches a black officer and says: 'We are not going to get in your way, but we want to follow you guys in. We'll stay behind you. Is that okay?'

'Sure, that's fine.'

When a burst of gunfire issues from the hostel, a soldier on top of one of the armoured vehicles returns fire. In the ensuing firefight, Marinovich is struck in the left breast and falls into the legs of two colleagues, João Silva and Sam Msibi.

The soldiers continue to fire at the hostel. Silva and Jim Nachtwey drag Marinovich to cover. Then Gary Bernard shouts: 'Ken O has been hit.' Nachtwey leaves Marinovich and heads to Bernard's position. He finds Bernard trying to get a response from Ken Oosterbroek, who has blood trickling from the side of his mouth, but who is in fact already dead.[33]

*

SAPA reports the following day, 19 April, that order has been restored to lower Khumalo Street by what appeared to reporters to be SADF troops. The arrival of the troops was cheered by the hostel dwellers in Mshaya'zafe, according to the report.

The dispatch adds that Christo Visser, spokesman of the SADF Wits Command, has confirmed that the SADF is lending 'limited support' to the peacekeepers – at the request of the National Peacekeeping Force itself.[34]

*

At a news conference in Pretoria on 19 April, President de Klerk announces: 'I am extremely pleased that after months of negotiations, intensive talks and intensive interaction and renegotiation of past days, we have reached agreement resulting in the participation in the elections on the scheduled dates of the IFP.'

He adds: 'The agreement also encompasses the amendment of the constitution in two respects with regard to the kingdom of KwaZulu, and Parliament will be called on Monday to consider those amendments.'

Sitting next to De Klerk are Nelson Mandela, Mangosuthu Buthelezi and the rotund, bespectacled Washington Okumu, who smiles throughout.

Chief Buthelezi says the agreements deal extensively with the existence of the Zulu kingdom and the rights of King Goodwill Zwelithini. The IFP believes that the provincial powers contained in the amendments set standards for other provinces.

The IFP has therefore recorded a 'negotiation victory', while the agreement 'on the role of the king and the existence of KwaZulu falls in line with the principles of self-determination'.

For Mandela, 'This agreement is a leap forward for peace, reconciliation, nation-building and an inclusive election process. Nothing is more precious than saving lives of human beings. Nothing is more urgent than the possibility that by making this process all-inclusive, we get all political parties to take part in this election. This deserves the support of all leaders and of all those who love South Africa.'[35]

*

'Go for the bottom,' Chief Buthelezi tells a crowd in Ulundi on 20 April 1994, referring to the position at the bottom of the ballot paper that the IFP will occupy owing to its delayed entry. He cautions that it will be 'a miracle' if Inkatha does well in the polls given its late start.[36]

*

Two days later, Sarel van der Walt from *Beeld* is part of the first group of journalists allowed to visit the South African Army's base at Wallmannstal outside Pretoria, where MK cadres have been assembling since 28 March 1994 in advance of their incorporation into the new army.

When the journalists arrive, there are about 2,550 MK soldiers present (out of the expected final total of 8,000). Petros Shecheshe, MK commander at the base, tells them cadres have come from across the land and also from Tanzania and Uganda. He says the process is advancing well: 'Despite what happened in the past we were received with open arms by the army. Most of us didn't expect it.'

SADF colonel Terence Murphy, the overall commander of the base, agrees, saying no problems have arisen. He adds that the MK soldiers will receive basic training in drill and the handling of weapons at the base. MK will be responsible for that, after which an evaluation team consisting of both SADF and MK members will judge whether they are ready to join the army.[37]

*

Just before midnight on the evening of 26 April, a multiracial crowd of several hundred gathers outside the Provincial Administration Buildings in Cape Town. On the balcony, a choir sings 'Die Stem' as the old South African flag is lowered. Then, amid cheers, tears and hugs, the choir sings the first verse of 'Nkosi Sikelel'iAfrika' while a new flag is raised.

While this is done, Albie Sachs, who is in the crowd, says: 'I've watched the Berlin Wall come down on television, and all the other changes in Europe. It's so nice that this change is happening here at home in our country.'

Asked about the new flag, he says: 'it's a mess'.[38]

*

At a press conference on the afternoon of the 27th, Johann Kriegler, the chairman of the Independent Electoral Commission, says an additional 8.6 million ballot papers will be printed by midnight in three parts of the country, and they will now include the IFP's name and logo.

He confirms that at some polling stations yesterday and today, voting began without IFP stickers attached to the ballot papers. In these instances, those who wanted to vote for the IFP had to write the IFP's name on their ballot paper and vote next to it. In some cases IFP officials asked IFP voters to do this.

Kriegler says: 'If Chief Minister Buthelezi were to phone me, I would be able to satisfy him that the procedure we have decided on won't prejudice the IFP.'

In a report appearing in the *Star* the following day, the voting on the 27th is described as having been peaceful but characterised by massive snaking queues at voting stations, amid continual reports of widespread ballot paper and IFP sticker shortages, leading to subsequent voting station closures.[39]

*

Radio South Africa's news bulletin at 11 p.m. on 2 May alleges that MK soldiers have stoned cars at the combined military centre of the new South African National Defence Force (SANDF) at Wallmannstal near Pretoria. The report claims it was a group of drunken soldiers, dissatisfied with their pay, who stoned the cars of MK officers who tried to mediate.[40]

The Associated Press follows up on the story the following day. It cites sources 'close to the ANC' that confirmed that 200 guerrillas were involved in the action, which was quelled after Siphiwe Nyanda called on SADF troops to restore order. Officers at Wallmannstal added that about 170 guerrillas were being held by military police following the incident.[41]

*

On 6 May the Independent Electoral Commission pronounces the country's elections free and fair and gives the results. The ANC has won 62.65 per cent of the nearly 20 million votes cast, while the National Party has won 20.4 per cent and the Inkatha Freedom Party 10.5 per cent.[42]

*

On 9 May, Nelson Mandela steps out onto the balcony of Cape Town's Grand Parade. An audience of 50,000 people greets him. Grown men are in tears, white police officers applaud.

'The people of South Africa have spoken in these elections,' Mandela says. 'They want change, and change is what they will get. Our plan is to create jobs, promote peace and reconciliation, and to guarantee freedom for all South Africans. We place our vision of a new constitutional order for South Africa on the table, not as conquerors, prescribing to the conquered.'[43]

*

In an interview broadcast on SABC television's *Newsline* programme that evening, new defence minister Joe Modise tells Leslie Mashokwe that his number-one priority will be to offer the various armies that became the SANDF on 27 April (primarily the SADF, MK, the PAC's military wing APLA, and the former defence forces of Bophuthatswana, the Transkei, the Ciskei and Venda) a uniform programme of training. He says the British have been asked to assist with both the training and the adjudication of the quality of the training (so as to avoid wrangling about standards when integration takes place).

Mashokwe says cynics will look at the experience with the National Peacekeeping Force and ask: 'will we be able to put together a national defence force if we failed at that level?'

Modise answers:

You must not forget that the Peacekeeping Force never had a chance. We had planned to put it together, train it for nine months. It was done in eight weeks. The training was completely inadequate. Time was too short and, what is more, the Peacekeeping Force was opposed long before its inception. The idea was opposed. It had a lot of enemies from within and from without. I've never seen a force that was criticised like the Peacekeeping Force. So, in other words, it was never given a chance. I don't think that attitude is going to prevail with the building of the new South African National Defence Force, and we are going to give ourselves time. We don't see integration as an overnight affair. We look at it as a process. We are going to start preparing our men now. We are going to put them through the necessary paces, until we feel that they are ready to be put together, because that's the only way in which we are going to have a legitimate force. The SADF cannot be transformed into the South African National Defence Force. It won't be accepted by the people. It will still remain an illegitimate force. To legitimise it we've got to bring in all these others and we've got to empower them.[44]

*

At 12.17 p.m the following day, another crowd of 50,000 gathers, this time on the front lawn of Pretoria's Union Buildings, watching two giant television screens as Nelson Mandela takes the oath of office.

Present at the swearing-in ceremony are representatives of over 200 governments and non-governmental organisations, including United States vice-president Al Gore, who is accompanied by first lady Hillary Rodham Clinton. Also there are United Nations secretary-general Boutros Boutros-Ghali, PLO chairman Yasser Arafat and Cuba's Fidel Castro.[45]

In his speech, Mandela declares that apartheid was 'an extraordinary human disaster that lasted too, too long'. He continues:

We have triumphed in the effort to implant hope in the breasts of the millions of our people. We enter into a covenant that we shall build the society in which all South Africans, both black and white, will be able to walk tall, without any fear in their hearts, assured of their inalienable right to human dignity – a rainbow nation at peace with itself and the world.

He concludes:

> Never, never and never again, shall it be that this beautiful land will again experience the oppression of one by another and suffer the indignity of being the skunk of the world.
>
> The sun shall never set on so glorious a human achievement!
>
> Let freedom reign!
>
> God bless Africa!
>
> I thank you.[46]

The new national anthem is played, consisting of the old one, 'Die Stem', followed by 'Nkosi Sikelel'iAfrika'. Mandela then turns and takes up position alongside Georg Meiring, the former chief of the South African Defence Force, who was directly behind him in the amphitheatre along with a number of ex-SADF generals in full military regalia, and MK officers, including Siphiwe Nyanda, in guerrilla fatigues.

(Meiring will be appointed SANDF chief by Joe Modise in May 1994, and in the following month Nyanda will be appointed lieutenant general and acting chief of staff in the SANDF pending his completion of a three-year training course. His appointment will be as one of nine MK officers promoted simultaneously by Modise to top positions in the army, amid objections from white generals about standards, and rumblings from MK cadres about the slow pace of integration.)[47]

Meiring and Mandela look through a glass screen at the rear of the amphitheatre as the SANDF puts on a show of its military might. A cannon salute is followed by a fly-past of helicopters carrying the new national flag, and warplanes trailing smoke in the new national colours of red, white, blue, black, green and gold.

This concludes the inauguration ceremony. Mandela holds the hand of his daughter Zenani Dlamini as he leaves the podium. They are accompanied by Thabo Mbeki and F.W. de Klerk, the deputy presidents of the new government of national unity. The group moves to a stage where a day-long concert is set to commence.

Mandela speaks from within a portable bulletproof box on the stage.

Referring to the struggle, he says: 'it has been costly in human lives but let us forget the past'. As for the future, 'We are now busy healing the wounds of the past and it is for you to support us in that task.'[48]

* * *

Notes

In these notes, where archival sources (whether in physical or electronic repositories) are referenced, all information appearing before a colon pertains to the document cited, while the information after the colon details the archival repository in which the document is to be found. The following is a list of abbreviations employed in the notes when referencing archival collections, internet databases, newspapers, press agencies and journals.

Archival Repositories
BL: Brenthurst Library
• PYP: Dr Percy Yutar Papers

BNA: Botswana National Archives and Records Service
• OP: Office of the President Record Group

ICS-RFP: Institute of Commonwealth Studies, University of London. Ruth First Papers

NARS: (South African) National Archives and Records Service
• NAB: Pietermaritzburg Archives Repository
• TAB: National Archives Repository (Pretoria)

NAZ: Zambian National Archives
• FA: Ministry of Foreign Affairs Collection

NMF(CM): Nelson Mandela Foundation Centre for Memory
• Mandela-Stengel Conversations: Transcripts of the audio recordings of conversations in 1992 and 1993 between Nelson Mandela and Richard Stengel during the making of *Long Walk to Freedom*
• NMPP: Nelson Mandela Private Papers (NMPP 2009/8)

OU-RHL: University of Oxford, Bodleian Library of Commonwealth and African Studies at Rhodes House
• *Barrell*: Research Papers of Howard Barrell (MSS. Afr. s. 2151 Barrell)

SANDF: (South African) Department of Defence, Documentation Centre

UFH-ANC: University of Fort Hare, African National Congress Archives
• CM: Canada Mission
• GM: German Mission (Bonn and Austria)
• LM: Lusaka Mission
• Lon.M: London Mission
• MO: Morogoro Office
• NMP: Nelson Mandela Papers
• ORT: Oliver Tambo Papers
• TM: Tanzania Mission

UCT: University of Cape Town Libraries
- AFT: Ashley Forbes Trial
- SC: Simons Collection

UKZN-AP: University of KwaZulu-Natal, Alan Paton Centre and Struggle Archive

UNIP: United National Independence Party Archives (Lusaka, Zambia)

UNISA(MF): University of South Africa Library, Microfilm Collection

UWC-MCA: University of the Western Cape, Robben Island Museum, Mayibuye Archives
- BC: Brian Bunting Collection
- MCA6: Mayibuye Centre: Oral History of Exiles Project

UWHP: University of the Witwatersrand, Historical Papers
- BH: Barbara Harmel interviews (A3301)
- C&N: Cambanis and Nicholls (AK2525)
- *Coetzee*: Coetzee, Dirk (A2790f)
- *Denton*: US Senate Subcommittee on Security and Terrorism (A1572)
- *Dumisa*: Diary of an MK operative (A3149f)
- EPCB: Ellis Park Car Bomb (H. Matshididi + others – AK2819)
- *Fischer*: State v Abram Fischer (AK2411)
- KGC: Karis-Gerhart Collection (A2675)
- *Harms*: Harms Commission (AK2300)
- HW: History Workshop audio interviews (A3191)
- *Kasrils*: Ronald Kasrils Papers (A3345)
- *Mapumulo*: Trials: W.M. Mapumulo & others vs the State, 1985 (AK2327)
- *Mathambo*: State v Mathambo (AK2371)
- *Mathabe/Nyanda*: State v Mathabe and Nyanda (AK2377)
- *Mncube&Nondula*: M.Z. Mncube and M.E. Nondula v The State – appeal (AK2228)
- *Modise*: S v Modise (AK2368)
- *Molobi*: Trials: Eric Molobi (AD1899)
- *Neame*: Sylvia Neame Papers (A2729)
- *Ngqungwana*: Trials: L.B. Ngqungwana & others vs the State (AK2307)
- *Nyembe*: State v Nyembe (A2372)
- *Passtoors*: S v H. Passtoors (AK 2426)
- PT: Political Trials (AD1901)
- PWI: Patti Waldmeir Interviews (A2508)
- *Rapholo*: J. Rapholo vs the State (AK2374)
- *Rivonia*: Rivonia Treason Trial (AD1844/A)
- RPP: Dr Ronald Press Papers (A3239)
- RT: Tucker, R (AK 3166)
- SAIRR: South African Institute of Race Relations Security Trials (AD2021)
- TLC: Tom Lodge Collection (A3104)
- TRC(CD): TRC Hearings and Amnesty Applications (Compact Disc – A3040)
- *Tsotsobe etc*: Trials: A.B. Tsotsobe and 2 others (AK2333)

- *Williams*: State v Williams (AK2395)
- WMT: State v Mkwayi, W and others, Record of Proceedings (AK2520)

ZNA: Zimbabwe National Archives

Internet Materials

O'Malley: Interviews conducted by Padraig O'Malley. The index page for the interviews can be found at: https://www.nelsonmandela.org/omalley/index.php/site/q/03lv00017.htm (Accessed 20 Nov. 2013)

RSC/*Aluka*: Raymond Suttner Collection (interviews available from the website www.aluka.org)

TRC2: South African Broadcasting Corporation website featuring material from the proceedings from the Truth and Reconciliation Commission process. The index page for the Amnesty Hearings transcripts is: http://www.sabctrc.saha.org.za/documents/amntrans.htm (Accessed 18 Nov. 2013)

UDW-'VR': University of Durban-Westville, Documentation Centre, Oral History Project ('Voices of Resistance'). The index page for the collection can be found at: http://scnc.ukzn.ac.za/doc/Audio/VOR/Transcript.htm (Accessed 6 Nov. 2013)

Newspapers and Press Agencies

AFP: Agence France Presse
AP: Associated Press
Argus: *Cape Argus*
BBC: British Broadcasting Corporation Summary of World Broadcasts
BDN: *Botswana Daily News* (Gaborone)
CSM: *Christian Science Monitor* (Boston, Massachusetts)
C.Times: *Cape Times*
DD: *Daily Dispatch* (East London)
FT: *Financial Times* (London, England)
Guardian: *Guardian* (London, England)
Independent: *Independent* (London, England)
IPS: Inter Press Service
M&G: *Mail & Guardian* (South Africa)
NDN: *Natal Daily News*
NM: *Natal Mercury*
NW: *Natal Witness*
NYT: *New York Times*
P.News: *Pretoria News*
RDM: *Rand Daily Mail*
R.Herald: *Rhodesia Herald*
SABC: South African Broadcasting Corporation
SAPA: South African Press Association
S.News: *Swazi News*

S.Observer: *Swazi Observer*
Star: *The Star* (Johannesburg)
S.Times: *Sunday Times* (South Africa)
TG&M: *The Globe and Mail* (Canada)
Times: *The Times* (London)
Times(Swz): *Times of Swaziland*
Times(Zam): Times of Zambia
TS: *Toronto Star*
UPI: United Press International
WM: *Weekly Mail* (South Africa)
WP: *Washington Post*
W.Times: *Washington Times*
Xinhua: Xinhua General News Service
ZDM: *Zambia Daily Mail*
ZM: *Zambia Mail*

Journals
Af.St: *African Studies*
S.Afr.Hist.Jnl: *South African Historical Journal*
Soc.D: *Social Dynamics*

PART I: THE STRUGGLE

Acts of Treason

1. 'P.E. rioting: policeman tells court of attack on station', *Star*, 8 Dec. 1952; '11 killed, 27 hurt in Native riots at P.E.', *RDM*, 20 Oct. 1952; 'Tin of paint was start of P.E. riots, say witnesses', *RDM*, 9 Dec. 1952.
2. M.F.B. Ntsangani/*Treason Trial: S v F. Adams et al.* (S.A. Supreme Court, Transvaal; *c.* 1961), p. 16215.
3. '11 killed, 27 hurt in Native riots'; 'Police statement on how riots started', *Star*, 20 Oct. 1952; 'Police stopped Natives from killing me', *RDM*, 20 Oct. 1952.
4. 'Fountainhead of "Defiance" is P.E. – Verwoerd', *RDM*, 21 Oct. 1952.
5. '"No outside country can help us" – Verwoerd', *Star*, 22 Oct. 1952.
6. 'Curfew, but not for New Brighton, proposed', *Star*, 29 Oct. 1952.
7. 'New Brighton Natives back up strike threat', *RDM*, 3 Nov. 1952.
8. 'More Police drafted to Eastern Cape', *RDM*, 8 Nov. 1952.
9. D. Card to C. Thomas, *Tangling the Lion's Tail* (Donald Card, 2007), pp. 34–5.
10. 'Border Native leader says location meeting authorized', *Star*, 11 Nov. 1952.
11. 'Three Europeans, 8 Natives killed in East London riots', *RDM*, 10 Nov. 1952.
12. '"Avoid trouble" appeal by African National Congress', *Star*, 10 Nov. 1952.
13. '10,000 Natives idle in P.E. strike: No Incidents', *Star*, 10 Nov. 1952.
14. 'One-day strike of Natives at P.E. ends quietly', *RDM*, 11 Nov. 1952.
15. 'Thousands of P.E. Natives dismissed', *Star*, 11 Nov. 1952.
16. A.J. Luthuli/*Treason Trial*, p. 11414; 'Chief deposed for sharing in "Defiance"; justifies himself', *RDM*, 13 Nov. 1952.
17. 'Equality Plan aim alleged by crown', *Star*, 26 Nov. 1952.
18. '20 resisters given right to appeal', *RDM*, 3 Dec. 1952; 'Defiance leaders guilty under anti-red act', *Star*, 2 Dec. 1952.
19. A.J. Luthuli/*Treason Trial*, p. 11412.
20. 'Public Safety Bill designed as a deterrent', *Star*, 11 Feb. 1953.
21. 'Government's "Earnest hope"', *RDM*, 12 Feb. 1953.
22. 'Defiance leaders in touch with Gold Coast – Swart', *Star*, 18 Mar. 1953.
23. 'United Front gained 130,000 more votes than Nat. "Volkswil"', *RDM*, 18 Apr. 1953.
24. A.J. Luthuli/*Treason Trial*, pp. 11440, 11442; 'Defiance Campaign to be continued, says Chief Luthuli', *RDM*, 21 Apr. 1953.
25. R. Resha/*Treason Trial*, pp. 16409, 16568–70; N. Mandela, *Long Walk to Freedom* (Abacus, 1995), p. 180; Mandela-Stengel Conversations, p. 405: NMF(CM); W. Sisulu to W. Kodesh, transcript: UWC-MCA/MCA6-371.
26. N. Mandela, *Long Walk to Freedom*, p. 184.
27. Z.K. Matthews speech, 'Exh. ZKM2'/*Treason Trial*, pp. 18274–5.
28. N. Mandela, *Long Walk to Freedom*, p. 184.
29. *Ibid.*, pp. 187, 189; 'Swart bans officials of African Congress', *Star*, 4 Sep. 1953; *Treason Trial*, pp. 13195–6.
30. N. Mandela, 'No Easy Walk to Freedom', in S. Johns and R. Hunt Davis (eds.), *Mandela, Tambo and the African National Congress* (Oxford University Press, 1991), p. 42; and Schedule 9, pp. 11–13/ *Treason Trial*.
31. W. Sisulu to B. Harmel, 04m15s–15m50s (audio): UWHP-BH/B21.6; W. Sisulu to W. Kodesh, transcript: MCA6-371.
32. R. Resha/*Treason Trial*, p. 16423.
33. *Ibid.*, pp. 16438, 16440–41; 'W. Areas families to be moved to-day', *RDM*, 9 Feb. 1955.
34. 'More than 100 Native families moved out from West Areas', *RDM*, 10 Feb. 1955.

35. 'It was a city within a city', S.Times, 14 Feb. 1960.

36. 'Freedom Charter – Full Text', 'Police throughout Union alerted to hinder Congress' and 'Freedom Charter adopted', New Age, 30 Jun. 1955; 'Congress of the People remembered 26th June 1955', Sechaba (Jun. 1985), p. 5; B. Turok, Nothing But the Truth: Behind the ANC's Struggle Politics (Jonathan Ball, 2003), p. 61.

37. T.E.E. Moeller, I. Maisels, and document content/Treason Trial, pp. 143–4, 11535–6, 11538–9, 13289.

38. 'Notes on the Transvaal A.N.C. Conference', New Age, 20 Oct. 1955.

39. 'More bans for Nelson Mandela', New Age, 29 Mar. 1956.

40. 'Freedom Charter adopted by A.N.C.', New Age, 5 Apr. 1956.

41. 'Swart's Treason Trial threat', New Age, 3 May 1956.

42. 'The Big Swoop: 53 come in by air', '52 remanded in custody on treason allegations', RDM, 6 Dec. 1956.

43. 'Ban on A.N.C. considered', S.Times, 3 Mar. 1957.

44. 'Leaders of A.N.C. may be banished', S.Times, 17 Mar. 1957.

45. '"No Sacrifice Too Great for Freedom": ANC Protests Against Banning Threat', New Age, 28 Mar. 1957.

46. 'Pass Laws Condemned at ANC Conference', New Age, 24 Oct. 1957; 'Tvl. ANC leaders move quickly to meet critics', New Age, 21 Nov. 1957.

47. 'ANC Conference: Great Advances', New Age, 26 Dec. 1957.

48. A.J. Luthuli/Treason Trial, pp. 11565–6.

49. 'United Party's firm line on A.N.C. demonstrations', Star, 25 Mar. 1958.

50. 'Verwoerd takes steps to ban A.N.C.', RDM, 15 Mar. 1958.

51. 'African nationalism cannot be banned', RDM, 19 Mar. 1958.

52. '"Ban" order on ANC gazetted', RDM, 18 Mar. 1958.

53. 'Native trouble at election designed to help Nats.', Star, 26 Mar. 1958.

54. 'A.N.C. split on protest plan', RDM, 2 Apr. 1958.

55. 'A.N.C. attitude to the election', RDM, 7 Apr. 1958.

56. 'Police chief tells Natives: My men will protect you', Star, 10 Apr. 1958.

57. 'Special Branch raids offices all over country', Star, 11 Apr. 1958.

58. 'Dr. Verwoerd bans gathering of more than 10 Natives', Star, 11 Apr. 1958.

59. 'A.N.C. call ignored – Natives go to work as usual', Star, 14 Apr. 1958.

60. 'A.N.C. calls off "stay home" protest', RDM, 15 Apr. 1958.

61. 'Nats. get 103 seats in new parliament, but U.P. voting strength is still greater', RDM, 18 Apr. 1958.

62. 'Mr. Strijdom dead', 'Brief tenure of office', 'Acting Premier', in S.Times, 24 Aug. 1958; B.J. Liebenberg and S.B. Spies (eds.), South Africa in the 20th Century (J.L. van Schaik, 1993), pp. 355–6.

63. 'Luthuli opposes Narrow Native Nationalism', S.Times, 2 Nov. 1958; 'Anti-Whiteism – It's a product of Apartheid', S.Times, 9 Nov. 1958; G.M. Gerhart, Black Power in South Africa (University of California Press, 1978), pp. 177–8; E. Sisulu, Walter & Albertina Sisulu: In our Lifetime (David Philip, 2002), pp. 201–2.

64. R. Sobukwe/R. Sobukwe et al. v The State, p. 457: UNISA(MF)-Sobukwe/FI4007.

65. M. Harmel, 'Revolutions are not abnormal', Afr.South, 3 (2), 1959, in M.J. Daymond and C. Sandwith (eds.), Africa South Viewpoints, 1956–1961 (University of KwaZulu-Natal Press, 2011), pp. 181–6.

66. 'Hero's welcome for Lutuli', New Age, 4 Jun. 1959.

67. 'They can ban me but spirit of freedom can't be banned says Tambo', New Age, 18 Jun. 1959.

68. 'We don't want Storm-Troops in S.A.!', New Age, 10 Dec. 1959.

69. 'Executive Report submitted to the African National Congress – Annual Conference', Dec. 1959, Durban, pp. 11–12: UKZN-AP/PC170/7/2/4/9.

70. 'Referendum for a Republic', RDM, 21 Jan. 1960.

71. 'Let me be very frank, says U.K. Premier', 'Macmillan: Merit, individual merit alone counts' and

'We listen, even if we differ – Dr. Verwoerd', *Star*, 3 Feb. 1960; 'Macmillan says U.K. "cannot support some aspects" of S.A. policy', *NDN*, 3 Feb. 1960.

72. 'The A.N.C. has 2 "boycott targets"', *RDM*, 22 Feb. 1960.
73. *New Age*, 24 Mar. 1960, read in *R. Sobukwe et al. v The State*, pp. 482–3: UNISA(MF)-Sobukwe/FI4007.

Violence and Non-Violence

1. 'Vereeniging Trouble: Police Move In', *Star*, 21 Mar. 1960.
2. P. Frankel, *An Ordinary Atrocity: Sharpeville and its Massacre* (Yale University Press, 2001), pp. 113–16; T. Lodge, *Sharpeville: A Massacre and its Consequences* (Oxford University Press, 2011), pp. 105–6.
3. '67 dead – the official figure', *RDM*, 23 Mar. 1960.
4. 'Riot Township Natives Stay at Home', *Star*, 22 Mar. 1960.
5. 'Verwoerd: revolt was planned', *RDM*, 23 Mar. 1960.
6. '"Day of mourning" call by Luthuli', *RDM*, 24 Mar. 1960.
7. 'Nats. rush bill for power to ban A.N.C.', *Star*, 25 Mar. 1960.
8. R.C. Mafeking to D.H.C., 28 Mar. 1960: BNA-OP/33/29.
9. District Commissioner's Office (Lobatsi), 'Report on Ronald Michael Segal and Oliver Tambo', 29 Mar. 1960: BNA-OP/33/29.
10. 'When a people go mad', *Star*, 29 Mar. 1960.
11. 'All was quiet until 4.30 – then came the mobs', *RDM*, 30 Mar. 1960.
12. 'On verge of revolution', *RDM*, 30 Mar. 1960.
13. W. Kodesh to H. Barrell, p. 340: OU-RHL/*Barrell*.
14. *Ibid.*, pp. 340–1; B. Turok, *Nothing But the Truth*, pp. 103–4; B. Turok to B. Harmel and P. Bonner, 18m55s–20m30s (audio): UWHP-BH/B23.1.
15. 'Cabinet discuss state of emergency', 'List of arrests in various centres', *Star*, 30 Mar. 1960; 'Drastic emergency laws', *RDM*, 31 Mar. 1960.
16. 'A.N.C. have gone underground', *Star*, 4 Apr. 1960.
17. 'A.N.C. and Pan-Africanists banned for year', *Star*, 8 Apr. 1960.
18. 'Prime Minister shot' and 'Latest: Condition Satisfactory', *Star*, 9 Apr. 1960; 'Dr. Verwoerd shot twice' and 'Arrested man a wealthy Transvaal farmer', *S.Times*, 10 Apr. 1960; 'Closer guard for cabinet', *RDM*, 11 Apr. 1960; 'Pratt tells why he shot Dr. Verwoerd', *S.Times*, 11 Sep. 1960.
19. 'Police reply to call for stay-at-home', *RDM*, 15 Apr. 1960.
20. 'Non-Whites go to work – as usual', *RDM*, 19 Apr. 1960.
21. 'Police preparing "riot plan"', *RDM*, 16 May 1960.
22. 'Planes, police watch June 26', *RDM*, 27 Jun. 1960.
23. B. Turok to B. Harmel and P. Bonner, 44m10s–45m25s, 46m05s–48m00s (audio): UWHP-BH/B23.1; 'South Africa What Next?', pp. 1, 4–5, 14–15: UWHP-*Neame*/B19.
24. 'State of Emergency will end today', *RDM*, 31 Aug. 1960.
25. 'The republicans win by 73,980', *RDM*, 7 Oct. 1960.
26. 'P.M. on republic date', *RDM*, 8 Oct. 1960.
27. 'African Leaders call for National Convention', *New Age*, 22 Dec. 1960; 'ANC elder statesmen: interviews with Govan Mbeki and Raymond Mhlaba', *Monitor*, Dec. 1989, p. 26: UWHP-KGC/III-93; Mandela, unpublished autobiography, pp. 405–6: NMF(CM).
28. B. Turok, *Nothing But the Truth*, pp. 122–3; B. Turok to H. Barrell, p. 1300; B. Hepple, *Young Man with a Red Tie* (Jacana, 2013), p. 36.
29. R. Bernstein to S. Neame, 21 Aug. 1986, pp. 29–30: UWHP-*Neame*/E1; R. Bernstein, *Memory Against Forgetting* (Viking, 1999), pp. 225–6; B. Turok to B. Bunting, Oct. 1973, p. 5: UWC-MCA/BC.
30. B. Turok, *Nothing But the Truth*, p. 123; B. Turok to B. Harmel and P. Bonner, 51m30s–51m50s; B. Turok to B. Bunting, Oct. 1973, p. 5; B. Hepple, *Young Man with a Red Tie*, p. 106.
31. Resolution cited in 'Memorandum', p. 1: UWHP-*Kasrils*/A6.1.4.1.
32. B. Turok to B. Harmel and P. Bonner, 51m55s–52m20s.
33. B. Turok to B. Bunting, Oct 1973, p.8: UWC-MCA/BC.

34. Report in the *Star* on 3 Feb. 1961 cited in 'Congress Alliance … A List of 14 admissions …', pp. 35–6: SANDF-HSI AMI/3/356 'A.N.C. General'.

35. 'Congress threatens government', *Contact*, 6 Apr. 1961: SANDF-HSI AMI/3/356 'ANC Policy'.

36. *Ibid.*; M.L. Marwa/*S v N. Mandela*, pp. 30–34 UNISA(MF)/Nelson Mandela Trial 1962 (hereafter *S v N. Mandela*).

37. J. Rumpff, 'Reasons for Verdict', p. 168/*Treason Trial*.

38. 'A night to remember', *RDM*, 30 Mar. 1961.

39. 'Mandela is asked not to become "difficult"', *RDM*, 25 Oct. 1962.

40. J.F. Barnard/*S v N. Mandela*, pp. 46–50.

41. 'Police raid homes and offices', *RDM*, 28 Apr. 1961.

42. 'Union-wide police action', *RDM*, 3 May 1961; '59 homes were raided in pre-dawn swoop', *RDM*, 4 May 1961.

43. P.B. Hazelhurst/*S v N. Mandela*, pp. 87–8.

44. 'Anti-R protest is not racial', *RDM*, 13 May 1961.

45. 'Non-white leaders on the run', *RDM*, 25 May 1961.

46. 'Mandela says: "We're not depressed"', *RDM*, 30 May 1961; N. Mandela, *Long Walk to Freedom*, p. 319.

47. A. Sampson, *Mandela: The Authorised Biography* (Harper Collins, 2000), p. 148; 'Nelson Mandela: the first call to arms', *Daily Telegraph*, 28 May 2010; Video of the Widlake-Mandela interview (http://www.itv.com/news/2013-12-06/nelson-mandelas-first-ever-tv-interview-in-1961-brian-widlake/) accessed 30 Apr. 2015.

48. 'Meetings ban may be lifted next week – Erasmus', *RDM*, 3 Jun. 1961.

49. Mandela-Stengel, p. 520; N. Mandela, *Long Walk to Freedom*, p. 320.

50. N. Mandela, *Long Walk to Freedom*, pp. 320–21.

51. *Ibid.*, p. 321; N. Mandela, *Conversations with Myself* (Macmillan, 2010), pp. 75–6.

52. N. Mandela, *Long Walk to Freedom*, p. 321; N. Mandela, *Conversations with Myself*, p. 76.

53. J.F. Barnard/*S v N. Mandela*, pp. 55–7.

54. W. Mkwayi to B. Harmel and P. Bonner, 1h6m20s–1h08m10s (audio): UWHP-BH/B9.1.

55. N. Naidoo, 'The "Indian Chap": Recollections of a South African Underground Trainee in Mao's China', *S.Afr.Hist.Jnl*, 64 (3), 2012, pp. 712–13.

56. I. Meer, *A Fortunate Man* (Zebra Press, 2002), p. 223; N. Mandela, unpublished autobiography, pp. 423–4; N. Mandela, *Long Walk to Freedom*, pp. 321–2.

57. I. Meer in R. Seedat and R. Saleh (eds.), *Men of Dynamite: Pen Portraits of MK Pioneers* (Ahmed Kathrada Foundation, 2009), p. 38; N. Mandela, unpublished autobiography, p. 423; N. Mandela, *Long Walk to Freedom*, pp. 323–4; N. Mandela, *Conversations with Myself*, p. 78; Mandela-Stengel, pp. 521–2, 621.

58. J. Slovo, *Slovo: The Unfinished Autobiography* (Ocean Press, 1997), pp. 173, 176–7.

59. R. Press, *To Change the World! Is Reason Enough?*, Ch. 1. 'Mists and Images': UWHP-RPP.

60. D. Goldberg, *The Mission* (STE, 2010), p. 85; D. Goldberg to H. Barrell, p. 192.

61. D.J. Smith, *Young Mandela* (Weidenfeld & Nicolson, 2010), pp. 219–22; 'Recollection of Nelson Mandela, Part One: the First Explosion', *Sechaba* (Mar. 1983), p. 14; 'The first known explosion', *Dawn* (Souvenir Issue, c. 1986), pp. 8–9 (in all these sources the account provided is by Wolfie Kodesh).

62. D. Goldberg to W. Kodesh, transcript: UWC-MCA/MCA6-279.

63. 'Nats' greatest lead' and '"Progs. on only true path" – Luthuli', *RDM*, 20 Oct. 1961.

64. 'Luthuli wins Nobel Prize' and 'Ex-chief will apply for passport', *RDM*, 24 Oct. 1961.

65. A. Mthembu/*S v W. Mkwayi et al.*, p. 115: UWHP-WMT; A. Mtembu/*S v N.G. Naidoo*, pp. 4, 11, 12: UWHP-PT/Box 35.

66. A. Mlangeni to P. Bonner, 2 Mar. 1994, pp. 22, 24–6: UWHP-BH/B.10.1; R. Mhlaba to T. Karis, Dec. 1989, p. 10: UWHP-KGC/I-22; R. Mhlaba to B. Harmel and P. Bonner, 56m30s–57m00s (audio): UWHP-BH/B8.1b; N. Parsons, 'The pipeline: Botswana's reception of refugees, 1956–68', *Soc.D*, 34 (1), 2008, p. 19.

67. B. Nair/*S v E. Ismail et al.*, pp. 2921–2: NARS-NAB/Case No: CC224/63.

68. B.M.S. Chaitow/*Ismail*, p. 296.
69. 'Way of violence still rejected', *RDM*, 12 Dec. 1961; 'Africa in revolt against oppression', *Star*, 12 Dec. 1961.
70. B.M. Hlapane/*S v A. Fischer*, pp. 211–12: UWHP-*Fischer*.
71. B. Mtolo in *S v N. Mandela et al.*, pp. 39–40: UWHP-*Rivonia*/Box 3 (hereafter *Rivonia*).
72. 'Lutulis are home', *NDN*, 16 Dec. 1961; 'Big welcome for Lutuli', *C.Times*, 16 Dec. 1961.
73. B. Mtolo/*Rivonia*, pp. 41–2; B. Mtolo/*S v T.H. Gwala et al.*, p. 235: NARS-NAB/Case No: CC108/76; S. Moodley to V. Reddy, 3 Jul. 2002: UDW-'VR'; 'Road blocks set up on all borders of Republic', *NM*, 18 Dec. 1961; 'Sabotage in Durban failed', *Star*, 18 Dec. 1961; R. Kasrils, *Armed and Dangerous: From Undercover Struggle to Freedom* (Jonathan Ball, 2004), p. 34.
74. B. Mtolo/*Rivonia*, p. 43.
75. B. Turok to H. Barrell, pp. 1305–6; B. Turok, *Nothing But the Truth*, pp. 128–30.
76. J. Slovo, 'The longest three minutes in my life', *Dawn* (Souvenir Issue, *c.* 1986), p. 7.
77. 'Mystery caller' and 'Sabotage outbreak in S.A.', *S.Times*, 17 Dec. 1961.
78. 'Mass police alert after ten bomb explosions', *C.Times*, 18 Dec. 1961.
79. 'Sabotage bid shakes P.E.', *S.Tribune*, 17 Dec. 1961; 'Bomb class in garage, court told', *C.Times*, 3 May 1962.
80. J. Slovo, 'The longest three minutes', p. 7.
81. R. Bernstein, *Memory Against Forgetting*, pp. 235–6.
82. R. Vandeyar/*Men of Dynamite*, p. 151.
83. 'Blast stopped the clock at 10.22', *S.Times*, 17 Dec. 1961.
84. J. Modise, 'The happiest moment in my life', *Dawn* (Souvenir Issue, *c.* 1986), p. 11.
85. T. Sigasa, F. Masinda and A. Dlepu in *S v B. Ramotsi*, pp. 18–23, 26–31, 45–6: NARS-TAB/Case No: CC323/62; 'More evidence in bomb explosion case', *New Age*, 8 Mar. 1962.
86. J. Modise, 'The happiest moment in my life'.
87. 'Mass police alert after ten bomb explosions'.
88. For details of this other incident, see *S v B. Turok*: NARS-TAB/Case No: CC284/62.

PART II: SABOTAGE

The Opening Phase

1. 'ANC elder statesmen: interviews with Govan Mbeki and Raymond Mhlaba', *Monitor*, Dec. 1989, p. 27: UWHP-KGC/III-93; 'New turn in P.E. explosives case', *New Age*, 19 Jul. 1962.
2. 'Arrests at Rivonia Described', *RDM*, 13 Feb. 1964.
3. 'Blanke agitators sit agter sabotasie', *Die Transvaler*, 19 Dec. 1961.
4. 'P.E. explosives case: court told of test tubes found in car', *Argus*, 5 May 1962.
5. *Ibid.*
6. 'No comment by Luthuli on sabotage report', *Argus*, 20 Dec. 1961.
7. 'Sabotage: death penalty foreshadowed', *S.Times*, 24 Dec. 1961.
8. N. Naidoo, 'The "Indian Chap": Recollections of a South African Underground Trainee in Mao's China', *S.Afr.Hist.Jnl*, 64 (3), 2012, p. 714; R. Mhlaba to T. Mufamadi, *Raymond Mhlaba's Personal Memoirs: Reminiscing from Rwanda and Uganda* (Human Sciences Research Council and Robben Island Museum, 2001), p. 115.
9. Mandela diary – African tour, 3 and 7 Jan. 1962, *Rivonia Exhibits* (Exhibit R17), p. 204: BL-PYP/MS.385/19-21; N. Mandela diary entry, 8 Jan. 1962: NMF(CM)/Box '1962 Diary + Notebook'; N. Mandela, *Long walk to Freedom* (Abacus, 1995), p. 342.
10. D.S.B.O. (Lobatsi) to O.C.S.B (Mafeking), 'Undesirables in the B.P.', 15 Jan. 1962: BNA-OP/33/6.
11. F. Keitseng, *Comrade Fish: Memories of a Motswana in the ANC Underground* (Pula, 1999), p. 54.
12. N. Mandela diary, 2 and 3 Feb. 1962: NMF(CM); N. Mandela, 'PAFMECSA', *Rivonia Exhibits* (Exhibit R13), p. 168: BL-PYP/MS.385/19-21; N. Mandela, *Long Walk to Freedom*, p. 351.
13. C. Ndlovu and B. Nair/*S v E. Ismail et al.*, pp. 2683–4, 2692, 2742, 2924, 2991: NARS-NAB/Case No: CC224/63.

14. N. Mandela, 'MAROC', p. 1, *Rivonia Exhibits* (Exhibit R16), p. 190: BL-PYP/MS.385/19-21; N. Mandela, notes titled 'Maroc', p. 77, in *Rivonia Trial: State's Concluding Address*, Part III: NARS-TAB/CC253/64; Mandela-Stengel Conversations, p. 591: NMF(CM).

15. D. Goldberg to H. Barrell, p. 211: OU-RHL/*Barrell* (Goldberg's account here of Mandela's conversation with 'the top Algerian military man … not Boummedienne' is based on a version Goldberg recalls being told by Mandela).

16. W. Kodesh to H. Barrell, p. 367.

17. 'Police evidence about December 16 document', *Star*, 29 Mar. 1962.

18. B. Mtolo in *S v N. Mandela et al.*, p. 46: UWHP-*Rivonia*/Box 3 (hereater *Rivonia*).

19. E. Isaacs and B. Nair/*Ismail*, pp. 658–65, 2943–4; R. Kasrils, 'Dynamite thieves', *Dawn* (Souvenir Issue, *c.* 1986), pp. 17–18; Letter from B. Nair to R. Kasrils, 20 Feb. 2002: UWHP-*Kasrils*/A6.2.1.2.4.

20. 'Death for sabotage in new S.A. bill', *NDN*, 12 May 1964.

21. O. Ngoza and J. Mtloko/*S v M. Magwayi et al.*, pp. 4–5, 54–5, 64–5: UWHP-PT/Box 43.

22. L.L. Dukashe and R.N. Mdube/*S v M.J.M. Kondoti et al.*, pp. 29–30, 253, 269–70: UWHP/PT-Box 32.

23. E.A. Suleiman/*S v S. Fadana*, pp. 22–3: UWHP-PT/Box 6.

24. I. Rani/*Rivonia*, pp. D21–2 (Box 2); I. Rani and A. Jantjies/*S v H. Fazzie et al.*, pp. 40–1, 43–4, 94–5: UWHP-PT/Box 13.

25. N. Mandela diary, 15 and 17 Jun. 1962; N. Mandela, *Long Walk to Freedom*, p. 361.

26. 'Motor cycle burnt in hunt for Mandela', *S. Times*, 24 Jun. 1962.

27. N. Mandela diary, 26, 28, 29 Jun. 1962; N. Mandela, *Long Walk to Freedom*, p. 362.

28. I. Rani, A. Jantjies and E. Suliman/*Fazzie*, pp. 46–8, 97–100, 140; I. Rhani Statement/'Sabotage Training', p. 1: BNA-OP/33/24; I. Rani/*S v B.M. Ngcobo et al.*, pp. 34–5: NARS-NAB/Case No: CC25/69.

29. J.J. Matoti, p. 21/*Kondoti*.

30. Mandela-Stengel, pp. 615–16.

31. R.C. Mafeking to H.C. Pretoria, 26 Jul. 1962: BNA-OP/33/21; P. Bapela, Declaration, p. 3/ *S v P. Baphela*: NARS-TAB/Case No: CC62/65.

32. T. Setumu, *Heeding the Call to Fight for the Fatherland: The Life and Struggle of T.T. Cholo* (Fortune-d Africa, 2011), p. 48.

33. F. Keitseng, *Comrade Fish*, p. 55.

34. R.C. Mafeking to H.C. Pretoria, 26 Jul. 1962; F. Keitseng, *Comrade Fish*, pp. 55–6; Mandela-Stengel, pp. 614, 616–17.

35. N. Mandela, *Long Walk to Freedom*, pp. 369–70; A. Kathrada, *Memoirs* (Zebra Press, 2004), p. 150; H.R. Slovo (Ruth First), Statement, pp. 10–11: UKZN-AP/170/7/4/2/7.

36. N. Mandela, *Long Walk to Freedom*, pp. 370–1; Mandela-Stengel, pp. 617–19.

37. C. Ndlovu/*Ismail*, p. 2776; B. Mtolo/*Rivonia*, pp. 71, 75–6; B. Mtolo/*Rivonia Trial: State's Concluding Address*, Part II, p. 22: NARS-TAB/CC253/64; B. Nair in M. Maharaj and A. Kathrada (editorial consultants), *Mandela: The Authorised Portrait* (Bloomsbury, 2006), p. 107.

38. Mandela-Stengel, pp. 621–2; N. Mandela, *Long Walk to Freedom*, pp. 371–2.

39. I. Rani, A. Jantjies and 'Judgement'/*Fazzie*, pp. 54–6, 106–111, 308.

Soldiers of Mandela

1. 'Emergency ANC conference in Tanganyika', *New Age*, 30 Aug. 1962.

2. J.T. Masupye/*S v A. Mashaba et al.*, pp. 13–15: UWHP-PT/Box 33.

3. B. Mtolo and B. Nair/*Ismail*, pp. 1689, 1745, 2927.

4. N. Babenia, S.T. Mbanjwa and D.V. Perumal/*Ismail*, pp. 80–1, 156, 392–3, 2797–8; B. Pillay [S. Singh], 'How MK grew', *Dawn* (Souvenir Issue, *c.* 1986), p. 20; N. Babenia, *Memoirs of a Saboteur* (Mayibuye, 1995), p. 73; T. Karis and G.M. Gerhart (eds.), *From Protest to Challenge: A Documentary History of African Politics in South Africa, 1882–1964*, Vol. 3 (Hoover Institution Press, 1977), p. 662.

5. S.T. Mbanjwa/*Ismail*, pp. 82, 158.

6. D.V. Perumal/*Ismail*, pp. 394, 396–7; B. Pillay, 'How MK grew', p. 20; N. Babenia, *Memoirs of a Saboteur*, pp. 73–4; 'Petrol bomb attacks in Cape and Natal', *Star*, 15 Oct. 1962.

7. A. Kathrada, *Memoirs*, p. 152; A. Kathrada in R. Seedat and R. Saleh (eds.), *Men of Dynamite*, p. 96; 'Police hunt Kathrada and Sisulu', *S.Times*, 21 Oct. 1962; 'House arrest order is served on Kathrada', *RDM*, 23 Oct. 1962; 'House arrest for Sisulu, Kathrada', *New Age*, 25 Oct. 1962.
8. 'Note on an interview with Walter Max Sisulu at Lobatsi on 24 October, 1962', pp. 1–2: BNA-OP/33/21.
9. R.C. Mafeking to H.C. Pretoria *et al.*, 26 Oct. 1962: BNA-OP/33/21.
10. J. Matthews, 'Memorandum to Prof. Tom Karis on the subject of the thinking and background to the decisions of the African National Congress (South Africa) in the period from 1964 onwards', p. 5: UWHP-KGC/III-95; B. Hlapane, Statement, 1 Oct. 1964, p. 16: UWHP-KGC/III-692; 'Exiles in secret meeting of A.N.C.', *RDM*, 29 Oct. 1962; F. Meli, *A History of the ANC: South Africa belongs to us* (James Currey, 1989), pp. 151–3.
11. 'Sisulu on "war"', *RDM*, 22 Apr. 1964.
12. R.N. Mdube/*Kondoti*, pp. 29, 50–51.
13. B. Mtolo/*Ismail*, pp. 1708–9.
14. S.T. Mbanjwa, G. Naicker, B. Nair/*Ismail*, pp. 84–5, 93–5, 102–3, 506–10, 2758–9; 'Saboteurs blast Natal power line', *RDM*, 2 Nov. 1962; 'Appendix I: Records of Acts of Sabotage', in E. Feit, *Urban Revolt in South Africa 1960–1964: A Case Study* (Northwestern University Press, 1971), p. 334.
15. '6 More house arrests', *RDM*, 10 Nov. 1962.
16. B.G.S. Magxengane, R.N. Mdube, S. Tanana and V. Tonjeni/*Kondoti*, pp. 34, 54, 297–9, 337–8.
17. I. Rani/*Fazzie*, p. 60.
18. B. Pillay, 'How MK grew', and E.I. Ebrahim, 'Though we had no AK47's nor revolvers', *Dawn* (Souvenir Issue, c. 1986), pp. 15, 20; 'Indictment', p. 9/*Ismail*; S.T. Mbanjwa/*Ismail*, pp. 113–18.
19. D. Card, I. Hoyi and T.T. Selani/*Kondoti*, pp. 3, 112–13, 316–17; C. Thomas, 'The entwined tale of Inkie Hoyi, Washington Bongco, Donald Card, and a "core group" of MK operatives – a foray into political intimidation and violence in Duncan Village 1959–1964', *Journal for Contemporary History* 30 (1), 2005, pp. 160, 165.
20. 'UMKONTO WE SIZWE greets the people of SOUTH AFRICA: A message from the High Command', BL-Edwin S. Munger Papers: PAM.MUN.701.
21. C.Z. Nboxele and C. Davids/*Rivonia*, pp. B2, D12–13; D. Goldberg to H. Barrell, p. 199; D. Singqomo/*S v K. Matshabe et al.*, p. 2: UWHP-PT/Box 15.
22. D. Goldberg, *The Mission* (STE, 2010), p. 91.
23. C.Z. Nboxele and C. Davids/*Rivonia*, pp. B4, D18; A. Sachs, 'The least dramatic contribution', *Dawn* (Souvenir Issue, c. 1986), p. 16.
24. J.P.F. van Wyk/*S v J.E. April*, pp. 30–32: NARS-NAB/Case No: CC84/71.
25. C.Z. Nboxele/*Rivonia*, p. D20; D. Goldberg, *The Mission*, p. 91; D. Goldberg to H. Barrell, p. 197.
26. A. Mthembu/*S v W. Mkwayi et al.*, pp. 115, 120–21, 122–4: UWHP-WMT; A. Mthembu/*S v M.G. Sexwale et al.*, p. 958: UWHP-PT/Box 62.
27. R. Mhlaba to T. Karis, Dec. 1989, p. 13: UWHP-KGC/I-22; R. Mhlaba to B. Harmel and P. Bonner, 04m00s–05m40s (audio): UWHP-BH/B8.2.
28. D.S.B.O. (Lobatsi) to O.C.S.B (Mafeking), 'A.N.C. Refugees', 11 Jan. 1963: BNA-OP/33/8.
29. Secretary for Justice to Registrar of the Supreme Court, 30 Oct. 1964: NARS-TAB/Criminal Case 1458; J. O'Hagan, statement of material findings against the accused, 16 Mar. 1964, p. 4/*S v Z. Mkaba et al.*: UWHP-PT/Box 19.
30. M. Mvula/*Ismail*, pp. 333–34, 359–60; S. Maphumulo, unpublished memoirs, p. 189: OU-RHL/*Barrell*; 'Blast hits newspaper', *RDM*, 19 Jan. 1963.
31. 'Blast hits newspaper'.
32. I. Rani and A. Jantjies/*Fazzie*, pp. 61, 115–16; I. Rani/*Ngcobo*, p. 43; I. Rhani Statement/'Sabotage Training', p. 4: BNA-OP/33/24.
33. A. Jantjies/*Fazzie*, pp. 116–17.
34. J.T. Masupye/*Mashaba*, pp. 29–34.
35. 'Dynamite sabotage bid at city's Treason Trial court', *P.News*, 24 Jan. 1963.
36. R.F. Ivy and D.R. McDermot/*Fazzie*, pp. 8–9, 20; 'Sabotage and military training: Refugees', 22 Feb. 1963: BNA-OP/33/24.

37. H. Bambane/*Rivonia*, p. D7; H. Bambani/*S v S.G. Hashe*, pp. 7–8: UWHP-PT/Box 23; F. Tyulu and G. Gaxkana, pp. 6, 9–10, 17/*S v W. Khanyile*: UWHP-PT/Box 36; G. Makamba, pp. 7–10, in *S v J. Gqabi*: UWHP-PT/Box 40.

38. P. Mfene to W. Kodesh: UWC-MCA/MCA6-317a.

39. G. Gaxkana , pp. 10, 12/*Khanyile*; H. Bambane/*Rivonia*, pp. D7–8; G. Makamba, p. 17/*Gqabi*.

40. F J. Glas/*Khanyile*, pp. 1–2; J. Glas/*Gqabi*, p. 3; J. Glas/*Tyulu*, p. 1: UWHP-PT/Box 6; J. Glas/ *S v S. Fadana*, p. 3: UWHP-PT/Box 6; J. Glas/*S v H. Makgothi*, p. 3: UWHP-PT/Box 16.

41. P. Mfene to W. Kodesh: MCA6-317a.

42. A. Masondo, 'Sawing electric pylons', *Dawn* (Souvenir Issue, *c.* 1986), pp. 22–3; 'Lecturer on charge of sabotage', *Spark*, 14 Mar. 1963.

43. A. Masondo, 'Sawing electric pylons'.

44. *Ibid.*; D. Card to C. Thomas, *Tangling the Lion's Tail* (Donald Card, 2007), pp. 89–91.

45. P. Mfene to W. Kodesh: MCA6-317a and b.

46. D. Card to C. Thomas, *Tangling the Lion's Tail*, pp. 123–4.

47. P. Mfene to W. Kodesh: MCA6-317a and b.

48. 'Sisulu can't even answer his phone', *RDM*, 4 Apr. 1963.

49. V. Shubin, *ANC: A view from Moscow* (Jacana, 2008), pp. 35, 37–8.

50. J.T. Masupye/*Mashaba.*, pp. 40–43.

51. '"Ambush of saboteurs" described', *RDM*, 10 May 1963; 'Sabotage only method of retaliation – guilty Indian', *RDM*, 11 May 1963; I. Naidoo, 'The longest night', *Dawn* (Souvenir Issue, *c.* 1986), p. 32; I. Naidoo to P. O'Malley, 14 Oct. 2002: *O'Malley*.

52. 'Tip-off led to raid on Rivonia', *RDM*, 19 Jun. 1964.

53. 'Sisulu disappears', *RDM*, 20 Apr. 1963.

54. 'Sisulu on "war"', *RDM*, 22 Apr. 1964.

55. 'Vorster's bill and – YOU', *RDM*, 24 Apr. 1963.

56. N. Mandela, *Long Walk to Freedom*, p. 334.

57. G. Mbeki and W. Sisulu/*Rivonia*, pp. 34, 85.

58. 'House ban Kathrada missing – the 10th', *RDM*, 6 May 1963; A. Kathrada/*Men of Dynamite*, p. 98; A. Kathrada, *Memoirs*, p. 156.

59. W.A. Knight to Chief Immigration Officer (Mafikeng), 'Mr and Mrs P.J. Hodgson', 1 May 1963: BNA-OP/33/20.

60. P.J. Hodgson, Statement, 1 May 1963: BNA-OP/33/20.

61. M. Maharaj to P. O'Malley, 8 Oct. 2002.

62. N. Naidoo, 'The "Indian Chap"', pp. 718–20.

63. G. Mbeki/*Rivonia*, pp. 87–8.

64. D. Goldberg to H. Barrell, p. 186; D. Goldberg, *The Mission*, p. 98.

65. (Bechuanaland) Commissioner of Police to Government Secretary, 'A.N.C. "Student Refugees"', 28 May 1963: OP/33/7.

66. L.M. Nkosi, Statement (Doc No: 683488), pp. 5–6: SANDF-AMI/HDI/15/125; A. Sibeko, *Freedom in our Lifetime* (Indicator, 1996), pp. 74–5.

67. UNIP/ANC press statement in A. Mbughuni, 'Tanzania and the Liberation Struggle in Southern Africa, 1958–1975' (DPhil, Howard University, 2006), pp. 157–8.

68. 'Federal Refugee Row', *RDM*, 24 May 1963.

69. A. Delius, 'African Summit Conference – II', *RDM*, 4 Jun. 1963 and 'African Summit Conference – III', *RDM*, 6 Jun. 1963; 'African leaders are preparing charter', *P.News*, 25 May 1963.

70. Exchange between B. Hlapane (citing Slovo) and A. Fischer (citing his own responses to Slovo)/ *S v A. Fischer*, pp. 43–4, 68–70: UWHP-Fischer.

71. B. Mtolo/*Rivonia*, pp. 90, 141–3.

72. S. Mbanjwa, pp. 10–11/*Matshabe*; S. Mbanjwa/*S v P. Ngakane*, pp. 764–5: UWHP-PT/Box 21.

73. H. Sitilo, pp. 38–9/*Matshabe*.

74. (Bechuanaland) Commissioner of Police to Govt. Sectretary, 'John Joseph MARKS alias J.B. Marks and Joe SLOVO', 4 Jun. 1963: BNA-OP/33/7.

75. B. Mtolo and W. Sisulu/*Rivonia*, pp. 44, 144–7.
76. E.A. Suliman/*Rivonia*, p. C5.
77. L.M. Nkosi, Statement, pp. 6–7.
78. P.A. Ferreira/*S v J.N. Majiba*, pp. 1–4: UWHP-PT/Box 19.
79. *Ibid.*, pp. 4–5.
80. *Ibid.*, p. 5; E.A. Sulliman, p. 12/*Matshabe*; E.A. Suliman/*Rivonia*, p. C5; W. Nyombo/*Matshabe*, pp. 1–2; S.T. Mbanjwa/*Ismail*, p. 282.
81. B. Hepple, *Young Man with a Red Tie* (Jacana, 2013), p. 114.
82. 'Guerrilla warfare will start soon – S.A. refugee', *Bulawayo Chronicle*, 21 Jun. 1963.
83. (Bechuanaland) Police Commissioner to Government Secretary, 5 Jul. 1963: BNA-OP/33/7.
84. L. Callinicos, *Oliver Tambo: Beyond the Engeli Mountains* (David Philip, 2004), pp. 291–2.
85. AFP dispatches '78' and '79', 24 Jun. 1963: SANDF-HSI AMI/3/357 'ANC Activities'.
86. E. Motsoaledi to P. Delius, n.d., p. 4: UWHP-BH/B11.2.
87. B. Hlapane, Testimony before the Senate Sub-Committee on Security and Terrorism, 25 Mar. 1982, p. 8: UWHP-*Denton*.
88. A. Mthembu/*Rivonia*, p. E33.
89. J. Nkadimeng to B. Harmel and P. Bonner, 17 May 1993, p. 34: UWHP-BH/B15.1.
90. 'Judgement', p. 694/*Mashaba*.
91. 'South African Freedom Day', NCNA, 26 Jun. 1963: SANDF-HSI AMI/3/357 'ANC Activities'.
92. K. Liang in 'South African Freedom Day', pp. 1–2, NCNA, 26 Jun. 1963: SANDF-HSI AMI/3/357 'ANC Activities'.
93. S.T. Mbanjwa/*Ismail*, p. 208.
94. L. Gay/*Mkwayi*, p. 213: UWHP-WMT; D. Goldberg to H. Barrell, p. 228; D. Goldberg to W. Kodesh, transcript: UWC-MCA/MCA6-279.
95. 'Police silent on "Freedom Radio" claim', *RDM*, 28 Jun. 1963; Text of inaugural 'Radio Liberation' broadcast/*Rivonia Exhibits* (Exhibit R60), pp. 498–9: BL-PYP/MS.385/19-21; W. Sisulu address/ *Rivonia Exhibits* (R222), p. 739: NARS-TAB/CC253/64; Text of broadcast/*Rivonia Trial: State's Concluding Address*, Part II, pp. 23–4: NARS-TAB/CC253/64.
96. (Bechuanaland) Police Commissioner to Government Secretary, 'Jack and Rica HODGSON', 27 Jun. 1963: BNA-OP/33/22.
97. 'Tip-off led to raid on Rivonia', *RDM*, 19 Jun. 1964.
98. Document and G. Mbeki contextualisation/*Rivonia*, pp. 45, 96–9.
99. L. Strydom, *Rivonia Unmasked!* (Voortrekkerpers, 1965), p. 16.
100. *Rivonia Trial: State's Concluding Address*, Part IV, p. 26: NARS-TAB/CC253/64.
101. *Ibid.*
102. (Bechuanaland) Police Commssioner to Government Secretary, 5 Jul. 1963: OP/33/7.
103. B. Nair to D. Shongwe, 12 Jul. 2002: UDW-'VR'.
104. I.D. Kitson to W. Kodesh, 6 Sep. 1993: UWC-MCA/MCA6-297a.
105. B. Hepple, 'Rivonia: The Story of Accused No. 11', *Soc.D*, 30 (1), 2004, p. 197.
106. D. Goldberg to H. Barrell, p. 227; A. Kathrada, *Memoirs*, p. 157.
107. R. Bernstein, *Memory against Forgetting* (Viking, 1999), p. 254.
108. L. Strydom, *Rivonia Unmasked!*, pp. 17–19.
109. B. Hepple, 'Rivonia', pp. 195–6.
110. L. Strydom, *Rivonia Unmasked!* p. 23.
111. R. Mhlaba, W. Sisulu/*Rivonia*, pp. 9–11, 49–51; D. Goldberg, *The Mission*, p. 109; D. Goldberg/'Era of sacrifice and solidarity', *Star*, 14 Mar. 2008.
112. 'Secret radio seized', *RDM*, 15 Jul. 1963; 'Arrests at Rivonia described', *RDM*, 13 Feb. 1964.
113. R. Bernstein, *Memory Against Forgetting*, p. 255; B. Hepple, 'Rivonia', p. 201.
114. W. Sisulu/*Rivonia*, p. 51; 'Secret radio seized'; 'Arrests at Rivonia described'; 'Era of sacrifice and solidarity'.
115. 'Operation Mayibuye'/*Rivonia Trial: State's Concluding Address*, Part I, pp. 1–2, 6: NARS-TAB/ CC253/64.

116. 'Secret radio seized'; 'Arrests at Rivonia described'; 'The Mandela I Knew', *The Jerusalem Post*, 16 Feb. 1990.
117. 'Freedom cry from Mandela's captor', *Sunday Herald*, 11 Feb. 1990; Mandela-Stengel, p. 59.

Adversity and Retreat

1. W. Mkwayi to B. Harmel and P. Bonner, 08m28s–14m48s (audio): UWHP-BH/B9.1.
2. 'Lawyer held at border on 90-day clause', *RDM*, 19 Jul. 1963.
3. G. Frankel, *Rivonia's Children: Three Families and the Price of Freedom in South Africa* (Jonathan Ball, 1999), pp. 114–15.
4. D. Card, p. 9/*Kondoti*; D. Card to C. Thomas, *Tangling the Lion's Tail*, pp. 148–9.
5. (Bechuanaland) Police Commissioner to The Govt. Secretary, 'P.J. Hodgson', 2 Aug. 1963: BNA-OP/33/20.
6. Extracts of letter in (Bechuanaland) Police Commissioner to The Govt. Secretary, 'P.J. Hodgson', 2 Aug. 1963: BNA-OP/33/20.
7. D. Card, p. 11/*Kondoti*; D. Card to C. Thomas, *Tangling the Lion's Tail*, p. 150.
8. N.J. Grobler and S. Seshemane [Mtshali]/*Ismail*, pp. 1030–31, 2258–9; S. Maphumulo, unpublished memoirs, p. 218.
9. B. Pillay, 'How MK grew', p. 21.
10. 'Mrs Slovo arrested in Wits Library', *RDM*, 10 Aug. 1963.
11. L.M. Phokanoka, Statement (Doc No: 673676), p. 6: SANDF-AMI/HDI/15/125; L.M. Nkosi, Statement, pp. 10–11.
12. A. Sibeko, *Freedom in our Lifetime*, p. 79.
13. G. Frankel, *Rivonia's Children*, pp. 123, 128.
14. 'Arrests at Rivonia described', *RDM*, 13 Feb. 1964.
15. D.S.B.O (Southern) to O.C.S.B. (Mafikeng), 'Arthur Joseph GOLDREICH, Harold WOLPE', 28 Aug. 1963: BNA-OP/33/12.
16. 'Goldreich: we were helped' and 'Police net "nowhere near us"', *RDM*, 29 Aug. 1963.
17. H. Ferreira and K. Munger, Statements, Appendix 'A' and 'B', 31 Aug. 1963: BNA-OP/33/32.
18. 'Looksmart had bomb material – evidence', *RDM*, 27 Nov. 1963; 'Solitary can be killer', *RDM*, 28 Nov. 1963; 'Looksmart death – nobody is responsible', *RDM*, 12 Feb. 1964; 'They were murdered', *Sechaba*, 6 (2), Feb. 1972, p. 2.
19. 'Refugee plane crashes', *RDM*, 6 Sep. 1963.
20. 'Third man of Rivonia free 45 minutes', *RDM*, 10 Sep. 1963; D. Goldberg, *The Mission*, p. 117.
21. 'Escapers get out', *RDM*, 9 Sep. 1963; (Bechuanaland) Police Commissioner to the Govt. Secretary, 'Arthur Joseph GOLDREICH and Harold WOLPE', 9 Sep. 1963: BNA-OP/33/12.
22. R.C. Mafikeng to H.C. Pretoria, 18 Sep. 1963: BNA-OP/33/20.
23. 'Hodgsons land safely in Tanganyika', *RDM*, 23 Sep. 1963; Commissioner of Police to the Government Secretary, 25 Sep. 1963: BNA-OP/33/11.
24. I.D. Kitson in *S v W. Mkwayi et al.*, p. 83: UWHP-PT/Box 29.
25. B. Hepple, 'Rivonia', pp. 211–15.
26. '11 arraigned in more than 200 sabotage acts' and 'Seven alleged members of High Command', *RDM*, 9 Oct. 1963; A. Kathrada, *Memoirs*, pp. 165–6.
27. 'ANC 8. Dit word beweer dat alreeds …', 21 Oct. 1963: SANDF-HSI AMI/3/357 'ANC Activities'.
28. Z.W. Nqose, Statement (Doc No: 682041), pp. 5–7: SANDF-AMI/HDI/15/124.
29. B. Hepple, 'Rivonia', pp. 215–16; 'No police protection for freed Bob Hepple', *RDM*, 31 Oct. 1963.
30. 'Reds flew S.A. refugees', *RDM*, 7 Nov. 1963.
31. B. Hepple, 'Rivonia', pp. 216–17.
32. L. Gay/*Mkwayi*, pp. 225, 308: UWHP-WMT; I.D. Kitson/*Mkwayi*, p. 83: UWHP-PT.
33. W.D. Luthuli, Statement (Doc No: 681925), p. 5: SANDF-AMI/HDI/15/126.
34. B. Mochesane/*S v A. Mashaba et al.*, pp. 225–6, 249–55: UWHP-PT/Box 33.
35. B. Mochesane and T. Kgwele/*Mashaba*, pp. 236–8, 240–41, 374–5.

36. P.A. Ferreira/*Mashaba*, pp. 433–7; 'Bomb may have "made Vorster listen"', *RDM*, 19 Aug. 1964; '"Fortuitous" arrest of chief witness', *RDM*, 27 Aug. 1964.
37. P. Bapela, Declaration, pp. 10–11/*Baphela*: NARS-TAB/Case No: CC62/65; P. Bapela in *S v P. Metshane et al.*, pp. 17–19: NARS-TAB/Case No: CC265/65.
38. R.K. Letsholongyane, Statement (Doc No: 673675), pp. 5–6: SANDF-AMI/HDI/15/125.
39. M. Mogotsi/*S v I. Heymann et al.*, Belt 12: NARS-TAB/Case No: 322/66.
40. 'My fight is for all', *RDM*, 21 Apr. 1964; A. Fischer and P. Yutar/*Rivonia*, p. 4 (Box 4).
41. N. Mandela, *No Easy Walk to Freedom: Articles, Speeches and Trial Addresses of Nelson Mandela* (Heinemann, 1980), pp. 167, 188–9; A. Sampson, *Mandela: The Authorised Biography* (Harper Collins, 2000), p. 193.
42. 'My fight is for all'.
43. P. Bapela/*Metshane*, pp. 20–21; P. Bapela, Declaration, pp. 12–13/*Baphela*.
44. 'Rivonia Trial: 8 are guilty', *RDM*, 11 Jun. 1964.
45. 'The 9 faced four charges', *RDM*, 11 Jun. 1964.
46. 'Rivonia Trial: 8 are guilty'.
47. 'Judge says it was treason', *RDM*, 13 Jun. 1964.
48. 'Lecturer held for 90 days', *RDM*, 30 Jun. 1964.
49. 'Wives hope to visit detainees', *RDM*, 3 Jul. 1964.
50. 'Police net 17 in swoop', *RDM*, 4 Jul. 1994.
51. 'Raids could end plots – Vorster', *RDM*, 6 Jul. 1964.
52. M. Maharaj to P. O'Malley, 8 and 9 Oct. 2002.
53. *Ibid.*; N. Naidoo, 'The "Indian Chap"', pp. 719, 721–3.
54. P. Bapela, Declaration, pp. 13–14/*Baphela*; J. Mathanoko [P. Metshane], Declaration, p. 7/*Metshane*.
55. M.K. Dingake, Statement, 25 Jan. 1965 [*sic.* 1966], p. 7: UWHP-KGC/III-12.
56. B. Hlapane, Statement, 1 Oct. 1964, p. 33–4: UWHP-KGC/III-692; B. Hlapane, Testimony 25 Mar. 1982, pp. 14–15: UWHP-*Denton*.
57. L.M. Nkosi, Statement, pp. 15–16; Z.W. Nqose, Statement, pp. 2, 6–8; A. Sibeko, *Freedom in our Lifetime*, p. 81.
58. M.K. Dingake, Statement, pp. 9–10.
59. J. Mathanoko [P. Metshane], Declaration, p. 8/*Metshane*; M. Mogotsi/*Heymann*, Belt 13; R.K. Letsholongyane, Statement, pp. 19–20; J.M. Metshane/*J.F.S. Tangala et al. v The State*, pp. 177, 182: UWHP-PT/Box 45.
60. J. Mathanoko [P. Metshane], Declaration, pp. 8–9/*Metshane*.
61. B. Hlapane, Statement, p. 24.
62. B. Hlapane, Testimony, 25 Mar. 1982, p. 10.
63. P. Bapela, Declaration, p. 14/*Baphela*.
64. L.M. Nkosi, Statement, pp. 16–19.
65. *Ibid.*, p. 34.
66. W.D. Luthuli, Statement, p. 10.
67. W. Mkwayi to B. Harmel and P. Bonner, 31m20s–31m30s, 34m25s–34m35s (audio): UWHP-BH/B9.1; 'Ex-A.N.C. man is held', *RDM*, 12 Oct. 1964.

External Mission in Command

1. M.K. Dingake, Statement, pp. 11–12.
2. A. Cajee, account of experiences in ANC training camp 1960s, p. 4: UWHP-KGC/III-16.
3. R.K. Letsholongyane, Statement, p. 20.
4. I. Mgaga [M. Hlaya], Declaration, p. 3/*Metshane*.
5. J. Mathanoko [P. Metshane], Declaration, pp. 10–11/*Metshane*.
6. P. Bapela, Declaration, p. 15/*Baphela*.
7. I. Mgaga [M. Hlaya], Declaration, p. 4/*Metshane*; F. Smith in *S v M. Masala*, pp. 21–2: NARS-TAB/Case No: CC63/65.
8. 'Father fled as I slept, says Ilse Fischer', *RDM*, 26 Jan. 1965.

9. H. Ramahadi/*Heymann*, Belt 5.
10. M.K. Dingake, Statement, p. 15.
11. T.J. Swanepoel/*Metshane*, pp. 25–6; I. Mgaga [M. Hlaya], Declaration, p. 4/*Metshane*.
12. M. Matimula, J.M. Metshane, P. Mohale, W. Senna, T.J. Swanepoel/*Tangala*, pp. 162, 164, 184, 186, 203–5, 222–3.
13. M.K. Dingake, Statement, pp. 23–4.
14. R.K. Letsholongyane, Statement, pp. 22–3.
15. J.C. Broodryk/*Fischer*, p. 14.
16. Documents/*R.I. Arenstein v The State*, pp. 390, 392: NARS-TAB/Case No: 431/66.
17. R.A. van Rensburg/*Fischer*, pp. 8–9.
18. 'Rhodesia under sanctions' and 'Disguised Abram Fischer arrested', *RDM*, 12 Nov. 1965.
19. A. Sibeko, *Freedom in our Lifetime*, p. 83.
20. Z.W. Nqose, Statement, pp. 15–16.
21. M.K. Dingake, Statement, p. 26; M. Dingake to P. O'Malley, 16 Mar. 2003.
22. M.K. Dingake, Statement, pp. 26–7; M. Dingaka/*Heymann*, pp. 2–4; B.G. McKay/*Heymann*, Belt 10; G. Bizos's address to the court (p. 1)/*Heymann*.

PART III: GUERRILLA WARFARE

Invasion

1. Police Commissioner to Senior Permanent Secretary, Ministry of Home Affairs, 'Tennyson Xola MAKIWANE', 24 Jan. 1966: BNA-OP/55/31.
2. Z.W. Nqose, Statement (Doc No: 682041), pp. 16–17: SANDF-AMI/HDI/15/124.
3. 'Zambia denies refusing entry to Turok', *RDM*, 1 Feb. 1966.
4. B. Turok, *Nothing But the Truth* (Jonathan Ball, 2003), pp. 186–7.
5. L.M. Phokanoka, Statement (Doc No: 673676), pp. 17–20: SANDF-AMI/HDI/15/125.
6. *Ibid.*, p. 10.
7. (Bechuanaland) Police Commissioner to Senior Permanent Secretary, Ministry of Home Affairs, 'Martin Tembesila HANI alias Christopher NKOSANA', 22 Feb. 1966: BNA-OP/55/31.
8. L.M. Phokanoka, Statement, p. 11.
9. Zambia High Commissioner (Dar es Salaam) to Permanent Secretary, Ministry of Foreign Affairs (Lusaka), 25 Apr. 1966: NAZ-FA/1/22.
10. M. Futha statement/'Mack FUTHA, aged 24 years …', pp. 3–4: BNA-OP/55/32.
11. OAU 'Executive Secretariat Report to the Standing Committee on Defence Meeting on the 12th May, 1966 in Dar es Salaam', p. 4: NAZ-FA/1/225.
12. Zambia High Commissioner (Tanzania), 'Africa Liberation Committee. Standing Committee on Defence …', 14 May 1966, pp. 1–3: NAZ-FA/1/225.
13. M. Futha statement, pp. 4–5.
14. *Ibid.*, p. 6; 'Saboteurs returning to R.S.A.', 30 May 1966: BNA-OP/55/32; (Bechuanaland) Police Commissioner to Senior Permanent Secretary, Ministry of Home Affairs, 'Mack FUTHA (alias Stephen HLIZIYO)', 1 Jun. 1966: BNA-OP/55/32.
15. 'How Dr. Verwoerd died' and 'A heinous crime', *RDM*, 7 Sep. 1966; B. Liebenberg and S.B. Spies (eds.), *South Africa in the 20th Century* (J.L. van Schaik, 1994), p. 421.
16. Z.W. Nqose, Statement, p. 17; 'S.A. agent tells of "invasion"', *RDM*, 24 Sep. 1970; (Bechuanaland) Police Commissioner to Senior Permanent Secretary, Office of the Prime Minister, 'Terrorists returning to Rhodesia through Bechuanaland', 27 Sep. 1966: BNA-OP/55/67; Botswana Government Cabinet Memorandum, 'Prohibited Immigrants, Guerrilla Activities against the Republic of South Africa and Rhodesia and generally refugee policy', p. 1, 4 Oct. 1996: BNA-OP/55/32. For Ramotse's escape from South Africa see 'Ramoutsi fails to appear for trial', *RDM*, 25 Sep. 1962; J. Modise, 'The happiest moment in my life', *Dawn* (Souvenir Issue, *c.* 1986), p. 12.
17. S. Williams, *Colour Bar: The Triumph of Seretse Khama and his Nation* (Penguin, 2007), p. 317.
18. 'Prohibited Immigrants, Guerrilla Activities', p. 5, 4 Oct. 1966; Botswana Office of the President to

Botswana High Commissioner to Zambia, p. 2, 25 Oct. 1966: BNA-OP/55/32; Presidential Directive to Police Commissioner and the Office of the President: BNA-OP/55/32.

19. K. Kaunda to J.D. Mobutu, 15 Jan. 1967: NAZ-FA/1/225.
20. K. Kaunda to M.J. Nyerere, 15 Jan. 1967: NAZ-FA/1/225.
21. Permanent Secretary, Ministry for Presidential Affairs (Zambia) to Permanent Secretary, Ministry of Foreign Affairs (Zambia), 22 Jun. 1967, and Permanent Secretary, Ministry for Presidential Affairs (Zambia) to The Secretary, Co-ordinating Committee for the OAU, 26 Jul. 1967: NAZ: NAZ-FA/1/225.
22. OAU Liberation Committee Standing Committee on Defence, 'Executive Secretary's Report' (14 Apr. 1967), p. 4, and 'Report on meeting held 14–18 Apr. 1967', p. 3: NAZ-FA/1/151.
23. L.M. Phokanoka, Statement, pp. 12–13.
24. J. Jele to W. Kodesh, transcript, p. 21: UWC-MCA/MCA6-290; S. Sijake, 'Political Education in the African National Congress at home, in exile and in prison: a personal view', p. 18. Paper presented at workshop on 'Liberation Struggles in Southern Africa', University of Cape Town, 4–6 Sep. 2008; 'Against Manipulation of the South African Revolution', sgd T.X. Makiwane, Oct. 1975, p. 17: UWHP-KGC/III-166.
25. Z.W. Nqose, Statement, pp. 17–18; 'Feitlike studie: Rhodesië soos op 1 Apr 68', pp. 105, 111: SANDF-HSI AMI/3/379.
26. W.D. Luthuli, Statement (Doc No: 681925), pp. 10–12: SANDF-AMI/HDI/15/126.
27. T.T. Nkobi, 'Crossing the Zambezi', Dawn (Souvenir Issue, c. 1986), p. 39.
28. J. Jele to W. Kodesh, transcript, p. 22.
29. 'Nobel Winner Luthuli dies after being hit by train', RDM, 22 Jul. 1967.
30. 'Tributes to Luthuli', ZM, 28 Jul. 1967.
31. Z.W. Nqose, Statement, p. 19; L.M. Nkosi, Statement (Doc No: 683488), p. 46: SANDF-AMI/HDI/15/125.
32. Z.W. Nqose, Statement, pp. 19–21.
33. L.M. Nkosi, Statement, pp. 48–9.
34. Z.W. Nqose, Statement, pp. 21–2; L.M. Phokanoka, Statement, p. 14; 'Feitlike Studie van die situasie in Zambië soos op 25 Mrt 68', p. 137: SANDF-HSI AMI/3/380.
35. L.M. Nkosi, Statement, p. 52; L. Nkosi/S v J.E. April, pp. 65, 87: NARS-NAB/Case No: CC84/71.
36. L.M. Phokanoka, Statement, pp. 14–15; L.M. Nkosi, Statement, p. 53.
37. 'Rhodesian forces begin new clamp on terrorists', RDM, 1 Aug. 1967.
38. L.M. Phokanoka, Statement, p. 15; W.D. Luthuli, Statement, p. 14.
39. L.M. Nkosi, Statement, p. 53; 'Honour for unsung heroes of MK's military campaign', Star, 2 Aug. 2012.
40. W.D. Luthuli, Statement, p. 14; Z.W. Nqose, Statement, p. 23; L. Nkosi/April, p. 69; T.T. Nkobi, 'Crossing the Zambezi', p. 39.
41. L.M. Nkosi, Statement, p. 53; L.M. Phokanoka, Statement, p. 16; P. Mfene to W. Kodesh: UWCMCA/MCA6-317b.
42. W.D. Luthuli, Statement, p. 14; L.M. Phokanoka, Statement, p. 16.

The Wankie and Sipolilo Campaigns
1. J. Moyo, Admission, Exh. 21, p. 2: ZNA-S3398/1967-11424.
2. W.D. Luthuli, Statement, p. 14; Z.W. Nqose, Statement, p. 23; L.M. Nkosi, Statement, p. 54; L. Nkosi/S v T.H. Gwala et al., pp. 251–2: NARS-NAB/Case No: CC108/76.
3. W.D. Luthuli, Statement, p. 14; L.M. Nkosi, Statement, p. 55; L.M. Phokanoka, Statement, p. 16; L. Phokanoka interview, Oct. 1993 (Part 2): UWHP-HW; G. Morodi to W. Kodesh, transcript, p. 11: UWC-MCA/MCA6-324.
4. G. Morodi to W. Kodesh, p. 11; L.M. Nkosi, Statement, p. 56; 'Indictment' and L.M. Nkosi in S v B.M. Ngcobo et al., p. 13: NARS-NAB/Case No: CC25/69.
5. 'Judgement'/Ngcobo, p. 21; J.R.T. Wood, A Matter of Weeks Rather than Months: The Impasse Between Harold Wilson and Ian Smith: Sanctions, Aborted Settlements and War (Trafford, 2008), p. 355.

6. J.R.T. Wood, *A Matter of Weeks*, p. 355.
7. G. Morodi to W. Kodesh, p. 12.
8. 'Basil February', *Dawn* (Souvenir Issue, c. 1986), p. 40.
9. C. Hani, 'The Wankie Campaign', *Dawn* (Souvenir Issue, c. 1986), p. 35.
10. J. Moyo, Admission, p. 2; 'Basil February', p. 40.
11. J.R.T. Wood, *A Matter of Weeks*, p. 356.
12. Z.W. Nqose, Statement, p. 24.
13. R. Dube, Warn and Caution Statement, Exh. 1, p. 1: ZNA-S3398/1967-11424.
14. Comrade Rogers, 'The Battle of Nyatuwe', *Dawn* (Souvenir Issue, c. 1986), p. 47.
15. 'Judgement', pp. 2, 7/*S v R. Dube et al.*: ZNA-S3398/1967-11424.
16. R. Shay and C. Vermaak, *The Silent War* (Galaxie, 1971), p. 51.
17. 'Judgement', p. 3/*Dube*; F. Mninzi, Warn and Caution Statement, Exh. 4, p. 1: ZNA-S3398/1967-11424; 'Basil February', p. 40; 'The Battle of Nyatuwe', p. 47.
18. J.R.T. Wood, *A Matter of Weeks*, p. 356.
19. 'The Battle of Nyatuwe', pp. 47–8.
20. 'Judgement', pp. 3–5/*Dube*.
21. 'The Battle of Nyatuwe', p. 48.
22. F. Mninzi, Warn and Caution Statement, p. 1; 'Details of terrorist clash', *R. Herald* (n.d. newspaper clipping): ZNA-MS717/1-10; 'The Battle of Nyatuwe', p. 48.
23. J. Moyo, Admission, p. 2; F. Mninzi, Warn and Caution Statement, p. 1; R. Dube, Warn and Caution Statement, p. 2; 'The Battle of Nyatuwe', p. 48.
24. 'Judgement', p. 3/*Dube*; J.R.T. Wood, *A Matter of Weeks*, p. 356.
25. 'Judgement'/*Ngcobo*, pp. 20–21; L.M. Phokanoka, Statement, pp. 16–17.
26. Z.W. Nqose, Statement, p. 24.
27. J.R.T. Wood, *A Matter of Weeks*, p. 359.
28. Z.W. Nqose, Statement, p. 24.
29. J. Moyo, Admission, p. 2; 'Judgement', pp. 3A, 8/*Dube*; 'Details of terrorist clash', *R. Herald*; K. Maxey, *The Fight for Zimbabwe* (Rex Collings, 1975), p. 65.
30. P. Mfene to W. Kodesh: MCA6-317b; G. Morodi to W. Kodesh, pp. 12–13; L.M. Nkosi, Statement, p. 56.
31. 'The Fight is On', *ANC: News* (1), p. 1: UWHP-KGC/III-13.
32. ZAPU-ANC Press Release, 19 Aug. 1967: SANDF-HVS(KG) DGAA/1/67.
33. L.M. Nkosi/*Ngcobo*, p. 5; G. Morodi to W. Kodesh, p. 13; P. Mfene to W. Kodesh: MCA6-317c; 'V.M.' (a pseudonym), 'Notes of a guerrilla', *Sechaba*, 4 (1), Jan. 1970, p. 14; N. Duka, *From Shantytown to Forest* (LSM Press, 1974), p. 74; A. Wana, 'Wankie Battles', Dawn, 2 (2), Aug. 1978, p. 15; T. Bopela and D. Luthuli, *Umkhonto we Sizwe* (Galago, 2005), p. 65.
34. O.E.T. Bopela, Warned and Cautioned Statement, Exh. 17, p. 1: ZNA-S3398/1967-11425B; T. Kumalo, Statement, p. 1: ZNA-S3398/1967-11425B; L.M. Nkosi, Statement, p. 58; 'The Mzimela Trial', *Sechaba*, 7 (2), Feb. 1973, p. 2; G. Morodi to W. Kodesh, p. 15.
35. T. Kumalo, Statement, p. 1; L.M. Nkosi, Statement, p. 58; 'Notes of a guerrilla', p. 14; A. Wana, 'Wankie Battles', p. 16; G. Morodi to W. Kodesh, p. 15; P. Mfene to W. Kodesh: MCA6-317c; T. Bopela and D. Luthuli, *Umkhonto we Sizwe*, p. 68.
36. T. Bopela and D. Luthuli, *Umkhonto we Sizwe*, pp. 68–9; T. Bophela, Statement, 'Lt Smith and a platoon …', p. 1: UCT-SC/P29.4; C. Hani, 'The Wankie Campaign', p. 36; 'Leaders – Chris Hani': https://www.youtube.com/watch?v=NGKhN2BL1-U (accessed 11 May 2015).
37. L.M. Nkosi, Statement, p. 58; T. Bopela and D. Luthuli, *Umkhonto we Sizwe*, p. 69; T. Bophela, Statement, 'Lt Smith and a platoon', p. 1; O.E.T. Bopela, Warned and Cautioned Statement, p. 1; N. Duka, *From Shantytown to Forest*, p. 75; H. Hadebe, Warned and Cautioned Statement, Exh. 22, p. 1: ZNA-S3398/1967-11425B.
38. L.M. Nkosi, Statement, pp. 58–9; P. Mfene to W. Kodesh: MCA6-317c; A. Wana, 'Wankie Battles', pp. 16–17.
39. A. Wana, 'Wankie Battles', pp. 16–17; P. Mfene to W. Kodesh: MCA6-317c.

40. M. Ncube, Warned and Cautioned Statement, Exh. 21, p. 1: ZNA-S3398/1967-11425B; H. Hadebe, Warned and Cautioned Statement, p. 1; O.E.T. Bopela, Warned and Cautioned Statement, p. 1; T. Bophela, Statement, 'Lt Smith and a platoon', p. 2; W.R. Winnall and L. Nkosi/*April*, pp. 78, 91–3; 'The Mzimela Trial', p. 2; N. Duka, *From Shantytown to Forest*, p. 76; P. Mfene to W. Kodesh: MCA6-317c.

41. 'Notes of a guerrilla', p. 15; C. Hani, 'The Wankie Campaign', p. 37; T. Bopela and D. Luthuli, *Umkhonto we Sizwe*, pp. 73–4.

42. L.M. Nkosi, Statement, p. 60; 'Notes of a guerrilla', p. 15; T. Bopela and D. Luthuli, *Umkhonto we Sizwe*, p. 73.

43. L.M. Nkosi, Statement, pp. 58, 60; W.D. Luthuli, Statement, p. 16; Botswana Police Commissioner to Senior Permanent Secretary 'Incursion of alien terrorists into Botswana', 4 Sep. 1967, and Botswana Police Commissioner to Senior Permanent Secretary, Office of the President, 'Alien Terrorists in Botswana', 6 Sep. 1967: BNA-OP/27/3.

44. P. Mfene to W. Kodesh: MCA6-317c.

45. G. Morodi to W. Kodesh, pp. 19–20.

46. L.M. Nkosi, Statement, p. 61.

47. P. Mfene to W. Kodesh: MCA6-317c.

48. J.R.T. Wood, *A Matter of Weeks*, p. 363; G. Morodi to W. Kodesh, pp. 20–21; Botswana Police Commissioner, 'Alien Terrorists in Botswana', 6 Sep. 1967: BNA-OP/27/3.

49. P. Mfene to W. Kodesh: MCA6-317c.

50. Botswana Police Commissioner, 'Alien Terrorists in Botswana', 6 Sep. 1967: BNA-OP/27/3.

51. J. Moyo, Admission, p. 2; 'Judgement', p. 3A/*Dube*.

52. Joint Planning Staff Rhodesia to Headquarters SAAF, OP SITREP, 2–3 Sep. 1967: SANDF-HVS(KG) DGAA/1/67.

53. S. Khama to K. Kaunda, 5 Sep. 1967: BNA-OP/27/3.

54. JPS Rhodesia to Headuarters SAAF, OP SITREP, 7–8 Sep. 1967: SANDF-HVS(KG) DGAA/1/67.

55. '"No S.A. troops in Rhodesia", reports exaggerated – Britain', *RDM*, 8 Sep. 1967.

56. 'S.A. fights in Rhodesia', *RDM*, 9 Sep. 1967.

57. 'Smith confirms entry of armoured cars', *S.Times*, 10 Sep. 1967.

58. N.H. Nsele statement/*S v A. Ndhlovu et al.*, Draft Judgement, Sec. 2, p. 6: ZNA-S3385/11580/68.

59. M. Nyoni statement/*Ndhlovu*, Draft Judgement, Sec. 2, p. 8.

60. 'Organisation of African Unity Co-Ordinating Committee for the Liberation of Africa (Committee of Eleven)', Appendix I, Standing Committee on Defence, Executive Secretary's Report, p. 5: NAZ-FA/1/42.

61. 'Organisation of African Unity Co-Ordinating Committee for the Liberation of Africa (Committee of Eleven)', Standing Committee on Defence Report on 4–5 Dec. 1967 meeting, p. 4: NAZ-FA/1/42.

62. 'Report from Ralph Mzamo on what happened in Sipholile battles', 8 Jun. 1980, p. 1: UCT-SC/ P29.4; 'Feitlike Studie: Rhodesië soos op 1 Apr 68', pp. 112–13: SANDF-HSI AMI/3/379.

63. 'Report from Ralph Mzamo', pp. 2–3; 'Feitlike Studie: Rhodesië soos op 1 Apr 68', p. 105.

64. 'R.M.T. Ngqungwana' (aka R. Mzamo), 'Zambezi took a share', *Dawn* (Souvenir Issue', c. 1986), pp. 41–2.

65. *Ibid.*; 'Report from Ralph Mzamo', pp. 3–4; A. Ndhlovu, Warn and Caution Statement, Exh. 3, p. 3: ZNA-S3385/11580/68; K.J. Ndima/*Ngcobo*, p. 84; 'We fought in Zimbabwe, part 1', *Sechaba*, Jan. 1981, p. 19; M. Morris, *Terrorism* (Howard Timmins, 1971), p. 56.

66. 'Accused hid on board ship to South Africa', *NM*, 28 Feb. 1969.

67. Z.W. Nqose, Statement, p. 26; 'Botswana Central Intelligence Committee', 4 (Apr. 1968), Part. II, p. 2: BNA-OP/58/5.

68. A.F. Kahiya, Warn and Caution Statement, Exh. 4, pp. 1–2: ZNA-S3385/11580/68; M. Tshuma, Warn and Caution Statement, Exh. 1, p. 1: ZNA-S3385/11580/68; M. Mandela and K.J. Ndima/ *Ngcobo*, pp. 12–13, 74.

69. Z.W. Nqose, Statement, p. 26; 'Feitlike studie van die situasie Zambië soos op 25 Mrt 68', p. 135; 'Botswana Central Intelligence Committee', Part. II, p. 2.

70. 'Accused hid on board ship'; A. Lengisi to W. Kodesh, transcript, p. 8: UWC-MCA/MCA6-437.

71. 'Report from Ralph Mzamo', p. 7; K.J. Ndima/*Ngcobo*, p. 77.

72. 'We fought in Zimbabwe, part 1', p. 20.

73. 'Report from Ralph Mzamo', p. 8.

74. 'Recent Terrorist Incursion: Zimbabwe African People's Union (ZAPU)/South African African National Congress (SAANC): Mashonaland, March 1968: Operation Cauldron' (Doc No: 681547), p. 1: SANDF-AMI/HDI/15/124; 'J.M.' (a pseudonym), 'A guerrilla speaks', *Sechaba*, 3 (11), Nov. 1969, p. 3; M. Morris, *Terrorism*, pp. 57–8; J.R.T. Wood, *A Matter of Weeks*, p. 428; A. Binda, *The Saints* (30° South, 2007), p. 64.

75. INRAP, 17 Mar. 1968: SANDF-HVS(KG) DGAA/1/67.

76. 'Report from Ralph Mzamo', p. 8.

77. INRAP, 17 Mar. 1968.

78. 'Report from Ralph Mzamo', p. 8; A. Ndhlovu, Warn and Caution Statement, p. 5.

79. I. Mapoto in 'Report from Ralph Mzamo', pp. 9–10.

80. INRAP, 17–18 Mar. 1968, pp. 1–2: SANDF-HVS(KG) DGAA/1/67.

81. I. Mapoto/'Report from Ralph Mzamo', p. 10.

82. A. Binda, *The Saints*, p. 68; J.R.T. Wood, *A Matter of Weeks*, p. 431.

83. JPS Rhodesia to Compol Pretoria, SITREP 18 Mar. 1968: SANDF-HVS(KG) DGAA/1/67.

84. M. Tshuma, Warn and Caution Statement, p. 2.

85. JPS Rhodesia to SAP Pretoria, SITREP, 18–19 Mar. 1968: SANDF-HVS(KG) DGAA/1/67.

86. HMI to Minister of Defence, INRAP, 20 Mar. 1968: SANDF-HVS(KG) DGAA/1/67.

87. Mr Knight in Draft Judgement, Pt. 1, p. 1/*Ndhlovu*.

88. Lt. Strong and G. Mpofu in Draft Judgement, Pt. 1, pp. 8–10/*Ndhlovu*; M. Tshuma, Warn and Caution Statement, p. 2.

89. A. Sibeko, *Freedom in our Lifetime* (Indicator, 1996), pp. 92–3.

90. I. Mapoto/'Report from Ralph Mzamo', p. 11.

91. I. Mapoto, Warn and Caution Statement, Exh. 13, p. 1: ZNA-S3385/11580/68.

92. JPS Rhodesia to SAP, SITREP, 20–21 Mar. 1968: SANDF-HVS(KG) DGAA/1/67.

93. INRAP, 22–25 Mar. 1968: SANDF-HVS(KG) DGAA/1/67.

94. M. Nkomo, Warn and Caution Statement, Exh. 4, p. 2: ZNA-S3385/11580/68; M. Zikali, Warn and Caution Statement, Exh. 5, pp. 2–3: ZNA-S3385/11580/68.

95. JPS Rhodesia to Compol Pretoria, SITREP, 25–26 Mar. 1968: SANDF-HVS(KG) DGAA/1/67.

96. JPS Rhodesia to Compol Pretoria, SITREP 26–27 Mar. 1968: SANDF-HVS(KG) DGAA/1/67.

97. I. Mapoto, Warn and Caution Statement, p. 2.

98. 'Freedom fighters' toll up', *Times(Zam)*, 2 Apr. 1968.

99. P.M. Sibanda, Warn and Caution Statement, Exh. 12, p. 1: ZNA-S3385/11580/68; *S v A. Ndhlovu et al.*, Draft Judgement, Pt. 1, p. 27: ZNA-S3385/11580/68.

100. *S v A. Ndhlovu et al.*, Draft Judgement, pt. 2, p. 9.

101. JPS Pretoria to Compol Pretora, SITREP, 2–3 Apr. 1968: SANDF-HVS(KG) DGAA/1/67.

102. I. Mapoto, Warn and Caution Statement, p. 2.

103. Sgt. Hutton/*Ndhlovu*, Draft Judgement, pt. 2, pp. 10–11.

104. JPS Rhodesia to Compol Pretoria, SITREP, 4–5 Apr. 1968: SANDF-HVS(KG) DGAA/1/67.

105. JPS Rhodesia to Compol Pretoria, SITREP, 5–6 Apr. 1968: SANDF-HVS(KG) DGAA/1/67.

106. INRAP, 6–8 Apr. 1968: SANDF-HVS(KG) DGAA/1/67.

107. INRAP, 10–16 Apr. 1968, pp. 2, 5: SANDF-HVS(KG) DGAA/1/68.

108. P. Menye/*S v A. Moumbaris et al.*, p. 104: NARS-TAB: Case No: 1/4/3/6/730/72.

109. 'Botswana Central Intelligence Committee', 5 (May 1968), Part II, p. 2: BNA-OP/58/5.

110. P.J. Heady (Permanent Secretray to the President) to Permanent Secretary, Ministry of Home Affairs, cc Attorney General, Commissioner of Police, 18 Jun. 1968: BNA-OP/27/3.

111. 'Decision of the Standing Committee on Defence involving expenditure to be submitted to the Standing Committee on Finance', 22 Jun. 1968, p. 3: NAZ-FA/1/30.

112. P. Menye/*Moumbaris*, p. 104.

113. (Zambia) Permanent Secretary, Presidential Affairs to Permanent Secretary, Ministry of Foreign Affairs, 9 Jul. 1968: NAZ-FA/1/261.
114. K.J.S. Kapepa, 'Warned and Cautioned Statement', Exh. 9: ZNA-S3385/1968-11664/68; M. Mpata, 'Warned and Cautioned Statement', Exh. 12: ZNA-S3385/1968-11664/68; M[oses] Tshuma, 'Warned and Cautioned Statement', Exh. 13: ZNA-S3385/1968-11664/68; J.R.T. Wood, *A Matter of Weeks*, p. 475.
115. 'Terrorists asked for Zululand chief's aid', *NM*, 20 Feb. 1969.
116. Judgement, pp. 3–4, *S v Ncube et al.*: S3385/1967-11658/68.
117. INRAP, 26–29 Jul. 1968: SANDF-HVS(KG) DGAA/1/68.
118. J.S.T. Fletcher in *S v F.F. Choga et al.* (Prep. Examination), pp. 4, 8–9: ZNA-S3385/1968-11665.
119. 'Judgement', pp. 4–5/*Choga*.
120. J.R.T. Wood, *A Matter of Weeks*, p. 491.
121. INRAP, 1–2 Aug. 1968: SANDF-HVS(KG) DGAA/1/68.
122. T. Power/*S v K.S.M. Mavingira et al.* (Prep. Statement), pp. 3–5: ZNA-S3385/1968-11664/68.
123. 'Judgement/*Ngcobo*, p. 32.
124. *Ibid.*, pp. 16–17; 'State case closed in terror trial', *NM*, 4 Mar. 1969.
125. A. Lengisi to W. Kodesh, transcript, p. 10: UWC-MCA/MCA6-437.
126. S. Sijake, 'Political Education in the African National Congress', p. 19.

By Land, Sea and Air

1. Document/*S v S.R. Ndou et al.*, pp. 233–5: NARS-TAB/Case No: CC27/70; 'People killed in fight for A.N.C. leadership – evidence', *RDM*, 11 Dec. 1969.
2. 'Memorandum (1969)' in J. Smith and B. Tromp, *Hani* (Jonathan Ball, 2009), pp. 307–14.
3. 'What the Group Feels' extracts in 'Against Manipulation of the South African Revolution', sgd T.X. Makiwane, Oct. 1975, pp. 17–18: UWHP-KGC/III-166.
4. 'Escaper from north reports A.N.C. strife', *S. Times*, 26 Jan. 1969.
5. J. Matthews, 'Memorandum to Prof. Tom Karis on the subject of the thinking and background to the decisions of the African National Congress (South Africa) in the period from 1964 onwards', pp. 70–71: UWHP-KGC/III-95.
6. ANC (S.A.), 'Directive Concerning Preparations for Conference', 18 Feb. 1969: UFH-ANC/Lon.M-28/66.
7. B. Turok to W. Kodesh, 8 Mar. 1993: UWC-MCA/MCA6-379a; B. Turok, *Nothing But the Truth*, p. 219.
8. *Mayibuye*, 3 (10), May 1969, pp. 6–7: UWHP-KGC/III-16.
9. J. Matthews, 'Memorandum to Prof. Tom Karis' p. 23.
10. 'Strategy and Tactics of the African National Congress', *Sechaba*, 3 (7), Jul. 1969, pp. 16–23.
11. *Mayibuye*, 3 (10), May 1969, p. 9.
12. *Ibid.*, p. 11.
13. 'Close Ranks: A call from the Consultative Conference of the African National Congress', *Sechaba*, 3 (7) Jul. 1969, p. 2; 'Report on Organisation' [Draft prepared by J.S.], *c.* 1972, p. 10: ICS-RFP/1/17/3.
14. B. Turok to W. Kodesh, 8 Mar. 1993: UWC-MCA/MCA6-379a and MCA6-379b.
15. ANC NEC, 'The Report of the Secretariat governing the last two years', p. 5: UWHP-AG2510/A2-2.12.
16. J. Matthews, 'Memorandum to Prof. Tom Karis', p. 31.
17. ANC NEC 'The Report of the Secretariat', p. 5.
18. P. Menye/*Moumbaris*, p. 14.
19. F. Mbali, *In Transit* (South African History Online, 2012), pp. 140–41.
20. 'Statement to Defence Counsel by Charles Anthony David Holiday', pp. 10–11: UWHP-RT/17.
21. *Ibid.*, pp. 11–12.
22. 'A.N.C. slogan blitz in 2 cities', *RDM*, 15 Nov. 1969.
23. 'Statement to Defence Counsel by Charles Anthony David Holiday', pp. 15–18.

24. 'Timol probe – friendship is denied', *RDM*, 23 May 1972; 'Timol "talked to police of Red training"', *RDM*, 27 Apr. 1972; I. Cajee, *Timol* (STE, 2005), pp. 73–5, 82.

25. Paasport discussed/*Moumbaris*, p. 57; A. Moumbaris to W. Kodesh: UWC-MCA/MCA6-325a; R. Kasrils, 'The Adventurer Episode', *Dawn* (Souvenir Issue, *c.* 1986), p. 43.

26. I. Cajee, *Timol* (STE, 2005), p. 88.

27. A. Moumbaris and document/*Moumbaris*, pp. 57, 809.

28. T.T. Nkobi, ANC (SA) report to Ministry of Provincial and Local Govt., Lusaka, Zambia, 19 Jan. 1970: UWHP-KGC/III-18; F. Mbali, *In Transit*, pp. 142–4.

29. H. Macmillan, 'The Story of a House – 250 Zambezi Road, Roma Township, Lusaka – The Simons, the ANC and OXFAM', in R. Palmer (ed.), *A House in Zambia: Recollections of the ANC and OXFAM at 250 Zambezi Road, Lusaka, 1967–97* (Bookworld, 2008), p. 15; H. Macmillan, *The Lusaka Years: The ANC in Exile in Zambia* (Jacana, 2013), p. 87.

30. A. Timol/I. Cajee, *Timol*, p. 98.

31. 'Explosions scatter pamphlets', 'Police scatter from blast' and 'Leaflets in other centres', *RDM*, 14 Aug. 1970; 'Bomme in vyf groot stede', *Die Transvaler*, 14 Aug. 1970.

32. Memo, 'Zimbabwe African People's Union (ZAPU): History of sabotage and terrorism', p. 10: SANDF-HSI AMI/3/582; F. Mbali, *In Transit*, p. 142.

33. J.P.J. Botha, A. Kutuwela and Hotel Invoice described/*April*, pp. 42–3, 49.

34. F. Mbali, *In Transit*, pp. 148–9.

35. N. Kombele and G. Mose/*Moumbaris*, pp. 161–2, 405–6.

36. K. Nayager and I. Coetzee/*April*, pp. 129, 142–6.

37. 'Dark Night of the Soul', *Inside* magazine, *S. Times*, 9 Jul. 1996 (accessed via http://www.ahmedtimol .co.za on 2 Aug. 2014); 'Essop pleads not guilty to charges', *RDM*, 14 Jun. 1972; 'Timol's Girlfriend: I'm no Red', *RDM*, 18 Jul. 1972; 'Essop: I'm no ANC man or communist', *RDM*, 3 Aug. 1972.

38. 'Detainee dies in police custody', *RDM*, 28 Oct. 1971.

39. 'ANC vliegbasis te Mogadishu', 31 Jan. 1972 (Doc No: 720361): SANDF-AMI/HDI/15/126.

40. N. Kombele and G. Mose/*Moumbaris*, pp. 163, 408–9.

41. A. Moumbaris and passport described/*Moumbaris*, pp. 57, 912–14, 924, 926–7.

42. Security Branch Head Office to the Director of Military Intelligence, 17 Feb. 1972: SANDF-AMI/ HDI/15/126.

43. N. Kombele/*Moumbaris*, p. 411.

44. N. Kombele, P. Menye and G. Mose/*Moumbaris*, pp. 21–2, 166, 224–6, 411–13; T. Setumu, *Heeding the Call to Fight for the Fatherland: The Life and Struggle of T.T. Cholo* (Fortune-d Africa, 2011), pp. 76–7.

45. P. Menye and G. Mose/*Moumbaris*, pp. 23, 164, 167; F. Mbali, *In Transit*, p. 152.

46. G. Mose/*Moumbaris*, p. 167.

47. N. Kombele/*Moumbaris*, p. 414.

48. N. Kombele and P. Menye/*Moumbaris*, pp. 23–4, 415.

49. N. Kombele and G. Mose/*Moumbaris*, pp. 169, 415.

50. Passport described, A. Moumbaris and 'Judgement'/*Moumbaris*, pp. 57, 928, 1615; R. Kasrils, *Armed and Dangerous* (Jonathan Ball, 2004), p. 88.

51. G. Mose, J. Mpanza and T.P. Mtembu/*Moumbaris*, pp. 179–1, 1110, 1169, 1175.

52. J.A. Liebenberg and A. Moumbaris/*Moumbaris*, pp. 59–60, 827.

53. N. Kombele/*Moumbaris*, p. 416.

54. A. Moumbaris, G. Mose and J. Mpanza/*Moumbaris*, pp. 172–4, 828–9, 1111; T. Setumu, *Heeding the Call*, pp. 84–5.

55. T.T. Cholo, N. Kombele and J. Mpanza/*Moumbaris*, pp. 422–3, 1002–3, 1111.

56. A. Moumbaris and G. Mose/*Moumbaris*, pp. 175–6, 829–31.

57. N. Kombele/*Moumbaris*, pp. 438, 440–41.

58. Document described/*Moumbaris*, p. 58.

59. 'Terror plot disclosures', *Sunday Express* (Johannesburg), 24 Jun. 1973.

60. P. Menye and 'Judgement'/*Moumbaris*, pp. 25–6(a), 1552; K. Keable (ed.), *London Recruits* (Merlin, 2012), p. 129.
61. J.Z. van Niekerk/*Moumbaris*, pp. 283–4.
62. '"I was told how to make a bomb"', *RDM*, 31 Mar. 1973.
63. T.T. Cholo and F.J.D. Pretorius/*Moumbaris*, pp. 250, 1003.
64. R.R. Reynolds/*Moumbaris*, pp. 43–4, 47, 49.
65. J.W. du Plessis/*Moumbaris*, p. 279.
66. P. Menye/*Moumbaris*, p. 27.
67. D. Wessels/*Moumbaris*, pp. 625–9.
68. J.W. Hosey/*Moumbaris*, pp. 1310–12.
69. *Ibid.*, p. 1313.
70. B.B.D. Nyathi and J.W. Hosey/*Moumbaris*, pp. 189–91, 1311–12, 1316–17.
71. S. Hosey/*London Recruits*, p. 282.
72. 'Judgement', p. 1562/*Moumbaris*.

Rebuilding the Underground

1. K. Motlanthe interview, 10 Oct. 2001: UWHP-HW.
2. 'Saso 5 plead to Botswana', *RDM*, 31 Jan. 1974; 'The long wait goes on for 4 SA refugees', *RDM*, 17 Apr. 1974.
3. 'Eric Molobi @ Maroy, states under oath', pp. 2–3: UWHP-*Molobi*.
4. R. Nkosi and B.H. Nxasana in *S v T.H. Gwala et al.*, pp. 778–9, 1148, 1150-51: NARS-NAB/Case No: CC108/76.
5. 'Bomb kills ex-Saso leader', *RDM*, 4 Feb. 1974.
6. 'ANC bombed' and 'Dream of book-bomb victim Dube', *RDM*, 13 Feb. 1974; 'Comrade Boy Mvemve (J.D.) murdered', *Sechaba*, 8 (5), May 1974, p. 2.
7. 'Thousands mourn as Tiro is buried', *RDM*, 18 Feb. 1974.
8. 'Eric Molobi @ Maroy, states under oath', p. 5.
9. X. Nuse in *E. Molobi v The State*, p. 69: UWHP/*Molobi*; 'Eric Molobi @ Maroy states further under oath', p. 3: UWHP-*Molobi*.
10. E. Molobi and X. Nuse/*Molobi*, pp. 79, 513; 'Eric Molobi @ Maroy states further under oath', p. 4; E. Molobi, 'The first group that I Eric Molobi …', p. 1: UWHP-*Molobi*.
11. Chris Hani, 'My Life', *c.* Feb. 1991, http://www.sacp.org.za/main.php?ID=2294 (accessed 6 Jan. 2015).
12. T. Jenkin to P. O'Malley, 25 Mar. 2002: *O'Malley*.
13. 'Lisbon: army seizes power', *Star*, 25 Apr. 1974.
14. L. Kuny, 'Five o'clock cars lined the streets …', p. 6, document in *S v T.H. Gwala et al.* box; R. Suttner to H. Barrell, pp. 1213–17: OU-RHL/*Barrell*.
15. 'Salazar looks on as Frelimo takes control', *RDM*, 21 Sep. 1974.
16. 'Give us six months, says Vorster' and 'Police will stay in Rhodesia to "protect SA"', *RDM*, 6 Nov. 1974.
17. L. Kuny, 'Five o'clock cars' p. 15.
18. B.H. Nxasana/*Gwala*, pp. 784–5.
19. 'Interim Report of the Commission of the RC Secretariat "On the State of Affairs in MK in East Africa"', pp. 1–5: UFH-ANC/MO-28/F9.
20. R. Suttner to H. Barrell, p. 1223.
21. S. Gamedze/*Gwala*, pp. 566–7.
22. L. Kuny, 'Five o'clock cars', p. 19.
23. (S.A.) Military Intelligence Directorate, 'RSA: SA-ANC-Bedrywighede', 17 Jun. 1975, pp. 3–4: SANDF-DIVERSE/2/81.
24. R. Suttner to H. Barrell, p. 1223; 'Suttner, Raymond, 30, law lecturer, 7½ years': UNISA(MF)-Karis-Gerhart Collection 'From Protest to Challenge'/Part 5, C.J.1.; L. Kuny, 'Five o'clock cars', p. 30.

25. 'Machel hits out' and 'Struggle goes on, says Machel', *RDM*, 26 Jun. 1975.
26. 'Statement by Joe Nzingo Gqabi', pp. 1A-2: UWHP-KGC/III-28.
27. M. Sexwale, Deposition, pp. 6–7: UWHP-KGC/III-25.
28. *Ibid.*, pp. 11–14.
29. I.D. Rwaxa/*S v M.G. Sexwale et al.*, pp. 1163, 1165: UWHP-PT/Box 62; Naledi Tsiki, statement to the court, 5 Apr. 1978, p. 2384/*S v M.G. Sexwale et al.*: UWHP-PT/Box 64; N. Tsiki to H. Barrell, pp. 1254–7.
30. P.K. Motlanthe, 'Confession', pp. 4–5/*S v S.N. Nkosi et al.*: NARS-TAB/Case No: CC318/77.
31. P. Gamedze and T.H. Gwala/*Gwala*, pp. 634–5, 1953.
32. P. Gamedze/*Gwala*, pp. 636–8.
33. P.F. Mokoena and A.N. Xaba/*Gwala*, pp. 1470–73, 2488.
34. A. Nzama/*Gwala*, pp. 1454–8.
35. A.N. Xaba/*Gwala*, pp. 2503–5.
36. J. Zuma to H. Barrell, p. 1363: OU-RHL/*Barrell*.
37. N. Tsiki to H. Barrell, pp. 1261–2.
38. N. Tsiki, Deposition, pp. 5–6: UWHP-KGC/III-26.
39. M. Sexwale, Deposition, pp. 15–16.
40. N. Tsiki to H. Barrell, pp. 1279–80.
41. T. Sexwale, 'Oliver Tambo: May our courage mirror his', *The Thinker*, 58 (Dec. 2013), p. 15.
42. M. Sexwale, Deposition, pp. 19–20; N. Tsiki, Deposition, p. 10; N. Tsiki to H. Barrell, p. 1264.
43. S. Nyanda to P. O'Malley, 27 Oct. 2001; S. Nyanda/E. Masilela, *Number 43, Trelawney Park, KwaMagogo* (David Philip, 2007), p. 106.
44. S.G. Lukele/*Gwala*, pp. 1556–7.
45. K. Motlanthe interview, 6 Nov. 2001: UWHP-HW; P.K. Motlanthe, 'Confession', p. 6/*Nkosi*; S.N. Nkosi, 'Confession', p. 5/*Nkosi*; T. Simpson, 'Military Combat Work: the Reconstitution of the ANC's Armed Underground, 1971–1976', *Af.St*, 70 (1), 2011, p. 118.
46. E. Zuma/*Gwala*, pp. 1237–40.
47. S.G. Lukele/*Gwala*, p. 1557.
48. 'Statement of Petrus Mampogoane Nchabeleng', p. 1: UWHP-KGC/III/29.
49. 'Bucket bomb gear in Rabkin garage', *RDM*, 23 Sep. 1976; 'Rabkins' counsel says they won't be called', *RDM*, 24 Sep. 1976.
50. P. Gleijeses, *Conflicting Missions: Havana, Washington, and Africa, 1959–1976* (The University of North Carolina Press, 2002), pp. 300-345.
51. S.G. Lukele/*Gwala*, pp. 1558–62.
52. S.D. Mapanza and J[abulani].O. Mdluli/*Gwala*, pp. 1693, 1792–3.
53. 'The Mdluli dossier', *RDM*, 7 Apr. 1976.
54. 'SAP smash guerrilla network', *RDM*, 24 Apr. 1976.
55. S.D. Mapanza and J[abulani].O. Mdluli/*Gwala*, pp. 1702, 1797.
56. S.G. Lukele/*Gwala*, p. 1570.
57. S.D. Mapanza/*Gwala*, p. 1800.
58. 'The Mdluli dossier'.
59. T. Jenkin to P. O'Malley, 25 Mar. 2002.
60. J[abulani].O. Mdluli/*Gwala*, pp. 1710-11.
61. M. Gevisser, *Thabo Mbeki: The Dream Deferred* (Jonathan Ball, 2007), p. 341.
62. J.J. de Swardt, H.J. Fourie, C.M. Ndhlovu and I. Winter/*Gwala*, pp. 108, 110–11, 144–5, 167, 3253; C.M. Ndhlovu, 'Affidavit', p. 2/*Gwala*; J.N. Nduli, 'Affidavit', pp. 4, 6/*Gwala*.
63. K. Motlanthe interview, 6 Nov. 2001: UWHP-HW.
64. S.N. Nkosi, 'Confession', p. 5/*Nkosi*.
65. P.K. Motlanthe, 'Confession', p. 7/*Nkosi*.
66. *Ibid.*
67. E. Harvey, *Kgalema Motlanthe: A Political Biography* (Jacana, 2012), p. 32.
68. N. Tsiki, Deposition, pp. 19–20; N. Tsiki to H. Barrell, p. 1267.

PART IV: ARMED PROPAGANDA

Soweto Generation

1. 'Cold sweat amid fire of revolt', *Sunday Independent*, 14 Jun. 1998; 'June 16 survivor recalls', *The New Age*, 15 Jun. 2012.
2. 'Cold sweat'; N. Serache, 'Police fired – then I saw four children fall', *RDM*, 17 Jun. 1976; 'Report of the Commission of Inquiry into the riots at Soweto and elsewhere from the 16th of June 1976 to the 28th of February 1977', Vol. ii, Annexure D, p. 6; J.A. Kleingeld, Testimony before the Cillié Commission (2), 27 Sep. 1976, http://www.gutenberg-e.org/pohlandt-mccormick/pmh02d.html (accessed 5 Feb. 2015); M. Morobe in TRC Human Rights Violations Submissions – Q&As, 23 Jul. 1996: UWHP-TRC(CD)/HRVtrans> Soweto> MOROBE.
3. 'June 16 survivor recalls'; 'Report of the Commission of Inquiry into the Riots at Soweto', Vol. ii, Annexure D, p. 6; J.A. Kleingeld, Cillié Commission Testimony (2), 27 Sep. 1976; 'Flaming night', *RDM*, 17 Jun. 1976; 'A merry march that ended in chaos and blood', *Star*, 14 Jun. 1996; 'How a 16-year old sacrificed his youth', *Saturday Star*, 10 Jun. 2006.
4. 'Statement of Elias Masinga', pp. 8–9: UWHP-RT/27; 'Op 'n dag in Junie …', *Beeld*, 16 Jun. 2006.
5. Head of Special Branch to Permanent Secretary to the President, 5 Jul. 1976: BNA-OP/26/46.
6. J. Tseto/*S v M.G. Sexwale et al.*, pp. 1802–3: UWHP-PT/Box 65-013.
7. J. Nkadimeng to W. Kodesh, transcript, p. 19: UWC-MCA/MCA6-240.
8. J. Tseto/*Sexwale*, pp. 1803, 1875.
9. P.J.J. Fourie/*S v C.A.D. Holiday*, pp. 39–40: NARS-TAB/Case No: CC618/76; 'Statement to Defence Counsel by Charles Anthony David Holiday', pp. 40–42: UWHP-RT/17.
10. 'Bucket bomb gear in Rabkin garage', *RDM*, 23 Sep. 1976.
11. N. Tsiki, Deposition, p. 22: UWHP-KGC/III-26.
12. E.T. Mfalapitsa, Interrogation Report, p. 2: SANDF-OAMI/10/154; S. Zikalala interview, 21 and 27 May 2002: UWHP-HW.
13. N. Tsiki, Deposition, p. 23.
14. S. Mahlangu/*S v S. Mahlangu*, p. 535: NARS-TAB: Case No: 558/77; T.G. Mnguni, *The Biography of Solomon Mahlangu* (Zamanguni, 2007), p. 10.
15. N. Tsiki, Deposition, pp. 25–6.
16. *Ibid.*, pp. 23–4, 27–8.
17. *Ibid.*, pp. 28–30; N. Tsiki to H. Barrell, p. 1269: OU-RHL/*Barrell*.
18. 'Admissions'/*Sexwale*, pp. 1752–5.
19. N. Tsiki to H. Barrell, pp. 1271, 1273–4, 1288.
20. N. Tsiki, Deposition, pp. 33–4.
21. N. Tsiki to H. Barrell, p. 1274.
22. 'Statement of Elias Masinga', p. 15: UWHP-RT/27; 'Statement of Elias Tieho Masinga', pp. 2–3: UWHP-KGC/III-28.
23. E.T. Mfalapitsa, Interrogation Report, pp. 3–4; 'SAANC Refugees in Zimbabwe/External Military Activity', 26 May 1982, p. 2: SANDF-HSI/AMI/DTI/21/175.
24. 'Addendum to Detailed Report. Area Q', *c.* late Nov. 1976: UCT-SC/P29.4.
25. I.D. Rwaxa/*Sexwale*, pp. 1199–1201; M. Morobe to R. Suttner, 26 Aug. 2003, p. 19: RSC/*Aluka*.
26. M. Sexwale, Deposition, pp. 48–9: UWHP-KGC/III-25.
27. 'Admissions'/*Sexwale*, p. 1750; M. Sexwale, Deposition, p. 51.
28. M. Sexwale, Deposition, pp. 51–4; 'Admissions'/*Sexwale*, p. 1751; Sgt Khoza in 'Judgement'/*Sexwale*, pp. 2280–81.
29. G.M. Basele, D.C. (Lobatse) to Permanent Secretary to the President, 'Confidential: Movement of Refugees', 2 Dec. 1976: BNA-OP/26/3/1/1.
30. M. Sexwale, Deposition, pp. 56–7; I.D. Rwaxa/*Sexwale*, p. 1209.
31. M. Sexwale, Deposition, p. 62.
32. M. Sexwale, Deposition, p. 63; 'Statement of Petrus Mampogoane Nchabeleng', p. 4: UWHP-KGC/III-29.

33. N. Tsiki, Deposition, p. 45.
34. N. Tsiki to H. Barrell, p. 1278.
35. I.D. Rwaxa/*Sexwale*, pp. 1165, 1225–7, 2124, 2131.
36. M. Sexwale, Deposition, pp. 70–71; 'Statement of Petrus Mampogoane Nchabeleng', p. 5.
37. M. Sexwale, Deposition, pp. 73–5.
38. I.D. Rwaxa/*Sexwale*, pp. 1345–6.
39. 'Admissions'/*Sexwale*, p. 1749.
40. M. Sexwale, Deposition, pp. 81–2.
41. M. Morobe to R. Suttner, 26 Aug. 2003, p. 15; 'Statement of Elias Masinga re the making of the police statement', p. 1: UWHP-RT/27.
42. 'Statement of Petrus Mampogoane Nchabeleng', p. 10.
43. N. Tsiki, Deposition, p. 47.
44. M. Moshele and T. Mavuso in L.K. von den Steinen, 'Soldiers in the struggle: Aspects of the Experiences of Umkhonto we Sizwe's rank and file soldiers – the Soweto Generation and after' (MA, University of Cape Town, 1999), pp. 97–8; S. Manong, *If We Must Die: An Autobiography of a Former Commander of uMkhonto we Sizwe* (Nkululeko Publishers, 2015), pp. 61–2.
45. S. Nyanda to P. O'Malley, 27 Oct. 2001: *O'Malley*.
46. 'Podgorny vows support for Black nationalists', *RDM*, 29 Mar. 1977.
47. '3 Nationalists expected to see Castro in Angola', *WP*, 30 Mar. 1977; 'Castro said to promise aid to Namibian guerrillas', *WP*, 2 Apr. 1977.
48. 'Army warns of terror in Tvl' and 'Soviet shadow looms larger', *RDM*, 1 Apr. 1977.
49. Indictment, p. 5, in *S v A. Ramudzuli et al.*: NARS-TAB: Case No: CC96/78; A. Ramudzuli/*Ramudzuli*, pp. 921, 925–6.
50. 'Draft MHQ report – Part One', p. 5: UFH-ANC/LM-128/245; S. Nyanda to P. O'Malley, 27 Oct. 2001.
51. S. Nyanda in C. Braam, *Operation Vula* (Jacana, 2004), p. 86.
52. S. Nyanda to P. O'Malley, 27 Oct. 2001.
53. S. Mahlangu/*Mahlangu*, pp. 550–52.
54. J.M. Bosigo, Testimony to Senate Sub-Committee on Security and Terrorism, p. 8: UWHP-*Denton*.
55. F. Lekaba/*Ramudzuli*, pp. 388–9.
56. E.S. Huma/*Ramudzuli*, p. 405; 'Uitspraak', p. 4/*Ramudzuli*.
57. J.M. Bosigo, Testimony to Senate Sub-Committee, pp. 8–9.
58. S. Mahlangu/*Mahlangu*, pp. 555–6.
59. *Ibid.*, pp. 560–62.
60. S. Mahlangu, M. Steenkamp and J.K. Loggerenberg/*Mahlangu*, pp. 4–9, 11–12, 563.
61. S. Mahlangu/*Mahlangu*, pp. 565–8.
62. R.F. Bagg and P.L. Hartogh/*Mahlangu*, pp. 74–9, 92, 94; 'Machine gun terror hits Jo'burg', *RDM*, 14 Jun. 1977.
63. R.F. Bagg and S. Mahlangu/*Mahlangu*, pp. 95, 572.

The Anvil and the Hammer

1. I. Pillay to P. O'Malley, 11 Dec. 2002.
2. M. Maharaj to H. Barrell, pp. 393–4; M. Maharaj to V. Butler, Feb. 1988, p. 5: UKZN-AP/PC170/7/4/1/2.
3. S. Maphumulo, unpublished memoirs, p. 390: OU-RHL/*Barrell*.
4. *Ibid.*, pp. 391–2.
5. I. Pillay to P. O'Malley, 11 Dec. 2002.
6. *Ibid.*
7. 'Terror plan to invade SA smashed', *RDM*, 29 Aug. 1977.
8. T. Khumalo/*Ramudzuli*, pp. 681–2.
9. L.M. Nkosi, Statement (Doc No: 683488), pp. 76, 87–8: SANDF-AMI/HDI/15/125; 'Assassins gun down policeman', *RDM*, 12 Sep. 1977; 'Nkosi "a marked man after terror evidence"', *RDM*, 12 May 1979.
10. T. Khumalo, M. Madi and S.A. Montshiwa/*Ramudzuli*, pp. 110–12, 144–5, 687–90.

11. 'Uitspraak', p. 6/*Ramudzuli*.
12. I.M. van Niekerk/*Ramudzuli*, pp. 540–54.
13. M.C. Tibone (Permanent Secretary to the President) to Botcom, Lusaka, 'ANC Representatives in Botswana', 29 Sep. 1977: BNA-OP/27/48.
14. T. Mavuso in L.K. von den Steinen, 'Soldiers in the struggle', p. 133.
15. T.E. Williams/TRC Human Rights Violations Submissions – Q&As, 18 Jun. 1996: UWHP-TRC(CD)/ HRVtrans > Umtata>WILLIAMS.
16. M.T. Mthembu, TRC Section 29 Inquiry, 3 Apr. 1998, p. 18: UWHP-TRC(CD)/documents> 110.
17. M. Petane in L.K. von den Steinen, 'Soldiers in the struggle', p. 133; J.M. Bosigo, Testimony to Senate Sub-Committee, p. 14.
18. 'Charge Sheet – Klagstaat', p. 3 in *S v B.P. Molefe*: NARS-TAB/CC147/78.
19. B.P. Molefe admissions, description and statement/*Molefe*, pp. 7–8, 10, 17, 28–9.
20. J.H. Cronje/*Molefe*, pp. 21–2.
21. M. Maharaj to H. Barrell, pp. 397–8.
22. D/I. Branfield (Bulawayo), 'South African National Congress involvement with ZAPU Botswana: Zambia', 1 May 1979, p. 2: SANDF-HSI/AMI/3/358.
23. V. Tshabalala to P. O'Malley, 2 Mar. 2002.
24. *Ibid*; T. Modise in 'The Knitting Needles Guerrilla', *WM*, 23 Mar. 1989 and 'On the streets of Jo'burg, old military habits die hard', *WM*, 31 Mar. 1989.
25. D/I. Branfield (Bulawayo), 'South African National Congress involvement with ZAPU', p. 2.
26. 'Bomb rocks Manzini PO', *Times(Swz)*, 23 Jan. 1978; 'Booby trap injures top ANC exile', *RDM*, 24 Jan. 1978.
27. 'On the streets of Jo'burg'.
28. S. Manong, *If We Must Die*, pp. 102–3.
29. M. Maharaj to H. Barrell, pp. 413–15.
30. 'Chronology of incidents relating to the armed struggle since 1976', p. 4: UFH-ANC/LM-157/54; 'Abel Mthembu and "Hlubi" Chaphi liquidated', *Sechaba*, 12 (Third Quarter), 1978, p. 23.
31. O. Masina, Statement, 16 Sep. 1986 read in *S v O. Masina et al.*, 'Uitspraak', pp. 620–21: NARS-TAB/ Case No: 400/88; D.S. Simelane, TRC Amnesty Hearing, 8 Jun. 1999 (Pretoria): TRC 2.
32. 'All-out hunt for killer', *RDM*, 27 Jun. 1978; O. Masina and Mr Tshabalala, statement and testimony/*Masina*, 'Uitspraak', pp. 617, 621; J.O. Masina, TRC Amnesty Hearing, 8 Jun. 1999 (Pretoria): TRC 2.
33. 'Sekete, John M., 24' and others: UNISA(MF)-Karis-Gerhart Collection 'From Protest to Challenge'/Part 5, C.J.1.
34. S. Manong, *If We Must Die*, pp. 112–22; E.T. Mfalapitsa, Interrogation Report, p. 11; 'Fear of more terror gangs', *S. Times*, 6 Aug. 1978; 'Terror trial youth jailed for 15 years', *RDM*, 30 Jan. 1979; WIP#10, 'The Treason Trial', Nov. 1979, p. 42, in 'Sekete, John M., 24' and others: UNISA(MF)-Karis-Gerhart Collection 'From Protest to Challenge'/Part 5, C.J.1; 'Richard "Barney" Molokoane', *Dawn* (Souvenir Issue, c. 1986), p. 54.
35. 'Tswana terror clash youth from Soweto', *Weekend Argus*, 5 Aug. 1978; 'Polisie, terro's in skietgeveg', *Die Transvaler*, 5 Aug. 1978; 'Geveg met terroriste', *Beeld*, 5 Aug. 1978; 'Helde daad', *Die Vaderland*, 9 Aug. 1978.
36. 'Geveg met terroriste'; 'Polisie, terro's in skietgeveg'; 'Helde daad'; 'Richard 'Barney' Molokoane', *Dawn*, p. 54; 'Schedule "A" – Accused No. 1' in *S v J.M. Sekete et al.*: NARS-NAB/Case No: CC106/79.
37. 'ANC eye trial', *Times(Swz)*, 21 Aug. 1978; 'Ramusi back inside on unknown charge', *Times(Swz)*, 23 Aug. 1978; E. Dilinga, 'The Situation in Swaziland': UFH-ANC/LM-5/31.
38. J.O. Masina/TRC-8 Jun. 1999-Pretoria.
39. S. Nyanda, 'Weapons infiltration by the Transvaal Urban Machinery', *The Thinker*, 58 (Dec. 2013), p. 29.
40. O.N. Ntombelo, Interrogation Report, 20 Aug. 1982, p. 2: SANDF-HSI AMI/DTI/21/175.
41. D/I. Branfield (Bulawayo), 'South African National Congress involvement with ZAPU', p. 3.

42. B.J. Liebenberg and S.B. Spies (eds.), *South Africa in the 20th Century* (J.L. van Schaik, 1993), p. 466.
43. Tambo notepad, 14 Oct. 1978: UFH-ANC/ORT-A11.3.4.
44. Tambo notepad, 21 Oct. 1978.
45. 'Traffic cops foiled terror suspect's plans', *NDN*, 28 Sep. 1979; 'Caught out … by a traffic offence', *NM*, 28 Sep. 1979; 'Witness tells of plan to kill', *NM*, 20 Oct. 1979; 'Doomed black poses South African issue', *NYT*, 19 Nov. 1979; 'Sekete, John M., 24' and others: UNISA(MF)-Karis-Gerhart Collection 'From Protest to Challenge'/Part 5, C.J.1.
46. 'Police hunt escaped terrorist', *RDM*, 30 Oct. 1978; 'Policeman recalls gunfire and gruesome death in the bush', *NM*, 11 Sep. 1979; 'Schedule "B" – Accused No. 2', in *S v J.M. Sekete et al.*: NARS-NAB/Case No: CC106/79; C. de Witt in 'Sekete, John M., 24' and others: UNISA(MF)-Karis-Gerhart Collection 'From Protest to Challenge'/Part 5, C.J.1; S. Manong, *If We Must Die*, p. 135.
47. *AP*, 30 Oct. 1978; 'Terrrorist ambush', *RDM*, 31 Oct. 1978; '"They could have picked us off"' and 'Blackened tin and cartridges litter the lair', *RDM*, 1 Nov. 1978; S. Manong, *If We Must Die*, pp. 136–7.
48. S. Manong, *If We Must Die*, p. 140.
49. O.N. Ntombelo, Interrogation Report, pp. 3–5.
50. A. Mapheto, Statement, pp. 2, 4–6, 22 Dec. 1978/*Sekete.*
51. Charge Sheet, p. 10: UWHP-TLC/E19; Witness 'I.C. X1'/*S v A.M. Maseko et al.*, pp. 2646–7: UWHP-C&N/Am3; ANC Second Submission to the TRC, 'Appendix One: ANC Structures and Personnel, 1960–1994', http://www.anc.org.za/show.php?id=2646 (accessed 27 May 2014).
52. 'Report and Recommendations of the Politico-Military and Strategy Commission to the NEC of the ANC' ['The Green Book'], p. 1: UWHP-KGC/III-31.
53. M. Maharaj to H. Barrell, p. 421.
54. *Ibid.*, pp. 409, 420–41.
55. Jack Simons' 2 Jan. and 5 Jan. 1979 diary entries in J. Simons, *Political Sociology for Umkhonto Students*, Ch. 3, p. 4: UCT-SC/P29.10.
56. T.P. Makgage/*N.J. Lubisi et al. v The State*, pp. 662–3, 684: UWHP-SAIRR/22; *RDM*, 8 Sep. 1979 and WIP#10, 'The Treason Trial', Nov. 1979, p. 42, in 'Sekete, John M., 24' and others; S. Manong, *If We Must Die*, p. 143.
57. A. Masondo, TRC Section 29 Hearing, 26 Mar. 1998, p. 13: UWHP-TRC(CD)/documents>18.
58. Jack Simons' 16 Jan. 79 diary entry.
59. 'On the streets of Jo'burg'.
60. Comrade Meshengu quoted in J. Simons, *Political Sociology for Umkhonto Students*, Ch. 2, p. 16: UCT-SC/P29.10; M. Saeboe, 'A State of exile: The ANC and Umkhonto we Sizwe in Angola, 1976–1989' (MA, University of Natal, 2002), pp. 82, 84; L.K. von den Steinen, 'Soldiers in the struggle', p. 134; D. Lord, *From Fledgling to Eagle: The South African Air Force in the Border War* (30° South, 2008), p. 109.
61. S. Thelle, Interrogation Report, p. 7: SANDF-OAMI/10/154; 'Sipho' [Solly Shoke] in C. Braam, *Operation Vula* (Jacana, 2004), p. 198; 'Heroes of our Revolution', *Dawn*, 12 (1), 1988, p. 23.
62. 'Terreur in Soweto dalk A.N.C.', *Die Volksblad*, 4 May 1979; 'Guerrillas make bold raid on South African Police Station', *WP*, 5 May 1979; 'Massive police hunt for Soweto killers', *RDM*, 5 May 1979; 'ANC terror hunt on', *RDM*, 7 May 1979; S. Mogoerane, testimony and statement, pp. 902, 1526–7/*S v T.S. Mogoerane et al.*: UWHP-SAIRR/34.
63. S. Shoke/*Operation Vula*, pp. 200–201.
64. 'President's Draft Report'. May 1979, pp. 3, 18, 19, 21–2, 23: UWHP-KGC/III-30; 'Minutes of the East NEC Meeting', p. 1: UWHP-KGC/III-34.
65. 'Op Santa: Verslag oor kontak met RSDF', 24 Jan. 1980, pp. 1–2: SANDF-HS OPS/5/145.
66. *Ibid.*, pp. 2–3.
67. *Ibid.*, p. 4.
68. 'Minutes of the East NEC Meeting', p. 7; 'PMC Organisational Report', *c.* May 1985, p. 7: UWHP-KGC/III-61.
69. 'The Green Book', pp. 4–10, and 'Annexure B', pp. 10–12.
70. 'Minutes of the East NEC Meeting', pp. 9–10.

71. *Ibid.*, pp. 1, 11.
72. A. Ismail, 'The ANC's Special Operations Unit', *The Thinker*, 58 (Dec. 2013), p. 33.
73. 'Op Santa: Verslag oor kontak met RSDF', pp. 10–12.
74. 'WC meeting 22/08/79', p. 10: UWHP-KGC/III-31; M. Gevisser, *Thabo Mbeki: The Dream Deferred* (Jonathan Ball, 2007), pp. 336–7; A. Jeffery, *People's War: New Light on the Struggle for South Africa* (Jonathan Ball, 2009), p. 51.
75. 'On the streets of Jo'burg' and 'The Knitting Needles Guerrilla'.
76. 'How 60 sleep-befuddled men escaped slaughter', *Star*, 2 Nov. 1979; 'Terror attack', *RDM*, 2 Nov. 1979; 'Massive hunt launched for terror gang', *RDM*, 3 Nov. 1979; 'Terros hit by own grenades?' *Citizen*, 3 Nov. 1979; S. Mogoerane testimony and statement/*Mogoerane*, pp. 903–5, 1527; S.Z. Shoke and M.J. Rasegatla, TRC Amnesty Hearing, 16 May 2000 (Johannesburg): TRC2.
77. D. Martin and P. Johnson, *The Struggle for Zimbabwe: The Chimurenga War* (Monthly Review Press, 1981), pp. 293, 300, 314–15.
78. Kmdmt N. Tvl to H Leer, 29 Nov. 1979: SANDF-OAMI/10/152.
79. INTREP139/79. 'Possible infiltration by SAANC terrorists', 20 Nov. 1979: SANDF-OAMI/10/152.
80. N Tvl Kmdmt Stam HK to H Leer, 4 Dec. 1979, pp. 1–3: SANDF-OAMI/10/152.
81. INRAP 141/79. 'SA ANC Bedrywighede', 22 Nov. 1979: SANDF-OAMI/10/152.
82. 'SA acts to guard its trade links', *RDM*, 1 Dec. 1979; 'South Africa has forces operating inside Rhodesia', *WP*, 1 Dec. 1979.
83. N.J. Lubisi and P.T. Mashigo/*Lubisi*, pp. 1102–3, 1203, 1209–10, 1229.
84. I.M. Molebatsi/*Lubisi*, p. 1393.
85. J.Z. Zulu/*Lubisi*, p. 227.
86. Identification and B. Tau/*Lubisi*, pp. 1488–9, 1511.
87. J.Z. Zulu/*Lubisi*, p. 230.
88. N.J. Lubisi, P.T. Mashigo and N. Manana/*Lubisi*, pp. 1104, 1234–6, 1239–41, 1273–6, 1324–6.
89. B. Tau/*Lubisi*, pp. 1493, 1514–16.
90. G.P. Shezi, Interrogation Report, p. 5: SANDF-OAMI/10/152.
91. 'Gunmen in city bank siege' and 'Terrorist siege', *P.News*, 25 Jan. 1980; 'Eye-witnesses tell of their ordeal', *RDM*, 26 Jan. 1980; 'Guns waved but hostage thought it was a joke', *P.News*, 26 Jan. 1980.
92. C.J. de Swardt/*Lubisi*, pp. 348–9.
93. P. Chatwind/*Lubisi*, pp. 345–7.
94. 'Terrorist siege'.
95. C.R. Brazelle and C.J. de Swardt/*Lubisi*, pp. 349–53, 357–8; 'Siege busters', *P.News*, 26 Jan. 1980; 'Bank bloodbath', *RDM*, 26 Jan. 1980.
96. C.R. Brazelle, I.W. Grobbelaar and H.J. Lombard/*Lubisi*, pp. 358–9, 364–5, 410–41.
97. F.J.P. Nel/*Lubisi*, pp. 873–4.
98. J. Ehlers, J.D. du Plooy and N.J. Lubisi/*Lubisi*, pp. 599–600, 623–6, 1110.
99. P.G. Shezi/*Lubisi*, p. 1534; G.P. Shezi, Interrogation Report, p. 6: SANDF-OAMI/10/152.
100. K. Phiri/'SAANC activities Matabeleland Province': SANDF-OAMI/10/153; D. Martin and P. Johnson, *The Struggle for Zimbabwe*, p. 321.
101. 'Police track the border terrorists', *RDM*, 19 Feb. 1980.
102. 'South Africa: In Brief; Weapons for ANC seized in Natal', 16 Feb. 1980: BBC-18 Feb. 1980.
103. 'Minutes of a meeting between Rhodesian Defence Force and SADF representatives to discuss and co-ordinate Op Melba, held in the command and control centre, Defence Headquarters at 08h00 on 25 February 1980': SANDF-AI(DIV)/292/GP28.
104. 'Poll result sends some popular myths crashing', 'Results of the election in full' and 'Result came as a shock to SA Govt', *RDM*, 5 Mar. 1980.
105. M. Maharaj to H. Barrell, pp. 498–501.
106. HSAW to SAMA Salisbury, 17 Mar. 1980: SANDF-OAMI/10/152.
107. Stam HK Kmdmt N Tvl to H Leer, 17 Mar. 1980: SANDF-OAMI/10/152.
108. Stam HK Kmdmt N Tvl to H Leer, 1 Apr. 1980: SANDF-OAMI/10/152.
109. Main HQ N Tvl Command to C Army, 2 Apr. 1980: SANDF-OAMI/10/152.

110. M.F. Ranoto, Interrogation, 'Madimetsa Frans Ranoto is gebore te …', pp. 6–7: SANDF-AMI/14/133; S. Ellis, *External Mission: The ANC in Exile* (Jonathan Ball, 2012), p. 135.

111. 'South Africa African National Congress (SA-ANC) activities in Zimbabwe', p. 3: SANDF-HSI/AMI/DTI/21/175.

112. K. Phiri/'SAANC activities in Matabeleland …'.

113. 'Aanhangsel "A" – Beskuldigde Nr. 1 (Hierna die Beskuldigde Genoem)', p. 13: UWHP-*Tsotsobe etc*/A1; Thabo Mbeki, 'Family to rebury a courageous fighter', *ANC Today*, 3 (29), 25–31 Jul. 2003, http://www.anc.org.za/docs/anctoday/2003/at29.htm (accessed 29 Dec. 2013).

114. 'Black Guerrillas Attack First Police Station in White Urban Area', *AP*, 4 Apr. 1980; 'Fighting back – with his .38', *RDM*, 4 Apr. 1980; 'Man tells of chasing terrorists to Soweto', *RDM*, 7 Apr. 1980; A. Beam [Tsotsobe], Statement, pp. 1120, 1122–3: UWHP-*Tsotsobe etc*/49; S. Shoke/*Operation Vula*, p. 204.

115. 'Drive towards socialism carries on in Mozambique', *RDM*, 14 May 1980.

116. RC HQ, 'Our Military Perspectives and Some Special Problems', pp. 1–3, 6–7, 15–16: UCT-SC/P29.1.

117. R.A.D.L. Ntshekang, Interrogation Report, pp. 10–11: SANDF-OAMI/10/153.

118. *Ibid.*, pp. 11–2.

119. D. Moisi, Statement, pp. 1196–7: UWHP-*Tsotsobe etc*/49; S.M. Thobela, Statement, TRC Amnesty Hearing, 8 May 1998: UWHP-TRC(CD)/amntrans > pta7> ISMAIL3.

120. .A.D.L. Ntshekang, Interrogation Report, p. 12.

121. 'Sasol inferno', *Star*, 2 Jun. 1980; 'Policeman had lucky escape', *Star*, 3 Jun. 1980.

122. 'Another Sasol sabotage attempt', *RDM*, 3 Jun. 1980.

123. *Ibid.*

124. 'What Tambo said – before', *Times(Swz)*, 5 Jun. 1980.

125. D. Coetzee, 'Hitsquads, Testimony of a South African Security Policeman: The Full Story', pp. 105–7: UWHP-*Coetzee*.

126. *Ibid.*

127. 'Two die in Manzini blasts', *Times(Swz)*, 4 Jun. 1980.

128. Stan to Comrade John, 5 Jun. 1980: UFH-ANC/LM-5/31.

129. R.A.D.L. Ntshekang, Interrogation Report, p. 13.

130. 'Message focuses UK interest on Mandela's future', *RDM*, 12 Jun. 1980.

131. 'We shall crush apartheid' Message from Robben Island prison. Made public by the ANC 10 Jun. 1980, in K. Asmal *et al.* (eds.), *Nelson Mandela in his own words* (Little, Brown, 2003), pp. 43–5.

Battlefield Southern Africa

1. Minutes of 11 Jul. 1980 ANC NEC Working Committee meeting in 'WC Meeting 22/08/79', p. 39: UWHP-KGC/III-31.

2. D. Coetzee, 'Hitsquads', pp. 70–71.

3. 'Report on our political situation in area Q', 13 Sep. 1980, pp. 17–18: UCT-SC/P29.5.

4. 'No. 1 – Q' to 'Comrade Mkhize or Secretary General', Q. – 23rd September, 1980: UFH-ANC/LM-5/31.

5. 'Guidelines for the development of our political machineries in TX', 20 Sep. 1980: UCT-SC/P29.1; 'PMC Organisational Report', *c.* May 1985, p. 9.

6. 'No. 1 – Q' to 'Comrade Mkhize or Secretary General'.

7. 'Aanhangsel "A" – Beskuldigde Nr. 1 (Hierna die Beskuldigde genoem)', p. 14: UWHP-*Tsotsobe etc*/A1; A. Beam [Tsotsobe], Statement, p. 1126: UWHP-*Tsotsobe etc*/49; 'S. Africa bomb blasts reflect black discontent in Soweto', *CSM*, 16 Oct. 1980.

8. A. Beam [Tsotsobe], Statement, p. 1127; A.B. Tsotsobe/*S v A.B. Tsotsobe et al.*, p. 64: UWHP-*Tsotsobe etc*/A1.

9. 'Grenade blast in Soweto shootout', *RDM*, 24 Nov. 1980; '"ANC" suspect dies in Soweto', *Star*, 24 Nov. 1980; 'December 16th: Our Heroes Day', *Sechaba*, Dec. 1982, p. 9.

10. D. Coetzee, 'Hitsquads', pp. 108–9.

11. Dr B.G. Fourie and J. Veloso/'Meeting between the Director-General of Foreign Affairs and the Mocambian Minister of State for Security Affairs: Paris, 5 December 1980', p. 9: SANDF-OAMI/10/200.

12. 'Mosambiek: Inligting en EEI's mbt Joe Slovo', 9 Dec. 1980, pp. 1–2: SANDF-OAMI/10/152.

13. 'Attack on ANC bases: Mozambique – 29th January 1981', p. 4: SANDF-OAMI/10/153; 'Report on the South African Defence Force raid on three houses in Matola, 5 Feb. 1981, pp. 1–3: SANDF-OAMI/10/152; S.M. Thobela, Statement/TRC-8 May 1998-Pretoria; R.A.D.L. Ntshekang, Interrogation Report, p. 16; 'Two ANC raid victims were ex-Rhodesians', *RDM*, 3 Feb. 1981.

14. 'Four who were Communists', *African Communist*, 87 (4th Quarter), 1981, pp. 47–8.

15. *Ibid.*, p. 45.

16. R.A.D.L. Ntshekang, Interrogation, pp. 16–17.

17. 'Four who were Communists', p. 47.

18. T.T. Nkobi to the Secretary to the President (Gaborone), 28 Feb. 1981: BNA-OP/27/49.

19. M. Maharaj to H. Barrell, p. 533; 'Restricted document. Some aspects of enemy counter guerrilla tactics compiled from our own experience', May 1984, p. 19: UWHP-KGC/III-55.

20. E.T. Mfalapitsa, Interrogation, pp. 16–17; T.E. Mfalapitsa, TRC Amnesty Hearing, 25 Jul. 2000 (Pretoria): TRC2.

21. M. Maharaj to P. O'Malley, 15 Jan. 2003.

22. J.S. Mosololi, Interrogation Report, pp. 11–12: SANDF-OAMI/10/154; ANC: Members Abroad: Identifications by Semano Jerry Mosololi (S.4/49413): MK: Dragon Mosepidi', 19 Mar. 1982: SANDF-AMI/DTI/21/174; 'Polisie soek nog na drie terro's', *Rapport*, 3 Jan. 1982.

23. M.M. Mbatha/*S v T.S. Mogoerane at al*, pp. 502–6: UWHP-SAIRR/33; M.M. Mbatha/ *S v S.N. Mokoena*, p. 150: NARS-TAB/Case No: CC659/82.

24. M.M. Mbatha/*Mokoena*, p. 92; M.M. Mbatha/*Mogoerane*, pp. 506–7; 'ANC: Members Abroad: Identifications by Semano Jerry Mosololi'; Office of the President (South Africa), 'The Order of Mendi for Bravery in Gold' awarded to the 'G5' unit, http://www.thepresidency.gov.za/pebble. asp?relid=7644 (accessed 7 Jan. 2014); 'Heroes of our Revolution', p. 24.

25. J.S. Mosololi, Interrogation Report, pp. 11–12; 'ANC claims role in big sabotage wave', *RDM*, 26 May 1981; 'Arrests imminent for wave of sabotage', *AP*, 26 May 1981.

26. M.M. Mbatha/*Mokoena*, pp. 94–6.

27. 'This man bombed PFP', *S. Tribune*, 12 Jul. 1981; 'I did bomb PFP, Geyer confesses – two ex-colleagues also flee', *S. Tribune*, 19 Jul. 1981; 'Twilight world of a bomber', *S. Tribune*, 26 Jul. 1981; 'Marion Sparg convicted of treason and arson charges', *Star*, 4 Nov. 1986; 'Judge: Abundantly clear Marion Sparg is guilty', *Citizen*, 4 Nov. 1986; 'Inside the tortured mind of Marion Sparg', *S. Times*, 9 Nov. 1986.

28. J. Mamasela to Harms Commission, p. 2484: UWHP-*Harms*; J.S. Mamasela, TRC Section 29 Investigative Inquiry, 1–2 Dec. 1996, pp. 13–15: UWHP-TRC(CD)/documents> 129; 'In unlikely Botswana, sinister spy plots unfold', *NYT*, 24 May 1982.

29. Salisbury Home Service, 1 Aug. 1981: BBC-5 Aug. 1981; 'Black Nationalist from South Africa slain in Zimbabwe', *WP*, 2 Aug. 1981.

30. 'Aboobaker Ismail and 6 others', TRC Amnesty Decision, 16 Jan. 2000 (Cape Town): TRC2; J. Mnisi, TRC Amnesty Hearing, 7 May 1998: UWHP-TRC(CD)/amntrans> pta7> ISMAIL2.

31. 'Aboobaker Ismail and 6 others'; J. Mnisi/TRC-7–8 May 1998-Pretoria; Z.I. Patel, Statement, TRC Amnesty Hearing, 8 May 1998: UWHP-TRC(CD)/amntrans > pta7> ISMAIL3; F.J.P. Nel, TRC Amnesty Hearing, 11 May 1999 (Johannesburg): TRC 2; 'Volgorde van gebeure vuurpylaanval te Voortrekkerhoogte nag 12 Aug 81': SANDF-HSI/AMI/DTI/21/174; 'Guerrillas rocket military installation', *AP*, 13 Aug. 1981; 'MK's brazen strike sent out a message of hope', *Sunday Independent* (South Africa), 10 May 1998.

32. 'Rocket blitz', *P.News*, 13 Aug. 1981.

33. E.T. Mfalapitsa, Interrogation Report, p. 17; E. Mfalapitsa to the Subcommittee on Security and Terrorism, United States Senate, 25 Mar. 1982, pp. 19–22: UWHP-*Denton*.

34. E. Mfalapitsa to the Subcommittee on Security and Terrorism, pp. 23–4; E.T. Mfalapitsa,

Interrogation Report, p. 19; T.E. Mfalapitsa, TRC Amnesty Hearing, 4 May 1999 (Johannesburg): TRC2; N. Serache biography as told to Matlapeng Pilane by Nat Serache, according to Pilane. See Pilane's Statement, p. 7: SANDF-HSI AMI/DTI/21/74.

35. S. Thelle, Interrogation Report, p. 9; M.T. Motaung, Statement, p. 1554/*Mogoerane.*

36. R.H. Chamusso in *S v R.H. Chamusso*, pp. 720, 804–6, 828, 868: NARS-TAB/Case No: CC504/82; 'Patrick's [Roggerio Chamusso] story', http://www.twosisters.org.za/patricks-story.html (accessed 22 Feb. 2015).

37. 'Patrick's story'; 'Sabotasie poging by Sasol', *Die Volksblad*, 22 Oct. 1981; 'Blasts in E Tvl hit pipeline, substation', *RDM*, 23 Oct. 1981.

38. 'Summary of substantial facts', p. 1/*Chamusso*; R. Chamusso, 'Ogies MR 77.10.81', p. 1/*Chamusso*; R.H. Chamusso, J.H.N. Dietricksen and A.A. Oberholzer/*Chamusso*, pp. 230–34, 285–6, 809–14.

39. U.M. Strydom/*Chamusso*, p. 238.

40. 'Hoofpunte van betoog namens die staat', p. 4/*Chamusso*.

41. F.J.P. Nel/TRC-11 May 1999-Johannesburg.

42. J.S. Mosololi, Interrogation Report, p. 12; 'ANC: Members Abroad: Identifications by Semano Jerry Mosololi'; J.S. Mosololi, Statement, pp. 1538–9/*S v T.S. Mogoerane et al.*: UWHP-SAIRR/34; 'Heroes of our Revolution', p. 24.

43. M.M. Mbatha/*Mokoena*, pp. 101–6.

44. F.J.P. Nel, S.J. Visser and Mr Prinsloo, TRC Amnesty Hearing, 11–12 May 1999 (Johannesburg): TRC 2.

45. This account, based on version of events given by Z. Nyanda to ANC authorities, appears in 'Report Compiled in Q on the 24-12-81', p. 4: UCT-SC/P15.

46. F.J.P. Nel and G. Visser/TRC-11–12 May 1999-Johannesburg.

47. INRAP 61/81, 3 Dec. 1981 (Doc No: 2097): SANDF-OAMI/10/153; 'Report Compiled in Q on the 24-12-81', p. 4: UCT-SC/P15.

48. A.J. Dercksen, D.G. Hope, F.J.P. Nel, D.J. Steenberg, J.J. Viktor and G. Visser/TRC-11–12 May 1999-Johannesburg; TRC Amnesty Decision, http://www.justice.gov.za/trc/decisions%5C2001/ac21186.htm (accessed 4 Mar. 2014).

49. 'Notas geneem tydens samesprekings te Swaziland op 10 Des 81', 11 Dec. 1981, pp. 1–3: SANDF-HS OPS/5/145.

50. 'ANC: Members Abroad: Identifications by Semano Jerry Mosololi'.

51. M.M. Mbatha/*Mokoena*, p. 110.

52. 'Report Compiled in Q on the 24-12-81', pp. 4–6.

53. J.S. Mosololi, Statement, pp. 1540–42/*Mogoerane*; S. Mogoerane/*Mogoerane*, p. 906; *UPI*, 31 Dec. 1981; 'Top ANC commissar captured, say police', *S. Times*, 3 Jan. 1982.

54. J.S. Mosololi/*Mogoerane*, p. 727; J.S. Mosololi and S. Mogoerane, Statements, pp. 1529–30, 1542–4/*Mogoerane*; 'Polisie soek nog na drie terro's'.

55. M.M. Mbatha/*Mokoena*, pp. 109–10; 'Judgement', p. 246/*Mokoena*.

56. SSO Op Santa to C Dir MI, 'Report on contact with the Royal Swazi Defence Force (USDF), 5 Feb. 1982, pp. 1, 3: SANDF-OAMI/10/153.

57. M.M. Mbatha/*Mogoerane*, p. 518.

58. J.C. Coetzee, A. Grobbelaar, ; T.E. Mfalapitsa, Z. Musi and C.S. Rorich, TRC Amnesty Hearing, 3–4 May 1999 (Johannesburg): TRC2; 'Tikane Heritage Projects – Mogale City Heritage Projects', http://tikaneheritageprojects.wozaonline. co.za/Township+Heritage+Project (accessed 8 Sep. 2014).

59. M.F. Dlamini to P.W. Botha, 17 Feb. 1982: SANDF-HS OPS/5/145.

60. 'Finding' and C.S. Mnisi, TRC Amnesty Hearing, 8 Jun. 1999 (Pretoria): TRC 2.

61. M.M. Mbatha, F.J.P. Nel and L.R. Ntshekang/*Mogoerane*, pp. 99–101, 111, 439–40, 513–4; M.M. Mbatha/*Mokoena*, pp. 110, 156; S. Shoke/*Operation Vula*, p. 206.

62. R. Kasrils, *Armed and Dangerous* (Jonathan Ball, 2004), p. 160.

63. 'Bombs kill three in South Africa and Swaziland', *NYT*, 5 Jun. 1982.

64. 'Swaziland to get key areas of SA', *RDM*, 15 Jun. 1982.

65. ANC NEC, 'Memorandum to the Government of Swaziland on the agreement between Swaziland and the Pretoria regime on Ka-Ngwane and Ngwavuma', Lusaka, 15 Jul. 1982: UWHP-KGC/III-43.

66. Witness 'I.C. X1'/*Maseko*, p. 3203.
67. S. Rabkin to H. Barrell, p. 890.
68. 'Operation Ingwavuma: Memoirs of a Political Commissar', *Dawn: Journal of Umkhonto we Sizwe* (Souvenir Issue, *c.* 1986), p. 50.
69. R. Lalla, TRC Amnesty Hearing, 5 Sep. 2000 (Durban): TRC2.
70. O.N. Ntombelo, Interrogation Report, pp. 14–15.
71. 'Bombs blow roof off house', *AP*, 2 Aug. 1982; 'Bombs explode at homes of exiled South Africans', *UPI*, 2 Aug. 1982.
72. 'Report on political cases faced by our cadres in Swaziland (Supplementary Report)', 7 Aug. 1982: UFH-ANC/LM-34/22.
73. O.N. Ntombelo, Interrogation Report, p. 16; 'Captured A.N.C. terrorist: Oscar Nkosinathi Ntombela': SANDF-HSI AMI/DTI/21/175; 'Ondervragingsverslag: SAANC Terroris', 26 Aug. 1982: SANDF-HSI AMI/DTI/21/175.
74. 'ANC in Lesotho' (Doc No: 82211840): SANDF-HSI AMI/DTI/21/175.
75. C.S. Mnisi/TRC-8 Jun. 1999-Pretoria.
76. *Ibid.*; M.B. Moloise ('Pleit')/*S v M.B. Moloise*, p. 2: NARS-TAB/Case No: CC214/83; 'Uitspraak', p. 2/*Moloise.*
77. 'Manhunt on for killers of security policeman', *RDM*, 9 Nov. 1982.
78. 'Gebuite Dokumente', 22 Nov. 1982: SANDF-HSI AMI/DTI/21/175.
79. Ivan to Comrade Willy, 'Greetings to you. The accompanying notes by Sally …', p. 1: SANDF-HSI AMI/DTI/21/175.
80. ANC Swaziland to ANC Headquarters, Lusaka, 25 Nov. 1982: UFH-ANC/LM-34/22.
81. 'How we blew up Koeberg', *M&G*, 15 Dec. 1995.
82. P. Naidoo, *Le Rona re Batho: An account of the 1982 Maseru massacre*, p. 5: UWHP-Box AK2335-2339.
83. A. Nzo, 'Below is a Brief Account of what happened during the criminal South African Invasion against Lesotho …', 10 Dec. 1982: UFH-ANC/CM-39/67.
84. 'How we blew up Koeberg'; D. Beresford, *Truth is a Strange Fruit* (Jacana, 2010), pp. 106–7.
85. 'At home abroad; living with neighbours', *NYT*, 20 Jan. 1983.
86. 'Former ANC leader slain, had testified before U.S. panel', *AP*, 18 Dec. 1982; *UPI*, 18 Dec. 1982.
87. 'Bombs damage atom plant site in South Africa', *NYT*, 20 Dec. 1982; 'Reactor Components Struck in Bombings at South Africa's Koeberg Station', *Nucleonics Week*, 23 Dec. 1982.
88. 'Bombs damage atom plant site'.
89. A. Ismail, TRC Amnesty Hearing, 6 May 1998: UWHP-TRC(CD)/amntrans > pta7> ISMAIL1.
90. M. Hadebe, Interrogation Report, pp. 13–15: SANDF-OAMI/10/155; A.M. Bhungane and G. Ngwenya in *S v S.E. Mahlobo et al.*, pp. 240–41, 384–6: NARS-NAB/Case No: CC79/84.
91. 'Lesotho: ANC en Politieke Situasie', 21 Feb. 1983: SANDF-HSI AMI/DTI/21/177.
92. L.B. Ngqungwana, (Background) Statement, p. 4: UWHP-*Ngqungwana*/Box 2.
93. A. Ismail and J. Mnisi/TRC-7–8 May 1988-Pretoria.
94. M.A. Ismail and M.I. Shaik, TRC Amnesty Hearing, 6–7 May 1998 (Pretoria): TRC2; A. Ismail, 'The ANC's Special Operations Unit', *The Thinker*, 58 (Dec. 2013), p. 34.
95. 'Indictment', p. 16/*Mahlobo.*
96. 'Judgement'/*Mahlobo*, p. 492; *UPI*, 22 Apr. 1983.
97. S.E. Mahlobo, 'Year of United Action report', 4 May 1983/*Mahlobo*, pp. 505, 507.
98. 'Heunis: Stability is priority', *C.Times*, 6 May 1983; 'Byzantine start', *C.Times*, 7 May 1983; 'Winner takes everything', *S.Times*, 8 May 1983.
99. *UPI*, 9 May 1983; 'Foreign Ministers of South Africa and Mozambique meet at border': BBC-7 May 1983.
100. J. Mnisi/TRC-7 May 1998-Pretoria; H. Passtoors/*S v H.T.J.M. Pastoors*, pp. 1–2, 10–12: UWHP/ *Pastoors.*
101. 'Ex-convicts caused Pretoria blast – court', *Citizen*, 26 Aug. 1983; 'Inquest told of bomb pair's final moves', *RDM*, 26 Aug. 1983.

102. 'Ex-convicts caused Pretoria blast'.
103. F. Steenkamp in *AP*, 2 Aug. 1983.
104. *Ibid.*; 'Bloedige chaos ná bom', *Beeld*, 21 May 1983; '15 die in terror blast', *RDM*, 21 May 1983; 'Pretoria carnage as huge bomb explodes', *Star*, 21 May 1983; 'The Church Street massacre', *Star*, 23 May 1983; A. Kirkby, 'The bomb that still goes off in my head, again and again', *P.News*, 21 May 2008.
105. 'Guerrilla chief warns Pretoria of new attacks', *NYT*, 22 May 1983.
106. 'Mozambique suffers South Africa's warning shots', *FT*, 25 May 1983; 'Damage in Mozambique Looks Surprisingly Light', *NYT*, 25 May 1983.
107. 'Foe relies on foe in Southern Africa', *NYT*, 30 May 1983.
108. E.A. de Kock, TRC Amnesty Hearing, 24 May 1999 (Pretoria): TRC2.
109. 'South Africa's Strategy: To isolate the rebels', *NYT*, 6 Jun. 1983.
110. M.F. Ranoto, Interrogation, 'Madimetsa Frans Ranoto is gebore te …', p. 9: SANDF-AMI/14/133; 'Militêre Strategie teen die ANC: Vorderingsverslag', 29 Jul. 1983, p. 5: SANDF-HS OPS/3/290; 'Morake, P., 28': UNISA(MF)-Karis-Gerhart Collection 'From Protest to Challenge'/Part 5, C.J.1.
111. HQ Special Forces, 'Source Report: ANC camps Mozambique', 14 Jun. 1983: SANDF-OAMI/10/155.
112. D.J. Bhengu/*Mahlobo*, pp. 330–31.
113. U. Mokeba to ANC International Department, 18 Jul. 1983: UFH-ANC/LM-32/2; M. Senzangakhona, E. Mabitse, U. Abrahamse and G. Molebatsi, 'Umkonto we sizwe: Within living memories (Part 3), in *Umrabulo*, 13 (2nd Quarter), 2002, http://www.anc.org.za/show.php ?id=2933 (accessed 21 Aug. 2014).
114. 'Tough task for the crowd marshals at Plain rally', *Argus*, 22 Aug. 1983; 'UDF plans course of action' and '6 000 cheer Boesak', *C. Times*, 22 Aug. 1983; 'Nothing's positive in apartheid, says Boesak', *RDM*, 22 Aug. 1983; 'UDF launched with call for end to forced removals', *Citizen*, 22 Aug. 1983; 'Huge crowd at UDF launch', *Sowetan*, 22 Aug. 1983; 'A new opposition', *The Economist*, 27 Aug. 1983.
115. U. Mokeba to the Head, Department of International Affairs (ANC), 22 Aug. 1983: ANC-UFH/LM-32/2.
116. M.I. Shaik/TRC-6 May 1998-Pretoria; 'ANC bombers leave widespread wreckage', *Sunday Express*, 28 Aug. 1983; 'ANC in war on Ciskei', *Sowetan*, 29 Aug. 1983.

Planning for People's War

1. 'Editorial: The New ANC struggle', *Sechaba*, Sep. 1983, pp. 1–2.
2. 'Bomb blasts at S. African spa the work of black nationalists', *TG&M*, 12 Oct. 1983; '5 hurt in Mozambique bombing', *NYT*, 18 Oct. 1983.
3. 'Sentence', pp. 11–12, in *S v T.P. Ngcobo*: NARS-NAB/Case No: CC13/84; T.P. Ngcobo 'Plea in the Magistrate's Court on a charge Justiciable in a Superior Court', 15 Dec. 1983, pp. 21/*T.P. Ngcobo*.
4. 'Go to the polls and vote!', *C. Times*, 2 Nov. 1983.
5. 'How the Nation voted', *Star*, 4 Nov. 1983.
6. 'PMC Organisational Report', *c.* May 1985, p. 20.
7. 'Planning for People's War Document', Nov. 1983, pp. 1–5: UCT-SC/29.1.
8. E.A. de Kock, TRC Amnesty Hearing, 14 Jun. 1999 (Pretoria): TRC2.
9. D.J. Bhengu/*Mahlobo*, pp. 331–4.
10. D.J. Bhengu, T.R. O'Connell and M.J. Radebe/*Mahlobo*, pp. 72–3, 124, 339.
11. D.J. Bhengu, R.A. du Rand, V.N. Gumede, T.R. O'Connell and M.J. Radebe/*Mahlobo*, pp. 72–3, 85, 114–15, 125–6, 339.
12. E.A. de Kock, F.J. Pienaar, P.J. van Dyk, TRC Amnesty Hearing, 14–15 Jun. 1999 (Pretoria): TRC2; E. de Kock, *A Long Night's Damage* (Contra, 1998), pp. 107–8, 110.
13. F.J. Pienaar/TRC-14 Jun. 1999-Pretoria.
14. S. Rabkin to H. Barrell, p. 889.
15. 'Reports of the Commission of Enquiry into certain allegations of cruelty and human rights abuse

against ANC prisoners and detainees by ANC members', 20 Aug. 1993 ['Motsuenyane Commission'], p. 108: UWHP-AG2918; 'Report: Commission of Inquiry into recent developments in the People's Republic of Angola' ['Stuart Commission'], 14 Mar. 1984, pp. 19–20.

16. 'Stuart Commission', pp. 19–20.

17. *Reuters*, 20 Dec. 1983 (Doc: 84000320): SANDF-HSI AMI/DTI/21/74.

18. 'Secret Summit', *Times(Swz)*, 21 Dec. 1983.

19. 'Motsuenyane Commission', p. 38.

20. A. Nzo to The Secretariat, ANC Politico-Military Council, 23 Dec. 1983: UFH-ANC/LM-124/204.

21. M. Saeboe, 'A state of exile', p. 128; 'Stuart Commission', p. 18.

22. J. Matakata, *Hills of Hope: The Autobiography of Jama Matakata* (Nutrend, 2004), pp. 43–4; J. Makhura in P. Harris, *In a Different Time* (Umuzi, 2008), p. 47.

23. 'Fraternal Message from the African National Congress to the Frelimo Party', p. 1: UWHP-KGC/III-54; S. Machel in 'Two reports on discussions between governments of Mozambique and Tanzania re impending signing of Nkomati Accord …', p. 12: UWHP-KGC/III-55.

24. B. Ketelo *et al.*, 'A Miscarriage of Democracy', in P. Trewhela (ed.), *Inside Quatro* (Jacana, 2009), pp. 8, 10; N.P. Phiri/'Motsuenyane Commission', p. 109.

25. 'Fraternal Message from the African National Congress to the Frelimo Party', pp. 1–2.

26. 'Decisions and suggestions from NEC/PMC Meeting of 25th Jan 84.': UWHP-KGC/III-54.

27. 'Motsuenyane Commission', pp. 38, 109.

28. 'Stuart Commission', pp. 21–2.

29. 'Motsuenyane Commission', pp. 39, 128; M. Twala, *Mbokodo* (Jonathan Ball, 1994), pp. 60–63.

30. D. Makhubedu in 'Motsuenyane Commission', p. 79; S. Phungulwa/'Fighting the Crazy War', 2 (3), pp. 5–6: UWHP-AG2918.

31. 'Motsuenyane Commission', p. 39; B. Ketelo *et al.*, 'A Miscarriage of Democracy', p. 21; L. Dyasop in TRC Human Rights Violations Submissions – Q&As, 25 Jul. 1996: UWHP-TRC(CD)/HRVtrans> Soweto> DYASON.

32. 'Motsuenyane Commission', p. 39; B. Ketelo *et al.*, 'A Miscarriage of Democracy', p. 21; M. Twala, *Mbokodo*, pp. 63–4.

33. B. Ketelo *et al.*, 'A Miscarriage of Democracy', pp. 21–2; W.W. Bottoman, *The Making of an MK Cadre* (LiNc, 2010), pp. 146–7.

34. HQ Natal Command, 'Ntunja Mngomezulu', 10 Feb. 1984 (Doc: 84003070): SANDF-HSI/AMI/DTI/21/75.

35. R. Lalla, TRC Amnesty Hearing, 5 Sep. 2000 (Durban): TRC2.

36. 'Mapumulo, Wilfred, 38' and others: UNISA(MF)-Karis-Gerhart Collection 'From Protest to Challenge'/Part 5, C.J.1.

37. 'Mandela rejects new offer of release to homeland base', *TG&M*, 12 Mar. 1984; 'Jailed ANC leader rejects offer of freedom', *CSM*, 12 Mar. 1984.

38. 'Mozambique, South Africa, sign peace pact', *UPI*, 16 Mar. 1984.

39. 'Mozambique seizes South Africa rebels', *NYT*, 26 Mar. 1984.

40. 'Bylae: Die beskuldigdes het op 'n datum of datums …', pp. 9–10/*S v A.M. Maseko et al.*: NARS-TAB/Case No: CC319/87.

41. R. Kasrils, *Armed and Dangerous*, p. 165.

42. 'Judge: Abundantly clear Marion Sparg is guilty', *Citizen*, 4 Nov. 1986; 'Sad end for ANC protégé', *S.Times*, 9 Nov. 1986.

43. '10 held in police swoop', *S. Observer*, 3 Apr. 1984.

44. *UPI*, 3 Apr. 1984; 'Bomb outrage', *NM*, 4 Apr. 1984; 'Rush hour blast horror at docks', *RDM*, 4 Apr. 1984.

45. R. Lalla/TRC-5 Sep. 2000-Durban.

46. Chris to the Chief of Operations, Lusaka, and Chris to Bra Simon, both 7 Apr. 1984: UFH-ANC/LM-125/218b.

47. '15 ANC men on the run', *Times(Swz)*, 11 Apr. 1984.

48. Capital Radio, Umtata, 11 Apr. 1984: BBC-13 Apr. 1984.

49. 'Police in ANC shootout', *Times(Swz)*, 12 Apr. 1984; 'Happy-trigger ANC man arrested', *S. Observer*, 12 Apr. 1984.

50. 'Police in ANC shootout'; 'Shootout erupts as police hunt suspected African National Congress members', *AP*, 11 Apr. 1984; '7 ANC members arrested', *S. Observer*, 12 Apr. 1984; 'Police fear ANC rescue plot', *Times(Swz)*, 15 May 1984.

51. 'Shot man was ANC member', *S.Observer*, 14 Apr. 1984.

52. 1'Policeman dies in Nationwide swoop on ANC sanctuaries', *AP*, 14 Apr. 1984; 'Guerrilla kills policeman, wounds five in Swaziland', *UPI*, 14 Apr. 1984; '"ANC must get out"' and '"No shooting to kill"', *Times(Swz)*, 16 Apr. 1984; 'Cop shot dead by ANC men', *S. Observer*, 16 Apr. 1984; 'Shiba's killer shot dead'. *Times(Swz)*, 18 Dec. 1984; 'Report by Duma', p. 1: UFH-ANC/LM-34/22.

53. '2 ANC men shot dead', *S. Observer*, 21 Apr. 1984.

54. V.Z. Nyawo, Statement/'Notes of Consultations with the Accused and Statements from the Accused', pp. 6, 13: UWHP-*Mapumulo*.

55. 'Indictment', p. 13 and 'Summary of Substantial Facts', p. 46/*Mapumulo*.

56. W.W. Bottoman, *The Making of an MK Cadre*, p. 152; B. Ketelo *et al.*, 'A Miscarriage of Democracy', p. 27.

57. W.W. Bottoman, *The Making of an MK Cadre*, p. 153; B. Ketelo *et al.*, 'A Miscarriage of Democracy', pp. 27–8.

58. B. Ketelo *et al.*, 'A Miscarriage of Democracy', p. 28.

59. 1'Xulu, Sipho Bridget, 25': UNISA(MF)-Karis-Gerhart Collection 'From Protest to Challenge'/ Part 5, C.J.1.

60. *Ibid.*

61. B. Ketelo *et al.*, 'A Miscarriage of Democracy', p. 28.

62. ANC National Consultative Conference, Jun. 1985, National Preparatory Committee Documents, 'NPC Composite and Organisational Report', p. 1: UFH-ANC/ORT-B10.7-B10.7.1.

63. 'You're free', *Times(Swz)*, 20 Jul. 1984; 'Last of 80 rebels to be flown out of country', *UPI*, 21 Jul. 1984.

64. B. Rostron, *Till Babylon Falls* (Coronet Books, 1991), pp. 86–7.

65. 'South Africa: Low turnout in Mixed-Race election', *IPS*, 23 Aug. 1984.

66. R. Dumisa, diary, 28 Aug. and 1 Sep. 1984: UWHP-*Dumisa*.

PART V: PEOPLE'S WAR

Township Rebellion

1. 'PW now acting President', *Citizen*, 4 Sep. 1984.

2. 'Violent night in Sharpeville', *Star*, 3 Sep. 1984; *Sowetan*, 3 Sep. 1984; Labour Monitoring Group, 'The November 1984 Stayaway', in J. Maree (ed.), *The Independent Trade Unions, 1974–1984: Ten Years of the South African Labour Bulletin* (Ravan, 1987), p. 260.

3. 'Cabinet Ministers tour riot areas', *AP*, 7 Sep. 1984.

4. 'Government accuses Anti-Apartheid group of promoting revolution', *AP*, 5 Oct. 1984; *UPI*, 5 Oct. 1984.

5. *AP*, 10 Oct. 1984.

6. Radio Freedom, 17 Oct. 1984: BBC-22 Oct. 1984.

7. Radio Freedom, 20 Oct. 1984: BBC-25 Oct. 1984.

8. 'Hundreds held in swoop', *Star*, 23 Oct. 1984; 'Army, police at Sharpeville', *Citizen*, 24 Oct. 1984; 'Troops pull out of Vaal townships', *Citizen*, 25 Oct. 1984.

9. 'Black Sash slams SADF role in raids', *Star*, 24 Oct. 1984.

10. 'Students continue boycott after massive raid', *AP*, 24 Oct. 1984.

11. *AP*, 1 Nov. 1984.

12. 'Guerrilla Leader: Crackdown exposes myth of reform in South Africa', *AP*, 26 Oct. 1984.

13. R. Dumisa, diary, 28 Oct., 10 Nov. and 13 Nov. 1984: UWHP-*Dumisa*.

14. 'Top cop gunned down', *S. News*, 8 Dec. 1984; 'Shiba's killer shot dead', *Times(Swz)*, 18 Dec. 1984.

15. 'Notes of Consultations with the Accused and Statements from the Accused', p. 6: UWHP-*Mapumulo*.

16. 'Indictment', pp. 18, 20/*Mapumulo*.
17. 'Summary of Substantial Facts', p. 48/*Mapumulo*.
18. 'Shiba's killer shot dead'.
19. 'Give up – or else!', *Times(Swz)*, 21 Dec. 1984.
20. 'ANC Swaziland, The conflict between certain ANC elements …', 7 Jan. 1985 (Doc No: 85000741): HIS/AMI/DTI/21/75.
21. '2 held as police open fire', *Times(Swz)*, 28 Dec. 1984.
22. 'ANC Swaziland, The conflict between certain ANC elements'; 'Terror leap', *Times(Swz)*, 31 Dec. 1984.
23. 'Swazi Police hunt ANC guerrillas', *Guardian*, 4 Jan. 1985.
24. 'oau asked to intercede between anc and swaziland', *Xinhua*, 4 Jan. 1985.
25. Y. Shaik to D. Shongwe, 13 Aug. 2002: UDW-'VR'.
26. J.T. Mofokeng/*S v D.C.B. Buthelezi et al.*, pp. 1036–8, 1082, 1130: NARS-NAB/Case No: CC70/86; 'Judgement', p. 2734/*Buthelezi*.
27. 'Imprisoned South African leader of black independence movement interviewed', *AP*, 26 Jan. 1985.
28. 'Pretoria may release Mandela', *FT*, 1 Feb. 1985.
29. 'Botha makes a renewed offer to free Mandela', *Guardian*, 1 Feb. 1985.
30. 'Charge Sheet', p. 13: UWHP-TLC/E19; Y. Shaik to D. Shongwe, 13 Aug. 2002.
31. 'Mandela rejects freedom offer', *UPI*, 10 Feb. 1985; 'Black leader refuses offer for conditional release', *AP*, 10 Feb. 1985; 'Jailed black leader rejects S. African offer; 'Mandela's first public statement in 21 years', *WP*, 11 Feb. 1985.
32. 'Bomb reduces Jinja house to rubble', *BDN*, 14 Feb. 1985; J.A. Steyn/TRC-10 Jul. 2000-Pretoria; L. Nyelele and E. Drake, *The Raid on Gaborone: June 14, 1985 – A Memorial*, p. 5: BNA-OP/13/14.
33. 'Meeting between ministers RF Botha and GKT Chiepe in Pretoria: 22 February 1985', pp. 1–5: SANDF-HS OPS/3/308.
34. 'ANC: verhoudinge met Botswana-regering': SANDF-HSI AMI/3/943; 'ANC samesprekings met Botswana regering', 29 Mar. 1985, p. 2: SANDF-AMI/14/133.
35. Q.D. Michels, Statement, pp. 1–2 and 'Schedule J', p. 6: UWHP-*Ngqungwana*.
36. 'Report on the meeting held between the SD authorities, the OAU delegation and the ANC delegation held on 8.3.85', pp. 1–3, 9–10, 12: ANC-UFH/LM-128/241.
37. 'Indictment', pp. 30, 44, 47/*Buthelezi*; 'Summary of Substantial Facts', pp. 37–8, in *S v T. Tshika et al.*: NARS-NAB/Case No: CC70/87.
38. 'Schedule J', p. 1, 'Q.D. Michels Statement, p. 2, 'Summary of substantial facts', pp. 3, 5, and L.B. Ngqungwana, (Background) Statement, p. 5/*Ngqungwana*.
39. L. Nyelele and E. Drake, *The Raid on Gaborone*, p. 5; 'Bomb blast rocks capital, kills one', *BDN*, 15 May 1985; S.A. Police Security Headquarters, 'Daaglikse Veiligheidsoorsig', 21 May 1985 , p. 2: SANDF-HSI/AMI/DTI/21/76; 'Statement by his Excellency Dr O.K.J. Masire following a South African military raid in Gaborone on 14th June 1985': BNA-OP/13/113.
40. Jacob Zuma to the NPC, Lusaka, 27 May 1985: UWHP-KGC/III-61.
41. Report of 'Unit "U"': UWHP-KGC/III-61.
42. U. Mokeba, ANC Chief Rep (Angola), 'Report of the Regional Preparatory Committee – Angola Region', pp. 2–3: UWHP-KGC/III-61.
43. S. Manong, *If We Must Die: An Autobiography of a Former Commander of uMkhonto we Sizwe* (Nkululeko Publishers, 2015), p. 227.
44. 'Blast wrecks army offices', *Citizen*, 29 May 1985; 'Race against time before blast', *C. Times*, 29 May 1985; M.I. Shaik, TRC Amnesty Hearing, 7 May 1998 (Pretoria): TRC2.
45. 'Bylae: Die beskuldigdes het op 'n datum of datums', p. 17/*S v A.M. Maseko et al.*: NARS-TAB/Case No: CC319/87.
46. L. Nyelele and E. Drake, *The Raid on Gaborone*, p. 34; 'U.S. recalls South African envoy in response to raid on Botswana; 16 are reported killed as commandos strike an insurgent "center"', *NYT*, 15 Jun. 1985; 'Keitumetse 8, heroine of tragic night of SA raid', *BDN*, 3 Jul. 1985.
47. L. Nyelele and E. Drake, *The Raid on Gaborone*, pp. 18, 33; 'The Botswana Massacre – Victims were very "soft" targets', *Sechaba*, Aug. 1985, pp. 26–7.

48. 'The Botswana Massacre', pp. 26–7.
49. *Ibid.*
50. *Ibid.*
51. U. Abrahamse, 'Just before I commenced my studies at the University of Botswana ...', unpublished memoirs, pp. 40–42.
52. 'Hamlyn was 1st class science student', *BDN*, 19 Jun. 1985.
53. 'Indictment', p. 52/*Buthelezi.*
54. 'Bomb blast in Durban injures two', *UPI*, 19 Jun. 1985.
55. S. Spetsiotis/*Buthelezi*, pp. 126–7.
56. *Documents of the Second National Consultative Conference of the African National Congress*, p. 3: UFH-ANC/ORT-B10.7-B10.7.1.
57. ANC National Consultative Conference, 'Report, Main Decisions and Recommendations of the Second National Consultative Conference', p. 1: UFH-ANC/ORT-B10.7-B10.7.1.
58. 'Conference Communique', *Sechaba*, Aug. 1985, pp. 4–5.
59. ANC National Consultative Conference, 'Report, Main Decisions and Recommendations', pp. 1–2: UFH-ANC/ORT-B10.7-B10.7.1; 'NPC Organisational and Composite Report', pp. 1, 6–7, in ANC National Consultative Conference June 1985 National Preparatory Committee Documents: UFH-ANC/ORT-B10.7-B10.7.1.
60. 'Report, Main Decisions and Recommendations', p. 2; Mzala (J. Nxumalo) to G. Gerhart, p. 15; B. Bunting to T. Karis and G. Gerhart, Mar. 1991, p. 2: UWHP-KGC/I-5.
61. 'Report, Main Decisions and Recommendations', p. 5.
62. *Ibid.*, p. 10; P. Jordan to H. Barrell, p. 241: OU-RHL/*Barrell.*
63. 'Report, Main Decisions and Recommendations', p. 6.
64. 'Bylae: Die beskuldigdes het op 'n datum of datums', p. 17/*A.M. Maseko.*
65. 'Judgement', p. 22/*S v H.T.J.M. Passtoors*: UWHP-*Passtoors.*
66. O. Tambo/*Documents of the Second National Consultative Conference of the African National Congress*, p. 44: UFH-ANC/ORT-B10.7-B10.7.1.
67. 1'Umtata bombing: Call to extradite ANC man', *Argus*, 12 Apr. 1988; 'Transkei wants to try ANC accused', *Star*, 13 Apr. 1988; '"Mpilo" is dead, but his ghost haunts our courts', *WM*, 28 Jul. 1988; 'Extradited to face terror charges', *City Press*, 4 Sep. 1988; 'Police evidence in Umtata terror case', *DD*, 8 Sep. 1989.
68. M. Shaik to D. Shongwe, 7 Jul. 2002: UDW-'VR'.
69. H. Passtoors in 'Prison Remembered', *Sechaba*, Oct. 1989, p. 26.
70. M. Shaik and Y. Shaik to D. Shongwe, 7 Jul. and 13 Aug. 2002.
71. Y. Shaik to D. Shongwe, 13 Aug. 2002.
72. R.M. Sakloo/*Buthelezi*, pp. 1530–32; 'Judgement', p. 2734/*Buthelezi.*
73. 'Violence in South Africa causing collapse of black township governments', *CSM*, 19 Jul. 1985.
74. 'Emergency power granted to police by South Africa', *NYT*, 21 Jul. 1985.
75. 'Scores arrested in late night raids in South Africa', *NYT*, 23 Jul. 1985; 'Human Rights: Apartheid foes charge that emergency deepens crisis', *IPS*, 23 Jul. 1985.

Taking the War to White Areas

1. R.M. Sakloo/*Buthelezi*, pp. 1558–63; 'Indictment', p. 37/*Buthelezi*; 'Blast rocks home of Minister Rajbansi', *Star*, 5 Aug. 1985.
2. S. Rabkin to H. Barrell, pp. 897–900.
3. R. Lalla, TRC Amnesty Hearing, 5 Sep. 2000 (Durban): TRC2.
4. 'SA envoy expects major statement', *Star*, 14 Aug. 1985.
5. 'Media people jostle for space as world hones in on congress', *Star*, 16 Aug. 1985.
6. 'Botha rules out wide concessions to black demands', *NYT*, 16 Aug. 1985; 'Botha talks of advice and dangerous games' and 'Mandela view unchanged', *Business Day*, 16 Aug. 1985.
7. 'Did PW Botha have to do a backdown?', *Star*, 17 Aug. 1985.
8. 'Fierce clashes', *Argus*, 28 Aug. 1985; '8 die in township riot', *C.Times*, 29 Aug. 1985.

9. N.L. Pedro (admissions)/*S v A.A. Forbes et al.*, p. 2130: UCT-AFT.

10. 'Summary of Discussions Between certain Representatives of Big Business and Opinion-Makers in South Africa and the ANC', 14 Sep. 1985, in G.M. Gerhart and C.L. Glaser (eds.), *From Protest to Challenge*, Vol. 6 (Indiana University Press, 2010), pp. 576–80.

11. D. Fingland and S. Jobling/*Tshika*, pp. 106–11; Indictment, 'Annexure A, Acts performed by Accused No. 1: Thuso Tshika', p. 18/*Tshika*; A.Q. Msomi and T. Tshika, TRC Amnesty Hearing, 5 Sep. 2000 (Durban): TRC2.

12. L.O. Moni/*Buthelezi*, pp. 1203–6.

13. 'The Commonwealth Accord on Southern Africa', in *Mission to South Africa: The Commonwealth Report* (Penguin, 1986), pp. 142–5.

14. L.O. Moni/*Buthelezi*, pp. 1208–10, 1272; Witness 'A'/*Tshika*, p. 559.

15. V. Ramlakan, TRC Amnesty Hearing, 4 Sep. 2000 (Durban): TRC2; 'Judgement', p. 2636/*Buthelezi*.

16. R.J. McBride in *S v R.J. McBride et al.*, pp. 1522–3, 1532: NARS-NAB: Case No: CC116/86.

17. J.S. Mbuli and M.E. Nondula, TRC Amnesty Hearing, 3 Jul. 2000 (Messina): TRC2.

18. M.E. Nondula/TRC-3 Jul. 2000-Messina; M.E. Nondula, Statement/*M.Z. Mncube et al. v The State*, pp. 2729–30: UWHP-*Mncube&Nondula*.

19. M.Z. Mncube, Statement/*Mncube*, pp. 3394–5.

20. E. Mokgamatha and G.J. de Villiers/*Mncube*, pp. 127–9, 189–90.

21. 'A Submission on the Question of Negotiations', Lusaka, 27 Nov. 1985, in G.M. Gerhart and C.L. Glaser (eds.), *From Protest to Challenge*, Vol. 6 (Indiana University Press, 2010), pp. 589–92.

22. S.P. Molokoane [Sullivan Molokoane's account here based on account told to him by Matthew Simelane, his uncle], TRC Human Rights Violations Hearing, 3 Jun. 1997 (Leandra): TRC2.

23. *Ibid.*; 'Rocket attack on Secunda', *C. Times*, 29 Nov. 1985; 'Three shot after failed rocket attack on Sasol', *Business Day*, 29 Nov. 1985; 'Seven terror suspects die in shoot-outs', *Star*, 29 Nov. 1985; 'Drie terroriste ná aanval geskiet naby Piet Retief' and 'Terreur-vlag breek uit', *Die Burger*, 29 Nov. 1985; 'Terro's gejag', *Die Vaderland*, 29 Nov. 1985; '5 ANC men die in shoot-outs', *Citizen*, 29 Nov. 1985; 'ANC claims its men attacked Sasol plants', *NM*, 30 Nov. 1985; 'New wave of guerrilla attacks', *WM*, 5 Dec. 1985; 'Missing in action', *Sowetan*, 27 Jan. 1995; 'MK award a fitting honour for the legendary Barney Molokoane', *Star*, 7 Nov. 1997; 'MK heroes reburied in Soweto', *Star*, 1 Dec. 1997; Office of the President (South Africa), 'The Order of Mendi for Bravery in Gold' awarded to 'Richard Barney Molokoane', http://www.thepresidency.gov.za/pebble.asp?relid=7627 (accessed 5 Mar. 2014).

24. 'Indictment', p. 33 and 'Summary of substantial facts', p. 71/*Buthelezi*.

25. 'Take the Struggle to White Areas!' *Sechaba*, Dec. 1985, p. 2.

26. J.T. Mofokeng/*Buthelezi*, pp. 1049, 1156–8.

27. 'Nine killed in Raid: Guerrilla group says 6 of its members died', *AP*, 20 Dec. 1985; 'Mystery hit squads swoop to kill nine in Maseru', *NM*, 21 Dec. 1985; *Truth and Reconciliation Commission of South Africa Report*, Vol. 2 (Juta, 1998), p. 109; 'Special Report Transcript, Episode 15, Section 6, Time 34:18' in http://sabctrc.saha.org.za/tvseries/episode15/section6/transcript2.htm?t=%2Bquin+%2Bphoenix&tab=tv (accessed 27 Jan. 2014); E. de Kock, *A Long Night's Damage* (Contra, 1998), pp. 126–7.

28. 'Judgement', p. 2734/*Buthelezi*, pp. 1036–7; A. Zondo in F. Meer, *The Trial of Andrew Zondo: A Sociological Insight* (Skotaville, 1987), p. 108.

29. 'Indictment', p. 45/*Buthelezi*; A.Q. Msomi, TRC Amnesty Hearing, 5 Sep. 2000 (Durban): TRC2.

30. Indictment, 'Annexure A, acts performed by Accused No. 1', pp. 21, 23/*Tshika*; A.Q. Msomi/TRC-5 Sep. 2000-Durban.

31. A. Zondo in *The Trial of Andrew Zondo*, pp. 46, 108.

32. H.J.P. Botha, TRC Amnesty Hearing, 16 Nov. 1998 (Durban): TRC2.

33. 'Bomb horror', *Citizen*, 24 Dec. 1985; 'Bomb atrocity', *NM*, 24 Dec. 1985; 'Police release names of the five who were killed', *NM*, 24 Dec. 1985; J.T. Mofokeng/*Buthelezi*, pp. 1071, 1117–18; J. Mofokeng and A. Zondo in *The Trial of Andrew Zondo*, pp. 46, 94–5, 109.

34. C.A.P. Robertshaw and A.R.C. Taylor/*Buthelezi*, pp. 371–3, 2015–6.

35. W.R. Bellingan, TRC Amnesty Hearing, 17 Nov. 1997: UWHP-TRC(CD)/amntrans> CT6> BELLING1; T.J. Mbelo, TRC Amnesty Hearing, 18 Nov. 1997: UWHP-TRC(CD)/amntrans > CT6 > MBELO; J. Mbane, TRC Amnesty Hearing, 3 Feb. 1988: UWHP-TRC(CD)/amntrans> Ct8> 2NDGUG1.

36. 'South Africa tightens border control with Lesotho', *AP*, 4 Jan. 1986.

37. R.J. McBride/*R.J. McBride*, p. 1675; 'Indictment'/*S v G.C. Webster*: NARS-NAB: Case No: CC8/88.

38. B. Rostron, *Till Babylon Falls* (Coronet Books, 1991), pp. 116–17.

39. J. Mbane/TRC-3 Feb. 1988-Cape Town.

40. SAPA, 17 Jan. 1986: BBC-20 Jan. 1986; *AP*, 20 Jan. 1986; 'South Africa lifts blockade of Lesotho', *UPI*, 25 Jan. 1986.

41. T. Yengeni to W. Kodesh, transcript, p. 11: UWC-MCA/MCA6-386.

42. L.B. Ngqungwana in S. Westcott, *The Trial of the Thirteen*, p. 55: UCT-SC/F9.4.

43. J. Mbane/TRC-3 Feb. 1988-Cape Town.

44. *Ibid.*

45. 1'Limpet mine courier jailed for ten years', *City Press*, 2 Nov. 1986; 'Former journalist guilty of treason', *C. Times*, 4 Nov. 1986; 'Marion Sparg convicted of treason and arson charges', *Star*, 4 Nov. 1986; 'Sentence', p. 2/*S v M.M. Sparg*: UWHP-C&N/As1.

46. O. Masina, Statement, 16 Sep. 1986/*S v O. Masina et al.*, 'Uitspraak', pp. 622–3: NARS-TAB/Case No: 400/88; F.T. Masango, TRC Amnesty Hearing, 8 Jun. 1999 (Pretoria): TRC2.

47. W.R. Bellingan and T.J. Mbelo/TRC-17–18 Nov. 1997-Cape Town.

48. J. Mbane/TRC-3 Feb. 1988-Cape Town.

49. W.R. Bellingan and T.J. Mbelo/TRC-17–18 Nov. 1997-Cape Town; J. Mbane/TRC-3 Feb. 1988-Cape Town.

50. 'Seven blacks die in police ambush', *Guardian*, 4 Mar. 1986.

51. 'Sentence', p. 2/*Sparg*; 'Statement of Marion Monica Sparg', p. 23: UWHP-TLC/E13.

52. 'Blast at police headquarters injures at least four', *UPI*, 4 Mar. 1986; 'Blasts: Second White woman is held', *Citizen*, 12 Mar. 1986.

53. 'Police fire tear gas at mourners, mine planted in police station', *AP*, 8 Mar. 1986.

54. 'Former journalist guilty of treason', *C. Times*, 4 Nov. 1986; 'Statement of Marion Monica Sparg', pp. 23–4.

55. F.T. Masango/TRC-8 Jun. 1999-Pretoria; 'Uitspraak', pp. 627–8/*Masina*.

56. M. Shaik to D. Shongwe, 7 Jul. 2002.

57. M. Shaik to P. O'Malley, 7 May 2004.

58. J.E. Makhura, TRC Amnesty Hearing, 9 Jun. 1999 (Pretoria): TRC2.

59. V.L. Sindane, TRC Amnesty Hearing, 13 Jul. 2000 (Pretoria): TRC2. For a biography of Glory Sedibe, see J. Dlamini, *Askari: A Story of Collaboration and Betrayal in the Anti-Apartheid Struggle* (Jacana, 2014).

60. Witness 'I.C. X1'/*S v A.M. Maseko et al.*, pp. 2647–8, 3070–72, 3105–6: UWHP-C&N/Am3 (hereafter ('*Maseko*').

61. 'Bylae: Die beskuldigdes het op 'n datum of datums', p. 24 and 'Opsomming van Wesenlike Feite Ingevolge Artikel 144 (3) (a) van Wet 51 van 1977', p. 1/*S v A.M. Maseko et al.*: NARS-TAB/Case No: CC319/87 (hereafter '*A.M. Maseko*').

62. 'Schedule A', p. 6, 'Schedule J', p. 2, 'Summary of substantial facts', p. 11/*Ngqungwana*; Q. Michels/*The Trial of the Thirteen*, p. 62.

63. P. Mayapi and I.N. Ndzamela, TRC Amnesty Hearing, 28 Apr. 1999 (East London): TRC2; 'Instant Amnesty for MK Bombers', http://www.justice.gov.za/trc/media%5C1999%5C9904/s990428.htm (accessed 28 Apr. 2015).

64. 'Limpet mine blitz on casino', *Daily News*, 19 Apr. 1986; 'Boy of 12 dies in casino blast', *Weekend Post*, 19 Apr. 1986; 'Casino blast did not scare gamblers', *Sunday Star*, 20 Apr. 1986; 'Casino-bom eis tweede slagoffer', *Rapport*, 20 Apr. 1986.

65. 'Schedule J', p. 2, 'Schedule K', p. 1, 'Aanhangsel "A". C. Esau', p. 1, C. Esau, Statement, p. 1/*Ngqungwana*.

66. 'Three blacks wounded by landmines, police blame ANC', *AP*, 21 Apr. 1986; 'Dragnet is thrown around Ermelo', *Star*, 22 Apr. 1986; 'Only an old habit saved farmer (68) from death', *Star*, 23 Apr. 1986; 'Bylae: Die beskuldigdes het op 'n datum of datums', p. 3/*A.M. Maseko*.

67. L.B. Ngqungwana, (Background) Statement, pp. 6–7; L.B. Ngqungwana, (Post Arrest) Statement, p. 1; 'Summary of substantial facts', p. 13; 'Schedule J', p. 3/*Ngqungwana*; 'Esau, Cecil, (31) (35)?': UNISA(MF)-Karis-Gerhart Collection 'From Protest to Challenge'/Part 5, C.J.1.

68. S. Gunn, '"A very lonely road": The Story of a former MK Commander', in D. Foster *et al.* (eds.), *The Theatre of Violence: Narratives of Protagonists in the South African Conflict* (Institute of Justice and Reconciliation, 2005), pp. 211–12; 'Getting her breath back', *Witness*, 2 Mar. 2011.

69. G.C. Webster/*R.J. McBride*, pp. 2–4; 'Summary of Substantial Facts', p. 25/*Webster*; B. Rostron, *Till Babylon Falls*, p. 137.

70. D.J. McBride in *S v A.A. du Preez* et al., pp. 531–2: NARS-NAB/Case No: CC4/87.

71. A.A. du Preez/*A.A. du Preez*, pp. 491–2.

72. D.J. McBride/*A.A. du Preez*, pp. 532–5; W.W. Khumalo/*R.J. McBride*, pp. 487–8.

73. D.J. McBride and E. Ngcobo/*A.A. du Preez*, pp. 220, 537–9; R.J. McBride and G.C. Webster/*R.J. McBride*, pp. 5–6, 1563–6.

74. M.A. le Cordier and G.C. Webster/*R.J. McBride*, pp. 7–15, 1356–7.

75. R.J. McBride and G.C. Webster/*R.J. McBride*, pp. 15, 91, 1572.

76. G.C. Webster and R.J. McBride/*R.J. McBride*, pp. 17, 86, 1772–3; G. Apelgren, Section 29 Statement: OU-RHL/MSS AAM 1835.

77. M. Maharaj to H. Barrell, p. 528.

78. M. Maharaj to P. O'Malley, 24 Aug. 1998.

79. *Ibid.*; M. Maharaj to H. Barrell, p. 529.

80. *Mission to South Africa: The Commonwealth Report*, pp. 112, 114–17 (The text of the 'Possible Negotiating Concept' is reproduced pp. 103–4).

81. 'Motswana dies in another SADF raid', *BDN*, 19 May 1986; 'South Africa: Raids alleged ANC targets in three countries', *IPS*, 19 May 1986; 'South Africa attacks rebels in three countries', *UPI*, 19 May 1986.

82. *Mission to South Africa: The Commonwealth Report*, pp. 118–19.

83. A.A. Forbes and P. Jacobs (admissions)/*Forbes*, pp. 1222–3.

84. F.T. Masango/TRC-8 Jun. 1999-Pretoria; F.T. Masango, Statement, 2 Oct. 1986/*Masina*, 'Uitspraak', p. 647.

85. B.F. Msibi, TRC Amnesty Hearing, 5 Sep. 2000 (Durban): TRC2; B.F. Msibi, TRC Amnesty Hearing, 28 Mar. 2000 (Pinetown): TRC2.

86. 'Schedule H – Accused Eight'/*S v T.S. Yengeni et al.*, p. 1: UKZN-AP/PC92/3/2/1.

87. 'Mxolisi Petane "destined for future greatness in SA"', *C. Times*, 29 Dec. 1987.

88. W.J. Coetzee, L. de Jager, A. Pretorius and J.V. van der Merwe, TRC Amnesty Hearing, 4 Oct. 1999 (Pretoria): TRC2.

89. E.M. Lukhele, O. Masina and N.G. Potsane/*Masina*, 'Uitspraak', pp. 635, 639–40, 642, 644.

90. G. Apelgren, Section 29 Statement: OU-RHL/MSS AAM 1835; B. Rostron, *Till Babylon Falls*, p. 190; R.J. McBride, TRC Amnesty Hearing, 5 Oct. 1999 (Durban): TRC2.

91. 'Mines hit Natal border', *Times*, 11 Jun. 1986; 'Army swarms into blast-hit Volksrust' and 'Father could not move for fear that his son was dead', *Star*, 11 Jun. 1986; 'Bylae: Die beskuldigdes het op 'n datum of datums', pp. 3–4/*A.M. Maseko*; 'Charge Sheet', p. 25: UWHP-TLC/E19; Evidence read into the record of the TRC Amnesty Hearing, 30 Nov. 1999 (Pretoria): TRC2.

92. P.W. Botha/*UPI*, 12 Jun. 1986.

93. R.J. McBride/*R.J. McBride*, pp. 1580–81.

94. *Ibid.*, p. 1593.

95. '3 die in Durban blast', *Citizen*, 16 Jun. 1986; 'Massive hunt after bomb blast', *NM*, 16 Jun. 1986; 'Durban car-bomb probe points to ANC', *Star*, 16 Jun. 1986; R.G. Davidson, M.A. le Cordier and R.J. McBride/*R.J. McBride*, pp. 790–91, 897–900, 1601.

96. 'Bylae: Die beskuldigdes het op 'n datum of datums', pp. 25–6 and 'Opsomming van Wesenlike

Feite Ingevolge Artikel 144 (3) (a) van Wet 51 van 1977', p. 2/*A.M. Maseko*; 'Editorial: Heroes, not criminals', *Sechaba*, Mar. 1989, p. 1.

97. 'Gunmen kill 5 officials', *S. Times*, 6 Jul. 1986; 'Bylae: Die beskuldigdes het op 'n datum of datums', p. 26/*A.M. Maseko*.

98. C. Baadjies and A. Dramat (admissions)/*Forbes*, pp. 1286, 1288.

99. M.A. le Cordier/*A.A. du Preez*, p. 122; *Till Babylon Falls*, pp. 227–8; Z. Narkedien (née G. Apelgren), TRC Amnesty Hearing, 7 Oct. 1999 (Durban): TRC2.

100. 'Bylae: Die beskuldigdes het op 'n datum of datums', p. 27/*A.M. Maseko*.

101. 'Man het beken hy't bom in motor geplant', *Die Burger*, 14 Nov. 1987; 'Terroris skreeu ná uitspraak', *Die Burger*, 2 Dec. 1987; 'ANC "soldier" found guilty of terrorism', *Citizen*, 2 Dec. 1987; 'ANC trialist salutes as he is convicted', *C. Times*, 2 Dec. 1987.

102. 'Bylae: Die beskuldigdes het op 'n datum of datums', p. 27/*A.M. Maseko*.

103. B.W. Nofamela, 'Affidavit', p. 3/*P.M. Williams v The State*: UWHP-*Williams*; Witness 'I.C. X1'/*Maseko*, p. 2597; C.P. Deetlefs and E.A. de Kock, TRC Amnesty Hearing, 14–15 Feb. 2000 (Pretoria): TRC2.

104. B.A. Nofemela to Harms Commission, p. 446: UWHP-*Harms*; B.W. Nofamela, 'Affidavit', pp. 3–5/*Williams*; E.A. de Kock and J. Koole/TRC-15 Feb. 2000-Pretoria; E. de Kock, *A Long Night's Damage*, p. 134.

105. E.A. de Kock, TRC Amnesty Hearings, 29 Nov. 1999 (Pretoria): TRC2; E.A. de Kock/TRC-15 Feb. 2000-Pretoria.

106. Indictment, p. 24 and T.P. Tshika, Statement ('Verklaring deur Thuso Paulos Tshika'), p. 2/*Tshika*; T. Tshika, TRC Amnesty Hearing, 28 Mar. 2000 (Pinetown): TRC2.

107. P. Harris, *In a Different Time* (Umuzi, 2008), p. 117.

108. K.D. Mkhwamubi, M. Mkhwamubi and T. Mpembe/*S v K.D. Mkhwamubi et al.*, pp. 13–14, 101–5, 128, 156: NARS-NAB/Case No: CC19/87; 'Summary of Substantial Facts', p. 9/*Mkhwamubi*.

109. G.S. Schoon and 'Judgement'/*Mkhwamubi*, pp. 80, 173.

110. 'Natal bomb blasts: two held', *NM*, 14 Nov. 1986; S.T. Hlubi and S.T. Ndwandwe/*Tshika*, pp. 210–12, 216–17; B.F. Msibi and T. Tshika/TRC-28 Mar. 2000-Pinetown.

111. B.F. Msibi and T. Tshika/TRC-5 Sep. 2000-Durban; B.M.T. Sithole, 'Declaration' (Exh.R1), p. 4/*Tshika*.

112. '24 hurt by twin Natal bomb blasts', *NM*, 12 Nov. 1986; '22 hurt in blast at Newcastle', *Citizen*, 12 Nov. 1986; 'Newcastle blasts leave 21 injured', *NW*, 12 Nov. 1986; 'Huge police search for Natal bombers', *Star*, 12 Nov. 1986; 'Two held after Newcastle blasts', *Star*, 14 Nov. 1986; 'Arrests after Natal blasts', *C. Times*, 14 Nov. 1986; M.M. Brown/*Tshika*, pp. 253–6.

113. 'Newcastle blasts leave 21 injured'; C. Davidson, T. Tshika, E.C. van Niekerk and H. Veldman/*Tshika*, pp. 1121, 1506–9, 1600, 1626–7.

114. 'Terroris skreeu ná uitspraak', *Die Burger*, 2 Dec. 1987; 'ANC "soldier" found guilty of terrorism', *Citizen*, 2 Dec. 1987; 'Mxolisi Petane "destined for future greatness in SA"', *C.Times*, 29 Dec. 1987.

115. 'Schedule B – Accused 2'/*Yengeni*, p. 3; '11 "ANC members" to face treason charges', *Argus*, 16 Mar. 1988.

116. '5 people abducted', *S. Observer*, 13 Dec. 1986; 'It was a 6 hour terror drive', *Times(Swz)*, 16 Dec. 1986.

117. '5 people abducted'; 'Nyoni grief', *Times(Swz)*, 17 Dec. 1986.

118. '5 people abducted'.

119. *Ibid.*; S. Maphumulo, unpublished memoirs, pp. 422–8: OU-RHL/*Barrell*.

120. 'It was a 6 hour terror drive'.

121. 'Samesprekings met RSDF op 12 Des 86': SANDF-AMI/14/127.

122. P.W. Botha/*UPI*, 12 Dec. 1986.

123. 'Raided again: who is this victim?', *Times(Swz)*, 17 Dec. 1986; 'Top African National Congress member Ebrahim Ismael Ebrahim tells the story of how he was abducted – "by South African agents" – from Swaziland to SA last year', *The New Nation*, 6–12 Aug. 1987.

124. M. Shaik to P. O'Malley, 7 May 2004: *O'Malley*.

125. 'Summary of Substantial Facts', p. 13/*A.A. Forbes*: UWHP-C&N/Af1-2 (hereafter *A.A. Forbes*); A. Forbes and N.L. Pedro (admissions)/*Forbes*, pp. 1275, 1280, 2209.

126. M.Z. Mncube and M.T. Mncube, Statement/*Mncube*, pp. 2362–5, 3372; M.Z. Mncube, TRC Amnesty Hearing, 3 Jul. 2000 (Messina): TRC2.

127. A.Z. Eloff, M.Z. Mncube, M.Z. Mncube Statement, and P.M. Oosthuizen/*Mncube*, pp. 510, 553–8, 554, 2370, 3397.

128. A.Z. Eloff, M.T. Mncube Statement, and M.Z. Mncube/*Mncube*, pp. 555–9, 2376–7, 2381–5, 3373.

129. J.V. Rall/*Mncube*, pp. 590–94.

130. H.H. Franken, M.T. Mncube and M.Z. Mncube Statement, M.Z. Mncube/*Mncube*, pp. 997–8, 2389–91, 3373, 3398.

131. T. Jenkin in 'The Vula Connection', documentary broadcast on e-News Africa, 20 Jul. 2014.

132. E. Goosen, TRC Amnesty Hearing, 21 Apr. 1999 (Pretoria): TRC2.

133. J.V. van der Merwe, TRC Amnesty Hearing, 22 Apr. 1999 (Pretoria): TRC2.

134. 'Police report land mine attack', *UPI*, 30 Mar. 1987; D. Mkhonto, TRC Amnesty Hearing, 2 May 2000 (White River): TRC2.

135. M. Shaik to P. O'Malley, 7 May 2004.

136. R.I. Aboobaker to P. O'Malley, 21 Feb. 2003.

137. *Ibid.*

138. W.J. Momberg, TRC Amnesty Hearing, 21 Apr. 1999 (Pretoria): TRC2.

139. 'Pretoria suspected of Botswana car bombing', *Guardian*, 10 Apr. 1987.

140. F.A. Dlodlo in TRC Human Rights Violations Submissions – Q&As, 3 May 1996: UWHP-TRC(CD)/HRVtrans> Methodis> DLODLO.

141. 'South African Guerrilla Chief Resigns', *AP*, 22 Apr. 1987.

142. A. Dramat, A. Forbes and P.A. Jacobs (admissions), and A. Dramat and N.L. Pedro testimony/*Forbes*, pp. 1273, 2176, 2178–9, 2400.

143. E.J. Elias/*Forbes*, pp. 1213–4.

144. 'South Africa vote strengthens hold of Botha's party', *NYT*, 7 May 1987.

145. *UPI*, 7 May 1987.

146. 'ANC fight must be stepped up, says Tambo'. *Guardian*, 9 May 1987.

Season of Violence

1. J.T. Benzien, W.R. Liebenberg, J.L. Nel, D.R. Roman, E.H. Stoffels/*Forbes*, pp. 673–4, 676–7, 684, 692–3, 797, 835–8.

2. J. Koetle (7500/97) *et al.*, Amnesty Decision: UWHP-TRC(CD)/AMNESTY>64.

3. S. Nyanda to P. O'Malley, 27 Oct. 2001.

4. F.A. Dlodlo/TRC-3 May 1996-Johannesburg.

5. *Ibid.*; 'Five gunned three dead' and 'Night of terror', *Times(Swz)*, 25 May 1987; 'Three die in cold blood', *S. Observer*, 25 May 1987; 'Survivor tells her story', *Times(Swz)*, 26 May 1987; 'Southern Africa's secret war: ANC guerrilla leaders slain by hit squads', *TS*, 19 Jul. 1987; C.S. Mhlalo [née Ntshontsho] in E. Masilela, *Number 43, Trelawney Park, KwaMagogo* (David Philip, 2007), p. 139.

6. S.M.M. Nyanda, Affidavit, pp. 1–4: UWHP-*Mathabe/Nyanda*.

7. S. Nyanda to P. O'Malley, 27 Oct. 2001; S. Nyanda in 'The Vula Connection', documentary broadcast on e-News Africa, 20 Jul. 2014.

8. S. Makana, 'Suggestions from the units', 4 Jun. 1987: UCT-SC/P29.4.

9. C. Braam, *Operation Vula* (Jacana, 2004), pp. 82–6.

10. S. Gunn, '"A very lonely road"', p. 215.

11. 'For First Time, Rebels in Angola Detain South African Guerrillas', *NYT*, 15 Sep. 1987.

12. 'What white ANC cell did', *P.News*, 12 Jun. 1989; 'Broederstroom three "inspired by idealism"', *Citizen*, 22 Jun. 1989.

13. R.A.M. Toka, TRC Amnesty Hearing, 26 Jan. 1999 (Pretoria): TRC2.

14. U. Abrahamse, 'Just before I commenced my studies at the University of Botswana ...', unpublished memoirs, p. 91.

15. 'Outrage! Three gunned down', *Times(Swz)*, 10 Jul. 1987; 'Dikeledi was most wanted', *Times(Swz)*, 13 Jul. 1987; 'ANC man named … and SA is blamed', *Times(Swz)*, 16 Jul. 1987; 'Southern Africa's secret war: ANC guerrillas slain by hit squads', *TS*, 19 Jul. 1987; 'ANCSA ZA45390': UFH-ANC/CM-47/123.

16. J.T. Benzien/*Forbes*, pp. 929–30; 'It was either the "terrorist" or the cops – one had to be killed', *M&G*, 25 Apr.–1 May, 2014; 'Expert describes police version of Kriel killing "Improbable"', *South*, 15–19 Dec. 1988.

17. 'Schedule A – Accused 1', and 'Schedule B – Accused 2'/*S v T.S. Yengeni et al.*, pp. 3–5: UKZN-AP/PC92/3/2/1; 'City car bomb: Search for clues', *Argus*, 21 Jul. 1987; 'Two blasts rock city', *C. Times*, 21 Jul. 1987; 'Bomb explodes at Cape Town airport', *UPI*, 22 Jul. 1987; 'DF Malan bomb blast', *Argus*, 22 Jul. 1987.

18. 'Police probe bomb claims', *C. Times*, 25 Jul. 1987.

19. 'ANC member was shot in the back post-mortem examination reveals', *Times*, 27 Jul. 1987.

20. S. Gunn, '"A very lonely road"', p. 215.

21. 'South African bomber sees "lots of death"', *TS*, 8 Oct. 1988; H.J. Grosskop, TRC Amnesty Hearing, 21 Nov. 2000 (Pretoria): TRC2.

22. M. Nchangasi/*S v G. Nyembe et al.*, pp. 136–7: UWHP-*Nyembe*.

23. 'Umtata bombing: Call to extradite ANC man', *Argus*, 12 Apr. 1988; '"Mpilo" is dead, but his ghost haunts our courts', *WM*, 28 Jul. 1988; 'Extradited to face terror charges', *City Press*, 4 Sep. 1988.

24. 'Sluier hang oor vierde man', *Die Transvaler*, 24 Oct. 1989; '"Lenin" and the Jo'burg kugel', *Sunday Star*, 5 May 1991.

25. W.J. de Lange, V.J. Gcaba and R. Ngwane/*Forbes*, pp. 433, 453–4, 465, 513, 519–20.

26. J.T. Benzien and A. Dramat/*Forbes*, pp. 964–6.

27. 'Schedule A – Accused 1'/*Yengeni*, p. 5; J.T. Benzien, TRC Amnesty Hearing, 14 Jul. 1997: UWHP-TRC(CD)/amntrans > ct3 > BENZIEN; T. Yengeni to W. Kodesh, transcript, p. 13: UWC-MCA/MCA6-386.

28. 'Schedule B – Accused 2'/*Yengeni*, p. 8; 'Umtata bombing: Call to extradite ANC man', *Argus*, 12 Apr. 1988.

29. B. Rostron, *Till Babylon Falls*, pp. 303–4; M. Nchangasi/*Nyembe*, pp. 136, 152.

30. 'ANC network "smashed"', *Argus*, 9 May 1988; E. Schreiner, 'Trial notes' for 'Sept 17th': UKZN-AP/PC92/3/2/1; I.P. Siyali, TRC Amnesty Hearing, 21 Oct. 1999 (Cape Town): TRC2.

31. 'Schedule I – Accused 9'/*Yengeni*, p. 3; G. Kruser and J.T. Benzien/TRC-14 Jul. 1997-Cape Town.

32. 'South Africa: Busts ANC cell, 49 in custody', *IPS*, 7 Oct. 1987.

33. G.C. Khwela, 'uMkonto we Sizwe's contribution to the defence of the African Revolution in Angola', *Journal for Contemporary History*, 28 (2), 2003, pp. 107–8; '1987 Military Report and 1988 Annual Military Programme', p. 10: UCT-SC/P29.5.

34. A. Kasrils to W. Kodesh, 23 Aug. 1993: UWC-MCA/MCA6-295b; M. Senzangakhone, E. Mabitse, U. Abrahamse and G. Molebatsi, 'Umkonto we sizwe: Within living memories (Part 3)', in *Umrabulo*, 13 (2nd Quarter), 2002, http://www.anc.org.za/show.php?id=2933 (accessed 21 Aug. 2014).

35. 'Radicals Promoted in ANC "Army"', *FT*, 29 Oct. 1987.

36. *UPS*, 6 Nov. 1987.

37. 'South African myth becomes a man again', *TS*, 15 Nov. 1987.

38. S. Tshwete, 'Politics and the Army', pp. 2–3, a paper presented to ANC Department of Political Education Workshop, 23–28 Feb. 1988, Lusaka: UCT-SC/P29.1.

39. 'Government clamp on opposition prompts criticism', *AP*, 25 Feb. 1988.

40. 'Bom-hel op Benoni beskryf', *Beeld*, 2 Mar. 1988; 'Remote-control mine may have blasted SAAF bus', *Citizen*, 2 Mar. 1988; 'What white ANC cell did', *P.News*, 12 Jun. 1989; D.M. de Lange, TRC Amnesty Hearing, 31 Jul. 2000 (Johannesburg): TRC2.

41. R.A.M. Toka, TRC Amnesty Hearing, 26 Jan. 1999 (Pretoria): TRC2.

42. M.I. Shaik/TRC-7 May 1998-Pretoria.

43. '2 limpet mines defused after massive car blast', *Star*, 18 Mar. 1988; 'Car bomb kills 3', *Sowetan*,

18 Mar. 1988; 'Manhunt for bombers is on', *C. Times*, 18 Mar. 1988; 'Bomber hunted, R50 000 reward', *Citizen*, 18 Mar. 1988; 'Search hots up', *Star*, 19 Mar. 1988.

44. J.T. Maleka, G. Mathe and F. Pitsi, TRC Amnesty Hearing, 26–27 Jan. 1999 (Pretoria): TRC2.

45. 'Govt slams SA's murderous acts', *BDN*, 29 Mar. 1988; 'President visits raided house', *BDN*, 6 Apr. 1988; 'South Africa changes version of its Botswana raid', *AP*, 7 Apr. 1988.

46. R.A.M. Toka/TRC-26 Jan. 1999-Pretoria.

47. 'Explosion kills man near crowded theatre', *AP*, 15 Apr. 1988; P. Maluleka, TRC Amnesty Hearing, 25 Jan. 1999 (Pretoria): TRC2.

48. 'SAP operated secret ANC radio station', *Star*, 13 May 1988; 'Fifth man escaped Broederstroom net', *C. Times*, 14 May 1988; 'Só is ANC verklap', *Die Burger*, 14 May 1988; D.M. de Lange/TRC-31 Jul. 2000-Johannesburg.

49. 'Blasts in City' and 'Four hurt', *P.News*, 26 May 1988; 'Timetable of terror', *P.News*, 27 May 1988; G. Mathe and F. Pitsi/TRC-26–27 Jan. 1999-Pretoria.

50. 'Late-night explosion in Jo'burg dustbin is still a mystery', *Sunday Star*, 29 May 1988; 'Bomb explodes in Egoli refuse truck', *City Press*, 29 May 1988; 'Woman injured in blast at Jo'burg Station', *Citizen*, 30 May 1988; *C. Times*, p. 2, 30 May 1988.

51. C. Hani and S. Tshwete to J. Battersby, Jun. 1998: UWHP-KGC/I-12.

52. A.J. Vlok, TRC Amnesty Hearing, 20 Jul. 1988 (Pretoria): TRC2.

53. E.A. de Kock and F.J. Pienaar, TRC Amnesty Hearing, 26 Jul. 1999 (Durban): TRC2; E. de Kock, *A Long Night's Damage*, pp. 147–8.

54. F.K. Theron, TRC Amnesty Hearing, 28 Jul. 1999 (Durban): TRC2.

55. E.A. de Kock/TRC-26 Jul. 1999-Durban.

56. C.J. Botha, M.D. Ras and J.H. Tait, TRC Amnesty Hearing, 28 Jul. 1999 (Durban): TRC2.

57. E.A. de Kock/TRC-26 Jul. 1999-Durban; E. de Kock, *A Long Night's Damage*, p. 150.

58. F. Pitsi/TRC-26 Jan. 1999-Pretoria.

59. A. Dlodlo in K.L. Makau, 'Aspects of the Experiences of 10 women in MK: 1976–1988' (MA thesis, University of Johannesburg, 2009), pp. 54–5; The Presidency, 'The Order of Mendi for Bravery in Silver' awarded to Phila Portia Ndwandwe, http://www.thepresidency.gov.za/pebble.asp?relid=7642 (accessed 8 Jul. 2014).

60. 'Report of a Commission of Inquiry set up in November 1989 by the National Working Committee of the National Executive Committee of the African National Congress to investigate the circumstances leading to the death of Mzwakhe Ngwenya (also known as Thami Zulu or TZ)', pp. 7–8.

61. F.K. Theron/TRC-28 Jul. 1999-Durban.

62. A. Dlodlo in K.L. Makau, 'Aspects of the Experiences of 10 women in MK', p. 55.

63. 'Ellis Park Rugby Stadium Car Bomb', memo on amnesty applications of A. Shoke *et al.*, pp. 5–6 and L. Dumakude, p. 98 of testimony to Truth and Reconciliation Commission Amnesty Hearing, 4 Aug. 1998: UWHP-EPCB.

64. 'Witnesses describe car-bomb scene', *Star*, 3 Jul. 1988; 'Ellis bomb kills 2', *Sowetan*, 4 Jul. 1988; 'Street resembled battlefield', *P.News*, 4 Jul. 1988.

65. S. Nyanda to P. O'Malley, 27 Oct. 2001; M. Maharaj to P. O'Malley, 19 Sep. 2003.

66. T. Memela to P. O'Malley, 27 Feb. 2002.

67. 'Mr X'/S v D.N. Mathambo, pp. 423, 434–5: UWHP-*Mathambo*; D. Mathambo, 'Contents of Statement to Magistrate Christiaan Johannes Botha made on the 26th July 1988 at the Johannesburg Magistrate's Court', p. 11/*Mathambo*.

68. ANC second submission to the TRC, Appendix Seven, 'Case Study 2'.

69. '57 hurt in restaurant bomb blast horror', *S. Times*, 21 Jul. 1988; 'Bomb blast baby's miracle', *Sunday Star*, 31 Jul. 1988; 'Victims tell of blast horror', *Citizen*, 1 Aug. 1988; 'Benoni blast victim named', *Business Day*, 1 Aug. 1988; Adv. Steenkamp and E.P. Sigasa, TRC Amnesty Hearing, 7 Sep. 1998: UWHP-TRC(CD)/amntrans> benoni2> BENONI1.

70. 'Report of a Commission of Inquiry … to investigate the circumstances leading to the death of Mzwakhe Ngwenya', pp. 7, 8, 15–6.

71. T. Memela to P. O'Malley, 27 Feb. 2002.

72. 'Farmer sees police kill five suspected insurgents', *Star*, 5 Aug 1988.

73. 'Protocol of Geneva', 5 Aug. 1988, in *Namibian Independence and Cuban Troop Withdrawal* (CTP Book Printers, 1989), pp. 30–31.

74. 'Pursuit after border shootout', *Star*, 10 Aug. 1988; M.J. Rapholo, Statement, p. 5: UWHP-*Rapholo*; J.M. Rapholo, TRC Amnesty Hearing, 18 Apr. 2000 (Johannesburg): TRC2.

75. M. Maharaj and S. Nyanda in 'The Vula Connection', documentary broadcast on e-News Africa, 20 Jul. 2014; T. Memela to R. Suttner, 20 Aug. 2003, pp. 17–18: RSC/*Aluka*; T. Memela to P. O'Malley, 27 Feb. 2002; M. Maharaj to P. O'Malley, 19 Sep. 2003.

76. G.N. Erasmus and W.F. Schoon, TRC Amnesty Hearing, 23 Jul. 1998 (Pretoria): TRC2; E.A. de Kock, TRC Amnesty Hearing, 29 Jul. 1998 (Pretoria): TRC2.

77. E.A. de Kock/TRC-29 Jul. 1998-Pretoria.

78. 'Huge blast at Council of Churches HQ', *Argus*, 31 Aug. 1988; 'Khotso probe is hampered by unsafe conditions', *Star*, 1 Sep. 1988; 'Khotso house blast caused by car-bomb?', *Citizen*, 1 Sep. 1988; 'Bombing of Khotso House condemned by church leaders', *Cape Times*, 1 Sep. 1988.

79. S. Modise, 'Mr X.1', 'Mr X.3' and 'Mr X.4'/*S v S. Modise*, pp. 84–8, 119–21, 123, 125, 132: UWHP-*Modise*; J. Mbane/TRC-3 Feb. 1988-Cape Town; L.P. Mntambo, TRC Amnesty Hearing, 1 Nov. 1999 (Johannesburg): TRC2.

80. 'Blast hurts man outside government building', *AP*, 28 Sep. 1988; S. Gunn, '"A very lonely road"', pp. 216–17; S. Hendricks and V.R. November, TRC Amnesty Hearing, 28 Oct. 1999 (Cape Town): TRC2.

81. Police spokesman/SAPA, 29 Sep. 1988: BBC-3 Oct. 1988.

82. Mr Visser/TRC Amnesty Hearing, 13 Nov. 1998 (Durban): TRC2; J.A. Forster, TRC Amnesty Hearing, 16 Nov. 1998 (Durban): TRC2; M. du Preez, *Of Warriors, Lovers and Prophets: Unusual Stories from South Africa's Past* (Zebra Press, 2004), pp. 206–7; 'NDWANDWE, Phila Portia (aka "Zandile" or "Zandi")', http://sabctrc.saha.org.za/victims/ndwandwe_phila_portia_aka_zandile_or_zandi.htm&tab=victims (accessed 8 Jul. 2014).

83. TRC Amnesty Application, AC/2001/112, http://www.justice.gov.za/trc/decisions/2001/ac21112.htm (accessed 8 Jul. 2014).

84. Mr Visser/TRC-13 Nov. 1998-Durban.

85. 'SA puts bounty on ANC guerrillas to ward off election disturbances', *Guardian*, 6 Oct. 1988; 'Police offer rewards for information on terrorists', *Star*, 8 Oct. 1988.

86. '29 bomb blasts in September', *Star*, 3 Oct. 1988.

87. 'Two blasts rock courts', *Star*, 6 Oct. 1988.

88. '6 injured in Tembisa bomb blast', *Star*, 7 Oct. 1988.

89. 'Four policemen hurt in latest blast', *Star*, 11 Oct. 1988.

90. 'Three hurt in blast on East Rand', *Star*, 14 Oct. 1988.

91. 'Police hold suspect assassin', *Star*, 24 Oct. 1988.

92. 'Did Witbank bombers die?', *Star*, 25 Oct. 1988.

93. 'Sunrise blast in Potch leaves policeman hurt', *Star*, 26 Oct. 1988.

94. 'Far-righters do well in local elections; black boycott keeps turn-out low', *AP*, 26 Oct. 1988.

95. Radio Freedom, 27 Oct. 1988: BBC-31 Oct. 1988.

96. H.J.P. Botha, TRC Amnesty Hearing, 13 Nov. 1998 (Durban): TRC2; C.A. van der Westhuizen, TRC Amnesty Hearing, 18 Nov. 1998 (Durban): TRC2.

97. H.J.P. Botha/TRC-13 Nov. 1998-Durban; S.J.G. du Preez, TRC Amnesty Hearing, 17 Nov. 1998 (Durban): TRC2.

98. 'Agreement among the People's Republic of Angola, the Republic of Cuba, and the Republic of South Africa', New York, 22 Dec. 1988, in *Namibian Independence and Cuban Troop Withdrawal* (CTP Book Printers, 1989), pp. 16–17.

99. 'ANC forces on way out of base', *Times(Zam)*, 9 Jan. 1989.

100. S. Gunn in TRC Human Rights Violations Submissions, 7 Aug. 1996 (Case No: CT/00792): UWHP-TRC(CD)/HRVtrans> Helder> CT00792.

101. 'Black bodies Umsa, Ucasa to join forces', *Star*, 19 Jan. 1989.
102. 'South Africa: Govt announces "National Forum" for urban blacks, *IPS*, 18 Jan. 1989; 'Windy promises', *NM*, 18 Jan. 1989.
103. 'President hospitalized with stroke', *AP*, 18 Jan. 1989.

Interregnum

1. 'Party crown passed to safe heir apparent', *FT*, 3 Feb. 1989.
2. 'New Party leader pledges Black rights, White segregation', *AP*, 8 Feb. 1989.
3. 'De Klerk sticks to Botha line', *Independent*, 9 Feb. 1989.
4. 'anc leader dismisses south africa's reform pledge', *Xinhua*, 9 Feb. 1989.
5. 'Moscow shifts ground on anti-apartheid struggle', *Guardian*, 18 Mar. 1989.
6. 'Soviets, in shift, press for accord in South Africa', *NYT*, 16 Mar. 1989.
7. SAPA, 15 Mar. 1989: BBC-17 Mar. 1989.
8. 'Thatcher expects Mandela to be freed soon', *Independent*, 17 Mar. 1989.
9. 'anc leader calls on oau to initiate strategy for south africa', *Xinhua*, 22 Mar. 1989.
10. P. Hlongwane and C. Mavundla to P. O'Malley, 21 Jul. 1992.
11. 'Gunmen shoot 2 ANC cadres', *Times(Zam)*, 21 Apr. 1989; 'Trigger-happy ANC cadres lambasted', *ZDM*, 24 Apr. 1989.
12. 'Suspected ANC guerrillas attack radar base', *UPI*, 3 May 1989; 'South Africa: Govt warns neighbor states; elections for Sept', *IPS*, 4 May 1989; 'South Africa: waving sabre at Zimbabwe as ANC shows muscle', *IPS*, 6 May 1989; D. Mdlulwa, TRC Amnesty Hearing, 22 May 2000 (Johannesburg): TRC2.
13. 'ANC urges civil disobedience in South Africa, says it fears assassinations', *WP*, 10 May 1989.
14. 'hijack of soviet plane foiled in tanzania', *Xinhua*, 18 May 1989; 'South Africans try to hijack ANC plane', *UPI*, 19 May 1989; 'South African pleads guilty after hijacking attempt' *AP*, 1 Jun. 1989; '"ANC"-kaper is bly hy is weer tuis', *Beeld*, 7 Nov. 1991.
15. 'ANC cadres disarmed', *Times(Zam)*, 26 May 1989.
16. 'bomb blasts rock zambia's capital', *Xinhua*, 19 Jun. 1989; 'Man blown to pieces', *ZDM*, 20 Jun. 1989; 'bomb blast rocks anc office building in lusaka', *Xinhua*, 21 Jun. 1989; 'ANC officials injured', *BDN*, 23 Jun. 1989.
17. 'ANC to consult its supporters on talks with Pretoria', *Independent*, 23 Jun. 1989.
18. 'Ruling Party to campaign on promise of Black national vote in 5 years', *AP*, 28 Jun. 1989.
19. 'ANC rejects reform plan, sees truce possible', *UPI*, 30 Jun. 1989; 'Pretoria must come to terms first – Tambo', *ZDM*, 1 Jul. 1989.
20. H. Suzman, *In No Uncertain Terms – Memoirs* (Sinclair-Stevenson, 1993), p. 163.
21. A. Sparks, *Tomorrow Is Another Country* (Struik, 1995), pp. 54–5; N. Mandela, *Long Walk to Freedom* (Abacus, 1995), pp. 658–9.
22. 'South Africa: Cape Town rocked by three bomb blasts', *IPS*, 24 Jul. 1989; 'Blown to pieces', *Argus*, 24 Jul. 1989; *UPI*, 5 Aug. 1989.
23. 'Blacks to seek treatment at White Hospitals in Defiance Campaign', *AP*, 26 Jul. 1989.
24. Shan Napier in TRC Human Rights Violations Submissions – Q&As, 26 Jul. 1996 (Soweto), http://www.justice.gov.za/trc/hrvtrans%5Csoweto/napier.htm (accessed 23 Jul. 2014).
25. 'Blacks launch Defiance Campaign by seeking care at White hospitals', *AP*, 2 Aug. 1989.
26. 'Police fire tear gas to break up activists' funeral', *AP*, 5 Aug. 1989; *UPI*, 5 Aug. 1989.
27. 'Zambia accuses ANC of abducting four', *Citizen*, 11 Aug. 1989; 'UN protests at ANC abduction of refugees', *Business Day*, 23 Aug. 1989; P. Trewhela, 'A Can of Worms: The Imprisonment of Hubert Sipho Mbeje', *Searchlight South Africa*, No. 9 (Aug. 1992), pp. 74–5.
28. 'ANC rounds up suspected bombers', *ZDM*, 11 Aug. 1989.
29. 'Zambia accuses ANC of abducting four', *Citizen*, 11 Aug. 1989; 'Tambo and ANC appear to be ailing', *Washington Times*, 14 Aug. 1989.
30. 'Tambo rests', *Times(Zam)*, 14 Aug. 1989.
31. 'De Klerk sworn in as Acting President, replaces Botha', *AP*, 15 Aug. 1989; 'Botha quits, criticizing

succesor', *WP*, 15 Aug. 1989; 'Botha quits after bitter showdown', *Times*, 15 Aug. 1989; 'Botha quits as president', *FT*, 15 Aug. 1989.

32. 'ANC hand over four ex-members to Zambia', *C.Times*, 24 Aug. 1989.

33. 'Anti-Apartheid groups call restrictions void', *NYT*, 18 Aug. 1989.

34. 'Anti-apartheid activists defy government crackdown', *UPI*, 21 Aug. 1989.

35. 'African leaders set conditions for talks in South Africa', *AP*, 21 Aug. 1989; 'Southern Africa: OAU Committee adopts "Harare" Declaration', *IPS*, 21 Aug. 1989; 'Strategy on SA endorsed', *Times(Zam)*, 23 Aug. 1989.

36. 'Declaration of the OAU Ad-Hoc Committee on Southern Africa on the Question of South Africa', Harare, Zimbabwe, 21 Aug. 1989: UWHP-AG2510/E4.4.2.

37. 'De Klerk and Kaunda avoid ANC issue', *Independent*, 29 Aug. 1989.

38. 'Tambo "recovering"', *Times*, 31 Aug. 1989.

39. 'Now Nats consider their options', *Star*, 8 Sep. 1989.

40. 'Pretoria's rulers lose many seats but retain power', *NYT*, 7 Sep. 1989.

41. 'SA marchers capitalize on success', *Guardian*, 14 Sep. 1989; '20,000 in Cape Town apartheid protest', *Independent*, 14 Sep. 1989; 'Thousands of Marchers conduct Multiracial Protest in Cape Town', *NYT*, 14 Sep. 1989.

42. 'De Klerk gives order for Sisulu release', *Independent*, 11 Oct. 1989.

43. 'Freed S African leaders seek ANC revival' and 'Grey-haired Sisulu goes home to continue the fight', *FT*, 16 Oct. 1989; 'Tribute to two dads – one dead, one alive', *Star*, 14 Dec. 2009.

44. 'First ANC rally for 29 years permitted', *FT*, 23 Oct. 1989.

45. MA Umtata, 'Spanning oor ANC in Transkei', 25 Oct. 1989: SANDF-AI/29/42.

46. 'Pretoria Gets a Goading From a Maverick Chief', *NYT*, 28 Dec. 1989.

47. W. Sisulu in SAPA, 29 Oct. 1989: BBC-31 Oct. 1989; '70,000 Greet Freed Anti-Apartheid Leaders at Record Rally', *AP*, 29 Oct. 1989; 'South Africa: "Today it is freedom"', *IPS*, 30 Oct. 1989; '70,000 Hail rebels in South Africa', *NYT*, 30 Oct. 1989; 'Soweto rally puts ANC on centre stage', *Guardian*, 30 Oct. 1989; '"Armed struggle" will continue, activists pledge', *TS*, 30 Oct. 1989; Shan Napier/TRC-26 Jul. 1996-Soweto.

48. 'Report of a Commission of Inquiry set up ... to investigate the circumstances leading to the death of Mzwakhe Ngwenya', pp. 1, 10, 12.

49. 'Meeting of the NWC held on 21/11/89 at 09:00 hours', pp. 1–2: UWHP-KGC/III-93.

50. E.A. de Kock, TRC Amnesty Hearing, 14–15 Feb. 2000 (Pretoria): TRC2.

51. A. Sparks, *Tomorrow Is Another Country*, pp. 103–6.

52. P. Waldmeir, *Anatomy of a Miracle* (Penguin, 1998), pp. 142–3.

53. J.M. Rapholo/TRC-18 Apr. 2000-Johannesburg.

54. 'Dood spoor by stasie', *Die Transvaler*, 12 Dec. 1989; 'Station blast is linked to strike', *P.News*, 12 Dec. 1989; Shan Napier/TRC-26 Jul. 1996-Soweto; 'Ahmed Timol MK unit', http://www.ahmedti mol.co.za/ahmed-timol-mk-unit (accessed 23 Jul. 2014); A. Kumar, *Husband of a Fanatic: A Personal Journey through India, Pakistan, Love, and Hate* (New Press, 2005), pp. 187–8 (thanks to Elizabeth Williams of Goldsmiths, University of London, for facilitating access to this edition of the book); 'Tribute to two dads – one dead, one alive', *Star*, 14 Dec. 2009.

55. Mandela-Stengel Conversations, pp. 204–5: NMF(CM).

56. Representations on behalf of Jacob Rapholo, 12 May 1991, pp. 6–7: UWHP-*Rapholo*.

57. 'South African Rebels vow new attacks', *TS*, 9 Jan. 1990.

58. J. Carlin, 'ANC clings to myth of the armed struggle', *Independent*, 9 Jan. 1990.

59. 'Leaders touch down to emotional welcome', *ZDM*, 16 Jan. 1990; 'Waiting for Mandela', *Newsweek* (U.S. ed.), 29 Jan. 1990.

60. J.M. Rapholo/TRC-18 Apr. 2000-Johannesburg.

61. 'ANC admits inability to intensify armed struggle', *UPI*, 18 Jan. 1990; 'ANC Prepares to Take the Initiative on Negotiations', *Guardian*, 19 Jan. 1990; 'ANC admit limits to armed struggle', *C.Times*, 19 Jan. 1990; 'ANC Admits Limits of Armed Struggle in South Africa', *Times*, 19 Jan. 1990; 'Let's boost armed struggle – Nzo', *ZDM*, 19 Jan. 1990; 'Frank Talking', *FT*, 2 Feb. 1990.

62. E. Sisulu, *Walter & Albertina Sisulu* (David Philip, 2002), p. 601.

63. B. Anderson to H. Barrell, pp. 30–31; Gavin Evans, 'Mbeki & Zuma – between devil and deep blue sea', 30 Dec. 2007, http://lists.fahamu.org/pipermail/debate-list/2008-January/010019.html (accessed 25 Mar. 2015).

64. C. Lubisi [recounting version told to him by H. Gwala] to R. Lundie, pp. 11–12: UKZN-AP/95APB7.

65. E. Sisulu, *Walter & Albertina Sisulu*, p. 602.

PART VI: ENDGAME

Homecoming

1. 'De Klerk's Peace Offer', *Independent*, 3 Feb. 1990.

2. 'ANC vows to continue armed struggle', *UPI*, 3 Feb. 1990; 'On first legal day, ANC reassesses strategy', *AP*, 3 Feb. 1990.

3. R. Kasrils to P. O'Malley, 12 Jun. 2003.

4. 'Jubilation as Mandela leaves', *C. Times*, 12 Feb. 1990.

5. 'Triumph and bloodshed', *NW*, 12 Feb. 1990; 'Schoolboy dies, 13 hurt in Parade violence', *C. Times*, 12 Feb. 1990.

6. 'Text of Nelson Mandela speech', *AP*, 12 Feb. 1990.

7. 'Mandela support for Nationalization worries Businessmen', *AP*, 12 Feb. 1990.

8. '50 killed in Natal as violence flares', *NW*, 13 Feb. 1990.

9. 'Operation Hunger campaign for refugees', *Star*, 14 Feb. 1990.

10. 'ANC rebels seek Mandela aid', *Times*, 11 Apr. 1990.

11. 'Killer hails ANC leader in 'Kei', *S. Times*, 22 Apr. 1990.

12. 'MK Commander Vena acquitted in Umtata', *New Nation*, 31 May 1990.

13. SAPA, 16 May 1990: BBC-19 May 1990; BBC-26 Apr. 1990, 'Dissident ANC members detained on return from exile'; R.V. Shange in 'Reports of the Commission of Enquiry into certain allegations of cruelty and human rights abuse against ANC prisoners and detainees by ANC members', 20 Aug. 1993 ['Motsuenyane Commission'], p. 117: UWHP-AG2918.

14. 'Jovial tone to ANC leaders' homecoming', *Independent*, 28 Apr. 1990.

15. 'ANC may suspend armed struggle', *FT*, 5 May 1990.

16. M. Maharaj to P. O'Malley, 22 Mar. and 12 Dec. 2002; M. Maharaj to H. Barrell, p. 400: OU-RHL/ *Barrell*.

17. SAPA, 16 May 1990: BBC-19 May 1990.

18. M. Matshaya, TRC Amnesty Hearing, 20 Apr. 1998: UWHP-TRC(CD)/amntrans > umtata1 >UMTATA.

19. S. Nyanda in 'The facts behind the fiction', *Mayibuye*, 1 (3), 1990, pp. 10–11.

20. 'FW challenges ANC', *Eastern Province Herald*, 8 Jun. 1990.

21. Amnesty International, 'South Africa: Torture, ill-treatment and executions in African National Congress camps', 2 Dec. 1992, p. 18: UWHP-AG2918; 'Motsuenyane Commission', p. 62; M. Matshaya/ TRC-20 Apr. 1998-Umtata.

22. 'AK-47 backs talks says ANC', *NM*, 18 Jun. 1990; 'French Govt aids ANC medically', *NW*, 18 Jun. 1990.

23. 'Battle looms at Nxamalala', *NW*, 19 Jun. 1990.

24. 'Inkatha people "cut off from Greytown by ANC"', *NW*, 21 Jun. 1990.

25. S. Gunn in TRC Human Rights Violations Submissions, 7 Aug. 1996 (Case No: CT/00792): UWHP-TRC(CD)/HRVtrans> Helder> CT00792; TRC Special Report, 'GUNN, Shirley Renee', http://sabctrc.saha.org.za/victims/gunn_shirley_renee.htm&tab=victims (accessed 7 Sep. 2015); S. Gunn, '"A very lonely road": The Story of a former MK Commander', in D. Foster *et al.* (eds.), *The Theatre of Violence: Narratives of Protagonists in the South African Conflict* (Institute of Justice and Reconciliation, 2005), p. 217.

26. 'Hani: talks could fix armed struggle issue', *DD*, 27 Jul. 1990.

27. 'MK chief promises "defence of people"', *C. Times*, 7 Jul. 1990.

28. 'Cop dies in shootout: no arrests', *C. Times*, 9 Jul. 1990; F. Booi, TRC Amnesty Hearing, 28 Oct. 1999 (Cape Town): TRC2.
29. H.J.P. Botha, TRC Amnesty Hearing, 19 Aug. 1999 (Durban): TRC2.
30. *Ibid.*
31. *Ibid.*
32. H.D. Stadler (compiled), *The other side of the story: a true perspective* (Contact, 1997), p. 97; J.A. Steyn, TRC Amnesty Hearing, 20 Aug. 1999 (Durban): TRC2; L.G. Wassermann, TRC Amnesty Hearing, 24 Aug. 1999 (Durban): TRC2; S. Nyanda to P. O'Malley, 27 Oct. 2001.
33. J. Mndebele, Statement, TRC Amnesty Hearing, 20–21 Jul. 1998: UWHP-TRC(CD)/amntrans> ermelo2> BLACAT1; N.M. Zwane, TRC Amnesty Hearing, 28 Jul. 1998: UWHP-TRC(CD)/ amntrans> ermelo2> BLACAT7; S. Nkonyane, TRC Amnesty Hearing, 29 Jul. 1998: UWHP-TRC(CD)/amntrans> ermelo2> BLACAT8.
34. M. Gushu, TRC Amnesty Hearing, 22 Jul. 1998: UWHP-TRC(CD)/amntrans> ermelo2> BLACAT2.
35. 'Mandela sees De Klerk after ANC threat', *Independent*, 21 Jul. 1990; M. Maharaj/TRC-23 Aug. 1999-Durban; M. Maharaj to P. O'Malley, 24 Aug. 1998.
36. SAPA, 18 Jul. 1990: BBC-20 Jul. 1990.
37. 'ANC intensifying all strategies, says Hani', *DD*, 19 Jul. 1990.
38. 'Mandela sees De Klerk after ANC threat'.
39. 'Hani: no regrets over speech', *DD*, 21 Jul. 1990.
40. 'ANC in crisis over links to communists', *Guardian*, 28 Jul. 1990.
41. 'Crackdown on communits', *Sunday Star*, 22 Jul. 1990.
42. 'The facts behind the fiction', pp. 10–11; M. Maharaj to N. Wrench and D. Price, 12 Dec. 2002: ['Vula-Other']/*O'Malley*; 'South Africa: ANC Executive Member Detained', *IPS*, 26 Jul. 1990.
43. 'Rooies se konkelary', *Beeld*, 26 Jul. 1990.
44. Mandela-Stengel Conversations, pp. 692–3: NMF(CM).
45. 'South Africa's red flag holds promise for the curious', *Independent*, 29 Jul. 1990.
46. 'Mandela distances himself from his Communist allies', *FT*, 30 Jul. 1990; 'ANC tightens links with communists', *Guardian*, 30 Jul. 1990; SAPA, 29 Jul. 1990: BBC-31 Jul. 1990.
47. 'De Klerk, Mandela avert crisis', *TS*, 2 Aug. 1990; 'South Africa: Stage set for "Groote Schuur II" August 6', *IPS*, 2 Aug. 1990.
48. 'African National Congress Suspends Its Guerrilla War', *NYT*, 7 Aug. 1990; SABC TV, 6 Aug. 1990: BBC-8 Aug. 1990.
49. Radio South Africa, 15 Aug. 1990: BBC-15 Aug. 1990.
50. 'Freedom by force "if needed"', *Citizen*, 13 Aug. 1990; 'Fighting talk by Gwala, Hani', *NW*, 13 Aug. 1990; 'ANC move a test for NP, says Gwala', *Sowetan*, 14 Aug. 1990.
51. 'Mandela and Buthelezi meeting now on the cards', *Times*, 21 Sep. 1990.
52. Radio Freedom, 21 Sep. 1990: BBC-24 Sep. 1990.
53. SAPA, 30 Sep. 1990: BBC-2 Oct. 1990.
54. S.W. Motaung, N.J. Sibisi and J.M. Sithole, TRC Amnesty Hearings, 29 Jul. 1997: UWHP-TRC(CD)/ amntrans > PMB3 > MOTAUNG and SIBISI.
55. M. Ras, TRC Amnesty Hearing, 20 Apr. 1999 (East London): TRC2.
56. *Ibid.*; 'Craig Duli killed', *DD*, 23 Nov. 1990; MA Transkei to Army Chief, INRAP 75/90 'Los Brokkies informasie ivm die mislukte staatsgreep in Transkei', pp. 2–5: SANDF-AI/29/43.
57. SAPA, 18 Dec. 1990: BBC-20 Dec. 1990.
58. 'DF Malan Accord: Report of the working group under paragraph three of the Pretoria Minute', http://www.anc.org.za/show.php?id=3890 (accessed 10 Apr. 2015).
59. 'anc-pretoria agreement released', *Xinhua*, 16 Feb. 1991; SAPA, 15 Feb. 1991: BBC-18 Feb. 1991.
60. SAPA, 15 Feb. 1991: BBC-18 Feb. 1991.
61. T. Mbeki to P. Waldmeir, 2nd interview, p. 8: UWHP-PWI.
62. SAPA, 16 Apr. 1991: BBC-18 Apr. 1991; 'ANC draws up plan for armed units to defend townships', *Times*, 17 Apr. 1991.

63. 'MK Man in court on arms charges', *DD*, 10 Jul. 1991; 'The Goldstone Commission: Submissions on behalf of the South African Defence Force regarding Umkhonto we Sizwe', p. 16: SANDF-AI(DIV)/28/221.
64. 'ANC bases in Transkei exposed', *Citizen*, 12 Jun. 1991.
65. 'ANC bases denied', *DD*, 13 Jun. 1991.
66. J.M. Makhanya, TRC Amnesty Hearing, 27 Mar. 2000 (Pinetown): TRC2; M.J. Majosi, TRC Amnesty Hearing, 21 Oct. 1998 (Durban): TRC2.
67. 'ANC National Conference July 1991 Durban Nelson Mandela's Closing Address', p. 4: UWHP-AG 2510/A2.2-2.2.2.2.
68. 'ANC leaders get mandate to pursue Pretoria talks', *Times*, 8 Jul. 1991.
69. M. Gushu and J. Mndebele Statement/TRC-20–22 Jul. 1998-Ermelo.
70. P. Mankahlana to P. Waldmeir, pp. 12–13: UWHP-PWI.
71. 'Police paid Inkatha to block ANC', *WM*, 19–25 Jul. 1991.
72. 'Mandela urges armed wing to restructure', *AFP*, 9 Aug. 1991; BBC-10 Aug. 1991, 'Mandela calls for national unity government; Senegal President supports De Klerk'.
73. SAPA, 10 Aug. 1991: BBC-13 Aug. 1991; 'MK comes clean', *Vrye Weekblad*, 23–29 Aug. 1991: UFH-ANC/GM-12/81.
74. 'MK warns Hani about leaving', *S. Times*, 11 Aug. 1991.
75. 'Compromise, but accord signed', 'Armed Zulus steal limelight' and 'War and Peace', *Sunday Star*, 15 Sep. 1991; See copy of 'National Peace Accord': UWHP-*Kasrils*/B4.1.
76. 'Hitches don't halt peace accord', *Star*, 16 Sep. 1991.
77. SABC TV, 15 Sep. 1991: BBC-17 Sep. 1991.
78. 'Buthelezi gloomy, despite peace accord', *AFP*, 16 Sep. 1991.

Transition

1. 'South Africa: ANC Military Delegation Heads for India', *IPS*, 17 Oct. 1991.
2. M. Gushu/TRC-22 Jul. 1998-Ermelo.
3. *Ibid.*; SAPA, 21 Jul. 1998.
4. 'Psychological win for Mandela in clash of SA heavyweights', *Guardian*, 23 Dec. 1991.
5. 'South Africa on path to new constitution', *AFP*, 20 Dec. 1991; 'Pretoria shifts towards power-sharing', *Independent*, 21 Dec. 1991; 'SA leaders clash over "bad faith"', *Guardian*, 21 Dec. 1991; 'South Africa: Talks Pave Way for Final Eradication of Apartheid', *IPS*, 23 Dec. 1991; SABC TV, 20 Dec. 1991: BBC-23 Dec. 1991.
6. SAPA, 8 Jan. 1992: BBC-11 Jan. 1992.
7. 'Big CP win', *Sowetan*, 20 Feb. 1992.
8. 'FW stakes future on vote for reform', *Business Day*, 21 Feb. 1992.
9. J.T. Radebe, TRC Amnesty Hearing, 1 Dec. 1998 (Durban): TRC2.
10. 'Report by Edwin Dlamini', 8 Feb. 1993: UFH-ANC/NMP-19to39.
11. Interview with ANC S. Natal Regional Chairman in 'Report of the Golela Commission', p. 5: UFH-ANC/NMP-165/165; 'Addendum to report submitted by the investigation team into the Golela border post incident', 14 Feb. 1993: UFH-ANC/NMP-19to39.
12. 'Report by Edwin Dlamini'; 'Addendum to report submitted by the investigation team into the Golela border post incident'.
13. A. Strauss, 'The 1992 Referendum in South Africa', *The Journal of Modern African Studies*, 31 (2), Jun. 1993, p. 339.
14. 'Whites close door on apartheid', *C. Times*, 19 Mar. 1992; '"Apartheid book closed"' and 'Real birthday of new SA', *Star*, 19 Mar. 1992.
15. 'Referendum results', *Star*, 19 Mar. 1992.
16. SAPA, 20 Mar. 1992: BBC-21 Mar. 1992.
17. J.T. Radebe and S.J. Sithole, TRC Amnesty Hearing, 1 Dec. 1998 (Durban): TRC2.
18. 'Report by Edwin Dlamini'; 'Report of the Golela Commission', p. 5; 'Addendum to the report submitted by the investigation team into the Golela border post incident'.

19. J. Mndebele, Statement/TRC-20–21 Jul. 1998-Ermelo; Mr Hattingh, TRC Amnesty Hearing, 23 Jul. 1988: UWHP-TRC(CD)/amntrans> ermelo2> BLACAT4; P.P. Nkonyane, TRC Amnesty Hearing, 29 Jul. 1998: UWHP-TRC(CD)/amntrans> ermelo2> BLACAT8.

20. SAPA, 20 Apr. 1992: BBC-23 Apr. 1992.

21. 'South Africa: New Twist in Black-on-Black violence', *IPS*, 29 May 1992.

22. 'South Africa: Communities Torn Apart by Power Struggles', *IPS*, 6 Jun. 1992.

23. 'The night that Boipatong bled', *Star*, 19 Jun. 1992.

24. 'ANC halts talks after Township massacre', *FT*, 22 Jun. 1992; 'As Black Anger Grows, Mandela Pulls ANC Out of Talks', *AP*, 22 Jun. 1992.

25. 'ANC halts talks', *Chicago Sun-Times*, 24 Jun. 1992; SAPA, 27 Jun. 1992, 'Mandela's Memorandum to de Klerk on future of negotiations': BBC-29 Jun. 1992.

26. 'Mandela maintains hard line on negotiations', *AFP*, 27 Jun. 1992; 'Nelson Mandela says no talks until demands met', *AP*, 27 Jun. 1992.

27. M. Gushu/TRC-22 Jul. 1998-Ermelo; L.P. Mbokane, TRC Amnesty Hearing, 28 Jul. 1998: UWHP-TRC(CD)/amntrans > ermelo2 > BLACAT7.

28. 'Eyewitness: Death beyond the razor wire', *Guardian*, 8 Sep. 1992.

29. 'De Klerk calls for urgent talks on violence', *AP*, 9 Sep. 1992; 'ANC sets conditions for meeting with De Klerk', *AP*, 10 Sep. 1992.

30. SABC TV, 26 Sep. 1992, '"Channels of Communication are open again" following de Klerk-Mandela meeting': BBC-28 Oct. 1992.

31. 'Declaration of support for Buthelezi', *Irish Times*, 30 Sep. 1992.

32. J. Slovo, 'Negotiations: What room for compromise', *African Communist*, 130 (3rd Quarter), 1992, pp. 36–40.

33. SABC TV, 12 Oct. 1992: BBC-14 Oct. 1992.

34. African National Congress, 'Negotiations: A Strategic Perspective' (as adopted by the National Executive Committee of the African National Congress – 25 Nov. 1992), pp. 2–5: OU-RHL/MSS AAM 681.

35. 'De Klerk sets timetable to democracy', *AFP*, 26 Nov. 1992.

36. 'ANC's secret Uganda army', *S. Times*, 29 Nov. 1992.

37. 'South Africa: Cadres Dissatisfied with their condition', *IPS*, 19 Aug. 1993.

38. N. Mandela notebook entry, 5.1.93: NMF(CM)-NMPP/Box 1-Notebook 2/6.

39. M. Phosa, S. Nyanda *et al.*, 'Arms Issue – interview with detainees', 8 Feb. 1993: ANC-UFH/NMP -19to39; http://www.justice.gov.za/trc/decisions%5C1999/990329_ngobesemakhoba.html (accessed 19 Feb. 2014).

40. 'Arms Issue'; S.J. Sithole/TRC-1 Dec. 1998-Durban.

41. N. Mandela notebook entry, n.d.: NMF(CM)-NMPP/Box 1-Notebook 2/6.

42. 'Brief Summary of findings of inquiry into Golela incident', 2 Mar. 1993: ANC-UFH/NMP-19to39.

43. 'Death comes to Dawn Park', *Manchester Guardian Weekly*, 18 Apr. 1993; 'Four bullets for a dream', *P.News*, 9 Apr. 2008; 'A Time to Die, A Time to Cry', *P.News*, 10 Apr. 2008.

44. SAPA, 19 Apr. 1993: BBC-21 Apr. 1993.

45. SABC TV, 16 Dec. 1993: BBC-18 Dec. 1993.

46. 'A small and subdued crowd attends Oliver Tambo's funeral', *UPI*, 2 May 1993; 'ANC's saint works a miracle', *Independent*, 3 May 1993.

47. L.K. Mbatha, TRC Amnesty Hearing, 27 Oct. 1997: UWHP-TRC(CD)/amntrans> KIM1> MBATHA; W. Smiles, TRC Amnesty Hearing, 28 Oct. 1997: UWHP-TRC(CD)/amntrans> KIM1>SMILES.

48. SAPA, 13 Jun. 1993: BBC-15 Jun. 1993.

49. 'Extremists storm SA talks', *Independent*, 26 Jun. 1993.

50. 'Attack by White Extremists Unites Many S. Africans', *CSM*, 28 Jun. 1993.

51. 'Buthelezi rejects joint peacekeeping force plan', *AFP*, 11 Aug. 1993; 'Buthelezi calls for peace but warns towns of civil war', *Independent*, 12 Aug. 1993.

52. 'ANC ex-guerrillas form security company', *AFP*, 24 Aug. 1993.

53. N. Mandela, Keynote Address to MK National Conference, 3–4 Sep. 1993, pp. 4–6: UFH-ANC/NMP
-174/238; L.K. von den Steinen, 'Soldiers in the Struggle: Aspects of the Experiences of Umkhonto
we Sizwe's Rank and File Soldiers – The Soweto Generation and After' (MA, University of Cape
Town, 2002), p. 232.

54. SAPA, 5 Sep. 1993: BBC-7 Sep. 1993.

Victory

1. 'Pretoria veto overhangs power sharing', *FT*, 8 Sep. 1993.

2. 'SA bill gives blacks a say', *Independent*, 24 Sep. 1993.

3. SAPA, 13 Dec. 1993: BBC-15 Dec. 1993.

4. *Xinhua*, 16 Dec. 1993.

5. SAPA, 16 Dec. 1993: BBC-18 Dec. 1993.

6. 'Joy, tears as MK bows out', *Star*, 17 Dec. 1993.

7. 'Afrikaners and Zulus denounce new S Africa', *FT*, 17 Dec. 1993.

8. Capital Radio, 4 Jan. 1994: BBC-6 Jan. 1994.

9. 'Former ANC guerrilla campaigns in Soweto for de Klerk's party', *Times*, 24 Jan. 1994.

10. SABC Radio, 24 Jan. 1994: BBC-26 Jan. 1994.

11. SAPA, 30 Jan. 1994: BBC-1 Feb. 1994.

12. 'Mandela threatens retaliation for attacks by far right', *Times*, 7 Feb. 1994.

13. '12 gunned down in Natal province', *TG&M*, 7 Feb. 1994.

14. 'Peace keepers' camp shambles', *S. Times*, 6 Feb. 1994.

15. 'South Africa Alive with dangerous talk', *AP*, 8 Feb. 1994.

16. SAPA, 10 Mar. 1994: BBC-12 Mar. 1994.

17. SABC Radio, 10 Mar. 1994: BBC-12 Mar. 1994.

18. O.B. Menyatsoe, TRC Amnesty Hearing, 21 Sep. 1998 (Mmabatho): TRC2.

19. SAPA, 10 Mar. 1994: BBC-12 Mar. 1994.

20. SAPA, 11 Mar. 1994: BBC-12 Mar. 1994.

21. SAPA, 11 Mar. 1994: BBC-12 Mar. 1994.

22. P.D. de Ionne and O.B. Menyatsoe, TRC Amnesty Hearing, 21–22 Sep. 1998 (Mmabatho): TRC2.

23. A. Sparks, *Tomorrow Is Another Country* (Struik, 1995), p. 219.

24. G.J. Kruser, TRC Amnesty Hearing, 11 May 1998: UWHP-TRC(CD)/amntrans> joburg5> SHELL1.

25. Captain Wilken and H. Ndlovu/TRC Amnesty Hearing, 11 May 1998: UWHP-TRC(CD)/amntrans
> joburg5> SHELL1.

26. G.J. Kruser/TRC-11 May 1998-Johannesburg.

27. CNN News; 28 Mar. 1994, 3:03 pm ET.

28. 'South African Elections: "The world is turning upside down"', *Independent*, 18 Apr. 1994.

29. 'Zulu anger builds against SA army', *Independent*, 9. Apr. 1994.

30. 'Many soldiers set to lose jobs', *Star*, 8 Apr. 1994; '12 000 MK's kry opleiding', *Beeld*, 8 Apr. 1994;
'Integrated army on way', *Sowetan*, 8 Apr. 1994; 'MK soldiers gather for new SA army', *C.Times*,
8 Apr. 1994; 'MK and Defence Force troops gather together', *Argus*, 8 Apr. 1994; 'Umkhonto men
report for duty', *Business Day*, 8 Apr. 1994; '16 000 MK cadres to muster for new SA force', *Citizen*,
8 Apr. 1994.

31. 'Zulu anger builds against SA army'; *FT*, 8 Apr. 1994.

32. M. Buthelezi to P. Waldmeir, p. 11: UWHP-PWI.

33. G. Marinovich and J. Silva, *The Bang-Bang Club* (Arrow, 2001), pp. 1–3, 195, 197–8, 200–204.

34. SAPA, 19 Apr. 1994: BBC-21 Apr. 1994.

35. 'Jet, "African solution" clinched deal – Prof', *Citizen*, 20 Apr. 1994; SAPA, 19 Apr. 1994: BBC-20
Apr. 1994.

36. 'Buthelezi looks to poll slogan to achieve a miracle', *FT*, 21 Apr. 1994.

37. 'MK, Weermag "werk goed saam"', *Beeld*, 23 Apr. 1994.

38. 'Eyewitness: Cheers, Tears and God Bless Africa as the new flag is raised', *Guardian*, 27 Apr. 1994.

39. 'Bold IEC operation to salvage election', *Star*, 28 Apr. 1994.

40. SABC Radio, 2 May 1994: BBC-5 May 1994.
41. 'Ex-ANC guerrillas riot in assembly camp', *AP*, 3 May 1994.
42. 'Final Results Announced, ANC Wins 62.65 Percent', *AP*, 6 May 1994.
43. 'Mandela Chosen First Black President; Buthelezi Gets Hug, Winnie Snub', *AP*, 9 May 1994.
44. SABC TV, 9 May 1994: BBC-12 May 1994.
45. 'Mandela sworn in as South African president', *UPI*, 10 May 1994; 'From Prisoner to President, Mandela Inaugurated', *AP*, 10 May 1994.
46. 'Focus on new hope', *Sowetan*, 11 May 1994.
47. SAPA, 24 May 1990: BBC-26 May 1990; 'Top SANDF posts for MK officers', *Citizen*, 29 Jun. 1994; 'South Africa-Politics: Affirmative Action visits the military', *IPS*, 30 Jun. 1994.
48. 'Mandela sworn in'; 'From Prisoner to President'; 'Nelson Mandela Inauguration', https://www.youtube.com/watch?v=CSorcrEN4tc (accessed 28 May 2015).

Abbreviations

ALN: Armée de Libération Nationale (National Liberation Army – Algeria)
ANC: African National Congress
APC: Area Political Committee
APC: armoured personnel carrier
APLA: Azanian People's Liberation Army
AWB: Afrikaner Weerstandsbeweging
AWOL: absent without leave
BBC: British Broadcasting Corporation
BPP: Bechuanaland People's Party
CHQ: Central Headquarters
CIA: Central Intelligence Agency
CID: Criminal Investigation Department
CNN: Cable News Network
CODESA: Convention for a Democratic South Africa
COREMO: Revolutionary Committee of Mozambique
COSAS: Congress of South African Students
COSATU: Congress of South African Trade Unions
CPSU: Communist Party of the Soviet Union
DCC: Directorate of Covert Collection
DPM: deputy prime minister
EPG: Eminent Persons Group
FAPLA: Forças Armadas Populares de Libertação de Angola (People's Armed Forces for the Liberation of Angola)
FNLA: Frente Nacional de a Libertação de Angola (National Front for the Liberation of Angola)
FRELIMO: Frente de Libertação de Moçambique (Mozambique Liberation Front)
GMT: Greenwich Mean Time
HQ: headquarters
IFP: Inkatha Freedom Party
IPS: Inter Press Service
IRD: Internal Reconstruction Department
JMCC: Joint Military Co-ordinating Council
LMG: light machine gun
MHQ: Military Headquarters
MK: Umkhonto we Sizwe
MPLA: Movimento Popular de Libertação de Angola (People's Movement for the Liberation of Angola)
NATREF: National Petroleum Refiners of South Africa
NBS: Natal Building Society
NEC: National Executive Committee
NP: National Party
NPC: National Preparatory Committee

OAU: Organisation for African Unity
PAC: Pan Africanist Congress
PAIGC: Partido Africano da Independência da Guiné e Cabo Verde (African Party for
    the Independence of Guinea and Cape Verde)
PFP: Progressive Federal Party
PLO: Palestine Liberation Organisation
PMC: Politico-Military Council
PMSC: Politico-Military Strategy Commission
RAR: Rhodesian African Rifles
RC: Revolutionary Council
RENAMO: Resistência Nacional Moçambicana (Mozambican National Resistance)
RHQ: Regional Headquarters
RLI: Rhodesian Light Infantry
RPG: rocket-propelled grenade
RPMC: Regional Politico-Military Committee
RSDF: Royal Swaziland Defence Force
SABC: South African Broadcasting Corporation
SACC: South African Council of Churches
SACP: South African Communist Party
SACTU: South African Congress of Trade Unions
SADF: South African Defence Force
SAIC: South African Indian Congress
SANDF: South African National Defence Force
SAP: South African Police
SAPA: South African Press Association
SAS: Special Air Service
SASM: South African Students' Movement
SDUs: self-defence units
sitrep: situation report
SSRC: Soweto Students' Representative Council
SWAPO: South West Africa People's Organisation
TDF: Transkei Defence Force
TEC: Transitional Executive Council
UANC: United African National Council
UBLS: University of Botswana, Lesotho and Swaziland
UDF: United Democratic Front
UN: United Nations
UNHCR: United Nations High Commission for Refugees
UNIP: United National Independence Party
UNITA: União Nacional para a Independência Total de Angola (National Union for
    the Total Independence of Angola)
ZANLA: Zimbabwe African National Liberation Army
ZANU: Zimbabwe African National Union
ZANU-PF: Zimbabwe African National Union – Patriotic Front
ZAPU: Zimbabwe African People's Union
ZIPRA: Zimbabwe People's Revolutionary Army

Index

'Aaron' 219
Abdelhanna, Si 48
'Abe' *see* Motaung, Thabo
Abels, Sergeant 408–409
'Abie' *see* Motaung, Thabo
Abrahamse, Uriel 349–350, 408
'Abrahams, Faizul' *see* Forbes,
  Ashley
Accord of Nkomati 325
Adams, Ivor 346
Adamson, Anton 365
Africa Confidential 449
African Aid Fund 103
African Communist 172, 209, 492
Africanists 12–14, 17, 20
African nationalism 19
Africa South 17
Afrikaans language 207–208
Afrikaner Weerstandsbeweging
  see AWB
Afrika, Sandy 367
Agence France-Presse 500
Agenda 482
'Agrippa' 361–362, 396–397
Ahmed Timol Unit 451
Aisem, Rudolf 166
Akhalwaya, Yusuf 447, 451
Alexander, Ray 174–175
Algeria 47–48, 82
'Ali' (MK cadre) 264
Ali (victim) 269–270
All-In African National Action
  Council 28–29
ALN (Armée de Libération
  Nationale) 47–48
Amanzimtoti bomb 366–367
amnesty 492
ANC
  Defiance Campaign 4–5, 7, 9
  violence vs non-violence debate
    8–19, 21–24, 30–33
  M-Plan 9, 18, 22, 188
  divisions in 13–17, 166–169,
    273, 318–319, 351, 443
  formation of MK 54–55, 76,
    83, 87
  setbacks 106–107
  infiltrations into South Africa
    126, 128, 166–174, 178–179
  Wankie and Sipolilo campaigns
    139–140, 150, 160, 163–164

  people's war 252–253,
    350–353
  Internal Reconstruction
    Department (IRD) 233–235,
    244–245
  Main Machinery 194, 200,
    209, 213
  National Preparatory
    Committee (NPC) 346–348,
    351
  Politico-Military Council
    (PMC) 311, 313, 318,
    320–321
  Politico-Military Strategy
    Commission (PMSC) 245,
    251–252
  Revolutionary Council (RC)
    171–172, 176, 191, 221,
    232–234, 244–245, 252, 263,
    266–267, 272–273, 311
  negotiations with government
    454–455, 459, 461–466,
    468–500
  1994 election 501–508
  as ruling party 511–513
ANC Women's League 473
ANC Youth League 3, 50–51,
  477, 498
Anderson, Cindy 260
'André' 406
Anglo American 359
Angola 200, 214, 220–222,
  309–310, 317–318, 320,
  329–331, 407, 414, 427,
  434, 437
Anti-Apartheid Committee,
  England 103
'Antony' 228
APC 272–273, 299, 352
Apelgren, Eric 386
Apelgren, Greta 377–378, 380,
  384–387
Apelgren, Jeanette 386
Apelgren, Penelope 385–386
April, James ('George Driver'/
  'Henry Dirk Marais') 119,
  128–129, 145–148, 163,
  175–177
Arafat, Yasser 512
Area Political Committees
  see APC

'Areff, Salim' *see* Ebrahim,
  Ebrahim Ismail
Arenstein, Reeve 91
'Arkimedes' 223
arms caches 482, 485, 491
Ashley Kriel Unit 410, 430,
  434, 441
askaris 271, 429
Assembly Point Juliet 262–264
Assembly Point Kilo 263
Associated Press 335, 337, 369,
  432–433, 442, 461, 511
Astor, David 51
Atjesi, Priscille 419
Aventura 180–181
AWB 464, 496, 498–499, 505
Ayob, Ismail 324

Baartman, K.B. 299
Baatjies, Clement 387
Babenia, Natoo 58–59, 64
'Babsy' 322
'Bafana' *see* Mohlanyaneng,
  Simon
Bagg, Robert 225–226
Balekeng, Samuel 102–103, 105
Baloyi, Robert 142–143
'Bam, Comrade' 478
Bambani, Harry 71
Bambeni, Warrant Officer 475
Banda, Vronda 502–503
Bandom, Gordon 160
Bantu National Congress 12
Bantustans 351–352
Banzi, Temba 243, 296
Baphela, Patrick 53, 102–103,
  105–106, 108, 110
Barber, Lord 381
'Barks, Buti' *see* Hlabane, Thomas
Barnard, Gerrie 421
Barnard, Jacobus F. 28, 31–32
Barnard, Niel 441, 451
Barron, Chris 503
Barrow, Nita 381
Bartaune, Herbert 36, 54
Bartlett, Nurudien 430
Base Five camp 153–156, 159
Base Four camp 160–161
Basele, G.M. 217
Base One camp 152
Base Three camp 153

Basil February MK Squad 410
Basutoland Congress Party 101
Bates, Gordon 473
Batman, Patrick 160
Battersby, John 419–420, 499
Battle of Blood River 502
Battle of Inyatuwe 135–138, 175
Battle of Swaziland 331
BBC 270, 507
Bechuanaland 79, 90, 103, 119, 123–124
  see also Botswana
Beck, Henry 337
Beeld 470, 510
Beeselaar, G. 466–467
Befikadu, Wondoni 52
Bekele, Colonel 52
'Beki' 319
'Belgium' see Sithole, Mduduzi
Bella, Ahmed Ben 47–48, 56, 82
Belle, Steve 81, 121
Bellingan, Riaan 367, 369–372, 376, 412
Bennun, Tolly 35
Bensisni, Irma 367
'Benson' see Kgwatlha, James
Benson, Poko 158
Benzien, Jeffrey 404, 408–409, 412
Bernard, Gary 509
Bernberg, L. 258
Bernstein, Rusty 26, 29, 38, 41, 55, 90–92, 99, 105, 190
Bethell, Lord 342
Beukes, Herbert 357
Beyela, Philemon 51, 127–128
Beyers, Andries 485
Beyleveld, Piet 11, 29
Bhekimpi, Prince 318
'Bhengu' 51
Bhengu, David Jiba ('Thomas Masiza') 309, 314–315
Bhengu, Siegfried 106, 108–110
Bhila, Sipho Stanley 345
Bhungane, Mathanzima 303
Bischoff, Corinne 394
Bizana, Justice 374, 383
Black Cat gang 468, 479
Black Chain gang 468, 490
Bloom, Tony 359
'Bob' 243
Boesak, Allan 310, 442, 446–447
Boipatong 337, 489
Bongco, Washington 50, 61, 63–65, 94
'Bonono' 412
Booi, Fumanikile 466–467

'Booi, Lammy' see Mbali, Fanele
Booyens, Dudley 368
Booysens Police Station attack 265–266, 273, 278
Bopela, Thula 142–143, 145–147
Bophuthatswana 238, 503–505
Boshielo, Flag 171, 174–175
Bosigo, Jeff 223, 314–316
Botha, Warrant Officer 312
Botha, Cornelius 363, 422–423
Botha, Hendrik 367, 431, 433, 467
Botha, Johannes P. 175
Botha, Louis 480
Botha, Pik (Roelof) 301, 305–306, 317–318, 343–344, 358, 436
Botha, P.W.
  ANC and 256, 275, 324, 342–343, 395, 441
  as leader 239, 335, 435, 444
  agreements with other countries 293, 325
  states of emergency 355, 373, 385
  'Rubicon speech' 357–358
  on election results 403
  Khotso House 416, 420–421, 429
Botha, Simon 322
Bothma, Peet 470
Bothma, Sharon 367
Botswana
  independence of 124
  ANC in 124, 127, 187–189, 217, 222, 243, 254–256, 277, 282–283
  Wankie and Sipolilo campaigns 138, 148–149, 163
  agreement with South Africa 343–346
  attacks in 348–350, 381–382, 400, 417–418
  see also Bechuanaland
Botswana Machinery 231, 234, 236, 242–243, 246, 282, 400
Bottoman, Wonga 329
Boutros-Ghali, Boutros 512
Bowman, Advocate 200
Boyle, Brendan 324–325
Braam, Conny 407
'Bra Simon' 326
'Braso, Comrade' see Lalla, Rayman
'Bra T' see Motaung, Lele
Brazelle, Charles 259–260, 371
Brewer, G. 4

British South Africa Police 138, 154, 159
Brits, Constable 215–216
Broederstroom cell 416
Broodryk, Johannes 113–114, 209
Brooklyn, Jumpy 155
'Brown' 288, 298
Brown, Maria 392–393
'Bruce' 285, 290–291
Buchner, Jack 461
bucket bombs see leaflet bombs
'Budis' 278–279, 286
Bulawayo Chronicle 86
Bulbring, Edith 494–495
Burger, Colonel 393
Burger, Major 229–230
Burger, J.F. 3
Bushmen 120
Buthelezi, Johanna 53
Buthelezi, Mangosuthu 164, 252–253, 295, 324, 480, 482, 491–492, 499, 507–510
Buthelezi, Norbert 324, 339

Cachalia, Yusuf 8, 33
Caculama camp 347–348, 407, 415
Cahoon, Dr 5
Cajee, Amin 109–110
Camp 32 see Quatro camp
'Can Can' see Luthuli, Daluxolo
Cape Argus 45–46
Cape Times 312–313, 410
Capital Radio 327, 502
'Captain, Comrade' 321
Card, Donald 4, 65, 74–75, 94–95
Cardoso, Helio 309
Carlin, John 452
Carneson, Fred 26, 34–35
Cary, Warrant Officer 312
Cassiem, Nazeem 368
Castro, Fidel 31, 221, 512
Cele, Grace 394–395
Cele, Pam 379
Cele, Zinto 345, 361
Central Headquarters, MK 221–222, 243, 245
Centre for Applied Social Sciences 355
Chabalala, George 212
'Chacho, Phuti' see Cholo, T.T.
Chaitow, Brian 37
Chakafa (MK cadre) 161
'Chama, Callaghan' see Shange, Vusi
Chamusso, Rogerio 284–285
Chand, Jameel 451

Chaphi, Orphan ('Hlubi') 235–236, 239, 371
Chatwind, Phoebe 259
Chauke, Richard 210
Chawe, Lucky 160
'Chen, Mr' 103
Chetty, Mr 200
Chiba, Laloo 41
Chief Albert Luthuli Medal for Valour 501
Chiepe, G.K.T. 343–344
Chikane, Frank 416
Chikerema, James 139–140
'Chilies' 361–362
Chiliza, Henry 210–211, 215–218, 314
Chiliza, Sipho 201–202
Chimboya, Karl 158
Chimunye, William 154
China 9–10, 36, 102–103, 105, 112
Chirau, Jeremiah 254
Chirwa, James 57, 70–71
Chissano, Joaquim 193, 305–306
Cholo, T.T. ('Motiranka'/'Phuti Chacho') 53, 102–103, 105, 176, 178–180, 182–184
Chona, Mainza 119
Choobe, Vinus 443
'Chris' see Dumakude, Lester; Tsiki, Naledi
Christian Science Monitor 355, 499
'Christie' 284
Christie, Danie 258
Christie, Margaretha 258
Church Street bombs 307
CIA 298
Cindes Plot (farm) 120–121, 130
Ciskei 311, 490–491, 505
Citizen 443, 478
Claassen, M.N. 428
Claassen, P.S. 6
Claassens, Sergeant 226
Claiborne, William 438
Clan Ross 152–153
'Clement' see Molapo, Michael Roller
Clementson, Albert 426
Clinton, Hillary 512
Clucas, Clive 424
CNN 507
CODESA 484–485, 492
Coetsee, Kobie 415, 441, 450–451
Coetzee, Lieutenant 219
Coetzee, A.J. 28

Coetzee, Dirk 269, 271, 274
Coetzee, Ignatius 177, 383
Coetzee, Jan 292
Coetzee, Johan 227–228, 372
Coetzee, Piet 52–53
Coetzee, Willem 383
Coetzer, Joe 367
Coetzer, Martin 385
Cold War 221
Coloured People's Congress 33
Commission on Internal Mass Mobilisation 352
Commission on Strategy and Tactics 351–352, 361
Committee of Ten 322–323
Commonwealth 254–255, 360, 381–382
Communist Party of the Soviet Union see CPSU
Congress Alliance 11–12, 14, 17, 33–34, 55, 89, 169
Congress of Democrats 11, 29, 33–34
Congress of South African Students see COSAS
Congress of South African Trade Unions see COSATU
Congress of the People 8–11
Conservative Party 402, 446, 485–486, 496, 501
constitution of South Africa 305, 310, 312–313, 363, 492–494
Consultative Conference of African leaders (1960) 25–26
Convention for a Democratic South Africa see CODESA
COSAS 292, 498
COSATU 416, 439, 446, 473, 476–477
Cotoza, June-Rose 422
councillors 355
Cowell, Alan 308
Coxon, Inspector 96
CP see Conservative Party
CPSU 76
Craucamp, Chris 426
Cronje, Colonel 314–316
Cronje, Jan 232
Croukamp, Dennis 155–156
Cuba 31, 214, 220–221, 223, 231, 245, 434, 512
'Cwele, Ma' 338
Czechoslovakia 103

Dabengwa, Dumiso 152, 264

Dadoo, Yusuf 6, 171, 176, 178, 232–233
Daily Dispatch 183
Daily Mail 437
Dalindyebo, Sabata 448
'Dan' see Ramusi, Selaelo
Dantile, Lulamile ('Morris Seabelo') 365, 401
Dasoo, Aslam 442
'David' (askari) 413–414
'David' see Ramusi, Selaelo
Davidson, Captain 393
Davidson, Pat 111
Davidson, Russell 386
Davis, Boetie 475
Davison, Captain 137
Davison, Corporal 136
Dawara, Jordaan 176
Day, Stephen 409
De Beer, Zach 359, 487
De Bruyn, Colonel 288
De Bruyn, David 490
Declaration of Intent 484–485, 492
Deetlefs, Christo 274, 388, 390, 422, 450
Defiance Campaign 4–5, 7, 9
De Ionno, Peter 505
De Jager, Lodewyk 383–384
De Jonge, Klaas 352–353
De Klerk, F.W.
    Tricameral Parliament 332
    township protests 335
    Commonwealth Eminent Persons Group 382
    as leader 435, 444, 513
    negotiations with ANC 440, 446–447, 449–452, 459, 461, 463–464, 469, 472, 474, 482, 484–487, 491, 493–494, 504, 506–509
De Kock, Eugene 308, 314–316, 365, 367, 383–384, 388–390, 421–423, 428–429, 450, 475
De Lange, Damian 279–280, 408, 411, 416, 418
De Lange, William 412
Delius, Anthony 82
Democratic Party 446
Democratic Republic of the Congo 124
Department of Native Affairs 6
Dercksen, Adriaan 288
Desai, R. 178
De Swardt, Christiaan 258–260
De Swardt, Jacobus 202–203
detention without trial 78–79, 113

De Villiers, Gert 362
De Wet, Quartus 104–105
De Witt, Christiaan 241–242
D.F. Malan Accord 476–477, 487
'Dhlamini' see Mbeki, Govan
Dhlamini, Roderick 214
'Dhlamini, Victor' see Mkapili,
    Theophilus
Dhlodhlo, Michael 161
Dhlomo, Albert 191, 193–195,
    197–198, 201–202
Dhlomo, Sibongiseni 360, 364
Diale, Nelson 70–71
'Dick' 353
Dick, Nelson 74
Dietricksen, Johannes 284
Dikeledi, Paul 374, 408
Dimande, Mandinkosi 361
Dingake, Michael 103–104,
    106–107, 109–112, 114–115,
    120, 127
Dipholo, Patrick 236
Dirker, Sergeant 59–60
Diro, Michael 102–103, 105
Dladla, Barney 187
Dladla, Simon 374, 385, 387
Dlamini, A. 288
Dlamini, Edwin 486–487, 496
Dlamini, Jabulane 328, 340
Dlamini, Mabandla Fred 293
Dlamini, Makhosini 193
Dlamini, Maphevu 250–251,
    271–272
Dlamini, Mbiela 176
Dlamini, Philemon 474
Dlamini, R.V. 318
Dlamini, S. 288
Dlamini, Sipho 384
Dlamini, Themba 130, 164, 166
Dlamini, Zenani 513
Dlamini-Zuma, Nkosazana 480
Dlepu, Detective Constable 42
Dlodlo, Ayanda 423–424
Dlodlo, Felicia Azande 401,
    404–405
Dlodlo, Sidumo Theophilus
    ('Viva Zenge'/'Victor'/
    'Sipho Victor Simelane'/
    'Viva') 278–279, 286, 340,
    400–402, 404–406
Dloi, Captain 184
Dlomo, Mapiki 341–342, 364–365
Dludlu, Elizabeth 384
dogs 145, 207, 349
Dolcin, Lucas 127
Dolny, Helena 400

Dolo, Castro 143, 152, 163,
    174–175
Dolphin Unit 304, 311, 348, 417
'Donda' 137–138
Donda, Nicholas 145–146
Dorasamy, Detective Constable
    377
'Douglas' see Sijake, Sandi
DP see Democratic Party
Dramat, Anwa 387, 402, 412
Driver, George see April, James
Duba, Pilot 161
Dube, Lieutenant Colonel 251, 288
Dube, Itumeleng 424
Dube, John 129, 131, 133–134,
    140–143, 145–148
Dube, Leslie 239
Dube, Ronnie 137–138
Dube's Farm see Luthuli Camp
Dukada, Sisa 45
Duka, Norman 140
Dukashe, Lizo Lenton 50
Duli, Craig 475–476
'Duma' 197
Duma, Detective Sergeant 315
Duma, Bafana 61–62, 197,
    232–233, 328
'Dumaklaba' 478–479
Dumakude, Lester ('Chris')
    399–401, 424
Dumisa, Robert 324, 329, 332,
    338–339
'Dunkin' 278
Dunn, Mervyn 368
Du Plessis, Barend 477
Du Plooy, Johan 261
Du Preez, Brigadier 288
Du Preez, Antonio 377–379
Du Preez, Johannes 185
Du Preez, Salmon 430–431,
    433, 467–468
Du Rand, Ranier A. 315
Duru, Iheukumere 443
Dutch Anti-Apartheid
    Movement 407
Dwaba, Lunglo 61
Dyantyi, Abel 129
Dyantyi, Thami 254
Dyasop, Luthando 322–323, 462,
    464–465

Earp, Major General 288–289
Ebrahim, Ebrahim Ismail
    ('Salim Areff'/'Roynie')
    58–59, 62, 64, 325, 341, 343,
    348, 352–354, 395–396

Edson, Rita 386
'Eduardo' 223
Ehlers, Johannes 260–261
elections 7, 14–16, 402–403,
    419–420, 430, 432–435, 446,
    494, 502–503, 510–511
electricity infrastructure sabotage
    40, 61–62, 74, 284–285, 289,
    353, 368, 375
Elias, Elizabeth 402
Eloff, A.Z. 397–398
Els, N.J. 466–467
'Engineering' camp 220
Erasmus, Captain 258–259, 399
Erasmus, E. 45
Erasmus, Frans 18, 21–23, 30
Erasmus, Gerrit 428–429
'Eric' 51, 228
Esau, Cecil 375
Essop, Mohammed 177–178
Essop, Salim 174
Ethiopia, training in 57, 63, 69–70
Evans, Gavin 483

'Fakude, George' see Ndlanzi,
    Sibusiso
FAPLA 214, 309–310, 319,
    322–323
Fazzie, Henry 57, 70–71
February, Basil ('Paul Petersen')
    119–120, 128–129, 135, 138
Federation of South African
    Women 33
female MK cadres 214, 231
Ferreira, Detective Sergeant 85–86
Ferreira, Hendrik 97
Ferreira, P. 96, 102
Filakazi, Amanzi 433
Financial Times 447, 471
Fingland, David 359
First, Ruth 12, 29, 54, 79, 91, 95,
    275, 400
Fischer, Bram 22, 26, 29, 83, 86,
    99–100, 104, 106–107, 111,
    113–114
Fischer, Ilse 111
Fisher, Don 375
Five Freedoms Forum 440
flag, new South African 510
Fletcher, John 165
'Flint' 236
Forbes, Ashley ('P. Philander'/
    'Faizul Abrahams') 346, 375,
    382–383, 396, 402, 404, 412
Forrest, G.A. 60
Forster, A. 5

Forster, Jakobus 430–431
For the Sake of our Lives 477
Fourie, Captain 203, 476
Fourie, Brand 274–275
Fourie, Eugene 390
Fourie, Wynand 490
Fouroux, Roger 483
Franca, Antonio dos Santos 322
France 87
Fraser, Malcolm 381
Freedom Charter 9, 11–12, 14, 17, 259, 363
Free Mandela campaign 270–271
FRELIMO 127–128, 168, 187, 197–198, 209, 266, 320
Fritz, J. 40
'functional units' 235
Funda base 252
Futha, Mack ('Stephen Hliziyo') 108, 121–123
'Fyre' 223

G-5 Unit 247, 253, 265, 273, 278
G-6 Unit 286, 289, 290, 291
G-7 Unit 278, 279, 286, 291, 294
Gadu, Commissioner 506–507
'Gagarin, Boston' 132, 151
Gaitskell, Hugh 51
Gamedze, Peter 192–195
Gamedze, Sipho 408
Gamedze, Sylvia 192, 194–195
Game stores 359
Garson, Philippa 488–489
Gaxkana, Gladstone 73
Gay, Lionel 88, 98, 100, 106
Gcaba, Vuyile 411–412
'Gebuza' *see* Nyanda, Siphiwe
Geldenhuys, Mike 259
General Laws Amendment Act 49, 105
'George' 141, 284, 287–288, 298
Gerasimov, Gennady 436
Gerber, Frans 3
Gerrard, Michelle 386
Geyer, Arnold 279–280
Gibson, John 359
Gilmore, Inigo 502–503
Ginwala, Frene 269
Glas, Jan 73
Gleeson, Ian R. 250
Goboza, Tamana (Mikza) 167
Goch Street incident 224–226
Goldberg, Denis 34–35, 66–68, 80–81, 88, 90–92, 97, 99, 105
Goldreich, Arthur 79–80, 89, 92–93, 96–98

Golela Incident 495–496
Gombela, Mlungisi 490
Goniwe, Jakes 76, 155
Goniwe, Vuyani 242
Gordhan, Pravin 354
Gordon, Sean 367
Gore, Al 512
Gqabi, Joe 29, 36, 46, 68, 72–73, 194, 218, 281
Gqozo, Oupa 491–492, 505
Gqubule, Duma 303
Graaff, Sir de Villiers 14
Grant, Mr 54
Gray, Heather 300
Greeff, Johannes 96
Green Book 251–252, 313
Green, Erica 326
Grimond, Jo 51
Grobbelaar, Sergeant 111
Grobbelaar, Abraham 292
Grobbelaar, Andrich 371–372
Grobbelaar, Igor 260
Grobler, Nicolaas J. 95
Groenewald, Fanie 478
Groote Schuur Minute 463, 469, 472
Grosskop, Heinrich 410–411
Grosvenor Girls' High School 361
Guardian 401
Guenon, Alain 483
guerrilla warfare 56, 76, 79–80, 83, 86–87, 89, 91, 105, 172, 241, 282, 314
Gugulethu 358
Gugulethu Seven 372–373, 430
'Guidelines for the development of our political machineries in TX' 272–273
'Guluva' 151
Guma, Mduduzi ('Inkululeko') 276
Gumede, Detective Sergeant 315
Gumede, Mr 208
Gunn, Shirley 376, 407, 410, 430, 434, 465–466
Gushu, Mzwandile 469, 479, 483–484, 488, 490
Gwala, Harry 195–196, 227, 453, 455, 465, 473, 476

Hadebe, Dennis 330
Hadebe, Harry 145
Hadebe, James 57, 102–103, 105, 107
Hadebe, Lancelot 276

Hadebe, Moffat 150, 154–156, 158–159, 165
Hadebe, Thamsanqa 302–303
Haggerty, Roger 424
Hala, Mike 477–478
Hamlyn, Michael 350
Hani, Chris ('Chris Nkosana')
    in exile 81, 95, 120–121, 128–130, 132, 167, 178–181, 189, 239, 303, 310, 320, 323–324, 326–327, 351, 371, 380, 415, 419–420, 432, 437, 449–450, 452–453
    Wankie and Sipolilo campaigns 133, 141–143, 145–148, 163
    attacks on 296, 301
    negotiations with government 359, 478–481
    back in South Africa 466, 468–470, 472–474, 486, 488
    assassination of 466, 496–497
    medal 501
Hanna, Mike 507
Harare Declaration 446, 454, 459
Harmel, Michael 17–18, 22, 24–26, 55, 63, 79
Harmse, Retha 496–497
Hartman, Sergeant 161
Hartogh, M.R. 13
Hartogh, Peter 225–226
Hartzenberg, Ferdi 499, 501
Hashe, Boy 29
Hattingh, Krappies 232. 269
Hayes, Jury 421
Hazelhurst, Peter Bruce 29
Healey, Denis 51
Heiberg, P.J. 45
Heinlen, Margaret 462
'Hempe, W.' 167
Hendricks, Sidney 430
Henry, Mark 383
Hepburn, Constable 229
Hepple, Bob 26, 37, 79, 86, 90–92, 98–100, 105
Hepple, Shirley 100
Heunis, Chris 305, 382, 434–435
Heymann, Issy 106
Heynes, Nik 442
'hidden force' 474, 480–481
Hilary, E. 288
Hirschfeldt, A. 344
Hirschfeldt, S. 344
Hlabane, Thomas ('Victor'/'Buti Barks') 223, 233, 239, 264
Hlapane, Bartholomew 37, 87, 90, 106–109, 302

Hlapane, Beverley 302
Hlapane, Brenda 302
Hlapane, Matilda 302
Hlatshwayo, Cyprian 242
Hlaya, Mnyamane 102–103, 105, 108, 110–111
Hlekani, Gandi 155
Hleza, Sithule 483–484
'Hliziyo, Stephen' see Futha, Mack
Hlongwane, Nicholas ('Commandant Ntziswa') 247–248, 265, 273, 283, 285–286, 290–291
Hlongwane, Pat 437
'Hlubi' see Chaphi, Orphan
Hlubi, Mrs 269
Hlubi, Timothy 392
Hoang-Minh Phuong, Colonel 240
Hobo, Thembile 330
Hodgson, Jack 22, 34–35, 38–39, 41, 63, 68, 79, 89–90, 94–95, 98, 172–173, 228
Hodgson, Rica ('Stephanie') 22, 98, 173
Holiday, Anthony 172–173, 209
Holman, Michael 447
Holmes, Warrant Officer 71
Holomisa, Bantu 448, 475–476, 478, 483
Hoohla, Setsomi 168–169
Hope, Douglas 288
Hopkins, Patrol Officer 135
Horwood, Owen 200
Hosey, John 'Sean' 185–186
Hosking, Peter 135–137
hospitals 442
hostage taking 266–267
Hoyi, Daphne 65
Hoyi, Inkie 65
Hoyi, Linda 65
Huddleston, Trevor 7–8
Hudson, Thomas 375
Huma, Edward 223
hunger strike 438
Hutchinson, Robert 276
Hutton, Sergeant Major 161

IFP
ANC and 252–253, 324, 464, 473–474, 476, 486, 505–511
violence in townships 461, 465, 468, 483–484, 490
'Inkathagate' 480
negotiations with government 482, 499, 501

IFP Women's League 488
IFP Youth League 488
Impirima camp 309
Independent 452
Independent Electoral Commission 510–511
Independent Television News 30
India 483
Indian Congress 33
Ingwavuma unit 338–339
Inkatha Freedom Party see IFP
'Inkululeko' see Guma, Mduduzi
Inkululeko 177
Innes-Kerr, Mr 54
Inter Press Service 331–332, 355, 382, 414, 435, 483, 488
'Iotola' 280
Isaacs, Emmanuel 49
Ismail, Aboobaker ('Rachid') 252, 267, 270, 284, 302–304, 384–385, 400–401, 486–487
Ismail, Mohamed 304
Ivy, Roderick 71

Jabane, Petros 265, 273–274
'Jabu'/'Jabulani' see Mahlobo, Sithabiso
'Jack' 267, 270
Jack, Joseph 52–53, 56–57, 105
Jackson, Jesse 434
Jacobs, L. 263
Jacobs, Pieter ('K. Samuels'/ 'David Samuels') 346, 382–383, 396, 402–404
Jamal, Commander 48
'James' 308
Janson, Punt 200
Jantjies, Alfred 50–53, 57, 70–71
Jantshi, Abel ('Eric Nduna') 133, 135
Jardien, Gammat 77–78
Jassat, Abdulhai 96
'Jeff' 319
Jele, Josiah 109, 111, 127–128
Jenkin, Tim 189, 202, 399, 460
'Jeqe' 167
Jergens, Donovan 382–383
'Jim' 243–244
'Jimmy' 204, 209
JMCC 507–508
'Joe, Comrade' see Nyanda, Siphiwe
Joint Military Co-ordinating Council see JMCC
'Jonas' see Ramudzuli, George
Jonas, Bongani 383, 413–414

Jonathan, Leabua 369
Jones, Constable 402
Jones, Cyril 37, 88, 106
Jones, Richard 431
Jordan, Michael 200
Jordan, Pallo 351–352, 359, 459, 477
Joseph, Paul 41
Joubert, Jaap 434
Journal le Geneve 473

Kahiya, Felix Arnold 150
Kajee, A.S. 58–59, 64
KaNgwane area 383
Kantor, James 99, 105
Kapwepwe, S.M. 125
'Karbahle' 223
Kasrils, Andrew 415
Kasrils, Ronnie ('Ronnie Reynolds'/ 'ANC Khumalo')
acts of sabotage 37–38, 49, 58, 61–62, 95
in exile 181, 185, 190, 228, 295, 325
back in South Africa 459–460, 491
Kassner, Rupert 225–226
Kathrada, Ahmed ('Pedro')
arrests and trials 6, 8, 29, 59–60, 63, 99, 105, 358
transport of cadres 50
at Liliesleaf Farm 55, 79, 84, 91–92
release of 447–448, 453
Kaunda, Kenneth 124–126, 382, 444–446, 453
'Kawawa, Rashidi' see Mhlawuli, Goodman
'Kawe' 341–342
Keevy, J.M. 94
'Keith' 276–278
Keitseng, Fish 47, 53–54, 60, 94–96, 98, 103, 110, 112
Kekoenyetsoe, Raymond 327
Kelapi, Gladys 349
Kembelo, Roy 188
Kennedy, J.H.J. 92–93
'Kenny' 256
Ketelo, Bandile 461
Keyter, Clarence 472
Kgongoane, Simon 229
'Kgope, Tebogo' see Nyanda, Siphiwe
'Kgotoki' 194
Kgwatlha, James ('Benson') 428
Kgwele, Thomas 101–102

Khama, Seretse 124, 149, 255
Khan, Yaseen 375
Khanyile, William 191, 276
Khayingo, Wilson 69
Khayiya, Felix 153
Khayiyana, Victor 267, 270, 276, 363–364
Khombisa, Alfred 81
Khonza, Alfred 51–53, 57, 70–71
Khotso House 416, 420–421, 428–429, 434, 466
Khoza, Sergeant 215–216
Khoza, Duncan 127–128, 158
'Khoza, Thom' 223
Khumalo, Mr 272
'Khumalo, ANC' see Kasrils, Ronnie
Khumalo, Ntu 195
Khumalo, Sandile 339
'Khumalo, Sihle' see Ndlanzi, Sibusiso
Khumalo, Sipho 277, 393
'Khumalo, Solomon' see Sexwale, Mosima
Khumalo, Tennis 141
Khumalo, Tyrone 228–229, 234
Khumalo, Vincent 167
Khumalo, Welcome 377–378
Khuzwayo, Bafana 201–202
Khuzwayo, Judson 227
'Kid' 278–279
'Kim' 113
King, Colbert 488
Kirkby, Arnold 306–307
Kitson, Ian David 90, 98, 100, 106
Klein, Sergeant 177
Kleingeld, Johannes 207
Klindt, George 89
Knight, Mr 157
Knight, W.A. 79
Kobole, Eugenia 349
Koch, Eddie 488
Kodesh, Wolfie 22, 34–35, 41, 48, 59
Koeberg nuclear power station 300–302
Koetle, Joseph 404
Komarov, Andrei 178
Kombele, Nicholas 176, 179, 182–183
Kondoti, Malcolmess 50, 53, 61, 95
Kongwa camp 107–110, 114, 119, 121–122, 171–172
Koole, Johannes 388–389
Koornhof, Piet 200, 295

Koroni, Captain 137
Kotane, Moses
    arrests and trials 6, 22
    violence vs non-violence debate 24–25, 27, 29–31, 33–34, 60
    at Liliesleaf Farm 55
    in exile 68, 114, 126–127, 167, 169, 171
    Wankie and Sipolilo campaigns 166
Kouchner, Bernard 465
Kriegler, Johann 510–511
Kriel, Ashley 358, 409, 410
Kritzinger, Wessels 508
'Kroestjoff' 283
Kruger, A.J. 45
Kruger, Jimmy 178, 200
Kruger, M.D. 77–78
Kruger, Theuns 485
Kruser, Gary 414, 506–507
'Kubana, Lieutenant' 57
Kubukeli, Pumlani 465
Kumano, Joel 152
Kunene, Andrew 9
Kunene, Raymond 87
Kuny, Lawrence 190–191, 193
Kutuwela, Alfred 176
KwaZulu-Natal see Natal
'Kweyama, Eisland' 178

Laas, Mr 3
Labour Party (Britain) 19, 51
Labuschagne, Mr 450
Labuschagne, Frans 390
'Lake' 278
Lalla, Rayman ('Comrade Braso') 296, 324, 357, 366, 468
Lamani, Dingo 191
Lamprecht, Warrant Officer 196
landmine attacks
    Messina 362
    Breyten 375–376, 383
    Volksrust 385
    Parow 388
    Jozini Experimental Farm 391
    Diepgesit mine 400
Langa, Benjamin 330, 345
'Langa, James' 124
Larbi, Captain 48
Laurence, Patrick 355
Lawrence, Edward ('Ralph'/ 'Leonard') 258, 302, 314, 317, 330, 356, 360, 390, 426, 450
'LCB' ('Lucha Contra Bandidos') 319

Leadership South Africa 359
leaflet bombs 172–173, 175, 202, 279
Leballo, Potlako 12, 15
Le Cordier, Matthew 377–379, 386–387
Lee, Stephen 189, 202, 399
Le Grange, Louis 268–269, 335–336, 382, 410, 485
Legum, Colin 51
Leibowitz, Jack 80
Lekaba, Festus 222–223
Lekhanya, Justin 369
Lemmer, J.C. 20
Lengisi, Amos 153, 166
'Lennox' see Tshali, Mongameli
Lentswe, Chief 122
'Leonard' see Lawrence, Edward
Lephoto, David 443–444
Lerabane, Baleni 489
Lerole, Vusi 242–243
'Les' 193
Lesotho 296–297, 300–301, 368–370
Lesotho Radio 296
Letele, Dr 60
Letoboko, Johannes 76–77
Letsholonyane, Ronald 103, 112
Letsholothebe, Chief 122
Levitan, Jack 88
Lewin, Julius 17–18
Liang, Kao 87–88
Liebenberg, William 369–370, 403–404, 408–409, 412
Liefeldt, Major 6
light machine guns see LMGs
Liliesleaf Farm 54–55, 78, 90–93, 99
'Lincoln' see Xate, Lulamile
Lindwa, Doctor 152
Lisbon Radio 318
Lloyd, Selwyn 19
LMGs 136–138, 141
Lobengula Detachment 132
Loggerenberg, Jan Karel 224
Lombard, Hendrik 259–260
Lombo, Lolo 474
Loots, Brigadier 399–401
Loubser, Professor 260
Louw, Mike 451
Louwrens, Mr 165
Loxton, Allen 41
Lubisi, Amos 211, 215–216
Lubisi, Ncimbithi 256–257, 261
Lugg, Hugh 418
Lukhele, David 383–384

Lukhele, Samson 198–203
'Lungile' 256–257
Lupane group 129, 134–136, 138–139
Lushaba, Lucas 385
Luthuli, Albert 6–7, 11–12, 14–18, 21–22, 26, 32–33, 35–38, 45–46, 55, 128–129
Luthuli, Daluxolo ('Can Can') 108, 127–128, 133, 147
Luthuli Camp 72, 85, 127–128, 150
Luthuli Detachment 129–130, 132–133, 135, 139–140

Maake, Abel 214
Mabanda, Beatta 227
Mabele, William 404
Mabena, J.J. 469
Mabhida, Moses
  arrests and trials 22
  in exile 32, 60, 103, 112, 171, 176, 178–180, 209–213, 215, 220, 222, 271–273
  at Liliesleaf Farm 68
  Wankie and Sipolilo campaigns 164
Mabhija, Greatwell 143, 152
Mabitse, Edwin 321
Mabizela, Stanley 195, 215, 238, 245, 270–272, 289, 311
Mabophiwa, Thatayaone 348–349
'Maboya' 244
Maboya, Eleazor 100–101, 108, 119
'Mabuya' 466
Mabuza, Enos 295
Mabuza, Henry 274
Mabuza, Jacob 273–274
Mabuza, Joyce 273–274
Mabuza, Michael 327
Macaskill, Elvis 365
Machel, Samora 127, 193, 271, 301, 318–320, 325
Macmillan, Harold 19, 81
Macozoma, Saki 442
Madela, Wilfred 256–257, 260
Madikela, Bimbo 292
Madikiza, Colonel 476
Madi, Mash 229
Maduna, P.M. 299
Maduray, David 355–356
'Madzimba, David' see Moyo, Jonathan
Mafoko, Fanie 256–257, 260
Mafole, Tomeka 187

Mafuna, Bokwe 187–188
'Magabula' 314
Magagula, Ms 248
Magoafela, Jimmy 75
Magoo's Bar bomb 386
Magubane, Jerry 298
Magwayi, Meglory 50
Magxengane, Bandile 63
Maharaj, Mac
  training in East Germany 32, 79–80
  arrests and trials 106–107, 226
  in exile 232–234, 244–245, 263–264, 270, 277–278, 352, 380–381, 399, 406, 424–428
  back in South Africa 460
  negotiations with government 359, 463–464, 469–470, 480
Maharaj, Tim 106
Mahero (mutineer) 330
Mahlangu, Lucky 222–225
Mahlangu, Samuel 311
Mahlangu, Solomon 210, 222–226
Mahlasela, Do 81, 84–85
Mahlasela, Gabula 106
Mahlobo, Sithabiso ('Jabu'/ 'Jabulani') 279, 302–305, 309, 314–315, 340, 353
Mahoney, Captain 219
Mail on Sunday 342
Majinga, Simon 102
'Majojo' 64
Majola, Busi ('Mzala') 133, 135, 384
Majola, Henry 152
Majosi, Mlungesi 478–479
Makama, Styles 128
Makamba, Gladstone 73
Makana, Simon 352, 406–407, 415
'Makao, Rodger' 217
Makasi, Shooter 145, 147, 263
'Makayi, Charles' see Mandela, Morris
Make, Cassius 408, 410
Makeleni, Chief 95
Makgage, Thabo 246
Makgoale, Omry 322
Makhalima, Matthews 51–53, 57, 70–71
Makhanya, Joel 478–479
Makhathini, Johnny 52–53, 75
Makhoba, Mandlenkosi 495
'Makhonya' 129
Makhosini, Ali 242–243
Makhubedu, David 322, 462

Makhubo, Humphrey 256–257, 260
Makhubo, Sipho 201–202
Makhubu, Lawrence 167
Makhura, Joseph 319, 374, 383, 390
Makiwane, Ambrose 107–110, 114, 167, 176
Makiwane, Jebese 143
Makiwane, Tennyson 32, 56–57, 60, 68–70, 82, 103, 106–108, 110, 112, 114, 119–122
Makoni, Daniel 164–165
Makopo, Isaac 209, 231, 344
Makushe, Jackson 215
'Makwakwa' 186–187
Makwanazi, Simon 376
Malala, Justice 502
Malama, Phiri 133, 135
Malan, Magnus 311, 335, 450
Malawi 125
Malaza, Joseph 349
Malecela, John 381
Malefo, Philemon 281, 285, 287
Malgaz, Ernest 51–53, 57, 70–71
Malherbe, Frans 500
Maliba, Julius ('Goodman Moloi'/ 'Mancheck') 120, 126–127, 130, 141, 143, 191, 361
Mali, Mgqala 50
Malinga, Kenneth 81, 84–85
Maloke, Abraham 130
Maluleka, Eric 367, 369–372
Maluleka, Peter 418
Malume, Tony 126–127
Mamasela, Joe 280–281, 292, 314
Mamba, P.A. 299
'Mambaso' see Mantayana, Patrick Sindili
Mampane, Joseph 76–77, 101–102
Mampuru, Chris 140
Mamre training camp 66–68
Manabalala, Simon 417
Manana, Naphtali 256–257
'Mancheck' see Maliba, Julius
Manci, Alois 194, 211, 213, 215–217, 220
'Mandela' 369
Mandela, Morris ('Charles Makayi') 123–124
Mandela, Nelson
  arrests and trials 5–9, 12, 22, 93, 99, 104–105
  formation of MK 18, 26–35, 46–48, 51–58

on Robben Island 270, 350
release of 324, 342–343,
    357–358, 436
Commonwealth Eminent
    Persons Group 381
negotiations with government
    441, 447, 451–452, 459–463,
    469–474, 484–485, 487,
    489–491, 495–497, 503, 506,
    508–511
MK conferences 479–480, 482,
    500–502
swearing-in ceremony 512–513
Mandela, Winnie 51–52, 167, 460
Mandela, Zinzi 343
Mandela Camp 107
'Mandisi, Willie' see Seakamela,
    Charles
Mandiwengerayi, John 165
'Mandla' 195–196, 211, 474
Mandla, Jackson 147–148
'Mange' 259
Mange, James 236, 241
Mangope, Lucas 491–492, 503, 505
Mango, Sipho Irving 69
'Maniki' 405
Mankahlana, Parks 480
Mann, George 109
Manong, Stanley 234, 236
Mantayana, Patrick Sindili ('Alfred
    Scott'/'Mambaso') 134
Mantyi, S. 478
Manuel, Trevor 336
Manye, Christopher 194, 197
Manzini, Detective Sergeant 423
Mao, Chairman 46
Mapanga, Russell 191, 227
Mapanza, Sifiso 201–202
Mapetla, Richard ('Patrick Opa
    Tawa'/'Authu Muzorewa')
    236–238, 246
Mapheto, Andrew 243–244
Maphosa, Fredi 155
Maphumulo, Shadrack 69, 227,
    394–395
Maphumulo, Wilfred 329
Maponya, Mishack 'Mensday'
    408, 416–418
Mapoto, Isaac 108, 155, 158,
    160–161
'Maputo, Johnson' see
    Mathambo, Douglas
Maqhekeza, Mzizi ('Mpilo') 353,
    375
Marais, Henry Dirk see April,
    James

Marais, J.J. 97
Marais, Stephen 370
Marcus, Gill 488
Maree, Lenus 424
Maré, Paul 78
Marino, Happyman 154
Marinovich, Greg 509
Marks, J.B. 55, 84, 86, 171
Marney, Cardiff 66–67
Maroe, Isaac 214
Maroga, Elliot 120
Martin, R.L. 124
Martins, Ben 304
Martins, Dino 265
Martins, George 330
Marume, Tony 161
Marupeng, James 339
Marwa, Maxwell Levy 27
Marwane, Wilford 236–238
Marxism-Leninism 251
Marydale farm see Luthuli Camp
Masala, Macdonald 51, 57, 76,
    106, 108, 110–111
Masango, Frans 'Ting-Ting' 371,
    373–374, 383, 390
Masango, Ronnie 461
Maseke, Abe 234
Maseko, Acton 374, 385, 387, 500
Maseko, Anna 306
Maseko, Don 133, 135, 139
Maseko, Duke 330
Maseko, Ezekial 303, 306–307
Maseko, Nasho 154
Maseko, Tim 199
Masemula, Sam 85
Maseru raids
    December 1982 300–301
    December 1985 365
Masetlha, Billy 214–215, 219–220
Mashaba, Andrew 76–77
Mashigo, Petrus 256–257,
    260–261
Mashinini, Cliff 340
Mashinini, Tsietsi 207
Mashobane, Duke 349
Mashobane, Rose 349
Mashokwe, Leslie 511–512
Masimini, James 119, 136–138
Masina, Elias 432
Masina, Obed 235–236, 239, 371,
    373–374, 383–384
Masinda, Frans 41–42
Masinga, Elias ('Roller') 208, 210,
    213–215, 219–220, 280, 282
Masipa, Barry 142–143
Masire, Quett 344

'Masiza, Thomas' see Bhengu,
    David Jiba
Masondo, Andrew 74, 246, 323,
    344
Masondo, Jacob 130–131
'Master' 360
Masuku, Thomas 210
Masupye, John 58, 70–71, 76–77,
    102
Masupye, Michael ('Jimmy
    Mpedi') 123–124
Matabane, Itumeleng 292
Matabata, Bobbie 478–479
Matanzima, George 475
Matanzima, Kaiser 475
'Mateio' 341
Mathabathe, Lekgau 207
Mathambo, Douglas ('Johnson
    Maputo') 425–426
Mathebula, Sipho 322
Mathe, George 417–419, 423
Mathusi, George 162
Matibela, Enoch 76–77
Matimula, Martin 111–112
Matjale, Elias 433
Matlaku, Ismail 122
Matlase, Elias 85, 109
Matlou, Jonas 54, 60, 75
Matola raid 275–277
Matoti, J.J. 53
'Matoto' 108
Matroos, Vuyisile 281–282
Matse, David 331
Matshabe, Caleb 84, 86
Matshaya, Mfanelo 464–465
Matshididi, Harold 424
Matshoba, Nosi 187
Matsinhe, Mariano 319–320
Matsuko, Samuel 432
Matthee, Vivian 365
Matthews, Agnes 348
Matthews, Joe 60, 82, 169, 171
Matthews, John Edward 106
Matthews, Z.K. 6–10
Matwa, Bongani 322
Matyobani, Eric 327
Mavisela, Solomon 160
Mavis (recruit) 197
Mavundla, Charlton 437
Mavuso, Thoko 187, 231
Mavuyo, Thabo 234, 236
Maxongo, Amos 461–462
Mayapi, Phumzile 375, 462, 464
Mayekiso, Maxwell 51–53, 57,
    70–71
Mayibuye 103

'Mayoli' *see* Monwabisi, Joseph
Mayona, Sidwell 155
'Mayona, Solly' 267, 270, 275–276
Mazibuko, Elliot 'Piper' 277–278
Mazibuko, Fanyana 207
Mazibuko, Seth 207
Mazibuko, Sibusiso 345, 361
Mazimba, Reddy 108, 120, 176, 210
'Mbali' 167
Mbali, Fanele ('Lammy Booi')
    174, 176, 179–180, 184
Mbali, Jackson 81
Mbane, Jimmy 369–372, 430
Mbanjwa, Solomon 58–59,
    61–62, 64, 84, 86, 88
Mbaqa, Sipho 497
Mbata, Morgan 111
Mbatha, Laurens 497–498
Mbatha, Levy 68, 84, 86
Mbatha, Madoda 286, 291–292,
    294
Mbatha, Moses 278–279
Mbeje, Sipho 443–444
Mbeki, Govan ('Dhlamini') 22,
    26, 55, 60–61, 78–79, 84,
    89–92, 99, 105, 415, 453
Mbeki, Thabo 188, 193–194, 202,
    235, 244–245, 337–338, 344,
    359, 438, 442–443, 462, 477,
    480, 513
Mbelo, Johannes 367, 371–372
Mbengo, Luvo 461–462
'Mbengwa, Z.R.' 167
Mbeya, Mike 109
Mbhejelwa (guerrilla) 158
Mbita, Hashim 344–345
Mbokane, Lucky 490
Mbona, Dexter 329
Mbuli, Abel 120
Mbuli, Jabulani 361–362
Mbumbulu, Bullet 330
'Mbuse' 64
Mbvomo, Nkosi 111
McBride, Derrick 377–378
McBride, Leslie 387
McBride, Robert 331, 361, 368,
    377–380, 384–386, 387, 411
McDermot, Duncan 71
McDonald, Sags 120
McFadden, Keith 314, 317
McGarry, Dave 350
McKay, Barry 115
McKenzie, Keith ('NP395')
    399–401
McQueen, Sergeant 403
Mdhladhla, Mzomdala 239

'Mdingi' 74, 227
Mdlalose, Zakhela 58, 64
Mdlethshe, Comrade 158
Mdluli, Jabulani 201–202
Mdluli, Joseph ('Mtukuzi')
    199–202, 408
Mdluli, Lydia 202
'Mdubane' *see* Nzama, Alson
Mdube, Reginald 50, 61, 63–64,
    75, 94
Meadowlands 10
Mebeke, Kenneth 327
medals 501
Mehlomakhulu, Mabala 239
Meiring, Georg 513
'Melamu, Comrade' 150
Mellet, Leon 262, 337
Melo, John 179
Meluba, Edward 362
Memela, Totsie 425–426, 428
Meninger, Steven 505
Menyatsoe, Ontlametse 504–505
Menye, Pumelele 162–163,
    184–185
Menyoke, Samuel 327
Merafe, Major General 344
Merrivale farm *see* Luthuli Camp
Meshengu, Comrade 247
Metshane, Peter 102–103,
    105–106, 108, 110–112
'Metsing' *see* Modise, Simon
Meyer, Leon ('Joe Quin') 365, 376
Meyer, Roelf 495, 499
Meyiwa, Matthews 58, 64
Mfalapitsa, Ephraim 209–210,
    214, 236, 277, 282–283, 292
Mfamana, Alfred 133, 147–148
Mfene, Peter 72, 75, 132, 143–144,
    147
'Mgakane, Natalio Sello'
    see Molefe, Bushy
Mgijima, Ralph 449
Mguduso, Siphiwe 303
'Mhambi' 137
Mhlaba, Raymond 22, 26, 36, 46,
    68, 90–91, 99, 105, 358,
    447–448, 453–454
Mhlari, Willie 397
Mhlawuli, Goodman ('Rashidi
    Kawawa') 119, 133, 135, 138
Mhlongo, Happy 479
Mhlongo, Kate 322
Mhlongo, Peter 142
Michaelis, Mike 94
Michels, Quentin 344, 346,
    374–376, 382

'Mike' 228
Milane, Lennon 126–127, 150
Miles, John 104
Miller, Victor 242
Minford, Leslie 104
Mini, Nomkhosi 365
Mini, Vuyisile 61, 69
Miya, Bheki 201–202
'Mjojo' *see* Tshali, Mongameli
Mjo, Zola 63
MK
    violence vs non-violence debate
        20–42
    formation of 45–93
    National High Command 56,
        61, 65–66, 79–80, 86, 89, 100
    setbacks 93–109
    commanders 109–115
    infiltrations into South Africa
        119–133, 166–186
    Wankie and Sipolilo campaigns
        133–166
    grievances 168, 320, 346–348,
        406–407
    underground units 186–204
    violence in townships 207–226,
        335–355
    Central Headquarters 221–222,
        243, 245
    people's war 226–271,
        311–332, 403–435
    presence in Southern Africa
        271–311
    violence in white areas
        355–403
    organisational chart 356–357
    negotiations with government
        435–455, 459–500
    restructuring 480–482
    integrated into combined
        defence force 501–513
Mkaba, Zinakile 69, 76
Mkalipi, Theophilus ('Victor
    Dhlamini') 120, 126–128,
    130, 132, 143, 147
Mkhanya, Petros 287
Mkhize, Samson 195
'Mkhize, Steve' 377
Mkhonta, Z.L. 345
Mkhonto, Dick 400
Mkhonto, Ndumiso 400
Mkhwamubi, Khahla 391
Mkhwamubi, Musk 391
Mkhwanazi, Jabi 468–469
'Mkoko' 108
Mkokwana, Mcebisi 81, 84–85

Mkona, Michael 407
Mkwanazi, Edwin 108–109
Mkwayi, Wilton 32, 36, 46, 68, 84,
    93, 100, 106, 108–109,
    447–448, 453
Mlangeni, Andrew 36, 46, 68,
    84, 99, 105, 358, 447–448,
    453
Mlangeni, Selinah 461
Mlangeni, Themba 484
Mlonzi, Khanja 147–148
Mncube, Mthetheleli 396–399,
    502
Mndebele, John 468
Mngade, Aubrey 388–389
Mngadi, police officer 203
Mngomezulu, Bernard 329
Mngomezulu, Busisiwe 338–339
Mngomezulu, Jameson 324, 329,
    332, 338
Mngomezulu, Ntunja 324, 332
Mngomezulu, Tindla 332
Mnguni, Mthunzi 407
Mninzi, Freddie ('Comrade
    Rogers') 119, 129, 136–137
Mnisi, Christopher 293, 298
Mnisi, Johannes ('Victor')
    281–282, 285, 287, 293, 303,
    399–401
Mnisi, M.M.P. 344–345
'Mnyaka, Huitsa' 223
'Moadira' 343
Mobutu, Joseph-Désiré 124
Mochesane, Bernard ('Lucas
    Mokele') 101–102
'Mochudi' 267, 270, 275–276
Modalise, Frans 417
Modise, Joe
    acts of sabotage 41–42, 47
    formation of MK 49–50
    transport of cadres 52–54, 72,
        100
    at Liliesleaf Farm 68
    in exile 114, 119–120, 123,
        126–131, 167–168, 204, 221,
        234, 282, 310, 323, 347, 437,
        449, 455
    Wankie and Sipolilo campaigns
        150–153, 162–163
    back in South Africa 462
    negotiations with government
        472, 481–482, 486, 500,
        511–513
Modise, Michael 'Fanie' 340
Modise, Simon ('Metsing')
    429–430

Modise, Thandi ('Zandile
    Simelane') 233–234, 247,
    253, 376
Modise, Victor 234, 236
Modulo, Ernest 140
Moeller, Theodore 11
'Moema, Robert' see Ramano,
    Gilbert
Mofoka, Peter 349
Mofokeng, Grace 322
Mofokeng, Jacob 341–342, 364,
    366
Mofolo, Jabu 322
Mogano, Peter 58, 76–77, 87,
    101–102
Mogoerane, Simon 247–248,
    253–254, 283, 286, 289–292
Mogotsi, Martiens 103–104, 108,
    110–111
Mohale, Petrus 112
Mohammed, Sheik Nazeem 446
Mohapi, Columbus 127
Mohatle, Mankahelang 365
Mohlanyaneng, Simon ('Bafana')
    210–211, 213, 215, 219
Moise, David 267, 270
Mokeba, Uriah 309–310, 347–348
'Mokele, Lucas' see Mochesane,
    Bernard
Mokgabudi, Montso ('Obadi'/
    'Dolphin Ngake') 252, 262,
    267, 270, 275–277, 304
Mokgamatha, Elijah 362
Mokgoro, George 111
Mokgosi, Ramatshwiritlha 103,
    110
Mokgotsi, John 127
Mokoape, Keith 194, 197, 199,
    208–209, 228, 231, 234,
    282, 340
Mokoena, Charles ('Solomon
    Molefi'/'Paul Naledi'/'Naledi
    Molefe') 417–418
Mokoena, Julius 191, 223,
    231–232, 309–310, 318,
    321, 330
Mokoena, Mike 428
Mokoena, Philemon 195
Mokoena, Suzman 278–279, 286,
    291–292
Mokoena, Thabo 327
Mokone, Basil 122
Mokone, Ezekiel 498
Mokwena, Reverend 84
Molapo, Michael Roller
    ('Clement') 387–388

Molebatsi, George 221
Molebatsi, Ikanyeng 256
Molefe, Bushy ('Natalio Sello
    Mgakane') 232
Molefe, Levy 70–71, 101–102
Molefe, Morgan 109
'Molefe, Naledi' see Mokoena,
    Charles
Molefe, Pat 81
Molefe, Petrus 42, 48
Molefe, Sydney ('Pindela')
    278–279, 285–286, 289–291
Molefe, Tladitsagae 242
'Molefi, Solomon' see Mokoena,
    Charles
'Molege' 219
Molekwane, Nicholas 221, 230
Molife, Blackie 161
Molobi, Eric 187–189
Molobi, Frank 187, 189
'Moloi, Goodman' see Maliba,
    Julius
Moloi, Lehlohonolo (Lambert)
    121, 130, 166, 243, 300, 320
'Moloi, Modise' 124
Moloi, Sparks 142–143
Moloi, Super 219–220
Molokoane, Barney 236–238, 252,
    267–268, 270, 281–282,
    363–364
Moloto, Audie 127
Moloto, Oupa 208
Mombehuri, Chris 155
Mompati, Ruth 462
'Monde' see Montampede,
    Chief
Moni, Linda 360
Montampede, Chief ('Monde')
    63, 280
'Monte' 64
'Montle, Mr' 256
Montshiwa, Sello 229
Montwedi, Solomon 84, 86
'Monwabisi' 353
Monwabisi, Joseph ('Mayoli')
    365
Moodley, I. 178
Moodley, Khandilal 50–51
Moodley, Subbiah 38
Moolla, Mosie 96
Moonsamy, Kisten 62
Moosa, Mohammed Valli 470
Mope, Barney 417
Morake, Philemon 308–309
Moreni, Edward 248
'Morgan' 218

Morobe, Murphy 207, 214–215, 219–220, 444, 448–449
Morodi, Graham 130, 134, 140, 147–148, 152, 163
Moroka, James 6
Moroka Police Station attack 248, 249, 265, 278
'Morris' 262, 264
Morris Isaacson High School, Soweto 207
Morris Seabelo Rehabilitation Centre see Quatro camp
Mose, Gladstone ('Jackson Mlenze'/ 'Captain Moss') 120, 126–127, 130, 167, 176, 178–183, 186, 367, 421
Moseu, Joseph 199
Moshuloane, Jan 375
Mosoetsa, Benjamin 489
Mosololi, Jerry 278–279, 285, 289–292
Mosomane, Christina 424
Moss, Ismael 344, 346
Motaung, Charles 282
Motaung, Lele ('Bra T'/'Peter') 213, 215, 397, 399
Motaung, Sipho 474
Motaung, Thabo ('Abe'/'Abie') 247–248, 253–254, 278–279, 283, 285–286, 289, 291–292, 294
Mothusi, George 81, 123, 150, 154, 161
'Motiranka' see Cholo, T.T.
Motlanthe, Kgalema 186–187, 194, 199, 204
Motloung, Mondy 222–226
Motsepe, Andries 129, 138
'Motsese, Herbert' 124
Motshabi, John 191–192, 233–235
Motsi, Edward 176, 179–180
Motsila, Spy 128
'Motsipe, James' 124
Motsoaledi, Elias 52–53, 68, 87, 90, 99, 105, 447–448, 453
Motsoaledi, Mooki 236
Moumbaris, Alexander 174, 179, 181–184
Mouton, H.A. 238
Moyema, Isaac 293
Moyo, Edward 147–148
Moyo, John 158
Moyo, Jonathan ('David Madzimba') 129, 133–135, 137–139, 149

Moyo, Josiah 155
Mozambique
  Zambia and 125
  ANC in 127–128, 197–198, 263, 266, 287, 308–309, 319–321, 331
  independence of 190–191, 193
  attacks in 274–275, 311
  South Africa and 301, 325
Mpanza, Justice ('Reuben Ntlabati') 69, 81, 95, 120, 123, 126–127, 130, 143, 146, 152, 163, 180–185
Mpata, Mkalalwa 164
'Mpedi, Jimmy' see Masupye, Michael
Mpembe, Themba 391
Mpetha, Oscar 447–448, 453
Mphahlele, Andrew 417
'Mpho' 323
Mpho, Motsamai 70, 90
'Mpilo' see Maqhekeza, Mzizi
MPLA 188, 200, 214
M-Plan 9, 18, 22, 188
Mpofu, Gilbert 157–158
Mpofu, Lusceni 150
Mpontshana, Ndandi 391
Mpotokwane, L.M. 208
Mrewa, John 158
Mshaya'zafe hostel 508–509
'Msibi' 299
Msibi, Constable 392
Msibi, Alpheus 483–484
Msibi, Fani Basil 383, 390–393
Msibi, John 236
Msibi, Sam 509
Msibi, Themba 327
Msibi, Titus 288–289, 318, 326
Msomi, Audway 345, 359, 365–366
Msomi, Mildred 405–406
Msomi, Patrick 227
Msomi, Ronald 330
'Msweli, Wilson' see Nqose, Zolile
Mtatene, Simon 175
Mthembu, Abel 36, 46, 68, 84, 87, 90, 235
Mthembu, Diliza 462
Mthembu, Joseph 423
Mthembu, Lindiwe 422
Mthembu, Mtunzi 231
Mthembu, Petrus 180–184
Mthethwa, Timothy 271–272
Mthunywa, Osborne 187–188

Mtimkulu, 'Dick' 267–268, 270, 275–276
Mtolo, Bruno 37–38, 49, 55, 58, 61–62, 83–84, 95
Mtshali, Eric 107, 198, 204
Mtshali, Stephen 95
'Mtukuzi' see Mdluli, Joseph
Mubarak, Hosni 445
Mukoka, Jefferey 109
Mulder, Connie 200
Muller, Hilgard 200
Munger, Keith 96–97
Murphy, Terence 510
Murray, Hugh 359
Museti, Patrick 109, 155
Musindane, Jerry 254
Musi, Zondisile 292–293
Mutshekwane, Simeon Richard 122–123
Muzorewa, Abel 254, 263
'Muzorewa, Authu' see Mapetla, Richard
Mvemve, Boy 188
Mvula, Michael 69
Mwalusi, John 123
'Mwema, Robert' 178
'Mwumeleni' 362
Myburgh, Tertius 359
Mynele, Thami 349
Mynute, John 64
'Mzala' see Majola, Busi
'Mzala, Comrade' see Nxumalo, Jabulani
Mzamo, Ralph 128, 150–151, 153, 155
Mzathi, Kenneth 127, 153–154
Mzatho, Kenneth 150
Mzimele, Tano 130
Mzimeli, Motyatyambo 462
Mzimonke, Faldiri 130
Mzolo, Solomon 465

Nachtwey, Jim 509
Naicker, George 49, 61–62
Naicker, M.P. 26
Naidoo, Derrick 355–356
Naidoo, Indres 77–78
Naidoo, Jay 446
Naidoo, M.D. 33
Naidoo, Nandha 32, 36, 46, 68, 79–80, 106
Naidoo, Phyllis 300
Naidoo, Richard 355–356, 367
Naidoo, Sadhan 437
Naidoo, 'Steve' 79
Naidoo, T.N. 8

Naidu, Lenny 355–356, 422
Nair, Billy 36–38, 47, 49, 55, 58, 61–62, 83, 90, 374
'Naledi, Paul' *see* Mokoena, Charles
Namibia 120, 363, 427, 434 *see also* South West Africa
Nanabhai, Shirish 77–78
Napier, Prakash 442, 447–448, 451
Napier, Shan 442, 451
Natal 295–296, 350, 356, 383, 386, 461, 464–465, 487, 508
Nataller 69
Natal Machinery 222, 276, 295–296, 302, 314–317, 324, 326, 360, 374, 390, 422–424, 426, 431, 495
Natal Mercury 435
Natal Urban Machinery 257–258, 287
Natal Witness 461, 465
nationalisation 487
National Party 7, 16, 35, 69, 402, 446, 477, 485, 502–503, 511
National Peace Accord 482, 491
National Peacekeeping Force 502–504, 507–509, 512
National People's Party 356
Nayager, Keith 177
Nboxele, Caswell 66
Nchabeleng, Elleck 218–219
Nchabeleng, Petrus 76–77, 200, 217–220
Nchangasi, Moses 411–413
Ncise military base 475
Ncube (guerrilla) 164–165
Ncube, Base 233
Ncube, Danger ('Nkosinathi Smith') 233
Ncube, Morris 145
Ncube, Patrick 160
Ncube, Peri 145
Ndaba, Charles ('MK Zwelake') 296, 357, 390, 422–423, 467–469
Ndaba, David 355
Ndaba, Victor 174–175
Ndamasa, President 448, 475
Ndhlovu, Archion 155, 157
Ndhlovu, George 243
Ndhlovu, Harold 160
Ndhlovu, Joseph Bothwell 138
Ndima, John 154
Ndlanzi, Sibusiso ('Sihle Khumalo'/ 'George Fakude') 360, 366–367

'Ndlela' 129
Ndlovu, Akim 150
Ndlovu, Alfas 426
Ndlovu, Amos 133, 135, 138–139
Ndlovu, Curnick 47, 55, 58, 61, 203
Ndlovu, Derrick 265
Ndlovu, Humphrey 506–507
Ndlovu, John 154
Ndlovu, Nicolas 262, 266
Ndlovu, Sibusiso 433
Ndluli, Ben 375
Nduli, Joseph ('Alfred Ngwane') 81, 127, 133, 135, 188, 198–201, 203
'Nduna, Eric' *see* Jantshi, Abel
Ndwandwe, Phila 367, 423, 431, 433
Ndwandwe, S.T. 392
Ndzamela, Ndibulele 375, 462, 464–465
Ndzimandze, Mangomeni 291–292, 318
Ndzuzo, Jack 51–53, 57, 70–71
NEC 244–245, 248–249, 251–252, 271, 320–321, 331, 336, 380–381, 439–440, 449, 473–474, 477, 493–494
Nel, Frederik 287–288, 294
Nel, Johannes 404
Nel, Thinus 242
Nene, Vusi 393
Nengwekulu, Randwedzi 187
Neto, Agostinho 193
Netshitenzhe, Joel 480
New Age 12–13, 18, 24, 29, 48
Newsline 511
New York Times 308, 325, 444, 448
'Ngake, Dolphin' *see* Mokgabudi, Montso
'Ngcobo, Andreas' ('Solly') 218, 340, 362
Ngcobo, Bifana Matthews 152–153, 166
Ngcobo, Edward 378
Ngcobo, Matthews 51
Ngcobo, Thembinkosi 312
Ngcongo, Zazi 84, 86
Ngisi, John 128
Ngobese, Derrick 487, 495
Ngoza, Oceanic 50
Ngqungwana, Lizo Bright 303, 346, 370, 374–376, 382
Ngubane, Bheki 377

'Ngubane, Fana' *see* Nkala, Sydney
Ngudle, Looksmart 50, 66–67, 86, 96–97
Nguqu, Bafo 359
'Ngwane, Alfred' *see* Nduli, Joseph
Ngwane, Rosewell 411–412
Ngwaxela, Badman 128
Ngwenya, Chris 488
Ngwenya, David 81
Ngwenya, Gabriel 302–303
Ngwenya, Moloyi 391
Ngwenya, Muziwakhe ('Zulu, Thami') 194, 223, 314, 324–325, 338, 340, 356, 360, 383, 392, 426, 449–450
Nhlanhla, Joe 320
Nhlanhla, Sibisi 474
Nhlapo, Fanyana 292
Nicholas, H.D. 98
Nicosi, Mandla 287
Nieuwoudt, Jan 475
Nikles, Leo 265–266
Ninela, Vusi 467
Ningiza, Mthunzi 437
Nissan, Mr 402
'Njongwe' 297
Nkaba, Nganzile 51
Nkabinde, James 330
Nkadimeng, John 26, 36, 87, 194, 200, 209, 215, 438, 442
Nkadimeng, Rodgers 346
Nkala, Sydney ('Fana Ngubane') 179
Nkambule, Thembisile 488
Nkiwane, Abraham 152, 164
Nkobe, William 154
Nkobi, Thomas 106, 112, 277
Nkobi, Tom 60, 131–132, 171
Nkoko (MK cadre) 63
Nkomati Accord 325
Nkomo camp 150
Nkomo, Joshua 194, 221
Nkomo, Miller 159
Nkondo, Ephraim 322
Nkonyane, Paulos 488
Nkonyane, Silos 468
'Nkosana, Chris' *see* Hani, Chris
'Nkosi' 133
Nkosi, Abel 393
Nkosi, Bernard 58, 64
Nkosi, Berry 128
Nkosi, D.M. 290
Nkosi, Doris 228
Nkosi, Eric 479

Nkosi, Leonard 81, 84–85, 95, 107, 127, 129–130, 132, 134, 141–143, 146–147, 228
Nkosi, Lewis 143
Nkosi, Lindiwe 488
Nkosi, Madoda Alex 203
Nkosi, Marwick 269–270
'Nkosi, Mthlaba' 223
Nkosi, Raymond 187–188
Nkosi, Samuel 175
Nkosi, Sibusiso 479
'Nkosi, Sipho' 223
Nkosi, Stanley 194, 199, 204
Nkosi, Stephen 210
Nkosi, Thembi 391–392
'Nkotheni' 141
Nkwanyane, Tutu 405–406
Nkwe, Isaac 241
Nobel Peace Prize 36
Nofamela, Almond 314–316, 388–389
Nokwe, Duma 18, 22, 29, 36, 55, 68, 82, 102–103, 105, 107, 112
Nondula, Mzondelele 361–362
'No Revolution Round the Corner' 17
'Norman' 108
Northern Rhodesia 73, 81–82, 85
Nortje, Willem 365, 475
Nota, G.S.K. 448
Nova Catengue camp 222–223, 231–232, 245–247
November, Vanessa 430
NP see National Party
'NP395' see McKenzie, Keith
Nqose, Zolile ('Wilson Msweli') 107, 119, 123–124, 127, 129, 133, 135, 138, 152–153
Nsele, Nzewu Henry 150
Ntakana, Bhekinkosi 375
Ntangala, Joe 111
'Ntasarashu' 184
'Ntlabati, Reuben' see Mpanza, Justice
Ntombela, David 476
Ntombela, Madi 195
Ntombelo, Oscar 239, 243, 296–297
Ntsangani, Milner 3
Ntsele, Benson 158
Ntsele, Mzewu 100
Ntshekang, Lati 267–268, 270, 275–277, 294
Ntshontsho, Candy 405–406
Ntsoane, Jackson 76–77
'Ntwana, Robert' 179

'Ntziswa, Commandant' see Hlongwane, Nicholas
Nujoma, Sam 194, 221
Nuse, Xola 188–189
Nxasana, Bhekisisa 187–188, 191
Nxiweni, Phumezo 350, 431, 433
Nxumalo, Jabulani ('Comrade Mzala') 351
Nxumalo, Richard 377
Nxumalo, Sifiso 423
Nyakonda, Elvis 160
Nyanda, Sheila 406
Nyanda, Siphiwe ('Gebuza'/'Tebogo Kgope'/'Comrade Joe')
  acts of sabotage 194, 278–279, 299, 314
  in exile 198, 220, 222, 239, 293, 325, 340–341, 404, 425–426
  attacks on 406–407
  back in South Africa 428, 460, 468, 488, 496
  negotiations with government 464, 472
  SANDF 498, 501–502, 508, 511, 513
Nyanda, Zweli ('Douglas') 257–258, 261, 287, 296, 299, 302–303, 314, 317, 357
Nyathi, Detective Sergeant 184
Nyathi, Billy Boy 185–186
Nyati, Manyali 159
Nyawo, Msongomane 324, 329, 332
Nyawo, Vuxumuzi 329, 339
Nyembe, Mr 27
Nyembe, Dorothy 164, 166
Nyerere, Julius 82, 125–126
Nyikadzino, Detective Sergeant 161
Nyoka, Makhosie ('Umakhosi') 422–423
Nyoni, Danger 394
Nyoni, Dumisani 394
Nyoni, Mathias 150
Nyoni, Oscar 166
Nzama, Alson ('Mdubane') 195–196
Nzima, Jabu 227, 295
Nzimandze, J. 288
Nzima, Petrus 226–227, 271–272, 289, 295
Nzo, Alfred 171, 297, 300, 318–320, 337, 341, 446, 453–454, 462–463

OAU 103, 121–122, 125–126, 150, 163, 341, 344, 437, 445–446
'Obadi' see Mokgabudi, Montso
Obasanjo, Olusegun 381
Observer 51
O'Connell, Thomas 315
'O'Gara, Ché' 223
OK Bazaars 359
Okumu, Washington J. 508–509
Oliver, Gordon 446
Ondala, Wandile 330
Oosterbroek, Ken 505, 509
Oosthuizen, Petrus 397–398
Operation Bible 373-4, 396, 400-401
Operation Bullrush see Operation Palmiet
Operation Butterfly 357, 360, 364, 367
Operation Cauldron 162, 165
Operation Crow 295–296
Operation Excess 165
Operation Kletshwayo 400–401
Operation Mango 352
Operation Mayibuye 79, 80, 83, 89, 92–93, 176
Operation Melba 263
Operation Nickel 134, 149
Operation P 282
Operation Palmiet 337, 358
Operation Santa 253, 291–292
Operation Sparrow 295–296
Operation Vula 380-381, 399, 406, 424-425, 426-427, 428, 459-460, 463-464, 469-474
Organisation of African Unity see OAU
Orlando Police Station attack 253–254
'Oshkosh' 277
'Oupa' see Pule, Ernest Lekoto
Owusu, Mr 327

PAC 20, 22–23, 55, 214
Pahad, Aziz 439–440
Pakendorf, Harold 359
Pamela (MK cadre) 371
pamphlet bombs see leaflet bombs
Pan-African Freedom Movement 47
Pan-Africanist Congress see PAC
'Pandy, Yasmina' 411–412
Pango camp 329–330
'Pantsu' 384
parachute drops 83

'Parker' 264
Parmidian, Colonel 47–48
pass system 19–20
Passtoors, Hélène 306, 348,
    352–354
Patel, Zahied 281–282
Patrick (MK cadre) 167, 197
Pattinden, Angelique 386
'Paul' 256
'Paulus' 113
Payi, Clarence 330
Pearce, Chris 155–156
'Pedro' see Kathrada, Ahmed
Pedro, Niklo ('Denver Pedro')
    358, 387, 396, 402, 411–412
Peko, Jerry 300
Penny Green Street 177
'People's War (Armed Struggle)'
    351
Percy (victim) 269–270
Perumal, Debanathan 58–59, 64
Petane, Mxolisi 383, 388, 393
'Peter' see Motaung, Lele
Peters, Colonel 369
'Petersen, Paul' see February, Basil
'Peterson, Dan' 223
PFP 280, 402, 424
Phahle, George 349
Phahle, Levi 349
Phahle, Lindie 349
Phakati, Norman 443–444
'Phalanyane, Johannes' see
    Tshibogo, Jack
Phatswane, Johannes 162–163
Phenyane, Nelson 417
Phetla, Ace 236
'Philander, P.' see Forbes, Ashley
Phillips, Frederick 136–137
Phiri, Dube 127
Phiri, Kenneth 262, 264
Phiri, Norman 317
Phokanoka, Lawrence ('Peter
    Tladi') 41–42, 95, 120,
    126–128, 130–132, 134, 138
Phosa, Mathews 477
'Photela' 187–188
Phungulwa, Sipho 462,
    464–465
Pienaar, Frederik 314–317,
    388–389, 421–422
Pietermaritzburg 304–305
Pieterson, Hector 207
Piliso, Mzwai 57, 60, 87, 153, 171,
    198, 220, 246, 449
Pillay, Ivan 226–227, 341,
    425–426, 428

Pillay, Joe 227, 341
Pillay, Vella 32
pilots 179
'Pindela' see Molefe, Sydney
Pinny, Bunny 191
'Piper' 223
Pitout, Detective Sergeant
    352–353
Pitsani, Molefe 152
Pitsi, Francis 417–419, 423
'Pitso, Leonard' 167
'Planning for People's War'
    313–314
'Plot' (MK facility) 321–322
Podgorny, Nikolai 221
Pogrund, Benjamin 29
police see South African Police
political prisoners, release of 324,
    415, 436, 447, 459–461
Pollsmoor Prison 358
Pondoland 169, 171
Pooe, Mike 158
Pooe, Sparks 150
Portugal 189
Posselt, Edgar 337
Post 173
Potgieter, Warrant Officer 261
Potsane, Neo 374, 383–384, 390
Power, Thomas 166
Pratt, David 23
Premier Group Holdings 359
Press, Ronald 13, 22, 34
Pretoria Minute 473, 476–477
Pretoria News 71
Pretorius, Anton 383–384
Pretorius, Frans 184
Prinsloo, Major 8
Prinsloo, P. 258
Priscilla (girlfriend of Mamasela)
    280
Progressive Federal Party see PFP
Pronibrakiz, Colonel 100–101
Protocol of Geneva 427
Public Safety Bill 6–7
Pule, Ernest Lekoto ('Oupa')
    399–401
Pungule, Zenzile 330

Quatro camp 329, 401, 437
'Quin, Joe' see Meyer, Leon
Quinlan, Elsie 5
Qwabe, Cromwell 330

Rabie, Pierre 335
Rabilal, Krishna 276
Rabkin, David 209

Rabkin, Sue 209, 356
'Rachid' see Ismail, Aboobaker
Radebe, Jeff 486–488
Radebe, Jeremia 257–258,
    261–262
Radebe, Mfeketho 184
Radebe, Mgqutshwa 314–315
Radebe, Simon 188–189
Radebe, Siphiwe 127
Rademeyer, Major General
    15–16
Radio Freedom 198, 336, 433,
    473–474
Radio Liberation 88–89
Radio South Africa 511
Rajbansi, Amichand 356
Rajie, Shaheed 234
Ralebitso, Matumo 300
Rall, John 398
'Ralph' see Lawrence, Edward
Ramadite, Ernest 417–419
Ramahadi, Hendrik 109, 111
Ramano, Gilbert ('Robert
    Moema') 244
Ramaphosa, Cyril 477, 489–491,
    499
Ramlakan, Vijay 354–356,
    360–361, 366–367
Ramokgadi, Martin 194, 200,
    208–209, 213, 217–218
Ramonye, Peter 229
Ramotse, Benjamin 41–42, 48–49,
    107, 123
Rampa, Papetsana 417
Ramphomane, Dennis 236
Ramudzuli, Aitken 221–223,
    228–229, 234
Ramudzuli, George ('Jonas')
    243–244
Ramushwana, Gabriel 504
Ramusi, Collins 244
Ramusi, Selaelo ('David'/'Dan')
    196–198, 204, 209–213,
    215–218, 223, 232, 235,
    238–239
Randall, Gene 507
Rand Daily Mail
    protests 4–5, 15, 19, 21–22, 24,
        28–29, 175, 207, 279
    election results 7, 35, 263
    arrests and trials 12–13, 94,
        106, 111, 114, 178, 227
    African nationalism 82
    escape of Goldreich and Wolpe
        96–97
    training in Russia 99

on ANC in exile 119, 131, 172–173, 266, 344
Wankie and Sipolilo campaigns 149
Randeree, Shaik 120, 126–127
Rangasami, Mr and Mrs 326
Rani, Isaac 50–53, 56–57, 70–71
Ranoto, Madimetsa 264, 308–309
Rantau, Johannes 103–104, 108, 110, 112
Rantau, Masibe 108
Rapholo, Jacob 427–428, 451–453
RAR 134–136, 138–139, 142–145, 154–156
Ras, M. 246, 421–423, 475
Rasegatla, Johannes 247, 253–254, 265, 278
'Rashidi' 76
'Rastaman, Chris' 370–372
Record of Understanding 491–492
Reeves, Detective Inspector 136–137
referendums 18, 25–27, 486–487
refugee policy 121–122, 125–126
Relly, Gavin 359
RENAMO 306
'Report Compiled in Q on the 24-12-81' 289
republic, South Africa as 28–30, 279
Resha, Robert 8, 10–11, 29, 47–48, 57, 60, 75, 82
Resolution 435 427, 434, 437
Reuters 99, 269
'Revolutions are not Abnormal' 17–18
Reynolds, Reginald 184
'Reynolds, Ronnie' see Kasrils, Ronnie
Rhodesia 114, 125, 127–131, 149–150, 190, 233, 249, 254–256, 262
see also Zimbabwe
Rhodesian African Rifles see RAR
Rhodesian Army 134, 149, 154, 156–157, 160, 165, 263
Rhodesian Joint Planning Staff sitrep 149, 159–162
Rhodesian Light Infantry see RLI
Rhodesian Security Forces 131, 139, 144, 233, 263–264
Riekert, Constable 230
Rivonia Trial 99, 104–105
RLI 155–157, 165
'Robert' 268

Robertshaw, Colin 367
Robertson, Ian 408, 411, 418
Robinson, Claude 355
Robinson, Freek 482
'Roger' 264
'Rogers, Comrade' see Mninzi, Freddie
'Roller' see Masinga, Elias
Roman, Sergeant 403
Rorich, Chris 269, 274, 292, 314–315
Roux, Eddie 451
Roxburgh, Jenny 193
Royal Swazi Defence Force see RSDF
'Roynie' see Ebrahim, Ebrahim Ismail
RSDF 250–251, 253, 298
'Rubicon speech' 357–358
'Rufus' 374, 383
Rumpff, Justice 6, 28
Russia 95–96, 99–101, 103, 109, 172, 176, 178–179, 198, 221, 436
Rwaxa, Ian Deway 194, 210–211, 213–215, 217–219

Saaiman, Colonel 288
Sabotage Act 105
SACC 200, 420–421, 442, 449
Sachs, Albie 67, 510
Sacks, Harold 24
SACP 17–18, 24, 26–27, 37, 54–55, 83, 172–173, 320, 464, 470–471
SACTU 11, 29, 33, 276
SADF
reorganisation of 18
Rhodesia and 263
attacks on ANC 274–277, 309, 338, 397, 401
attacks on 281, 285, 303, 307–308
intercepted documents 298
in townships 336
SASOL attacks 363–364
integration with MK 497–499, 501, 504, 508–509
SAIC 4, 11, 36
Saker, Lindsay 209
Sakloo, Raymond ('Revaleno Singh'/'Rev') 354–356
Salie, Aneez 410, 430, 434
Salomane, M.B. 267, 270
Saloojee, Babla 8
'Samuels, David' see Jacobs, Pieter

'Samuels, K.' see Jacobs, Pieter
SANDF 510–513
'Sandile' 364
SAPA 5, 476–477, 504–505, 509
Sartre, Jean-Paul 87
SASM 207–208, 215
SASOL attacks
June 1980 267–269, 276
October 1981 284–285
November 1985 363–364
Saula, Goodman 50–51
Scammell, David 154
Schalkwyk, P.J. 250
Scheepers, Coen 74
Schermbrucker, Ivan 88
Scheurer, Anna 367
Schneider, Mr 398
Schneider, Danny 394–395
Schoon, Brigadier 288, 383
Schoon, Gerhardus 391
Schoon, Willem 428
Schreiner, Denys 393
Schreiner, Jenny 393, 409, 411–412
Schwartz, J.D. 98
'Scott, Alfred' see Mantayana, Patrick Sindili
Scott, Edward 381
Scott, Michael 51
SDUs see self-defence units
'Seabelo, Morris' see Dantile, Lulamile
seaborne invasion 176–181
Seakamela, Charles ('Willie Mandisi') 451–453
Searchlight 173
Sebastiao, Senior Lieutenant 310
Sebastiao, Jose 344
Sebe, Charles 279
Sebina, Tom 439
Sebokeng 335–337
Sechaba 311, 364
Section C1, Security Branch see Vlakplaas
Security Branch 51–52, 179, 184, 229–230, 274, 281, 322
security company, Johannesburg 500
Sedibe, Glory ('September') 243–244, 340, 374, 383, 388–390, 404–405, 450
Sefako, Mrs 348
Sefako, Keitumetse 348–349
Segal, Ronald 21
Segoale, Koos 188–189
Sehume, Solomon 237–238

Seiso (victim) 269–270
Sekete, John 236, 238
Sekete, Vincent 363–364
Selabogo, Morris 191
Selani, Tamsanqa 64–65
Selanto, Vincent 188–189
Selassie, Haile 47
selection of cadres 245
Selepe, Julia 298
Selepe, Phillipus 287, 298
self-defence units (SDUs) 468,
    476–477, 479, 486–489,
    508–509
Seloro, Levy 83
Senekal, Lieutenant 284–285
Senior Organs (SOs) 252
Senna, Simon 108
Senna, William 104, 109, 111–112
Senzangakhona, Vaku 267, 270,
    276, 363
Sepal, Ralph 22
'September' see Sedibe, Glory
'September Machinery' 383–384
September, Reg 325–326
Serache, Nat 207, 283, 343
Serfontein, J.H.P. 168–169
Serrano, Mary-Ann 426
Sethlapelo, Salathiel 239
Sexwale, Johnny 282
Sexwale, Joseph 197
Sexwale, Magirly 196
Sexwale, Mosima ('Solomon
    Khumalo') 194, 197–198,
    213, 215–220, 483
Shabangu, Mr 272
Shabangu, Elias 385
Shabangu, Jerry 306
Shaik, Moe 353–354, 373–374,
    396, 400
Shaik, Mohammed 304, 311,
    348, 417
Shaik, Yunis 341, 343, 354, 396
Shange, Vusi ('Callaghan Chama')
    322, 462
Shang, Lee 103
Sharpeville 20–21, 202, 335–337
Shecheshe, Petros 510
Shell House massacre 506–507
'Shezi' 405–406
Shezi, Grant 257–258, 261–262
Shiba, Petros 339–340
Shilubane, Paul 238
Shoke, Aggie 424
Shoke, Solly ('Jabu') 247–248,
    253–254, 265, 278–279, 286,
    289, 292, 294

Shongwe, Freddie 293, 298, 303,
    306–307
Shongwe, Zakhele 328
Shongweni, Mr 248
Shope, Mark 55, 60, 81, 95, 223
Shumo, Joseph 191
Sibanda, Elliot 239
Sibanda, Patrick 150, 160–161
Sibanyoni, Delmas 136–138
Sibanyoni, Piet 376
Sibanyoni, Stoel 376
Sibasa group 141–143, 361
Sibeko, Archie 35, 81, 85, 95, 107,
    128, 130, 158, 167
Sibeko, Joel 131
Sibepe, Sidney 281–282
Sibisi, Jabulani 423
Sibiya, Joseph 175
Sibiya, Vezimuni 200
Sibongi, Lawrence 81, 84–85
Sigasa, Thomas 42
Sigwela, Ezra 476
Sijake, Nimrod 107
Sijake, Sandi ('Douglas') 127, 166,
    176, 178, 182–183, 185
Sikhakhane, Bonnie 217
Sikhosana, Doris 227
Sikhosana, Mandla 195–196
Sikhosana, Richard 443–444
Silva, João 509
Silverton siege 258–260,
    266–267
Simelane, Commissioner 341
Simelane, David 235, 239, 298
Simelane, Jack 120, 145–146
Simelane, Johannes 393
Simelane, Majaji 340, 344–345
Simelane, Matthew 363
'Simelane, Sipho Victor' see
    Dlodlo, Sidumo Theophilus
'Simelane, Zandile' see Modise,
    Thandi
Simons, Jack 174, 245
Simumba, Musyani 443
Sindane, Vusimusi 374
Sindelo, Thami 76
Singh, J.N. 33
'Singh, Revaleno' see Sakloo,
    Raymond
Singh, Sonny 58–59, 64, 95, 226
Singh, Swaran 381
Siphuma, police officer 399
Sipolilo campaign 133–167, 249
Sishuba, Charles 142–143
Sisulu, Albertina 78, 336
Sisulu, Max 188

Sisulu, Walter
    arrests and trials 6–10, 22, 29,
        59–60, 63, 76, 92, 105, 358
    violence vs non-violence debate
        26, 31
    formation of MK 50, 79
    at Liliesleaf Farm 55, 84,
        88–92, 98–99
    release of 441, 447–449, 453
    negotiations with government
        455, 469
Sithole, Anna 248
Sithole, Basil 392
Sithole, Johannes 474
'Sithole, Kwazi' 367
Sithole, Mduduzi ('Trevor Vilakazi'/
    'Belgium') 299, 345, 359
Sithole, Ndabaningi 254
Sithole, Peter 132, 147
Sithole, Sipho 487, 495
Sithole, Wilson 330
Sitilo, Herbert 84, 86
Sitole, Lucky 102–103, 105
Siyali, Isaiah 413–414
Sizane, Zweli 207
'Sizwe' 264
'Sizwe, Ruben' 124
'Skatau' 110
'Slabbie' 255
Slovo, Joe
    formation of MK 26, 34, 37,
        68, 83–84, 86–87, 90
    arrests and trials 29
    acts of sabotage 39–41,
        80–81
    at Liliesleaf Farm 54, 99
    in exile 169–173, 176, 178–180,
        204, 221, 228, 234, 245, 268,
        270, 275, 284, 302, 320, 325,
        351–352, 380, 400–402,
        406, 460
    negotiations with government
        471–472, 492, 499, 505
    back in South Africa 462–464
Smiles, Walter 497–498
Smit, Albertus 237–238
Smit, Corneo 367
Smit, Hennie 200
Smith, Inspector 96
Smith, Francis 110–111
Smith, François 73
Smith, Ian 150, 254
Smith, James F. 337
Smith, Nicholas 142–143
'Smith, Nkosinathi' see Ncube,
    Danger

smuggling of arms 131, 243, 269, 399–400, 478, 487–488, 496
Snyders, Detective Sergeant 212
Snyman, Lionel 475
Soal, Peter 424
Sobhuza II, King 250–251, 289–290, 293
Sobukwe, Robert 20
Sodo, Patheka 462
Soekmekaar Police Station 256–257, 260–261
'Solly' see 'Ngcobo, Andreas'
Solodovnikov, Dr 268–269
Solomon Mahlangu Unit 270
Sols, Seth 253
Somalia 178–179
Somana, Brian 29, 84
Sondezi, Leslie 81, 84–85
Sophiatown 10
Sordor, J. de L. Peter 359
Sotsu, Ernest 488–489
South African Air Force 149, 307–308, 416
South African Communist Party see SACP
South African Congress of Trade Unions see SACTU
South African Council of Churches see SACC
South African Defence Force see SADF
South African Indian Congress see SAIC
'South African Liberation Support Cadre' 279–280, 325, 408
South African Military Intelligence 99, 159, 162, 165–166, 178, 193, 250, 253, 255, 303, 309, 395, 450
South African National Defence Force see SANDF
South African Police 238, 259–260, 262, 288, 308, 468, 506
South African Press Association see SAPA
South African Students' Movement see SASM
South African Students' Organisation 217
'South Africa What's Next?' 24–27
South West Africa 125 see also Namibia
South West Africa People's Organisation see SWAPO

Souza, Pendray 309
Soviet Union see Russia
Sowetan 335
Soweto 41–42, 278–279
Soweto Students' Representative Council see SSRC
Sparg, Marion 279–280, 325–326, 370, 373
Sparks, Allister 96
Sparks, Douglas 61
Special Operations Unit 270, 275–276, 281, 284, 301–302, 361, 370, 399, 411, 424
'Speedo' 346
Spetsiotis, Sotiris 350
'Sponi' 283
Spotlight 103
SSRC 215, 219
Stacey, Bradley Richard 438–439
Stadler, Herman 166, 461
Stanley, Mrs 69
Stanley, Eric 69
Star 5–6, 15–16, 20–21, 23, 27, 189, 313, 335, 357–358, 487, 502, 505, 511
State Security Council 420
states of emergency 23, 355, 358, 373, 385, 438, 459, 464–465, 507
Steenkamp, Lieutenant 95
Steenkamp, Frans 228
Steenkamp, Manie 224
'Stephanie' see Hodgson, Rica
Steyn, Brigadier 430–431
Steyn, Section Officer 138
Steyn, Johannes 467
Steyn, Marais 200
Steyn, P.M. 175
Stirling, Tony 478
Stoffels, Edward 403
Stopper (mutineer) 330
Strachan, Harold 35–36, 45
'Strategy and Tactics of the African National Congress' 170–171
Strijdom, J.G. 14, 16
Strong, Jerry 157–158, 165
Strydom, Captain 393
Strydom, Colonel 212
Strydom, M.B. 288
Strydom, Urban 285
Stuart, James 119, 359
Sudan 74–75
Suleiman, Ebrahim 52–53
Suleiman, Essop 50, 52–53, 84, 86

Sunday Express 29
Sunday Star 415, 470
Sunday Times 13, 40–41, 46, 52, 59, 168–169, 359, 462, 494, 503, 505
sunset clauses 477, 480, 492, 494
Suppression of Communism Act 6, 9, 12–13, 24, 105
Sutill, Ian 276
Suttner, Raymond 190–193
Suzman, Helen 440–441
Swanepoel, Dawid 427
Swanepoel, F.C. 11
Swanepoel, Theunis 78, 111–112
SWAPO 120, 194, 221
Swart, C.R. 6–7, 12–13, 16
Swaziland
    ANC in 181–182, 193–195, 214, 222, 238, 249–251, 271–274, 287–293, 314, 325–329, 338–341, 344–345, 374, 388, 394–395, 401–402
    attacks in 269–270, 317–318, 331, 408
    South Africa and 253, 295–299
Swazi Observer 328
'SWT180' 384
'Sylvester' 239

'Tabane' 362
'Tabu' 239
Tadesse, Colonel 52
Tait, Johan 422
'Tallman' see Xate, Lulamile
Tamane, Bothwell ('Zami') 136–137
Tambo, Oliver
    protests 16, 336, 355
    arrests and trials 18
    formation of MK 21, 52–53, 55, 57, 60, 68–70, 76, 82, 87
    in exile 103, 105, 112–114, 126–132, 169–172, 174, 178–181, 198, 245, 248–249, 263–264, 289, 350–351, 403, 415, 424
    Wankie and Sipolilo campaigns 139–140, 162
    discussions with southern African countries 193, 194, 272, 319–320
    in Soviet Union 176, 221
    in Cuba 221
    in Vietnam 240–241
    on targets for sabotage 269, 307, 353

withdrawal of MK 344, 434
Operation Vula 380–381, 406
negotiations with government
359, 435–437, 440–441, 443,
448–449
Harare Declaration 446
funeral of 497
Tamsen, Oscar 21
Tanana, Siduma 63
Tanganyika 32, 82
Tanzania 119, 121–122, 125–126,
171–172, 198, 331, 481–482,
508
Tatane, Henry 287
Tau, Benjamin 256–257
Tau-Tau, Johannes 100
Tavimbo, Chigobesintayka 155
'Tawa, Patrick Opa' see Mapetla,
Richard
Taylor, Andrew 367, 430–431, 433
Tazuwinga, Corporal 135
TEC 501, 504–505, 507
Tema, Hudson 212
Temba, Brian 248
Temple, Melodie 392
Tengwa, Eric 176
'Terence' 362
Terre'Blanche, Eugène 499
Thabethe, Lucky 154
'Thabo' 256, 308
Thatcher, Margaret 436–437
Thebe, Goliati 145
Thema, Moses 322
'Themba' 264
Thenjekwayo, Nkosi 423
Theron, Flip 421–422
Thia, Akga 465
'third force' 474, 480–481
Thobela, Sipho 267, 270, 275–276
Thomas, Patrol Officer 145
Thunzi, Sydney 81
Tibone, M.C. 231
Tichafa, Raymond 153–154
Times, The 410, 462, 502–503
Times of Swaziland 233, 326–327
Times of Zambia 160, 439, 443
Timitiya, C.S.M. 142
Timol, Ahmed 173–174,
177–178
Timol, Hawa 174
Tiro, Onkgopotse Abraham
187–188
Titana, Mthetheleli 383
'Titus' 223
'Tladi, Peter' see Phokanoka,
Lawrence

Tladise, Mthebe 228–229
'Tlhapelo, Frans' 223
Tloome, Dan 5–6, 26, 55, 60, 109,
112
Toka, Rodney 408, 416–417, 423
Tonjeni, Victor 63
'Tonkie' 332
'total national strategy' 221
training
opening phase 71–77
camps 66–68, 228
in China 36, 102–103, 105, 112
in Ethiopia 53, 57, 63, 69–70
in Russia 95–96, 99–101, 109,
172
via Swaziland 194–195
in Angola 320–321
in Uganda 494–495
for political work 235
in transition phase 483
transit camps 169, 415–416
Transitional Executive Council
see TEC
Transkei 169, 243, 353, 375,
447–448, 462, 475–476, 478
Transvaal Implementation
Machinery 374, 383, 385, 395
Transvaal Indian Congress 12–13,
16
Transvaal Rural Machinery 222,
244, 256
Transvaal Urban Machinery
222–223, 232–233, 239, 247,
253–254, 273, 278, 286, 289,
291, 307–308
Transvaler, Die 45
Travallyn Farm 90–91
Treason Trial 28
Treurnicht, Andries 200, 486
Tricameral Parliament 331–332,
335, 501
Tripartite Agreement 434
'Truter' 96
Tsafendas, Dimitri 123
Tseto, Joe 208–209, 219–220
Tshabalala, Mr 236, 248
Tshabalala, Mbuso 467, 469
Tshabalala, Norman 213, 216, 218
Tshabalala, Vuso 233
Tshali, Mongameli ('Mjojo'/
'Lennox') 130, 132–134,
142, 146–147, 197, 209–210,
221, 317
Tshepe, Henderson 103, 112
Tshibogo, Jack ('Johannes
Phalanyane') 123

Tshika, Thuso 345, 359, 365–366,
390–393
Tsholotsho group 129, 135,
139–140
Tshona, Zamuxolo 461–462
Tshuma, Mabeli 152, 156–157
Tshuma, Moses 163–164
Tshwete, Steve 50, 61, 415–416,
419–420, 432, 441
Tsiki, Naledi ('Chris') 194,
196–198, 204, 209–213, 215,
217–218, 220
Tsinini, Eliza 408
Tsotsi, Stanley 155
Tsotsobe, Anthony 265, 273
Turok, Ben 22, 24–27, 29, 38–39,
42, 119–120, 169, 171, 176
Turok, Mary 22
Tutu, Desmond 416, 442–444,
446–447
Twala, Mwezi 321–322, 462
Tyron, Terence 356, 364
Tyulu, Freddie 72

UDF 310, 313, 331–332, 335–336,
416, 438–439, 442, 444, 461,
468, 473
Uganda 481–482, 494–495, 508
'Umakhosi' see Nyoka, Makhosie
Umkhonto we Sizwe see MK
Umkhonto 48–49
unbanning of organisations 381,
438, 448–449, 454, 459
uniforms 130, 255
UNIP 82, 84–85
UNITA 200, 309, 317, 319,
407–408, 414
United Democratic Front
see UDF
United National Independence
Party see UNIP
United Nations 327, 434, 437, 443
United Party 7, 14, 16
United Press International
305–306, 324–325, 369
Unit U 346–347
University of Natal 296, 360
Unlawful Organisations Act
22–23
Uys, Detective Sergeant 85
Uys, Sergeant 102

Vaal Triangle 335–337, 358
Vaderland, Die 359
'Vakala' 74
Valla, Eric 469

Van den Berg, Anton 388
Van den Bergh, Hendrik 156
Van der Linde, Julie 386
Van der Merwe, Johan 383, 399–400, 421, 428, 467
Van der Merwe, Roelof 368
Van der Merwe, Stoffel 415, 440
Van der Walt, May 392
Van der Walt, Sarel 510
Van der Westhuizen, Casper 433, 467
Vandeyar, Reggie 41, 77–78
Van Dyk, Lieutenant 281
Van Dyk, Sergeant 393
Van Dyk, Paul 269, 274, 314–316, 383–384, 388–389, 422
Van Heerden, Constable 230
Van Heerden, Neil 369
Van Jaarsveld, Petrus 234
Van Niekerk, Colonel 85
Van Niekerk, Sergeant 111
Van Niekerk, Warrant Officer 219
Van Niekerk, C.J. 250
Van Niekerk, Ignatius 229–230
Van Niekerk, Johannes 184
Van Niekerk, Michael 166–167
Van Rensburg, Lieutenant 111
Van Rensburg, Major 184
Van Rensburg, Nick 269
Van Rensburg, Rudolf 113–114
Van Rooyen, Dina 258
Van Tonder, Major 209
Van Tonder, Warrant Officer 292
Van Wyk, Constable 291
Van Wyk, Major 260
Van Wyk, Johannes 67–68
Van Wyk, Willem 367
Van Wyk, Willie 89, 91, 96
Van Zweel, James 314–316
Van Zyl, Lieutenant 92
Veloso, Jacinto 274–275, 301
Vena, Mzwandile 353, 411–412, 462, 477–478
Venter, Mr 177
Venter, H.A. 234
Vera, Simon 154
Vermaak, T.J. 251
Vermeulen, Snor 293, 475
Verwoerd, H.F. 3–4, 7, 14–16, 18–21, 23, 25, 123
Viana camp 321–324
'Vicks' 281–282
'Victor' see Dlodlo, Sidumo Theophilus; Hlabane, Thomas; Mnisi, Johannes
Viera, Sergio 301

Vietnam 240–241, 244–245
Viktor, J.J. 269, 274, 287–288
Vilakazi, Sibongiseni 201–202
'Vilakazi, Trevor' see Sithole, Mduduzi
Viljoen, Constand 308, 499, 502
Viljoen, Gerrit 335
Visagie, Jacobus 48–49
Visser, Christo 509
Visser, Schalk 287–288
'Viva' see Dlodlo, Sidumo Theophilus
Viviers, J.C. 175
Vlakplaas 271, 292, 308, 367, 371
Vlok, Adriaan 414, 416, 420–421, 429–430, 432, 438, 470
Voice of Women 325–326
Voortrekkerhoogte military base 281, 285, 303
Vorster, Sergeant 56
Vorster, John 45–46, 106, 123, 149, 190, 239, 246
Vuma, Senki 373
Vundla, E. 299
'Vusi' 264, 302
Vũ Xuân Chiêm, Major General 240

Waldmeir, Patti 471
Wallmannstal base 508, 510–511
Waluś, Janusz 496–497
Wana, Douglas 145
Wanda (victim) 269–270
Wandrag, Bert 287–288
Wankie campaign 133–167, 249
Wardle, Lieutenant 138–139
Warmbaths attack 311
Washington Post 438, 442
Washington Times 443
Wassermann, Lawrence 430–431, 433, 467–468
Waterwitch, Robbie 441–442
weapons and equipment 35, 37–38, 45, 76–77, 123, 136–138, 141, 211, 255, 303, 495–496
see also arms caches; smuggling of arms
Webster, Gordon 331, 361, 368, 377–380, 384, 411–413
Webster, Trevor 379
Weekly Mail 480
Wehr, Graham 265–266
Weinberg, Eli 107
Weinberg, Violet 113
Welman, Robert 368

Wessels, Officer 95
Wessels, Daan 185
Westcott, Susan 411, 418
Western Cape Machinery 388, 393
'What the Group Feels' 168
white areas, taking struggle to 419–420
Widlake, Brian 30
Wilken, Captain 506
Wilkinson, Rodney 300–301
Willemse, General 441, 451
Willemse, Douw 383
Williams, Cecil 54–56
Williams, Coline 430, 441–442
Williams, Teddy 'Mwase' 231
Wimpy attacks 392–393, 426
Winnal, William Rodney 144–145
Winter, Lieutenant 203
'Wiseman' 466–467
Witmore, J.S. 259
Wolfendale, Kenneth 225–226
Wolpe, Harold 94, 96–98
Wonderboom Police Station attack 290
World Economic Forum 487
World Festival of Youth and Students for Peace and Friendship 8
World Trade Centre attack 498–499
Wren, Christopher 448
Wurayayi, Platoon Warrant Officer 134

'X, Mr' see Xate, Lulamile
Xaba, Anton 195–196
Xaba, Mbulelo 475–476
Xate, Lulamile ('Tallman'/ 'Lincoln'/'Mr X') 341–342, 354, 360–361, 364–365, 466
Xinhua 87
Xulu, Sipho 330

Yamile, Chief 370
Yates, Constable 393
Yengeni, Tony 369–370, 393, 409, 412–414
Yengwa, Mr 164
Yukalov, Yuri 436
Yutar, Percy 98–99, 104

Zabane, April 187
Zambia 119, 121–126, 163, 172, 264, 359, 382, 439, 443, 481
Zambia Mail 128
'Zami' see Tamane, Bothwell

ZANLA 262–263
ZANU 262–263
ZAPU
  in Rhodesia 127
  ANC and 129, 132, 221, 255, 262–265
  Wankie and Sipolilo campaigns 133, 139–140, 150, 160, 163–164, 249
  in Mozambique 194
  in Botswana 239
'Zenge, Viva' see Dlodlo, Sidumo Theophilus
Zibi, Christopher 254
Zikalala, Snuki 209–210, 228, 231, 234
Zikali, Michael 159
Zimbabwe 249, 254–256, 263–265, 308–309, 382
  see also Rhodesia

Zimbabwe African People's Union see ZAPU
Zimbabwe People's Revolutionary Army see ZIPRA
Zimmerman, Vincent 368
ZIPRA 233, 249, 263–264
'Zola' 64, 304
Zondi, Detective Warrant Officer 315
Zondi, Bessie 106, 108, 110
Zondi, Edgar 195
Zondi, Timothy 465
Zondo, Andrew 364–367
Zondo, Elliot 109
'Zoni' 76
Zovira, Aaron 158
Zscizserin, Colonel 100–101
Zulu, Benny 176
Zulu, Bob 174–175
Zulu, Fanwell 439

Zulu, Joseph Zakile 256, 261–262
Zulu, Joshua 58, 64
Zulu, Matthews 152–153
Zulu, Midian 365
Zulu, Raymond 264
'Zulu, Thami' see Ngwenya, Muziwakhe
Zuma, Edna 199
Zuma, Jacob 84, 86, 191, 196, 198–202, 227, 327, 344–347, 356, 380, 480
Zungu, Sipho 254
Zwane, Dumisani 395–396
Zwane, Jwi 479
Zwane, Lungile 405–406
Zwane, Nicolas 468
Zwane, Nimrod 109
'Zwelake, MK' see Ndaba, Charles
Zwelithini, Goodwill 502, 509